# The
# ADIRONDACK
## Book
### *A Complete Guide*

Nancie Battaglia

# THE ADIRONDACK BOOK

## A Complete Guide

ELIZABETH FOLWELL

*with Neal S. Burdick*

Berkshire House Publishers
Stockbridge, Massachusetts

**On the cover and frontispiece: Photographs by Nancie Battaglia.** *Frontispiece:* Adirondack chair on an Adirondack lake. *Front cover background:* Big Slide via the Brothers, Keene. *Front cover insets:* Wooden boats on shore, Blue Mountain Lake, in the "No-Octane Regatta." Adirondack chair and birches, autumn. "Pulkka Tupa" and skis, Lapland Lake Cross-Country Ski & Vacation Center, **Benson.** Breakfast overlooking Lake Placid; Whiteface Mountain in distance. *Back cover insets:* Lake Placid Sinfonietta at Mirror Lake. Fort Ticonderoga. Adirondack packbaskets, Keene Valley.

The Adirondack Book: A Complete Guide
© 1992 by Berkshire House Publishers
Photographs © 1992 by credited photographers.
Maps designed by NRC Graphics Inc.

Library of Congress Cataloging-in-Publication Data

Folwell, Elizabeth, 1953-
      The Adirondack book : a complete guide / Elizabeth Folwell.
            p. cm. — (The Great destinations series, ISSN 1056-7968)
      Includes bibliographical references and index.
      ISBN 0-936399-30-9
      1. Adirondack Mountains Region (N.Y.)—Guidebooks. 2. Adirondack Park (N.Y.)—
Guidebooks. I. Title. II. Series: Great destinations.
F127.A2F55 1992
917.47'50443—dc20

ISBN: 0-936399-30-9
ISSN: 1056-7968 (series)

Editors: Sarah Novak, Elizabeth Tinsley. Original design for Great Destinations series: Janice Lindstrom. Original design for Great Destinations cover: Jane McWhorter. Production services by Ripinsky & Company, Connecticut.

"Allen's Bear Fight Up In Keene" from BODY, BOOTS AND BRITCHES by Harold W. Thompson. Copyright 1939 by Harold W. Thompson. Copyright renewed 1967 by Dr. Marion Thompson. Reprinted by permission of HarperCollins Publishers.

Berkshire House books are available at substantial discounts for bulk purchases by corporations and other organizations for promotions and premiums. Special personalized editions can also be produced in large quantities. For more information, contact:

Berkshire House Publishers
Box 297, Stockbridge MA 01262
800-321-8526

Manufactured in the United States of America
First printing 1992
10 9 8 7 6 5 4 3 2

*No complimentary meals or lodgings were accepted by the author and reviewers in gathering information for this work.*

# The GREAT DESTINATIONS Series

The Berkshire Book: A Complete Guide
The Santa Fe & Taos Book: A Complete Guide
The Napa & Sonoma Book: A Complete Guide
The Chesapeake Bay Book: A Complete Guide
The Coast of Maine: A Complete Guide
The Adirondack Book: A Complete Guide
The Aspen Book: A Complete Guide
The Charleston & Savannah Book
    With Coastal Islands: A Complete Guide (Spring 1993)

# Contents

CHAPTER ONE
*The People's Park*
**HISTORY**
1


CHAPTER TWO
*Over the Rivers and Through the Woods*
**TRANSPORTATION**
22


CHAPTER THREE
*Rustic, Classic, and Basic*
**LODGING**
41


CHAPTER FOUR
*From Highbrow to Downhome*
**CULTURE**
133


CHAPTER FIVE
*Always in Good Taste*
**RESTAURANTS & FOOD PURVEYORS**
186


CHAPTER SIX
*A Land for All Seasons*
**RECREATION**
275

CHAPTER SEVEN
*Woodsy Whimsy to Practical Gear*
**SHOPPING**
379


CHAPTER EIGHT
*Nuts, Bolts, and Free Advice*
**INFORMATION**
439

July 15, 1992

Dear Reader:

Berkshire House has chosen an appropriate time to introduce its readers to the wonderful diversity of the Adirondacks. This year New Yorkers and visitors from around the globe celebrate the centennial of the creation of the Adirondack Park, one of the largest and oldest State parks in America.

As the readers of this richly informative guide book will quickly discover, the Adirondack Park is unlike any other Park in this country, or indeed the world. Contained within its "Blue Line" are six million acres of public and private lands, an area the size of Vermont with a population of 130,000 permanent residents, 70,000 seasonal residents, and environmental treasures of international proportions — the largest wilderness lands east of the Mississippi where a visitor can still step where no human has ever walked before, 46 mountains over 4,000 feet, 2,800 lakes and ponds, 1,500 miles of rivers, towering forest full of bear and deer and some of the most breathtaking scenery on earth.

As Governor of New York State, I am proud of New York's Adirondack heritage. As with many great enterprises, the history of the Adirondack Park has involved, at times, conflict and controversy. That history continues to be written every day as we strive to maintain a park which is a unique and complex mixture of both public and private interests.

Millions of New York's families share lasting and important memories of good times in these mountains, some spanning generations. For those New Yorkers who make the region their home, life in the Adirondacks, though often demanding, reflects a fierce independent spirit and enduring love for the outdoors.

I have traveled to the Adirondacks more than any Governor since Theodore Roosevelt. It is difficult not to be humble in the Park. It is difficult not to admire the harmony of nature, a harmony that eludes us so frequently in our personal and our political lives.

This book serves as an enticing invitation to visitors to share in this harmony, to share in all that the Park has to offer.

Sincerely,

Mario M. Cuomo

# *Acknowledgments*

Writing is a solitary job, but putting a book together is always the sum of many individuals' efforts. This guidebook came about in a relatively short period of time, thanks to a lot of good people who gave cheerful, generous, speedy help.

I'm particularly indebted to Neal Burdick, editor of *Adirondac* magazine and publications director at St. Lawrence University, in Canton, New York, for writing the History and Transportation chapters. Neal's knowledge of the Adirondack past and politics is rock solid, and I'm surely glad that he was willing to help in the early stages of this project. Thanks to Neal, I was only slightly, rather than completely, overwhelmed.

Special thanks are in order to Nancie Battaglia for her excellent photographs in these pages. Nancie's photos are frequently featured in the *New York Times*, *Newsweek*, *USA Today*, and many other national publications; not only does she take great pictures, she's a marvel of organization.

Kudos, hats off, forks aloft, and many thanks to the crew of gourmets, gourmands, and good eaters who were the Adirondack Diners' Club, my intrepid team of restaurant reviewers who ranged from Au Sable Forks to Big Moose in search of anything edible served up with a smile: Sue Halpern and Bill McKibben, Lohr McKinstry, Dennis Aprill, Joan and Roy Potter, Margaret Lamy, Peter O'Shea, Jim Gies and Kenn Sprague, Laurel Massé and Greg Palestri, and Tom Akstens.

A word of appreciation is due my *Adirondack Life* co-workers Tom Hughes, editor, and Ann Eastman, art director, for their interest, patience, and support. Jerry Pepper and Alice Gilborn at the Adirondack Museum, in Blue Mountain Lake, were also quite helpful from the beginning. My husband, Tom Warrington, was a constant source of advice when I found myself in unfamiliar waters (like when writing about golf, for example); Tom was ever the willing adventurer, happy to hit the road in search of another diner, another bed and breakfast, another corner of the park that we hadn't seen in years.

I'm grateful to Sarah Novak, the managing editor at Berkshire House, for her serene composure throughout this project; to Carmen Elliott, the fact checker, for performing a painstaking job with grace and skill; and to Elizabeth Tinsley, editor, for helping to pull it all together. Mary Osak, Berkshire House staff, also contributed many hours and much cheerfulness.

When I began compiling material for the book, I sent out hundreds of letters to innkeepers, craftspeople, antique dealers, tourism directors, and many others, requesting information. I was surprised by the quantity and quality of responses; folks were genuinely interested in seeing this book be published. It's only fair that the last word of thanks goes to all of those strangers and friends who responded with the encouragement, ideas, and leads that became the core of this book.

# Introduction

New York's Adirondack Park is a big park — bigger than Yellowstone, Yosemite, or any of the national parks in the lower forty-eight. This park is better than national parks in many ways, too: you don't have to pay an entry fee when you cross the park's boundaries (known to one and all as the Blue Line, since the first map describing the park a century ago showed the area delineated in blue); you don't need a special permit to canoe or hike or climb a mountain; and people live here, making the region far more diverse, and offering far more options and services, than you'd find within any federal park. There's a deep human history to discover in this park, beside the natural world and its wonders.

Just how big the park is seems very abstract when you hear numbers like six million acres (which includes the private and public lands put together), or two-and-a-half million acres (which is the public land, in large and small parcels). About another million acres belong to timber companies; not only do their lands look wild and undeveloped from the highways, the industry is a major contributor to the local economy. Think of the Adirondack Park as about the same size as either the state of Vermont or Connecticut, with about 130,000 year-round residents. Hamilton County, which is where I live, has fewer people per square mile than interior Alaska.

I've been in the Adirondacks for all of my adult life, and I've visited many different communities, explored numerous wild places, and learned about North Country culture. Every day I discover something new and surprising about the place; it's always a pleasure to go to some new destination and find a beautiful vista, a cluster of rare wildflowers, a hidden waterfall, a quiet back road through a peaceful valley, a pretty little town.

And even though I'm rather attached to Blue Mountain (where I live), and think that Blue Mountain Lake is near perfect at times, I'll admit that Lake George is a gorgeous body of water, that the Champlain Valley hills and farms are very pretty, that Union Falls Pond has a terrific view, and that the High Peaks are spectacular. All these places are different too, so that the park is like a visual smorgasbord where you can pick and choose among the different elements.

All this fine scenery encourages you to get out in the woods, on the waters, up the mountains. But if you'd prefer to see the countryside from the comfort of a car, that's entirely possible. Just sampling the regional arts and museum scene makes a great pastime: the Adirondack Museum rivals any of the country's great outdoor museums for interpreting people within a region, and there are dozens of charming historic places to see. And if it's good food, fine company, great music, professional theater, quality crafts, or interesting places to stay that you're after, well, I hope that this book sets you on the right track.

Betsy Folwell
Blue Mountain Lake

# The Way This Book Works

There are eight chapters in this book, including History, Culture, Recreation, Transportation, Information, and Shopping, plus many maps and indexes. Within each chapter, you'll find a subheading — such as "Fishing," for example — and under that topic is general information that's true for the whole park. Then specific services and businesses are grouped geographically by region: **Lake George and Southeastern Adirondacks, Champlain Valley, High Peaks and Northern Adirondacks, Northwest Lakes Region,** and **Central and Southwestern Adirondacks,** with appropriate towns listed alphabetically in the regions. So, Bolton Landing may the first town listed in the Lake George area, and pertinent businesses in that town will then be listed alphabetically.

Many of the entries have information blocks in the left-hand margin of the page, listing phone numbers, addresses, and so forth. We've checked these facts as close to the book's publication date as possible, but businesses do change hands and change policies. It's always a good idea to call ahead — a long-distance call is a whole lot cheaper than a tank of gas.

For the same reason, you won't find specific prices listed for restaurants, lodgings, greens fees, and so forth; we indicated a range of prices, which you'll find at the beginnings of the chapters or directly under the specific heading. Lodging prices are based on a per-room rate, double occupancy, during the high season, so that we had a consistent standard for comparison; off-season and mid-week rates are generally cheaper. Restaurant-price ratings show the cost of one meal including appetizer, entree, and dessert, but not cocktails, wine, tax, or tip.

**Price Codes**

|  | *Lodging* | *Dining* |
|---|---|---|
| Very Inexpensive | Under $35 | Under $10 |
| Inexpensive | $35 to $65 | Under $15 |
| Moderate | $65 to $95 | $15 to $20 |
| Expensive | $95 to $130 | $20 to $30 |
| Very Expensive | Over $130 | Over $30 |

Credit cards are abbreviated as follows:

AE: American Express

CB: Carte Blanche

D: Discover Card

DC: Diner's Club

MC: Master Card

V: Visa

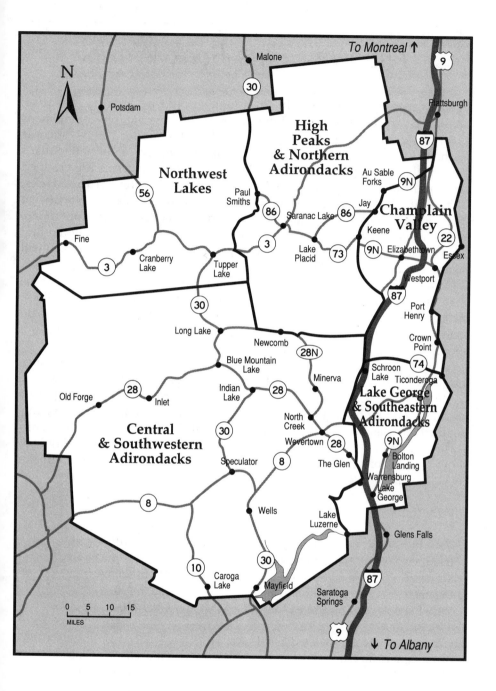

# The
# ADIRONDACK
# Book
*A Complete Guide*

# CHAPTER ONE

# *The People's Park*

## HISTORY

**A**gainst the majestic backdrop of deep forests, brooding mountains, and crystal clear lakes, explorers, patriots, fortune hunters, dreamers, and schemers all tried to shape the Adirondacks into something that could be managed and subdued, but the wilderness resolutely resisted their attempts. As small settlements flourished in the Northeast and great cities

"Mount Haystack," from the *Seventh Report of the Adirondack Survey*, 1880

*New York State Surveyor Verplanck Colvin and his crew explored the unmapped Adirondack wilds from 1872 to 1900.*

grew along the coast, this region remained a blank spot on the map. Along Lake Champlain's western shore, military outposts and clusters of homes were built in the mid-18th century, but only a few trappers, scouts, hunters, and surveyors penetrated the woods and waters beyond the lake's gentle valley. Slightly more than two centuries ago, when New York City was the political and commercial center of our new nation, mapmaker Thomas Pownall labeled the state's upper corner as "the Dismal Wilderness," and in 1784 fretted, "It is said to be a broken, unpracticable tract. I own I could never learn any thing about it."

Within a hundred years, how much all that changed. By 1884, there were thriving towns, a network of roads, railroads, and steamers, and a tourism business that rivaled that of any Gilded Age destination. Numerous guidebooks and publications trumpeted the scenic beauty and fine acccommodations to be found in the Adirondacks. The region's rare beauty, so close to the urban centers, stirred new ideas of conservation and preservation: a *New York Times* editorial suggested that "Within an easy day's ride of our great city ... is a tract of country fitted to make a Central Park for the world"; another writer said, "Had I my way, I would mark out a circle of a hundred miles in diameter and throw around it the protecting aegis of the constitution. I would make it a forest forever." At the same time, the vast natural resources — timber, minerals, and waterpower — led to bursts of activity and economic boom. How humans first came into the country and made their own discoveries about this place is best understood in the context of the region's natural history, so we'll begin our own exploration there, with the very roots of these mountains.

## NATURAL HISTORY

A common misperception about the Adirondacks is that they're part of the Appalachian Mountain range. In fact, the Adirondacks are the only eastern mountains that are not Appalachian. They're of a completely different geologic family, twice as old as the Appalachians and more resistant to the forces that perpetually wear mountains down.

### THE ADIRONDACK DOME

The Adirondacks are a southern appendix of the great Canadian Shield, a vast complex of billion-year-old Precambrian igneous and metamorphic rock shaped like a knight's shield that is the nucleus of the North American continent. While most of it underlies Canada, a portion dives under the St. Lawrence River in the vicinity of Alexandria Bay, New York, where it becomes visible as the Thousand Islands, and surfaces as a dome-shaped uplift, the Adirondacks.

Today, this dome lies generally between 1000 and 2000 feet above sea level, with higher mountain peaks, while the surrounding valleys (Champlain on the east, Mohawk River on the south, Black River on the west, and St. Lawrence on the north) range from less than 100 to more than 500 feet above sea level. While the slope of the dome is quite gradual from most directions, the eastern elevation change from Lake Champlain (95 feet above sea level) to the summit of Mt. Marcy (5,344 feet) occurs more abruptly, in about 25 air miles.

The dome gives rise to dozens of rivers — 6000 miles of them — which

---

#### *"Where Are the Mountains??"*

Many people think the whole Adirondack region is mountainous. Not exactly true, as you'll discover if you enter from anywhere except the east. Only about a quarter of the 6.1-million-acre Adirondack Park is what most of us, by Eastern standards, would consider mountainous. That's the northeast sector, the area around Lake Placid and home of the High Peaks — the highest, Mt. Marcy; the most famous, Whiteface (fifth highest, not first as some people think); and other 4000-footers such as Gothics, Giant-of-the-Valley, Skylight, Haystack, and so on. The rest of the park is mostly rolling upland forest, with collections of lower peaks (around Lake George and in ridges from Indian Lake to Old Forge, for example) and several isolated summits such as Crane Mt. in the south, the Jay Range in the east, and Azure Mt. in the north.

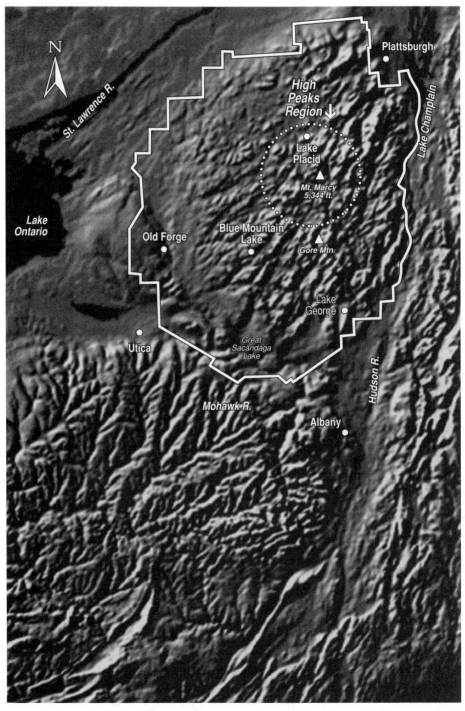

TOPOGRAPHY OF THE ADIRONDACKS

more or less radiate out from its center like spokes on a wheel. The Hudson, whose highest source is the lyrically named Lake Tear of the Clouds, on the upper slopes of Mt. Marcy, flows southeast before turning due south as it leaves the Adirondack Park. The Raquette (French for "snowshoe") begins virtually dead center in the park at Blue Mountain Lake, only a couple of miles

Nancie Battaglia

*The rounded mountains near Marcy Dam show the effects of the glaciers of 10,000 years ago.*

from a tributary of the Hudson, and drains much of the northwest Adirondacks into the St. Lawrence River. Not too far away the Saranac and Ausable rivers start their tumble through the northeast quarter. The Sacandaga flows to the south; the West Canada, Moose, Independence, and Beaver drain the southwest and west. Around the clock from about 10 a.m. (northwest) to 2 p.m. (northeast) are the Oswegatchie, Grass, St. Regis, Salmon, Chateaugay, and Chazy.

The Adirondack dome continues to rebound from the weight of glaciers, at the rate of a few centimeters a century. This upward thrusting has eroded the younger rock cover and exposed the ancient bedrock, which is among the oldest exposed bedrock in the world. Part of the bedrock is composed of anorthosite, a rare feldspar nearly identical to some of the rocks brought back from the moon; it has a bluish cast that you can pick out in some highway rock cuts.

In contrast to the ancient skeleton of the region, the face of the Adirondacks you see today is remarkably young by geologic standards, having been most recently carved and sculpted by glaciers only about 10,000 years ago. The southwest-to-northeast trend of many rivers and lakes is the result of this latest glacial action, as are such features as the shapes of the mountains and the locations of ponds. You may spot eskers — tall, narrow, sandy ridges created when meltwater tunneling beneath the glaciers left sediment in its wake.

From the roads and trails you can also see immense boulders that appear to have been plopped down where they sit. In fact, that's just how these "erratics" got there, carried by the glaciers and left behind when the glaciers receded. They're completely unrelated to the rock upon which they repose, and they'll likely stay where they are until the next glacier comes along.

## FLORA AND FAUNA

The Adirondacks straddle the border between the northern, largely coniferous boreal forest (from Boreas, the Greek god of the north wind) and the midcontinental mixed forest. Dominant tree species of the boreal forest are spruces and firs, while the mixed forest is characterized by deciduous maples, beeches, ashes, birches, and coniferous pines. Along the frontier between these forest types their representative species mingle, presenting an ecologically complex and visually pleasing mix. In the Adirondacks, you can find within a few miles of each other oak groves suggestive of the southern states and bogs typical of northern Canada. Adirondack slopes in autumn are decorated not only by the brilliant reds, oranges, and yellows of the maple and beech woods but also by the deep, rich, everlasting greens of the conifers.

You can cross ecological zones by gaining elevation, also; a rise of 1000 feet in altitude is equivalent to driving about 300 miles north. A drive up the Whiteface Memorial Highway or a hike to the top of a comparably high peak will carry you through vegetation bands until at the summit you would find yourself above tree line in an arctic zone inhabited only by mosses, lichens, and tundra-hardy plants.

Wildlife is abundant in most of the Adirondacks, ranging from that ubiquitous picnic interloper, the chipmunk, to the reclusive moose, which has reintroduced itself into the region slowly over the last few years. Among the larger animals, you're most likely to see the prolific whitetail deer, all too frequently in the middle of the road directly ahead of you. Black bears have learned where humans camp, and often rummage for food near campsites and dumps. (While generally harmless, they are wild animals and should not be

*A few dozen bull moose have moved back to the Adirondacks in recent years; some are being monitored with radio collars.*

Nancie Battaglia

approached.) Species such as the mountain lion and wolf were hunted out of the region in the 1800s; some environmentalists would like to see them reintroduced, as has happened, with some apparent success, with the lynx. The opportunistic coyote has filled the niche vacated by the wolf; you may hear its call some night.

Of more concern to you will be considerably smaller beasts, particularly blackflies and no-see-ums, that appear as if on cue on the second warm day of early summer and can make pests of themselves until around the first of August. The secret is to keep moving, stay where there's a breeze, pursue indoor activities, or muster your resolve to stoically ignore the creatures. Many repellents make extravagant claims about shielding you against bug bites of all kinds; the active ingredients of these elixers range from pleasant-smelling pennyroyal oil to DEET. Although it's possible to get "jungle formula" repellents with a high concentration of that chemical compound, it's best to avoid those with more than 30% DEET.

Loons, revered for their haunting songs, inhabit many Adirondack lakes and ponds. With luck you may see an osprey, peregrine falcon, or bald eagle soaring on warm air currents over a lakeshore or cliff. Hawks are fairly easy to spot, and varieties of ducks too numerous to list populate the waterways of the park.

Fishing used to be not just popular but downright famous in the Adirondacks, but overfishing and acid-rain pollution have dramatically diminished the size and number of fish in recent years in formerly productive lakes and rivers. However, sportsmen (and women) still find brook, brown, and rainbow trout; landlocked salmon; walleye and northern pike; and large- and smallmouth bass. In many areas, aggressive scientific stocking programs by the Department of Environmental Conservation have helped bring back sportfishing; research continues in park ponds and streams on how best to cope with acid precipitation.

While most of the Adirondacks do not harbor snakes of any number or consequence, Tongue Mountain, overlooking Lake George, shelters colonies of Eastern timber rattlesnake. While they should be treated with respect, they should not be a compelling reason to avoid this area with its excellent hiking and marvelous views. Take proper precautions (wear sturdy boots and long pants and stay on the trails), and remember that the mountain is their home and you're the intruder.

## SOCIAL HISTORY

### HUNTERS, EXPLORERS, TRADERS, AND SETTLERS

Adirondack wildlife, notably deer, attracts hunters by the thousands each fall, and animals were what attracted the first humans to the region, so far as we know. Conventional wisdom holds that no native Americans lived year-round in the Adirondacks; being agricultural peoples, they apparently avoided these mountains and forests except to hunt or fish or gather special plants such as medicinal herbs, sweetgrass, bark and roots for baskets and boats, and berries of all kinds.

---

*A Little Traveling Etymology*

Where did the name come from? Most people think "Adirondacks" is a corruption of an Iroquois word for their enemies the Algonquins, whom they called "rat-i-ron-tacks" or "eaters of bark" in derisive reference to the Algonquins' supposed inability to farm well. This, of course, has never been proven, and some native Americans of this writer's acquaintance dismiss it as white man's fantasy. The word was first applied by a surveyor, Ebenezer Emmons, in 1837.

Adirondack or Adirondacks — singular or plural? Depends if you're talking about the region (singular) or the mountains in it (plural), which are interchangeable in many people's minds. But "Adirondacks is..." sounds strange, so most people use the plural most of the time.

---

The native Americans who penetrated the region were enemies (the Iroquois from the south and the Hurons and Algonquins from the north), and they fought at any chance encounter. Arrowheads and other artifacts from the scenes of their battles, and from their campsites along the rivers, are the principal record of their presence in the region. Their legacy resides mostly in names, such as Oswegatchie (a long river in the northwestern Adirondacks, meaning "black water" or "'orse, we got ye," attributable to some settlers whose horse had unsuccessfully tried to escape, if you prefer tall tales); Couchsachraga, which roughly means "dismal wilderness" (the 18th-century mapmaker mentioned at the beginning of this chapter was not alone in his assessment); and Ticonderoga, supposedly "the place where waters sing as they swiftly cascade over the rocks into the lake." One should be careful of these names, though; the supposed "Indian" name for Mt. Marcy, Tahawus ("cloud-splitter"), was purportedly invented by a disgruntled New York City newspaperman shortly after the peak was named for a governor of the state.

Dominating the view from the junction of Adirondak Loj Road and Rte. 73 between Keene and Lake Placid is Algonquin Peak, second highest in the Adirondacks; just beyond it to the south and hidden from view is Boundary Peak, and south of that, barely visible over a shoulder of Algonquin, is Iroquois Peak. Perhaps apocryphal, the story is that the two nations named the two prominent summits as "border monuments" to their parts of the Adirondacks, the Algonquins in the north and the Iroquois in the south, with the lesser mountain between them marking the actual boundary.

Nicaolo Visscher's 1685 map of "New Belgium" shows northern New York as a land of bumpy mountains and large beavers; present-day Lake Champlain is called "Lacus Irocoisi."

To the best of our knowledge, the first European to see the Adirondacks was Jacques Cartier, who in 1535 climbed what later was named Mont Royal, now in the heart of Montreal in the Canadian province of Quebec, and noted in his journal that he could discern "hilles to the south." (You can do this yourself, although you may have to peer around buildings and through urban smog.) It took 74 years for another European to see the Adirondacks. In 1609 Samuel de Champlain, another French explorer, journeyed south from Canada up the lake that he named for himself (south is upstream on Lake Champlain, to the distress of those who believe water must flow down a map) and reported on the marvelous rocky scenery spilling at times directly into the lake.

Near Ticonderoga, Champlain and his Huron guides came upon a party of Iroquois. A battle ensued; Champlain, armed with an arquebus, killed several warriors and vanquished the astonished Iroquois. They never forgave the French for violating a cardinal rule of Eastern-woodland native American warfare (don't use a weapon your opponent doesn't know about), and sided with the British against the French in later contests for control of North America.

It's possible that a third European explorer, Henry Hudson, spied the Adirondack foothills on the northern horizon from the future site of Albany in that same year of 1609. Whether he did or not, for the next century and a half the Adirondacks went virtually ignored while the perimeter valleys filled slowly with settlers, and wars came and went. Lying north of the Mohawk Valley, which was the most northerly travel route to the interior of the continent, the mountains were largely bypassed by the westering pioneers. Those few who did penetrate the interior were interested not in settling but in extracting resources: beaver for fur and white pines for ship's masts.

---

### What's The Adirondacks?

What do we mean when we say "the Adirondacks"? Some possibilities:

• **The Adirondack Park.** Established in 1892, it covers 6.1 million acres of public and private land in a polygonal configuration occupying much of the northern third of New York State. It's the largest state park in the nation, larger even than our smallest states. Its boundary is known as the Blue Line because it was first drawn on a state map with a blue pencil. It's not all wilderness; everything within, from the summits of the highest peaks to the most remote bog to Main Street in Lake Placid, is in the park. It will probably show up as a great green lumpy circle on your road map.

• **The Adirondack Forest Preserve.** Established in 1885, this is now the 42% of the Adirondack Park that is public land and preserved as wilderness. It's many scattered parcels of land, not one contiguous unit, and it won't appear at all on your road map. In a nutshell, if you're on Forest Preserve land you're free to hike, hunt, fish, canoe, and do whatever else you want, although some parts are off-limits to motorized vehicles (e.g. snowmobiles and motorboats); if you're not on public land, you're trespassing on somebody's property, unless you have permission to be there. Odd as it may seem to come across private land inside a state park, please respect it. If you want to go for a walk in the woods, look for trailheads with state Department of Environmental Conservation signs; they are on public land.

• **The Adirondack Mountains.** For the most part they occupy the northeast quarter of the Adirondack Park. Not all of them are on public land. Forty-plus are more than 4000 feet above sea level, although this number changes each time some of the borderline summits get remeasured.

• **And ...** There's a town called Adirondack near Schroon Lake. There's a Loj called Adirondak (the spellings attributable to Melvil Dewey, champion of simplified spelling, who owned the site in the 19th century) near Lake Placid. And there's a magazine called *Adirondac* — no one knows why it's spelled like that, although a long-since-abandoned mining town near Mt. Marcy was so spelled. There's a different magazine called *Adirondack Life*, and these are the two best magazines specific to the region.

In fact, these white pines helped spur the Americans to win their independence. After the British drove the French forever into Quebec in 1759, the Crown sent timber cruisers into the Adirondack forests to mark the tallest and straightest white pines. These were to be used for British naval and commercial ships' masts, and the colonists were not to touch them. That the colonists not only could not harvest these giants but also had to stand by and watch while they were taken, perhaps to be turned against them in naval battles, was more than they could accept. The "king's trees" became a rallying point for the region's freedom fighters.

Although little Adirondack land was known in the late 18th century, most of it was owned. First the British and then the American government, short of cash, used this "waste and unappropriated" real estate as payment to soldiers, the idea being that the soldiers would either settle it or sell it. Few settled here; most sold their holdings to other nonresidents or speculators. In one such transaction, in 1771, two ship's carpenters named Totten and Crossfield, acting as front men for a coalition of financiers, came into possession of nearly a million acres in what is now the middle of the Adirondack Park. The tract was never properly surveyed, and even now the "Totten and Crossfield Purchase" confounds assessors and real estate agents.

Emblematic of the problems faced by those who did try to civilize their holdings is the case of John Brown (not the abolitionist; he comes later), who in 1798 came into possession of some 200,000 acres of wilderness west of Old Forge. He and his family struggled for years. Farming proved futile against a cold climate and soil whose most reliable issue was rocks. Lumbering didn't pan out; it was too far to markets and roads were abysmal. Iron ore was discovered and a forge built, but that enterprise also failed. Later, one of Brown's sons-in-law, Charles Frederick Herreshoff, attempted to revitalize the "old forge," but after a series of setbacks put a bullet through his brain before the year 1819 ended. He had told his family he would settle the land or it would settle him.

## ONCE MORE A'LUMBERING GO

It was the forest itself, at first a hindrance to settlement, that finally brought human progress into the Adirondacks. As the nation's demand for wood grew in the early 1800s, loggers advanced farther into the region. Little explored in 1830 (the source of the Nile River was discovered before the Hudson's, and Pike's Peak was climbed before Mt. Marcy), by 1850 the Adirondacks made New York the leading lumber-producing state in the nation. Lumber barons sought the white pine for its strength and straight grain, and were so successful at finding it that today only a few isolated tracts retain giant "virgin" white pines. Hemlocks were stripped of their bark for its tannin, critical in the leather tanning industry, and the logs were left behind in the forest to rot. When in 1867 it was discovered that spruce made the best pulp for paper, that species was doomed to the ax and saw.

*Lumberjacks pose for Seneca Ray Stoddard's camera, 1888.*

Courtesy Adirondack Museum, Blue Mountain Lake, NY

Customarily, logs were lashed together to form rafts and floated to markets, but Adirondackers discovered you could simply push the logs into the rivers, particularly at "ice out" in the spring, and let the current carry them to mills. Thus was the river drive born in 1813. For the rest of the 19th century, and into the 20th, Adirondack rivers — declared public highways for the purpose — were choked with tumbling logs every spring. The drives gave rise to a romantic chapter in American folklore, replete with songs and stories of drama, danger, and death in the icy rushing waters.

Later, railroads penetrated even the most remote parts of the wilderness to haul out logs year-round. Tupper Lake, a hub of logging activity in the northern Adirondacks, also became a major railroad center, with main lines extending in several directions and branches reaching out from them like tentacles.

Not surprisingly, the harvest of timber was so successful in that pre-conservation era that by 1910 the Adirondack forest was almost a memory. Mile after mile of woodland lay in waste, clearcut and buried in brush. Slopes denuded of vegetation were washed away by rain. Railroad locomotives started conflagrations when sparks from their smokestacks landed on the dead slash left behind by "cut and run" loggers.

Adirondack visitors now see mile after mile of mature mixed hardwood forests with very little evidence of this wholesale cutting. How the woods recovered is part of a later story of enlightened ideas of forest management. Today, the forest-products industry ranks second behind tourism as an economic force in the Adirondacks. Furniture, pallets, and the famous Adirondack baseball bats, as well as raw lumber and pulp for paper, are among the products of this enterprise.

### Presidents in Residence

Although we can't claim that George Washington slept here, the father of our country was certainly aware of the vital importance of fortifications at Ticonderoga and Crown Point along Lake Champlain's western shore. **Thomas Jefferson** and **James Madison** visited Lake George in 1791, on a summer reconnoiter to Vermont that doubled as a vacation; Jefferson, a seasoned world traveler, described the lake as one of the most beautiful he'd ever seen.

In 1817, **James Monroe** skirted the wild edge of what would become the Adirondack Park in a trip from Champlain to Sackets Harbor, on the St. Lawrence River. **Andrew Jackson**, a.k.a. "Old Hickory," was a close friend of Richard Keese II, after whom the village of Keeseville is named. Jackson went north to see Keese, and in honor of the occasion, a hickory sapling was sought to plant in the front yard of the homestead. But no hickories could be found for miles around, so a bitter walnut was substituted. It thrived.

**Chester A. Arthur** stayed at Mart Moody's Mount Morris House, near Tupper Lake, in 1869, and slept on the floor like everyone else. When he was president, in 1881, Arthur named the guide and innkeeper postmaster of a new settlement named — surprisingly enough — Moody.

**Grover Cleveland** also knew Moody as a guide. While hunting near Big Wolf Pond, Cleveland reportedly said to him, "There's no wolves here, darn it! But — there ain't a hundred pencils here, either, goin' every minute to take down everything I say." The president returned to the Adirondacks for his honeymoon, and also stayed at posh places like the Grand View, in Lake Placid, and Saranac Inn.

President **Benjamin Harrison** visited his vice-presidential candidate Whitelaw Reid at Loon Lake during the 1892 campaign, and he whistle-stopped in Crown Point, Lyon Mountain, Bloomingdale, and Saranac Lake. Along the way, he was feted with band concerts and pageants, and given gifts of iron ore and wildflower arrangements. In 1895, Harrison built a rustic log camp named Berkeley Lodge on Second Lake, near Old Forge.

**William McKinley** made a special trip here to John Brown's grave in 1897, but it was his assassination that led to one of the most exciting footnotes in Adirondack history. **Theodore Roosevelt**, who first came to the mountains as a teenager in 1871, was climbing Mount Marcy when news of McKinley's imminent demise was cabled north. A guide scrambled up the peak to tell T.R., who made it down in record time. Three relays of teams and wagons whisked him from the Tahawus Club to North Creek, and Roosevelt was sworn in as the 26th president on September 14, 1901, in the North Creek railroad station.

**Calvin Coolidge** established a summer White House at White Pine Camp, on Osgood Pond in 1926. This was at the height of Prohibition; silent Cal's place was a mere stone's throw away from Gabriels, a hotbed of bootleg activity. He never knew.

**Franklin D. Roosevelt** was no stranger to the North Country. He officiated at the opening of the 1932 Winter Olympics, dedicated the Whiteface Memorial Highway in 1935, and celebrated the fiftieth anniversary of the Forest Preserve in Lake Placid that same year.

## DAYS OF ORE

**M**eanwhile, although it never achieved the stature of lumbering, mining was another important element in the 19th-century opening of the Adirondacks. Iron was always a temptress in the Adirondacks — it was there, sometimes in abundance, but hard to get at, hard to transport, and full of an impurity that rendered it costly to process. Mining operations sprang up near Port Henry, Crown Point, Chateaugay Lake, Lake Placid, Star Lake, and Lyon Mountain. All of these have since ceased, in some cases leaving behind struggling "company towns."

Yet another operation's misfortunes seemed to prophesy the fate of the entire mining industry in the Adirondacks. Iron ore was discovered near Sanford Lake in 1826, and for decades the operators fought against bad roads, lack of water (necessary in the ore-separation process), too much water in the form of floods, economic ups and downs, the accidental shooting death of one of the principals at a spot ever since called Calamity Pond, and most of all, that maddening impurity.

Ironically, that impurity turned out to be ilmenite, the ore of titanium, and when this was discovered to have applications in the paint and aerospace industries the mine flourished for a period in the mid-20th century. Iron was then the unwanted intruder. In the face of declining markets and competition from abroad, the mine shut down in 1989. The story is not all bad for mining, though: garnet near North Creek, zinc and talc in the northwest, and wollastonite near Willsboro have been profitably extracted in recent years. Mining is for the most part a minor player in the Adirondack economic picture, though.

## ADVENTURES IN THE WILDERNESS: THE RECREATION INDUSTRY

**B**y far the major player in Adirondack economics is, as it has been for more than a century and probably will be for the foreseeable future, tourism. This industry came about as the result of a fortuitous combination of a number of factors: a changing attitude toward wilderness, more affluence, and the increasing acceptability of leisure activities in the middle decades of the 19th century.

Early in the century, as had been true for most of human history, wilderness was seen as a thing to be subdued, an enemy of progress, the abode of darkness and evil. Europeans brought this notion to the New World with them; it justified the conquering of the wilderness, along with its animal and human inhabitants. But by the 1840s, as the frontier was pushed farther from most people's consciousness, and life became more than a struggle to stay alive, Americans — particularly Easterners — became less antagonistic toward wild nature. Indeed, as conditions in the cities worsened folks became nostalgic for a simpler, cleaner time.

Simultaneously, the philosophical movement called Transcendentalism took

*A pre-Civil War Adirondack hunting party brought along all the comforts of home in "A Good Time Coming," by the English artist A.F. Tait.*

hold of a small but significant portion of the population. One of its principal tenets was that nature, especially wild nature, is the source of spiritual, emotional, and even physical well-being. Leading lights of Transcendentalism such as Thoreau and Emerson glorified nature; Emerson, Louis Agassiz, James Russell Lowell, and several others spent part of the summer of 1858 in the Adirondacks, in an idyllic setting later dubbed "The Philosophers' Camp," and Emerson's poem "The Adirondacs" was one of the most popular pieces of writing during its time. Meanwhile, artists such as Charles Ingham, Thomas Cole, and A.F. Tait brought visual images of the Adirondacks to the public.

The economic boom in the North during and after the Civil War provided expendable cash for such pursuits as vacations, and as the Puritan work ethic was tempered over time the idea of relaxation became socially acceptable. It remained only for someone to suggest that people visit the Adirondacks.

That someone was a Boston minister, William H.H. Murray, who in 1869 published *Adventures in the Wilderness*, a boldly embellished account of his experiences camping, fishing, and boating in the Adirondacks. Although not the first to extoll the virtues of such an outing, this book was a hit, the rush was on, and, for better or worse, the region was forever changed. An entire industry was born, spawning rustic inns with guides who took the "city sports" hunting and fishing, then more and more lavish hotels and better transportation.

The 1870s through 1910 have been called the Gilded Years of the vacation business in the Adirondacks. Hotels rivaled those in major cities for their opulence; the first one in the world to have electricity throughout was the Prospect House, overlooking Blue Mountain Lake. (It also had a two-story outhouse, which we'll leave to your imagination.) Along Lake George, Lake Placid, the Saranacs, and into the interior, the fashionable summer scene was on a par with Newport or Saratoga, although here the emphasis was not on sailing or spas, but the great outdoors. Men hunted, fished, told lies, and smoked cigars; ladies took to the woods and waters shaded by parasols, gloves, hats, and veils. For some women, that backwoods experience translated into a quiet cruise across a peaceful pond with a patient guide pulling at the oars, but for the more adventuresome, tramping on the trails was perfect sport.

Charles Hallock, a travel writer for *Harper's, Forest and Stream,* and other publications, captured all the hustle and bustle at Paul Smith's Hotel in the 1870s: "Great is the stir at these caravanseries on the long summer evenings — ribbons fluttering on the piazzas; silks rustling in dress promenade; ladies in short mountain suits, fresh from an afternoon picnic; embryo sportsmen in velveteen and courduroys of approved cut; descanting learnedly of backwoods experience; excursion parties returning, laden with trophies of trout and pond lilies; stages arriving top-heavy with trunks, rifle-cases, and hampers.... After dinner there is a generous flow of champagne to a selected few ... and the exploits of the day are recounted and compared. The parlors grow noisy with music and dancing; silence and smoke prevail in the cardroom."

Families came for the entire summer, bringing trunkfuls of fine china and

*Blue Mountain Lake's Prospect House, built in 1881, was the first hotel in the world with electric lights; Thomas Edison himself designed the twin dynamos that powered the building.*

*Steamboats cruised the length of Lake George between towns and resorts.*

From *The Northern Tourist*, 1882

linen as well as household servants; some stayed in their own "camps," actually veritable villages of well-appointed buildings along a remote lake. US presidents relaxed in the region. Most people came and went via luxurious overnight trains from New York and Boston. Steamboats plied Adirondack lakes, making regular stops at the lodges on their shores.

*Decorative touches in an Adirondack Great Camp often included everything from twig-mosaic tables to Japanese lanterns and parasols, as this 1880 interior view of Camp Cedars shows.*

Courtesy Adirondack Museum, Blue Mountain Lake, NY

## THE ADIRONDACK CURE

Others came to the Adirondacks not for fun, but literally to save their lives. Thanks to the pioneering work of Dr. Edward Livingston Trudeau, the Adirondacks became a mecca for tuberculosis sufferers. Trudeau, himself a victim of the disease, believed the best treatment was rest and clean air. "Sanitaria" in the Saranac Lake area were the destination of thousands of people from the 1880s to the 1950s. Robert Louis Stevenson, Philippines president Manual Quezon, baseball great Christy Mathewson, gangster "Legs" Diamond (who brought his bodyguards), Bela Bartok, and Mrs. Fiorello

LaGuardia were among those who came to "take the cure." By the mid-20th century, "miracle drugs" made treatment at home easier, but medical research remains a significant part of Saranac Lake's Trudeau Institute in the 1990s.

*An idyllic vista of Lake George, looking toward Long Island.*

From *The Northern Tourist*, 1882

## THE CONSERVATION MOVEMENT

Whether seeking game, a sunny hotel verandah, or a sanitarium, these people came to the Adirondacks not to see burned-over wastelands of clearcut forests, but green and healthy woods. They began to clamor for some sort of protection for the Adirondack wilderness.

Indeed, such a movement had begun almost simultaneously with the beginnings of the recreation industry. Conservation was alien to most Americans, living in the midst of such superabundance, but in Europe, where a denser population had put more pressure on fewer resources for much longer, conservation had become a necessity. A bookish Vermont lawyer named George Perkins Marsh, U.S. ambassador to Italy, saw what steps the Italians had taken to preserve forest lands, and what value they had for an America fast churning its way through its natural resources. In 1864 he published *Man and Nature*, a daunting tome that is credited as the first salvo of the American conservation movement. In it he suggested that Americans adopt European conservation practices, such as forest management, and that the Adirondacks would be a good place to start.

*Happy campers, 1890s-style.*

Stanley Harris

*A little snow never deterred surveyor Verplanck Colvin (left) and his assistant, Mills Blake, from measuring mountains and charting unknown waters.*

Even earlier than that, a few voices had called for some action to stem the destruction of the forests. But Marsh's book provided a practical reason to do so: healthy forests, he said, retained rainfall, regulating its runoff into streams and rivers that supplied "Downstate" with water. "Downstate" meant not only New York's cities, but also its commercial lifeline, the Erie Canal. Suddenly the state's powerful business community had a reason for conservation.

Marsh's call was taken up by many, none more eloquently than Verplanck Colvin, who from 1872 until 1900 took it upon himself, with the irregular support of the state, to survey the entire Adirondack region. In annual reports to the state legislature he argued passionately for creation of some sort of "park or preserve" to save the forests for watersheds and, almost as an off-the-cuff aside, recreation. Eventually, he got both, plus a little more:

• In 1885, the state established in the core of the region the Adirondack Forest Preserve to protect the supply of water to cities and the Erie Canal.

• In 1892, in large part because of continuing abuses of the Forest Preserve by logging interests, the state provided a second layer of armor, the Adirondack Park, which encompassed the Forest Preserve and thousands of acres of private lands ringing it. Thus the park consisted of a mix of public and private lands, an unusual situation that continues to this day, causing countless management headaches.

• In 1894, because abuses still had not ceased, the legistature allowed the voters of New York to amend their constitution to dictate that the Forest Preserve should remain "forever wild." In other words, there would be not conservation but *preservation* in the Forest Preserve. The woods would not be managed; they would be left to nature. Nowhere else in the world does wilderness have such a triple-ply sheath of protection.

## THE ADIRONDACKS IN THE 20TH CENTURY

After the excitement of the 1880s and 1890s, the Adirondacks went into relative dormancy for the first few decades of the 20th century. Ironically, in the years immediately after protective steps were implemented, rampaging fires destroyed much of whatever forest the loggers had left. (The careful observer can still find scars from these fires, although the forests have largely recovered.) Reforestation and other elements of scientific forestry gradually caught on.

Tourism grew steadily, particularly after World War I, as other industries receded. Although towns such as Saranac Lake and Lake Placid celebrated the coming of cold weather in carnivals replete with ice palaces, parades, and innumerable sporting competitions, it was Melvil Dewey's Lake Placid Club that launched winter as a time for tourism, too. The club's full roster of organized programs, from toboganning and skating to skiing and sleigh riding, packed visitors' days and nights with action that anyone — athlete or not — could enjoy. The 1932 Winter Olympics in Lake Placid, in which Sonia Henie once again took the gold for figure skating, and the Americans triumphed in bobsledding — also put the Adirondacks on the map for skiers.

More and more people came to camp, hike, and climb the mountains, departing from the more sedate vacationing style of the late 1800s. The state responded by building campgrounds on principal highways, along with wilderness trails with three-sided log shelters called lean-tos. The Adirondack Mountain Club was formed by outdoor enthusiasts in 1922. In the booming 1950s and '60s, the notion of vacation homes came into vogue, and the

*Songstress and part-time Adirondacker Kate Smith joined with other Lake Placid Club skiers for a snapshot.*

Irving Steadman

Adirondacks, within a day's drive of millions of urbanites and suburbanites, was a choice location.

However, by the late 1960s, overconsumption, this time by vacationers, was as real a concern as overconsumption by loggers had been 80 years earlier. Completion of Interstate 87, the Adirondack Northway, in 1967, promised only to exacerbate the problem.

Since then, Adirondack history has been dominated by a debate, sometimes heated, over how the region should be managed to serve the best interests of residents, visitors, and the environment. In broadest terms, those concerned most about the future of the Adirondack ecosystem have promoted levels of controls on growth by various government agencies, and have supported additional wild-land purchases by the state, while advocates of free-market economic growth and "home rule" have fought such proposals.

The proliferation of vacation homes prompted conservationist Laurance Rockefeller to propose a national park in the Adirondacks in 1967. That unpopular idea went nowhere, but it did spur his brother, Governor Nelson Rockefeller, to appoint a state commission to study the region's future. Among the commission's proposals for better management released in 1970 was an Adirondack Park Agency (APA) to regulate land use by zoning all land in the park.

When the APA brought out its plan for zoning on state land, which included such steps as banning motorized vehicles in wilderness areas, there was an outburst of protest. A state agency, it was argued, should not tell people what they could and could not do on public property. But when in 1973 the APA issued its plan for restrictions on the use of *private* land, the outburst became an eruption. This time, the state was telling people what they could and could not do with their own land. Much of this control was vested in zoning laws that regulate the density of buildings per square mile; in some areas, which are designated as "resource management" lands, 42 acres are required for each principal dwelling. Other regulations include building setbacks from shorelines and permitted economic activities within different zoning areas. Towns were encouraged to draft their own local zoning ordinances, but very few actually did, due to lack of funds to prepare the plans.

The existence of the APA, and more abstractly its role as guardian of the character of the Adirondacks — a definition of which there is no agreement — has colored all subsequent discussions about what to do with the region. Some argue that development can, and should, increase to bolster local business, while others counter that the area's natural assets should not be sacrificed for short-term gain.

As the disagreement over the fundamentals of managing the Adirondack Park has waxed and waned, one thing has remained constant: the undeniable beauty of the landscape. Behind all that wrangling that stays a basic truth, and something that folks on all sides of the issue can agree on.

In 1992, the centennial year of the Adirondack Park, there's much to discover and appreciate about this special place, regardless of the bugs, rain, ice, snow, and political discussions you may encounter. Read on; if you don't already, perhaps you'll learn to love the Adirondacks, too. Not just in summer, or when the leaves blaze away on the hillsides, but during mud season, blackfly hatches, and when the cold winds blow off Whiteface. If this were an easy place to love, well, it just wouldn't be the Adirondacks.

Nancie Battaglia

*A view from the air on a frosty morning, with Whiteface Mountain in the background.*

# CHAPTER TWO

## *Over the Rivers and Through the Woods*

# TRANSPORTATION

The rivers were the first travel corridors in the Adirondacks. By canoe or by snowshoe over the ice, native Americans and the first Europeans followed these paths of least resistance. Although no river provided passage through the entire immense and rugged region, it was possible to travel from the southwest to northeast corners via the Moose, Raquette, and Saranac river systems with but a few short "carries," the Adirondack word for "portage." The importance of the rivers is underscored by the fact that in the early 1800s they were declared public highways for the purpose of floating logs to market on them.

Courtesy Natalie and Maude Bryt

*Arriving in style at the Fort William Henry Hotel, Lake George, 1885.*

The first roads were literally hacked out of the forest in the early 1800s, usually to get at iron ore. Later, some of these dirt tracks were corduroyed (paved with logs), but they were never very good, being not much more than wide trails. A stagecoach ride on one could be a life-threatening experience.

Even into the beginnings of the tourist era, the waterways remained the principal routes of conveyance. Craft indigenous to the Adirondacks were designed to suit their environment: the guideboat, light, fast, and maneuverable, with oars rather than paddles, marvelous for fishing and hunting on

Adirondack ponds; and tiny steamboats, built to fit the small lakes of the interior.

The first popular overland means of movement was the railroad. Originally built to haul timber out, the railroads quickly became a profitable and convenient way to haul tourists in. In the heyday of the vacation era, a spiderweb of lines throughout the region saw several passenger trains a day speeding north from East Coast cities to destinations in the park. One of the most popular targets, Blue Mountain Lake, could be reached by a remarkable trip that involved an overnight train ride from New York via Utica, transfer to a steamboat, change to the world's shortest standard-gauge railroad (less than a mile long), and a final transfer to another steamboat for delivery to your hotel of choice.

With the growing popularity of the automobile as the 20th century progressed, roads were gradually improved until they eventually surpassed the railroads, although such special offerings as ski trains enabled passenger service to struggle along until well after World War II.

The late 1960s were a watershed time; the last passenger train serving the interior, the Adirondack Division of the New York Central (the Utica-to-Lake Placid line), rolled to a stop in 1965, and the Adirondack Northway, the only interstate highway in the region, was completed along the eastern edge of the park in 1967. This event seemed at once to assure that the family car would be the way the vast majority of people would travel to the Adirondacks for years to come, and to discourage the development of a public transportation system.

So, if you want to get around in the Adirondacks, heed this advice: buy, rent, beg, or borrow a car. Even if you get here by some other means, once you arrive it can be difficult to do much without one, and renting a car is no mean feat in most places. The region has fewer people than a few blocks in Manhattan do, yet it takes in all or part of 12 counties.Thus, public transportation comes in one of two stripes — slim and none — so be forewarned. Please also note, however, that a few of the places to stay we've reviewed in Chapter Three, *Lodging*, are accessible by public transportation; you'll find a short list of those places in the index at the back of the book.

The following information gives you the best routes for access to the Adirondacks, and for getting around once you're here. We start with the most practical means of transportation — your car — and also provide details on bus, train, and air service. Routes that incorporate a ferry crossing are also described. A selection of taxi services in principal communities is listed as well. For car rentals within the Adirondacks, we suggest you contact the chamber of commerce or visitor information center of the the area you plan to visit; you'll find phone numbers and addresses in this book's *Information* chapter under "Tourist Information."

# BY CAR

## HIGHWAYS TO GET YOU HERE

Major highways can get you to the perimeter of the Adirondack Park from all points:

• *From New York:* Take I-87 north. This is the New York State (or Thomas E. Dewey) Thruway, a toll road, to Albany (Exit 24); then it becomes the toll-free Adirondack Northway. Principal exits off the Northway for the interior are 21 (Lake George), roughly four hours from metro New York; 23 (Warrensburg), about 15 minutes farther north; 28 (Schroon Lake, Paradox Lake, and Ticonderoga), about five hours from New York; and 30 (for Lake Placid, Saranac Lake, and the High Peaks), another 15 minutes up the line.

Nancie Battaglia

*The Adirondack Northway, Interstate Route 87, allows speedy access to the eastern part of the park.*

• *From Philadelphia and South:* Good news: you can miss New York City altogether. Take the Northeast Extension of the Pennsylvania Turnpike and then I-81 north to Syracuse. From Syracuse take I-90 east to entry points such as Utica and Amsterdam, or I-81 farther north and then east on Rte. 3 at Watertown to reach the northern areas. Either way, it's not as far as you might think — you can reach the southwestern edge of the park in about six hours from Philadelphia. Or you can take I-88 from Binghamton to Schenectady, go east two exits on I-90 and head north on I-87 from Albany; see above, "From New York." And there's always the Garden State Parkway to the New York Thruway, then proceed as above.

• *From Buffalo, Cleveland, and West:* Take I-90 east to Syracuse, then proceed as directed above ("From Philadelphia"). From Buffalo to the edge of the park north of Utica is a little over four hours.

• *From Toronto and Detroit:* Take Rte. 401 toward Montreal. Three toll bridges cross the St. Lawrence River. The one that provides the most direct access not only to the edge of the park but also to such interior locations as Lake Placid and Blue Mountain Lake leaps from Prescott (Highway 16 exit) to

# ADIRONDACK ACCESS

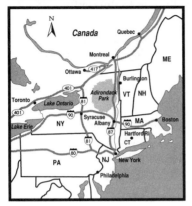

**B**lue Mountain Lake is central — it's 1-1/2 to 2 hours to the edge of the park in every direction — so this location will serve as a reference point in determining about how long a drive to the Adirondacks will take.

| CITY | MILES TO BLUE MOUNTAIN LAKE | APPROXIMATE TIME TO BLUE MOUNTAIN LAKE |
|------|------|------|
| Albany | 105 | 2 hrs |
| Binghamton | 220 | 4 hrs |
| Boston (via Albany) | 270 | 5 1/2 hrs |
| Buffalo | 280 | 5 1/2 hrs |
| Burlington, VT | 100 | 3 hrs (with ferry) |
| Montreal | 165 | 3 hrs* |
| New York | 260 | 5 1/2 hrs |
| Ottawa | 150 | 4 hrs* |
| Philadelphia | 390 | 8 hrs |
| Rochester | 210 | 4 1/2 hrs |
| Syracuse | 140 | 3 hrs |
| Toronto | 320 | 7 hrs* |
| Utica | 90 | 2 hrs |

*plus possible delays crossing border

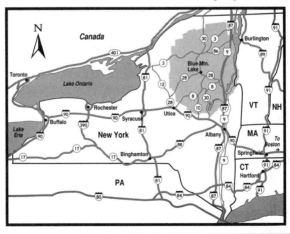

Ogdensburg; the toll is $2.00 one way. On the US side, take Rte. 37 west a couple of miles to Rte. 68 south to Colton, and Rte. 56 into the park. From Toronto it's about five hours to the edge of the park and seven to the center.

• *From Ottawa:* Take Highway 16 to the Prescott-Ogdensburg toll bridge and proceed as directed above ("From Toronto"). Allow two hours to the edge of the park, four to central points.

---

### Deer Crossing

Keep your eyes peeled for deer as you drive through the Adirondacks — not only to see them, which will be a pleasant memory of your trip, but also to avoid hitting them.

Deer are most active in the late afternoon and evening, and particularly just after sunset, when they're hardest to see. They often travel in pairs or small groups; if one crosses the road ahead of you, others are likely to follow. They're especially mobile during the fall for several reasons: that's their breeding season; they have to travel more to find food; and hunters disrupt their daily routines. In winter deer seek out plowed roads since the going is easier.

One more thing: the instinctive reaction of a deer caught by car headlights is to freeze, not to scramble out of the way. It's up to you to miss, if you have time and can do it safely. Your best bet: drive alertly, obey speed limits — and take those "DEER CROSSING, X MILES" signs seriously.

---

• *From Montreal:* Take Highway 15 south; this becomes I-87, the Adirondack Northway, at the border. Principal jumping-off exits for the interior are 38 (Plattsburgh), only an hour (plus customs wait, which can be lengthy) from the outskirts of Montreal, and 34 (Keeseville), 20 minutes south of Exit 38.

• *From Boston:* Take the Mass. Pike, I-90, to I-87, then head north and follow the directions given under "From New York," above, to get past Albany. Or, take I-93 north to I-89, to one of the Lake Champlain ferry crossings described below. Via Albany, the Adirondacks are about four hours from Boston; via the ferries they're closer to five, but the ferries are fun.

## HIGHWAYS TO GET YOU AROUND ONCE YOU GET HERE

### North and South

Not surprisingly, four of the five north-south highways that traverse the Adirondacks do so in the narrow corridor between Lake Champlain and the mountains. This is where, or close to where, much of the region's population and many of its attractions are located, and it's also on a direct line between two dense concentrations of population: New York City and Montreal. These routes are as follows:

• *NY Rte. 9N*, which makes a scenic ramble from Saratoga Springs north-west to Corinth and Lake Luzerne, then east to Lake George village, then up to Hague, and to Lake Champlain at Ticonderoga.

• *NY Rte. 22* hugs Lake Champlain all the way from Whitehall, up to Ticonderoga, where it joins 9N. The combined routes have magificent views of the lake on the east, and farmland in the valley beneath the High Peaks on the west, passing through Crown Point and Port Henry. At Westport, Rte. 22 fol-lows the shoreline north to Willsboro, while 9N heads west to Elizabethtown, over Spruce Hill and on to Keene. This historic route passes through Upper Jay, Jay, and Au Sable Forks, paralleling the Ausable River, and connects again with Rte. 22 at Keeseville. Just east of Keeseville, Rtes. 9N and 22 pass directly over Ausable Chasm, there's a parking pull-out so you can take a look down, down, down.

• *US Rte. 9* begins in the park at Warrensburg and skirts Schroon Lake and the Schroon River, but its route has been mostly supplanted by ...

• *I-87, the Adirondack Northway*, a full-blown interstate highway that won an award as "America's Most Scenic Highway" in 1966-67.

The fifth north-south route, • *NY Rte. 30*, bisects the region from Gloversville to Malone via Speculator, Indian Lake, Blue Mountain Lake, Long Lake, Tupper Lake, and Paul Smiths. It's famous for some surprising four-lanes-wide segments between Long Lake and Tupper. (Resist the temptation to speed; log trucks, deer, or a trooper may pop out of the woods at any time.) The remote and lightly populated western half of the region has no north-south highways.

### East and West

Reflecting the reality that most travel in the Adirondacks is and always has been north-south, only three highways traverse the entire region on the east-west axis, and two of them cover some of the same territory. These are

• *NY Rte. 28*, which forms a huge semicircle from Warrensburg through North Creek, Indian Lake, Blue Mountain Lake, Inlet, Old Forge, and down to Utica.

• *NY Rte. 8*, which zigzags west from Hague, on Lake George, through Brant Lake, Chestertown, Johnsburg, Speculator, Lake Pleasant, Piseco, Hoffmeister, and southwest to Utica.

• *NY Rte. 3*, which crosses the northern part of the park from Plattsburgh, to

Cadyville, Redford, Vermontville, Bloomingdale, Saranac Lake, Tupper Lake, Piercefield, Childwold, Cranberry Lake, Star Lake, and exiting the Blue Line west to Watertown.

### Additional Routes

Other shorter but scenic routes in the Adirondacks include

• *Northeast on NY Rte. 73* from Underwood (Exit 30 of the Northway) to Lake Placid, which offers a 45-minute panorama of the High Peaks.

• *West on NY Rte. 86* from Jay, past the foot of Whiteface Mt. and through dramatic Wilmington Notch to Lake Placid.

• *East on NY Rte. 374* from Chateaugay, past the Chateaugay lakes and Lyon Mt. to Plattsburgh, which, in addition to views of the Adirondacks, provides a long-distance scan across silvery Lake Champlain to the Green Mountains of Vermont as it drops down Dannemora Mountain.

• *Northwest on NY Rte. 28N* from North Creek to Long Lake. Be sure to stop at the roadside rest area at Newcomb, where a display identifies the High Peaks arrayed to the north.

---

### Winter Driving

All those feet of snow the Adirondacks are famed for may be great news for skiers and snowmobilers, but what about the road conditions, you might wonder. Throughout the park, the state and county highway departments have prowling fleets of snowplows that toil night and day to keep roads clear; it's probably a good bet that Adirondack roads after a deep snow are in better condition than suburban streets after a modest flurry. For several years, a "bare roads" policy has been in effect for the North Country, meaning that sand and salt are applied liberally when roads may be slippery. Another plus for winter driving these days is the prevalence of four-wheel and front-wheel-drive cars, which both handle better on slick roads than the traditional rear-wheel-drive vehicles. (If you're coming to the wintry Adirondacks in a pick-up truck or a van or passenger car with rear-wheel drive, try putting at least 150 pounds of weight — concrete blocks, sandbags, whatever — over your rear axle to help traction.)

The worst driving scenarios often occur at the beginning or end of winter, when temperatures hovering at the freezing point can cause a mixture of snow, rain, and sleet, with perhaps a little fog near lakes and low, cold spots. Then it's best to consider your options: can you wait out the storm at your lodgings, or are you prepared to rest at a remote pull-out if conditions deteriorate? Every winter traveler's car should carry a sleeping bag, a small shovel, a snow scraper, extra windshield-washing fluid, a powerful flashlight, and some candy bars, just in case you need to dig out of a snowbank, or sit quietly beside the road for a few hours as the weather takes its course.

• *East on the "Number Four" Road* from Lowville, past Stillwater Reservoir and on to Big Moose and Eagle Bay, which is on NY Rte. 28. This drive offers not so much great views as a sense of the forest depths of the western Adirondacks. About half of the 45 miles is unpaved, and there are no services over the full distance.

The Adirondack North Country Association (ANCA) has designed several driving tours both in and around the Adirondacks. These are arranged so as to hit scenic vistas, historic markers, craft shops, and so on. You can pick up a map of these routes at tourist centers and chambers of commerce, or call ANCA at 518-891-6200.

---

### BUMP!

As winter turns to spring, and longer, sunnier days warm the black asphalt highway surfaces, the frost begins to melt below the roads. During cold nights, underground moisture freezes again, and a cycle of expansion and contraction in the ground begins. With bedrock not too far beneath the soil, the ice can only expand upward, sometimes pushing rocks along with it, and "frost heaves" in the roads are the result. These bumps can range from minor humps that are barely noticeable, to deep dips that can send cars airborne. Usually, the bumps occur in roughly the same spots each year, and highway crews are diligent about marking these hazards. Watch for the large, diamond-shape "BUMP" signs as a warning to slow down; the treacherous spot itself may be marked with orange flagging on sticks placed on the shoulder of the road, or smaller, plain yellow diamonds set back on the right-of-way. Be alert; try to brake well before you reach the bump.

---

## BY BUS

Considering the size of the Adirondack region — you could fit New Jersey inside it — it's astonishing how little bus service exists. There's only one round trip a day that's of any use, and once you get off the bus you're dependent on traveling by foot, or finding sparse taxi service and even sparser rental car possibilities. If you do plan to use bus service, however, here are your options:

• *Greyhound Lines, Inc.* plies the I-87 ("Northway") route on the eastern edge of the park several times a day, but declines to stop anywhere in the park. The best you can do is Glens Falls or Plattsburgh. For more information: 518-434-8095 (Albany terminal).

• *CHAMP Express* offers service within Essex County and between Lake Placid and Plattsburgh, connecting with Greyhound buses there. For more information: 518-523-4431.

• *Adirondack Trailways* is your best bet for bus access, and offers the following routes:

**The daily single trip into the interior:** This run leaves from New York City's Trailways terminal, gates 30, 32, 34, 36, and 38 at the Port Authority, 41st St. and 8th Ave. (212-947-5300), at 10 a.m. daily and, being decidedly a "local" north of Albany, stops in Clifton Park, Saratoga Springs, Glens Falls, Lake George, Warrensburg, Chestertown, Pottersville, Schroon Lake, Keene Valley, Keene, Lake Placid ("rest stop"), Saranac Lake, Paul Smiths, and Malone, continuing to Massena and Potsdam before terminating in Canton at 8:05 p.m. The southbound trip leaves Canton at 8:30 a.m. daily and arrives in New York at 6:50 p.m.

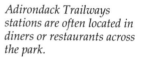

*Adirondack Trailways stations are often located in diners or restaurants across the park.*

Nancie Battaglia

Some of the stops on this run help you realize you're not in urban America anymore. The "bus station" in Keene Valley, for example, is the Noon Mark Diner: in Lake Placid, it's the Main Street Deli; and in Warrensburg, L.D.'s Pharmacy.

Parts of this trip were inaugurated on a trial basis in 1992 and had no "track record" on our publication date; check while you're planning your visit to be sure what their status is.

**The weekend special** also operates on this route as far as Saranac Lake, where it splits off to end in Tupper Lake. It goes north on Friday only, leaving New York at 5:45 p.m. and arriving in Tupper Lake at 12:55 a.m., and returns on Sunday only, leaving Tupper Lake at 4:00 p.m. and arriving in New York at 11:20 p.m.

**Five other buses from New York/Albany north:** Two penetrate the Adirondacks as far as Warrensburg and the other three give it up in Glens Falls, just outside the Adirondack Park. There's also summer-only service along the west shore of Lake George to Ticonderoga.

**Once-a-day service between Plattsburgh and Ogdensburg,** with stops in the Adirondacks at Dannemora, Lyon Mountain, Merrill, and Brainardsville. This run leaves Plattsburgh (call 518-563-1480; address: 570 Cornelia St.) where connections from Greyhound can be made, at 5:05 p.m.

For more information: Adirondack Trailways, 1-800-225-6815, or at the New York City number, at 212-947-5300.

## BY TRAIN

### AMTRAK

Amtrak operates one train a day each way between New York City and Montreal. *"The Adirondack"* leaves each city in midmorning and reaches its destination the same evening (schedules are different on Sundays), closely following the west shore of Lake Champlain for the better part of 90 miles through the park. The New York departure is from Penn Station (212-582-6875), not Grand Central as it was for years. It makes several stops in the Adirondacks, but how to get around once you are deposited at these places is problematic. You can arrange, in advance, for shuttle service from the story-book Victorian depot in Westport to Lake Placid (or Elizabethtown or Keene) by calling 518-523-4431 or 518-523-1475. A cafe car on the train offers plastic-wrapped sandwiches, sodas, and such that are tolerable but expensive, and there's even "Custom Class," which means deluxe reserved seating with complimentary coffee, tea or juice, and newspaper. It may not be what it once was, but compared to buses and puddle-jumper airplanes, this remains the snazziest way to get to the Adirondacks.

The trip is spectacular, involving tunnels, high trestles, rocky ledges 150 feet above the waters of Lake Champlain, and vistas of farm and forest, river, lake, and mountain that simply cannot be had any other way. You might consider a two-day excursion involving the train ride north from a point such as Fort

H.M. Beach. Courtesy Adirondack Museum, Blue Mountain Lake, NY

*A busy day at the Thendara station of the New York Central, 1920s.*

Edward (the stop for Glens Falls), a layover in Plattsburgh, and a return the next day. As this entails an evening and morning in Plattsburgh, you could further consider making Montreal your layover, although this would incur far greater expense plus the bother of two customs inspections. Do it soon, though; "The Adirondack" is dependent on strapped state and federal budgets, and may be axed at any time. In early 1992 the Fort Edward-Plattsburgh round trip fare was $31 if tickets were purchased within four days of the trip, or S33 if purchased up to six months ahead.

In addition, *Amtrak's Empire Service* leaves New York's Penn Station several times a day and stops in Albany-Rensselaer, Schenectady, and Utica, where you can arrange to rent a car by calling 1-800-654-3131 (Hertz) or 1-800-331-1212 (Avis). One train a day from Boston hooks up with this route at Albany-Rensselaer. Coming from the west, Empire Service originates in Buffalo; Chicago-Boston/New York and Toronto-New York Amtrak trains also ply this route.

For more information: 1-800-USA-RAIL (872-7245) or 1-800-523-5700.

### THE SKI TRAIN

The ski train is not just a memory; Gore Mt. offers packages from several northeast corridor cities, with pick-up at and return to the Fort Edward station. So does Whiteface, via Westport. For more information: 1-800-333-3454.

## BY FERRY

The only way to get to the Adirondacks from the east is to cross Lake Champlain, largest freshwater lake in America after the Great Lakes. You can do that on the bridge at Port Henry, which has a nice view that lasts for about 30 seconds, but why not enjoy yourself and take one of the Lake Champlain ferries? The views last for up to an hour and you don't have to steer. Three of the four crossings are operated by the oldest continuously running inland navigation company in America. Rates vary depending upon type of vehicle, number and age of persons in it, etc.; those shown are for car and driver, one way.

• *From Charlotte, Vermont, to Essex:* This may be the most scenic route, seeming to deliver you literally into the mountains. Crossing time is 20 minutes; trips run from approximately April 1 to New Year's, departing Charlotte on the hour and on the half hour, from 8:30 a.m. to 7:30 p.m. during the summer season. $6.75.

• *From Burlington, Vermont, to Port Kent*: This is almost as scenic, and delightful for its relaxing one-hour crossing of the widest part of the lake.

*The Essex ferry is one of four car ferries that cross Lake Champlain between the Adirondacks and Vermont.*

Nancie Battaglia

Trips run several times a day from mid-May through mid-October. Snacks and light meals, including a continental breakfast for $1.50, can be had on board. $12.00.

• *From Grand Isle, Vermont, north of Burlington, to Plattsburgh:* A ways north of the Adirondacks, this route provides a decent if long-distance view of them. It operates year-round, blasting through ice packs in even the coldest snaps, generally every 20 minutes from 5:00 a.m. to 1:20 a.m. Crossing time is 12 minutes. $6.75. For more information: 802-864-9804.

• *From Orwell, Vermont, to Fort Ticonderoga*: This crossing is a living museum. Following a route that's been in use since the British army arrived in the 1700s, it brings you to the foot of the promontory on which the restored fort reposes. This is one of the few cable-guided ferries left in America: the cable is attached at each landing and power is provided by a tugboat. Crossing time is six minutes; the one-way fare is $5 per car, and trips run from 8 a.m. to 6 p.m., from early May through late October, and until 9 p.m., from July 1 through Labor Day. There's no schedule; "We just go back and forth," the operator says. For more information: 802-897-7999.

A variation on the two-day train excursion (see above) is to take the train north to Port Kent, walk down the hill to the ferry dock, purchase round-trip pedestrian passage, ride the ferry to Burlington (the early evening crossing can be a pure delight), lay over in that interesting city — accommodations and such are within an easy walk of the dock — and return to Port Kent in time to catch the early afternoon southbound train. You may have to wave your arms and generally make a scene to get the train to stop for you, since Port Kent has no station, but it will stop. Remind the conductor to look out for your for your return trip, when you get off the train.

# BY AIR

## COMMERCIAL AIRPORTS

In all this vast territory there's only one commercial airport: Adirondack Airport at Lake Clear, about 15 minutes from Saranac Lake and 30 from Lake Placid. In early 1992 it was served by Commutair (1-800-428-4322), a subsidiary of USAir Express, flying 19-seater Beechcraft planes that look like cigars with wings. Service consisted of three direct round trips (two morning, one evening) from Albany, scene of USAir connections. Forget weekends, though; none of these goes on Saturdays, and only one on Sundays. Fares are all over the lot, depending on the time of year, how far ahead you purchase your ticket, and so forth. Persistent inquiry about the cost of a flight from New York (actually Newark in most cases) finally elicited a brave "about $200."

As these "commuter" airlines come and go like fireflies on a summer night, it's best to call first to make sure this one's still airborne. The airport number is 518-891-4600. If you're calling another airport or a travel agent, ask about "Saranac Lake," not "Adirondack." Car rentals are available at the airport: 518-891-4075.

Cities just outside the Adirondacks that offer air service are Albany, Syracuse, and Burlington (amenities such as jets and car rentals), and Watertown and Plattsburgh (puddle-jumpers). The best source of up-to-date information about these options is your travel agent.

## PRIVATE AIRPORTS

If you pilot your own plane, and are comfortable with flying in hilly terrain with sometimes unpredictable winds and weather, and feel confident landing on short runways, there are several airports for private craft across the park. Most of these airfields are open only May—October during daylight hours. Consult a good navigational map to locate these. Perhaps the most significant is on the outskirts of Lake Placid, with a 4300-foot runway and complete facilities: 518-523-2473. A couple of small airports with on-site telephone information available includes the fields in Ticonderoga (518-585-9779; Shanahan Rd., Ticonderoga, NY 12883); and Piseco (518-548-8794; Airport Rd., Piseco, NY 12134).

There are also airports in Westport, Keene, and Schroon Lake (call Essex County Tourism, 518-942-7794, for information) and North Creek (check with the Gore Mountain Region Chamber of Commerce for information, 518-251-2612). Another is at Speculator, at which pick-up can be arranged by calling Don Bird's taxi service, fifty miles away in Inlet, 315-357-3631. Better be prepared to be met at most of the others; taxi service and cars to rent are nowhere to be found in most cases.

For the truly adventuresome, you can charter a seaplane to pick you up on the East River, at 23rd St. and Waterside Plaza; check under "Scenic Flights" in the *Recreation* chapter for seaplane services.

## BY TAXIS AND SUCH

Taxi and other livery service in the Adirondacks varies radically in terms of availability (or even existence). Services in principal communities do include the following:

| | |
|---|---|
| Lake George | Lake George Taxi, 518-668-9600 |
| | Adirondack Limousine, 518-668-5466 |
| Lake Placid | Eddie's Taxi, 518-523-2024 |
| | Gene's Taxi, 518-523-3161 |
| | Jan's Taxi, 518-523-1891 |
| | Thomas Pelkey, 518-523-9797/2324 |
| Saranac Lake | Lavigne Taxi, 518-891-2444 |
| | Corrow Taxi, 518-891-5082 |
| | Northway Limousine, 518-891-0338 |
| Tupper Lake | Kennedy's Taxi, 518-359-2193 |
| | Lucky 8 (taxi and limo), 518-359-3849 |
| Inlet/Old Forge area | Don Bird, 315-357-3631 |

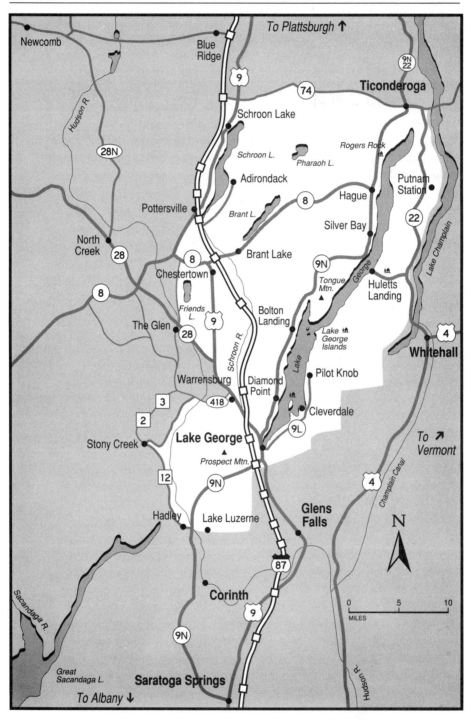

LAKE GEORGE AND SOUTHEASTERN ADIRONDACKS

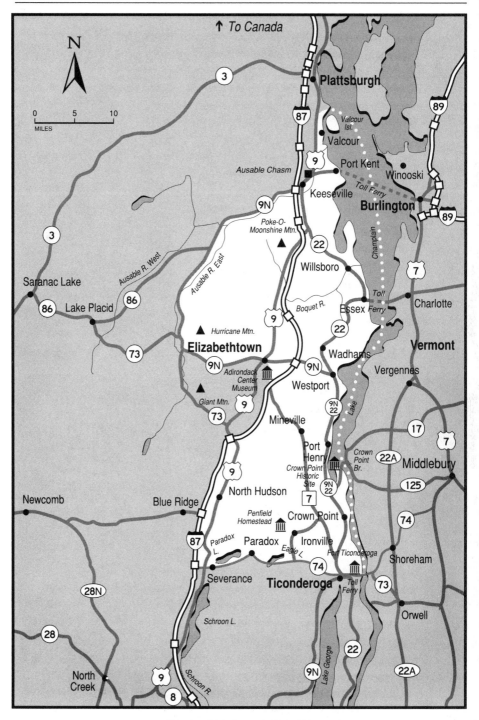

CHAMPLAIN VALLEY

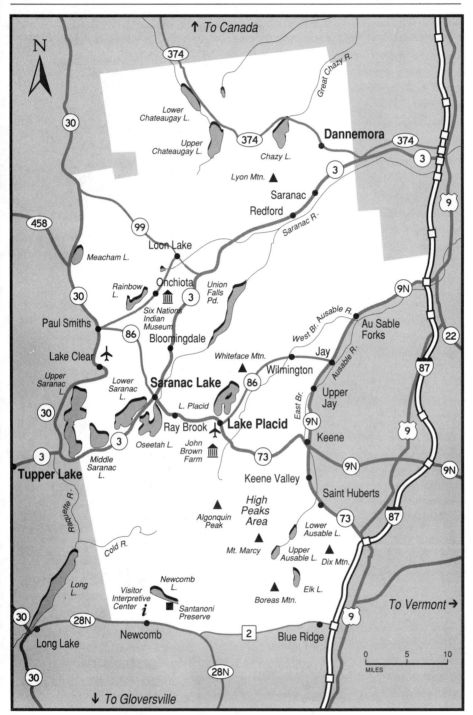

HIGH PEAKS AND NORTHERN ADIRONDACKS

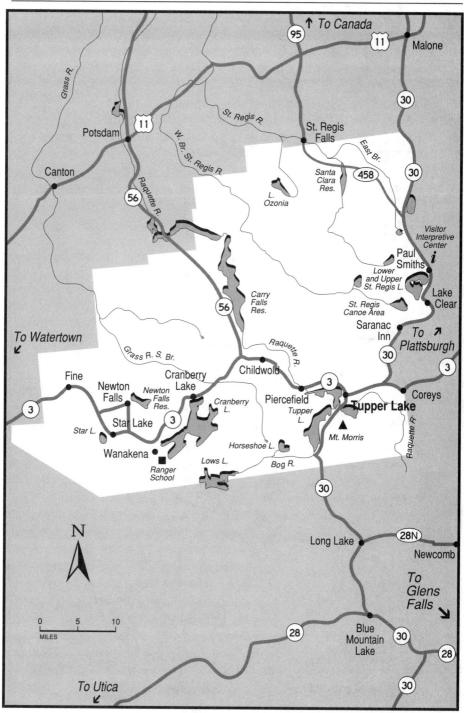

NORTHWEST LAKES REGION

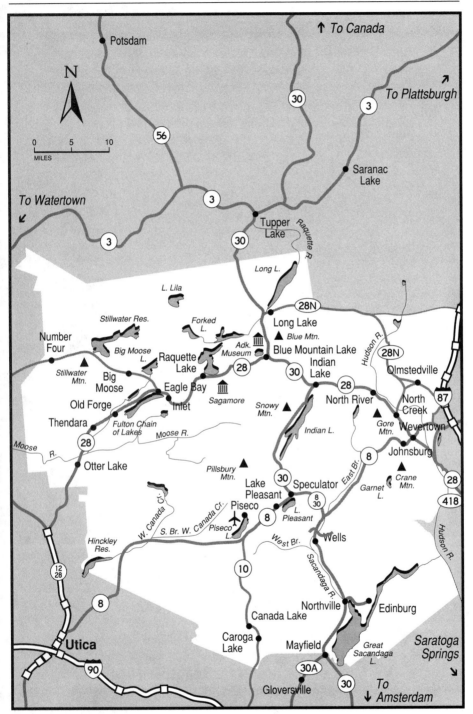

CENTRAL AND SOUTHWESTERN ADIRONDACKS

# CHAPTER THREE
## *Rustic, Classic, and Basic*
# LODGING

Early Adirondack visitors relied on the hospitality of families living along the backwoods lanes: country folks felt obligated to take in travelers, knowing that someday they, too, might need a roof over their heads and a hot meal from strangers. These casual arrangements were not unlike today's bed and breakfasts. By the mid-1800s, in the more settled parts of the region, there were numerous local businesses set up

Courtesy the Barry Collection, Lake Placid Center for the Arts

*Adirondack visitors were to "Rest & be Thankful" according to the sign in front of the original White Face Inn, near Lake Placid.*

as hostelries and boardinghouses for single or transient workers, with taverns and beds (or at least straw mattresses) for guests. The settings were resolutely rustic, and we don't mean "rustic" in today's tasteful, architectural sense of the word.

After the Civil War and the publication of *Adventures in the Wilderness* by William H.H. Murray, the region became highly acclaimed as a tourist destination. The demand for lodging increased, particularly for luxurious accommodations that could compare with Newport's or Saratoga's, and huge frame hotels multiplied on the lakeshores from Bolton Landing to Westport, Lake Placid to Schroon Lake. Seneca Ray Stoddard's 1874 guidebook, *The Adirondacks Illustrated*, lists dozens of such places: Rockwell's Hotel, in Luzerne, could accommodate 150; Lake George's Fort William Henry Hotel was four to six stories high, with scores of rooms and tiers of piazzas; the Mansion House, in Elizabethtown, claimed that 200 could lodge there; Martin's, at Lower Saranac Lake, even had telegraph service; Paul Smith's St. Regis House was described as "first class in every respect, and patronized by the very best class of people in the country." Families came to spend months at a time at these hotels, arriving by train, steamboat, stagecoach, and buckboard, complete with nannies, valets, and trunks full of clothing for all occasions.

Those vast hotels one by one succumbed to fire and/or the changing tastes of the traveling public. The Adirondacks in the late 19th century were an exclusive place, a destination that was hard to get to, and with modern steamship travel, the spas and cities of Europe became accessible to the moneyed classes and thus were perceived as offering a tonier kind of vacation. As

*A fine porch with a view remains an Adirondack essential.*

Courtesy the Barry Collection, Lake Placid Center for the Arts

the 20th century progressed, the middle class was increasing in numbers, automobiles were becoming affordable, and ordinary people started taking vacations. They said no thanks to the stodgy old hotels, and headed for tent campgrounds, resorts, and roadside cabins.

The 1920s-vintage resorts combined common dining rooms and group activities like dances, waterfront contests, singalongs, and games for kids, with private sleeping arrangements in individual cabins. The housekeeping-cottage colonies, groups of buildings without a central dining facility, took that notion of privacy a step further, and money could be saved by having Mom prepare all the meals. Motels, designed for people who just wanted a clean place to rest for a few hours, were built on the edges of many towns.

The coming of the 1980 Winter Olympics to Lake Placid led state economic planners to worry that not enough lodgings would be available for the thousands of anticipated spectators. Workshops on how to turn your home into a bed and breakfast were held across the park, and many private homeowners took the plunge. The Olympic legacy is many newly renovated B&Bs with truly homey atmospheres, most of which are along the major highway routes.

A word here differentiating the various lodging terms: generally, in New York, a *bed and breakfast* is defined as a place that holds 10 or fewer guests. Breakfast is served, the owner usually lives on the premises, and the business has relatively little contact with the state health department or other regulatory agencies. An *inn* is larger, often serves dinner or lunch as well as breakfast, and has to comply with certain state mandates for public safety and food service. Then there is the *bed and breakfast inn*, which means a place that's bigger than a B&B, is regularly inspected by the state, and includes the morning meal

*Near Port Henry, a typical 1930s lakeside and roadside tourist camp.*

Courtesy Adirondack Museum, Blue Mountain Lake, NY

in the price of a night's stay. As long as we're on the subject of definitions, a *housekeeping cabin* includes a kitchen or kitchen area, so guests can cook meals. Maybe not bake a cake, but at least boil water.

Nowadays the variety of Adirondack lodgings covers the full spectrum: there are cozy bed and breakfasts stamped with the owners' interests and style; country lodges that offer hearty meals, clean beds, and access to hiking, canoeing, or skiing; vast old hotels filled with antiques; lakeside resorts with a full roster of planned activities; housekeeping cottages on the beach; and motels. For many visitors, the classic Adirondack vacation is a week by the lake in the same housekeeping cottage that they enjoyed as children. Some families come back the same week every year; their kids play with the same summer friends every season and build lasting friendships. For that reason, many of the nicest places are booked years in advance. If you want to try a housekeeping cabin and have some flexibility in your vacation time, you may think about late June or early fall.

Listed in this chapter you'll find a whole range of accommodations. Our criteria for selection included such intangibles as style and personality, and also such basics as comfort, cleanliness, and hospitality. For some listings, the setting is a primary consideration; for others, it's wonderful architecture and beautiful rooms; some sites offer lots of first-class amenities and services; in still others, it's the hosts and hostesses that set the place apart. With this kind of intuitive categorization, you'll find positive notes on a few modest, inexpensive places that succeed at what they're trying to do, just as you'll find perhaps briefer notes on the popular, highly acclaimed spots. We've also identified a few places accessible by the somewhat sketchy public transportation system in the Adirondacks — check the index in the back of the book for a complete list. Above all, we try to offer a range of prices and options so that you'll see anyone can stay in the Adirondack Park.

At the end of the chapter, you'll find a brief listing of motels. There are many, many more places to stay in the Adirondacks than you'll read about in this book (if we listed all the places in Lake George village alone it would fill most of the pages); phone numbers for tourist information offices can be found in Chapter Eight, *Information*.

# ADIRONDACK LODGING NOTES

## RATES

Some cottages and resorts are available by the week only in July and August, and this is indicated in the "Min. Stay" section of the information box. Multiply the per-night, double-occupancy rate by seven, and you should get an idea of what a week's visit costs. Or just take our word for inexpensive, moderate, and so on. It's possible to rent a remote log cabin on Cranberry Lake for less than $200 per week, just as a couple can spend upwards of $700 for one night at The Point.

Rates quoted are for per-room, double occupancy during the tourist main season, which in most cases is July and August. Some places that are open year-round charge more January through March because of increased heating costs. You can usually expect lower rates for midweek stays, off-season rentals, or package deals; it's always worthwhile to ask. In places described as bed and breakfasts, you can expect breakfast to be included in the price of your room; many resorts and inns offer — or insist upon — full or modified American meal plans. You'll see that information listed as MAP or full American plan after the rate category.

Currently in New York there's a 5% room tax on accommodations costing more than $100 per night, which keeps rates for many places hovering around the $95 mark. There's talk of having this tax repealed, but so far there's been no action in the state legislature. You'll also have to pay 7% sales tax on overnight stays, and some places add 10% to 15% gratuity to the bill. The rates that are listed here don't reflect those additional charges since they vary quite a bit; again, inquire.

| Very Inexpensive | Under $35 (per night, double occupancy) |
| Inexpensive | $35 - $65 |
| Moderate | $65 - $95 |
| Expensive | $95 - $150 |
| Very Expensive | Over $150 |

## MINIMUM STAY

**M**any of the resorts and housekeeping cabins rent units by the week only in the summer, with guests arriving and leaving on a Saturday or Sunday. In the winter, some accommodations ask for a two-night minimum stay in order to make it worthwhile to turn up the heat in the cabin. Midweek in the off-season many places will happily welcome overnight guests; if no minimum stay is specified, you can assume that one night is fine.

## DEPOSIT/CANCELLATION

**R**eservation arrangements vary greatly from place to place. Some resorts and cottages that rent by the week ask for a 50% deposit; many winter-season places have a "no-snow" cancellation policy so that guests don't get stuck if the weather fails to cooperate. When you request information from lodgings, the details on deposits and cancellations are usually spelled out clearly, but don't be afraid to ask.

## OTHER OPTIONS

**L**ocal real-estate agents often handle private summer-home rentals. These places might be anything from backwoods camps to new condominiums to lovely old houses with plenty of private lakefront, boats, and all the up-to-date creature comforts. Check locally, or look on bulletin boards, in newspapers, and so on. This kind of renting takes considerable advance planning: you should start inquiring many months or even a year ahead.

There's also the brand-new parkwide *Adirondack Bed and Breakfast Reservation Service* (Nadia Korths; 1-800-552-BNBS or 518-891-1632; 10 Park Pl., Saranac Lake, NY 12983). About twenty inns and bed and breakfasts are offered under this service; Nadia has inspected each one.

Some private campgrounds are listed in this chapter, but you'll find all of the Department of Environmental Conservation Adirondack campgrounds in Chapter Six, *Recreation*.

## CREDIT CARDS

**C**redit cards are abbreviated as follows: AE, American Express; CB, Carte Blanche; D, Discover; DC, Diners Club; MC, Master Card; V, Visa.

# LODGING IN THE ADIRONDACKS

## LAKE GEORGE AND SOUTHEASTERN ADIRONDACKS

### Baldwin

**THE RANCHOUSE AT BALDWIN ON NORTHERN LAKE GEORGE**
Hosts: Chattie and Jeff Van Wert.
518-585-6596.
79 Baldwin Rd., Baldwin/Mail: RR 1, Ticonderoga, NY 12883.
Closed: Nov.—Apr.
Price: Moderate.
Min. Stay: 2 nights.
Credit Cards: MC, V.
Handicap Access: 4 units; inquire.
Special Features: Private beach, boats for guests, free dockage; children welcome; no pets.

Since 1966, the Van Wert family has operated these lakefront accommodations, which are motel rooms and suites with kitchens. Guests staying in rooms without kitchens are welcome to use the communal kitchen/dining area, or cook out on the gas grills. A few canoes and rowboats are on hand for guests to use; this is one of the few places on Lake George that offers free dock space for guests' boats.

### Bolton Landing

**ADIRONDACK PARK MOTEL**
Hosts: Gena and Jan Lindyberg.
518-644-9800.
Rte. 9N, Bolton Landing, NY 12814.
Closed: Oct. 15—May 15.
Price: Moderate.
Credit Cards: MC, V.
Special Features: Private beach; pool; boats for guests; play area; children welcome; no pets.

The Lake House, a five-bedroom woodsy lodge with knotty pine interiors and a vintage stone fireplace, is one of the options at this family-run resort. There are also two-bedroom housekeeping cottages, efficiencies, and motel units, all with direct access to Lake George.

There's a pool, picnic area, playground, and private beach; guests have free use of canoes, rowboats, small sailboats, and docks. To start your vacation day off right, the Lindybergs even serve a complimentary continental breakfast.

**BONNIE VIEW ON LAKE GEORGE**
518-644-5591/before May 15: 518-644-3611.

Set on nine wooded lakefront acres, Bonnie View offers a variety of accommodations from knotty-pine-paneled housekeeping cottages with fireplaces

Lake Shore Dr., Bolton
 Landing, NY 12814.
Closed: Late Sept.–mid-May.
Price: Inexpensive to
 Expensive; depends on
 season.
Credit Cards: MC, V.
Special Features: Children
 welcome; private beach;
 heated pool; no pets.

to motel units with sundecks cantilevered over the water. Besides a private sandy beach, there's a heated pool, tennis court, and rowboats for guests. Rates here for mid-May through late June and Labor Day through foliage season are very reasonable; even though folks call that the off-season, most of the Bolton-area restaurants and shops are open, and it's a good time to explore the lake. Cabins generally rent by the week only in July and August.

### HILLTOP COTTAGE BED & BREAKFAST

Owners: Anita and Charlie
 Richards.
518-644-2492.
6883 Lakeshore Dr., Bolton
 Landing, NY 12814.
1/2 mile south of the traffic light on Rte. 9.
Open: Year-round.
Price: Inexpensive.
Credit Cards: None.
Special Features: No pets;
 no small children; smoking in public rooms only.

A former caretaker's farmhouse on "Millionaire's Row," the Bolton Landing to Lake George road, Hilltop Cottage is directly across the street from the Marcella Sembrich Memorial Studio, a museum honoring the Polish-born diva. The clapboard cottage has three guest rooms upstairs, all sharing a bath, and a guest cabin in the backyard available May—October. Anita, a former German teacher, and Charlie, a retired guidance counselor, bought the 11-room house in 1985 and opened it as a B&B three years later. Hilltop Cottage is a friendly, homey place within easy walking distance of Bolton's beach, tennis courts, and public parks.

### THE OMNI SAGAMORE HOTEL

Managing Director: W.
 Robert McIntosh.
518-644-9400.
Sagamore Rd., Bolton
 Landing, NY 12814.
Open: Year-round.
Price: Expensive to Very
 Expensive.
Credit Cards: AE, DC, MC, V.
Handicap Access: Several
 units; elevators in hotel.
Special Features: 2
 gourmet restaurants;
 sandy beach; indoor
 pool; spa; fitness center;
 tennis courts; conference
 facilities; children welcome; no pets.

For years the old Sagamore Hotel lingered on its own private island, neglected and overgrown. The 1883 hotel survived two fires, weathered the Depression — it was carefully rebuilt in 1930 — drew convention crowds in the '50s, but gradually declined through the seventies. In 1981, real estate developer Norman Wolgin bought the hotel and began a long restoration process; today's Omni Classic Resort is thoroughly elegant and immaculate.

The elegantly appointed public areas include a conservatory with lake views, the Trillium Dining Room, the Sagamore Dining Room, Mr. Brown's Pub, an art gallery, and a gift shop. Guests have 350 deluxe units to choose from, including suites, hotel bedrooms, eight lodges, and executive retreats with lofts. The list of amenities is impressive: a huge indoor pool, a fitness center, miniature

*Aerial view of the Sagamore, Bolton Landing, 1950s.*

golf, an indoor tennis and racquetball facility, outdoor tennis courts, a playground, a beautiful sandy beach, docks for guests' boats, and a Donald Ross-designed championship golf course two miles away. Guests can go for complimentary Lake George cruises aboard the *Morgan*, a charming wooden tour boat, and any kind of water sport, from snorkeling to sailboarding, can be arranged.

The Sagamore is a popular spot for conferences, offering top-notch facilities for large and small groups. There's no need to leave the kids at home if one or both parents are attending meetings: the social department has plenty of supervised activities for children.

The view of Lake George from the Sagamore's waterfront is stunning in any season.

### *Chestertown*

**THE BALSAM HOUSE INN AND RESTAURANT**
Managers: Bruce Robbins, Jr. and Helena Edmark.
1-800-441-6856.
Atateka Dr., Chestertown, NY 12817.
Closed: Nov.
Price: MAP: Expensive.
Credit Cards: MC, V, AE, DC.
Special Features: Children welcome; award-winning restaurant; fishing guide service; mountain bikes and boats for guests; special weekend packages.

The Valentine family built the original farmhouse near Friends Lake in 1845, and after Victorian-era additions such as a three-story tower and a full-length veranda were added, the Valentine Hotel opened to much fanfare in 1891. Operating off and on as a summer resort for many years, the inn was modernized once again and renamed the Balsam House following World War II. The hostelry underwent significant restoration in 1980; today's guests have 20 elegant, spacious rooms, all with private baths, to choose from.

The Balsam House was among the first of the old Adirondack inns to spruce up for current tastes, and thus set a high standard for subsequent attempts. Antiques, old prints, and fresh flowers can be found throughout the building; the restaurant wins rave reviews from critics and visitors alike. The secluded location on Friends Lake is a bonus, and guests will find that there is good antique hunting in the neighborhood. In the winter, you can enjoy sleigh rides around the property; in summer, there's a private beach with canoes and rowboats.

**THE CHESTER INN**
Owners: Bruce and
  Suzanne Robbins.
518-494-4148.
Main St., Chestertown, NY
  12817.
Rte. 9, near the town hall.
Open: Year-round.
Price: Moderate.
Credit Cards: MC, V.
Special Features: No pets;
  children over 12 wel-
  come; smoking in desig-
  nated areas only.

One of Chestertown's beautiful homes that is listed in the National Register of Historic Places, this Greek Revival inn dates back to 1837. Beyond the grand hall, with its mahogany railings and grain-painted woodwork, there are four lovely second-floor guest rooms with private baths, including the Victorian Suite, which has its own sitting room and bath with a deep, old-fashioned tub. Guests are welcome to explore the 13-acre property, which has gardens, a horse barn, a smokehouse, and an early cemetery, and it's a short walk to

Nancie Battaglia

The Greek Revival architecture of the Chester Inn, Chestertown, offers elegance and comfort.

another of Bruce and Suzanne's projects, the Main Street Ice Cream Parlor, or to a movie at the newly restored Carol Theatre. Nondrivers take note: Chestertown is a regular stop on the Adirondack Trailways bus line, and this inn is just a block from the station.

**THE FRIENDS LAKE INN**
Owners: Sharon and Greg
  Taylor.
518-494-4751.
Friends Lake Rd.,
  Chestertown, NY 12817.
Open: Year-round.
Price: MAP: Expensive.
  B&B: Moderate.
Credit Cards: MC, V.
Min. Stay: 2 nights on
  weekends; 3 nights on

For most of its 130-year history, the Friends Lake Inn has been a hostelry of one kind or another, although its first tenants, the tannery workers, would marvel to see people rather than cowhides soaking in the enormous wooden hot tub outdoors. Sharon and Greg have completed extensive renovations on the building and guests now enjoy 16 comfortable rooms, all with private baths. Bedrooms have brass or iron bedsteads, patchwork quilts, and antiques; many have views of nearby

holiday weekends; 1 night midweek.
Special Features: Outdoor hot tub; cross-country ski and mountain-bike rentals; guide service for outdoor treks; extensive wine list.

Friends Lake, while eight rooms even have their very own hot tubs. There are common areas with fireplaces and couches; a wide, shady porch; and a pleasant bar for relaxing.

This is truly an inn for all seasons. Guests can enjoy sleigh rides and cross-country skiing here in the winter, fishing in the spring, swimming and mountain biking in the summer, and hiking in the fall. From time to time, there are wine- or beer-tasting parties, or murder-mystery weekends. There's no need to travel far for dinner — the restaurant on the first floor is top-notch. The Taylors offer numerous seasonal packages combining lodging with golfing, rafting, or skiing; mid-week bed-and-breakfast rates in effect during spring and November are quite reasonable.

*Sharon and Greg Taylor, innkeepers at Friends Lake Inn, Chestertown.*

Nancie Battaglia

## *Diamond Point*

**CANOE ISLAND LODGE**
Owners: Jane and William Busch.
518-668-5592.
Lake Shore Dr., Diamond Point, NY 12824; Rte. 9N.
Closed: Nov.—Apr.
Price: Expensive.
Min. Stay: 3 nights.
Credit Cards: None.
Special Features: Private island; private sandy beach; sailboats; row-

**W**ith cheerful log cabins, waterfront chalets, an old-fashioned carriage house, and a massive rustic main lodge, this 16-acre complex offers all kinds of family-vacation options. At Canoe Island Lodge, there are clay tennis courts, a sandy beach on Lake George, and numerous excellent boats to sail, including a pair of custom-designed Canoe Island 30s, which are fleet, elegant sloops. For a small extra fee, guests can go waterskiing or rent windsurfers. Perhaps the best part of a stay here, though, is the chance to enjoy the lodge's very own five-acre island, about 3/4 mile offshore. Regular shuttle boats take guests to the island where they

boats; windsurfers; tennis courts; some planned activities; children welcome.

can swim, snorkle, fish, and explore a beautiful, secluded, undeveloped part of the lake.

The Busch family, which opened the lodge in 1946, takes great pride in offering genuine hospitality and hearty European-style meals with home-grown vegetables, homemade bread and pastries, and treasured old-country dishes. On Thursdays, there are beach-side chicken barbecues; there are also dances and special children's programs on certain evenings, although there's no pressure to join in if that's not to your taste. The lodge accommodates 175 people at peak capacity. In spring and fall, rates include breakfast, lunch, and dinner; from July 1 to Sept. 7, a modified American plan is in effect.

## CHELKA LODGE

Owners: Maureen and
  Tom Mikan.
Rte. 9N, Diamond Pt., NY
  12824.
518-668-4677.
Closed: Mid-Oct.—mid-
  Apr.
Price: Moderate.
Credit Cards: None.
Min. Stay: 2 nights on
  summer weekends.
Special features: Sandy
  beach; boats; tennis;
  children welcome.

Guests at this resort can enjoy the lodge's canoes, rowboats, and sailboats, play tennis, and swim at the private sandy beach. There are 25 motel and efficiency units on the shady, well-kept grounds; guests with motorboats may reserve dock space for an added fee. Fishermen take note: Chelka opens soon after the ice goes out, and off-season rates are reasonable. Breakfast is available in the main lodge from late June through Labor Day.

## *Hadley*

## SARATOGA ROSE

Owners: Nancy and
  Anthony Merlino.
518-696-2861/1-800-942-
  5025.
Rockwell St., Hadley, NY
  12835.
Open: Year-round.
Price: Moderate to
  Expensive.
Credit Cards: MC, V, D.
Special Features:
  Fireplaces; no pets; no
  children under 12;
  smoking permitted
  downstairs only.

In its heyday Hadley was a thriving community, its industry based largely on water-powered mills along the Hudson River. Well-to-do mill owners built some elaborate Victorian mansions in town, and today, one of them has been restored to its former glory by Nancy and Anthony Merlino. Saratoga Rose — on sedate, tree-lined Rockwell Street, it's a surprising sight in exuberant shades of buff, shocking pink, and mauve — is now a bed and breakfast inn with four second-floor guest rooms, each with private bath. The Queen Anne Room has its own working fireplace; the Garden Room has a private sun porch and Jacuzzi spa. All rooms are decorated with period antiques and prints. Several different packages are available to guests, with options such as clubhouse passes to the Saratoga harness-racing track, guided horseback-riding trips, scenic airplane flights, or a visit to Crystal Spa for a Saratoga mineral-water bath and massage.

Saratoga Rose has a very good restaurant that's open to the public year-round, and a small pub room; in the summer, the wide, geranium-draped veranda is a pleasant spot to enjoy tea or supper. Tony Merlino suggests that the inn is also suitable for private parties, board meetings, and small corporate retreats.

## Hague

**TROUT HOUSE VILLAGE RESORT**
Owners: The Patchett Family Partnership.
518-543-6088/1-800-368-6088.
Lake Shore Dr., Hague, NY 12836; Rte. 9N.
Open: Year-round.
Price: Moderate.
Credit Cards: MC, V, AE, D.
Special Features: 400-foot sandy beach; boats and bikes for guests; fireplaces; cable TV with HBO; children welcome.

One of the few four-season resorts on the peaceful northern end of Lake George, Trout House is a spotlessly maintained complex of log cabins and chalets. Many of the cabins have fireplaces, decks, and complete kitchen facilities; there are nine rooms in the main lodge, all with private baths. In the summer, there are canoes, rowboats, sailboats, kayaks, bikes, and even a nine-hole putting green for guests. Trout House is a short distance from historic sites like Fort Ticonderoga, Crown Point, and the Penfield Homestead, and the Ticonderoga Country Club — a scenic and challenging 18-hole course — is just up the road.

By January, the atmosphere changes from that of an active resort to that of a quiet country inn. Cross-country skiers, skaters, ice fishermen, and snowmobilers can go out right from the front or back doors to explore miles of countryside. For indoor-minded folks, there's a game room with ping pong, foosball, shuffleboard table, and a BYOB bar. Numerous package options and winter discounts are available.

## Lake George

**ALPINE VILLAGE**
Owners: Lil and Ernest Ippisch.
518-668-2193.
Rte. 9N, Lake George, NY 12845.
Open: Year-round.
Price: Moderate to Expensive.
Min. Stay: 3 nights midweek in summer; 4 nights weekend in summer.

Log cabins of all sizes, from the spacious main lodge to cute duplex cottages with fireplaces, characterize this lakeside resort complex. The grounds are nicely landscaped, leading down to a private beach; other amenities include rowboats and canoes for guests, a recreation room, tennis court, and some dock space for visitors' boats. In the summer, breakfast is included in the room rate. Folks here will even pick you up at the bus station if you make advance arrangements.

Credit Cards: MC, V.
Special Features: Private
  beach; tennis; boats
  for guests; children
  welcome; no pets.

*Log lodge at Alpine Village,
Lake George.*

Courtesy Alpine Village

**THE BALSAM MOTEL**
Owner: Cynthia Ferrone.
518-668-3865.
430 Canada St., Lake
  George, NY 12845.
Closed: Oct. 12—May 14.
Price: Moderate.
Credit Cards: MC, V.
Special Features: Heated
  pool; children welcome;
  no pets.

Within easy walking distance of Lake George's Canada St., with its restaurants and shopping, the Balsam offers a surprising oasis of quiet. Homey little cottages and new motel units are located along a shady lane; there's a picnic grove and a heated pool with hydrotherapy jets. In July and August guests are treated to continental breakfasts.

**CLINTON INN**
Owner: Don Clinton.
518-668-2412/winter: 201-
  461-8487.
Lake Shore Dr., Lake
  George, NY 12845.
Closed: Late Oct.—early
  May.
Price: Moderate.
Credit Cards: MC, V.
Special Features: Sandy
  beach; extensive recre-
  ational facilities; restau-
  rant; grocery store; cock-
  tail lounge; children
  welcome; no pets.

At this new lakefront resort, there are 13 housekeeping cabins and numerous spacious motel rooms. There's a big heated pool — a rarity in the Adirondacks despite the fact that the lakes here tend to be cool — plus a sandy beach on Lake George, clay tennis courts, basketball and volleyball courts, boat docks, and an 18-hole putting green. Folks here will help arrange baby-sitters if parents want to go out to dinner, and there's a self-service laundry on the premises.

Housekeeping cabins, with complete kitchens, barbecue grills, picnic tables, and cable TV are rented by the week only in high season, and may be reserved for shorter periods in spring and fall. After Labor Day, motel rooms are offered at a three-nights-for-the-price-of-two rate.

## CORNER BIRCHES BED & BREAKFAST GUEST HOUSE

Owners: Janice and Ray Dunklee.
518-668-2837.
86 Montcalm St., Lake George, NY 12845.
Open: Year-round.
Price: Very Inexpensive.
Credit Cards: None.
Special Features: Cable TV; well-behaved children welcome; no pets.

While the rest of Lake George seems to have been swept away in recent times by the need to modernize and create dozens of strip motels, the Dunklees have kept their guest house pretty much as it was in 1957; even the rates reflect another era. Says Janice, "We like children, senior citizens, and anyone else in between, and stress those elusive, lost qualities of the past like courtesy, cleanliness, and personal service." There are four guest rooms, which share bathrooms, "just like at home."

This place is suited for folks who are traveling without a car: Corner Birches is just four blocks from the bus station. In summer, guests can saunter over to Shepard Park for free concerts, head down to the pier for a cruise on the tour boats, or walk a bit further to Million Dollar Beach for a swim (admission fee). Of course, if you have a car, there's private parking and access to many nearby museums and attractions, and in winter, downhill skiing at Gore Mountain is about a half an hour away.

## DUNHAM'S BAY LODGE

Managers: Kathy and John Salvador.
518-656-9242.
Rte. 9L, Lake George, NY 12845.
On the east side of the lake at Dunham's Bay.
Closed: Mid-Oct.—late May.
Price: Expensive.
Credit Cards: MC, V.
Min. Stay: 3 days on summer weekends.
Special Features: Sandy beach; rowboats and canoes for guests; tennis; pool; play area; sailing school; restaurant; children welcome; no pets.

The centerpiece of this very stylish resort located on a quiet Lake George bay a few miles outside of town is a massive stone lodge built by a well-to-do Glens Falls dentist in 1911. The lobby and restaurant are spacious and sunlit; there's a new indoor/outdoor pool complex with a Jacuzzi, and for a cool drink at the end of the day, there's a swank cocktail lounge with a pool table. Amidst all the mirrors, skylights, and ferns, managers John and Kathy Salvador greet the public with the same genuine warmth and friendliness, just as they did twenty years ago when the lodge first opened.

Accommodations range from one- or two-bedroom housekeeping cabins in a shady grove to large, modern rooms in the main lodge or motel. Cottages rent by the week only in the summer, but during the off-season, from Memorial Day to mid-June, there's a two-night minimum stay and daily rates are considerably less. A restaurant and snack bar on the premises offer breakfast, lunch, and dinner.

## FORT WILLIAM HENRY MOTOR INN

518-668-3081 / 1-800-234-0267.
Canada St., Lake George, NY 12845.
On Rte. 9.
Open: Year-round.
Price: Inexpensive to Expensive, depending on season.
Credit Cards: AE, DC, D, MC, V.
Handicap Access: 1 room.
Special Features: Restaurants; lake view; in-room phones; children welcome.

For more than 125 years there's been a hotel named Fort William Henry on this bluff overlooking Lake George. The current edition is a brand-new resort with 99 motel and hotel rooms, an indoor pool, a heated outdoor pool, and 18 acres of manicured grounds. The complex has three restaurants, including the Lookout Cafe, which serves lunch in a pleasant outdoor setting, and the Trolley, which specializes in steak and seafood.

Right next door is the Fort William Henry museum, portraying French and Indian War history on the site of the original fort; cannons boom, muskets blaze, and uniformed soldiers go through their drills. If modern amusements are more to your taste, there's miniature golf and the Million Dollar Beach a short walk away.

The motor inn offers special packages for retired persons and couples in spring and fall, with some meals plus free admission to the museum included. Rates for Labor Day—late June are considerably less than summer-season prices.

*The original Fort William Henry Hotel occupied the site of the present-day motor inn from 1855-1908.*

**LAKE GEORGE
   AMERICAN YOUTH
   HOSTEL**
518-668-2634.
Corner Iroquois and
   Montcalm Sts., Lake
   George, NY 12845.
Closed: Labor Day—May
   20.
Price: Very Inexpensive.
Credit Cards: None.
Special features: Children
   welcome; no pets.

At the St. James Episcopal Parish Hall, guests can stay in a clean, quiet bunkhouse for a mere 10 bucks a night. The hostel is located close to Canada St., for shopping and people watching, and an easy walk away from the battlefield park and public beach. The maximum stay is three nights.

**ROCKLEDGE**
Owners: Jack and Pat
   Barry.
518-668-5348.
Lake Shore Dr., Lake
   George, NY 12845.
Closed: Labor Day—
   Memorial Day.
Price: Moderate to
   Expensive.
Credit Cards: MC, V.
Special Features: 540 feet of
   lakefront; sandy beach;
   pool; restaurant; chil-
   dren welcome; no pets.

The original Rockledge, a three-story mansion built by the Rev. Isaac Tuttle in 1886, stands guard under the pines on this 14-acre lakefront property. Although the historic house isn't open to guests, the building's gracious presence adds a special touch to this otherwise thoroughly modern resort.

Rockledge offers one- or two-bedroom house-keeping cottages, motel rooms, and suites. Cottages are generally available by the week only, although in summer 1992 the Barrys are offering a few summer short-term rentals. There's an outdoor pool, a sandy beach, play area, and room for badminton, volleyball, and shuffleboard. The Wayside Inn Restaurant, open for breakfast, lunch, and dinner, serves hearty family fare, which can be enjoyed on a sunny deck.

**STILL BAY**
Hosts: Carolyn and Bob
   Brown.
518-668-2584.
Rte. 9N, Lake George, NY
   12845.
Closed: Oct.—May.
Price: Moderate to
   Expensive.
Credit Cards: None.
Special Features: Private
   beach; rowboats and
   canoes for guests; dock-
   age for guests' boats;
   children welcome; no
   pets.

The lovely white-pillared boathouse at Still Bay gives a clue to the property's past — it was another of the turn-of-the-century estates along Millionaire's Row. Now the seven acres are home to modern motel and efficiency units and house-keeping cottages.

There's a 325-foot-long swath of natural, sandy beach, nicely landscaped grounds, dock space for guests' boats, a play area, and a recreation room for rainy days and evenings. During July and August, guests receive complimentary continental breakfasts, and rowboats, canoes, and pedal boats are available at no extra charge.

## Lake Luzerne

**THE ELMS
WATERFRONT
COTTAGES AND
LODGE**
Owners: Denise and Dave
  Paddock.
518-696-3072.
1981 Bay Rd., Lake
  Luzerne, NY 12846.
Closed: Nov.—Apr.
Price: Inexpensive.
Credit Cards: None.
Special Features: Sandy
  beach; children wel-
  come; inquire about
  pets.

For more than forty years, families have been returning to the Elms every summer, and it's no wonder why they come back. There's a nice sandy beach on a tranquil bay of the Hudson River, rowboats for fishing, and just 15 housekeeping cabins and lodge suites. For a couple of families vacationing together, the Sacandaga Lodge has three different two-bedroom units, plus decks and a fireplace. Next door there's the popular Waterhouse Restaurant, and for amusement there's horseback riding, white-water rafting on the Sacandaga River, golf, and small museums all within a short drive.

In summer, cottages are available by the week only; from May through June and Sept. 7 to Oct. 31, special group rates are available for five cottages or more for school, church, or social groups, or family reunions, and there's no minimum stay for midweek guests.

**KASTNER'S**
Owner: Mary Moeller.
518-696-2715.
RR 2, Box 227, Lake
  Luzerne, NY 12846.
Open: Year-round.
Price: Inexpensive.
Min. Stay: 2 nights; house-
  keeping units rent by
  the week only July—
  August.
Credit Cards: MC, V.
Special Features:
  Lakefront; children wel-
  come.

Located on the the piney shores of Lake Vanare, Kastner's has simple, affordable housekeeping cabins and motel units. You can swim, go out for a cruise in one of the pedal boats, relax in the shade in the summer, or rent a snowmobile, or cross-country ski in the winter. There's no restaurant on the premises, but there are outdoor grills and picnic tables for guests, and plenty of eateries from funky to fancy within a few miles.

**THE LAMPLIGHT INN
BED & BREAKFAST**
Owners: Linda and Gene
  Merlino.
518-696-5294.
2129 Lake Ave., Lake
  Luzerne, NY 12846.

Voted "Inn of the Year" for 1992 by readers of *The Complete Guide to Bed & Breakfasts, Inns and Guesthouses in the United States and Canada* by Pamela Lanier, the Lamplight Inn is an elegant, tasteful retreat. Built a century ago as the bachelor "cottage" for a wealthy lumberman, the inn has

Open: Year-round.
Price: Moderate to
  Expensive.
Credit Cards: MC, V, AE.
Special Features:
  Fireplaces in bedrooms;
  no pets; smoking per-
  mitted in parlor only;
  children over 12 wel-
  come.

been carefully refurbished by Gene and Linda
Merlino. The public room has rich chestnut wainscoting; high, beamed ceilings; two fireplaces;
Oriental rugs, lace curtains, and lots of antiques
throughout. Just off the hallway is a tiny gift shop
with antiques, vintage clothing, and packages of
Linda's tasty granola to take home. The spacious,
sunny dining room, although a recent addition, is
entirely in keeping with the overall Victorian style.
Lunch is open to the public on weekends and some
weekdays, and the dining room is available for private parties and meetings.

An ornate keyhole staircase leads upstairs to the 10 guest bedrooms, all with
private baths. Five of the rooms have gas-burning fireplaces — "instant
romance," says Gene, as a flick of a wall-mounted switch sets the ceramic logs
blazing. The furniture and decor are quite different and delightful in each

*The Lamplight Inn, Lake
Luzerne, "Inn of the Year"
in 1992.*

Courtesy the Lamplight Inn

room: for example, the Skylight Room has a high coffered ceiling, skylight,
and a high-back old-fashioned oak bedstead, while the Victoria Room has a
queen-size canopied four-poster bed. Breakfast, which is included in the room
rate, features fresh fruit and sweet breads or cake, some of that homemade
granola, omelets, and daily specials like apple crepes or Belgian waffles.

The Lamplight Inn is close to the Saratoga Racetrack and tends to be quite
busy during the month of August. From November through April room rates
are offered at special savings, with packages for leaf-peepers, holiday shop-
pers, cross-country and downhill skiers, and mud-season gourmet-dinner
fans. The inn is also becoming a popular choice for corporate gatherings; the
directors from Ben & Jerry's Homemade Ice Cream were recent guests.

## *Paradox*

**ROLLING HILL BED & BREAKFAST**
Owners: Jewel and Lou Ady.
518-532-9286.
Rte. 74, Paradox, NY 12858/ Mail: Box 32, Severance, NY 12872.
Closed: Winter.
Price: Inexpensive.
Credit Cards: None.
Special Features: Children over 5 welcome; no pets.

A pleasant farmhouse located near Paradox Lake, Pyramid Lake, and Eagle Lake, Rolling Hill offers old-time country hospitality and a hearty homemade breakfast. Guests in the four rooms upstairs share bathrooms. Just off the dining room there's a spacious screen porch, a real plus during bug season. For hikers and fishermen, the Pharaoh Lake Wilderness Area, with miles of trails and dozens of trout ponds, is close by. This is good terrain for bicyclists, too, with lots of quiet back roads to explore.

## *Schroon Lake*

**SCHROON LAKE INN**
Owners: Louise Cronin and Pat Savarie.
518-532-7042.
Rte. 9, Schroon Lake, NY 12870.
Bed & breakfast open year-round.
Price: Moderate.
Credit Cards: MC, V.
Min. Stay: 2 nights on weekends.
Handicap Access: 1 room with private bath.
Special Features: Fireplace; no smoking; no pets; children over 12 welcome.

Only minutes off the Northway (Exit 28) is Louise Cronin and Pat Savarie's lovely country inn, with seven guest rooms sharing five baths. One room with attached bath is completely accessible to the mobility impaired. The living room has a stone fireplace, shelves and shelves of books and magazines, and comfortable sofas for curling up with the novel of your choice. In fine weather, the long front porch is decorated with hanging baskets of lush flowers; from a vintage wicker chair or a classic rocker, you can look out over the Schroon River valley to the east. Rooms have polished hardwood floors, Oriental rugs, antiques, patchwork quilts, and thick terrycloth robes in the closet.

Just across the lawn is the inn's gourmet restaurant. Guests receive a full breakfast with their lodging, and dinner is available on weekends in the fall and spring, daily in the summer. Also on the same property is a charming gift shop that opened in June 1992, featuring Victoriana, imported hand-painted Christmas ornaments, wreaths and floral arrangements, and Fitz & Floyd porcelain.

**THE SCHROON LAKE PLACE**
Owner: Ellen Egglefield.
518-532-9832 summer/

Located in town, on the lake, and on a quiet beach, Ellen Egglefield's place is a favorite with families. It's a short walk to the Strand Theater, the public beach, the tennis courts, and the shops on

518-873-9832 winter.
Closed: Oct.—May.
Price: Inexpensive.
Credit Cards: None.

Main Street, so kids don't need to bother their folks to take them to amusements. Accommodations include efficiencies and housekeeping cabins, most of which have lake views or decks.

**SCHROON RIVER RANCH MOTEL**
Owners: Theresa and Paul Morris.
518-532-9006.
Rte. 9, Schroon Lake, NY 12870.
Closed: May—Nov.
Price: Very Inexpensive to Inexpensive.
Credit Cards: MC, V.
Special Features: Riverfront; children welcome; private hiking trails.

With simple log cabins under tall white pines, a network of hiking trails crisscrossing a hundred acres, and frontage along one of the classic Adirondack fishing streams, the Schroon River Ranch Motel is a quiet, family-oriented retreat. Folks catch trout and bass in the Schroon, look for wildflowers along horse trails that date back to the time when the ranch was still active, or read mysteries on the porches. Just like in the old days, guests gather around the community campfire on summer evenings. There are outdoor grills, picnic tables, and a pool. As Paul Morris says, "Try a day — you'll stay a week."

*The Lake House, part of Wood's Lodge, in Schroon Lake, has welcomed travelers since the 1880s.*

Courtesy Catherine Wood Querns

**WOOD'S LODGE**
Owner: Catherine Wood Querns.
518-532-7529 May—Oct./518-462-1641 Nov.—Apr.

The Lake House, a wonderful white wedding cake of a cottage perched out over Schroon Lake, is just one part of the complex at Wood's Lodge, a waterfront hostelry that's been owned and operated by the same family since 1912. The Lake

Closed: Mid-Oct.—May 14.
Price: Moderate.
Credit Cards: None.
Special Features: Private beach; children welcome; no pets.

House has two tiers of gingerbread-trimmed porches wrapping all around the building, and antiques in every room. There's also a chalet with several suites and private rooms, a main lodge with two-room suites, and five lakeside cabins. Many of the accommodations have kitchen facilities, but for those without, there's a large, modern community kitchen and an elegant dining room with a beautiful lake view. As an added bonus, there's an old-fashioned Adirondack camp on the east side of the lake called Tali Chito that's available by the week.

Wood's Lodge is a short walk from all that downtown Schroon Lake has to offer, and there's a private beach, tennis court, and shuffleboard court on the property. Around 5:00 p.m., one of the staff comes around with ice, spring water, and glasses for happy hour on the porch, another gracious Wood's Lodge tradition.

**WORD OF LIFE INN**
Manager: Don Lough.
518-532-7771.
Rte. 9, Schroon Lake, NY 12870.
Open: Year-round.
Price: Inexpensive to Expensive.
Credit Cards: MC, V.
Handicap Access: 6 rooms available.
Special Features: Children welcome; Christian atmosphere; recreational facilities; separate summer camps for youth.

A huge Christian resort, the Word of Life Inn offers all kinds of accommodations from chalets and rustic lakeside cabins to deluxe executive and honeymoon suites. There's a complete roster of regularly scheduled activities and inspirational speakers, plus tennis, miniature golf, swimming, boating, hiking, and special events. Besides the inn, which is located just south of Schroon Lake village, there's a family campground farther down the lake with sites for tents, travel trailers, and motor homes (some sites have electrical, water, and sewer hook-ups), plus several housekeeping cabins.

## *Severance*

**LAKE PARADOX CLUB AND THE RED HOUSE ON SAWMILL ROAD**
Owner: Helen Wildman.
518-532-7734.
River Rd., Paradox Lake, NY/Mail: Box 125, Severance, NY 12872.
Closed: Most cabins mid-Oct.—mid-May;

Helen Wildman's family has owned 150 acres on the western end of Paradox Lake for more than a century; eight of the 10 lakefront rental houses were built by her grandfather. These places are big — four to six bedrooms — and have old-fashioned stone fireplaces and screened porches, but most of the cottages have one bathroom. There's nice swimming at the club's private beach, canoes and rowboats for exploring pretty Paradox Lake, plus tennis, horseshoes, and a baseball field.

Westward open year-round; B&B closed Nov.—March.

Price: Inexpensive to Moderate.

Credit Cards: None.

Min. Stay: 1 week for houses July—Aug.; inquire about B&B.

Special Features: Children welcome; private sand beach; boats; guests must supply linens, towels, and eating utensils for some cabins.

Guests can rent outboards for fishing or Sunfish for sailing around the lake. Helen says, "Many of our tenants return regularly, year after year, and sometimes for several generations, but there's always room for newcomers, especially if your vacation plans are flexible."

In spring and fall, weekly rental rates are about half the July—August fees. Westward, one of the houses, is completely winterized, and a favorite spot with ice fishermen and cross-country skiers.

Nearby, and under the same ownership as the Lake Paradox Club, is a charming old farmhouse now operating as a B&B. The Red House on Sawmill Road is next to Paradox Brook and close to excellent fishing, hiking, and canoeing; guests here can enjoy the club's waterfront amenities, too. Sixteen miles down the road is Fort Ticonderoga, and Schroon Lake is just four miles away.

## Silver Bay

**NORTHERN LAKE GEORGE RESORT**

Manager: Mark Martucci. 518-543-6528.

Rte. 9N, Silver Bay, NY 12874.

Closed: Lodge and motel closed Nov.—Apr.; villas open year-round.

Price: Inexpensive to Expensive.

Credit Cards: MC, V.

Handicap Access: Some accommodations.

Special Features: 400 feet of lakefront with sandy beach; free rowboats and canoes for guests; children welcome; dive shop; docks for guests' boats.

Opened as the Hotel Uncas in 1896, the Northern Lake George Resort bills itself as the last of the lake's original old hotels still open to the public. The main lodge has been changed significantly over the years, though: the third floor with dormer windows was removed in the 1950s, and balconies and porches were added. The Great Room still maintains the appeal of an old Adirondack lodge with its stone fireplace and polished wood floors.

Inn guests can select from rooms on the lodge's second floor with private balconies providing views of the lake and the cliff; modern winterized lakeside villas with fireplaces, kitchens, cable TV, and decks; or motel rooms. There's a cocktail lounge and restaurant on the premises that's open to the public, July—August. Summertime visitors can arrange for MAP rates.

James Fenimore Cooper fans please note that the mountain overlooking the property is purportedly the very cliff from which Chief Uncas leapt to his death in *The Last of the Mohicans*. And the depths of Lake George hold numerous 18th- and 19th-century shipwrecks, from French and Indian War bateaux to sidewheel steamboats. The Northern Lake George

Resort has a full-service dive shop offering tank fills and supplies; special dive charters to underwater historic sites can be arranged for groups.

## *Warrensburg*

**BENT FINIAL MANOR**
Owners: Patricia and Paul
  Scully.
518-623-3308.
194 Main St.,
  Warrensburg, NY 12885.
Open: Year-round.
Price: Moderate to
  Expensive.
Credit Cards: None.
Special Features:
  Fireplaces; children wel-
  come.

An impressive Queen Anne-style mansion, complete with three fireplaces, numerous stained-glass windows, a wraparound porch, a conservatory, a tower, and the trademark "bent finial," this Main Street bed and breakfast is elegant indeed. There are four guest rooms with private baths and queen-size beds, all on the second floor. The Master Chamber is delightful year-round: it has a wood-burning fireplace and a secluded veranda overlooking the garden behind the house. The Eastlake Chamber is decorated with Eastlake furniture, and the Turret Room has curved walls, lovely windows, plenty of ruffles and lace.

Guests enjoy early-morning coffee and afternoon tea or perhaps a glass of wine in the conservatory. Breakfast is a candlelit, leisurely affair; Pat bakes every day, with souffles, cinnamon buns, and Belgian waffles special favorites. "We've had guests from seventeen countries, including Manchuria and Nepal," says Pat.

**COUNTRY ROAD
  LODGE**
Owners: Sandi and Steve
  Parisi.
518-623-2207.
Hickory Hill Rd.,
  Warrensburg, NY 12885.
Open: Year-round.
Price: Inexpensive.
Credit Cards: None.
Special Features: Cross-
  country ski trails; no
  pets; no electronic
  games.

In 1974, Steve Parisi began transforming an old farmhouse on the banks of the Hudson River into a haven for cross-country skiers and a year-round bed and breakfast. The Country Road Lodge is decidedly off the beaten path, well suited to bird-watchers, hikers, and others who want to explore the secluded 35-acre property and adjacent state lands. Hickory Hill downhill ski center, sort of a mom-and-pop hill with an impressive vertical drop of 1200 feet, is right next door. The lodge is also a short distance from the antique shops in Warrensburg, the tour boats on Lake George, and the Saratoga flat track.

There are four comfortable guest rooms, two with private baths. Special winter weekend packages include meals plus apres-ski treats. There's no TV at Country Road Lodge, but plenty of books, magazines, a piano, and board games. Monopoly, anyone?

### CRONIN'S GOLF RESORT

Owner: James P. Cronin.
518-623-9336.
Golf Course Rd.,
  Warrensburg, NY 12885.
Closed: Late Nov.—early
  Apr.
Price: Inexpensive to
  Moderate.
Credit Cards: None.
Special Features: 18-hole
  golf course; children and
  small pets welcome.

One of the few places in the southern Adirondacks where you can stay right at the golf course, Cronin's offers modest housekeeping cabins and a motel with frontage along the Hudson River. The family-run 18-hole course was first developed in the 1930s; it's usually one of the last golf courses to close up in the fall.

### CRYSTAL LAKE TOWNHOUSES

Owners: Susan and Andy
  Beadnell.
518-494-2742.
Crystal Lake/Mail: Box
  369, Warrensburg, NY
  12885.
Open: Year-round.
Price: Expensive.
Credit Cards: MC, V, AE,
  D.
Min. Stay: 2 nights.
Special Features: Private
  lake; children welcome.

These attractive new log townhouses have all the amenities — dishwasher, microwave, washer-dryer, full kitchen, and Jacuzzi — and are ideal for a family or two couples vacationing together, whether it's ski season or high summer. Some units have three floors and a cathedral ceiling with balcony; all the townhouses have decks. Crystal Lake is a small spring-fed lake with good fishing, and guests have exclusive use of its waters for canoeing, rowing, and sailing.

### DONEGAL MANOR BED & BREAKFAST

Owner: Dorothy Dill
  Wright.
518-623-3549.
117 Main St.,
  Warrensburg, NY 12885.
Open: Year-round.
Price: Moderate.
Credit Cards: MC, V.
Min. Stay: 2 nights on holiday weekends and dur-
  ing August.
Special Features: Fireplace;
  antique shop in barn;
  smoking permitted in
  parlor only; children over
  10 welcome; no pets.

Local lore says that James Fenimore Cooper was a guest at Peletiah Richards' house when he was researching *The Last of the Mohicans*. In those days, the house was among the grandest in town, and later in the 19th century it became more elaborate still, with the addition of an Italianate tower, a long veranda, and a bay window. Details inside Donegal Manor are lovely: there's an ornate fireplace in the parlor, a beautiful coffered wood ceiling above the staircase, lace curtains, and antiques throughout.

There are four guest rooms, two of which share a bath. The Victorian Suite, on the second floor, has its own sun room and modern private bath; the Rose Room, on the first floor, also has a private

*Irish hospitality in an Italianate mansion sets Donegal Manor apart.*

Nancie Battaglia

bath. An older portion of the house is currently under renovation to create another suite.

The best part about Donegal Manor can't be described in architectural or decorative terms — it's Dorothy Dill Wright, the innkeeper, and her warm, genuine Irish charm. We suspect she's the real reason that folks return time and again to this bed and breakfast.

**THE HOUSE ON THE HILL**
Owners: Lynn and Joe Rubino.
518-623-9390/1-800-221-9390.
Rte. 28, Warrensburg, NY 12885.
Open: Year-round.
Price: Moderate.
Credit Cards: MC, V.
Special Features: No smoking; antique shop on premises; French and Italian spoken.

Just outside Warrensburg is a nicely restored 14-room Federal-style farmhouse set on 176 acres. Joe and Lynn Rubino bought the place in 1969 and have spent years fine-tuning the property. Throughout the parlor, hallways, and living room, there are lots of Victorian antiques and interesting ephemera, especially opera items like autographed scores, playbills, and letters. There's an eclectic assortment of artwork on the walls, from signed Peter Max lithos to 19th-century engravings, all collected by Joe, a retired graphic-design expert.

Four spacious, sunlit guest rooms, and three baths, are on the second floor. One room, with its own kitchenette and private staircase, can be combined with another bedroom to form a suite. There's a spectacular Venetian porcelain chandelier in the Rose Room. In the mornings, Lynn slips upstairs to leave fresh pastries and hot coffee outside the guest rooms.

The Rubinos pride themselves on offering a dust-free, smoke-free, relaxed atmosphere. Breakfast — as much you'd like and whatever you please —is served at any time up to 11:00 a.m., and dinners may be arranged by special request. "Romantic getaway" packages are available, and the Rubinos know just when to light the candles and disappear.

*The House on the Hill, a restored 14-room Federal-style farmhouse.*

Joe Rubino

**THE MERRILL MAGEE HOUSE**
Owners: Florence and Ken Carrington.
518-623-2449.
2 Hudson St.,
    Warrensburg, NY 12885.
Closed: March.
Price: Moderate to
    Expensive.
Credit Cards: MC, V, AE, D.
Min. Stay: 2 nights on
    weekends.
Special Feature:
    Restaurant; tavern; pool;
    cross-country ski
    rentals.

Until Florence and Ken Carrington purchased this lovely Greek Revival house in the center of town in 1981, the property had remained in the same family since 1839. The oldest part of the orginal house is now the tavern and reception rooms; the back portion of the restaurant, circa 1812, actually came from another homestead some miles away. Merrill Magee House is listed in the National Register of Historic Places.

Three cozy, old-fashioned rooms with double beds and shared bath are upstairs in the inn. The new Peletiah Richards Guest House, located behind the inn, combines 20th-century conveniences like private baths with 19th-century decor: each room has its own fireplace, brass or four-poster bed, and handmade quilt. These rooms are all named after herbs, and "Parsley" is wheelchair-accessible. There's also a three-room family suite with television, refrigerator, and sitting room.

Merrill Magee's grounds are beautifully landscaped, with flower gardens, shady nooks, and a swimming pool. In the summer you can sit on the porch and listen to evening concerts held in the bandshell just on the other side of the white picket fence. The restaurant wins rave reviews, and the English-style tavern is a great place to linger over a pint of imported ale.

## RIDIN'-HY RANCH RESORT

Managers: Andy and Susan Beadnell.
518-494-2742.
Sherman Lake, Warrensburg, NY 12885.
Located several miles north of Warrensburg, and west of Bolton Landing.
Open: Year-round.
Price: Moderate to Expensive.
Credit Cards: AE, MC, V, D.
Min. Stay: 2 nights.
Special Features: Entertainment; horseback riding; downhill and cross-country skiing; snowmobiling; private lake; indoor pool; restaurant; cocktail lounge; children welcome; no pets.

Western-style dude ranches were once abundant in the southeastern Adirondacks, but many have closed in the last few years. Ridin'-Hy, an 800-acre complex on Sherman Lake, continues to prosper, offering everything from a private intermediate-level downhill ski area to rodeos. There are 50 miles of trails for snowmobiling, cross-country skiing, or horseback riding: you can ride Old Paint year-round, for as many hours or days as you please. In warmer weather guests can swim, row, or water ski on Sherman Lake, and fish in Burnt Pond or the Schroon River.

The centerpiece of the ranch is an enormous two-story log cabin that contains a cocktail lounge, living room, game room, and restaurant. Accommodations include new chalet cabins, lodge rooms, and motel units, all finished with natural wood. Numerous midweek and off-season packages are available, such as "Learn to Love Winter," which includes rental ski equipment and lessons.

## RIVER WILLOWS FARM

Owners: Theresa and Raymond Whalen.
518-623-9570.
Schroon River Rd., Warrensburg, NY 12885.
Open: Year-round.
Price: Expensive.
Credit Cards: MC, V, AE.
Min. Stay: Summer or holiday weekends: 2 nights.
Handicap Access: Yes.
Special Features: Telephone, fax, and copier; cable TV and VCR in Great Room; children and pets welcome.

Combining guest-cabin privacy with bed-and-breakfast hospitality, River Willows opened in spring 1992. Cabins — tastefully decorated with regional antiques — all have two bedrooms and private baths, plus porches with old-fashioned rocking chairs. Breakfast is served in the Great Room, which has a massive cut-stone fireplace, a vintage Steinway grand piano, and a pre-Civil War Brunswick Balke Collander pool table. The beautiful farm covers 62 acres; guests are free to climb nearby Kelm Mountain and picnic on a private beach on the Schroon River. The "Bell Walk," fountains, gardens, and greenhouse are lovely from May through the fall.

## CHAMPLAIN VALLEY

### Crown Point

**CROWN POINT BED &
BREAKFAST**
Managers: Doreen and
Tom Plantier.
518-597-3651.
3A Main St., Crown Point,
NY 12928.
Open: Year-round.
Price: Inexpensive to
Moderate.
Credit Cards: MC, V.
Special Features: Children
welcome; no smoking;
no pets permitted
indoors.

**B**uilt by a local banker in 1887, this stately 18-room mansion is a testament to Victorian craftsmanship. The woodwork — cherry, mahogany, oak, chestnut, walnut, and pine — gleams in paneling, window trim, pocket doors, floors, and an ornate staircase. There are three parlors, three porches, four fireplaces, and five acres of gardens and grounds for guests to enjoy. It's a five-minute walk to Lake Champlain, a short drive to the historic ruins at Crown Point.

There are five guest rooms, all decorated with antique bedsteads and dressers. The Crown Room and the Garden Room each have private baths; the Master Bedroom Suite, decorated with antique wicker and a high-back walnut bed, has a small attached room with a daybed. Breakfast, with homemade breads, muffins, and fresh fruit, is served in the oak-paneled dining room.

### Elizabethtown

**STONELEIGH BED &
BREAKFAST**
Owners: Rosemary
Remington and William
Ames.
518-873-2669/1-800-445-
0696.
Water St., Elizabethtown,
NY 12932.
Open: Year-round.
Price: Inexpensive.
Credit Cards: MC, V.
Special Features: Fireplace;
older children welcome.

**R**ichard Harrison, a Boston-based architect who left his mark on Wichita, Kansas, designed this impressive Germanic-style stone building for New York State Supreme Court Justice Arthur Smith in 1882. The house has a fine library, as befits a country judge, and several porches and balconies look out over the tree-shaded, secluded grounds. (From the road, the place might look a bit as if Morticia and Gomez could be lurking around the corner, but not to worry — the Addams family doesn't live here.) There's also a TV room and a living room for guests.

Downstairs, there's a bedroom with private bath that is wheelchair-accessible; upstairs, four rooms share a bath at the present, although there are plans to build an extra half-bath in the near future.

**STONY WATER BED
& BREAKFAST**
Owners: Winifred
Thomas and Sandra
Murphy.

**R**obert Frost slept here. Rockwell Kent designed the library. Louis Untermeyer owned the place. Stony Water, a beautifully restored Federal-style house located on 87 acres of rolling hills outside Elizabethtown, is simply wonderful.

518-873-9125.
Roscoe Rd.,
  Elizabethtown, NY
  12932.
Closed: April.
Price: Moderate.
Credit Cards: MC, V; prefer cash or personal check.
Special Features: Fireplace; library; pool; gardens; dinner available by special arrangement; children welcome; no smoking; no pets.

In the main house, a grand piano in the parlor invites guests to play. Upstairs there are two guest rooms decorated with antiques, and over the garage, there's a spacious, sunlit apartment that accommodates up to four people. Off in the woods a few hundred yards away is Untermeyer's former writing studio, which was recently remodeled into an attractive two-bedroom house. Called Trillium Cottage, it has natural wood paneling throughout, cathedral ceilings, a fireplace, and a screen porch. Rental is by the week. In the backyard, Winifred and Sandy — ever the genial hosts, even with paintbrushes or trowels in hand — are transforming a gardener's shed into a wheelchair-accessible cottage.

Stony Water is located on a very quiet country road ideal for mountain biking; there are also hiking trails on the property to explore, and there's an in-ground pool if those activities generate too much warmth. The perennial and herb gardens are lovely from late spring through fall.

Courtesy Winifred Thomas and Sandra Murphy

*Stony Water Bed & Breakfast, just outside of Elizabethtown, is on 87 acres.*

### Essex

**ESSEX INN**
Owner: David Millhouse.
518-963-8821.
Lake Shore Rd., Essex, NY 12936.
Open: Year-round.
Price: Moderate.
Credit Cards: MC, V.
Handicap Access: 2 downstairs suites.
Special Features: Arts center and gallery on premises; Pizzaz by Z clothing shop; cafe; children welcome.

This authentic, nicely restored 180-year-old inn stretches along Main Street with two tiers of porches. The building is surprisingly narrow — just one room and the hallway wide — with a casual cafe, courtyard, dining room (open for breakfast year-round, for dinner in July and August), and two spacious guest suites downstairs. Upstairs there are three bedrooms, plus two more suites: one includes a bedroom, bath, and kitchenette, and the other has two bedrooms, a sitting room, and bath.

The inn is full of antiques, as well as an eclectic array of art ranging from 19th-century engravings to modern paintings; this gallery is actually the Millhouse Bundy Performing and Fine Arts Center, which began in Waitsfield, Vermont, more than 20 years ago. Under the arts center's sponsorship, the inn hosts a half-dozen or so jazz concerts in the summer.

*The Essex Inn first opened to travelers in 1810.*

Nancie Battaglia

On the lakefront, and under the same ownership are the Shipyard Point Cottages, six fully equipped cabins that also have private docks.

The entire hamlet of Essex is a historic-preservation buff's dream: there are dozens of beautiful early to mid-19th-century buildings. For information about the town, see Chapter Four, *Culture.*

### North Hudson

**PINE TREE INN B&B**
Owners: Pat and Pete
  Schoch.
518-532-9255.
Rte. 9, North Hudson, NY
  12855.
Open: Year-round.
Price: Inexpensive.
Credit Cards: MC, V.
Min. Stay: 2 nights on holi-
  day weekends.
Special Features: Children
  over 6 welcome.

Oak floors, tin ceilings, and old-fashioned hospitality mark this country lodge, which opened as the Schroon River Inn in 1911. It's a short walk to the Schroon River, where there are a beach and a tennis court, and the yard has picnic tables and grills for guests. Pat and Pete Schoch have welcomed families and couples here since 1984.

Five guest rooms, which share two full baths, are located upstairs. Downstairs is a lounge area with plenty of books, magazines, and a television, although, Pat says, watching TV isn't all that popular: "Folks come here for the peace and quiet." We'd agree, although we bet they return in part because of the delicious, hearty breakfasts with homemade sticky buns, muffins, and pancakes served with real Adirondack maple syrup.

### Ticonderoga

**BONNIE VIEW ACRES**
  **BED & BREAKFAST**
Owners: Bonnie and Orley
  Dixon.

Picture this on a snow-covered January day: a sleigh ride over the fields followed by a candlelight dinner in the farmhouse dining room. Bonnie View is a family farm with Belgian draft horses,

518-585-6098.
Canfield Rd., Ticonderoga,
NY 12883.
Open: Year-round.
Price: Inexpensive.
Credit Cards: None.
Special Features: Sleigh
and wagon rides; farm
animals; well-behaved
children welcome.

sheep, chickens, ducks, a cat, and a dog. Guests may walk or cross-country ski on hiking trails, there's good fishing nearby, and Orley will hitch up the team for a twilight wagon ride in summer or fall.

There are four guest rooms outfitted with old-fashioned iron bedsteads and patchwork quilts; one room has a private bath. Family antiques, including ancestral portraits, decorate the rooms. For breakfast, fresh eggs from the Bonnie View's flock, buttermilk biscuits, and jams made from local wild berries are on the menu.

## Westport

### BRADAMANT CORPORATION

Manager: Sandra Goodroe.
518-962-8313.
36 S. Main St., Westport,
NY 12993.
Garden Cottage available
year-round; Knolls
Cottage closed Oct.–Apr.
Price: Moderate to
Expensive.
Min. Stay: 1 week.
Credit Cards: MC, V.
Special Features: Lake
views; children and well-
behaved pets welcome.

The Bradamant Corporation, a Westport real-estate concern, has two very nice, fully equipped guest houses located in the center of town. The Garden Cottage, which is available year-round, and Knolls Cottage, available May through the foliage season, both have four bedrooms. The cottages are side-by-side near the Westport Yacht Club, and they have old-fashioned porches with stunning lake views. Ballard Park, with a nice beach on Lake Champlain, is close by, as are public tennis courts; the 18-hole golf course is about a third of a mile away.

### THE GRAY GOOSE GUEST HOUSE

Owner: Elizabeth
Kroeplin.
518-962-4562.
Box N, 42 N. Main St.,
Westport, NY 12993.
Open all year, but advance
reservations are
required Oct. 15—May
15.
Price: Moderate.
Credit Cards: None.
Special Features: Children
welcome; no smoking
indoors.

A sprightly Victorian cottage with views of the lake, Gray Goose has two first-floor rooms, each with private baths and a private entry off the front porch. There's one room upstairs with twin beds, its own bath, and a small sitting room. For a small extra charge, guests can enjoy a continental breakfast in the dining room, which does double-duty as the Gifted Goose, a craft shop offering balsam pillows, handmade cloth dolls, and wreaths. All of Westport's attractions, from good restaurants to swimming, tennis, and golf, are within walking distance.

## THE INN ON THE LIBRARY LAWN

Owners: Christine and
  Bernard DeLisle.
518-962-8666.
Box K, 1 Washington St.,
  Westport, NY 12993.
Closed: Jan.—mid-Apr.
Price: Moderate.
Credit Cards: AE, MC, V.
Special Features: Lake
  view; children welcome.

A pair of beautifully restored buildings — the Inn on the Library Lawn and the Gables, the first a classic old country inn, circa 1875, and the second a gracious turn-of-the-century home two doors away — comprise these lodgings on Main Street. Both places feature ten guest rooms, every room with private bath, with assorted antiques, and Victorian-style wallpapers and trims. Guests can enjoy breakfast downstairs or on the outdoor deck overlooking Westport's library and lakefront. The main floor of the inn is also home to an excellent antique shop and children's bookstore.

Although the Inn on the Library Lawn no longer serves lunch and dinner, several nearby restaurants serve everything from burgers to gourmet fare. Lake Champlain boaters take note: the inn is just a couple of blocks from the Westport Marina. Tennis, golf, swimming, and the weekly farmers' market are all within walking distance.

## THE WESTPORT HOTEL

Innkeepers: Rita and
  Ralph Warren.
518-962-4501.
Pleasant St., Westport, NY
  12993.

When the railroad came to Westport in 1876, Albert Gates opened his hotel on the other side of the tracks. Ever since, the spacious clapboard building has been operated as an inn. Guests

B. Folwell

*The wraparound porch at the Westport Hotel is a good place for watching the world go by or enjoying a meal.*

On Rte. 9N near the
Amtrak station.
Open: Year-round.
Price: Inexpensive to
Moderate.
Credit Cards: MC, V.
Special Features:
Restaurant; off-season
packages with meals
available; children and
leashed pets welcome.

can now choose from **ten recently renovated rooms**
decorated with antiques and hand-stenciled walls;
most rooms have private baths. In warm weather,
there's a breezy wraparound porch for watching
the world go by on Route 9N or enjoying a meal
from the hotel's fine kitchen.

Folks who are traveling without a car should
note that there's daily Amtrak service to Westport,
and many of the town's charms, from the Essex
County Fair and the Depot Theater to the lake-
front, are nearby. Rita can direct you to local historic sights or send you out on
a walking tour.

## Willsboro

**1852 INN**
Owner: Lil Iten.
518-963-4075.
277 Lake Shore Rd.,
Willsboro, NY 12996.
On Rte. 22 between Essex
and Willsboro.
Open: Year-round.
Price: Inexpensive.
Credit Cards: MC, V.
Special Features: Lake
view; children and well-
behaved pets welcome.

Just up the road from Essex is a lovely Greek
Revival home opened by Lil Iten and her late
husband, Gusti, as a bed and breakfast. The 1852
Inn has a sweeping view of Lake Champlain and
four upstairs guest rooms that share baths.

Guided fishing trips or sunset boat tours of the
lake can be easily arranged, and guests may walk
to the lakefront from the front door or bicycle on
back roads with the inn's bikes. From May through
the fall, the perennial beds are beautiful, and vegetables from the garden appear at the table. Lil, who
once ran a wonderful restaurant featuring Swiss
and French cuisine, prepares dinners for guests with
one-day advance notice. She says, "We offer what's completely fresh and in season, whether it's local strawberries in June or wild mushrooms later on. Dinners
might include lamb in springtime, or venison in the fall." Besides good food, the
inn also serves up true hospitality in a very pleasant setting.

**LONG POND CABINS**
Owner: John Wintermute.
518-963-7269.
Rte. 22, Willsboro, NY 12996.
Closed: Oct. 20—Apr. 15.
Price: Moderate.
Credit Cards: None.
Handicap Access: Some cot-
tages have ramps.
Special Features: Sandy beach;
convenience store; boats;
children and pets welcome.

Lakefront housekeeping cottages are a relative
rarity in the Champlain Valley, and on the
shores of Long Pond — actually a good-sized lake
— John Wintermute operates a cluster of homey
two- and three-bedroom cabins. There's swimming
and fishing in the pond, plus tennis, horseshoes, a
play area, a convenience store, and a game room
all on the property. Guests can rent canoes, fishing
boats and motors, or pedal boats for exploring the
pond.

## HIGH PEAKS AND NORTHERN ADIRONDACKS

### *Elk Lake*

**ELK LAKE LODGE**
Innkeeper: Peter Sanders.
518-532-7616.
Elk Lake Rd., Elk
  Lake/Mail: North
  Hudson, NY 12855.
Off Blue Ridge Rd.
Closed: Late Nov.—early
  May.
Price: Expensive; includes
  all meals.
Credit Cards: None.
Min. Stay: 2 nights.
Special Features: Private
  lake and pond; 12,000-
  acre preserve; hiking
  trails; canoes and row-
  boats for guests; fishing;
  children welcome; no
  pets.

In a nutshell, Elk Lake Lodge is the quintessential Adirondack lodge. Set on a breathtaking private lake ringed by the High Peaks, in the midst of a 12,000-acre preserve, the lodge offers everything an outdoors person could ask for: great fishing, unlimited wilderness hiking, big-game hunting, and canoeing on an island-studded lake that's off-limits to motorboats. Of course, if just hanging out, listening to the loons, and admiring the view are your kinds of recreation, this place has that in spades, too.

There are six rooms in the turn-of-the-century lodge, all with twin beds and private baths. Around the lakeshore there are seven cottages, ranging from Little Tom, a cozy spot under the trees for two, to Emerson Lodge, which sleeps up to 12. Several of the cabins are completely equipped with kitchens and have fireplaces; some

Michael Flecky

*The view from Elk Lake Lodge.*

have decks overlooking the lake; all are nicely decorated with classic, clean-lined furniture. The price of a stay at Elk Lake includes all meals, which are served in a dining room with huge picture windows looking out on the mountains and lake.

Guests can use the lodge's canoes and rowboats on either Elk Lake or another private water body, Clear Pond. Brook trout, lake trout, and landlocked salmon are regularly stocked in the preserve.

## *Keene*

**BARK EATER INN**
Owner: Joe Pete Wilson;
   manager: Jodi Downs.
518-576-2221.
Alstead Hill Rd., Keene,
   NY 12942
Open: Year-round.
Price: Moderate to
   Expensive.
Credit Cards: AE, MC, V.
Min. Stay: 2 nights on
   weekends and holidays.
Special Features: cross-country skiing; horse-back riding; dinners available; children welcome; special packages.

The stagecoach carrying folks from Lake Champlain to Lake Placid used to stop here more than 150 years ago, and since the 1940s, members of the Wilson family have taken in guests. The main part of this country inn is a beautiful farmhouse with two stone fireplaces and wide-board floors, packed with antiques. There are seven rooms upstairs that share baths, plus four rooms in the new Carriage House with private baths. The Log Cottage has two three-bedroom suites and two guest rooms with private baths. Breakfast is served family-style in the dining room; full five-course gourmet meals are available.

Guests seek out the Bark Eater not just for the surroundings and the friendly staff, but for horse-back riding, hiking, and cross-country skiing. The lodge has dozens of well-mannered English and Western mounts and many miles of woodland trails. Polo games are held in a nearby field on Sunday

*The Bark Eater Inn, Keene, has miles of woodland trails for horseback riding and cross-country skiing.*

B. Folwell

afternoons during July and August. In winter, the bridle trails become groomed ski trails; Bark Eater's 20 kilometers connect with the Jackrabbit system, so you could ski for days and never cover the same territory. Owner Joe Pete Wilson was an Olympic biathlete, and he has outfitted a complete ski-rental shop on the premises.

The inn offers several different midweek and weekend ski or horseback-riding packages; there are facilities for small conferences or board retreats, too.

## *Keene Valley*

**CHAMPAGNE'S HIGH PEAKS INN**
Owners: Sherry and Norman Champagne.
518-576-2003.
Rte. 73, Keene Valley, NY 12943.
Open: Year-round.
Price: Moderate.
Min. Stay: 2 nights.
Credit Cards: MC, V.
Special Features: Fireplace; mountain views; children welcome.

Kagan, a friendly Newfoundland, is the unofficial greeter at this spacious lodge located on Keene Valley's main street. At the High Peaks Inn, there are three guest rooms with private bath, including one on the first floor, and five rooms that share baths upstairs. Guests can lounge in two enormous yet cozy living rooms, reading books by the fireplace or watching cable TV. There are old-time rocking chairs on the front porch and Adirondack chairs in the side yard, from which you can see Spread Eagle Mountain.

Breakfast at Champagne's gets you off to a good start for hiking, cross-country skiing, fishing, or touring the Olympic village. "Everything's made from scratch," Sherry says, "even the bread for the French toast." For that very toast, there's real maple syrup, too.

**TRAIL'S END FAMILY INN & HIKER'S LODGE**
Owners: Laura and Ray Nardelli.
518-576-9860.
Trail's End Rd., Keene Valley, NY 12943.
Off Rte. 73.
Open: Year-round.
Price: Moderate.
Credit Cards: MC, V.
Min. Stay: 2 nights on holiday weekends.
Special Features: Fireplaces; hiking trails; children welcome.

A rambling gambrel-roofed house with eyebrow windows on a quiet road, Trail's End calls itself a hiker's lodge, implying that the accommodations aren't so fancy that you need to worry about washing off yesterday's bug dope before you come to breakfast. Downstairs, the lodge has a large, comfortable living room with a fireplace and VCR, plus a winterized sun porch full of toys and games for kids. The breakfast room looks out over a field bordered by a stone wall; in May the lilacs are lovely.

Guest rooms upstairs include Catamount, which has a corner fireplace, a private porch, and a sink, and Marcy, a two-room suite with private bath and sleeping porch. There are two single and four double rooms, sharing baths, plus a separate coed bunkhouse that accommodates ten. At times, hiking clubs or family groups take over the entire place, which can hold 38 comfortably. Meals can be arranged for large groups.

You don't need a car to enjoy Trail's End. The bus stops every day at the Noon Mark Diner, a five-minute walk away, and from the inn, there's easy access to numerous High Peaks hiking trails.

## Lake Placid

**ADIRONDAK LOJ**
Manager: Rob Bond.
518-523-3441.
Adirondak Loj Rd., Lake Placid, NY 12946.
Off Rte. 73, three miles south of Lake Placid village.
Open: Year-round.
Price: Very Inexpensive to Inexpensive.
Credit Cards: MC, V.
Special Features: Swimming; fishing; hiking trails; tent campground; backcountry cabins; meals; nature museum; High Peaks Information Center; store.

The drive into Adirondak Loj, with its sweeping panorama of Mount Marcy and Indian Pass, sets you up for a visit to the Adirondack Mountain Club's (ADK) wilderness retreat. Located on pretty Heart Lake in the midst of the High Peaks, the 1920s-era lodge is a rustic, comfortable place. In the living room, you can rock in an Old Hickory chair in front of the vast stone fireplace and choose from the shelves practically any book that's ever been written on the Adirondacks. Breakfast — the wake-up bell rings bright and early, folks — is served family-style at picnic tables in an adjoining room. Trail lunches are available by arrangement, and plain, home-cooked dinners are served most evenings when the lodge is busy.

You don't need to be a member of the ADK to stay at the Loj, but you must make advance reservations. There are four private rooms, four bunk rooms, and a huge coed loft. The bunk rooms, which have four built-in log beds, are snug and cozy, like cabins on a ship, and during late fall and spring when the hiking and skiing aren't prime, you may have one all to yourself. The management refers to the bathrooms as

Nancie Battaglia

*Entrance to the Adirondack Mountain Club's campground at Adirondack Loj, outside Lake Placid.*

"semiprivate," but they're more akin to the facilities in a college dorm, with separate toilets and showers, and rows of sinks.

Nearby, there's a wilderness campground for tents. Ten lean-tos are available on a first-come, first-served basis; there's a wash house with showers, toilets, and sinks for campers. Heart Lake has good swimming and fishing, and numerous hiking and cross-country ski trails are accessible from the property.

For the intrepid traveler, ADK has three backcountry cabins that are accessible by foot and available year-round: Johns Brook Lodge is three and a half miles in, and has meals available in the summer months. Farther away are Grace Camp and Camp Peggy O'Brien, which have tiers of bunks, gas lights, and wood heat; they're excellent bases for hiking, snowshoe, or ski weekends.

**BLACKBERRY INN**
Owners: Gail and Bill
  Billerman.
518-523-3419.
59 Sentinel Rd., Lake
  Placid, NY 12946.
Open: Year-round.
Price: Inexpensive to
  Moderate.
Credit Cards: None.
Min. Stay: 2 nights on
  prime winter weekends
  and holidays.
Special Features: Children
  welcome; walking dis-
  tance to downtown and
  Olympic Arena.

A country-style home near the heart of town, the Blackberry Inn offers five guest rooms that share two baths. The Billermans provide slippers and bathrobes for guests so that no awkward towel-draping or indoor-overcoat-wearing need occur. There are other nice touches here too, like a front-porch swing, a comfortable living room with cable TV, and terrific breakfasts. Gail's specialties include apple and raisin crepes, cheese souffles, and French toast made with homemade bread.

**HIGHLAND HOUSE INN**
Owners: Cathy and Ted
  Blazer.
518-523-2377.
3 Highland Place, Lake
  Placid, NY 12946
Off Hillcrest Ave., near the
  Holiday Inn.
Open: Year-round.
Price: Moderate.
Credit Cards: MC, V.
Min. Stay: 2 nights on
  weekends.
Special Features: Children
  welcome; mountain-bike
  rentals.

Secluded but central, Highland House looks and feels like an authentic Adirondack inn, which it assuredly is. The main house, with antiques and rustic details, opened to guests in 1910. Downstairs, there's a large living room with a wood-stove, a piano room, a dining room, and a deck with benches built around two big clumps of white birch trees. In nice weather, guests enjoy breakfast (which is included in the nightly rate) in a glass-enclosed garden room.

The inn has seven rooms, all with private baths; most bedrooms have an extra-long double bed, plus a bunk bed, so that two to four people can rest comfortably. Next door to the inn is Highland Cottage, a perky little spot complete with kitchen, fireplace, and balcony deck. There's a two-night minimum reservation for the cottage.

It's only a five-minute walk from this residential neighborhood to Main Street, but if you'd prefer not to stroll, Highland House also rents mountain bikes to guests.

**THE INTERLAKEN INN**
Owners: Carol and Roy Johnson.
518-523-3180.
15 Interlaken Ave., Lake Placid, NY 12946.
Around the corner from the Mirror Lake Inn.
Closed: April.
Price: MAP: Expensive. B&B: Moderate.
Credit Cards: AE, MC, V.
Min. Stay: 2 nights on holiday weekends.
Special Features: Fireplace; restaurant; children over 5 welcome.

With walnut-paneled walls, tin ceilings, a fireplace, a winding staircase, and all kinds of antiques, the Interlaken is a true gem tucked away from Lake Placid's busy streets. Built in 1906 by one of the founders of the Bank of Lake Placid, the place has been operated as an inn for most of its existence. Downstairs, the dining room is elegant, yet casual; guests can eat on the porch during nice weather. Off the living room is a cozy little bar, with club chairs, card table, VCR, and TV — the perfect place for reliving that golf match or discussing the fall foliage.

There are a dozen lovely guest rooms on the second and third floors, most with queen-size beds, all with private baths and decorated with antiques. The "Honeymoon Suite" has a canopy bed and its own private balcony. The third-floor rooms are especially charming; even the bathrooms, with clawfoot tubs tucked under the eaves, are romantic. During

*Antique bird's eye maple furniture is found throughout the Interlaken Inn's guest rooms.*

Nancie Battaglia

most of the year, rooms are available on the Modified American Plan. On Sundays and Mondays, except for holiday weekends, no dinner is served and the bed-and-breakfast rate applies.

The Interlaken Inn is a family affair. Carol and her son, Kevin, who graduated from the Culinary Institute of America, do the cooking, and dinners are wonderful, with menus that change every day. You'd never find the same combination of gourmet soups, salads, entrees, and desserts if you stayed here for months. Roy, whose Texas accent has resolutely resisted six years in the North Country, is the consummate innkeeper.

**LAKE PLACID MANOR**
Owners and Managers:
Carolyn and Robert
Hardy.
518-523-2573/1-800-822-
8579.
Whiteface Inn Rd., Lake
Placid, NY 12946.
Open: Year-round.
Price: Inexpensive to
Expensive; MAP available.
Credit Cards: AE, MC, V.
Min. Stay: Inquire.
Special Features:
Restaurant; lakefront;
boats for guests; fireplace in main lodge;
children welcome; pets
may stay in cottages for
nominal charge.

First, a geography lesson: the village of Lake Placid is located on tiny Mirror Lake; the lake named Placid is slightly west of town, and it's a big body of water with a couple of islands, acres of wild lands on the northeastern shore, and gorgeous views. Only a few lodgings are located on the secluded western banks of Lake Placid; the Manor sits in a particularly magical spot.

Built as a private summer home at the turn of the century, the building has been enlarged over the years, with a wing added here, a porch there, and the rooflines changed, but the heart of the building has been left intact. In 1946, Mae and Teddy Frankel opened the place as a hotel, and for nearly 40 years ran it with a personal touch. Carolyn and Robert Hardy purchased the manor in 1986.

It's not just the view from the porch — which is spectacular — or the excellent restaurant, or the wonderfully rustic bar, or the living room, with its huge stone fireplace and classic Adirondack look; besides the sum of all its charming parts, Lake Placid Manor offers old-fashioned comfort and service.

In the Main Lodge, there are 13 guest rooms, all with private baths; Swiss Cottage, near the lake, has six rooms, all with private baths; Cedar Cottage has two connecting rooms with private baths; Pine Cottage has six rooms with baths. There's a postage-stamp-size sandy beach, and canoes, sailboards, pedal boats, and rowboats are available to guests at a small rental fee. The Whiteface Inn golf course is located on the adjacent property, an easy walk from the Manor.

**LAKESHORE MOTEL**
Owner: Susanne Praeger.
518-523-2261.
54 Saranac Ave., Lake
Placid, NY 12946.
Open: Year-round.
Price: Moderate to

This quiet chalet-style motel has features that set it apart from the rest: a large private beach on Lake Placid, free rowboats and canoes for guests, picnic tables and a barbecue grill, and a great view of Whiteface Mountain. Guests can choose such walking destinations as the nearby Peninsula

Expensive.
Credit Cards: AE, MC, V.
Handicap Access: 1 unit.
Special Features: Private
sandy beach; boats for
guests; children and
pets welcome.

Nature Trails or Main Street shopping. There are eight double rooms with balconies overlooking the lake, eight ground-floor units, and eight efficiency units with kitchenettes, ideal for families. Off-season rates are inexpensive.

**MIRROR LAKE INN**
Owner: Edwin Weibrecht.
518-523-2544.
5 Mirror Lake Dr., Lake
Placid, NY 12946.
Open: Year-round.
Price: Moderate to Very
Expensive.
Credit Cards: AE, DC, MC,
V.
Handicap Access: 2 units.
Special Features: Spa;
restaurant; private
beach; heated pools;
conference facilities; ten-
nis; hair and skin-care
salon; children welcome.

On a hillside overlooking Mirror Lake, this elegant, modern resort hotel offers guests an array of amenities and services. There's a spa for workouts and fitness walks, or you can engage a personal trainer; a hair and skin-care salon is open five days a week; there's even a nutritional counselor on staff. There are tennis courts, indoor and outdoor heated pools, and a private beach on the lake. In the winter, a skating rink is cleared for guests.

The best accommodations, the "Placid Suites," are split-level rooms connected by an oak spiral staircase, with king-size beds, huge whirlpool baths, and private balconies overlooking the lake; suite guests receive champagne and flowers upon arrival, and nightly turn-down service. There's a full range of private rooms, from country-furnished doubles with private balconies to the comfortable "Colonial Bedrooms," which give guests a chance to

*The Mirror Lake Inn at Christmas time, Lake Placid.*

Nancie Battaglia

enjoy all that the inn offers at an economical price. Even the least expensive rooms have refrigerators, hair dryers, clock radios, cable TV, and magnifying make-up mirrors.

Mirror Lake Inn has an excellent restaurant (with a dress code for dinner), a cozy bar, and various nooks and crannies for guests to relax in. The inn is an exceptional facility for conferences, with plenty of attractive meeting rooms for large or small groups.

### SOUTH MEADOW FARM LODGE

Owners: Nancy and Tony Corwin.
518-523-9369/1-800-523-9369 outside 518 area code.
Cascade Rd., Lake Placid, NY 12946.
Off Rte. 73, 3 miles south of Lake Placid village.
Open: Year-round.
Price: Moderate.
Credit Cards: MC, V.
Min. Stay: 2 nights on holiday weekends; inquire.
Special Features: Farm animals; cross-country ski trails; fireplace; meals available; children welcome; no smoking.

Near Mount Van Hoevenberg is a small family farm that operates as a homey bed and breakfast. The Corwins produce much of the food that appears on the table, including maple syrup. The lodge property contains cross-country ski trails that are part of the 50-km Olympic complex, and is close to the trails up Cascade and Pitchoff mountains, so this is an ideal spot for outdoors people. There's even an outdoor sauna for relaxing after your ski or hike.

Accommodations include private rooms with half baths, rooms in the loft with shared baths, and four mountain cabins for the "soft camper," which have sleeping lofts, woodstoves, candlelight, and running water and privies nearby. The lodge's living room is quite attractive, and centers around a big fireplace. Breakfast is included in the nightly rate; family-style dinners with delicious country chow and trail lunches are available at an extra charge.

### SPRUCE LODGE BED & BREAKFAST

Owners: Guy Westcott, Carol and Doug Hoffman.
518-523-9350.
31 Sentinel Rd., Lake Placid, NY 12946.
Open: Year-round.
Price: Inexpensive to Moderate.
Credit Cards: MC, V.
Min. Stay: 2 nights on some weekends; inquire.
Special Features: Children welcome.

The Westcott family has run Spruce Lodge for more than 40 years. The place is a comfortable, rambling old house with seven rooms for guests, two of which have private baths. A continental breakfast is included in the nightly rate for these rooms. On the property is also a housekeeping cottage with two bedrooms and a full kitchen; a two-night minimum stay is required in the cottage. Spruce Lodge is on the eastern end of town, within walking distance of the Olympic Arena, the speed-skating oval, and the town beach on Mirror Lake.

### STAGECOACH INN

Owner: Lyn Witte.

With its dormers, full-length front porch, and antique weathervane, the Stagecoach Inn is

518-523-9474.
370 Old Military Rd., Lake
  Placid, NY 12946.
Open: Year-round.
Price: Moderate.
Credit Cards: None.
Min. Stay: 2 nights;
  inquire.
Special Features:
  Fireplaces; children over
  10 welcome; pets wel-
  come in 2 rooms.

an authentic Adirondack lodge located on the outskirts of town. Built in the 1830s, the inn has beautiful wainscoting throughout, and the stairway and
balcony in the Great Room are trimmed with rustic
yellow birch logs. The porch has a row of old-fashioned rocking chairs and a swing.

Five of the guest rooms have private baths; two
even have their own fireplaces. Four rooms share
baths. Some of the first floor rooms have wide
doors that would allow wheelchair access. Lyn
serves a full breakfast, with crisp French toast and
puffy cheese souffle as her specialties.

**WHITEFACE INN
RESORT & CLUB**
Assistant General
  Manager: Robert
  Vojnich.
518-523-2551/1-800-422-
  6757.
Whiteface Inn Rd., Lake
  Placid, NY 12946.
Off Rte. 86 west of Lake
  Placid village.
Open: Year-round.
Price: Moderate to
  Expensive. MAP avail-
  able.
Credit Cards: AE, DC, MC,
  V.
Min. Stay: 2 nights.
Handicap Access: Several
  units.
Special Features: Golf
  course; lakefront; pool;
  boats for guests; non-
  smoking rooms avail-
  able; restaurant; cross-
  country ski trails; chil-
  dren welcome.

L ocated between a championship 18-hole golf
course and the shores of Lake Placid, Whiteface
Inn presents a wide range of accommodations in a
lovely setting. There are 19 nicely appointed log
cabins on the lakefront, each with a fieldstone fireplace; luxury condominiums; hotel and motel
rooms; suites; two- or three-bedroom chalets with
kitchens; and a trio of vintage Adirondack lodges
perfect for large families or groups wishing to rusticate together.

There's a pool and a small private beach, and
canoes, rowboats, and windsurfers are available to
guests for a small charge. The Walter Hagen-
designed golf course is one of the best in the park.
In the winter, there are groomed cross-country ski
trails on the property that connect with the
Jackrabbit Trail, and Whiteface Inn has all kinds of
seasonal sports packages the include lift tickets,
greens fees, tennis, or sailing, plus meals.

## *Newcomb*

**MURDIE'S BED AND
BREAKFAST**
Owner: Raymond Murdie.
518-582-3531.
Rte. 28N, Newcomb, NY

I n the Winebrook Hills section of Newcomb, near
the town park, which has an awesome High
Peaks vista, friendly Ray Murdie has opened his
home to guests. "Folks from all over the world —

12852.
Open: Year-round.
Price: Inexpensive.
Credit Cards: None.
Special Features: Children
welcome.

Israel, Holland, West Germany — have stayed here with me," he says. Three bedrooms, which share a bath, are all upstairs, and there's a shower downstairs for guests. The whole house is open to visitors, with the enclosed back porch a favorite spot for relaxing near the woodstove or watching the birds at the feeder. Breakfast is ham and eggs, all you want, whenever you want. Murdie's is a convenient spot from which to hike, cross-country ski, check out the Visitor Interpretive Center, or explore the upper Hudson River.

### *Onchiota*

**YEMASSE LODGE**
Owner: Laura Williams.
518-891-0498.
Rainbow Lake, Onchiota,
    NY/Mail: HCR 1, Box
    50, Onchiota, NY 12968.
Closed: Sept. 15—May 31.
Price: Inexpensive.
Min. Stay: 1 week.
Credit Cards: None.
Special Features: Sandy
    beach; rowboats; children welcome; no pets.

A couple of housekeeping cottages on a secluded part of Rainbow Lake, Yemasse Lodge has a sandy beach for swimming and provides a rowboat for each cabin.

### *Owls Head*

**PEEBLES INDIAN AND
    MOUNTAIN VIEW
    LAKE COTTAGES**
Owners: Pat and Wayne
    Peebles.
518-483-0306 summer/
    514-626-7857 winter.
Owls Head, NY 12969.
Closed: Oct. 1—May 15.
Price: Inexpensive.
Credit Cards: No
Min. Stay: 1 week.
Special Features: Sandy
    beach; boats for guests;
    children and pets welcome.

The Peebles choice: pick a housekeeping cabin on either Indian or Mountain View Lake. On Indian Lake, there are three cabins, two of which have fireplaces, and on Mountain View Lake, there's one cabin on the lakeshore. All the cottages come with either a rowboat or canoe, and have nice screen porches, color televisions, telephones, gas grills, and outdoor barbecue pits. "Guests need to bring sheets and towels," says Pat Peebles, but everything else is supplied.

## Saranac Lake

**AMPERSAND BAY
  BOAT CLUB**
Hosts: Keti and John
  Zuliani.
518-891-3001.
12 Ampersand Bay Rd.,
  Saranac Lake, NY 12983.
Off Rte. 3.
Open: Year-round.
Price: Moderate to
  Expensive.
Credit Cards: None.
Min. Stay: 1 week in cabins
  and suites during sum-
  mer; inquire.
Special Features: Private
  sandy beach; canoes;
  boat launch and dock-
  age; children welcome;
  no pets.

A short distance from town, but directly on beautiful Lower Saranac Lake, Ampersand Bay has five nice two-bedroom log cabins with screen porches and complete kitchens; studio apartments; two two-bedroom boathouse suites directly on the water; six motel rooms; and assorted large and small cottages. If you're traveling with your own boat, you can handily launch and dock here; there's a fee for slips. The lodging includes a private sandy beach and free canoes so that guests can explore the many state-owned islands in the lake. From Lower Saranac you can travel through the locks to Middle Saranac Lake, or to Oseetah, Kiwassa, and Lake Flower, with great fishing throughout.

**HARBOR HILL
  COTTAGES**
Hosts: Denise and Wayne
  Bujold.
518-891-2784.
104 Riverside Dr., Saranac
  Lake, NY 12983.
Closed: Nov.—Apr.;
  inquire about winter-
  ized cabins in fall 1992.
Price: Moderate.
Min. Stay: 1 week late
  June—Labor Day; 2
  nights in spring and fall.
Special Features: Sandy
  beach; fireplaces; boats
  for guests; dockage; chil-
  dren and pets welcome.

A cluster of cozy Adirondack cabins on Lake Flower, Harbor Hill provides waterfront tranquility in a residential neighborhood. On a July or August Friday night, guests sitting on the docks can enjoy the free outdoor folk music concerts from across the water, or they can canoe over to the bandshell in one of the Bujolds' boats.

Four of the five cabins have fireplaces; they range in size from one to three bedrooms, and all have picture windows and decks overlooking the water. The cabins are completely outfitted with all kitchen gear, linens, and even Weber grills. There's a private beach for swimming, dock space for visiting boats (the public launch is nearby), motorboats available to rent, or free rowboats, pedal boats, and canoes. Denise says that plans are underway to winterize a couple of the cottages in fall 1992; inquire if you'd like to visit during ski season.

**HILLMAN'S COTTAGES**
Owners: Mr. and Mrs.
  Theodore Hillman.
518-891-2263.
Lake Colby Dr., Saranac

A short distance from Lake Colby, which has excellent fishing, a public boat launch, and a nice swimming beach, the Hillmans have housekeeping cottages and a small motel comprising ten

Lake, NY 12983.
On Rte. 86, near the
　Adirondack Medical
　Center.
Closed: Oct.—May.
Price: Inexpensive.
Credit Cards: None.
Handicap Access: All
　units have ground-floor
　entrances.
Special Features: Children
　welcome; no pets.

**THE HOTEL SARANAC
OF PAUL SMITH'S
COLLEGE**
General Manager: Don
　Kirche.
518-891-2200/1-800-937-
　0211.
101 Main St., Saranac
　Lake, NY 12983.
Open: Year-round.
Price: Inexpensive to
　Moderate; B&B or MAP
　available.
Credit Cards: AE, DC,
　MC, V.
Handicap Access:
　Elevators; most rooms.
Special Features:
　Restaurants; cocktail
　lounge; gift shop on
　premises; children, and
　pets on leash, welcome.

**THE POINT**
Owners: Christie and
　David Garrett;
　Managers: Claudia and
　Bill McNamee.
518-891-5674/1-800-255-
　3530.
Mail: Star Rte., Box 65,
　Saranac Lake, NY 12983.
Closed: April.
Price: Very Expensive.
Credit Cards: AE.
Min. Stay: 2 nights.
Special Features: Great

units altogether. Overnight guests are welcome throughout spring, summer, and fall.

For more than 30 years, the Hospitality Management students of Paul Smith's College have gotten on-the-job training at this landmark downtown hotel. As a result, the staff here is competent, friendly, and helpful at all hours of the day or night. There are 92 air-conditioned guest rooms, all with private baths; rooms are pleasant in a nondescript way, but the second-floor lobby, with beautiful painted wood beams, a grand piano, and potted plants, is quite nice. Lydia's Dining Room, named after the wife of North Country hotelier and college founder Paul Smith, is open from breakfast to dinner, while the Boathouse Lounge — a quiet, pleasant tavern — serves light meals as well. The Hotel Saranac offers numerous packages for golf or skiing, and tour groups or conferences are cheerfully accommodated.

William Avery Rockefeller built a drop-deadgorgeous Great Camp named Wonundra on an Upper Saranac Lake peninsula in the thirties, and if you've read any recent articles about the Adirondacks, chances are you've seen The Point, that Rockefeller place that's now open to guests. A roundup of comments from the press gives you a glimpse of what's so special here: "Simply the most attractive private home in America whose owners welcome paying guests in the European tradition," said the *New York Times*. "A private estate that sweeps all honors as the most enchant-

Camp; private 10-acre lakefront peninsula; gourmet meals; boats for guests; member *Relais et Chateaux*; no children under 18.

ing lakefront sanctuary of its kind in America," stated *The Hideaway Report*. "It's rather like those European castles where one can arrange to spend a week as the guest of the duke and duchess," commented the *Yale Alumni Magazine*. "The Point: the wilderness at its most luxurious," summarized *Vogue* magazine.

The 11 rooms, located in four different buildings, each have vast beds, lake views, and fireplaces, and are filled with a well-planned mixture of antiques, Adirondack furniture, Oriental rugs, old prints, and stuffed beasts. The Boathouse is a special gem, with its own private dining alcove and wrap-around balcony, but all the rooms are lovely.

In the Main Lodge, The Great Hall measures 30 by 50 feet; fireplaces of astonishing proportions blaze away. The atmosphere here is that of a truly elegant house party; black tie is suggested for dinner on Wednesday and Saturday nights. The food warrants that treatment too — Master Chef Albert Roux deftly combines native bounty, fine herbs, exquisite seafood, and imported ingredients in an imaginative kaleidoscope of flavors. The wine list is unsurpassed, and the bar is always open.

There are all kinds of boats to enjoy, from vintage Adirondack guideboats to canoes, sailboards, and a gleaming mahogany HackerCraft. The lake is delightful for swimming, and the lodge has plenty of rods and reels for guests; licensed guides are available to help you find elusive brook trout or trophy bass.

All this elegance and hedonism comes at a price; two nights (the minimum stay) for a couple at The Point costs about as much as a week for two at Elk Lake Lodge. But *Forbes* magazine sums it up well: "There are no telephones, no newspapers, and no menu choice. You partake of what is prepared each day and sit down to dine at the appointed hour. If you don't like the hosts, the food, the guests or the digs, tough luck ... [yet] for those in search of sybaritic creature comforts, there is only one destination — The Point."

A final note: don't expect to be able to drive in for just a look at the place. No signs mark the way to The Point, and only registered guests get the secret directions.

**THE PORCHES**
Hosts: Susan and Glenn Arnold.
518-891-2973.
16 Helen St., Saranac Lake, NY 12983.
Closed: Christmas holidays.
Price: Inexpensive.

This nicely restored Queen Anne house bristles with seven assorted glass-enclosed sun porches where tuberculosis patients once took "the cure," which was basically lots of fresh air all year-round. Staying here has equally restorative effects today, especially if you start with one of Glenn's scrumptious homemade breakfasts (pineapple souffle, deep-dish bread pudding with blueberry

Credit Cards: None.
Special Features:
  Fireplace; children over
  12 welcome.

sauce, Belgian waffles topped with fresh strawber-ries, to name a few), and take to the outdoors.

All the rooms are surprisingly private, and are on the third floor of the house, with views of the village and nearby mountains. There are two dou-bles and a single, which share a bath. The guests' living room has shelves and shelves of books and great music to play; there's a fireplace in the foyer. The cobblestone-enclosed yard has nice perennial gar-dens, and it's an easy walk to Moody Pond or downtown.

*The Porches Bed & Breakfast, in Saranac lake, has seven different glass-enclosed "cure porches."*

Courtesy Susan Arnold

## Upper Jay

**THE ARK/CONSTITUTION TRAIL INN**
Hosts: Edelgard and Klaus Todte.
518-946-2276.
Rte. 9N, Upper Jay, NY 12987.
Open: Year-round.
Price: Inexpensive.
Credit Cards: MC, V.
Handicap Access: 1 room.
Special Features: Meals available; children and pets welcome.

On a swift-flowing stretch of the Ausable River, the Ark has quiet motel-style rooms and offers breakfast and dinner to guests. This is a good spot for fly fishermen, downhill skiers (Whiteface Mountain is only a few miles away), and hikers who plan to explore the High Peaks; on summer Saturday evenings, there are free folk- and classical-music concerts on the village green in Jay, a short drive away.

**HIGH PEAKS BASE CAMP**
Managers: Julie Ward and

With cozy one-room sleeping cabins, a spa-cious bed and breakfast lodge, and a primi-tive campground, the Base Camp offers many

Nancy Fallica.
518-946-2133.
Springfield Rd., Upper Jay, NY 12946.
Open: Year-round.
Price: Inexpensive.
Credit Cards: AE, MC, V.
Handicap Access: Some units.
Special Features: Primitive campground; cross-country ski trails; occasional live music and theater; restaurant; children welcome; pets welcome in campground; group packages available.

lodging opportunities for folks traveling solo or in large groups. Within the lodge, which also contains the Wood Parlor Restaurant, there are private rooms with shared baths, and a huge, inexpensive hostel-style bunk room. All linens are provided, but guests need to bring towels.

The Base Camp is located on a 200-acre farm, with horses in the fields and trout and salmon in the pond. (These fish can be caught for your dinner, but there's no recreational fishing in the pond.) From time to time there are special events, like Frog Pond Theater performances or folk-music festivals. When the snow's deep enough, guests can cross-country ski here; complete ski rentals are available. For alpine skiers, Whiteface Mountain is nearby. If you'd like to travel farther afield for hunting and fishing, ask about guide service.

## *Wilmington*

### WILKOMMEN HOF

Owners: Heike and Bert Yost.
Rte. 86, Wilmington, NY 12997.
518-946-SNOW/1-800-541-9919.
Closed: Apr. 15—May 31; Oct. 15—Nov. 15.
Price: Inexpensive to Moderate. MAP available.
Credit Cards: MC, V.
Special Features: Meals available; sauna; children welcome; midweek ski packages.

Heike and Bert have recently renovated their turn-of-the-century farmhouse, adding two new bathrooms and a sauna, and redecorating the dining room. Wilkommen Hof houses a maximum of 24 guests; full breakfasts and after-ski treats are included in the room rate. Dinners are often available on winter weekends, and may be arranged at other times. The fabled Ausable River trout waters are nearby, as are numerous state-marked trails for cross-country skiing and hiking. Wilkommen Hof is quite popular with Whiteface Mountain downhill skiers as it's just minutes away from the slopes.

## NORTHWEST LAKES REGION

### *Cranberry Lake*

### CRANBERRY LAKE INN

Owners: Genie and Mike Coleman.
315-848-3301.
Rte. 3, Cranberry Lake, NY 12927.

Look down the lake from the motel/restaurant complex and you get a feel for just how wild and vast the Adirondacks are. This clean, homey place is a good jumping-off spot for exploring Cranberry Lake or the Five Ponds Wilderness Area

Closed: March 21—Apr. 30.
Price: Inexpensive.
Credit Cards: MC, V.
Handicap Access: Some units; inquire.
Special Features: Children and well-behaved pets welcome.

several miles to the southwest, or heading out on the network of nearby snowmobile trails. There are 23 units for guests, including two apartments; many rooms have views of the lake. The restaurant here is one of the best in the area, and the antiques, stuffed animals, and old photographs give a good introduction to this uncrowded part of the park.

**WILDCLIFFE LODGE**
Owners: Barb and Vern Peterson.
No phone.
Mail: Box 526, Cranberry Lake, NY 12927.
Closed: Nov. 15—June 1.
Price: Inexpensive to Moderate; lodge rooms are MAP.
Credit Cards: None.
Special Features: Remote location; access by boat only; children welcome.

Says Vern, "Unless you want to hike about thirteen miles, the only access to the lodge is across the lake, by boat, six miles from the village." Everything comes by boat, as a matter of fact, from soup to nuts, including the mail. Forget about phones or TV; electricity is supplied by a generator.

The main lodge is a big log building, housing a dining room, a bar that's open to the public (it's a Cranberry Lake tradition for folks to visit Wildcliffe at least once in the summer for a beer), and a long porch. There are four rooms upstairs in the lodge, sharing baths, and two log cabins, which have cold running water but no showers or tubs. For the cabins, you need to supply all your own bed linens, blankets, and towels, but the weekly rate is very inexpensive. The Petersons serve plain, hearty, home-cooked fare such as T-bone steaks, pork chops, and ham; the annual Fourth of July Chicken Barbecue and the mid-September Pig Roast are jolly affairs.

From Wildcliffe, there are many miles of wilderness hiking trails to explore. Fishing and canoeing are very good in Cranberry Lake, and the lodge is open during the first couple weeks of big game season if you'd like to hunt far from the roads.

## *Lake Clear*

**CHARLIE'S INN & JUNCTION CAMPGROUND**
Owner: Charles Elwyn, Sr.
518-891-9858.
Junction Rd., Lake Clear, NY 12945.
Just off Rte. 30.
Open: Year-round; restaurant closed Tues.
Price: Inexpensive.
Credit Cards: MC, V.

Charlie's offers mainly a full-service campground with complete hookups, a laundromat, picnic and play area, showers, and hiking trails; in the inn there are a half-dozen rooms, which are popular with snowmobilers, fishermen, and hunters. There's plenty of good, home-style chow in the restaurant and bar.

**THE LODGE AT LAKE CLEAR**
Manager: Cathy Lee Fisher; Owners: Ellen and Ernest Hohmeyer, Sr.
518-891-1489.
Rts. 30 & 186, Lake Clear/Mail: Box 46, Lake Clear, NY 12945.
Open: Year-round; restaurant closed Nov. 15—30; March—Apr.
Price: Moderate to Expensive; MAP available.
Min. Stay: 2 nights in chalets; 2 nights on holiday weekends.
Credit Cards: MC, V.
Special Features: Fireplaces; restaurant; children welcome in some accommodations; pets allowed in chalets (deposit required).

People for miles around beat a path to the Lodge for its excellent German cuisine, and overnight guests have enjoyed the Hohmeyers' true hospitality for more than a quarter century. On 20 secluded lakeshore acres, the accommodations are spotless and attractive.

There are four upstairs rooms in the inn, each with private bath. Two brand-new chalets are completely outfitted with good kitchens, nicely decorated living rooms, and cozy fireplaces; at 900 square feet, they're far bigger than the usual housekeeping cabin. There's an outdoor deck on each chalet. Also on the grounds is a one-bedroom summer cabin. All of these buildings are spread out enough so that families can enjoy some woodsy privacy.

Guests have use of canoes, rowboats, picnic area, and beach; Cathy is happy to arrange mountain-bike rentals, guide service, or overnight canoe trips. Recently, the Lodge has begun offering special weekend packages that include dog-sled adventures, jazz or theater tickets, and sleigh rides.

Nancie Battaglia

*The parlor at The Lodge on Lake Clear.*

## Paul Smiths

**NORTHBROOK LODGE**
Manager: William Schwartau.
518-327-3279.
Off Rte. 86, Paul Smiths, NY 12970

A former Adirondack Great Camp on a ten-acre peninsula on Osgood Lake, Northbrook Lodge has 15 nice rooms for guests, all on the main floor, and each with private baths. The place is rustic and peaceful — "No organized activities,"

Closed: Sept. 15—June 15.
Price: Expensive. MAP.
Min. Stay: 3 nights.
Credit Cards: None.
Special Features: Fireplace;
   lakefront; sandy beach;
   boats for guests; chil-
   dren welcome.

states Bill firmly. Instead, guests can swim, fish, take out one of the inn's canoes or rowboats, or relax in an Adirondack chair. Breakfast and dinner are included in the room rate, and the food is plentiful and tasty.

*Lounging by the boathouse at Northbrook Lodge.*

Nancie Battaglia

## *Saranac Inn*

**SUNDAY POND BED
AND BREAKFAST**
Owners: Lesley and Dick
   Lyon.
518-891-1531.
Rte. 30, Saranac Inn, NY
   /Mail: Star Rte., Box
   150, Saranac Lake, NY
   12983.
Open: Year-round.
Price: Inexpensive.
Credit Cards: None.
Special features: Fireplace;

Say you're a canoeist and you want to explore the St. Regis Canoe Area with its dozens of lakes and ponds, but you hate the thought of camping out. Or say you're a cross-country skier and you'd like to make a long day-trip up St. Regis Mountain, but you can't face leaving home at 4:00 a.m. for that four-hour drive to the trailhead. Look no further: Sunday Pond is located smack where you can start all those adventures right from the front door.

Lesley and Dick's house — one of very few in this corner of the park — is quite nice, with a long

guide service available; children over 8 welcome.

porch, skylights, a fireplace, and a big family room. Guests can choose from two rooms that share a bath, a room with a private bath, or a spacious sleeping loft with its own bath. Breakfasts are ample and healthy.

## *Tupper Lake*

**COLD RIVER RANCH**
Hosts: Marie and John Fontana.
518-359-7559.
Rte. 3, Coreys, NY/Mail: Coreys, Tupper Lake, NY 12986.
Open: Year-round.
Price: B&B: Moderate; MAP available.
Credit Cards: MC, V.
Special Features: Horseback riding; cross-country ski trails; canoe rentals; children welcome.

Cold River is famous for wilderness trail rides and overnight pack trips, and the huge old farmhouse is a very comfortable bed and breakfast as well. Nine guests are accommodated in four rooms with shared baths. Breakfast, which John describes as "fancy home cooking," can include cheesecake still warm from the oven. Full board is an option, too.

In the winter, the horse trails are endless backcountry ski trails. Guides, instructors, and rental equipment are available, and the Fontanas are happy to arrange custom ski tours for guests.

Nancie Battaglia

*Marie and John Fontana with one of the Cold River Ranch horses.*

**CURTINGAY COVE**
Owners: Gail and Morris Weissbrot.
518-359-9612/winter: 904-753-8296.

On a quiet bay of Little Wolf Lake, which is just east of Tupper Lake village, the Weissbrots offer four fully equipped housekeeping cottages. "Our customers from the city always tell us, 'This is exactly what we were looking for.' And they

South Little Wolf Rd., Tupper Lake, NY 12986/Winter mail: 508 Rainbow Blvd., Lady Lake, FL 32159.
Closed: Oct. 1—June 1.
Price: Inexpensive to Moderate.
Min. Stay: 1 week July— Aug.; weekend in off-season.
Credit Cards: None.
Handicap Access: Yes; inquire.
Special Features: Sandy beach; canoe rentals for guests; children welcome; small well-behaved pets allowed.

always comment about how clean our cottages are," says Gail.

All the cottages have sun decks, picnic tables, and outdoor fireplaces. Canoes are available for guests to rent. Curtingay Cove is the kind of place that families return to every year, with kids building friendships that last beyond the summer.

## SHAHEEN'S MOTEL

Manager: Ken Horn.
518-359-3384.
310 Park St., Tupper Lake, NY 12986.
Open: Year-round.
Price: Inexpensive to Moderate.
Credit Cards: AE, DC, MC, V.
Special Features: Heated pool; cable TV; children welcome; no pets.

With a heated pool, copier and fax service, free continental breakfast, balconies, a picnic area, and a few other touches, Shaheen's is a pleasant place to stay near the center of town. The Park Restaurant is nearby, and miniature golf is a short walk away. There are 33 units.

## THREE PILLARS

Owners: Bob and Neil Shofi.
518-359-9093/Winter: 914-835-2900.
Moody Rd., Tupper Lake, NY 12986/Off-season mail: 231 Halstead Ave., Harrison, NY 10528.
Closed: Late Sept.—June.
Price: Moderate.
Min. Stay: Inquire.
Credit Cards: None.
Special Features: Private beach; lakefront; boat dockage for guests; children welcome.

With nearly a thousand feet of shoreline on Big Tupper Lake, the secluded cabins at Three Pillars have a great view. The location, on the southern end of Big Tupper Lake and close to Bog River Falls, is one of the best you'll find on this large lake.

There are three pine-paneled housekeeping cottages with fireplaces and screen porches, comfortably furnished with homey touches and complete kitchens, plus a three-bedroom apartment. There's a nice sandy beach and a long dock for guests' boats. Ask about where to find the walleyes.

## THE WAWBEEK RESORT

Owner: Wawbeek Realty Associates.
518-359-2656.
553 Panther Mountain Rd., Tupper Lake, NY 12986.
Just off Rte. 30.
Open: Year-round.
Price: Moderate to Expensive; MAP available.
Min. Stay: 1 week in some accommodations in summer; inquire.
Credit Cards: MC, V.
Special Features: Lakefront; sandy beach; boats for guests; boat launch and dockage for guests; tennis; restaurant.

Sharing the same Upper Saranac bay as the classic Great Camps, Wenonah Lodge and Sekon Lodge, the Wawbeek Resort has an authentic Adirondack style. The original Wawbeek, itself a Great Camp, burned down about 12 years ago, and new owners consolidated that property with a former boys' camp next door. One of the buildings, Mountain House Lodge, is a wonderful turn-of-the-century structure with double-deck porches, stone fireplace, and great room; it's the kind of place that would be ideal for several couples or an extended family to share for a week. Scattered under the trees are comfortable one-bedroom log cabins and modern housekeeping cabins of various sizes.

Guests have all of gorgeous Upper Saranac Lake to explore if they choose. The lodge offers sailboats, rowboats, and canoes for guests; there's a beach, tennis court, game room, basketball court, and boat launch on the premises. In the winter, cross-country skiers can try the Deer Pond cross-country trails just a short distance away. The Wawbeek's restaurant is one of the nicest in the Adirondack Park.

## CENTRAL AND SOUTHWESTERN ADIRONDACKS

### *Arietta*

## AVERY'S INN

Manager: Darla Oathout.
518-835-4014.
Rte. 10, Arietta/Mail: Box 48A, Caroga Lake, NY 12032.
Closed: Lodgings, summer; restaurant open winter, spring, and fall weekends; Wed.—Sun. in July—Aug.
Price: Inexpensive to Moderate.
Credit Cards: None.
Special Features: Fireplaces; restaurant and bar; access to snowmobile trails.

A huge old hotel on a less traveled stretch of highway, Avery's has been operated by the same family for more than a hundred years. The West Branch of the Sacandaga meanders across the way; snowmobile and hiking trails are nearby. It's an out-of-the-way spot, so much so that the inn has to generate its own electricity.

There are 17 rooms for guests, offered mainly from hunting season through spring thaw, and Darla says that availablity can be limited at times because of the high rate of return visits. Special weekend packages with meals and lodgings are designed for cross-country skiers and snowmobilers. The main business here is a restaurant, which easily seats 125, and a bar; there are two big stone fireplaces and a friendly, casual atmosphere.

## *Benson*

**LAPLAND LAKE CROSS-COUNTRY SKI & VACATION CENTER**
Owners: Ann and Olavi Hirvonen.
518-863-4974.
Storer Rd., Benson, NY/Mail: RD 2, Box 2053, Northville, NY 12134
Open: Year-round.
Price: Moderate to Expensive.
Min. Stay: 2 nights.
Credit Cards: MC, V.
Special Features: 50 km cross-country ski trails; private lake; restaurant in winter; sauna; ski-rental shop; ski lessons; children welcome; no pets.

Just when you think you got the directions wrong to this rather remote spot, you see road signs in ... *Finnish*? Quickly, the view opens up to a brand-new ski shop and a bunch of neat little cottages. In winter there's always lots of snow here; the 50 km of trails are meticulously groomed by Olavi, a former Olympic skier. *Snow Country* magazine readers recently rated Lapland Lake among the top 10 Nordic ski centers in the East.

Summertime is nice at Lapland Lake, too. Ann says that families celebrating reunions are a growing clientele; the separate cottages allow folks to have privacy and proximity at the same time. There's a small spring-fed lake on the 300-acre property where guests can swim, canoe, and fish. The trails here connect with state-owned hiking trails; you can pick up the Northville-Placid Trail less than a mile away, or climb Cathead Mountain.

The 10 housekeeping cottages range in size from two to four bedrooms, and are called *tupas*, which means "cabins" in Finnish. They're spotless and homey; most have woodstoves or screen porches. The biggest cabin, *Lapin Tupa*, is the property's original farmhouse. It has a formal dining room with a nice view of the pond, a big eat-in kitchen, living room with piano, four bedrooms, and two full baths.

The Hirvonens pride themselves on offering all kinds of services for guests. There's a sauna, a small wintertime restaurant serving Finnish dishes along with American fare, and a full ski-rental shop. Guide service can be arranged for spring through fall outings; from December through March, there are dozens of special ski events and workshops for folks of all ages and abilities.

*A familiar scene in front of a Lapland Lake tupa.*

Nancie Battaglia

## TRAILHEAD LODGE

Owner: John Washburn.
518-863-2198.
Washburn Rd., Benson, NY/Mail: RD 2, Box 2047A, Northville, NY 12134.
Open: Year-round.
Price: B&B: Inexpensive.
Min. Stay: 2 nights winter weekends; 3 nights holiday weekends.
Credit Cards: None.
Special Features: Outfitting and guide service; canoe rentals; fireplace; outdoor-skill workshops; adjacent to Lapland Lake Cross-Country Ski and Vacation Center; children over 5 welcome.

In the 1880s, John Washburn's great-grandfather took in hunters and fishermen here, and guided them to the big ones; nowadays you can expect much the same thing in rather a bit more comfort at Trailhead Lodge. On the outside the building looks like a typical farmhouse, and inside, the walls are finished with new pine boards and decorative Adirondack touches, like snowshoes, packbaskets, and such. There are four guest rooms that share baths. Public areas downstairs include a spacious living room with a fireplace, a dining room, and a game room. Guests may choose bed and breakfast or modified American plan arrangements.

John, a licensed Adirondack guide, is very knowledgeable about the woods and wildlife; he often leads map-and-compass workshops for groups, or takes folks on hikes, canoe trips, backcountry ski adventures, and snowshoeing trips. By the roaring fire on a chill night, you might coax him to recite Robert Service poems or tall tales.

From Trailhead Lodge you can easily get to the Silver Lake Wilderness Area, which is peppered with lakes, ponds, and trout streams. Chances are if you hike in a mile or two you may not see another person all day.

*A classic winter view of Trailhead Lodge, Benson.*                    B. Folwell

*Doug and Bonnie Bennett at the Big Moose Inn.*

Nancie Battaglia

## Big Moose Lake

**BIG MOOSE INN**
Innkeepers: Bonnie and
   Doug Bennett.
315-357-2042.
Big Moose Rd., Big Moose
   Lake, NY; Mail: Eagle
   Bay, NY 13331.
Closed: April.
Price: Inexpensive to
   Moderate; MAP avail-
   able.
Min. Stay: 2 nights on
   weekends.
Credit Cards: AE, MC, V.
Special Features: Fireplace
   in living room; restau-
   rant and lounge; snow-
   mobile trails; lakefront;
   canoes for guests; chil-
   dren welcome.

**M**ud season is about the only time you can't enjoy Big Moose Inn. In the late spring, you can canoe and fish in peace on Big Moose Lake; in the summer you can hike around Pigeon Lake Wilderness Area, or visit nearby towns like Eagle Bay, Inlet, and Old Forge; in the fall you can see beautiful foliage or hunt; when the snows arrive, there's snowmobiling or cross-country skiing prac-tically right to the front door.

There are 16 rooms upstairs in the inn, some with private baths. Midweek packages for May—June 15 and mid-September—early December are quite reasonable.

If you've avoided staying at an Adirondack inn because you're not sure about the quality of the food, be assured that the meals here are delicious. Folks come from miles around to enjoy dinner, and someone once described the Big Moose Inn as "a restaurant so good you want to spend the night."

**COVEWOOD LODGE**
Owner: C. V. Bowes, Jr.
315-357-3041.
Big Moose Lake, Eagle
   Bay, NY 13331.
Open: Year-round.
Price: Moderate to
   Expensive;

**O**ne of the all-time great woodsy Adirondack retreats, Covewood was built as a hotel back in the days when guests stayed all summer long. Even in today's busy world, you'd probably wish you could stay from Independence Day to Labor Day, the place is so nice and peaceful. Major Bowes keeps it that way.

depends on cottage size.
Credit Cards: None.
Special Features: Sandy
     beach; lakefront; boats
     for guests; cross-country
     ski trails; children wel-
     come; no meals.

There are 17 housekeeping cabins along the lake and under the pines, ranging in size from one room to seven bedrooms plus kitchen, living room, and porches. All the cabins have fireplaces and furnaces. There's a big rustic lodge with stone fireplace for guests to enjoy; weekly square dances used to be held here. In the summer, there are special programs for children so that parents can have some time alone together.

There's a private beach on Big Moose Lake. Guests can rent canoes, small outboards, and sailboats. Covewood is also a popular spot with cross-country skiers, as miles of backcountry trails are accessible right from the cabins.

**THE WALDHEIM**
Owner: Wanda Martin.
315-357-2353.
Big Moose Rd., Big Moose,
     NY/Mail: Eagle Bay, NY
     13331.
Closed: Columbus Day—
     late June.
Price: Expensive; includes
     all meals.
Credit Cards: None.
Special Features: Sandy
     beach; boats for guests;
     children welcome; extra
     daily charge for pets.

The Waldheim was built back in 1904 by E. J. Martin from logs cut on the property, and there's still a wonderful old-time feel to the place. Many of the 15 cabins are made of logs and have twig-work railings on the porches; they all look out on the lake. The places are aptly named "Cozy," "Comfort," "Heart's Content," and so on. Every one has a fireplace, and early in the morning the "wood boy" slips in to start a fire. The gracious dining room is paneled with knotty pine and furnished with antique chairs and tables. Rates include three full meals a day.

Just about the time the cottages open, lovely wild azaleas bloom along the pathways. Guests can hike, canoe, swim, and fish; arrangements can be made to have a seaplane pick you up at the dock for a scenic flight. There are no planned activities except the weekly "camp picnic," which is a moveable feast taken to a remote part of the lake by boat. The 300-acre property is adjacent to state land so the location is secluded indeed.

### Blue Mountain Lake

**CURRY'S COTTAGES**
Owners: Carrie Moodie
     and Robert Curry.
518-352-7354/Winter: 518-
     352-7355.
Rte. 28, Blue Mountain
     Lake, NY 12812.
Closed: Nov.—Apr.
Price: Inexpensive to

These charming barn-red housekeeping cottages are a familiar sight to Blue Mountain Lake visitors; photographs of the chorus line of white Adirondack chairs near the beach have appeared in numerous national magazines. Three generations of Currys have operated the cottages, and Bob, the current Curry, is always at work making improvements.

Moderate.
Credit Cards: None.
Min. Stay: 1 week in
 July—Aug.; overnights
 welcome May—June,
 Sept.
Special Features: Sandy
 beach; boat launch; chil-
 dren welcome.

There are 11 cottages that accommodate couples to families of eight; four cottages are on the water and the remainder are on the edge of the woods across the road. The beach at Curry's is a favorite with families; it's safe and shallow for kids to play in. There's a boat launch for guests. When guests tire of waterfront fun, it's a short walk to the Adirondack Lakes Center for the Arts, the post office, and fine crafts shops. The Adirondack Museum is about a mile away.

## THE HEDGES

Owner: Richard Van
 Yperen.
518-352-7325/518-352-
 7672.
Hedges Rd., off Rte. 28,
 Blue Mountain Lake,
 NY 12812.
Closed: Oct. 15—June 15.
Price: Expensive; MAP.
Credit Cards: None.
Special Features: Private
 sandy beach; boats for
 guests; tennis; meals;
 children welcome; no
 pets.

Col. Hiram Duryea, a Civil War veteran and millionaire industrialist, began building the Hedges in 1880. The main house, with four wonderful guest rooms all with private baths, has an unusual mansard roofline that sweeps onto a rustic, wraparound porch. The lovely Stone House, built about 1890, has a three-bedroom suite with fireplace on the first floor, and six rooms with private baths upstairs. Antiques and fine woodwork are found throughout these two lodges.

There are 14 one- to four-bedroom sleeping cottages along the secluded lakeshore. All accommodations are modified American plan; picnic lunches are available at a small charge. Guests have use

*The Hedges, Blue Mountain Lake: a secluded spot on a quiet lake.*

Courtesy Richard Van Yperen

of canoes, rowboats, a clay tennis court, and the library; the game room, with lots of antique rustic detailing, is worth a visit even if you don't play ping pong.

Meals are served in the Dining Room Lodge, another appealing old building, which has stamped-tin walls and ceilings and a stone fireplace. Guests get their own tables for the duration of their stay, so there's no need to try to make new friends over dinner every night. After dinner, desserts and coffee are put out so that folks can linger over those treats in their own cabins or rooms.

Blue Mountain Lake is a very beautiful, quiet lake; the Hedges is in a particularly lovely, private spot. Generations of families have returned since the hotel opened to guests more than 70 years ago; three generations of the Van Yperen family work hard at making sure folks feel comfortable.

**HEMLOCK HALL**
Owner: Paul Provost.
518-352-7706.
Maple Lodge Rd., Blue Mountain Lake, NY 12812.
Closed: Mid-Oct.—mid-May.
Price: Expensive; MAP.
Min. Stay: 2 nights; inquire.
Credit Cards: None.
Special Features: Private beach; boats for guests; meals; children welcome; no pets.

On the Maple Lodge Road, a mile off the main highway, is another stunning Adirondack hostelry. Hemlock Hall was carefully restored by Eleanor and Monty Webb in the 1950s, and the results of their hard work are evident everywhere. The woodwork in the main lodge — a complicated pattern of wainscoting on the walls and ceilings — still gleams, and there are numerous antiques throughout. The stone fireplace has hearths on two sides, opening onto part of the living room and a wing of the dining room. There's even a fireplace in an upstairs hallway.

There are 23 rooms for guests, in accommodations ranging from lodge rooms with shared baths to motel units to two- or three-bedroom cottages. The "tower suite" in the main lodge has its own private screen porch and charming window seats; several of the lodge rooms have nice lake views; you can even rent the top floor of the boathouse. Breakfast and dinner are included in the room charges.

There's a nice sandy beach, plenty of rowboats and canoes, fishing gear, and a play area. Hiking trails into Minnow Pond or up Castle Rock begin at Hemlock Hall.

The dining room serves wholesome, plentiful food in a family-style arrangement. There's one entree offered each evening, so if corned beef and cabbage isn't to your taste, well then, have some more of that tasty homemade bread. Nonguests can dine with prior reservations. Folks are seated at different tables each night so they get to mingle with the other visitors; alcoholic beverages, which might make all this mingling a bit easier, are not permitted in the dining room.

## POTTER'S RESORT

Owners: Laura and Ralph Faxon.
518-352-7331.
Rts. 28 & 30, Blue Mountain Lake, NY 12812.
Closed: Sept. 30—May 10.
Price: Moderate; depends on cabin or motel unit.
Min. Stay: 1 week for housekeeping cottages July—Aug.
Credit Cards: AE, D, MC, V.
Handicap Access: 1 cottage.
Special Features: Private beach; dockage for guests' boats; tennis; restaurant; children welcome; no pets.

**A**s you enter the hamlet of Blue Mountain Lake, Potter's Resort is one of the first places you'll see. Along the lakeshore, there's a string of 12 cozy housekeeping cottages, and in the woods across from the lake, six more cabins are nestled in the shade. Most cabins have porches; several have fireplaces; some are huge, with cathedral ceilings. There are eight nice motel units near the road that all have porches; four even have fireplaces.

Potter's has a great beach, dock space for visitors' boats, and a tennis court. The dining room is open for breakfast, lunch, and dinner from late June through Labor Day.

Enjoy this place while you can. Plans are underway to subdivide the property across the road for building lots, and as the land is developed, some of the lakeshore cottages will be torn down to make a private beach for the new homeowners.

## PROSPECT POINT COTTAGES

Manager: Bob Webb.
518-352-7378.
Rte. 28, Blue Mountain Lake, NY 12812
Closed: Oct. 10—May 10.
Price: Moderate.
Min. Stay: 1 week July—Aug.; 3 nights spring and fall.
Credit Cards: None.
Special Features: Private sandy beach; children welcome; no pets.

**T**his beautiful point on Blue Mountain Lake was once the site of the three-story, hundred-room Prospect House, the first hotel in the world to have electricity. (Never mind that technology only went so far — guests had to use outhouses.) Now, five recently renovated two- and three-bedroom housekeeping cottages occupy the point. They're under new management as of 1991, and are spotlessly clean and ship-shape. All linens and kitchen gear are provided.

The view of Blue Mountain from the lawn or the big sandy beach is simply magnificent. From Prospect Point, which is close to town but off the road, it's an easy walk to the arts center, the summer store, or the post office to mail those picture postcards of the lake.

## *Brantingham*

## BATES COTTAGES

Owners: Jerry and Doug Bates.
315-348-8811.
Long Point Rd., Brantingham, NY 13312.

**W**ith fully equipped three-bedroom housekeeping accommodations, the Bates Cottages are popular year-round. There's great snowmobiling on free, groomed trails that connect with Stillwater, Old Forge, and all points in the southwest-

Open: Year-round.
Price: Moderate.
Min. Stay: 2 nights in winter; 1 week July—Aug.
Credit Cards: None.
Special Features: Private beach; rowboats for guests; snowmobile trails nearby; children welcome; no pets.

**BRANTINGHAM BEACH CLUB, INC.**
Manager: Beatrice Kalen.
315-348-8076.
Lodge Rd., Brantingham, NY.
Open: Year-round.
Price: Inexpensive to Moderate.
Credit Cards: None.
Min. Stay: 1 week July—Aug.; inquire about other months.
Handicap Access: 1 cottage; inquire.
Special Features: Large private beach; tennis courts; playground; children welcome; small dogs may stay for an extra charge.

## *Indian Lake/Sabael*

**BURKE'S COTTAGES**
Owners: Rose and Bruce Burke.
518-648-5258/Winter: 516-281-4983.
Lake Shore Dr., Sabael, NY 12864.
Open: Year-round.
Price: Moderate.
Min. Stay: 2 nights; 1 week July—Aug.
Credit Cards: None.
Special Features: Private beach; dock; children welcome; no pets.

ern Adirondacks or Tug Hill, ice fishing on the lake, and downhill or cross-country skiing nearby. In summer, guests can swim from the safe, sandy beach on Brantingham Lake. Each cabin has its own rowboat and picnic table. From the cottages, it's a quick drive to the 18-hole Brantingham Golf Club, where you can play all day long for about 10 bucks.

With a big beach area, tennis courts, playground, and basketball court, the Brantingham Beach Club offers lots of summer fun. The four housekeeping cottages here are open in the winter, too, for snowmobiling and other winter sports. Four restaurants are within walking or sledding distance of the club.

On Indian Lake a few miles south of the village, the Burkes rent six newly renovated housekeeping cabins throughout the seasons. Most have two bedrooms, fireplaces, and comfortable furnishings; some have decks or screen porches. You can see Indian Lake from all the cottages.

There's a private beach for swimming, and a dock for boats, and Rose and Bruce are around from spring through fall to help you select the perfect hike, that undiscovered restaurant, or something to do on a rainy day.

## CAMP DRIFTWOOD
Owners: Doris, Jon, and A. E. Voorhees.
518-648-5111/Winter: 813-355-3535.
199 Sabael Rd., Indian Lake, NY 12842/Winter mail: 2712 59th St., Sarasota, FL. 34243.
Closed: Mid-Oct.—mid-June.
Price: Inexpensive to Moderate.
Min. Stay: 1 week July—Aug.; inquire about spring and fall.
Credit Cards: None.
Special Features: Private beach; boats for guests; children and well-behaved pets welcome.

Indian Lake is about 13 miles long, with numerous bays and publicly owned islands to explore, and Camp Driftwood is a good base from which to plan short excursions or day trips, or simply to relax in a pretty, secluded spot. Nick and Doris Voorhees rent eight housekeeping cabins all along the shore and tucked back in the woods. "Maple" is an old lodge, with three bedrooms, a fireplace, screen porch, and deck; "Birch" also has three bedrooms, and you can practically roll out of bed in the morning for a dip in the lake. All cottages have full kitchens and woodstoves for cool mornings, plus outdoor fireplaces for barbecues. Guests need to bring bed linens and towels.

There's a sandy beach for wading, a float for advanced swimmers, canoes and rowboats, and genuine hospitality from the Voorhees family. This is the kind of place where families settle in for two weeks or more and pretend they're at home.

## CHIEF SABAEL COTTAGES
Owners: Cynthia and Robert Kluin.
518-648-5200.
Lake Shore Dr., Sabael, NY 12864.
Cottages closed: Columbus Day—Memorial Day; efficiencies open all year.
Price: Inexpensive to Moderate.
Min. Stay: 1 week in cottages and efficiencies July-Aug.; inquire about remainder of year.
Credit Cards: None.
Special Features: Private sandy beach; tennis; dockage for guests' boats; children welcome; extra charge for pets.

Four miles south of town, on a quiet stretch of the lake, Chief Sabael Cottages offer privacy and convenience: it's a short walk to the Lake Store for that root beer float at the soda fountain, or for resupplying the refrigerator. The Kluins rent six housekeeping cottages that accommodate from two to seven people; many have fireplaces and porches with lake views. The cabins are available by the week only (two weeks preferred) during July and August; visitors may arrange for three-day stays in spring and fall. Additionally, there are winterized efficiency units open year-round, so that skiers, snowmobilers, fishermen, white-water rafters, and others can stay near all those activities.

This is one of the few places in the immediate area with a private tennis court. There's also a log lean-to by the lake, a sandy beach, and dock space available for guests' boats at an extra charge.

*1870 Bed & Breakfast, Indian Lake, is set in gardens and farmland near the center of town.*

B. Folwell

**1870 BED & BREAKFAST**
Host: Bill Zullo.
518-648-5377.
Main St., Indian Lake, NY 12842.
Rte. 28, near the health center.
Open: Year-round.
Price: Inexpensive.
Credit Cards: None.
Special Features: Fireplace; gardens; cable TV; children welcome; no pets.

Folks passing through Indian Lake hamlet always comment on a beautiful perennial garden on Main Street; from May through the fall there's a constant display of daffodils, irises, peonies, lilies, asters, and fall flowers. The garden was tended by Lilias Cross, who took in guests beginning in the sixties, and now her grandson, Bill Zullo, is doing the same.

Guestbooks from 30 years ago still capture the flavor of the place: "Our stay here was wonderful as usual. In the past 16 years, nothing has changed," commented one repeat visitor 20 years ago. You'll still find real braided rugs on the floors, tatted spreads on the antique beds, ruffled curtains in the windows, family pictures dating back to the turn of the century on the walls, and a homey, quiet atmosphere.

There is one bedroom with a private bath on the first floor, and four nice rooms upstairs that share a bath and a sitting room. The living room has comfortable Grandma's-house-type furniture, a fireplace, cable TV, and shelves of board games and puzzles. From the shady front porch you can look out over the garden, and farther back on the old 40-acre farm, there's a big raspberry patch that's open for grazing. Town tennis courts are kitty-corner from the house. There are a couple of new bikes in the barn that guests can use, and there's a private right-of-way to Lake Adirondack for fishing or canoeing about a half-mile away.

**GEANDREAU'S CABINS**
Owners: Dotty and Bob Geandreau.
518-648-5500.

When you enter the hamlet of Indian Lake from the east, one of the first places that comes into view is Geandreau's cluster of tidy cabins on Route 28 across from Lake Adirondack. In

Rte. 28, Indian Lake, NY
  12842.
Closed: Dec. 5—21.
Price: Inexpensive.
Min. Stay: 2 nights.
Credit Cards: None.
Special Features: Boats for
  guests; children wel-
  come.

the summer, the border of bright red dahlias in the front yard might catch your eye. For more than a quarter-century Dot and Bob have built up a year-round business, accommodating everyone from adventure-seekers to folks looking for a peaceful place to rest.

The cabins sleep up to five people, and are fully outfitted with kitchen equipment, linens, towels, and so on. There are screened porches on all the cottages, making them particularly enjoyable during bug season. Rowboats and canoes for exploring the nearby lake are provided; there's a swimming beach a short distance away.

### GALUSHA'S COTTAGES

Owners: Dorothy and
  Lynn Galusha.
518-648-5365.
Rte. 30, Indian Lake, NY
  12842.
Closed: Nov.—May; 2 cot-
  tages open in winter.
Price: Moderate.
Min. Stay: 1 week in July—
  Aug.; 2 nights off-sea-
  son.
Credit Cards: None.
Handicap Access: 2 cot-
  tages.
Special Features: Private
  beach; rental boats for
  guests; children wel-
  come; inquire about pets.

Lewey Lake, ringed by 3900-foot mountains, is a pretty spot, and besides the state campground at the northern end, Galusha's cottage colony offers the only accommodations on this lake. There are 18 housekeeping cottages here, ranging in size from one to three bedrooms — nothing fancy, but offering all the creature comforts. Two of the cottages are available in the winter, too.

There's a gradually sloping sandy beach and good fishing, and guests can rent rowboats and canoes. Galusha's is located midway between the towns of Indian Lake and Speculator, so it's an easy drive to grocery stores, movie theaters, and the laundromat.

### MCCANE'S

Owners: Fran and Royce
  Wells.
518-648-5125.
Cedar River Rd., Indian
  Lake, NY 12842.
5 miles off Rte. 28/30.
Closed: April.
Price: Inexpensive.
Min. Stay: 1 week July—
  Aug.; inquire about rest
  of year.

The Cedar River valley has an almost western look to it, with a beautiful, rocky trout stream flowing through a broad plain surrounded by rolling hills and peaked mountains. In large clearings in the valley are a few of the original settlers' farmsteads, and at one of these, there's a 75-year-old log cabin that you can rent. McCane's is right on the Northville-Lake Placid Trail, which is great for hiking and cross-country skiing, and it's also on Indian Lake's snowmobile trail system that leads

Credit Cards: None.
Handicap Access: Yes.
Special Features: On
Northville-Placid Trail;
RV hookups; children
and pets welcome.

**SNOWSHOE HILL
COTTAGES**
Owners: Helen and John
Feeney.
518-648-5207.
Cedar River Rd., Indian
Lake, NY 12842.
Open: Year-round.
Price: Inexpensive.
Min. Stay: 2 nights.
Credit Cards: None.
Special Features: Children
welcome.

**TIMBERLOCK**
Owner: Richard Catlin.
518-648-5494/Winter: 802-
457-1621.
Indian Lake; Sabael, NY
12864.
Closed: Oct. 1—June 20.
Price: Expensive to Very
Expensive. Full
American plan.
Min. Stay: 2 nights.
Credit Cards: None.
Special Features: Private
beach; boats for guests;
horseback riding; tennis;
archery; meals; nature
programs; adventure
camp for teens; photog-
raphy workshops for
adults; Elderhostel pro-
grams; children wel-
come; no pets.

to the Moose River Plains and surrounding towns. The cabin is completely furnished with kitchen equipment, linens, and towels. There are also two complete RV hookups at this site with water, electricity, and sewer.

Also in the Cedar River area, and near the Northville-Placid trail, is Snowshoe Hill Cottages, two year-round, fully equipped housekeeping cottages, plus an apartment (with a private entrance) in the Feeneys' house. Just up the road is good fishing on the Cedar River Flow, good hiking up Wakely Mountain, or mountain biking along the dirt roads of the Moose River Recreation Area. In the other direction, about two miles away, is Wakely Lodge Golf Course. In the winter you can cross-country ski or snowmobile right from the front door.

For more than 90 years Timberlock has welcomed guests. Not much has changed since those early days: all the buildings and the guests' log cabins are still equipped with gaslights and woodstoves, so don't expect to find outlets for blow dryers and curling irons. The atmosphere here is rustic, relaxed, and peaceful, yet the resort offers a surprising variety of activities and amenities.

There are four Hartru tennis courts; easy-going horses for guided trail rides; an excellent sandy beach; numerous boats to sail, paddle, or row on Indian Lake; and trails on the property for hiking and birding. Timberlock is home to Elderhostel seminars in the fall that make use of the Adirondack Museum and local experts for history and nature-lore presentations; there are photography workshops, adventure-camp sessions for teens, inn-to-inn canoe trips, and other outdoors or educational programs offered from year to year. If you'd prefer to discover the Adirondacks on your own, the Catlins have assembled a 120-page book outlining car trips, picnic spots, mountain climbs, museums, and other sites to explore.

B. Folwell

*One of many log buildings at Timberlock, overlooking Indian Lake.*

"Timberlock is not for everyone," says Dick Catlin. "We are not a luxury place and have not paved away the wildlife." There are a dozen "family cottages," with full baths, screen porches, and lake views, plus some small cabins without baths. Rates include three hearty meals a day and use of all the facilities and activities except horseback riding. There are no neighbors within miles of Timberlock, and your wake-up call in the morning may well be a loon's yodel from the lake.

## Inlet

**THE CINNAMON BEAR**
Owners: Jane and Bob
   Fowlston.
315-357-6013.
Rte. 28, Inlet, NY 13360.
Open: Year-round.
Price: Inexpensive.
Credit Cards: None.

Jane and Bob Fowlston opened the Cinnamon Bear, the area's first bed and breakfast, in 1988. Upstairs in their home there are four guest rooms that share baths, each room decorated differently with floral wallpapers and country accessories. Downstairs, guests can enjoy the comfortable living room with a fireplace, television, books, and games.

## CLAYTON'S COTTAGES

Owner: David Gribneau.
315-357-3394.
Seventh Lake Rd., Inlet,
NY 13360.
Just off Rte. 28.
Price: Inexpensive to
Moderate.
Min. Stay: 2 nights; prefer
to rent cottages by the
week July—Aug.
Credit Cards: None.
Handicap Access: Some
units; inquire.
Special Features: Private
beach; docks for guests'
boats; boats available;
children welcome; no
pets.

On Sixth Lake, the Gribneaus rent fourteen housekeeping cabins, ranging in size from one to three bedrooms. All the units have full kitchens, screen porches, cable TV, and fireplaces. Guests can enjoy a private sandy beach, a picnic and play area, and two docks for their own boats in the summertime; there's direct access to Inlet trails for snowmobilers in the winter. A year-round restaurant is next door to these cabins.

## THE CROSSWINDS

Owners: Jan and Bill
Burwell.
315-357-4500.
Rte. 28, Inlet, NY 13360.
Closed: Mid-Oct.—late
May.
Price: Inexpensive to
Moderate.
Min. Stay: 1 week July—
Aug.; overnights wel-
come in off-season.
Credit Cards: None.
Special Features: Private
beach; dockage for
guests; boat rentals; chil-
dren welcome; no pets.

Near Rocky Point, on Fourth Lake, the Burwells rent five attractive two-bedroom housekeeping cottages. All the places have completely equipped kitchens; guests need to supply their own linens and towels. There's a 200-foot private sandy beach and a large dock for guests' boats (extra charge for dock space). Canoes, rowboats, and motorboats can be rented on the premises. It's a short walk from the Crosswinds to downtown Inlet, which has a movie theater, restaurants, tennis courts, and shops.

## DEER MEADOWS

Owners: Linda and Robert
Gordon.
315-357-3274.
Rte. 28, Inlet, NY 13360.
Open: Year-round.
Price: Inexpensive.
Min. Stay: 2 nights on holi-
day weekends; cottages
rent by the week July—
Aug.

At Deer Meadows there's a 10-unit motel on Route 28, with queen-size beds, cable TV, and in-room coffee, and on a private drive across the highway, there are six pleasant housekeeping cottages ranging in size from one to three bedrooms. All the cottages have fireplaces and complete kitchens; guests need to bring bed linens and towels.

There's a nice little beach and picnic area on Seventh Lake, free rowboats for guests, and plenty

Credit Cards: D, MC, V.
Handicap Access: Yes.
Special Features: Private
beach; game room; row-
boats for guests; heated
garage for snowmobil-
ers; children welcome.

of friendly mallard ducks to feed in the summer. The accommodations are open year-round, and snow-mobilers in particular appreciate the heated garage the Gordons make available for minor repairs.

**HOLL'S INN**
Innkeeper: Rosemary Holl.
315-357-2941/Winter: 315-
733-2748.
South Shore Rd., Inlet, NY
13360/Winter mail: 615
Ravine Dr., Utica, NY
13502.
Closed: Sept.—June.
Price: Moderate to
Expensive; full
American plan.
Min. Stay: 2 nights.
Credit Cards: None.
Handicap Access: 25
rooms have ramps.
Special Features: Private
beach; free canoes and
rowboats for guests;
restaurant and bar; ten-
nis; movie theater for
guests; library.

**R**osemary Holl says, "The way we were is the way we still are!" This spacious resort — 150 acres on the shores of Fourth Lake — dates back to the 1920s, and the Holl family has been in charge since 1935. The buildings and grounds are beautifully maintained and quite secluded; white-tail deer often cross the lawn to drink from the lake.

There are numerous rooms, all with private baths, in the original hotel building; twenty-five rooms with private baths in the Annex, and two apartments in the Alpine House. Guests get three hearty meals a day in the lovely dining room, which is also open to the public with advance reservations. An especially charming nook of the inn is the Tyrolean Bar, done up in Dresden blue, yellow, and red, with cozy booths and hand-decorated plates commemorating all the honeymooners who have stayed at Holl's over the years. After all that food and drink, there are plenty of ways to work off the extra calories: there's a large private beach, tennis court, canoes, and rowboats for guests to enjoy.

**RICHARD KNIGHT RENTALS**
315-369-6242.
P.O. Box 525, Inlet, NY
13360.
Numerous private homes
available to rent.

**D**ick Knight is a matchmaker: he'll match your interests and needs with just the right cottage, camp, or house. Want a small camp near a hiking trail? Log cabin with a loft and a fireplace? Big lodge for a family gathering? Chances are that Dick can find them all. He's the exclusive agent for dozens of private homes that are available by the week, year-round in the Inlet, Eagle Bay, and Old Forge area.

**ROCKY POINT TOWNHOUSES**
315-357-3751/1-800-442-2251.

**T**he original Rocky Point, an enormous old hotel, was run by several generations of the DeCamp family, and recently the place was razed

Rte. 28, Inlet, NY 13360.
Open: Year-round.
Price: Expensive to Very
Expensive.
Min. Stay: 1 week July—
Aug.
Credit Cards: None.
Special Features: Private
beach; dockage for
guests' boats; tennis
courts; children wel-
come.

**WOODHOLME**
Owners: Muriel and Bill
Campbell; Jean and
Jean-Pierre Fortier.
315-357-2161/Winter: 613-
233-2459.
Seventh Lake, Inlet, NY
13360/Winter mail: 205
Daly Ave., Ottawa, Ont.,
Canada K1N 6G1.
Closed: Sept.—June.
Price: Moderate.
Min. Stay: 2 weeks.
Credit Cards: None.
Special Features: Private
lakefront; boats for
guests; children welcome.

## Johnsburg

**GARNET LAKE LODGE**
Owners: Joyce and Pete
Parker.
518-251-2582/Winter: 518-
251-2273.
Garnet Lake, Johnsburg,
NY 12843/Winter mail:
Box 68, North Creek, NY
12853.
Closed: Oct. 12—June 15.
Price: Moderate.
Min. Stay: 1 week July—
Aug.; 2 nights off-season.
Credit Cards: None.
Special Features: Private
beach; rowboats for
guests; children wel-
come; inquire about pets.

to make room for big, new, three-bedroom lake-side townhouses. Although there's a certain sameness to the way they look, each one is quite nicely furnished and has a fireplace. Kitchens have microwaves, dishwashers, and new appliances all around. The beach is excellent, nearly 1200 feet long, and there are three tennis courts.

On the north shore of Seventh Lake, sharing a boundary with state lands, Woodholme is in a lovely, quiet setting. On the same property as the two large housekeeping cottages is a historic Adirondack lodge, which once operated as a hotel; that building is not open to guests, but adds a distinctly rustic air to the place. There's private waterfront, with a boat and motor for each cottage, and a canoe is available for trips on Sixth and Seventh Lakes. From Woodholme, there's a hiking trail up Black Bear Mountain — take a container for the blueberries you may find along the way.

Garnet Lake is mostly surrounded by wild state lands, and has only about two dozen residences around it. There's very good fishing, nice swimming, and plenty of peace and quiet. The Parkers offer a total of five two- and three-bedroom cottages, each of which comes with a rowboat for finding those lunker bass. The cabins are completely furnished except that guests need to bring sheets, towels, and a toaster.

## *Long Lake*

**CAMP HILARY**
Owners: Dixie and Joe
  LeBlanc.
518-624-2233.
Deerland Rd., Long Lake,
  NY 12847.
Closed: Dec.—late May.
Price: Inexpensive to
  Moderate.
Credit Cards: None.
Min. Stay: 1 week.
Special Features: Private
  sandy beach; canoes to
  rent; docks for guests'
  boats; game room; chil-
  dren welcome; inquire
  about pets.

There's plenty to do at Camp Hilary — swimming, boating, waterskiing, canoeing, fishing
— but we have a feeling that families keep coming
back mostly because they like Joe and Dixie, who
are down-to-earth, friendly folks. Dixie's a wildlife
rehabilitator for the Department of Environmental
Conservation, and often has raccoons, fawns, and
other creatures that she's nursing back to health so
they can be returned to the woods. Joe's Joe; you'll
just have to meet him.

There are more than a dozen housekeeping cottages here, ranging in size from one to three bedrooms, plus a two-room log cabin, a tiny one-room
cabin, and a mobile home. Many of the cottages
have fireplaces or screen porches, and are equipped
with full kitchens — nothing fancy, but certainly
adequate. Guests need to bring towels, but everything else is supplied.

**INN ON THE HILL**
Innkeepers: Pat Fehr and
  Jerry Fletcher.
518-624-4684.
Deerland Rd., Long Lake,
  NY 12847.
Open: Year-round.
Price: Inexpensive.
Credit Cards: None.
Special Features: Fireplace;
  children over 5 wel-
  come; no pets.

A brilliant yellow swath of coreopsis growing
alongside Route 28/30 greets summer visitors
to the Inn on the Hill, a big Bavarian-style house
located a couple of miles southwest of Long Lake
hamlet. The place is thoroughly charming inside:
the living room is set up with small tables and
chairs as if great-aunt Martha's bridge club is coming for the afternoon. There's a stone fireplace,
couches, lacy curtains, and chandeliers. In nice
weather, you can see Long Lake and Owl's Head
Mountain from the Adirondack chairs on the front
porch. Upstairs are four spacious, newly redecorated bedrooms sharing two
baths; two rooms have king-size beds.

**LONG VIEW LODGE**
Owners: Ruth and Don
  Howe.
518-624-2862.
Deerland Rd., Long Lake,
  NY 12847.
Closed: Dec. 1—May 15.
Price: Inexpensive.

Four generations of the Emerson family have
run the Long View, which is right on Long
Lake. There's a private beach for swimming, and
Coddington's Boathouse, a full-service boat livery
and marina, is right next door.

The inn has 14 bedrooms, most of which have
private baths; Ruth says that the adjoining rooms

Min. Stay: 2 nights on
weekends.
Credit Cards: MC, V.
Special Features: Private
beach; restaurant and
bar; children welcome.

with shared baths are ideal for families. There are
two sleeping cottages on the property as well. The
restaurant, which is also open to the public, serves
breakfast and dinner daily during July and
August. The Long View is a popular spot for wedding receptions, private parties, and family
reunions.

## STONEGATE LODGE

Owners: Susan and Marc
Katz.
518-624-4831/Winter: 914-
693-7111/Reservations:
1-800-767-7111.
Walker Rd., Long Lake,
NY 12847.
Closed: July 1—Aug. 21.
Price: Moderate to
Expensive; inquire.
Min. Stay: Weekend.
Credit Cards: None.
Special Features: Half-mile
private lakefront; tennis
courts; canoes, row-
boats, and sailboats;
auditorium; meeting
rooms; children wel-
come.

Have you ever wondered what happens to children's camps in the off-season? At Stonegate
Lodge, you can rent an entire fully equipped camp,
complete with canoes, sailboats, and tennis courts,
and have a party for 150 of your best friends, or
you can book a housekeeping cabin for two, or you
can arrange any combination in between. This is an
ideal spot for a conference or board retreat, with
meeting rooms, an auditorium that seats several
hundred, and a large dining hall.

The 100-acre property includes nearly a half-
mile of shoreline on Long Lake and an assortment
of historic stone and wood buildings. In the winter,
there's cross-country skiing from the lawns out
onto the frozen lake, and snowmobilers can easily
travel to the town trail system.

## WATER'S EDGE
## CABINS

Owners: Lesley and Tom
Knoll.
518-624-5825.
Deerland Rd., Long Lake,
NY 12847.
Closed: Mid-Oct.—mid-
May; 1 cabin available in
winter.
Price: Inexpensive to
Moderate.
Min. Stay: 2 nights; prefer to
rent by week July—Aug.
Credit Cards: MC, V.
Special Features: Private
beach; boats for guests;
dock; fireplaces; chil-
dren welcome; inquire
about pets.

On Long Lake but convenient to the highway,
Water's Edge is a cluster of four housekeeping cottages, all recently redone and nicely decorated. The cabins are all named after Adirondack
birds: Osprey is a large two-bedroom unit,
Sandpiper is a cozy place for a couple, and Loon
and Chickadee are the in-between sizes. Each cottage has a full-sized kitchen, fireplace or glass-
doored woodstove, picnic table, and cable TV.
There's a private beach and a dock; guests share an
aluminum canoe and a pedal boat.

## WHISPERING WOODS
Owners: Margaret and
  Bob Sauerhafer.
518-624-5121.
Walker Rd., Long Lake,
  NY 12847.
Open: Year-round.
Price: Inexpensive to
  Moderate; depends on
  cottage or apartment.
Min. Stay: 2 nights; cot-
  tages rent by the week
  July—Aug.
Credit Cards: MC, V.
Special Features: Private
  beach; canoes and
  rowboats to rent; fire-
  places; grocery store;
  game room; RV hook-
  ups; children wel-
  come; leashed pets
  welcome.

A large sandy beach on a quiet shore of Long Lake is one of the major attractions at Whispering Woods, but the campground and cottage complex also has a well-stocked grocery store, game room, playground, and canoes and rowboats to rent. There are numerous options for lodging, from the five-bedroom Farmhouse and assorted cabins to second-floor apartments in the Main Lodge. All the cottages have kitchens equipped with the basics; guests need to bring bed linens and towels. For recreational vehicles and travel trailers, there are wooded and lakeside sites with complete water, electric, and sewer hookups available from May through November.

Cross-country skiers find that Whispering Woods is close to the loop trails around Lake Eaton, and snowmobilers can use the frozen lake to get to the Long Lake/Raquette Lake network of trails.

## *Minerva*

## MORNINGSIDE CAMPS AND COTTAGES
Owners: Sandy and
  Frank LaBar.
518-251-2694.
Minerva Lake, Minerva,
  NY 12851.
Closed: Winter.
Price: Inexpensive to
  Moderate.
Min. Stay: 1 week in
  summer; 2 nights
  spring and fall.
Credit Cards: None.
Special Features: Private
  beach; tennis; boats
  for guests; fireplaces;
  children welcome;
  no pets.

L ocated on 80 acres of land accessible by a pri-vate road, Morningside Camps offer water-front seclusion on an undeveloped lake. There are 10 nice log cabins with stone fireplaces and five chalets, all of which have complete kitchens, bathrooms, and decks or screen porches. The property features a private beach, a play area with a treehouse for the kids, a tennis court, sev-eral docks for canoes and rowboats, and a series of hiking trails through the woods that lead you to the general store, the town beach, or just around the shoreline. Each cabin comes with its own boat.

Understandably, there's often a waiting list for the LaBars' cabins in July and August; they are generally easier to book before the Fourth of July and after Labor Day. Don't be afraid to ask.

## North Creek

**THE COPPERFIELD INN**
518-251-2500.
Main St., North Creek, NY
  12853.
Closed: Nov.; inquire.
Price: Moderate to
  Expensive.
Credit Cards: AE, D, DC,
  MC, V.
Special Features: Heated
  pool; tennis court,
  restaurant; lounge;
  nightclub; shuttle bus;
  children welcome; no
  pets.

A brand-new, elegant motor inn that comes as quite a surprise after you've driven down North Creek's modest Main Street, the Copperfield has all the amenities you'd expect at a real ski resort: heated pool, health club, tennis court, fancy restaurant, lounge, shuttle bus to the slopes. You can arrange to use a boat on Loon Lake, about 10 miles away, and numerous package deals for white-water rafters, golfers, senior citizens, and midweek guests are available. There are 25 huge rooms, and they come with terrycloth bathrobes, no less.

**GOOSE POND INN**
Innkeepers: Beverly and
  Jim Englert.
518-251-3434.
Main St., North Creek, NY
  12853.
Open: Year-round.
Price: Moderate.
Credit Cards: None.
Special Features: Fireplace;
  children over 10 wel-
  come; no pets.

A beautifully restored Victorian home set back on a shady lawn off Main Street, Goose Pond Inn has four lovely bedrooms, each with its own bath. Antiques, old prints, and amusing details are found throughout. Jim cooks up superb breakfasts, such as brandied French toast with sautéed apples, crepes with rhubarb sauce, or Belgian waffles with flambéed bananas. From the inn, it's a five-minute drive to downhill skiing at Gore Mountain or to any of the white-water rafting headquarters for trips down the Hudson Gorge. If adventure isn't your thing, you can always commune with the resident geese at their pond here, or curl up by the fire with a good book.

## North River

**GARNET HILL LODGE**
Manager: Peter Fitting;
  owner: George Heim.
518-251-2444.
Thirteenth Lake Rd.,
  North River, NY 12856.
Closed: Nov. 15—30.
Price: Expensive; MAP.
Credit Cards: None.
Special Features: Cross-
  country ski trails;

Cross-country skiers flock to Garnet Hill: there are some 35 miles of groomed trails, a full shop, and reliable snow cover. In fact, readers of *Snow Country* magazine just named the place one of the 10 best Nordic ski centers in the country.

But you don't have to ski to enjoy this country inn, and you don't have to wait for winter, either. Except for two weeks in November, Garnet Hill is open all year. In early spring you can observe

full ski shop; restaurant and lounge; fireplaces; private lakefront; mountain bike, canoe, and rowboat rentals for guests; children welcome; no pets.

maple-syrup making at the sugarbush, or later on, join in a bird-watching program with a local forest ranger. Elderhostel, the international educational organization, has a couple of week-long Adirondack-history sessions at the lodge before summer begins. When the weather's settled, you can mountain bike or hike on the trails, or plan a trip into Siamese Ponds Wilderness Area, or just watch the days pass in a beautiful setting from a comfortable chair near Thirteenth Lake.

The Log House, built in 1936, has sixteen upstairs guest rooms, all with private baths. Downstairs is the restaurant, a game room, a massive fireplace made of local garnet, and two lounges for guests. Guests can also stay in Big Shanty, which was the home of Frank Hooper, developer of the original garnet mines in the area. Big Shanty, with another great stone fireplace, many rustic details, and a traditional Adirondack flavor, overlooks Thirteenth Lake and has seven guest rooms. A new building on the property, the Tea House, has just two luxurious rooms with king-size beds, whirlpool baths, and its own private lounge.

Garnet Hill visitors can swim at the private beach, play tennis at the inn's courts, or rent canoes, rowboats, and sailboats. Numerous packages are available for white-water rafters, fishermen, inn-to-inn skiers, and groups.

**HIGHWINDS INN**
Innkeeper: Kimberly
    Repscha.
518-251-3760.
Barton Mines Rd., North
    River, NY 12856.
Closed: Apr., Nov.
Price: B&B: Moderate;
    MAP: Expensive.
Credit Cards: MC, V.
Special Features: Cross-
    country ski trails; moun-
    tain bikes for guests;
    canoes; tennis; fire-
    places; restaurant;
    wilderness cabin; chil-
    dren over 6 welcome; no
    pets.

The former home of the president of Barton's Mines, Highwinds Inn is a surprisingly elegant place in a very out-of-the-way spot, some five miles off the main highway. The house is lovely, with a beautifully furnished living room centered around a rough-hewn garnet fireplace. Four lovely guest rooms, each with private bath, are upstairs, and rooms all look out on a sweeping vista of the ponds and hills in the Siamese Ponds Wilderness Area. The elevation here is 2500 feet above sea level, so Highwinds is probably the highest accommodations you can find anywhere in the state.

There are 1600 acres that guests can explore on skis over 25 km of cross-country trails, on mountain bike along old woods roads, or by canoe on small private ponds stocked with trout. Hikers are welcome to tour the old garnet mines with guides in the summer. On Pete Gay Mountain, which faces the downhill area on Gore Mountain, there's a wilderness cabin made of logs that's available for two-night stays.

One word summarizes the food at Highwinds: excellent. Breakfast is often whole-grain blueberry pancakes, sour cream waffles with maple syrup, or fresh-baked pastries of all kinds. Dinners offer a varying menu, with several choices for appetizer, salad, entree, and dessert, and everything is prepared at the inn. Guests can opt for a bed-and-breakfast plan or modified American plan, at varying rates for weekend or midweek, summer or winter stays.

### HUDSON HOUSE

Owners: George and John Riding; Manager: Linda McCane.
518-251-3339.
North River Rd., (Rte. 28), North River, NY 12856.
Open: Year-round.
Price: Inquire.
Credit Cards: None.
Special Features: Fireplace; children welcome.

A large guesthouse suitable for an extended family gathering or two families vacationing together, Hudson House has North River's trademark garnet fireplace, a fully equipped kitchen, and room for 15 guests. From Hudson House it's a short walk across the highway to trophy trout fishing on the river, an easy drive to Thirteenth Lake or Siamese Ponds trailheads, or a five-minute excursion into North Creek for groceries, restaurants, and a taste of civilization.

### TOAG'S LODGE

Owner: Cynthia Cormack.
518-251-2496.
Rte. 28, North River, NY 12856.
Open: Year-round.
Price: Inexpensive.
Credit Cards: None.
Special Features: Fireplace; children welcome.

River drivers on the Hudson a century ago visited Toag's Lodge for the female company within rather than the quality of the accommodations; in recent memory, the building quietly sank into disrepair with only its colorful reputation intact. After a thorough remodeling in 1991, the place is now a charming, antique-filled bed and breakfast run by Cynthia Cormack.

There are five guest rooms with shared baths, and a pleasant living room with a fireplace. Cynthia prides herself on baking bread, muffins, and pastries that make a hearty breakfast ideal for launching a day of skiing, rafting, fishing, hiking, or exploring.

## Northville

### INN AT THE BRIDGE

Owners: Patricia and William Eschler.
518-863-2240.
641 Bridge St., Northville, NY 12134.
Open: Year-round.

An exuberant Queen Anne-style cottage with porches, gables, and a tower, the Inn at the Bridge is stylish indeed. All of the five bedrooms have queen-size beds and are furnished with Victorian antiques; the rooms share two baths. There's a lovely fireplace in the family room,

Price: Inexpensive to Moderate.
Min. Stay: 2 nights on weekends.
Credit Cards: MC, V.
Special Features: Fireplace; lakefront; children over 10 welcome; no pets.

which also has comfortable couches, television, and books galore. Breakfast includes an assortment of homemade breads, muffins, and strudel, bagels, fruit, and so forth. There's frontage on Great Sacandaga Lake, and visitors can stroll through town to the Adirondack Country Store, the Alhambra, or other stops along Main Street.

## Old Forge/Thendara

### CAMP LAWRENCE RESORTS

Owner: Theresa Winslow.
315-357-2889.
Lawrence Point, Fourth Lake/Mail: Old Forge, NY 13420.
7.6 miles north of the Tourist Information Center in Old Forge.
Closed: Winter.
Price: Expensive to Very Expensive.
Min. Stay: 1 week June 20—Sept. 7; weekends in spring and fall.
Credit Cards: None.
Special Features: Private lakefront; docks; fireplaces; children welcome; no pets.

Lewis Lawrence, a member of the North Woods Walton Club, built Camp Lawrence in the late 1800s, and it's a huge, comfortable Adirondack lodge suitable for an extended family or a group traveling together. There are two living rooms, two family rooms, two porches, a main kitchen and a luncheon kitchen, three and a half baths, and seven bedrooms. The lodge is usually booked for the summer months, but inquire about June or September rentals.

If you don't need quite so much space, on the same Fourth Lake shoreline property there's a very nice new house, Lakesedge, which has three bedrooms, two baths, living room, kitchen, family room, patio, and private dock. Lakesedge is only 40 feet from the water.

### THE KENMORE

Owners: Joyce and Ron Leszyk, Dave Harradine.
315-357-5285.
Fourth Lake, Old Forge, NY 13420.
Off Rte. 28.
Open: Year-round.
Price: Moderate in summer; winter rates reflect heating costs.
Min. Stay: 1 week July—Aug.; 3 nights in winter.

A cottage colony off the main highway on the north shore of Fourth Lake, the Kenmore welcomed its first guests in 1901. Fourteen modern housekeeping cottages ranging in size from one to three bedrooms are available by the week in summer and for three-night stays in spring and fall; five of the cabins are completely winterized and conveniently located for snowmobilers and cross-country skiers. Almost all the cottages have lake views; many have fireplaces.

There's a shallow sandy beach and play area for the kids, free canoes and rowboats, picnic tables

Credit Cards: None.
Special Features: Private beach; canoes, rowboats for guests; children welcome; no pets.

and outdoor grills, a volleyball court, and a campfire area. Says Joyce, "A family can enjoy a relaxing, fun-filled week and never leave our premises." But if the urge hits to explore farther afield, Old Forge's numerous attractions — from the newly restored Strand Theater to the Enchanted Forest/Water Safari park to the Fulton Chain of Lakes tour boats — are nearby.

**MOOSE COUNTRY CABINS**
Owners: Shirley and Larry Garbett.
315-369-6447.
Main St., Old Forge, NY 13420.
Open: Year-round.
Price: Moderate.
Credit Cards: MC, V.

Near town, and a stone's throw from the Moose River, the Garbetts rent several housekeeping cabins that sleep from two to eight people. Two of the cabins are completely winterized. Skiers like this spot because McCauley Mountain is just two miles away, and snowmobilers appreciate the fact that the trails start virtually at the doorstep. Want to find out more? Ask for a copy of the latest "Moosepaper" describing these cottages.

Nancie Battaglia

*The front porch at the Moose River House, Thendara.*

**MOOSE RIVER HOUSE**
Owner: Frederick Fox; host: Allyn Gardner.

This elegant, stately Victorian house on the banks of the Moose River was owned by the DeCamp family for more than a century, and has

315-369-3104/1-800-241-
6188.
12 Birch St., Thendara, NY
13472.
Off Rte. 28 behind Van
Auken's Inne.
Closed: Nov.—May 15.
Price: Moderate.
Min. Stay: Prefer 2 nights.
Credit Cards: None.
Special Features:
Riverfront; fireplace;
children over 6 wel-
come; no pets.

been recently restored by its first non-DeCamp occupant. On the first floor, there's a lovely parlor with a baby grand piano; the living room has French doors that open out to a porch overlooking the river. The guest accommodations are first-rate: two rooms with queen-size beds have private baths; two rooms, each with vanities, share a bath, and there's a suite with its own living room, kitchen, and bath.

Breakfast here is a sumptuous sit-down affair, often featuring *pain perdu* stuffed with lemon curd, eggs Benedict, wholegrain pancakes, or special omelets. Homemade muffins and breads are in ample supply.

You can launch a canoe from the back door, and state-marked hiking trails to Nick's Lake and Otter Lake are close by. If you don't have your own canoe, Tickner's Moose River Canoe Rentals will bring one over for you.

## PALMER POINT
315-357-5594.
South Shore Rd., Old
Forge, NY 13420.
Closed: Oct. 15—May 25.
Price: Inexpensive to
Moderate.
Min. Stay: 1 week July—
Aug.
Credit Cards: AE, MC, V.
Special Features: Private
beach; boat rentals; chil-
dren welcome; no pets.

Located on Fourth Lake, and next to state land, the assorted housekeeping cottages at Palmer Point accommodate couples and families of up to six people. There's an excellent sandy beach, hiking trails, a lean-to, and boats of all kinds to rent.

## VAN AUKEN'S INNE
Innkeepers: Jayne and
George Taylor.
315-369-3033.
Forge St., Thendara, NY
13472.
Off Rte. 28 by the
Adirondack Railroad
station.
Closed: March 17—May
30; Oct. 15—Dec. 1
Price: Moderate; B&B.

This stately old hotel was a year old when the Adirondack branch of the New York Central made its first stop in Thendara station in 1892. Over the years, the trains have come and gone (and are back again in summer 1992 for short excursions from Thendara to Minnehaha), while Van Auken's has remained an enduring presence across the way. Jayne and George Taylor began working on the hotel in 1988, and the place has been restored to much of its 19th-century charm.

Min. Stay: 2 nights on weekends.
Credit Cards: MC, V.
Special Features: Restaurant and bar; children welcome; no pets.

The second floor, where 20 bedrooms used to share two baths, has been remodeled into 12 guest rooms, each with private bath. Original details and antique furniture have been incorporated into these modern accommodations. The public areas downstairs, like the taproom and the lobby, once again have polished wood floors, stamped-tin ceilings, and other elegant touches. The restaurant is open for breakfast, lunch, and dinner, offering imaginative cuisine and good service.

*Van Auken's Inne, Thendara, an enduring presence since 1891.*

Nancie Battaglia

## Olmstedville

**FAIRVIEW HOUSE**
Owners: Karen and Brian Barosi.
518-251-4160.
Main St. and Donnelly Rd., Olmstedville, NY 12857.
Open: Year-round.
Price: Inexpensive.
Credit Cards: None.
Special Features: Children welcome; no pets.

Olmstedville is a quiet little town off the major highways, yet close to North Creek and Chestertown. The Fairview House, an impressive-looking 150-year-old white farmhouse on Main Street, opened in 1990 as a bed and breakfast, but it was originally a boardinghouse for tannery workers. There are three guest bedrooms, furnished with white iron bedsteads, old-fashioned floral wallpaper, and polished wood floors; the rooms share two baths. Downstairs is a library full of books, with rocking chairs, couches, and a VCR. Breakfast is served in the dining room, which is furnished with an antique cherrywood table, chairs, and sideboard; for lunch or dinner, it's a short stroll down to Betsy's Steak House or the Country Diner.

## Piseco

**IRONDEQUOIT INN**
Innkeeper: Jim Abbott.
518-548-5500.
Old Piseco Rd., Piseco, NY
 12164.
Open: Year-round.
Price: Moderate; MAP.
Credit Cards: None.
Special Features: Private
 beach; private island;
 tennis court; restaurant;
 tent campsites; canoes
 to rent; children wel-
 come; no pets.

This landmark inn — actually two adjacent buildings — celebrated its centennial in 1992. From the front porches, you can look down the lawns to Piseco Lake and see Oxbow, Rogers, and Piseco mountains. The inn owns 600 acres you can explore; as Sherry says, "It's like a summer camp for adults." There's even a private undeveloped island in the lake that guests can canoe to for picnics, swimming, or sleeping out under the stars.

There are nine rooms, which share three baths, and three housekeeping cabins. There's also a campground by the lake with tree-shaded sites for 13 tents.

Room rates include full breakfast and dinner, all hearty, home-cooked fare. New in summer 1992 is a more complete menu that offers four or five entree choices each evening, and the restaurant will be open to the public by advance reservation. "BYOB," suggests Jim.

**PISECO LAKE LODGE**
Owners and managers:
 Jean and Chet Blessing.
518-548-8552.
67 Old Piseco Rd., Piseco,
 NY 12134.
Closed: Thanksgiving to
 Christmas; mid-
 March—mid-May.
Price: Inexpensive.
Min. Stay: 2 nights in win-
 ter.
Credit Cards: MC, V.
Special Features:
 Lakefront; boat livery;
 convenience store;
 restaurant; bar; children
 welcome; no pets.

Located on the Piseco Lake inlet, this facility is a year-round resort complex with a motel, campers' store, boat livery, restaurant, and bar with package license. The lodge is popular with hunters, hikers, snowmobilers, and fishermen, and it's near the trails for Panther Mountain and T Lake Falls.

## Raquette Lake

**CUMMINGS COVE
 COTTAGES**
Owners: Kris and Jay
 Cummings.

At Cummings Cove, you can pretend that either of the two cottages is your own private second home; there's ample space between the buildings and it doesn't feel like a colony. Both two-bed-

315-354-4631 summer/315-354-5783 school year.
Brightside Rd., Raquette Lake, NY 13436.
Closed: Mar.—Apr.; Nov.
Price: Moderate.
Min. Stay: 1 week July—Aug.; 3 nights in winter.
Credit Cards: None.
Special Features: Private lakefront; children welcome; no pets.

room cottages are completely modernized and winterized, with fully equipped kitchens and heating systems. Guests need to bring linens and towels, and that's about it. There's a hundred feet of private lakeshore for swimming, canoeing, and fishing, or ice fishing, snowmobiling, and cross-country skiing in the winter.

### RIGHT EYE COTTAGES
Owner: Robert Skiba.
No phone.
Rte. 28, Raquette Lake/Mail: Box 514, Raquette Lake, NY 13436
Closed: Oct.—May.
Price: Inexpensive.
Min. Stay: 1 week July—Aug.
Credit Cards: None.
Special Features: Private lakefront; dock for guests' boats; children welcome.

In a secluded yet easily accessible spot on Raquette Lake, Bob rents three housekeeping cottages from Memorial Day to foliage season. There's a private beach, a long dock for guests' boats (a boat livery is next door), and a great mountain vista to the east toward Blue Mountain.

### RISLEY'S RUSH POINT
Manager: Barbara Risley Allen.
315-354-5211/School year: 315-429-9239.
Rte. 28, Raquette Lake/Winter: 3 E. Spofford Ave., Dolgeville, NY 13329.
Closed: During the school year.
Price: Moderate.
Min. Stay: 1 week.
Credit Cards: None.
Special Features: Private sandy beach; dock for guests' boats; fireplaces; playground; children welcome; no pets.

Several of the cottages here — part of the original 1891 Adirondack camp — are rustic gems with stockade-style log siding, stone fireplaces, and long spacious porches under big pines and spruces. There are also several newer three-bedroom cottages, for a total of nine cabins on the 27-acre property. Each has a complete kitchen and bathroom; guests need to supply bed linens and towels.

A special attraction at Risley's is a sandy natural beach that slopes gradually for a hundred yards into deep water. There's a dock for guests' boats, a dock for sunbathers, outdoor fireplaces, picnic tables, a playground, and two lean-tos.

## *Speculator*

**BEARHURST**
Owners: Helen and Dick
 Armstrong.
518-548-6427/Winter: 518-
 842-6609.
South Shore Rd.,
 Speculator, NY 12164.
Closed: Oct.—May.
Price: Moderate to
 Expensive.
Min. Stay: 1 week July—
 Aug.; 2 nights June,
 Sept.
Credit Cards: None.
Special Features: Private
 lakefront; dockage for
 guests' boats; fireplaces;
 gazebo on the water;
 children welcome; no
 pets.

Most folks associate Great Camps with Raquette Lake or the Upper Saranac or Upper St. Regis lakes, but in other parts of the park, there are some smaller estates that are equally nice. One of these is Bearhurst, which was built in 1894 by Herman Meyrowitz (fashionable optical shops in Paris, Geneva, and Milan still carry his name), and it occupies a quarter-mile of lakefront on Lake Pleasant.

Guests stay in five of the original outbuildings: the ice house, pump house, summer kitchen, horse shed, and boathouse, all of which have been converted into delightful modern accommodations while still maintaining historical details and charm. The living rooms in each have fireplaces, and the fully outfitted kitchens even have dishwashers.

*The lakeside gazebo at Bearhurst, on Lake Pleasant.*

B. Folwell

A centerpiece of the property is the main lodge, a stunning log building with lovely leaded glass windows and gracious porches; the stonework is especially intricate, with spiral stone staircases leading down from the front porch. One fireplace has an inset oval leaded-glass window on the second floor. The Armstrongs live in the main lodge, but guests can certainly enjoy the building from the outside.

There's a private beach, dock space for guests' boats, and a pretty little rustic gazebo for watching the sunset over the lake. If you visit in June, the grounds are covered with pinksters, the graceful wild azaleas.

**THE INN AT SPECULATOR**
Innkeeper: Neil McGovern.
518-548-3811.
Rte. 8, Speculator, NY 12164.
Open: Year-round.
Price: Inexpensive; MAP.
Min. Stay: 2 nights on weekends.
Credit Cards: AE, CB, DC, MC, V.
Special Features: Fireplace; restaurant and bar.

Joe Buck, a German immigrant who had been headwaiter at Luchow's and maitre d' at the Waldorf Astoria, "retired" to Speculator in 1946. He built the inn, with a bar and restaurant downstairs, his apartment on the second floor, and tiny garret cells for hunters and fishermen on the third floor.

Neil McGovern bought the place in 1979 and has been working on it practically nonstop ever since. Guests now stay on the second floor in homey, spacious quarters, some of which have private baths. There's a big living room with a fireplace, television, telephone, and a piano, just above the main dining room.

The inn's property includes frontage on Lake Pleasant, so there's easy access to the lake for canoeists and fishermen, and the ice is generally safe for cross-country skiing and snowmobiling from January through March. In the summer, you can walk down to the Adirondack Picture Show for a movie.

**MELODY LODGE**
Owners: Susan and George Swift.
518-548-6562.
Rte. 30, Speculator, NY 12164.
Closed: Apr.
Price: Inexpensive.
Credit Cards: MC, V.
Special features: Restaurant; bar; children welcome; no pets.

Built in 1912 as a singing school for young girls, Melody Lodge opened to the public as a restaurant and inn in 1937. For decades, Frances and Hamilton Chequer ran the place, and now Susan and George Swift are the innkeepers. From the lodge, there's a view down Page Hill to Lake Pleasant and Sacandaga Lake; look out the windows toward the lawn and you might see rabbits of all shapes and colors hopping around — the Swifts started out with a couple of pets, and they just multiplied on their own.

There are ten comfortable rooms upstairs that share four baths. Downstairs is a nice restaurant open to the public that serves dinner in the summer and lunch and dinner in the winter.

## *Stillwater Reservoir*

**STILLWATER**
Owners: Marian and Walt
  Stroehmer.
315-376-6470.
Stillwater Rd., Stillwater
  Reservoir/Mail: Star
  Rte., Box 258M,
  Lowville, NY 13367.
Closed: Apr.; Mon.—
  Thurs. May, Nov., Dec.
Price: Inexpensive.
Min. Stay: 2 nights in peak
  seasons.
Credit Cards: AE, MC, V.
Special features: Boat
  launch; lakefront;
  restaurant and bar; chil-
  dren welcome; no pets.

Stillwater Reservoir, which is several miles back from the main highways via a winding gravel road, has 117 miles of shoreline, 45 islands, and thousands of acres of public land for you to explore. Once you're out in a canoe, it seems that there are more loons here than anywhere else in the Adirondacks, and the fishing's not too bad, either.

At the western end of the lake is the Stroehmer hotel/restaurant complex, the only accommodations you can drive to on the reservoir. (If you want to visit the Norridgewock, in Beaver River, New York's most remote settlement, you have to take a water taxi.) There are seven comfortable, winterized motel rooms, and a restaurant and bar open to the public. The menu is quite extensive, with offerings from Cajun shrimp to veal saltimbocca, plus prime rib, steaks, and chicken.

Stillwater is popular with snowmobilers in the winter, since the snow cover is generally excellent and several trail systems are accessible right from the property.

## *Wells*

**ABNER GREENFIELD'S
  COUNTRY INN**
Hosts: Kathleen and Brian
  Towers.
518-924-2206.
Rte. 30, Wells, NY 12190.
Open: Year-round.
Price: Inexpensive.
Credit Cards: MC, V.
Special Features: Fireplace;
  children welcome; no
  pets.

Kathy Tower's great-grandmother took in boarders at her farmhouse near the East Branch of the Sacandaga River in the 1880s; after many years, the house has been restored to its original purpose, but considerably improved. (The bed and breakfast is named after Abner Greenfield, a colorful local character prone to pranksmanship and storytelling, who lived in the 1850s.)

Upstairs there are four bright bedrooms, each beautifully furnished with antique beds and heirloom quilts, which share two recently renovated baths. Downstairs is a big living room with hunter-green velvet wing chairs around the stone fireplace, and on the other side of the stairway is a cozy nook with a CD stereo system and piano for musically inclined guests. Breakfast (homemade everything, even jams) is served in a sunny dining room where a small army of teddy bears rests in a window seat. In the summer you can sip iced tea on the veranda and watch occasional cars go by; in the winter after a long cross-country ski, you can soak in what's reputed to be the first bathtub to have arrived in the town of Wells.

**ADIRONDACK MOUNTAIN CHALET**
Host: Jeffree Trudeau.
518-924-2112.
Griffin Gorge Commons, Rte. 30, Wells, NY 12190.
Open: Year-round.
Price: Moderate to Expensive.
Min. Stay: Weekend.
Credit Cards: None.
Special Features: Holistic community; children welcome.

Griffin Gorge Commons, a 40-acre community with a dozen or so residents who share holistic health and environmental beliefs, also rents a unique lodge on their property. The attractive figure-8-shaped building, which was constructed from materials salvaged from an old hotel and a barn, sleeps four adults comfortably. There's a full kitchen, bathroom, gas lamps, a woodstove, and a deck overlooking a pond; kids are welcome to explore the treehouses and play areas nearby. Adult guests may participate in the community's sweat lodge or seasonal celebrations.

**WINTERLOCK COTTAGES**
Owners: Dolores and Frank Lekstutis.
518-924-3600.
Lt. Amsterdam Rd., Wells, NY 12190.
Closed: Nov. 1—May 15.
Price: Moderate.
Min. Stay: 2 nights.
Credit Cards: None.
Special Features: Private lakefront; rowboats for guests; fireplaces; children welcome; no pets.

On Lake Algonquin, which is an impounded stretch of the Sacandaga River's east branch, are Winterlock Cottages, two nicely maintained two-bedroom housekeeping units. The knotty-pine paneled cottages have screen porches and either a fireplace or a Franklin stove. Rowboats are provided for guests. Kitchens are completely equipped; guests need to bring bed linens and towels.

## Wevertown

**MOUNTAINAIRE ADVENTURES**
Host: Doug Cole.
518-251-2194/1-800-950-2194.

Doug Cole, a licensed Adirondack guide, manages a variety of accommodations at Mountainaire. In the main lodge, there are four rooms upstairs with private baths; nearby, there's a hostel

Rte. 28, Wevertown, NY
12886.
Open: Year-round.
Price: Hostel: Inexpensive;
B&B: Moderate; MAP:
Expensive.
Credit Cards: AE, MC, V.
Special Features: Hot tub;
sauna; meals; fireplace;
guided trips and out-
door instruction; moun-
tain-bike and canoe
rentals; children wel-
come; no pets.

that sleeps 16, a new three-bedroom chalet with complete kitchen, and an efficiency apartment. The main lodge has a dining room and lounge, a sauna, and a hot tub. Guests may choose bed-and-breakfast or MAP arrangements for meals.

From the lodge, it's only a few minutes to Gore Mountain for downhill skiing, the Hudson River for white-water rafting, or Siamese Ponds Wilderness area for exploring 150,000 acres of backcountry. Outdoor-sports packages for fly fishing, rafting, mountain biking, and skiing are available.

# MOTELS AND CAMPGROUNDS

## LAKE GEORGE AND SOUTHEASTERN ADIRONDACKS

For a complete list of accommodations in the Lake George-Chestertown-Warrensburg area, contact Warren County Tourism (1-800-365-1050). A sampling of motel and campground accommodations is listed below.

### *Bolton Landing*

**Melody Manor** (518-644-9750; Rte. 9N, Bolton Landing, NY 12814) Price: Moderate to Expensive. 40 rooms. Private beach; pool; boats; tennis; no pets. Closed: Oct. 15—May 1.

**Victorian Village** (518-644-9401; Rte. 9N, Bolton Landing, NY 12814) Price: Moderate. 30 units. Private beach; boats; tennis; no pets. Closed: Nov. 1—May 1.

### *Lake George*

**Colonial Manor** (518-668-4884; Rte. 9N, Lake George, NY 12845) Price: Moderate to Expensive. Motel and cottages. Heated pool; playground; no pets. Closed: Oct. 15—May 1.

**The Georgian** (518-668-5401; 384 Canada St., Lake George, NY 12845) Price: Moderate to Expensive. Huge, modern motor inn complex. Heated pool; private beach; docks for guests' boats; restaurants. Open: Year-round.

**Lake Crest** (518-668-3374; 366 Canada St., Lake George) Price: Moderate to Expensive. 40 rooms. Heated pool; private beach. Closed: Oct. 22—Apr. 1.

**Tea Island** (518-668-2776; Lake Shore Dr., Lake George) Price: Moderate. Motel, efficiencies, and cottages. Private beach; cafe. Closed: Oct. 15—May 1.

## CHAMPLAIN VALLEY

For a complete list of accommodations in the area, contact Essex County Tourism (518-942-7794; Box 10, Mineville, NY 12956).

### *Elizabethtown*

**Crest of the Hill Motel** (518-873-6529; Rte. 9, Elizabethtown, NY 12932) Price: Inexpensive. Friendly Mom-and-Pop motel with barbecue grills and picnic tables, 1.5 miles outside town. Closed: Dec. 1—May 15.

## *Keeseville*

**Ausable Chasm KOA Campground** (518-834-9990; Rte. 9, Keeseville, NY 12944) 89 tent and RV sites; some full hook-ups. Short walk to Ausable Chasm. Closed: Mid-Oct.—mid-May.

## *Port Kent*

**Yogi Bear's Jellystone Park Camp Resorts** (518-834-9011; Rte. 373, Port Kent, NY 12975) Numerous RV hookups and tent sites, overlooking Lake Champlain at the Port Kent Ferry. Pool; nature trails; activities for kids; camping cabins; playground; laundromat. Closed: Mid-Oct.—mid-May.

## HIGH PEAKS AND NORTHERN ADIRONDACKS

Lake Placid has lodging information available at 1-800-44P-LACI, or you can contact the Visitors Bureau (518-523-2445; Main St., Lake Placid, NY 12946). A sampling of motels in the area is listed below.

## *Blue Ridge*

**Blue Ridge Falls Campground** (518-532-7863; Blue Ridge Rd., Blue Ridge, NY 12855) Off the main highway. Pool; walk to waterfalls.

## *Lake Placid*

**Best Western Golden Arrow** (518-523-3353; 150 Main St., Lake Placid) Price: Moderate to Expensive. Huge modern motor inn on the lakefront in the heart of downtown. Health club; heated pool; private beach; shopping arcade. Open: Year-round.

**Howard Johnson Lodge** (518-523-9555; Saranac Ave., Lake Placid) Price: Moderate to Expensive. Surprisingly good restaurant — HoJo goes homemade. Tennis; indoor pool. Open: Year-round.

**Lake Placid Hilton** (518-523-1120; 1 Mirror Lake Dr., Lake Placid) Price: Moderate to Expensive. Large, new motor inn complex across from the lake in downtown. Heated pool; restaurant and lounge; shops. Open: Year-round.

**Holiday Inn Grandview** (518-523-2556; 1 Olympic Dr., Lake Placid) Price: Moderate to Very Expensive. 200+ rooms. Overlooking the Olympic Arena. Heated pool; access to Jackrabbit cross-country ski trails; lake view; restaurant and lounge. Open: Year-round.

**Prague Motor Inn** (518-523-2587; 25 Sentinel Rd., Lake Placid) Price: Inexpensive to Moderate. Quiet, folksy Mom-and-Pop place with an amusing Queen Anne house in front of the motel units.

## *Wilmington*

**Hungry Trout Motor Lodge** (518-946-2217; Rte. 86, Wilmington, NY 12997) Price: Moderate to Expensive. 20 rooms. Great view; nice restaurant and tavern; excellent fishing; fly-fishing guide service and lessons. Closed: Mid-Apr.—late June; Nov.—Dec.

**Ledge Rock Motel** (518-946-2302; Rte. 86, Wilmington) Price: Moderate. Pool; nice grounds; view of Whiteface Mountain. Closed: Apr., Nov.

**Whiteface Chalet** (518-946-2207; Springfield Rd., Wilmington) Price: Inexpensive to Moderate. 18 rooms. Quiet, off-highway location. Tennis; cafe and lounge. Closed: Apr., Nov.

## NORTHWEST LAKES REGION

For a complete list of lodgings in the immediate area, contact the Tupper Lake Chamber of Commerce (518-359-3328; Park St., Tupper Lake, NY 12986).

## *Tupper Lake*

**Pine Terrace Motel & Tennis Club** (518-359-9258; Rte. 30, Tupper Lake, NY 12986) Price: Inexpensive to Moderate. Pool; lighted tennis courts; beach across the road; picnic area; lake view; near downhill ski area. Open: Year-round.

**Red Top Inn** (518-359-9209; Rte. 30, Tupper Lake) Price: Inexpensive. 18 rooms. Lake view; private beach across the road; fishing dock. Close to Big Tupper Ski Area. Open: Year-round.

**Sunset Park** (518-359-3995; DeMars Blvd., Tupper Lake) Price: Inexpensive. 11 rooms. Near McDonald's, A&P, and the municipal park (site of the Woodsmen's Days, an excellent flea market, and night ballgames). Lake view; private beach; picnic tables. Open: Year-round.

## CENTRAL AND SOUTHWESTERN ADIRONDACKS

The Central Adirondack Association (315-369-6983; Main St., Old Forge, NY 13420) lists many accommodations in the Inlet, Eagle Bay, Old Forge, Raquette Lake, and Blue Mountain Lake area. Information on lodgings in Hamilton County is available from the county tourism office (518-648-5239; White Birch Lane, Indian Lake, NY 12842). For the Great Sacandaga Lake region and Caroga-Canada lakes, contact the Fulton County Regional Chamber of Commerce (518-725-0641; 18 Cayadutta St., Gloversville, NY 12078).

A sampling of motels, campgrounds, and cottages is listed below.

### Canada and Caroga Lakes

**Canada Lake Cottages** (518-835-6069; Rte. 10, Canada Lake, NY 12032) Lakefront cottages. Private beach; boat rentals; general store nearby. Open: Year-round.

**Lakeside Motel** (518-835-2331; Rte. 10, Canada Lake) Motel and cottages. Lakefront; Closed: Oct.—May.

### Long Lake

**Sandy Point Motel** (518-624-3871; Rte. 28/30, Long Lake, NY 12847) Price: Inexpensive to Moderate. Motel units and efficiencies. Private beach; docks; rental boats; cross-country skiing, snowmobiling. Open: Year-round.

**Shamrock Motel** (518-624-3861; Rte. 28/30, Long Lake) Price: Inexpensive to Moderate. Motel and cottages. Private beach; picnic area. Closed: mid-Oct.—Memorial Day.

### Northville

**Park Motel** (518-863-4644; Sacandaga Park, Rte. 30, Northville, NY 12134) Price: Inexpensive to Moderate. 11 units. Lakefront; near golf course. Closed: Mid-Oct.—May.

### Old Forge

**Clark's Beach Motel** (315-369-3026; Main St., Old Forge, NY 13420) Price: Moderate. 42 units. Lake view; next to public beach; indoor pool. Open: Year-round.

**The Forge Motel** (315-369-3313; Main St., Old Forge) Price: Moderate. 61 units. Lake view, the best from Room 13; pool; next to public beach; walk to restaurants. Open: Year-round.

**Old Forge KOA** (315-369-6011; Rte. 28, Old Forge) Campground. 200 sites on 116 acres. Private lake; laundromat; showers; convenience store; dumping station; canoes; movies. Open: Year-round.

**Sunset Motel** (315-369-6836; Rte. 30, Thendara, NY 13472) Price: Moderate. 50 rooms. Indoor pool; tennis; putting green. Open: Year-round.

**Water's Edge Inn and Conference Center** (315-369-2484; Rte. 30, Old Forge) Price: Moderate. 42 rooms. Lakefront; indoor pool; sauna; dock; across from Enchanted Forest/Water Safari park. Open: Year-round.

# CHAPTER FOUR

# From Highbrow to Downhome
## CULTURE

Culture as a collection of the noble things in life — fine arts, architecture, literature, classical music, theater, ballet — may have been out of reach of the hardscrabble 19th-century Adirondack woodsman and his family, but the wild Adirondack landscape inspired many a visiting writer, painter, and composer. It could be argued, too, that because of the images of the Adirondacks in the popular fiction of that time, in the weekly national magazines like

Seneca Ray Stoddard. Courtesy Adirondack Museum, Blue Mountain Lake, NY

*A fiddler entertains Raquette Lake Hotel guests, 1888.*

*Harper's*, *Frank Lesley's*, and *Every Saturday*, and in Currier & Ives prints, the Adirondacks were much better known as a particular place a hundred years ago than they are today. In contrast, Adirondack folk culture, represented by the guideboat, rustic furniture, packbaskets, and other crafts, by fiddle tunes and backwoods ballads, and by "epic" poems and tall tales, is finally in the spotlight as something worthy of preservation and presentation to a larger audience.

But let's go back to the Adirondacks' place in the 19th-century world for a moment. Take *The Last of the Mohicans*, for example. The harrowing trip from what's now called Cooper's Cave, in Glens Falls, to the fort at Ticonderoga went along the Hudson River, crossed over the Tongue Mountain Range, skirted the western side of Lake George, and reached Lake Champlain where it begins to narrow. The adventure is now part of practically every high-school graduate's memory, but few of us connect the journey with actual places that happen to be in the Adirondacks. James Fenimore Cooper visited Warrensburg and Lake George in 1824 to research his story and meticulously record the landscape. Many of the landmarks are inaccessible or hidden today, but you may catch a few glimpses if you follow in his tracks, on modern-day Rte. 9.

Artists also recorded the Adirondacks in a state of bucolic grace, before the charcoal kilns of the iron industry darkened the skies and lumbermen cut the forests; beginning in 1830, and on up to the turn of the century, the countryside practically swarmed with painters. Thomas Cole, Frederic Church, and other Hudson River School artists depicted an allegorical region with glowing mountains, silvery shimmering lakes, and perfect little villages. Frederic Remington, who was born just north of the Adirondacks, in Canton, NY, sketched trapper's cabins and lumbercamps: "The Tragedy of the Trees," published in *Every Saturday*, was a documentary of a rough-and-tumble way of life in the Adirondack lumber woods that paralleled his western works. The English painter A.F. Tait also showed the manly side of the wilderness, in oil paintings of groups of hunters and fishermen, and portraits of their prey: bucks, bears, and trout. Many of Tait's images were used for Currier & Ives lithographs, but the popularity of those Adirondack prints also created a demand for Tait imitators; more than 120 different Currier & Ives images show scenes of the region, from maple-sugaring parties to trappers' travails to humble log farmsteads. Throughout the country, these Adirondack visions hung on parlor walls.

Winslow Homer painted scenes of guides in Keene Valley and at the North Woods Club, near Minerva, in a luminous, impressionistic style that helped cinch his career as America's premier watercolorist. His illustrations of hunters and lumberjacks that appeared in popular weeklies brought the Adirondack backwoods into urban homes. Harold Weston, who lived most of his life in Keene Valley, made bold, burly oils of the High Peaks that were exhibited widely from the 1920s to the 1970s, and are now in permanent major collections throughout the world. Rockwell Kent spent his last decades at his farm near Au Sable Forks, painting the Ausable River valley, designing buildings, and expressing his radical politics to a nonplussed yet tolerant set of neighbors. David Smith, one of the best-known sculptors of the modern age, lived in Bolton Landing; today, in a field overlooking Lake George, many of his abstract sculptures remain, but unfortunately the property is rarely open to the public.

Composers found inspiration in the woods and waters, too. A few godawful parlor ditties and tone poems made the rounds in the late 19th century, like "Floating for Deer" and "The Adirondacks: A Gallop." The immense popularity of recreational canoeing at the turn of the century created a whole new genre of songs celebrating the sport; "Paddlin' Madeline Home" is just one example. But, more importantly, two of the finest modern composers, Charles Ives and Bela Bartok, both spent extended periods of time working in the Adirondacks. Ives composed the *Concord* piano sonata while visiting Elk Lake, and began the *Universe Symphony*, one of his last major works, while at his wife's family's summer home in Keene Valley. Bartok wrote the *Concerto for Orchestra* in Saranac Lake, where he was taking the "cure" for tuberculosis.

Women are notably absent from this list of resident and visiting artists. There's one exception. Jeanne Robert Foster grew up in grinding poverty in Johnsburg, and went on to become an editor of the *Transatlantic Review*. Her circle of friends included Ezra Pound, T.S. Eliot, and John Butler Yeats, father of the Irish poet. Recently her poetry-and-prose memories of her youth were published in *Adirondack Portraits* (Syracuse University Press, 1989).

Folk arts from the 19th-century Adirondacks reflect the lumbering days, in songs and tall tales, and the Gilded Age, in the rustic furniture and decorative items local carpenters built for the Great Camps. Traditional music can be heard in many of the summer arts-performance series listed elsewhere in this chapter; the best place to see rustic furniture in quantity and quality is at the Adirondack Museum, in Blue Mountain Lake. And throughout the park, the icons of North Country material culture are ubiquitous: the guideboat, the packbasket, the lean-to, and the Adirondack chair. The fine art of storytelling is also alive and well in local diners and gathering places, and occasionally onstage.

Today, the cultural scene in the Adirondacks is remarkably diverse, showcasing native skills and crafts and honoring the fine artists who have visited the region. There's real community pride in local libraries, arts centers, theater companies, historic-preservation groups, museums, and musical ensembles. But beyond the good feelings and active schedules, there's also a level of professionalism and excellence that rises above the sometimes humble settings.

The following descriptions will tell you where to go in search of history and the arts throughout the park. We suggest you call or write in order to get a current schedule of events. Many local radio stations and weekly papers offer calendars of events for a small region within the park; the *Adirondack Daily Enterprise* has a weekly calendar that extends from Blue Mountain Lake to Keene. *Adirondack Life* has a bimonthly calendar in each issue, "Inside & Out," which does cover the entire Adirondack Park, but it's always a good idea to call ahead to confirm ticket availability or location of an event.

## ARCHITECTURE

Compared to touring Vermont, with its many postcard-pretty villages, old-house hunting in the Adirondack Park may be a little disappointing to the historic-preservation buff. Bear in mind that settlements in the North Country, especially in the central Adirondacks, are considerably newer than New England towns, and that the communities which date back to the 1700s along lakes George and Champlain generally were destroyed during the French and Indian and Revolutionary wars. Devastating fires before the turn of the centu-

Topridge, on Upper St. Regis Lake, was built by Marjorie Merriweather Post, the Post Toasties heiress.

Nancie Battaglia

ry in towns such as Tupper Lake and Indian Lake obliterated hundreds of prosperous businesses and substantial homes. However, especially along the eastern edge of the park, there are several lovely towns to see with fine buildings dating back to 1790 or so.

The celebrated Adirondack rustic style of architecture, which borrowed designs from Swiss chalets, English half-timber buildings, pioneer cabins, and even Japanese pagodas, isn't easy to find from the comfort of an automobile. You'll find rustic lodges and boathouses in all their twiggy glory mainly on remote lakeshores: *Sagamore*, the former Vanderbilt summer estate near Raquette Lake, is the only "Great Camp" you can easily visit. *Santanoni Preserve*, near Newcomb, is a 10-mile walk, round-trip, but it's well worth the trip. By walking, biking, or taking a wagon ride in, you get a real sense of the isolation of the estate.

## LAKE GEORGE AND SOUTHEASTERN ADIRONDACKS

For many travelers, **Warrensburg** is the gateway to the Adirondacks. Along Main Street (Rte. 9), there are several stately 19th-century homes — practically wall-to-wall — from Greek Revival and Gothic cottages to Italianate villas and Queen Anne monsters with towers and turrets. The oldest building in Warrensburg, near the stoplight for the Schroon River Road, is a modest stone structure housing Frances Antiques; it was once a blacksmith shop and dates back to about 1814. Along the Schroon River (Rte. 418 west), you can see remnants of the village's industrial center in several old mill buildings; the *Grist Mill*, now a restaurant, still has all the grindstones, chutes, and grain-milling apparatus visible. Also on Rte. 9, *Chestertown* has a historic district with colorful Greek Revival houses and restored storefronts. The local historical society plans to publish a walking-tour map/guide to notable buildings in summer 1992 (for information write to Historical Society, Town of Chester, Chestertown, NY 12817).

*Lake Luzerne* remains a community with quiet side streets, many well-kept Victorian homes, and some nine or so churches, including fine examples of Greek Revival style. *St. Mary's Episcopal Church*, built about 1860, is an unusual mix of Gothic stone-and-stick work, with complex slate rooflines and stunning stained-glass windows (across from the Lamplight Inn, on Lake Ave.). There's a walking-tour guide for Lake Luzerne slated for publication in summer 1992 (518-696-4520 for information).

In the rolling hills of **Washington County**, between Lake Champlain and Lake George, a few late 18th- and early 19th-century buildings can be seen along roads branching off Rte. 22. Near **Putnam**, follow the signs to the *United Presbyterian Church* and you'll be rewarded with a view of a classic Greek Revival Church. There's a tidy cemetery and a lovely perennial garden in the churchyard. On Rte. 9L, which goes up the east side of Lake George, you'll see the quaint stone *Harrisena Community Church* and several early farmhouses

B. Folwell

*The United Presbyterian Church in Putnam was built in 1857.*

near the southern end of the lake. Near *Pilot Knob*, there's an 1867 Mansard-Italianate church in immaculate condition, but you'll have to admire it from the road since it is now a private residence.

## CHAMPLAIN VALLEY

Essex County is especially rich in architectural sights. In *Ticonderoga*, even the modern water-treatment plant has a pentagonal 18th-century-fort shape. *Fort Ticonderoga* is about 2.5 miles south of the village on Rte. 22, but you can find the tumbledown walls and old cannons of *Fort Mount Hope* by exploring near the old cemetery on Burgoyne St. At the head of Montcalm St. is a replica of John Hancock's Boston home, built by Horace Moses in 1926. Moses made his fortune with the Strathmore Paper Company and funded many town beautification projects, including the *Liberty Monument*, a bronze statue by Charles Keck. A walking tour that highlights Ticonderoga's bustling 19th-century industrial history and stately homes is available from PRIDE (518-585-6366).

At *Crown Point*, there once were several 18th-century fortifications along the lake; what remains visible today can be seen at a state historic site near the bridge to Vermont, on Rte. 8, marking a 1750s-vintage trading post and settlement and, of course, *Fort Crown Point*. West of Crown Point is *Ironville*, a perfect gem of an early 19th-century community, described more completely in "Historic Homes and Districts" elsewhere in this chapter. On the way to Ironville, in *Factoryville*, you'll see the only octagonal house in the Adirondacks.

Historic markers erected by New York State abound along Rte. 22 as you approach *Port Henry*. The original settlement here supplied lumber for the forts at Crown Point and for Benedict Arnold's naval fleet. Later, the discovery of abundant iron ore shaped the town. Evidence of this prosperity shows up in an ornate downtown block, elaborate churches, and the exuberant high-Victorian *Moriah Town Office* building, formerly the headquarters of the Witherbee-Sherman Iron Company, near the Amtrak station.

Continuing north along Champlain's shore you'll find *Westport*, which was first settled in 1770. Buildings from that era have all disappeared, but a few homes near the lake on Washington St., off Rts. 9N and 22, date back to the 1820s, when a ferry to Vermont began service. Westport was a vital port, shipping out native iron, lumber, wool, and other farm products before the Civil War, and a thriving summer community afterward.

Following Rte. 22, you pass Gothic cottages and impressive stone houses with inviting porches overlooking the lake. Between Westport and Essex on that route is the tiny farm community of *Boquet*, with its odd little octagonal schoolhouse. The stone school, complete with bell tower, is slowly being restored. On the Camp Dudley Rd., off 9N and 22, is a stone one-room schoolhouse built in 1816.

The Adirondack community richest in architectural treasures is undoubtedly *Essex*; it's as if the clock stopped here in 1856. There are wonderful Dutch Colonial, Georgian, Federal, and Greek Revival buildings in excellent repair throughout the town: check under "Historic Buildings and Districts" for specific sites. Continuing on Rte. 22, *Willsboro* and *Keeseville* are both rich in historic buildings. Keeseville has several unusual homes made of buff-pink native sandstone, dating from the 1830s, and other buildings in the full range of 19th-century architectural styles from Dutch Colonial to Federal and Greek Revival to Gothic Revival and Romanesque.

The *Stone Arch Bridge* over the Ausable River, built in 1842, is the largest single-span-arch bridge in the country. *Crossing the River*, a monograph published by the Friends of Keeseville (518-834-9606), highlights historic bridges in *Essex County* and outlines an excellent driving tour. Another excellent driving tour for the historic *Boquet River* is published by the Boquet River Association (518-873-6301). The loop begins at Euba Mills, not far west of the Northway, and follows the river through Elizabethtown, Wadhams, Whallonsburg, Boquet, and Essex to its northernmost point at Willsboro, and then goes south to Reber and Lewis. In *Elizabethtown*, *Hand House* and *Hale House* are beautifully maintained early 19th-century Greek Revival homes found along Rte. 9.

## HIGH PEAKS AND NORTHERN ADIRONDACKS

Still in Essex County, and still east of Lake Placid, the Ausable River valley holds many historic buildings that are visible along the roadways. South of Keene Valley, it's worth a quick detour off Rte. 73 at *St. Hubert's* to see the *Ausable Club*, a massive Victorian inn. It's "members only" inside the building, but you can get a rare glimpse of the kind of hostelry that 19th-century visitors once enjoyed throughout the Adirondacks. North on Rte. 9, between *Upper Jay, Jay*, and *Au Sable Forks*, there are some fine Federal-style stone and brick houses and churches; the sole remaining Adirondack *Covered Bridge* spans the Ausable River in Jay (Mill Hill Rd., 1/4 mi. off Rte. 9).

The Olympic Village — *Lake Placid*, that is — has only a few buildings left from its earliest days, when the settlement of *North Elba*, near the ski jumps, was an iron-mining center; one that's easy to spot on the *Old Military Road* is the *Stagecoach Inn*. On the shore of Mirror Lake, a short walk from downtown Lake Placid, is the *Lake Placid Club*. The sprawling, titanic complex defies any succinct architectural categorizing; some call it "Adirondack Victorian." The club hasn't been used since the 1980 Winter Olympics, and attempts to revitalize the extensive property have failed for one reason or another.

In *Saranac Lake*, which was incorporated in 1892, the tuberculosis "industry" inspired its own architecture, manifested in "cure porches" and "cure cottages." The group Historic Saranac Lake sponsors lectures and tours from time to time highlighting buildings of note (518-891-0971).

*The covered bridge over Ausable River, Jay*

On **Upper Saranac Lake**, there are several fine examples of rustic architecture, but you'll need a canoe to quietly paddle by *Knollwood, Wenonah Lodge, Prospect Point* (now Young Life's summer camp), *Camp Wonundra* (now The Point, a guest lodge; see Chapter Three, *Lodging*), *Pinebrook, Eagle Island* (now a Girl Scout camp), and *Sekon Lodge.* Don't expect more than a tantalizing peek at these places hidden by the trees, and for heaven's sake, don't go ashore on private lands. Another vehicle for touring the lake may be the summer mail boat; check at the Saranac Lake post office, on Broadway downtown, to learn if the contract mail-delivery person is taking passengers.

Tucked back in the woods at **Loon Lake**, partly visible from County Rd. 99, is a surprising collection of cottages and larger buildings designed by Stanford White. The best way to see these haunting structures is by playing a round of golf at the Loon Lake course.

*The boathouse at Knollwood, a Great Camp on Upper Saranac Lake.*

Nancie Battaglia

## NORTHWEST LAKES REGION

For boathouse fans, **Upper St. Regis Lake**, near Paul Smiths, has many love-ly waterfront buildings, in high rustic, cobblestone, and shingle style. Again, you'll need your own boat to make this tour, and you'll have to paddle several miles from the public put-in on the Keese Mill Rd., west of Paul Smith's College. Also, a reminder — respect the landowners' privacy by stay-ing away from docks and shore.

## CENTRAL AND SOUTHWESTERN ADIRONDACKS

The heart of the Adirondacks has relatively few buildings dating from before the Civil War. **Olmstedville**, off Rte. 28N, has a cluster of Greek Revival storefronts and homes from the 1840s. Farther south, on Rte. 30, **Wells** has several nicely restored classical and Victorian homes along the Sacandaga River. For rustic architecture, in **Raquette Lake**, a boat tour of the lake either on Bird's mail boat (315-354-4441) or the *W.W. Durant*, a replica of an old steamboat (315-354-5532), allows glimpses of Great Camps like *Pine Knot* (the first rustic camp designed by William West Durant), *Camp Echo*, and *Bluff Point* (the former Collier estate). Occasionally, the former J.P. Morgan place, *Camp Uncas*, is open to the public for tours; check with the staff at *Sagamore* (315-354-5301) for information.

## ARTS CENTERS AND ARTS COUNCILS

The arts scene is surprisingly lively in this, New York's most rural area, thanks in part to the long-time leadership of the New York State Council on the Arts. Through grants from the state council to arts presenters, producers, and nonprofit galleries, and a re-grant program to fledgling and volunteer organizations, all kinds of arts programs in all kinds of towns flourished throughout the '70s and '80s. Now, with New York's budget in disarray, there have been some funding cutbacks, but the myriad programs continue with local support.

*The 1992 Adirondack Park Centennial Quilt Exhibition was a highlight of the season at the Adirondack Lakes Center for the Arts.*

Nancie Battaglia

**ADIRONDACK LAKES CENTER FOR THE ARTS**
518-352-7715.
P.O. Box 101, Blue Mountain Lake, NY 12812 (mail).
Rte. 28, next to the post office, Blue Mountain Lake, NY 12812.
Season: Year-round.
Fee: Concert, film, and theater tickets $5—$12. Discounts for seniors, children. Workshop fees vary.
Gift Shop: Open 7 days in summer, 9—5 and intermissions.

**B**ack in 1967, when tie dye and fringe were all the rage, two young Tupper Lakers, Jim and Sheila Hutt, were brought to town for a noble experiment — to bring a full palette of the arts to Blue Mountain Lake, population 150 (give or take). Since then, the Adirondack Lakes Center for the Arts (ALCA), housed in a former garage, has presented hundreds of concerts, including performances by the Tokyo String Quartet, Doc Watson, the Dixie Hummingbirds, Janos Starker, the Seldom Scene, Odetta, Livingston Taylor, and many others. About 8,000 people participate in ALCA visual, performing, and literary arts programs each year.

Exhibitions now include traditional and pictorial quilts; contemporary paintings, photography, and pottery; Adirondack furniture; children's art; and traveling shows. Complementing the exhibitions are intensive courses for adults, scheduled on weekends in fall and winter, and weekdays in summer (see the "Crafts Instruction" listing elsewhere in this chapter). There are numerous programs for kids, from crafts, dance, and music workshops to films and family theater presentations with storytelling, New Vaudeville, and magic.

*The Arts Center/Old Forge organizes several major exhibitions each year, including photography, watercolor, and quilt shows.*

Nancie Battaglia

**ARTS CENTER/OLD FORGE**
315-369-6411.
Rte. 28, Old Forge, NY 13420.
Season: Year-round.
Fees: Concert and theater tickets $5—$12. Donations suggested for special exhibitions.
Gift Shop: Open 7 days in July and August, and during special exhibitions rest of year.

The Arts Center/Old Forge is the oldest multi-arts group in the Adirondacks, founded in the early '50s, but the organization continues to grow, change, and pursue new directions. The facility is a rather homely Butler building — a former boat-storage barn — but it's truly transformed by annual events such as the Adirondacks National Exhibition of Watercolors (September) and the October quilt show. The same space hosts live theater by Pendragon, a touring company from Saranac Lake (see "Theater" elsewhere in this chapter), and children's performances. Classical concerts are often held in the Nichols Memorial Church, a few miles away, while bluegrass, folk, or jazz programs may be presented at McCauley Mountain Ski Area, at the Old Forge beachfront, or in the center's black box theater.

In the summer, the center offers Adirondack Discovery programs, which range from local history outings and lectures to presentations by artists and writers. The Audubon lecture series covers the natural world. Throughout the year, the arts center shows contemporary American and foreign films in different venues (see "Cinema" elsewhere in this chapter), and offers crafts workshops for adults, from boat-building to basketry. There is a raft of kids' programs for ages 5 and up. The center also has a satellite gallery in the old bank, on Main Street in Old Forge, and a cooperative crafts shop, also on Main Street.

**ESSEX COUNTY ARTS COUNCIL**
518-873-6301, ext. 359.
P.O. Box 805,
Elizabethtown, NY
12932 (mail).
Hubbard Hall,
Elizabethtown, NY
12932.
Season: Year-round.

Originally an advocacy group for local artists and craftspeople, the Essex County Arts Council now publishes an extensive summer-events calendar for arts exhibitions; lectures; fairs and festivals; music, theater, and dance performances; and children's programs for the eastern Adirondacks. The organization also presents traditional and contemporary musicians from the region in different settings such as the Lake Placid Center for the Arts and town bandshells, and sponsors special juried arts exhibitions.

**LAKE GEORGE ARTS PROJECT**
518-668-2616.
Canada St., Lake George, NY 12845.
Season: Year-round.
Fees: Concerts are free.

Of all the Adirondack arts institutions, the Lake George Arts Project (LGAP) is decidedly the hippest. Over the years, LGAP has organized outdoor contemporary sculpture shows on the frozen lake, in tree-shaded Shepard Park, and alongside the popular tourist highway up Prospect Mountain. The offices and indoor gallery are on the ground floor of the old courthouse in the center of town; special exhibitions featuring regional artists of national renown are scheduled monthly. Oscar Hijuelos, author of the Pulitzer Prize winner *The Mambo Kings Play Songs of Love*, was an artist-in-residence in 1990. Ongoing programs include fiction and poetry workshops, weekly summer concerts in the park, the hot Lake George Jazz Festival (see "Music" elsewhere in this chapter), and the Black Velvet Art Party, a paean to tackiness complete with Elvis doppelgänger, usually held on the Friday closest to Halloween.

**LAKE PLACID CENTER FOR THE ARTS**
518-523-2512.
Saranac Ave., Lake Placid, NY 12946.
Season: Year-round.
Tickets: Concerts and theater $6—$12. Discounts for seniors and students.

The Lake Placid Center for the Arts (LPCA) has been through a couple of identities: as the Center for Music, Drama, and Art; as an accredited two-year arts school; and as the summer campus for the Parsons School of Design. The facility is top-notch, with a beautiful theater that seats about 300, well-equipped studios, and a bright, airy gallery. In front of the current LPCA complex is the old art school's library, which now houses the Adirondack North Country Crafts Center.

Music and dance presentations here include the Jazz Festival in February, winter dance performances and summer dance-company residencies, and a summer series by the Lake Placid Sinfonietta (see "Music" elsewhere in this

chapter). The LPCA also is home to the Community Theater Players, who offer three or four shows annually. For kids, in July and August, there's the free "Young and Fun" performance series on weekday mornings.

*An artist in residence works on a monumental sculpture at the Lake Placid Center for the Arts.*

Courtesy Lake Placid Center for the Arts

## CINEMA

**D**uring the silent-film era, the Adirondacks provided a backdrop for numerous popular films including *The Shooting of Dan McGrew, Janice Meredith, The Wilderness Woman, The Tiger, Glorious Youth,* and dozens more;

*Heading for a movie on a summer night, Lake Placid.*

Nancie Battaglia

the movie industry thrived for more than a decade in such unlikely places as Saranac Lake, Plattsburgh, and Port Henry. There were cowboy chase scenes at Ausable Chasm, "Alaskan" trapper cabins throughout Essex County, and adventures supposedly set in South America, Siberia, Switzerland; as the cameras rolled, Washington crossed the frozen Delaware — somewhere on the Saranac River.

In 1941, Alfred Hitchcock's only comedy, *Mr. and Mrs. Smith*, was filmed at the Lake Placid Club. A few years later, *Lake Placid Serenade*, which featured lots of figure skating and Roy Rogers (without Trigger or Dale) as king of the Placid winter carnival, was a commercial success. In 1958, portions of *Marjorie Morningstar* were shot in Schroon Lake; local extras were paid the princely sum of $125 per day. Today, the Adirondack movie scene isn't nearly so lively, but there are many places where you can catch foreign, classic, and first-run films. Besides locations listed below, check with local libraries.

## LAKE GEORGE AND SOUTHEASTERN ADIRONDACKS

**Carol Theater** (518-494-7744; Main St., Chestertown) Recently restored and reopened after a long hiatus. First- and second-run films; children's matinees.

**Strand Theater** (518-532-9300; Main St., Schroon Lake) Vintage Art Deco moviehouse, open June through Labor Day. First- and second-run films, some live performances.

## HIGH PEAKS AND NORTHERN ADIRONDACKS

**Berkeley Theater** (518-891-5470; Broadway and Berkeley Square, Saranac Lake) New theater, first-run films.

**Lake Placid Center for the Arts** (518-523-2512; Saranac Ave., Lake Placid) Foreign and contemporary American film series in fall, winter, and spring.

**Lake Placid Public Library** (518-523-3200; 67 Main St., Lake Placid) Kids' film series outdoors in the summer, on the lawn behind the library overlooking Mirror Lake. Bring a blanket or beach chair and plenty of popcorn — if you don't like the movie, you can always feed the ducks.

**Palace Theater** (518-523-9271; Main St., Lake Placid) Recently redone moviehouse, with restored Art Deco stenciling in the lobby and displays of Lake Placid movie memorabilia. Mostly current American stuff, three screens.

## NORTHWEST LAKES REGION

**State Theater** (518-359-3593; Park St., Tupper Lake) Recent commercial films.

## CENTRAL AND SOUTHWESTERN ADIRONDACKS

**Adirondack Picture Show** (518-548-6199; Rte. 8, Speculator) A huge barn, probably the oldest movie theater in the park still operating (circa 1926). Recent films every night in the summer.

**Lake Theater** (518-648-5950; Main St., Indian Lake) Recent films nightly from late May through mid-September in a Quonset hut; occasional classic and foreign films on winter weekends in conjunction with the Adirondack Lakes Center for the Arts.

**Last Waltz Cinema** (315-357-4552; Rte. 28, Inlet) Recent films nightly, Memorial Day through Labor Day; weekends in fall and winter. Occasional classic and modern American films in conjunction with the Arts Center/Old Forge. A Quonset hut; try the balcony if it's open.

**Strand Theater** (315-369-6703; Main St., Old Forge) Under new management and carefully restored. Two or three shows nightly; cult classics at midnight in the summer; children's matinees; foreign films in cooperation with the Arts Center/Old Forge.

# CRAFTS INSTRUCTION

Weave a traditional Adirondack packbasket, spin a skein of wool, tie a dry fly, build a log cabin — you can learn these old-time skills, as well as contemporary crafts, in several centers across the park. Classes for adults range from one- or two-day intensive programs to weeklong sessions; prices vary. Always call ahead to register for these workshops.

*Stitching up a storm at a Sagamore quilting weekend.*

Courtesy Sagamore, Raquette Lake

## CHAMPLAIN VALLEY

**Northern Expressions Gallery & Studio** (518-834-2093; Rte. 22, Port Kent, NY 12975) Basketry, watercolor painting, dried-flower workshops and demonstrations.

## HIGH PEAKS AND NORTHERN ADIRONDACKS

**Adirondack Mountain Club** (518-523-3441; Adirondak Loj Rd., Lake Placid, NY 12946) Painting, photography, and traditional crafts classes in a spectacular natural setting that provides both materials and inspiration.

**Lake Placid Center for the Arts** (518-523-2512; Saranac Ave., Lake Placid) Stained glass, pottery, photography, quilting, furniture making, and other classes for adults, year-round. Some courses are co-sponsored by North Country Community College.

**Newcomb Visitor Interpretive Center** (518-582-2000; Rte. 28N, Newcomb, NY 12852) Weekend classes year-round in traditional Adirondack basket-making, taxidermy, fly tying, watercolor painting, nature photography, and other skills. Also children's nature-crafts programs on Saturdays.

## NORTHWEST LAKES REGION

**Paul Smiths Visitor Interpretive Center** (518-327-3000; Rte. 30, Paul Smiths, NY 12970) Similar offerings to the Newcomb center, above.

## CENTRAL AND SOUTHWESTERN ADIRONDACKS

**Adirondack Lakes Center for the Arts** (518-352-7715; Rte. 28, Blue Mountain Lake, NY 12812) Workshops in quilting, log-cabin and Adirondack lean-to building, wood carving, rustic furniture making, basketry, and other crafts, year-round.

**Arts Center/Old Forge** (315-369-6411; Rte. 28, Old Forge, NY 13420) Classes in watercolor painting, traditional wooden boat building, quilting, pottery, rug making, weaving, basketry, and other skills, year-round.

**Sagamore** (315-354-5311; Sagamore Rd., Raquette Lake, NY 13436). Weekend courses in traditional music and dance, basketry, wood carving, rustic furniture, blacksmithing, quilting, nature illustration, fly tying, paper making, and other skills. Fees include room and board.

# DANCE

## LAKE PLACID CENTER FOR THE ARTS
518-523-2512.
Saranac Ave., Lake Placid, NY 12946.

For three or more weeks each spring or summer, the Lake Placid Center for the Arts (LPCA) features a modern dance company in residence: in 1991, the Rebecca Kelly Dance Company; and in 1992, Rosalind Newman and Dancers in June, and the Kelly group in July. Part of the residency includes classes for adults and children; usually two evening performances and one children's daytime program are scheduled. The LPCA also presents occasional dance concerts throughout the year, such as native American tribal dance performances by the North American Indian Traveling College, and traditional American clogging and step dancing by regional troupes.

*Beth Ann Lacomb and Willie Hinton, members of the Rebecca Kelly Dance Company, which appeared at the Lake Placid Center for the Arts in 1991 and 1992.*

Courtesy Lake Placid Center for the Arts

---

### North Country Dancing

Square, round, and altogether shapeless dancing to the fiddle and banjo is a North Country tradition. Neophytes are welcome at community square dances, and callers will usually walk each dance through. In the summer, there are weekly dances on the tennis courts in *Schroon Lake* (518-532-7650; Chamber of Commerce, Schroon Lake, NY 12870); **Stony Creek Mountain Days** (see "Seasonal Events" in this chapter) also features old-time dancing. Check locally for dances at other festivals, firehalls, and community centers from Saranac Lake to Warrensburg.

**BEYOND THE BLUE LINE**

You'll have to venture outside the Adirondack Park for a full calendar of professional dance, but by traveling not too far afield you can catch rehearsals and performances of the **New York City Ballet** at Saratoga Performing Arts Center (518-587-3330; Saratoga Spa State Park, Saratoga Springs, NY 12866). At rehearsals, seating is usually open so you can get up close, and get a sense of the sheer physical strength of the dancers. At the other end of the spectrum, the annual ballet gala in July is an elegant, magical evening. Also to the south, **Margaret Wagner & Dancers**, a modern-dance company based in Cambridge, NY, holds performances at Hubbard Hall, in Cambridge, and elsewhere (518-677-5606; 9 W. Main St., Cambridge, NY 12816).

## ELDERHOSTEL

The Adirondack Park is a favorite learning laboratory for Elderhostel, the international educational organization for people over age 60. Generally, Elderhostel's informal, non-credit courses last five or six days and cover history, nature, folklore, even culinary arts, in sessions led by local experts; the price for lodging, meals, and instruction is usually less than $300 per person for the entire session. In 1992, Elderhostel topics included spring bird-watching, maple-sugar making, garnet-mining history, Lake George shipwrecks, canoeing, 18th-century social dancing, Great Camps, and ecology.

Adirondack sites for Elderhostel programs include *Sagamore Lodge*, in Raquette Lake (315-354-5311); *Paul Smith's College*, at Paul Smiths (518-327-6249); *Adirondack Lakes Center for the Arts*, in Blue Mountain Lake (518-352-7715; *Adirondack Mountain Club*, at Adirondak Loj, outside Lake Placid (518-523-3441); *Silver Bay Conference Center*, on the northern end of Lake George (518-543-8833); the *Adirondack Museum*, in Blue Mountain Lake (518-352-7311); *Sonrise Conference Center*, near Schroon Lake (518-494-2620); and the *State University of New York's Star Lake Campus* (315-267-2000). For more information on the Elderhostel organization, write to 75 Federal St., Boston, MA 02110.

## HISTORIC BUILDINGS AND DISTRICTS

About two dozen sites in the Adirondack Park are in the National Register of Historic Places; oddly enough, all of the state land — the Adirondack Forest Preserve — is a historic district. And when private land here becomes public property, the terrain is to be returned to a natural condition, and buildings must be destroyed. At least, that's the usual scenario. *Santanoni Preserve*, a hundred-year-old rustic estate described below, will not meet this fate thanks in large part of the efforts of *Adirondack Architectural Heritage* (315-354-5832; AARCH, Box 159, Raquette Lake, NY 13436), a park-wide preservation group. Besides advocacy for endangered properties, AARCH provides technical assistance to towns, inventories historic properties, and offers tours and lectures.

Listed below are a selection of architecturally significant places, old forts, industrial sites, interesting homes, and local preservation organizations, located in towns, villages, and in some fairly remote corners of the park. You'll find the region's major museums plus county and town historical societies described elsewhere in this chapter, under the heading "Museums."

## LAKE GEORGE AND SOUTHEASTERN ADIRONDACKS

**MARCELLA SEMBRICH MEMORIAL STUDIO**
518-644-2492.
Lakeshore Dr. (Rte. 9N),
Bolton Landing, NY
12814.
Season: July—Labor Day;
daily 10—5.

In the early decades of this century, Bolton Landing was a mecca for opera stars and composers, such as Samuel Barber and Gian-Carlo Menotti. From 1921 to 1935, Marcella Sembrich, a Polish soprano, made her home here. Born Marcella Kochanska, Sembrich was a European sensation, and in 1898 she joined the Metropolitan Opera. She founded the vocal departments of the Juilliard School and the Curtis Institute; during the summers, a select group of students came with her to Bolton. Her cottage-studio under the pines now houses a collection of music, furniture, costumes, and opera ephemera related to Sembrich's brilliant career. Music history lectures and concerts are held on summer afternoons and evenings.

## CHAMPLAIN VALLEY

**CROWN POINT STATE HISTORIC SITE**
518-597-3666.
Rte. 17, off Rts. 9N and 22.,
Crown Point, NY 12928.
Season: May—October;
Wed.—Sat. 10—5, Sun.
1—5
Fee: Free.
Handicap Access: Yes.

In Lake Champlain there's a thumb-shaped point that parts the waters, with big Bulwagga Bay to the west and the long reach of the lake on the east: the sweeping view to the north once provided an ideal spot for guarding the territory. The French built Fort St. Frederic here in 1734, which was attacked repeatedly by the British in 1755-58 and finally captured by them in 1759; colonial forces launched their assault on the British ships in Lake Champlain from Crown Point in 1775.

In 1910, the ruins of the French, British, and colonial forts were given to the state of New York. There's a new visitor center that explains the archaeology and political history of this haunting promontory through exhibits, audiovisu-

*Ruins of the soldiers' barracks at Fort Crown Point.*

al programs, and several miles of interpretive trails winding around stone walls and redoubts.

**ESSEX COMMUNITY HERITAGE ORGANIZATION**
518- 963-7088.
Rte. 22, Essex, NY 12936.
Season: Year-round.

During that brief quiet period between the French and Indian War and the American Revolution, William Gilliland, a successful Manhattan merchant, bought up huge tracts of land along Lake Champlain. He had an empire of prosperous farming communities in mind, and by 1770, present-day Essex was established. Unfortunately the town lay smack in the path of General Burgoyne as he marched from Canada to Saratoga, and, just a decade after the settlers arrived, all that remained there was cellar holes and ashes.

By 1800, though, the town was once again thriving, thanks to iron mining, stone quarrying, shipbuilding, and other commerce up and down the lake. Boats built in Essex were tailor-made for the Champlain Canal. By 1850 the population of the town was 2,351; that era was the peak of the town's prosperity.

However, when the railroads came to eastern New York, bypassing these waterways, the fortunes of Essex and other such lakeside towns declined. Its population has since dropped steadily to its current level of about a thousand residents. Because of this decline and the lack of economic opportunities, there was little need for new housing, and old buildings were preserved out of necessity. Today Essex contains one of the most intact collections of pre-Civil War buildings in the Northeast.

Through the *Essex Community Heritage Organization* (ECHO), you can get an excellent booklet describing the dozens of fine homes, inns, and commercial

The Harmon Noble House (circa 1835), in Essex.

Courtesy Essex Community Heritage Association

buildings in town ($3). A self-guided walk through Essex in late spring, summer, or fall is a delightful way to spend a day. Just a few examples to whet your appetite: the town offices are in Wright's Inn, which served as a tavern and inn as early as 1790. Down the street is the Essex Inn, which opened in 1810. Greystone, located near the ferry slip, is a wonderful stone Greek Revival mansion; next door is the Harmon Noble house, a handsome brick Federal-style building, with a tiny octagonal, gingerbread-trimmed one-room schoolhouse that looks like a gazebo. Even the firehouse is charming. (A few of the historic buildings listed in the guide are shops and restaurants open to the public, but many are private homes.)

ECHO also is a leader in roll-up-your-sleeves historic preservation to find new uses for old buildings, and sponsors lectures, workshops, and special house tours from time to time.

**PENFIELD HOME- STEAD MUSEUM**
518-597-3804.
Old Furnace Rd., off Rte. 74, Ironville, Crown Point, NY 12928.
Season: Mid-May— Columbus Day; 9—4 daily.
Handicap Access: Partial

A sign in the picket-fenced front yard of the homestead makes an astonishing claim: the site is the birthplace of the Electrical Age. In 1831 Allen Penfield used a crude electromagnet to separate iron ore from its base rock, thus using electricity in an industrial application for the first time.

Ironville today is a lovely, quiet, otherworldly spot so different from what it was in its heyday, the center of a major iron industry from 1830 to '80.

The complex is an open-air museum dedicated to the local mines, forges, and old railroads, with an eclectic historical collection in the homestead itself, a white-clapboard Federal building circa 1826. The other buildings along the lane in town are mainly Greek Revival, in excellent condition; there's a self-guided walking tour of the 550-acre grounds that takes you into the woods to find remnants of the days of iron. In mid-August, Heritage Day is a festival of traditional crafts and skills, with wagon rides and a chicken barbecue.

## HIGH PEAKS AND NORTHERN ADIRONDACKS

**JOHN BROWN FARM**
518-523-3900.
John Brown Rd., off Old
    Military Rd., Lake
    Placid, NY 12946.
Season: mid-May—
    October: Wed.—Sun, 10-
    5.
Fee: Free.
Handicap Access: Yes

In 1849, abolitionist John Brown came to North Elba, near Lake Placid, to help Gerrit Smith launch a self-sufficient community for free blacks. Smith owned more than 100,000 acres across northern New York, and his plan was to give 40 acres to each would-be black homesteader. Regardless of the community's charismatic leadership, the idea may have been doomed from the start, because the families were not prepared to farm in the harsh climate. Most of the residents of "Timbuctoo," as it became known, left within a few years of their arrival. Brown himself lived only a few years at the farm, abandoning his family for months at a time in order to pursue a failing wool business and antislavery concerns. Before heading out on his final adventure in Harpers Ferry, Brown brought his grandfather's gravestone over from Connecticut, and carved the letters "J.B." in a boulder in the front yard. Brown was executed on December 2, 1859, in Charlestown, Virginia.

In 1870 the property was acquired by a group of the abolitionist's admirers, including the pioneering journalist Kate Field. Today the farmhouse and outbuildings, managed by New York as a state historic site, contain exhibits related to John Brown's life, and his "body lies a-mouldering in the grave" nearby.

*The John Brown Farm, Lake Placid.*

Courtesy John Brown Farm Historic Site

## ROBERT LOUIS STEVENSON MEMORIAL COTTAGE

518-891-4480.
11 Stevenson Lane.
Saranac Lake, NY 12986.
Season: July 1—Sept. 15,
daily exc. Mon., 10—4.
Fee: $2.

In 1887-88, Robert Louis Stevenson took the "cure" for tuberculosis in Saranac Lake, sleeping in an unheated porch all winter, and taking in lots of fresh ozone- and balsam-laden air while hiking and figure skating. During his Saranac Lake years, Stevenson wrote a dozen essays for Scribners, started *The Master of Ballantrae*, and worked on *The Wrong Box*, a collaborative effort with Lloyd Osbourne. In a letter to Henry James, the Scotsman described his tiny cottage: "Our house — emphatically 'Baker's' — is on a hill, and has sight of a stream turning a corner in the valley — bless the face of running water! — and sees some hills too, and the paganly prosaic roofs of Saranac itself; the Lake it does not see, nor do I regret that; I like water (fresh water, I mean) either running swiftly among stones, or else largely qualified with whiskey."

In 1916, the Stevenson Society was founded to commemorate the writer's life and works; one of the group's original projects was to interest sculptor Gutzon Borglum in designing a bronze bas-relief dedicated to RLS. Since then, the society has managed the former Baker cottage, with displays of original Stevenson letters and first editions, and sponsored public readings and lectures. The annual Stevenson Day, with visiting writers, is in early September.

## HISTORIC SARANAC LAKE

518-891-0971.
132 River St., North Elba
Town Hall, Saranac
Lake, NY 12983.
Season: Year-round.

The history of the health-care industry in Saranac Lake is unique, and in 1980, this historic preservation organization was founded to commemorate the special architecture that evolved locally to help tuberculosis patients get more fresh air and sunlight. Numerous cure cottages and sanatorium-related buildings have now been recognized in the National Register of Historic Places.

Historic Saranac Lake has published a walking tour of selected structures and operates a warehouse of salvaged building materials available to the public at low cost. The organization has also sponsored "TB Reunions" for former patients and staff, and presents lectures and conferences year-round.

## ADIRONDAC BLAST FURNACE

No phone.
Tahawus Rd., off Blue
Ridge Rd., off 28N,
Newcomb, NY 12852.
Season: Year-round.

Miles from nowhere on the Tahawus road, which ends at the Upper Works hiking trails parking lot, the startling 50-foot-tall hulk of a blast furnace looms. The stone monolith was built in 1854 to make iron for the McIntyre Iron Works, and on the banks of the Hudson River below the furnace you can easily see the rusty remnants of the blowers that supplied the "blast" of forced air

*By the 1880s, the massive blast furnace at Adirondac was already abandoned.*

Seneca Ray Stoddard. Courtesy the Adirondack Museum, Blue Mountain Lake, NY

that helped the furnace reach high temperatures. For a brief period, pig iron of the highest quality was produced in this remote place, taken by oxcart and sled to Lake Champlain. (Note that the furnace is on private land: visitors are welcome to look, but please leave the site undisturbed for future historians.)

Continuing on the road to the north, you come to a series of deserted structures; the first building on the right, a faded white farmhouse with a porch, was the office of the mining company circa 1840. (The brown buildings were summer cottages for the Tahawus Club, and are considerably more recent.) From 1826 to about 1845, this valley rang with the sound of rock crushers and forge hammers. Workers collected the ore and stoked the fires; farmers provided food for the families; woodsmen cut an acre of hardwood a day for making charcoal to fuel the forges. Today, there are few obvious signs of this commerce, but if you look carefully in the woods on the edge of the parking lot for the High Peaks trails, you can find lumps of 150-year-old charcoal from the mining days.

**SANTANONI PRESERVE**
No phone.
Santanoni Rd. (no cars permitted), Newcomb, NY 12852.

Five miles off Rte. 28N, in the shadow of the High Peaks, there's a deserted Great Camp on the shore of Newcomb Lake. Camp Santanoni was built from native logs in 1892 by a wealthy Albany industrialist, Robert C. Pruyn, and in the early days, Theodore Roosevelt was among the numerous guests who came to hunt, fish, and rusticate in comfort.

You'll have to travel to the camp by muscle power — human or horse — along a wonderful old road with stone bridges over clear brooks. About 1.5 miles from the gate, you come to a fine clearing and the farmstead that once supplied milk, meat, and eggs for the Pruyns. The barn and stone creamery shed are in excellent condition, but the farm cottages are fairly dilapidated and shouldn't be explored. Look up in the woods beyond the last house, and you'll see a cobblestone smokehouse that furnished hams and bacon for summertime meals. Feel free to hike behind the houses up into the old pastures; this is state land.

The main camp complex includes a boathouse, a lakeside studio, and several buildings connected by some 5,000 square feet of veranda. Peek in the window of the main lodge and you'll see an enormous fireplace, rustic railings, split cedar-log wainscoting, and birch bark applied as wallpaper. (The building interior is not open to the public.) The architecture shows Japanese and European influences in its complex rooflines and numerous nooks and crannies.

Santanoni Preserve, about 12,000 acres, was acquired by New York State in the 1970s, and for several years the buildings' fate was in jeopardy; under provisions of the state constitution, public lands in the Adirondacks are to be kept "forever wild," which has been interpreted to mean that structures should be destroyed. But, for one reason or another, the state never got around to razing Santanoni, and now, through the efforts of Adirondack Architectural Heritage (AARCH) and the Town of Newcomb, it appears that Santanoni will be stabilized and left standing. Occasionally there are guided tours of the property sponsored by AARCH, the Visitor Interpretive Center in Newcomb, or other groups; check with the Newcomb town offices (518-582-3211) for information.

## NORTHWEST LAKES REGION

**BETH JOSEPH SYNA-
GOGUE**
518-359-7229.
Lake St., Tupper Lake, NY
12986.
Season: July—Aug.

**B**uilt in 1905, this symmetrical, modest structure is made of simple pine boards and tall arched windows. Beth Joseph once served an active congregation of dozens of families, but after the 1930s, attendance declined. Boy and Girl Scout troops met in the basement, and for a time, a group of Baptists without a church of their own worshiped there. In 1959, the synagogue closed, and stood vacant for 25 years.

Community interest in the historic building was rekindled by a summer resident who encouraged former temple members to get the structure listed on the National Register of Historic Places and begin restoration work. People of all faiths pitched in with donated labor, materials, and funds; the ornate embroidered velvet Torah covers were painstakingly restored by a local weaver. In 1991 work was completed, and now the facility hosts art exhibitions, concerts, and other events.

## CENTRAL AND SOUTHWESTERN ADIRONDACKS

**SAGAMORE LODGE**
315-354-5311.
Sagamore Rd., off Rte. 28,
Raquette Lake, NY
13436.

**W**illiam West Durant built the massive rustic lodge along the lines of a Swiss music box in 1897, and sold it to Alfred G. Vanderbilt, Sr., in 1901. Even though the Vanderbilts spent much of their time elsewhere, Sagamore was like a self-suf-

Season: late June—Oct.;
daily in July and Aug.,
weekends in fall, 9-4.
Fee: $5; $2.50 children.
Gift shop.

ficient village in the heart of the wilderness, with its own farm and a crew of craftsmen to supply furniture, hardware, and boats. Today, the millionaires' enclave — main lodge, dining hall, rustic guest cottages, casino playhouse, open-air bowling alley, and boathouse — and the artisans' complex with blacksmith shop, barns, carriage house, and workshops are open to the public for tours. The contrast between the playful rustic ornamentation on the Vanderbilt structures and the utilitarian work buildings gives a good picture of life here at the turn of the century; a narrated slide program provides a larger context for this upstairs/downstairs theme.

Courtesy Sagamore Lodge

*The Main Lodge at Sagamore.*

Sagamore is in a gorgeous setting on the shore of Sagamore Lake, four miles off the main road on a rough dirt road. Besides tours for the public, the Great Camp sponsors many workshops and conferences and is available for overnight accommodations.

## LECTURE SERIES

With just a little bit of effort, it's easy to get an Adirondack education through numerous public lectures at libraries, museums, and town halls (check the listings under libraries and museums elsewhere in this chapter). *The Atmospheric Science Research Center* (518-946-2142) on Whiteface Mountain presents natural history and environmental science lectures on Tuesdays in July and August. At the *Visitor Interpretive Centers* in Paul Smiths (518-327-3000) and Newcomb (518-582-2000) there are numerous nature, history, and arts lectures and presentations by Adirondack photographers year-round. *The Huntington Lecture Series*, presented in July and August at the Newcomb center by the Adirondack Ecological Center — a major research facility associated with the State University of New York's College of Environmental Science and Forestry — is an excellent assortment of programs on environmental topics of current concern.

**ADIRONDACK DISCOVERY**
315-357-3598.
Mail: Box 545, Inlet, NY 13360.
Season: Summer.

In 1978, Joan Payne and Sue Beck, both Inlet residents, began an informal lecture series in the town hall, presenting local experts on nature, history, transportation, and the arts. Then, as now, speakers volunteered their time; most programs still are free. The lectures became quite popular, attracting a dedicated audience, and soon other towns asked for Adirondack Discovery to provide programs for them.

Now the nonprofit organization has become a sort of mobile Chautauqua, offering guided canoe trips and hikes to historic sites and along old railroad routes, evening lectures on topics ranging from aerial photography to old postcard collections, hands-on workshops by local craftspeople, and special gala occasions in Inlet, Indian Lake, Raquette Lake, Speculator, Old Forge, Saranac Lake, Westport, and beyond. In 1992, for example, Adirondack Discovery presented 98 different programs during July and August, and the group now serves as the educational outreach for the Adirondack Museum and both Visitor Interpretive Centers.

## LIBRARIES

There are 30-some public libraries inside the Blue Line of the Adirondack Park, and visitors are always welcome, rain or shine. Several libraries have special collections of books of regional interest, and some even have mini-museums. Most libraries offer children's programs, readings by regional poets and writers, films, travel lectures, how-to sessions, and even concerts; pick up a schedule locally for the details. Also, hours vary from summer to winter in many places, so it is advisable to write or call ahead. A selection of libraries with noteworthy collections, exemplary programs, or fine buildings follows.

Outside the park, *Crandall Library* (518-792-6508; City Park, Glens Falls, NY 12801) has a special Adirondack collection and a reference staff well versed in North Country lore; the *Adirondack Research Center* (518-377-1452; Association for the Protection of the Adirondacks, P.O. Box 951, Schenectady, NY 12301) also has a collection of archival materials open to scholars.

Within the park, the most complete research library is housed at the *Adirondack Museum* (518-352-7311; Rtes. 28 and 30, Blue Mountain Lake, NY 12812; Jerry Pepper, Librarian). Note that appointments are essential for undertaking projects at these three repositories, and that browsing through stacks is not permitted.

## LAKE GEORGE AND SOUTHEASTERN ADIRONDACKS

### *Brant Lake*

**Horicon Free Library** (No phone; Rte. 8, Brant Lake, NY 12814) Tiny, picturesque cobblestone building perched over the lake; bring your camera.

### *Lake George*

**Caldwell Lake George Library** (518-668-2528; 340 Canada St., Lake George, NY 12845) Crafts workshops for adults and children; films; lectures. Catch a performance by Shirley McPherson, the librarian, if you can — she's an expert on local ghost stories.

## CHAMPLAIN VALLEY

### *Ticonderoga*

**Black Watch Library** (518-585-7380; Montcalm St., Ticonderoga, NY 12883) Designed as a medieval-looking "shrine to literacy" in 1905, and named after the 42nd Highland Regiment, which fought at Ticonderoga in 1758.

### *Westport*

**Westport Library Association** (518-962-8219; Washington St., Westport, NY 12993) Great old bell-towered building with fireplaces, warm woodwork, natural lighting, high ceilings, and comfy couches for reading Victorian novels. Lecture series and occasional summer concerts on the library lawn.

### *Willsboro*

**Paine Memorial Free Library** (518-963-4478; 1 School St., Willsboro, NY 12996) Lovely brick building overlooking the Boquet River. The Paine Jordan bird-skin collection is here for ornithologists to study; there's also a good selection of local history books. Numerous summer programs, from art exhibits to traditional crafts demonstrations.

## HIGH PEAKS AND NORTHERN ADIRONDACKS

### *Keene Valley*

**Keene Valley Library** (518-576-4335; Main St., Keene Valley, NY 12943) Excellent local history and mountaineering collection with monographs, maps,

photographs, and rare books. Lectures, readings, special exhibitions on local history and by regional artists. Call for hours.

### Lake Placid

**Lake Placid Library** (518-523-3200; 67 Main St., Lake Placid, NY 12946) Story hours and outdoor films for children; good general collection.

### Saranac Lake

**Saranac Lake Free Library** (518-891-4190; 100 Main St., Saranac Lake, NY 12983) Extensive Adirondack collection in the William Chapman White Room, open by appointment. Brown-bag-lunch lecture series, evening lectures; gallery featuring local artists; Charles Dickert Wildlife Museum open in July and August.

## NORTHWEST LAKES REGION

### Paul Smiths

**Cubley Library** (518-327-6313; Paul Smith's College, Paul Smiths, NY 12970) College reference library, with fall and winter concert series open to the public.

### Tupper Lake

**Goff Nelson Memorial Library** (518-359-9421; 41 Lake St., Tupper Lake, NY 12986) Good Adirondack collection available to readers whenever the library is open; art and local history exhibits; lectures.

## CENTRAL AND SOUTHWESTERN ADIRONDACKS

*Indian Lake*

**Indian Lake Public Library** (518-648-5444; Pelon Rd., Indian Lake, NY 12842) General collection, with lectures and special programs year-round.

*Inlet*

**Little Schoolhouse Library** (315-357-6494; Rte. 28, Inlet, NY 13360) Small community library.

*Old Forge*

**Old Forge Library** (315-369-6008; Crosby Blvd., Old Forge, NY 13420) Adirondack collection, lecture series, writers' workshops, children's programs, performances by Adirondack storytellers.

*Raquette Lake*

**Raquette Lake Library** (315-354-4005; Dillon Rd., Raquette Lake, NY 13436) Charming turn-of-the-century building with window seats and fireplace; lectures and special programs.

# MUSEUMS

**THE ADIRONDACK MUSEUM**
518-352-7311.
Rtes. 28 and 30, Blue Mountain Lake, NY 12812.
Season: Late May—Oct. 15: daily 9:30—5:30.
Fee: $10 adults; discounts for children, seniors, and groups.
Handicap Access: Yes.
Book and gift shop; snack bar.

Simply put, no visit to the Adirondacks is complete without a trip to the Adirondack Museum; even if you've been there within the last few years, you ought to go back again to see what's new and improved. If you've never seen the complex, described by the *New York Times* as "the best museum of its kind in the world," you're in for a surprise. Perched on the side of Blue Mountain, and overlooking the island-studded lake, is a major outdoor museum that is user-friendly, scholarly, beautiful, amusing, and superlative in every way.

The museum's theme is interpreting man's relationship to the Adirondacks, and it does so in twenty exhibit buildings on a lovely campus. Adjacent to the Gatehouse is a theater and conference building

*The rustic summer house overlooking Blue Mountain Lake is one of many buildings and exhibits at the Adirondack Museum.*

Nancie Battaglia

showing "The Adirondacks: The Lives and Times of an American Wilderness," a recent award-winning film about people living and working in a special place. In the galleries of the main building, there are changing exhibits of landscapes by 19th-century painters such as Thomas Cole, Winslow Homer, and Levi Wells Prentice, plus a series of displays to introduce Adirondack history spanning from the glacial epochs to the present day.

There are scores of wooden boats, including fine examples of the native watercraft, the Adirondack guideboat, and a Gold Cup racer; there are also dozens of carriages, sleighs, and wagons. You can glide through August Belmont's private railroad car, "Oriental," and imagine yourself en route to your very own Great Camp, or you can picture the other extreme of Adirondack life, in exhibits depicting logging and mining. In "Woods and Waters: Outdoor Recreation in the Adirondacks," you'll find hunting and fishing paraphernalia and natural history exhibits. On Merwin Hill, in Bull Cottage, there is room after room of rustic furniture, from twig-mosaic tables to white birch-bark pieces that resemble Louis XIV furniture. If all this seems like too much walking, there's a building where you can sit down and watch 300 or so old photographs parade by.

The museum is a great place for children who can read and understand historical ideas; there are plenty of audio- and videotape stations that add depth to the displays. One suggestion, though: parents should keep a close eye on young ones who may be tempted to climb and touch fragile artifacts. The Marion River Carry locomotive, located in the center of the campus, is a good place to let active kids explore.

In July and August, there are history lectures on Monday nights. Craftspeople demonstrating skills from fly tying to birch-bark canoe building are scheduled from time to time. The Rustic Furniture Makers' Fair in the fall showcases 40 or so builders so that visitors can decide how to begin their own Adirondack collections. There are numerous other events from special conferences to the "No-Octane Regatta: A Wooden Boat Classic," held in Blue Mountain Lake in June.

It's probably a natural response to plan a visit to the Adirondack Museum on a rainy day, but thousands of other folks think along the same lines, and the place can get crowded. Far better to pick a gorgeous day when you can savor the exhibits, the many outdoor displays, and the view.

### Vintage Watercraft

In 1843, John Todd visited the handful of lonely settlers in Long Lake and wrote, "Their little boats were their horses, and the lake their only path." Traditional wooden boats, especially the guideboat — a light, fast rowboat made of native spruce, pine, and cedar — performed a major role in 19th-century work and play. At several boat gatherings across the park, you can get a taste of this era, and enjoy beautifully restored guideboats, canoes, sailboats, and early powerboats.

The **No-Octane Regatta** (518-352-7311) held in Blue Mountain Lake in late June attracts hundreds of boat nuts who bring a glorious array of muscle- and wind-powered watercraft. There are boat-builders' displays at the Adirondack Lakes Center for the Arts, workshops and lectures at the Adirondack Museum, and toy boat events for kids at both locations, but the main attraction is near the public beach on Rte. 28, where the visiting boats are displayed. There are numerous old-fashioned races and contests, including canoe jousting, where standing contestants try to knock each other out of canoes with long, padded poles, and the hurry-scurry race, in which boats are anchored out in the lake: competitors must run from the beach, swim to the boats, clamber into the boat, then paddle or row to the finish line. Of course, all this action generates appetites, so there's a chicken barbecue at the firehall across the street.

In Saranac Lake, the annual **Guideboat Show** (518-891-1990) at the Civic Center in early July presents restored antique and fine new guideboats by regional builders. The event brackets the one-day Willard Hanmer Guideboat and Canoe Races held on Lake Flower.

The **Wooden Canoe Heritage Association Assembly** (no phone; Box 226, Blue Mountain Lake, NY 12812) is a four-day canoe confabulation held at Paul Smith's College, in Paul Smiths, in late July. There are demonstrations and workshops by boat builders, lectures on historic voyages and techniques, and opportunities for the public to paddle and sail traditional canoes.

The **Adirondack Chapter of the Antique and Classic Boat Society** (315-369-3552) will hold its annual show and rendezvous at Old Forge's lakefront on July 24, 1993; visitors should be able to get a good look at all that mahogany, brass, and class when the boats are tied up at the public docks, or folks can watch the parade through the Fulton Chain of Lakes in the afternoon.

In Cleverdale, on the quieter eastern side of Lake George, Castaway Marina hosts its annual **Antique and Classic Boat Show** (518-585-6472) in late August. This is another place to see gleaming old Fay & Bowens, Chris Crafts, HackerCrafts, Garwoods, and even Gold Cup racers.

*Seen from the air,
Fort Ticonderoga commands
a broad sweep of
Lake Champlain.*

Courtesy Fort Ticonderoga Museum

**FORT TICONDEROGA**
518-585-2821.
Fort Rd., off Rte. 22,
   Ticonderoga, NY 12883.
Season: mid-May—mid-
   Oct.: daily 9—5.
Fee: $6; children 10—13 $5;
   under 10 free.
Handicap Access: Yes.
Museum shop; snack bar;
   picnic grove.

High above Lake Champlain is another must-see for Adirondack visitors: Fort Ticonderoga. In 1755, the French built a fort, *Carillon*, on the site, and for the next quarter-century the stone fortification was a key location in the struggle to claim North America. The Marquis de Montcalm defended the site against numerous British invaders until 1759, when Lord Jeffrey Amherst captured the fort. Ticonderoga was British territory until Ethan Allen and the Green Mountain Boys took the fort by surprise, "in the name of Jehovah and the great Continental Congress."

In the early 1800s, the Pell family acquired the ruins and fields where the soldiers once camped. Restoration was begun in 1908 to rebuild the barracks and parade grounds, making Fort Ticonderoga the nation's first restored historic site (in contrast, Colonial Williamsburg restoration dates back only to the '30s).

Inside the barracks are exhibits and artifacts pertaining to the French and Indian War and the American Revolution, from intricately inscribed powder horns to blunderbusses, cannons, and swords. The grim side of winter warfare becomes fairly clear, and there's little glorification of the ordeal of battle. On the barracks' walls there are some surprisingly familiar-looking paintings, including Thomas Cole's "Gelyna," depicting a wounded British officer. Below the barracks is the subterranean kitchen, which once supplied thousands of loaves of bread every day to the standing army.

Events and activities are scheduled at the fort throughout the summer, including demonstrations of black-powder shooting and cannon firing, and fife-and-drum drills. On selected weekends, there are encampments of regiments reenacting battles, or bagpipe-band concerts. There's also a boat tour available every day in July and August on the *Carillon*, which goes from Fort Ti on historic Lake Champlain cruises for an extra fee.

The fort is set in a spectacular spot with a magnificent view of the lake, but don't end your visit there. It's worth a side trip up Mount Defiance, near town, to get an even higher perspective. From the top of that hill, a show of British cannons so intimidated the brass at Ticonderoga and Mount Independence, a fort across the lake in Vermont, that the colonials fled both fortifications in 1777. (Shots were never fired.) Bring a pair of binoculars and a picnic lunch.

**ADIRONDACK CENTER MUSEUM**
518-873-6466.
Court St. (Rte. 9), Elizabethtown, NY 12932.
Season: Mid-May—mid-Oct.: Mon.—Sat. 9—5, Sun. 1—5 p.m.
Fee: $3; $2 seniors; $1 children 6—16.
Handicap Access: Yes.
Gift Shop.

If all the military skirmishes along Lake Champlain have blurred into one confusing cloud of cannon smoke, the Essex County Historical Society's museum has a nifty sound-and-light show that puts the various wars and individual battles into a geographical and chronological context. That's not the only reason to visit: the Adirondack Center Museum describes local pioneer life — mining, farming, trapping, logging — with its informative permanent exhibits, and showcases contemporary local artists during the spring and summer.

There's a stagecoach that once carried passengers from Elizabethtown to Keene, a fire tower that you don't have to climb a mountain to enjoy, a roomful of dolls, and the wonderful Colonial Garden, with a formal design of perennials and herbs. For Adirondack and genealogical scholars, there's an excellent library open by appointment year-round. On the second Saturday of October, there's the annual Forest, Field, and Stream Festival, with traditional music and storytelling, a fiddle contest, craft demonstrations, a black-powder shoot, native foods, and activities for kids.

**SIX NATIONS INDIAN MUSEUM**
518-891-0769.
Buck Pond Campsite Rd., Onchiota, NY 12968.
Season: July 1—Labor Day, daily 9:30—6; May—June, Sept.—Oct. by appointment.
Fee: $1; 50 cents, children.

Native people did travel to the North County for spring fishing, summer gathering, and fall hunting: the mountains, forests, and lakes were a veritable supermarket of riches. At many local institutions this information is overshadowed by all the other stories those museums have to tell, but in Ray Fadden's museum, the kaleidoscopic collection of baskets, beadwork, quillwork, tools, weapons, paintings, drums, cradle boards, hats, pottery, and clothing celebrates the Iroquois tribes' lives and times in and around the Adirondacks. Inside the main exhibit building, there are dioramas of Abenaki, Mohican, and other villages, while outdoors, on the grounds, there are bark and log shelters and camp settings to explore.

Ray Fadden recounts an
Iroquois legend at his Six
Nations Indian Museum.

Nancie Battaglia

Fadden meets with museum visitors to explain native culture, "read" a beaded record belt, or discuss how our democratic government has its roots in the Iroquois Confederacy and the Great Law. He's an impassioned teacher and an interesting storyteller, and the museum's message is definitely a life-long commitment for him.

## LAKE GEORGE AND SOUTHEASTERN ADIRONDACKS

In Warren County you'll find numerous small museums to visit. In **Bolton Landing**, the *Bolton Historical Museum* (518-644-9960; Rte. 9N, Bolton Landing, NY 12814) is housed in a former Catholic church with lovely stained glass windows. Nineteenth-century photos of Lake George hotels by Seneca Ray Stoddard give a taste of the Gilded Age; more contemporary photos show sculptor David Smith at work in his Bolton Landing studio. There's an assortment of furniture, clothing, agricultural implements and so forth.

In **Brant Lake**, the *Horicon Museum* (518-494-7286; Rte. 8, Brant Lake, NY 12815) is a nine-room farmhouse full of antiques, agricultural implements, prints, photos, toys, and dolls, and is open from Memorial Day through Labor Day. The *Frances Kinnear Museum*, open year-round in a historic **Lake Luzerne** home (518-696-4520; 2144 Main St., Lake Luzerne, NY 12846) is similarly chock-full of local memorabilia. The town is also home to two summer museums: the *Mill Museum*, set in a park near the lake (no phone; Mill St.), and the *Schoolhouse Museum* (518-696-3500; Main St., near the Norstar Bank). Another museum, in **Chestertown**, open July—August, is the *Town of Chester Museum of Local History* (518-494-3758; Town Hall, Main St., Chestertown, NY 12815), with displays on village life.

In **Lake George**, in the old Court House, the *Lake George Historical Museum* (518-668-5044; Canada St., Lake George, NY 12845) is three floors of exhibits,

### Allen's Bear Fight Up in Keene

This heroic poem has been recited in Essex County since the Civil War; folklorist Harold W. Thompson recorded it in *Body, Boots and Britches* (Philadelphia: Lippincott, 1939, and reprinted in 1979 by Syracuse University Press). The incident took place in 1840, when newspaper editor Anson Allen was appointed census taker for the million-acre county, which held less than 25,000 residents in widely scattered settlements. The punchline, in the fifth stanza, is a venerable classic of American folklore. *Reprinted courtesy of HarperCollins.*

Of all the wonders of the day,
There's one that I can safely say
Will stand upon the walls of fame
To let all know bold Allen's fame.
The greatest fight that e'er was seen
Was Allen's bear fight up in Keene.

In 1840, as I've heard
To take the census off he steered
Through bush and wood for little gain,
He walked from Keene to Abram's plain.
But naught of this, it is not well
His secret motives thus to tell.

As through the woods he trudged his way,
His mind unruffled as the day,
He heard a deep, convulsive sound
Which shook the earth and trees around;
And looking up with dread amaze,
An old she-bear there met his gaze.

The bear with threatening aspect stood
To prove her title to the wood.
This Allen saw with darkening frown;
He reached and pulled a young tree down,
Then, on his guard with cautious care,
He watched the movements of the bear.

Against the rock with giant strength
He held her out at his arm's length.
*"Oh God!* he cried in deep despair,
*"If you don't help me, don't help the bear!"*
'Twas rough and tumble, tit for tat;

The nut-cakes fell from Allen's hat.
Then from his pockets forth he drew
A large jack-knife for her to view;
He raised his arm high in the air,
And, butcher-like, he stabbed the bear.

Let old men talk of courage bold,
Of battles fought in days of old
Ten times as bad; but none, I ween,
Can match a bear-fight up in Keene.

from the 1845-vintage jail cells in the basement to "the church that cheated the hangman." The detailed folk-art model was carved by George Ouellet, a convicted murderer, in 1881; he whittled the church, sold it for a good sum, hired a new lawyer, appealed his conviction, and was acquitted. In July and August, there are Monday evening lectures on the history of the Lake George basin. Also in Lake George is *Fort William Henry* (518-668-5471; Canada St.), a restored fort with life-size dioramas, assorted armaments, and lots of action: military drills, musket and cannon firing, fife and drum bands.

The *Schroon-North Hudson Historical Society* in **Schroon Lake** (518-532-7798; Olden Dr., Schroon Lake, NY 12870) is open Thursday—Sunday in July and August; in **Warrensburg**, the *Warrensburg Museum of Local History* (518-623-9826; 47 Main St., Warrensburg, NY 12883) highlights the town's early industries, from garment factories to sawmills.

## CHAMPLAIN VALLEY

In **Ticonderoga** are two local-history museums: the *Heritage Museum* (518-585-6366; Bicentennial Park, Montcalm St., Ticonderoga, NY 12883) and the *Historical Society* (518-585-7868; Hancock House), located in a replica of John Hancock's Boston Home. The Heritage Museum depicts 19th-century industries, including paper- and pencil-making, in a brick and terra cotta Victorian office building that's open daily in July and August and on fall weekends. Hancock House was the first home of the New York State Historical Association (now based in Cooperstown), and the historical society's museum has several period rooms illustrating social history from the 1700s to the turn of the century. There's an extensive research library open by appointment year-round.

## HIGH PEAKS AND NORTHERN ADIRONDACKS

In **Lake Placid**, the old train station for the Adirondack Division of the New York Central is home to the *Lake Placid-North Elba Historical Society Museum* (518-523-1608; Averyville Rd., Lake Placid, NY 12946). There's a nostalgic country store display, sporting gear and memorabilia from the 1932 Olympics, and a music room; the place is pretty lively in the summer with lectures and concerts. Open June—September, Tuesday—Sunday afternoons.

In the **Saranac Lake** Free Library, the *Charles Dickert Memorial Wildlife Museum* (518-891-4190; 100 Main St., Saranac Lake, NY 12983) is open July and August, with displays of stuffed mammals, birds, and fish native to the Adirondacks.

## CENTRAL AND SOUTHWESTERN ADIRONDACKS

Riley's Tavern in **Piseco** is home to the *Piseco Lake Historical Society* (518-548-6401; Piseco Lake Rd., Piseco, NY 12139), a local collection of antiques and ephemera open in the summer. In *Edinburg*, the *Nellie Tyrell Edinburg Museum* (no phone; RD 1, Edinburg, NY 12134) is an old schoolhouse with displays showing life before the creation of the Great Sacandaga Reservoir. *Northville* is home to two museums located right on South Main Street: the *Gifford Valley Schoolhouse*, behind the municipal offices, and the *Paul Bradt Museum*, which is filled with North American wildlife and housed inside the village office complex. Museum isn't exactly the word to describe the *Lawrence R. Faust Art Park* (518-863-2530; Sacandaga Park, off Rte. 30, Northville, NY 12134); it's a sculpture garden that even kids love, since it's not at all a static, academic, hands-off kind of place. Nearby on Mountain Road, in *Mayfield*, is the *Tamarack Bird and Wildlife Museum*. It's open most days except Sunday, but you do need to call Arthur Ginter (518-863-6796) for an appointment to see this private collection.

*Caroga's* outdoor museum complex near the lake, the *Caroga Historical Museum* (518-835-4400; London Bridge Rd., Caroga, NY 12032) re-creates pioneer life in the southern Adirondacks in a farmstead, schoolhouse, and country store, and hosts changing exhibits of quilts, paintings, and photographs.

In *Olmstedville*, the *Minerva Historical Society* (518-251-2229; Main St., Olmstedville, NY 12857) is open July and August; occasional special exhibits honor artists who visited the area, such as Winslow Homer.

In *Old Forge*, the *Town of Webb Historical Association* (315-369-3838; Crosby Blvd., Old Forge, NY 13420), in the Cohen Memorial Building above the library, has exhibits on Adirondack railroads, rustic furniture, and early industry; the museum is open Tuesday, Wednesday, and Friday, year-round. Just east of Old Forge is the *Forest Industries Exhibit Hall* (315-369-3078; Rte. 28, Old Forge, NY 13420), with exhibits on forest management, logging history, and dioramas open Memorial Day—Labor Day; the building is also a showcase for dozens of species of native woods in the ceilings, beams, walls, floors, railings, and display cases.

## BEYOND THE BLUE LINE

In *Glens Falls*, the *Hyde Collection* (518-792-1761; 161 Warren St., Glens Falls, NY 12801), an exceptional private art collection, includes works by da Vinci, Botticelli, El Greco, Rembrandt, Rubens, Degas, Renoir, Cezanne, and Picasso, along with famous American artists, amid 16th- through 19th-century antique furnishings, in a handsomely restored villa. There's a new wing with changing exhibits, and many participatory programs. Also in Glens Falls is the *Chapman Historical Museum* (518-793-2826; 348 Glen St., Glens Falls, NY 12801), a historic house with a modern gallery highlighting photographs by Seneca Ray Stoddard.

Southeast of the Adirondacks, in *Granville*, the *Pember Museum of Natural History* (518-642-1515; 33 W. Main St., Granville, NY 12832) houses a wonderfully preserved Victorian gentleman's collection of hundreds of birds, butterflies, and trophy heads in polished wood cases. In *Saratoga,* next door to Lincoln Baths, a public spa, is the *National Museum of Dance* (518-584-2225; Rte. 9, Saratoga Springs, NY 12866). Open from Memorial Day through the fall, the museum's collection includes lovely ballet costumes and sets, hundreds of photographs, and special exhibitions highlighting international dance history; programs include lectures, demonstrations, and classes for adults and children.

North of the park, in *Chazy,* is another private museum, the *Alice T. Miner Colonial Collection* (518-846-7336; Main St., Chazy, NY 12921), set in a three-story mansion, with a fine textile collection, good china and glass, rare books, colonial furniture, and strange curiosities from around the world. In *Plattsburgh,* the *Kent-DeLord House Museum* (518-561-1035; 17 Cumberland Ave., Plattsburgh, NY 12901) is a nicely restored late 18th-century home with period furnishings. Near *Malone* is the *Farmer Boy's Home* (518-483-1207; Stacy Rd., Burke, NY 12953), the setting for *Farmer Boy,* by Laura Ingalls Wilder. The farmstead, which is gradually being restored, was the home of Almanzo Wilder in the mid-19th century.

South of the park, in *Johnstown,* but pertinent to Adirondack studies, is *Johnson Hall State Historic Site* (518-762-8712; Hall Ave., Johnstown, NY 12095). The restored 1763 Georgian mansion was the home of Sir William Johnson, who served as superintendent of Indian affairs for the northern colonies; the Adirondack fur trade was a mainstay of his wealth. The Colonial Market Fair is a popular event, and the site hosts historic encampments of frontiersmen, Canadian fur traders, and native people.

## MUSIC

Virtually every American of a certain age knows a piece of popular music written about the Adirondacks: "Indian Lake," the seventies bubble-gum hit by the Cowsills. The group vacationed in the village, had a great time, and immortalized their summer experience on vinyl. Fortunately for us, there's no annual Cowsill Festival attracting dozens of bell-bottomed Cow Heads, but the music scene across the park is truly rich and varied.

There's traditional North Country music, represented by a particular style of dance and fiddle tunes that have roots in French Canadian and Irish music, and by the ballads of the lumber woods, like "Blue Mountain Lake," "The Jam on Gerry's Rocks," "The Wild Mustard River," and "Once More A-Lumbering Go," sung unaccompanied or with a simple guitar back-up. To hear authentic old-time instrumental music, look for the occasional fiddle jamborees, contests, or square dances, sponsored by arts groups and towns. The **Adirondack Lakes Center for the Arts** (518-352-7715) in *Blue Mountain Lake* usually hosts an informal contest in June; the **Forest, Field, and Stream Festival** in October at the **Adirondack Center Museum** (518-873-6466) has featured local fiddlers. **Long Lake Parks and Recreation** (518-624-5112) sponsors fiddlers' gatherings once in a while; you can dance like a wave of the sea at **Stony Creek Mountain Days** (518-696-2332) in August. The **Adirondack Fiddlers Association** meets the second Sunday of every month in the *Lake Luzerne* Community Center (518-696-4545; Rte. 9N); arrive by 12:30 p.m. for a good seat. To hear the folksongs and ballads, check with music presenters listed below. The **Schroon Lake Arts Council** (518-532-7675) stages an annual Adirondack folk festival in August, and the **Essex County Arts Council** (518-873-6301) schedules local singers in various concert settings. Besides traditional music, there are many excellent summer chamber-music series outlined in the following pages.

## LAKE GEORGE AND SOUTHEASTERN ADIRONDACKS

**LUZERNE CHAMBER MUSIC FESTIVAL**
Luzerne Music Center
518-696-2771
Lake Tour Rd., 1.3 miles off Rte. 9N, Lake Luzerne, NY 12846.
Season: July—Aug.
Tickets: $10.

Members of the Philadelphia Orchestra (who also perform at the Saratoga Performing Arts Center in July and August) present a superb chamber-music concert series on Monday nights. Artistic directors of the center are Toby Blumenthal, piano, and Bert Phillips, cello, and they pride themselves on bringing internationally acclaimed soloists to join the resident ensembles. The music center is also a summer camp for gifted young musicians, and the free student/faculty recitals held Fridays, Saturdays, and Sundays are definitely worth a listen. A sampling from past concert programs includes Beethoven's "Archduke" Trio for violin, cello, and piano; Mendelssohn's String Quartet Opus 12 in E Flat Major; Gabrielli's Canzoni for Brass Quartet; Brahms's Trio in A Minor, Opus 114, for clarinet, cello, and piano.

**SEAGLE COLONY**
518-532-7875.
Charley Hill Rd., Schroon Lake, NY 12870.
Season: July—Aug.
Tickets: Vary.

Oscar Seagle, famed tenor and voice teacher, established this rural retreat in 1915. Vocal music is still the primary program, with coaching and master classes in opera and musical theater for conservatory students and aspiring performers. Every Sunday evening in the summer, the nondenominational Vespers concerts feature exceptional choral singing; public concerts featuring scenes from opera and musical theater are held in July.

**SCHROON LAKE ARTS COUNCIL**
518-532-7675.

On the lakeshore, yet within walking distance of downtown Schroon Lake, the Boat House Theater is a fitting spot to hear traditional Adiron-

Boat House Theater,
  Schroon Lake.
Mail: Box 668, Schroon
  Lake, NY 12870.
Season: July—Aug.
Tickets: $5; $3 children.

dack music. The arts council presents several evening concerts and dance performances each summer in the 1860s building, and a daylong festival of folk music and storytelling each August. Featured folk artists have included Chris Shaw, whose Adirondack recordings were recently accepted in the Library of Congress; Dan Berggren; storyteller Bill Smith; and Roy "Poncho" Hurd.

*Tunes under the trees at the Lake George Jazz Festival in September.*

Courtesy Lake George Arts Project

### Hot Rods and Cool Jazz

After Labor Day, hustling, bustling Lake George village calms down a bit, but during the second weekend in September there's a burst of color and sound: the **Adirondack Nationals Car Show** (518-785-9432) at the Fort William Henry Motor Inn, and the **Lake George Jazz Festival** (518-668-2616), in Shepard Park on Canada St., the main drag (especially for these two days). On Saturday and Sunday, chopped and channeled street rods and trucks in a rainbow of hues cruise up and down the street, while under the trees, there's dancing and grooving to some great tunes. The free jazz festival is sponsored by the Lake George Arts Project, and rising stars and legendary performers share the stage. Past players include Bobby Sanabria, Nestor Torres, Orange Then Blue, Richie Cole, David Leonhardt, Manhattan Tap, and Dakota Staton.

## CHAMPLAIN VALLEY

**MEADOWMOUNT
  SCHOOL OF MUSIC**
518-873-2063.
Lewis-Wadhams Rd.,
  Lewis.
Mail: RFD 2, Westport, NY
  12993.
Season: July—Aug.
Tickets: Vary.

A short list of some of Meadowmount's alumni gives a hint of the talent that can be found in the summery hills of the Boquet Valley: Yo-Yo Ma, Itzhak Perlman, Pinchas Zukerman, Michael Rabin, Lynn Harrell. Distinguished faculty and promising students give free concerts at the camp on Wednesdays and Sundays, while the annual special benefit concert features world-famous string players in a cozy, informal setting. Meadowmount student chamber groups also play in free outdoor concerts in nearby towns such as Jay and Elizabethtown, so check locally for scheduling; the alumni concert series at the Lake Placid Center for the Arts is held on weeknights beginning in early July.

**TICONDEROGA FESTIVAL GUILD**
518-585-6716.
Montcalm St.,
Ticonderoga.
Mail: Box 125,
Ticonderoga, NY 12883.
Season: July—August.
Tickets: Vary.

An enormous striped tent in the center of town is the festival guild's summer home; under the big top there are weekly performances of music, dance, and theater, with concerts on Tuesday nights and kids' shows on Wednesday mornings. Past guests have included the Berkshire Ballet, the Empire Brass Quintet, the Lake Placid Sinfonietta, and the Tommy Gallant Allstars.

## HIGH PEAKS AND NORTHERN ADIRONDACKS

**ADIRONDACK FESTIVAL OF AMERICAN MUSIC**
518-891-1057.
Various locations, Saranac
Lake.
Mail: Box 562, Saranac
Lake, NY 12983.
Season: July.
Tickets: Vary.

Since 1973, Gregg Smith, one of the country's premiere choral leaders, and the Grammy-award-winning Gregg Smith Singers, have called Saranac Lake their summer home. Their gift to the community is music, music, music. The month-long festival includes workshops for music teachers, composers, and schoolkids, and there are literally dozens of choral, chamber, jazz and pops concerts sprinkled throughout the village in churches, parks, and the town hall. Resident ensembles are the ConSpirito wind quintet, the Adirondack Chamber Orchestra, and others; guest artists have included the Dave Brubeck quintet.

**LAKE PLACID SINFONIETTA**
518-523-2051.
Various locations.
Mail: Box 1303, Lake
Placid, NY 12946.
Season: July—Aug.
Tickets: Vary.

Back in 1917, the Sinfonietta was established as the resident orchestra at the Lake Placid Club, playing for the guests at that exclusive resort. Now the 18-member chamber orchestra is a valued community resource, presenting free Wednesday night concerts in the bandshell overlooking Mirror Lake in the center of town (7 p.m.; bring a beach chair or cushion), free children's programs at the Lake Placid Center for the Arts (LPCA), the free Pops and Picnic at the Horseshoe Grounds on Old Military Rd., and the annual Train Station Concert at the Lake Placid-North Elba Historical Society in August. On Sunday nights, the Sinfonietta performs in the art center's theater with selected guest artists; the programs range from newly commissioned works by American composers to pieces by Mozart, Haydn, Bach, and Schubert. Vienna Night is a Strauss celebration usually held in early August; the annual gala features dinner, dancing, and music through the night. Tickets for the LPCA concerts are $12 for adults.

*On Wednesday evenings in the summer, the Lake Placid Sinfonetta performs by the shore of Mirror Lake.*

Nancie Battaglia

---

### Music Under the Stars

Many towns offer free summer outdoor concerts in pretty little parks; you're welcome to bring a picnic basket, blanket, beach chair, and mosquito repellent. In *Lake George* village's Shepard Park, there's music sponsored by the town on Tuesdays at 7 p.m., and an excellent acoustic and jazz series organized by the Lake George Arts Project (518-668-2616) on Wednesdays at 8 p.m. The Glens Falls City Band plays on Wednesdays in *Warrensburg's* downtown bandshell at 7 p.m. (518-761-6366).

In *Port Henry's* bandshell, there are biweekly folk concerts (518-546-3502), and in Riverside Park in *Keeseville*, blues and folk music shows a few nights in July and August (518-834-7292). The weekly classical, folk, jazz, or puppet performances start at 6:30 Saturday evening in *Jay* on the village green (518-946-7348). *Saranac Lake* presents an excellent lineup of jazz, blues, Latin, and folk musicians on Fridays in the Anderson Bandshell on Lake Flower (518-891-1990).

In the central Adirondacks, there are Saturday bluegrass, folk, and jazz concerts at Arrowhead Park in *Inlet* (315-357-5501), and on Sundays in *Old Forge* in the town park overlooking First Lake (315-369-6983).

---

## BEYOND THE BLUE LINE

Yes, it's confusing, but the *Lake George Opera Festival* (518-793-3866; Box 2172, Glens Falls, NY 12801), isn't there anymore. From its original home in a tin-roofed barn in Diamond Point, the summer opera festival has moved (to *Glens Falls*, a few miles down the road), and matured to become one of the country's most prestigious series. Performances — always in English — are staged at the Queensbury High School Auditorium.

*Saratoga Springs* isn't too far beyond the Adirondack Park, and the *Saratoga*

*Performing Arts Center* (518-587-3330; Saratoga Springs, NY 12866) is a wonderful outdoor setting for the New York City Opera, the Philadelphia Orchestra, the Newport Jazz Festival-Saratoga, and the new Saratoga Chamber Music Festival. From mid-June through Labor Day, SPAC is busy practically every night. There are seats in the amphitheater as well as on the sloping green lawns; an added plus is that children under 12 (accompanied by an adult) are admitted free for lawn seats to opera, ballet, and orchestra concerts, courtesy of the Freihofer Baking Company.

**Washington County**, east of Lake George and just this side of the Vermont border, is home to two fine chamber groups, *Music from Salem* (518-677-2495; Hubbard Hall, Cambridge, NY 12816), with the Lydian String Quartet in residence, and *L'Ensemble* (518-677-5455; Content Farm Rd., Cambridge, NY 12816).

# NIGHTLIFE

Let's face it, the after-dark scene in the Adirondacks was more lively fifty or sixty years ago, when practically every hotel or resort had its resident band for dances; Duke Ellington, Count Basie, and other top band leaders brought their sidemen up for gigs at places like the Pine Cone Bowl in Speculator, while Rudy Vallee was a familiar face at the Lake Placid Club. Today, our vacation patterns are different — we just don't stay at a resort for a month or longer, so hostelries can't afford to entertain guests quite so lavishly.

You'll find the North Country is devoid of fern bars, has only one or two sports bars (try *Mud Puddles* in **Lake Placid**, 518-523-4446, or check out Canada St. in **Lake George**), has only occasional karaoke evenings (try the *Jager House* in **Warrensburg**, 518-623-2727) and decidedly lacks a reliable assortment of decent jazz bars ... well, only one place jumps to mind for occasional blues or jazz, and that's the *Lady of the Lake* in **Edinburg** (518-863-4390; S. Shore Rd., Edinburg, NY 12134). In the dead of winter in 1992, they had the spunk to present Alligator Records' bluesman, Lefty Peterson, but the ambiance of the bar is borderline gloomy.

A few places in the southeastern Adirondacks offer live country-western or country-rock music on a regular basis in winter and summer: *Jimbo's Club at the Point* (518-494-4460; **Brant Lake**) and *Stony Creek Inn* (518-696-2394; **Stony Creek**) are two possibilities. There's a Polynesian floor show at the *Howard Johnson Tiki Resort*, complete with fire routines and sword dancing; to find the place, just look for the only giant palm trees in **Lake George** (518-668-5744; Rte. 9, Lake George). Bars in other towns frequently have live music on summer weekends, so your best bet is to ask locally and consult area newspapers to find out who's playing what where. The *Chronicle* from Glens Falls has a good weekly listing.

In **Lake Placid**, there are occasional rock concerts at the Olympic Arena in the summer; Bonnie Raitt has played there twice (518-523-1655; Main St., Lake

SOCIAL DANCE

AT

Allen's Hall,

North Elba, N. Y.,

Tuesday Evening, Dec. 25th, 1877.

Yourself and Ladies are Invited.

FLOOR MANAGERS :

Ed. Kennedy, D. Cameron, Orrin Holt.

Good Music in Attendance,

TICKETS, $2.00.

Courtesy Natalie and Maude Bryt

Placid, NY 12946). Occasionally there are free outdoor concerts in the Olympic village — C.J. Chenier rocked the speed-skating oval on the 4th of July in 1992 — but check ahead with the Lake Placid Visitors Bureau for special offerings (518-523-2445; Main St., Lake Placid).

Many tour-boat operators offer moonlight cruises with live music; on *Lake George*, you can try either the paddlewheeler *Minne-Ha-Ha* or the enormous and opulent *Lac du Saint Sacrement* (518-668-5777; Beach Rd., Lake George, NY 12845). Check under "Boat Tours" in Chapter Six, *Recreation*, for more listings, in the central Adirondacks and Lake Placid.

Don't overlook the numerous programs presented by arts centers, arts councils, and chambers of commerce; although you won't be able to enjoy an alcoholic drink at these affairs, the music can be outstanding, and the price — sometimes free — is right.

## SEASONAL EVENTS

Throughout the Adirondack Park, many special events celebrate local ways and old-time North Country culture. The programs listed below, in roughly chronological order, emphasize history, music, storytelling, traditional crafts and skills, or a combination of the arts. You'll find annual athletic events, such as the White Water Derby and the Whiteface Mountain Uphill Footrace listed in Chapter Six, *Recreation*; craft fairs, flea markets, and antique shows are listed in Chapter Seven, *Shopping*; and affairs with a gustatory focus, like the Newcomb Steak Roast, are outlined in Chapter Five, *Restaurants and Food Purveyors*.

*The Ice Palace of the 1901 Saranac Lake Winter Carnival.*

Courtesy Adirondack Collection, Saranac Lake Free Library

### LAKE GEORGE AND SOUTHEASTERN ADIRONDACKS

**Lake George Winter Carnival** spans several weekends beginning in early February, with lots of kid-oriented activities, like the "Frostbite Theater" shows in Shepard Park and horse-drawn sleigh rides on the ice. The annual Polar Bear Swim provides some vicarious chills and thrills; there are flag-football and softball games on the frozen lake, plus all kinds of contests and races (518-668-5755).

**Lake Luzerne Winter Extravaganza** is usually the first weekend in February, with a particular highlight being the outhouse races. There are snow-sculpture contests, sleigh rides, snowshoe races, and a craft fair (518-696-3500).

**Hague Winter Carnival** is slated for the second full weekend in February, starting off with a torchlight parade on Friday evening. Daytime action includes the National Ice Auger and Chisel Contest, which involves boring through frozen Lake George, and plenty of other competitions for adults and children, from broom hockey to ice fishing to cross-country skiing (518-761-6366).

**Americade** is reportedly the world's largest motorcycle touring rally. Held in and around Lake George in early June, the event includes guided scenic rides on Adirondack back roads, seminars, swap meets, and banquets. Bikes range from tasteful special-edition Harleys worth tens of thousands of dollars to strange, rusty "rat bikes" that look like found-object sculptures, which of course they are, in a sense. The participants aren't scary; they're just ordinary folks who love motorcycles (518-656-9367).

**Summerfest** features live music, arts and crafts, and games for kids in Shepard Park on Canada St. in Lake George, during the last weekend in June (518-668-5755).

**Smokeeaters Jamboree** combines exciting firefighting-skill competitions with carnival games, music, dancing, and events for children in the recreation field on Library Ave. in Warrensburg, in late July (518-623-9598).

**Stony Creek Mountain Days** highlight old-time Adirondack skills and pastimes. There are lumberjack contests, crafts demonstrations, square dancing, wagon rides, and plenty of barbecue, followed by fireworks, held the first weekend in August (518-696-2332).

**Warren County Country Fair** is a family-oriented fair, with the usual 4-H and agricultural exhibits, a horse show, historical displays, traditional music, a pony pull, carnival rides, and fish-and-wildlife exhibits, held in mid-August at the fairground on Horicon Ave. outside Warrensburg (518-623-3291).

## CHAMPLAIN VALLEY

**Explore & Discover Days** at Adirondak Loj, near Lake Placid, concentrate on learning in and about the outdoors through storytelling, nature crafts, map and compass sessions, adventure hikes, and other programs for families with children 6 to 12. Preregistration is required; programs are in July. Sponsored by the New York State Outdoor Education Association and the Adirondack Mountain Club (518-523-3441).

**Old-Time Folkcraft Fair**, on the lawn of the Paine Memorial Library in Willsboro, is a showcase for local artisans and a chance to learn traditional North Country skills, in late July (518-963-4478).

**Essex County Fair**, in Westport, features harness racing, livestock and agricultural displays, a midway, educational programs by the Cooperative

Extension, and lots of cotton candy. Novelist Russell Banks wrote about the annual Demolition Derby in *The Sweet Hereafter*, published in 1991 by HarperCollins. The fair runs for five days in mid-August (518-962-4810).

**Heritage Day**, under the tent in downtown Ticonderoga, is sponsored by the Ticonderoga Heritage Museum (518-585-6366), and is usually in early August. A highlight of the annual festival is the Adirondack Memorabilia Show, with displays of historic maps, photos, prints, books, and ephemera, and a show of contemporary rustic furniture, taxidermy, quilts, and other crafts.

**Downtown Essex Day** is the second Saturday in August, featuring boat races in Lake Champlain, music, crafts, games for kids, and an evening outdoor performance with giant puppets by the Mettawee River Theatre Company, in Beggs Point Park, Essex (518-963-7088).

**Forest, Field, and Stream Festival**, at the Adirondack Center Museum in Elizabethtown, is the second Saturday in October, with a full slate of storytelling, old-time music, crafts demonstrations, black-powder shooting, and participatory programs for children (518-873-6466).

## HIGH PEAKS AND NORTHERN ADIRONDACKS

**Saranac Lake Winter Carnival**, in February, is reputedly the oldest winter carnival in the country. On the shore of Lake Flower, there's an awesome ice palace, dramatically lit by colored spotlights each evening; events include ski races, a parade, concerts, and special activities for kids (518-891-1990).

**Round the Mountain Festival** in Saranac Lake is a spring celebration with an afternoon of bluegrass bands, a barbecue, and a canoe race, all on the second Saturday in May (518-891-1990).

## NORTHWEST LAKES REGION

**Woodsmen's Field Days** in Tupper Lake highlight old-time lumber skills and underline the importance of logging in the Adirondack economy today. There's a parade with polished and pinstriped log trucks hauling the year's biggest, best logs; contests for man (ax-throwing, log-rolling, and speed-chopping), beast (skidding logs with draft horses), and heavy equipment (precision drills for skidders and loaders); clowns and games for kids. It's all on the second weekend in July, in the municipal park on the lakefront in Tupper Lake (518-359-3328).

**Adirondack Wildflower Festival** at the Visitor Interpretive Center in Paul Smiths offers guided wildflower walks, wildflower craft workshops, wildflower cooking demonstrations, and art programs for kids, in late July (518-327-3000).

### CENTRAL AND SOUTHWESTERN ADIRONDACKS

**Indian Lake Winter Festival**, on Presidents' Weekend in February, mixes local history (films, lectures, tours) with outdoor events such as cross-country ski treks, downhill races at the town ski area, snowmobile poker runs, and snowshoe softball throughout Indian Lake and Blue Mountain Lake. A sampling of the goofier programs includes bed races, pie-eating contests, and golfing on snow. There's music and sometimes square dancing in the evenings, plus plenty of community suppers (518-648-5112).

**Neighbor Day** opens the summer season in Old Forge, with music, crafts, kids' performances, and special art exhibitions across town, in early June (315-369-6411).

**Minerva Day**, at the town beach on Minerva Lake and in downtown Olmstedville, features a parade, crafts demonstrations, and activities for kids on the last Saturday in June (518-251-2869).

**Old Home Days** in Wells are held the first full weekend in August, with a parade featuring horse-drawn wagons, antique cars, floats, and marching bands. There's all kinds of music, plus a carnival and a crafts fair (518-924-7912).

**Bluegrass Festival** in Long Lake's Sabattis Park brings top upstate bands and dancers for an outdoor show on the third Saturday in August (518-624-3077).

**Gore Mountain Oktoberfest** is the last weekend in September in North Creek, with plenty of oom-pah-pah and *gemütlichkeit*. There's live music and German-style dancing, a crafts fair, ethnic food and beer booths, children's activities, and rides on the ski area's chairlift to view the fall foliage (518-251-2612).

**Apple Festival,** also in Long Lake's Sabattis Park, is family fun with performances and games for kids, apple-cider making, a crafts show, and apple pies galore, usually on the Saturday before Columbus Day (518-624-3077).

## STORYTELLING

Stretching the truth and telling outright lies as social entertainment is a North Country tradition going back to the earliest days. Every town had its favorite storyteller: Mart Moody, from Tupper Lake; Pants Lawrence, from Speculator; Abner and Bill Greenfield, from Wells; Bob Glassbrooks from North Point; and many more.

Some of the well-worn stories told in the Adirondacks also appear as familiar Paul Bunyan sagas, such as the lumberman's new harness that shrank so much overnight that the load of logs was drawn out of the woods without a single tug on the traces. Life in the Blue Line lumber camps spawned yarns about all kinds of insects, from body lice as fierce as bobcats to mosquitoes capable of biting through iron axes or carrying off iron kettles. Then there are the hunting stories, with bear chases and hand-to-paw wrestling matches, or accounts of bucks bearing antlers so broad they could only walk backwards through the woods. Fishing tales describe highly intelligent, ambulatory trout or astonishing catches made without baiting a hook — by following a specially trained trout hound or by gathering fish from the ice of a pond after a rapid freeze. Agricultural yarns include an early ploy to attract potential settlers by showing them a sackful of beechnuts and telling them the objects were enormous grains of buckwheat; a recent incarnation of the farmers' fib is that here zucchinis grow so large they can be carved into dugout canoes.

Occasionally the members of the *Adirondack Liars' Club* appear at local arts centers, fairs, festivals, or weekend programs at Sagamore Lodge (see "Historic Buildings and Districts" elsewhere in this chapter). This group (the members now live mostly outside the Blue Line) tells old and new Adirondack-flavored tall tales in an informal, conversational style, with each teller trying to outdo the next. Greenfield Review Press, based in Greenfield Center, NY, has published a few collections of these stories, most recently *I Was on the Wrong Bear*, all told by the late Blue Mountain Lake liar Harvey Carr.

## THEATER

### LAKE GEORGE AND SOUTHEASTERN ADIRONDACKS

**LAKE GEORGE DIN-NER THEATER**
518-761-1092 year-round information; 518-668-5781 summer reservations.
Holiday Inn, Rte. 9, Lake George, NY 12845.
Season: mid-June—mid-Oct.
Tickets: Dinner and play $39; Wednesday lunch and matinee $26; theater only $21.
Handicap Access: Yes.

This Actors Equity company presents one show a season in a semi-proscenium setting; a sample from past playbills includes *Oil City Symphony, Dames at Sea, Little Mary Sunshine,* and *On Golden Pond.* In 1992, the group's 25th-anniversary summer, the show was *I Ought to Be in Pictures* by Neil Simon. Productions are thoroughly competent, as is the food.

## CHAMPLAIN VALLEY

**DEPOT THEATER**
518-962-4449.
Delaware & Hudson
Depot, Rte. 9N,
Westport, NY 12993.
Mail: Box 414, Westport,
NY 12993.
Season: June—Sept.
Tickets: $12.50; $11.50
students, seniors.
Handicap Access: Yes.

In the late 1970s, as transportation by train declined, the Westport D&H depot found a surprising new life as home to a fine professional equity acting company directed by Westport native Shami McCormick. Now the former freight room comes alive with four or five shows each summer. Past plays included Alan Ayckbourn comedies, *Driving Miss Daisy*, *Nunsense*, and David Mamet's A *Life in the Theatre*. Each year, a new musical debuts, and performance art pieces by visiting artists are scheduled midweek. Depot Theater offers matinees for each of its shows — a nice option on a rainy day — but be sure to call ahead for ticket reservations.

Nancie Battaglia

*Nowadays, folks come to the D&H freight room for great shows — courtesy of the Depot Theater — rather than to pick up their bags.*

The group and the facility remain active year-round, through arts-in-education programs for regional schools, residencies at North Country arts centers, workshops, and exhibitions by local artists. During the summer season, there's a theater apprentice program for students interested in acting, directing, set design, lighting, and theater management.

In Port Henry, the local theater group, *Harmony House Players* (518-546-7539; c/o Henry Dubois, Port Henry, NY 12974) present shows almost every Saturday in the summer.

## HIGH PEAKS AND NORTHERN ADIRONDACKS

**PENDRAGON THEATER**
518-891-1854.
148 River St., Saranac Lake, NY 12983.
Season: Year-round.
Tickets: $12; $10 students, seniors.
Handicap Access: Yes.

**B**ob Pettee and Susan Neal have forged a truly professional year-round theater company that's not content to present the tired warhorses of small-town theater; Pendragon's active calendar always includes adventuresome new works designed to challenge actors and audience alike. The company was begun in 1981, but Pettee's Adirondack roots go back a decade more, to Mountain Echo Theater, in Long Lake, and other local touring companies. In 1983, Pendragon performed at the Edinburgh International Arts Festival and garnered a prestigious Fringe First Award, for *Third Class Carriage* by Jack Kendrick, a Lake Placid poet and playwright.

Each summer, Pendragon presents three plays in repertory format; in 1992, the plays were *The Boys Next Door* by Tom Griffin, *Our Country's Good* by Timberlake Wertenbaker, and *Crimes of the Heart* by Beth Henley. Also during July and August, Pendragon actors offer works in progress, one-man shows, and readings. The fall season usually produces a classic show, while in February and March, the Prop Trunk Players tour local schools and the ensemble presents a contemporary work. Home base is in a converted warehouse near Lake Flower in Saranac Lake, but the company also visits the Arts

*In July 1992, Ginger Lee McDermott and Bob Pettee of Pendragon Theater, performed the world premiere of the drama* In the Charge of an Angel, *by Hal Corley.*

Courtesy Pendragon Theater

Center/Old Forge and the Adirondack Lakes Center for the Arts, in Blue Mountain Lake, for two or more summer plays.

**COMMUNITY THEATER PLAYERS**
518-523-3438.
Saranac Ave., Lake Placid/Mail: Box 12, Lake Placid, NY 12946
Season: Year-round.
Tickets: Vary.
Handicap Access: Yes.

Since 1972, the Community Theater Players have presented shows at the Lake Placid Center for the Arts such as *Annie, Fiddler on the Roof, South Pacific, The Odd Couple*, and other mainstream musicals and comedies. The usual schedule includes a fall, winter, and summer play, plus a children's production; recent productions have been of a very high caliber and nicely staged.

**FROG POND THEATRE**
518-946-2133.
High Peaks Base Camp, Springfield Rd., Upper Jay, NY 12987.
Season: Year-round.
Tickets: Vary.
Handicap Access: Yes.

At the base camp, a rambling lodge on the edge of the Sentinel Range, the Frog Pond Theatre has a number of faces: a free children's theater school; music, dance, and storytelling performances by Adirondack folk; daylong multi-arts festivals in summer and winter, and evening programs for teenagers. Music is presented coffeehouse style in the restaurant, while summer events are often outdoors.

## CENTRAL AND SOUTHWESTERN ADIRONDACKS

**ACT, INC.**
315-369-6411.
c/o Arts Center/Old Forge, Rte. 28, Old Forge, NY 13420.
Season: Spring and winter.
Tickets: Vary.
Handicap Access: Yes.

Musicals are on the menu for this spirited local group; past shows include *Annie, Oklahoma!*, and *Hello, Dolly*. Folks with surprisingly rich voices come from miles around to be onstage at the Arts Center in Old Forge during mud and snow season. In wintertime, there's usually a special children's show besides the Broadway plays.

# WRITERS' PROGRAMS

The Writer's Voice, a nationwide program of the YMCA, opened a literary arts center in 1991 at Silver Bay Association, on the quiet northern end of Lake George. In June and July each summer, there are weeklong workshops in children's literature; nature, travel, and journal writing; and in fiction, poetry, and prose, led by regional writers with national reputations. On Thursday evenings from June through August, there are Readings by the Bay, featuring such authors as James Howard Kunstler, Ed Vega, Anne LaBastille, Joseph Bruchac, and Emily Neville. For information, contact the Writer's Voice at Silver Bay, Sharon Ofner, Director; 518-543-8833; Silver Bay, NY 12874.

# CHAPTER FIVE

# *Always in Good Taste*

# RESTAURANTS & FOOD PURVEYORS

**B**eans, spuds, turnips, and cabbage — the cornerstones of archetypal Adirondack cuisine — were utilitarian fuel for the body, not an opportunity to exercise kitchen creativity. The earliest taverns and hostelries offered travelers what grew grudgingly from the ground, along with a little bit of salt pork, perhaps a haunch of venison, or maybe, if the guests were particularly blessed, a freshly caught speckled trout. Food was food; you ate it because you were hungry, and it was fine.

Courtesy Adirondack Museum, Blue Mountain Lake, NY

*Jack's Camp, near Elizabethtown, 1930s.*

The arrival of railroad service to many North Country towns enlivened dining options considerably. Oysters, packed in barrels, were plentiful and cheap; local churches and clubs held oyster suppers almost as often as their seaside equivalents did. By the 1880s, the humble woodsmen's lodges had given way to grand hotels, which had an elite clientele to please. Menus became elaborate affairs listing *quenelles, duxelles,* and *mirepois* alongside the caviar, fresh figs, sweetbreads, and lobster. Meals lasted for hours on end, as course after course stacked one rich dish atop another. Fresh venison appeared in a variety of guises and in all seasons; many establishments prided themselves on offering brook trout at every meal.

The grand hotels and their attendant style fell out of favor by the 1920s. Vacations became family car trips, and a new kind of restaurant, specializing in unadorned, hearty, eat-and-run chow, sprang up along the highways. Diners proliferated at the crossroads. Resorts with individual sleeping cabins, and dining buildings where guests could gather for breakfast and dinner, became the standard for lodgings.

Today many towns still have a diner, where men gather most mornings for coffee and local women have lunch together occasionally. The original screen-door, street-level roadside places are rarer; two examples come to mind: Tail O' the Pup, on Route 86 in Ray Brook, which hasn't changed much from when it started in 1945, and Burke-Towne, a summer-only breakfast-and-lunch place in Raquette Lake. (Listed under *Lodging*, Chapter Three, are those resorts which still offer meals to guests under full or modified American plans.)

In the 1980s, the restaurant scene in the Adirondack Park underwent a revival. Many places, especially near Lake Placid, spruced up a bit before the Olympics; others, buoyed by a growing tourist business, revamped their kitchens, fired their cooks for chefs, wrote new menus, and started afresh. Today there's a surprising variety of food establishments for what remains basically a very rural area. Across the park there are a few city-style delicatessens, some old-timey ice cream parlors, lots of decent family restaurants, plus many places with spotless white tablecloths, real flowers, and color-coordinated candles on the tables; waiters and waitresses who can adroitly pronounce the names of foreign foods; and imaginative, excellent cuisine.

In preparation for this chapter about a dozen Adirondack residents from different towns took to the byways in search of good places to eat. We visited pizzerias, rustic lodges, country inns, swank hotels, and greasy spoons from mid-February through early May 1992. We were looking for restaurants that operate with a clear sense of what they're trying to do and which apply that vision through good service, quality food, and fair prices. So you'll find some very cheap places as well as some very fancy places, and all kinds of choices in between. We hope that the listings in this chapter give you an accurate idea of what to expect when you walk in the door of any given restaurant, or lead you to explore a new part of the region.

The list that follows is long, but it's by no means exhaustive. The Lake George area alone has scores of restaurants, including nearly two dozen that advertise home-cooked Italian food. So if you're a veteran Adirondack eater, you may not find your favorite place in these pages. Maybe we didn't get a chance to eat there during the three months we were conducting this research, or maybe we did try the place, were disappointed, and felt that no write-up was better than a negative review. Also, just at press time, we learned that a handful of landmark Adirondack restaurants reopened in summer 1992 after a long hiatus, most notably **Steak & Stinger** (518-523-9927; 15 Cascade Rd., Lake Placid, NY 12946), **The Pinnacle** (518-835-4121; Rte. 10, Canada Lake, NY 12032), and the historic **Nick Stoner Inn** (518-835-2211; Rte. 29A, Caroga Lake, NY 12032).

We present here everything from neighborhood joints where five bucks gets you a satisfying bellyful, and the company's good to boot, to thoroughly elegant restaurants of well-deserved international renown. Each restaurant is designated with a price code that summarizes the cost of one meal (appetizer, entree, and dessert) but does not include wine, cocktails, sales tax, and tip.

The restaurants are grouped by region starting with Lake George and the southeastern portion of the Adirondack Park and proceeding counterclockwise. Within the regions you'll find the towns in alphabetical order, with restaurants named alphabetically under each town. In the back of the chapter, you'll find a sampling of bakeries, candy makers, delicatessens, gourmet shops, farm stands, orchards, maple-syrup makers, and other food purveyors. You'll also find a calendar of community barbecues and suppers that offer great chow at low prices. All these places and events are listed in the index, too.

| _Dining Price Codes_ | Inexpensive | up to $15 |
|---|---|---|
| | Moderate | $15 to $20 |
| | Expensive | $20 to $30 |
| | Very Expensive | over $30 |

| _Credit Cards_ | AE: | American Express |
|---|---|---|
| | CB: | Carte Blanche |
| | D: | Discover |
| | DC: | Diners Club |
| | MC: | Master Card |
| | V: | Visa |

| _Meals_ | B: | Breakfast |
|---|---|---|
| | L: | Lunch |
| | SB: | Sunday Brunch |
| | D: | Dinner |

# RESTAURANTS

## LAKE GEORGE AND SOUTHEASTERN ADIRONDACKS

### _Bolton Landing_

**THE CLUB GRILL**
518-644-9400.
Frank Cameron Rd., off
   Riverbank Rd., Bolton
   Landing.
Open: Daily mid-May—
   Oct.; weekends only
   Nov.—early May.
Price: Expensive.
Cuisine: American grill,
   Continental.
Serving: L, D.
Credit Cards: AE, D, MC,
   V.

This place inspires fantasy. Suddenly, it's 1932. Walter Hagen's Pierce-Arrow gleams near the entrance of the tidy stone clubhouse. Walter himself is about to finish the round. He hits an easy six iron to the elevated 18th green. It lands pin-high, about 12 feet from the cup — an excellent chance at a birdie. There's warm applause from the gallery.

The Club Grill, which is part of the Sagamore Hotel complex, has class. It also has an expensive menu and wine list. But then again, who cares what it costs? Would you really quibble about the check if you were given the chance to eat a decent meal at the Newport Casino or the Ausable Club?

Handicap Access: Yes.
Special Features: Lake and golf course view; outdoor dining.

The sensible approach here is to simply surrender to the atmosphere. Grab one of bartender Geoff's fine dry martinis and do some fairway rambling before you settle down to a session of the kind of grill cooking that nobody does anymore — the filet mignon is as thick as your hand is wide, and ditto for the lamb and veal chops. The salads and desserts won't win any prizes, but at least you're eating them in one of the truly impressive rooms inside the Blue Line — a hunting lodge/golf club fantasy that will make you smile, not wince, when you plop down your gold card. Ten-dollar Nassau, anyone?

**JULE'S SERVICE DINER**
No phone.
Main St., Bolton Landing.
Closed: Tues.
Price: Inexpensive.
Cuisine: American.
Serving: B, L.
Credit Cards: None.
Handicap Access: No.

A classic diner that did yeoman duty for years in Attleboro, Massachusetts, Jule's Service Diner now occupies a place of honor in downtown Bolton, where the Bill Gates Diner (which is now displayed at the Adirondack Museum) once stood. It's a perky place, tricked out in butter yellow with blue trim, and authentic inside down to the tiny two-person booths and counter. The food here is far better than the usual diner chow, not so much fried stuff, more herbs and spices, distinctive soups; baked goods, like pies and muffins, are excellent.

**THE TRILLIUM**
518-644-9400.
At the Sagamore Omni Classic Resort, Sagamore Rd., Bolton Landing.
Open year-round.
Price: Very Expensive.
Cuisine: Continental.
Serving: D, SB.
Credit Cards: AE, DC, MC, V.
Handicap Access: Yes.

The Trillium, one of several restaurants at the Sagamore Hotel, is a pretty exclusive place — no jeans or collarless shirts allowed, jackets required, as are reservations. In the elegant, high-ceilinged dining room a musician unobtrusively strums classical guitar pieces; attractive guests seated at nicely appointed tables murmur in hushed tones. It seems as though there is a waiter or waitress at every corner, greeting you, thanking you for coming, offering assistance with this or that.

At a recent dinner, we started with appetizers of exotic fruits served in a light cream, and an excellent salmon and caviar plate. These were followed by a pheasant salad and tomato cachepot salad, both very well prepared and beautifully presented. For the main course we chose beef tournedos, two delicate fillets served with bordelaise sauce over onions and mushrooms, and meltingly tender lamb in a rich, creamy sauce. Other entrees include scrupulously fresh seafood, milk-fed veal, duckling, and occasional game like venison or quail.

A separate dessert menu includes a selection of fruit sorbets and sweets baked on the premises. We had the chocolate cake, which came two slices to a plate, napped with a delectable sauce. It was excellent.

There's also a delightful Sunday brunch at the Trillium, drawing guests from as far away as Albany. The selection of fresh and smoked fish, fresh fruits, vegetable salads, and entrees (paupiettes of sole with lobster mousse, sauce Nantua; breast of chicken with black beans, Spanish rice, and roasted corn; sirloin of beef with Madeira and wild mushrooms, to name a few) are tastefully arrayed, and invite hours of sampling.

Dinner or brunch here is not for anyone on a limited budget: Our dinner total for two people came to $123; the only drinks we ordered were two glasses of the house white wine. An "American plan" five-course dinner is available for $47 a person and you can order just about anything off the menu. The house automatically adds 17% for gratuity.

The Trillium is one of several restaurants within the Sagamore Hotel, an Omni Resort located on Lake George. The recently restored, historic old hotel has hundreds of rooms and acres of gardens. After your meal, take a stroll down to the waterfront and admire the view.

### *Chestertown*

**BALSAM HOUSE**
518-494-2828/
  1-800-441-6856.
Friends Lake Rd.,
  Chestertown.
Price: Expensive.
Cuisine: French.
Serving: D.
Credit Cards: AE, DC, MC,
  V.
Reservations:
  Recommended.
Special Features: Historic
  inn; fireplace.
Handicap Access: Ramp in
  back.

Start a romantic evening at the brass bar in the Balsam House's 1891 Lounge sipping a fresh Bass Ale or, in winter, a hot buttered rum beside the fire, and before long you will feel yourself transported to the Adirondacks of a much earlier, more stately era. The Balsam House is old — except for a brief hiatus in the 1970s, it has been run as an inn for over a century. It feels authentic because it is.

Meanwhile, innkeepers Helena Edmark and Bruce Robbins, Jr., and their new chef, Gerard Moser, have kept the menu up-to-date. Almost everything is homemade, from the puffed rolls and pheasant paté to the raspberry cheesecake and rum-raisin shortbread. The French country cuisine is inventive and delightful. Chef Moser has his own smokehouse, and his smoked fish salé, with oysters and salmon, is not to be missed. Some of the smoked fish also finds its way into his seafood sausage, served with caviar and capers. His roast duckling with raspberry sauce is tender and hearty. The wine cellar, which has consistently received awards from the *Wine Spectator*, boasts more than 3000 bottles.

After dinner, follow the short path to Friends Lake and walk along the shore. As with everything else at the Balsam House, you'll be enchanted.

*Friends Lake Inn owners Greg and Sharon Taylor in the dining room.*

Nancie Battaglia

**FRIENDS LAKE INN**
518-494-4751.
Friends Lake Rd., west
  side, Chestertown.
Closed: Mon.—Wed., Mar.
  15—Memorial Day.
Price: Expensive.
Cuisine: Regional.
Serving: B, L (in winter
  only), D.
Credit Cards: MC, V.
Reservations:
  Recommended.
Handicap Access: Yes.
Special Features: Extensive
  wine and beer lists;
  country inn; fireplace.

The superlatives first: a wine list 375 bottles long; perhaps the best selection of beers in all of New York State; and food, described by the owners as "imaginative regional," that compares with any in the Adirondacks. But Friends Lake Inn is more than the sum of its superb parts. It is a casually elegant, gracefully homey, altogether delightful spot to spend an evening.

Tucked on the western shore of pretty Friends Lake, the inn opened in 1860 as a boardinghouse for tannery workers. Its first real glory days were during Prohibition, when it was a popular retreat; its modern renaissance began a few years ago when Sharon and Greg Taylor refurbished it as a top-notch restaurant, hotel, and cross-country ski center. Occasionally you have to wait for a dinner table on the weekends (start at the bar with Sierra Nevada Pale Ale, available almost nowhere else in the Northeast), but most week nights a table by the fire or the window is yours for the asking. Much of the food is locally (and organically) grown, and even the seafood, which must travel some distance, tastes impeccably fresh. The sauteed shrimp in hazelnut honey butter makes an excellent starter; the smoked chicken and salmon strudel are two of the best entrees. End your meal with a glass of port or a winter beer, and be sure to pet Zack, the house yellow lab, as you leave. You'll want him to remember you on your next visit.

**MAIN STREET ICE
  CREAM PARLOR**
518-494-7940.

If the haute cuisine found on the edge of town just doesn't appeal to you, try Suzanne and Bruce Robbins's deli and ice cream parlor. Besides

Main and Church Sts.,
Chestertown.
Open: Daily.
Price: Inexpensive.
Cuisine: Deli, Ice cream
parlor.
Serving: L, D.
Handicap Access: Yes.

some terrific ice cream concoctions, like the Dusty Road Sundae — a hot butterscotch sundae sprinkled with malt powder — or the maple walnut sundae, topped with locally made syrup, there's a fine assortment of deli sandwiches and salads, good homemade soups, and spicy, meaty chili. The Main Street Melt, which is grilled rye filled with tuna salad, tomatoes, bacon, Russian dressing, and Swiss cheese, is certainly enough to satisfy all but the hungriest. From May to October, the parlor is open daily from 10 a.m. to 9 p.m.

Besides offering good food at reasonable prices, the building is a feast for the eyes. There's a full-size wagon in the window, assorted farm implements, and old photographs of the town. Lots of local advertising art covers the walls: ads for clothing, chicken feed, horse races, and stagecoach lines. The original telephone switchboard, a console not much bigger than a modern phone booth, which once served the area from Chestertown to Blue Mountain Lake, is near the front of the store. Just on the other side of the ice cream parlor, sharing the entrance, is Miss Hester's Emporium, with antiques, contemporary quilts from local seamstresses, baskets, and stationery.

*Sampling a soda at the Main Street Ice Cream Parlor, Chestertown.*

Nancie Battaglia

**THE PLACE**
518-494-3390.
Rte. 8, Chestertown, 3 miles west of Chestertown on Rte. 8/9, near Loon Lake.
Closed: Winter.
Price: Moderate.
Cuisine: Italian.

The Place, nestled halfway between Chestertown and Loon Lake, is one of the best, and least expensive, Italian restaurants in the Adirondacks. This family-owned business features excellent service and moderate prices on a full menu of dishes.

On a recent trip, a garden salad was 95 cents and an ample portion of lasagna cost $8.20. You can't

Serving: D.
Credit Cards: None.
Handicap Access: Yes.

beat those prices, and hot homemade bread is included with every meal. Linguine comes in a creamy cheese sauce with tiny bits of bacon, and the spaghetti is served in huge allotments, with generous helpings of meatballs or sausage. The spaghetti sauce is perfect family fare — not too spicy, not too wimpy.

People who eat at The Place are usually too full for dessert but several homemade treats are available, including cheesecake and a selection of pies.

**RENE'S MOUNTAIN VIEW HOUSE**
518-494-2904.
White Schoolhouse Rd., 1 mile east of Rte. 8, Chestertown.
Open year-round.
Price: Moderate to Expensive.
Cuisine: Swiss, Continental.
Serving: D.
Credit Cards: MC, V.
Reservations: Recommended.
Handicap Access: Yes.

Chef Rene Plattner has cooked in the great hotels of Switzerland, for the late Shah of Iran, and alongside Chef "Tell" Erhardt; his wife, Barbara, is an accomplished pastry chef. The pair revitalized the nearby Balsam House in the early 1980s, and opened the Mountain View House in 1989. The place is rambling and casual; there's no need for neckties here, although the quality of the service and the superb food would warrant dressier attire in a more self-conscious setting.

The menu reflects the seasons. In the winter, for example, appetizers include baked raclette cheese, Cajun barbecued shrimp, and hearty vegetable soups. Entrees include venison served with homemade spaetzel and sliced breast of duck Cassis.

Fresh fish is prepared simply and well, often accompanied by pasta. Dessert is a must: the menu changes daily, but you can count on tortes, trifles, or truffles. Even the ice cream is made in the kitchen here. Try the banana.

## *Hadley*

**SARATOGA ROSE**
518-696-2861.
Rockwell St., Hadley.
Closed: Mon.—Wed. fall, winter, and spring.
Open daily in summer.
Price: Moderate to Expensive.
Cuisine: Italian, Continental.
Serving: L, D.
Credit Cards: D, MC, V.
Reservations: Recommended.
Handicap Access: Ramp in rear.

The Van Zandt mansion in Hadley has been through several incarnations in its century of existence, including a brief stint as a funeral home. In April 1988 Nancy and Anthony Merlino bought the rambling Victorian house with an eye toward creating a modern bed and breakfast in an old-fashioned setting. Recently, they've begun serving lunch and dinner to the public.

The parlor, library, and living room, plus the veranda in nice weather, are the dining areas. There are marble fireplaces, chandeliers, hardwood floors, and lots of antiques throughout; whimsical folk-art-style paintings by Cate Mandigo, a local

Special Features: Dining on the porch; fireplaces; old Victorian inn.

artist of national renown, line the walls. The overall effect is a pleasant, unpretentious atmosphere, enhanced by prompt, friendly service.

Anthony performs double duty as chef and innkeeper. The menu is quite extensive, offering tasty Italian fare like eggplant and sausage Parmigiana, fettucini and scallops Segretta (sautéed scallops and fresh broccoli in a cream sauce), shrimp scampi, and veal picatta, but Saratoga Rose is far more than a good Italian restaurant in a big pink house. Many of the entrees are unusual and hearty, such as the spinach-stuffed pork loin sautéed in anisette, roast duckling, and chicken Lena, a breast of chicken with asparagus, feta cheese, and a light cream sauce.

Appetizers are sizable: a recent order of mussels marinara, served with a very good homemade tomato sauce, was certainly enough for a dinner. If you'd rather save room for dinner and dessert, you still get a chance to point your palate with the homemade paté, crackers, and gherkins that are brought to the table before the salad course. After dinner, you can settle in with a cup of cinnamon-scented coffee and a homemade parfait layered with Chambord or Amaretto. If you're planning to hike home, you can always go for the ultra-rich chocolate mousse truffle cake.

## Hague

**INDIAN KETTLES**
518-543-6576.
Rte. 9N, Hague (south on Rte. 9N, 8 miles from Ticonderoga village).
Closed: Winter.
Price: Moderate.
Cuisine: American.
Serving: L, D.
Credit Cards: None.
Handicap Access: No.

Indian Kettles, a roadside and waterfront restaurant with slightly hokey Indian pictographs on the siding, is famed for its spectacular view of northern Lake George. The kettles are natural depressions in the nearby rocks formed by glacial action and supposedly used by native Americans for cooking. You can arrive by boat and tie up to the restaurant's protected docks on the lake, and there's a nice deck overlooking the lake for summertime dining.

Hamburgers, salads, and fried seafood platters are served in ample portions. Recently, a chef's salad was so large it seemed to take up half the table and was even served on a platter. The service could be speedier, however.

On high-season Saturday nights, there's live music on tap at the Kettles.

## Lake George

**BARNSIDER BBQ & GRILL**
518-668-5268.

Look for the restored buggy just south of town on Rte. 9, and you'll find Ed Pagnotta's pleasant restaurant, a newcomer to the Lake George

Rte. 9, Lake George, near
  Water Slide World.
Closed: Tues., except in
  July and Aug.
Price: Moderate.
Cuisine: Barbecue,
  American.
Serving: B, L, D. (B on
  weekends only except
  July—Aug.)
Credit Cards: D, MC, V.
Reservations: No.
Handicap Access: Yes.

dining scene that offers three square meals a day. Breakfast is the usual eggs, bacon, toast, and such, but at lunch the barbecue grill comes into service for plump burgers topped with blue cheese, bacon, mushrooms, or whatever; tasty ribs; and chicken with teriyaki, barbecue, or Italian sauces. Homemade Italian-style sandwiches like eggplant parmesan or sausage and peppers are available, as are Philly-style cheese steaks, Reubens, or barbecue beef on a hero roll. For dinner, add grilled entrees such as swordfish, chicken kebabs, strip steak, shrimp en brochette, and nightly specials to the list. The shrimp and spareribs come highly recommended. There's a modest wine list and draft beer by the mug or pitcher.

In the back of the place is a nice, shady deck where you can enjoy your meal in quiet surroundings. The Barnsider's just off the Warren County Bike Trail, or you can arrive in style by horse-drawn carriage after you tour the town.

**GARRISON KOOOM
  CAFE**
518-668-5281.
Beach Rd., past the Lake
  George Battlefield State
  Park, Lake George.
Open Year-round.
Price: Inexpensive.
Cuisine: Tavern.
Serving: L, D, late-night.
Credit Cards: None.
Reservations: No.
Handicap Access: One
  step up.

A no-frills neighborhood bar and eatery, the Garrison serves good homemade soups and burgers from noon until whenever. The pine-paneled walls display hundreds of college pennants; look hard and you'll find Hamburger University, Ronald McDonald's alma mater, somewhere between Clemson and Sweet Briar. There's a jukebox with individual selection stations at each booth, and a woodstove for chilly days.

The menu's not too elaborate, but you'll find plenty of choices at non-tourist-town prices. Daily lunch specials include hot soup and cold sandwich combos, chef salads, and the like; the Monte Cristo, which usually is available on Tuesdays, is sliced turkey with cranberry sauce, with the bread dipped in batter and grilled. Dinners include fish fry, London broil, chicken teriyaki, burgers, and sandwiches, with nothing more costly than $6.95. For regulars, the "bonus dining card" gets you a free meal for every five.

**LUIGI'S RISTORANTE**
518-668-2158.
462 Canada St. (Rte. 9),
  Lake George.
Open year-round.
Price: Moderate.
Cuisine: Italian.

To understand Luigi's, you need to understand Lake George, a resort town seemingly preserved in amber since the Eisenhower administration: the Million Dollar Beach, the wax museum with figures from Dr. Zhivago, the world's oldest miniature golf course (just 18 of the 162 miniature

Serving: B, L May—Sept.;
   D year-round.
Credit Cards: AE, DC, MC,
   V.
Reservations: No.
Handicap Access: Yes.

holes the town offers). And a downtown strip of restaurants that stress big plates full of dinner. Forget *nouvelle cuisine* — this town offers *ancien food.*

Luigi's, which can seat 185 in its red-tableclothed dining rooms, anchors the southern end of the strip. From its front door you can survey the honky-tonk spreading out before you; but at the back, the restaurant is cantilevered over a waterfall on English Brook. In midsummer, when no reservations are accepted, chances are you won't get a table with a view; the rest of the year, they're usually free, and a good spot to have a drink. ("A cocktail before dinner will add zest to your dinner appetite," the menu proclaims — this *is* an old-fashioned restaurant.)

Sadly, the food is not as fine as the scenery. The baked clams are forgettable, the pasta sometimes gummy, the tomato sauce insipid, the shrimp rubbery. Stick with the chicken dishes and the crisp salads, enjoy that cocktail ("Martini, Manhattan, Gimlet, Gin and Tonic or What You Will — Expertly Mixed and Served"), and pretend that it's 1957.

### MAMA RISO ITALIAN RESTAURANT
518-668-2550.
Rte. 9, Lake George.
Closed: Winter; open daily
   from Mother's Day to
   Halloween, and week-
   ends in spring.
Price: Moderate.
Cuisine: Italian.
Serving: D.
Credit Cards: AE, MC, V.
Handicap Access: Ramp in
   back.

If you are driving north through Lake George you may be tempted to pass up Mama Riso's, at its southern end, for the promise of what the village may hold. While it is true that Mama Riso's new al fresco eating porch offers box seats from which to view nothing more than the traffic heading into town, the atmosphere inside is homey, as if the owners, Antoinetta and Sinibaldi Rossi, just happened to invite you and a roomful of strangers over for a bottle of chianti and a plate of scungilli. This is the sort of restaurant that has regulars who come week after week, year after year, and they come as much for the feel of the place (friendly and warm) as they do for the food (good). It makes sense that the Rossis once ran a diner called the Family Restaurant, another Lake George institution.

Sinibaldi Rossi is an attentive chef, and if your meal seems to take a long time coming, it's because he really is in the kitchen preparing it. While you're waiting you'll have time to appreciate the menu itself: "Broiled Scallops — No skin or what have you, just total goodness"; "Lobster Tails (2) — This succulent tail meat says 'eat me.'" Make sure that you try the minestrone and the linguine, both of which are made fresh every day. Like the Rossis themselves, the helpings here are generous. So generous, in fact, that we can't tell you anything about dessert.

**S. J. GARCIA'S**
518-668-2190.
192 Canada St., Lake George.
Open Year-round.
Price: Moderate.
Cuisine: Mexican, American.
Serving: L, D.
Credit Cards: CB, DC, MC, V.
Handicap Access: Yes.
Special Features: Carry-out available.

Across the street from Frankenstein's Haunted Castle, tucked in amongst innumerable T-shirt shops, and kitty-corner from Movieland Wax Museum — which displays a skinny, pallid Elvis in the lobby — is a pretty decent Mexican restaurant. At Garcia's you can make believe that you're quaffing your tasty margarita in some slightly more exotic hideaway than the hustling scene on Lake George's Canada Street.

You can get the usual spicy Mexican appetizers here, and the vegetarian black bean soup is quite good. Lunch and dinner entrees include competently prepared chimichangas, tostadas, enchiladas, burritos; there are mucho mix-and-match plates like La Carumba, which features a beef chimichanga, cheese burrito, rice, beans, and greens, and the combination dinner for two, *Mira Aquí! Madre Mía!*, which seems to be everything but the *cocina* sink. Prices are reasonable, and the service is quick.

## *Lake Luzerne*

*Waiting for a doggy bag at De Fino's.*

B. Folwell

**DE FINO'S HERITAGE INN**
518-696-3733.
Northwoods Rd., Lake Luzerne, off Rte. 9N.
Closed: Mid-Oct.—mid-May; Mon.—Wed. in spring and fall. Open daily late June—Labor Day.

Back in the thirties, this log cabin was the North Woods Dude Ranch, one of the first cowboy-style resorts in the Northeast. The location is pretty, on the shore of tiny Lake Forest, with huge pines shading gardens of cascading spirea and pink impatiens.

People don't come to De Fino's for the view from the bar, though — they come back year after

Price: Moderate.
Cuisine: Italian.
Serving: D.
Credit Cards: MC, V.
Handicap Access: Yes.
Reservations: Suggested
   for July and August
   weekends.

year because the food's terrific, and because every-one here makes you feel like you're one of the family. One evening, the waitress came around with a bowl of macaroni salad and said, "Dot made a little extra for everybody tonight. Enjoy!"

Everything is made from scratch at De Fino's, from the feathery-crusted hot bread to the creamy garlic salad dressing to the carrot cake. Phil, the owner, says that one of the best offerings on the menu is the linguine with white clam sauce, and we'd agree: there's lots of garlic, lots of clams, lots of al dente pasta, in a portion that could make two adults feel pleasantly stuffed. Another specialty is baked ziti Siciliano, a meat-less dish with layers of fried eggplant, ricotta cheese, ziti, homemade red sauce, and mozzarella. Other entree choices are various veal dishes, chicken cacciatore, pork chops Pizziola, pot roast, and stuffed cabbage. Our only com-plaint on a recent visit was that there seemed to be an endless Tom Jones tape on the stereo, but by the time coffee came around, Nat King Cole smoothly took his place.

**PAPA'S**
518-696-3667.
2117 Main St., Lake
   Luzerne, NY.
Closed: Oct.—late May.
Price: Inexpensive.
Cuisine: Ice cream parlor.
Serving: B, L. (until 8 p.m.;
   ice cream until 10 p.m.).
Credit Cards: None.
Handicap Access: No.

Papa's Old-Fashioned Ice Cream Parlor is adver-tised as "the area's most charming ice cream parlor." It more than lives up to that promise, with turn-of-the-century decor that would look just right on the set of *The Music Man*. Shelves of glass milk bottles ring the walls; old photos and post-cards of the Lake Luzerne/Stony Creek area cover every other available surface. A long counter flanks the soda fountain; there are also comfortable wooden booths, and outdoor seating on the back porch overlooks the Hudson River.

The food is simple, fresh, and good. Pure maple syrup is available at break-fast (50 cents extra), and the menu includes such treasures as corn on the cob — "when the best is available" — peanut butter and bacon sandwiches, and chocolate egg creams.

But it is as an ice cream parlor that Papa's really shines. Delicious ice-cream sodas, shakes, malts, sundaes, and creamy frozen yogurt make this the perfect stop during a long day's mosey along the Dude Ranch Trail. Remember how sweet and cold and special ice cream in the summer used to be? At Papa's, it still is.

**RUSTIC INN**
518-696-2318.
Rte. 9N, Lake Luzerne.

The cowboy flavor of this part of the Adiron-dacks — "big hat country" — is epitomized by the Rustic Inn. The bar is faced with logs, the back

Open year-round.
Price: Moderate.
Cuisine: American.
Serving: L, D (bar menu
   after 10 p.m.).
Credit Cards: CB, DC, MC,
   V.
Handicap Access: Yes.

windows offer a lake view, and there's live country-western music for dancing on Saturday nights. There are no surprises on the menu, just competent tavern food at reasonable prices. The pizza is maybe a bit disappointing, but the "rustic burger" is great.

## Warrensburg

**ANTHONY'S
RISTORANTE
ITALIANO**
518-623-2162.
Rte. 9, north of
   Warrensburg, next to
   the North Country
   Lodge.
Open: Wed.—Mon. in
   summer; Thurs.—Sun.
   in winter.
Price: Moderate to
   Expensive.
Cuisine: Italian.
Serving: D.
Credit Cards: MC, V.
Handicap Access: Yes.

The pasta palaces of Lake George are fine for an evening of boisterous dining. But for the same price, and only six or seven miles farther up Rte. 9, you can eat Italian food that matches the best of Manhattan's Little Italy in one of the Adirondacks' most memorable restaurants.

From the outside Anthony's Ristorante Italiano looks like an utterly typical spaghetti parlor. The minute you cross the threshold, though, you know you're someplace special. The walls are lined with the proof of chef Anthony Sapienza's other talent — wonderful, enormous celebrity portraits, most of them depicting his pantheon of movie heroes.

The handsome, boyish Anthony knows some of them personally, since he's had small parts in Martin Scorsese and Spike Lee features, and he's hoping for more. In the meantime, he keeps busy in the kitchen. His special antipasto and the crusty bread make a fine beginning, but his real talent is for the sauces he heaps on his pasta: the pasta con sarde, with its deep combination of sardines and fennel, is without peer.

Asked if his family had moved north from Brooklyn's Canarsie neighborhood along with him, Anthony said, "No — just my mother and father and sister." The Sapienzas are in evidence throughout the dining room, full of good suggestions about the solid wine list and the many special dinners the restaurant presents. (Private parties, too — when Oscar Hijuelos won the Pulitzer Prize for his novel *The Mambo Kings Play Songs of Love*, Anthony hosted the festivities.) One piece of advice: save room for dessert, especially the perfect cannolis made fresh on the premises. And a cup of espresso, then back out into the woods.

**BILL'S RESTAURANT**
518-623-2669.
190 Main St.,
   Warrensburg.

At Bill's, there's a table in the middle more or less reserved for regulars — as one leaves, another takes his place in an endless round of coffee-drinking and chat. But they're nice to strangers,

Open daily.
Price: Inexpensive.
Cuisine: American.
Serving: B, L, D.
Credit Cards: None.
Reservations: No.
Handicap Access: Ramp in
rear.

too. Sit at the table in the window, looking across Warrensburg's Main Street at the cliffs on Hackensack Mountain, and order something filling from the menu. Not hard to do — almost everything is filling, especially the hot turkey sandwich carved with an actual knife off an actual bird and enthroned on the most absorbent white bread. The turkey vegetable soup is mined with big chunks of turkey, too.

Bill's claim to fame is that it serves breakfast all day long — "one of the very few places in town that do," says the waitress. They charge four bits more for your eggs or pancakes after 11 a.m., but it's still a bargain — a dinner of three slices of French toast and two eggs for $3.

**DRAGON LEE**
518-623-3796.
35 Main St., Warrensburg
(Next to Stewart's Shop.)
Open year-round.
Price: Inexpensive.
Cuisine: Chinese:
Cantonese, Hunan,
Szechuan.
Serving: L, D.
Credit Cards: MC, V.
Handicap Access: Yes.

The Adirondacks is among the most sparsely settled places in the East — few people, few roads, few Hunan shrimp. Which is why Dragon Lee, a quite decent Chinese take-out restaurant, received such a warm welcome from locals when it opened in 1991. Its enormous menu lists 154 dishes; refugees from the crowded metropolises "down below" can enjoy their first taste in years of General Tso's Chicken, or hot and sour soup (deliciously packed), while visitors need no longer avoid the area for fear of a sudden craving for moo shu pork. An added plus is that the restaurant is open until 11 p.m. on Fridays and Saturdays.

In fact, the main difference between this and your average everyday urban Chinese take-out (besides the lower prices) is the list of places you can take out to. Within a few minutes' drive of Dragon Lee, you can be sitting on the banks of the Schroon or the Hudson (the ducks in Warrensburg's small riverside park will probably be all too happy for a bite of moo goo gai pan); before the lo mein cools you could be dangling your feet in Lake George.

**THE GRIST MILL**
518-623-3949.
River St. (Rte. 418, just
beyond the iron bridge),
Warrensburg.
Closed: Winter.
Price: Expensive.
Cuisine: American regional.
Serving: D.
Credit Cards: AE, DC, MC,
V.

For a restaurant in the middle of town — not an especially beautiful town — to have a view as scenic as this suggests how deliberately Shane Newell, the owner and chef of the Grist Mill, is trying to set it apart. Perched over the Schroon River rapids, which are illuminated after dark, the place feels like the inside of a well-appointed boathouse. In fact, it was a working mill until not that long ago, and the interior is artfully decorated with the cogs and barrels and tools of the miller's trade.

Reservations:
Recommended.
Handicap Access: No.
Special Features: Historic
building; fireplace in
bar.

"Everything is fresh," declares a promotional brochure. "Everything on your plate is edible," declares the menu. Both are true. The oysters in the corn and oyster stew were tender, succulent, and not long out of the shell. The lightly grilled swordfish was delicate; there was no attempt to cook it as if it were a cut of beef that just happened to be hauled from the sea. The chocolate in the chocolate torte was just about carnal.

But the freshness and edibility come at an unwarranted price: the Grist Mill is one of the most expensive restaurants in the southern Adirondacks. At $19.50, the swordfish is one of the cheaper entrees. Expect to pay more than that for lamb or steak. And that's just the beginning. Appetizers, soups, and desserts are not only not included in the price of the entree, but are pricey themselves. If you order one of the restaurant's featured American wines, you can easily drop $100 for a dinner for two, and while the dinner itself will not disappoint you, the bill might make you, too, fresh.

*The Grist Mill, Warrensburg, was once a working mill.*

Nancie Battaglia

### MERRILL MAGEE HOUSE

518-623-2449.
2 Hudson St. (near the band-
shell), Warrensburg.
Closed: Mar.
Price: Expensive.
Cuisine: Continental.
Serving: D, 7 nights; L,
May—Oct.
Credit Cards: AE, D, MC, V.
Reservations: Suggested.
Handicap Access: Yes.
Special Features: Historic
building; pub.

The Lions meet every Wednesday at the Merrill Magee House, and that would be reason alone to join the club if you lived in Warrensburg. Tucked behind a white picket fence, across the street from the Meat Store of the North and the ancient soda fountain at LD's Drug Store, the Merrill Magee House is a mainly Victorian gem. Its cozy, wood-planked bar has the feel of a Cotswold pub, and indeed a wide array of English ales, lagers, and stouts are available, as is Pimm's No. 1 Cup in summer.

The bar is part of the original, early-19th-century homestead that the first Magee, a timber merchant by the name of Stephen Griffin II, bought in 1839. Over time the house was added to; one section of the dining room was imported from an even older house several miles away. The resulting architectural patchwork is not only quaint (without being cloying), it's listed in the National Register of Historic Places.

Dinner at the Merrill Magee House, once you tune out "Born Free" and "The Sound of Music" being piped into the candlelit, otherwise intimate dining room, is uncommonly good. Delicious homemade breads, a house appetizer, and green salad are all included with the meal, and each is something to look forward to. An entree of crisp roast duck can be a bit too crisp, but the green peppercorn and plum sauce accompanying it cancels all debts. The fish is cooked with absolute care. There is even a vegetarian entree of stir-fried vegetables with potatoes or rice. The wine list is long and reasonably priced. Desserts are the standard sweets.

**RODNEY'S**
518-623-3246.
214 Main St. (across the road from Oscar's Smokehouse), Warrensburg.
Open year-round.
Price: Inexpensive.
Cuisine: Italian, American diner food.
Serving: B, L, D (open at 5 a.m.).
Credit Cards: None.
Reservations: No.
Handicap Access: Yes.

You begin to get the idea at Rodney's when you notice that the tall high-school boys eating dinner are asking for doggie bags. Rodney's is a relative newcomer to the Warren County diner scene, but it is already setting the new standard for quantity, and in some cases quality, as well.

Seven or eight dollars at dinner will buy you a heaping platter of eggplant parmigiana or fried fish; the steaks and chops run a buck or two more, but all come with large and fresh green salads. Begin with the chilled fruit cup, because the rest of the menu is not exactly loaded with vitamins, and avoid the bland fried clams and scallops. It's the Italian food they really do best, and it draws a crowd at lunch. At dinner, the place is a little less jammed; if you're by yourself, buy a Glens Falls paper from the rack by the cash register, take a few deep breaths, and then get to work on the Adirondack mountain of spaghetti.

*Schroon Lake*

**PITKIN'S RESTAURANT**
518-532-7918.
Main St., Schroon Lake.
Open year-round.
Price: Inexpensive.
Cuisine: American.
Serving: B, L, D.
Credit Cards: None.

Since the Depression, this modest storefront eatery has served generations of summer and winter folk, but the Texas-style barbecue — beef, pork ribs, and chicken — is a new twist. The beef brisket is delicious, lightly smoked and tucked under a thin, not-too-sweet, tangy sauce; at $6.95 for a plateful, with chunky homemade potato salad

Reservations: No.
Handicap Access: Street-
  level entry.
Special Features: Texas-
  style barbecue; chil-
  dren's menu.

and coleslaw, it could be one of the best cheap meals found anywhere inside the Blue Line. Homemade soups are good, too, and the hand-hewn-looking pies are excellent.

Thursday is ribs night, and be advised that this joint can be jumping in July and August, with lines of hopeful diners stretching down Main Street. The good news is that Pitkin's is open year-round, and the barbecue's always going.

**SCHROON LAKE INN**
518-532-7042.
Rte. 9, Schroon Lake,
  about 2 miles north of
  town.
Closed: Mar.; Mon.—
  Thurs. mid-Sept.—June;
  open daily July—Aug.
Price: Expensive.
Cuisine: Continental.
Serving: L, D, SB.
Credit Cards: MC, V.
Reservations: Suggested.
Handicap Access: Yes.
Special Features: Dining
  on the porch.

Louise Cronin and Pat Savarie have built a very classy place from the ground up; the Schroon Lake Inn looks and feels like an 1890s estate, but it's brand-new throughout. On a summer evening, you can enjoy dinner on the capacious veranda set with wrought-iron tables, and gaze out at views of distant hills and the Schroon River valley, or in the winter, you can curl up on the camel-back sofa in front of the fireplace in the bar, brandy snifter in hand.

An eye to details makes all the difference here. The dining room is lovely, with deep-green wall-paper and carpeting and cabbage-rose-print table-cloths on the tables. The waitresses' dresses match the table linens, and botanical prints line the walls. Candle lanterns and a wreath of dried flowers are centerpieces on each table.

The food displays that same attention to detail, changing with the seasons. Appetizers include shrimp Darington, jumbo shrimp wrapped in bacon with a honey-mustard sauce; stuffed mushrooms; Swiss Alps pie, which is chicken

*The veranda of the Schroon Lake Inn offers a view of the river valley and distant hills.*

Nancie Battaglia

breast, wild mushrooms, and Gruyère cheese in puff paste; and calamari salad, a tangled twirl of purple squid (tentacles and all) in a garlic vinaigrette. Entrees range from a grilled chicken breast with Mornay sauce to beef tournedos napped in an Armagnac-flavored demi-glace to duckling à l'orange to broiled or poached salmon with lemon parsley butter; if all this sounds too rich, you can ask for the sauces to be held. There are also steaks, pork chops, and lamb. The pace is relaxed, the service attentive, so that just when you're thinking about what a nice meal you've had, the desserts (tarts, layer cakes, and pies) come around on a mahogany cart.

Schroon Lake Inn serves a leisurely lunch, and an elegant, yet reasonably priced Sunday brunch buffet.

## CHAMPLAIN VALLEY

### Elizabethtown

**CONNELL'S COUNTRY KITCHEN**
518-873-9920.
Court St., Elizabethtown.
Open year-round.
Price: Inexpensive to moderate.
Cuisine: American.
Serving: B, L, D.
Credit Cards: None.
Reservations: No.
Handicap Access: Yes.

The Connells, Lucy and Dan, run this family-style restaurant, and one of their attractive children might be waiting tables during college vacations. It's the kind of friendly, small-town place where, as a citified visitor noted with awe, "people talk to each other from table to table."

Connell's food is plain and usually satisfying, especially the breakfasts. Selections include nicely prepared eggs with bacon, ham, or sausage, home fries, toast, and coffee; pancakes; French toast; western, eastern, ham, and cheese omelets, all in the $3 to $4 range. The lunch menu offers hot and cold sandwiches and a daily special, such as tuna melt with soup or french fries.

For dinner, there's fried chicken or shrimp, and roast turkey, more specials, including baked scrod and chicken cordon bleu. Every Wednesday, spaghetti with meatballs or meat sauce, tossed salad, garlic toast, and coffee is priced at $5.99. Along with ice cream and pies, Connell's has two outstanding desserts, a cinnamony apple crisp served warm with whipped cream, and a creation called Brownie Nut Supreme, drenched with hot fudge sauce and whipped cream.

The restaurant has a take-out window, and picnic tables are set up outdoors for warm-weather snacking.

**DEER'S HEAD INN**
518-873-9903.
Court St., across from the Essex County Courthouse, Elizabethtown.
Closed: Some weekdays in winter.

The Deer's Head Inn, a rambling white frame building that dates back to 1808, is reputed to be the oldest inn in the Adirondacks. In warm weather, you can have pre-dinner drinks on the wide front porch and watch the cars and pickups that drift by. Inside the Deer's Head there's a cozy,

*The Deer's Head is reputed to be the oldest inn in the Adirondacks.*

B. Folwell

Price: Moderate to
  Expensive.
Cuisine: Continental.
Serving: L, D.
Credit Cards: AE, MC, V.
Handicap Access: Yes.

book-lined cocktail lounge and three adjoining dining rooms. Two of the rooms are attractively decorated in blue and white, with floral wallpaper, blue tablecloths, and willow-ware china, reflecting, perhaps, the English tearoom memories of the inn's British owners. A fireplace warms the smaller front room on winter days; the third dining room, in the back, is casual, with wood-paneled walls and more shelves of books.

Lunches at the Deer's Head are relatively modest: soup, salad, quiche, and grilled sandwiches, such as turkey with melted cheese and cranberry sauce. The evening menu is more ambitious, sometimes overly so. Appetizers might include escargots sautéed with garlic, herbs, and Pernod, or grilled shrimp brochette with Cajun seasoning. Entrees feature rack of lamb baked with rosemary, veal Marsala, various chicken dishes, and pasta with shrimp, scallops, and crabmeat in marinara sauce. Save room for desserts like Heathbar crunch pie and cranberry apple granny.

**MOUNTAIN SHADOWS**
518-873-6712.
Rte. 9N between Elizabeth-
  town and Westport.
Closed: Mon.
Price: Moderate.
Cuisine: American,
  Continental.
Serving: L, D.
Credit Cards: None.
Reservations: No.
Handicap Access: Yes,
  with assistance (one
  step).

This rustic restaurant on the shore of a small tree-fringed pond has been an E'town landmark for years, but when Debbie and Jim Kneiper took over in 1992 they brightened up the decor and lightened the cuisine. Their chef, Lewis Axtell, prepares seafood, chicken, and meat dishes that are attractively presented with delicate but well-seasoned sauces. The regular dinner menu includes fresh fish, charbroiled, fried, or blackened; pork schnitzel; several chicken and beef dishes; and pizza with a variety of toppings. At the salad bar, diners can choose from fresh-baked bread and rolls, green salad, potato salad with dill, pickled beets, and assorted crunchy items. Lunch offerings lean toward sandwiches and homemade soups.

Mountain Shadows also features dinner specials. One weekend evening, after starting our meal with a delicious tomato bisque, we ordered the special, a generous mound of fried calamari, which was so light and tasty we didn't give a thought to our usual low-fat diets. "It looked like too much calamari," remarked our companion, "but I ate it anyway."

The cozy dining room invites lingering over dessert and coffee and, in summer, diners can relax in a screened patio that overlooks the pond. The silence is broken only by the murmuring of contented eaters, the quack of ducks on the pond, and occasional bursts of cheery laughter from the adjoining bar, which attracts a large and lively crowd.

### *Essex*

**LE BISTRO DU LAC**
518-963-8111.
Essex Shipyard, off Rte. 22,
  Essex (3 blocks south of
  the Essex Ferry).
Closed: Mid-Oct.—
  Memorial Day weekend.
Price: Expensive.
Cuisine: Continental,
  French.
Serving: L, D.
Credit Cards: AE, MC, V.
Reservations:
  Recommended in July
  and August.
Handicap Access: Yes.

A casual restaurant that serves elegant food, Le Bistro du Lac is housed in a rambling white clapboard building overlooking the Essex Shipyard on Lake Champlain. Bright marigolds and geraniums fill the window boxes, and boat owners wearing equally brilliant attire pass to and fro, some stopping in for a meal. A few tables are set up near the bar and in two small, pine-paneled rooms on the main floor. Up a short flight of stairs is another, larger dining room. All have windows with lake views.

Le Bistro's lunches include soups, salads, hamburgers, and such entrees as paté with salad and mussels marinière. At dinner, chef Bradford Barker becomes more daring. One pleasant June evening, we happily devoured appetizers of lobster on puff pastry with leeks and shiitake mushrooms, and poached salmon surrounded by endive, arugula, and radicchio, topped with a roasted-red-pepper sauce. One entree, lovely golden-brown roasted chicken breast in a delicate tarragon sauce, was accompanied by new potatoes, green beans, broccoli, mushrooms, and leeks; linguine with seafood, tossed in a delicate, creamy sauce, got high marks except for a mild complaint about dryish chunks of lobster. The menu also offers such entrees as filet of beef with béarnaise or pepper sauce, rack of lamb with rosemary herb sauce, and veal sautéed with shiitake mushrooms. The crème caramel we shared for dessert was served with raspberries and whipped cream — absolutely delicious. Foolishly, we passed up the chocolate-covered strawberries, chocolate mousse, and apple tart that were also on the dessert list.

Le Bistro's prices are somewhat higher than many other restaurants in the region, but after enjoying the satisfying food, pleasant surroundings, efficient service, and charming personality of the owner, Bernard Perillat, you hardly flinch when you see the check.

**THE OLD DOCK RESTAURANT**
518-962-4232.
Lake Shore Rd., Essex, adjacent to the Essex ferry landing.
Closed: Early Oct.—mid-May.
Price: Lunch: Moderate; Dinner: Moderate to Expensive.
Cuisine: American.
Serving: L, D.
Credit Cards: MC, V.
Handicap Access: Indoor dining room only.

The Old Dock's menu is a bit pricey and the food is uneven, but the lovely lakeside setting may make up for any minor dissatisfactions. If you dine on the outdoor deck you can watch the comings and goings of various craft, from small speedboats to the car-laden Essex ferry, while seagulls circle overhead. The breezes rippling the waters of Lake Champlain and the sunlight filtering through the leaves of tall old trees are pleasantly lulling. From the inside of the restaurant, the windows of the large dining room provide a more sheltered view of the surroundings.

Lunch at the Old Dock includes salads, barbecue ribs, crab cakes, and burgers, along with a kids' menu at $4.95. Recently, we enjoyed a charcoal-broiled burger, but the impressive-looking taco salad turned out to be largely iceberg lettuce and an inedible flour tortilla. At 3 in the afternoon, an outdoor grill is lit and light entrees — burgers and ribs again — are served on the deck through the evening. The more elaborate dinner menu offers steak, fish, and chicken dinners, and a popular Shore Platter, with scrod, scallops, and shrimp, beer-battered and deep-fried.

Old Dock's wine list ranges from California zinfandel and chardonnay to a Taittinger Brut. For dessert, there's cheesecake, ice cream, and peaches-and-cream pie.

*The Old Dock Restaurant and Marina enjoys a view of Lake Champlain.*

Nancie Battaglia

## Keeseville

**BLAISE'S BARNSTEAD**
518-834-7578.
Rte. 9, Keeseville.
Open year-round.
Price: Moderate to
   Expensive.
Cuisine: American, Italian,
   Seafood.
Serving: B, L, D.
Credit Cards: AE, CB, DC,
   MC, V.
Reservations:
   Recommended.
Handicap Access: No.
Special Features:
   Children's menu; deliv-
   ery available.

Aptly named, Blaise's resembles a barn both inside and out, but an elegant one at that. Pleasant country antiques and prints adorn the weathered walls of the large dining room.

The menu ranges from homemade pizza to broiled Alaskan king crab legs. Appetizers are eclectic: fried cauliflower, egg rolls, potato skins, hot chicken wings. Dinner selections range from the Fisherman's Platter to chicken Marsala to calves' liver. Broiled scallops and strip steak, a regular offering, includes a succulent piece of aged steak and tender, buttery bay scallops. The children's menu offers more options than most places; there are a half-dozen entree choices, such as roast turkey, three fried shrimp, or spaghetti with one meatball, all accompanied by a cup of soup, potatoes, and a simple, kid-size dessert.

The Barnstead also includes Italian entrees, among them a tender veal Parmesan topped with a spicy tomato and cheese sauce and generous side helping of spaghetti. The thick-crusted pizza is among the best in the North Country and is made exactly to your specifications: at a child's request we asked for, and got, an interesting pizza without cheese but topped instead with strips of bacon.

**NORTH COUNTRY CLUB**
518-834-7255.
26 N. Ausable St. (near the
   Keeseville Fire Dept.),
   Keeseville.
Open year-round.
Price: Moderate.
Cuisine: American, Italian.
Serving: L, D.
Credit Cards: MC, V.
Handicap Access: Yes.
Special Features: Pizza and
   sandwiches available
   after 11 p.m.

Founded in 1958, the North Country Club prides itself on being a family restaurant, and claims its pizza is the best in all the North Country. That claim is hotly contested (see Blaise's, above), but the club's pie is fresh and tasty for sure.

Don't be fooled into thinking "family" refers to just a noisy kids' place, though. On the contrary, the moderate-size dining area, with center tables and surrounding booths, is accented by paintings, plenty of warm-toned wood, and soft lighting — not your average formica-and-fluorescent fast-food decor. The menu is elaborate by northeastern New York norms, offering the usual prime rib/filet mignon fare but also an extensive and authentic-tasting Italian cuisine featuring dishes like baked lasagna, manicotti, and linguine with red or white clam sauce. Fresh green salads and homemade soups round out the meal.

## *Port Henry*

**THE AMBER LANTERN**
518-546-3624.
141 Broad St., Port Henry.
Open year-round.
Price: Inexpensive to
 Moderate.
Cuisine: American.
Serving: B, L, D.
Credit Cards: MC. V.
Handicap Access: Yes.

This pleasant restaurant, with its light, airy dining room, is a recent and welcome addition to the Port Henry area. There's nothing unfamiliar on the breakfast and lunch menus, but standard dishes are given a special touch by the chef and co-owner, Stella Mildon, who runs the business with her daughter and son-in-law, Pam and Rick Norton. The hot roast beef sandwich, for example, consists of a mound of tender, thinly sliced beef on toasted bread with a dark, rich gravy. It's accompanied by "jo-jos" — baked potatoes sliced thickly, seasoned, and lightly fried — and a dish of crunchy, fresh coleslaw.

Dinner entrees, which come with salad, homemade bread, potato, and a vegetable, include a 16-ounce New York sirloin, baked stuffed haddock, ham steak, and liver and onions. There are some Italian dishes on the menu, like stuffed shells and manicotti, even a few "low-cal" plates, and every night features a special entree, like swordfish on Friday, prime rib on Saturday, and Mexican treats midweek.

Desserts at the Amber Lantern are homemade and delicious. The raisin-studded rice pudding is creamy and mellow, and the bread pudding and strawberry shortcake are equally tempting.

## *Ticonderoga*

**THE CARILLON**
518-585-7657.
61 Hague Road,
 Ticonderoga, 1/2 mile
 south of the Liberty
 Monument circle.
Open year-round.
Price: Expensive.
Cuisine: French, Seafood.
Serving: L, D.
Credit Cards: AE, MC, V.
Handicap Access: No.

*Carillon* was the original French name of Fort Ticonderoga, located about three miles away. The restaurant is a modest-looking red wooden building on a hill, just off the state highway. After your meal you can follow the signs to the fort, which is open May through October. Think of Ticonderoga restaurants this way: Benedict Arnold would have eaten at the Carillon, while Ethan Allen would be back with the Green Mountain Boys at the Wagon Wheel.

Owners Russ and Lori Slater pride themselves on offering fresh seafood, and the catch of the day is usually a good bet. The scallops are great, with just the right seasoning and buttery sauce. Soups and dessert at the Carillon are excellent. If you come for dinner, be prepared to spend some time here, though; if the restaurant is busy, the service can be a bit slow.

## EDDIE'S
518-585-7030.
Hague Road (Rte. 9N), 5
    miles south of Ticonder-
    oga village on Rte. 9N.
Open year-round.
Price: Moderate.
Cuisine: American, Italian.
Serving: L, D.
Credit Cards: AE, MC, V.
Handicap Access: Yes.

Eddie's is a nice little place halfway between Ticonderoga and Hague. The Rogers Rock State Campground, on Lake George, is only a mile farther south. This is where Major Robert Rogers, without his famed rangers, escaped the French and Indians in 1758 by tricking them into thinking he'd leaped onto the frozen lake from an impossibly great height. He survived.

Try the pasta at Eddie's: spaghetti or linguine with sausage is excellent here. Homemade soups and salads are also quite good. For dessert, the peach cobbler with ice cream is worth saving room for. The restaurant has plenty of seating, yet still offers a warm, cozy atmosphere; the service is excellent.

## THE OLDE
## SCHOOLHOUSE
518-585-4044.
Rte. 9N, Streetroad, 3
    miles north of
    Ticonderoga village on
    Rte. 9N.
Open year-round.
Price: Moderate.
Cuisine: American.
Serving: L, D.
Credit Cards: AE, MC, V.
Handicap Access: No.

The Olde Schoolhouse, not surprisingly, used to be a school in bygone days. It's located across from the Streetroad Cemetery, where the inventor of the modern lead pencil, Guy Baldwin, is buried. An Off Track Betting parlor is stuck in one side of the building, but it doesn't seem to do much business, at least not enough to have any impact on dining. The restaurant is downstairs, where the schoolhouse motif is largely intact — daily specials are scrawled on the original classroom chalkboard, and there are antiquated maps on the walls. Lunches, the usual sandwich, soup, and burger fare, are inexpensive; dinners, while not particularly imaginative, are good values. A nice touch is the sizable salad bar, with plenty of extras and embellishments. The steaks are excellent: the dinner sirloin is thick, juicy, and prepared with care. For dessert, try the cheesecake.

## ROBERT'S RESTAURANT
518-585-4024.
155 Montcalm St.,
    Ticonderoga, next to the
    Black Watch Library.
Open year-round.
Price: Inexpensive.
Cuisine: American,
    Seafood.
Serving: L, D.
Credit Cards: None.
Handicap Access: Yes.

Some days it seems as if everybody in town goes to Robert's Restaurant. The owner is a retired local politician who just loves the food business. The service is great; meals — in abundant portions — are well prepared. Go here if you're hungry.

For lunch, try a club sandwich or a burger; for dinner, the seafood is very good. A bowl of cream of mushroom soup here is excellent as a prelude to a sauerkraut-stuffed Reuben for lunch. Have some homemade cherry pie for dessert and stroll down to the LaChute Falls and Bicentennial Park, a couple of blocks away, to work it off.

*Everybody who's anybody goes to Robert's Restaurant, Ticonderoga.*

Lohr McKinstry

**THE WAGON WHEEL**
518-585-9700.
Wicker St. (Rte. 9N),
 Ticonderoga.
Open year-round.
Price: Inexpensive.
Cuisine: American.
Serving: B, L, D.
Credit Cards: MC, V.
Handicap Access: Yes.

A *huge* wagon wheel in front sets the theme for Patricia Thatcher's restaurant: no matter which meal you eat here, expect large portions. Breakfasts at "The Wheel" are unforgettable: the Grizzly Bear Special features two eggs, home fries, sausage, toast, a short stack of pancakes, and plenty of coffee. Better forget lunch after that.

In case you've skipped breakfast, for lunch the cheeseburger club sandwich is excellent, washed down with some real homemade iced tea and followed by chocolate pudding. The Wagon Wheel is a stand-out with its simple, good food and excellent service. Even when the place is packed, food is ready quickly. Try this one out.

## *Valcour*

**ROYAL SAVAGE INN**
518-561-5140.
Rte. 9, Valcour, 3 miles
 south of Plattsburgh.
Open year-round.
Price: Expensive.
Cuisine: Continental,
 American.
Serving: L, D.
Credit Cards: D, MC, V.
Reservations:
 Recommended.
Handicap Access: Yes.
Special Features: Gift
 shop, cocktail lounge.

Named for Benedict Arnold's flagship, sunk in 1776 off Valcour Island, the Royal Savage Inn sits directly across from that historic island. The restaurant is situated at the northern end of the Adirondack Park, on a knoll between the Salmon River, which diners can see from the lower-level dining room, and Lake Champlain, at its front door. This inn, a former hay barn which began a second career as a tearoom in 1919, should be savored slowly, both for its interesting and historic scenery and its excellent cuisine. Antiques, including bull's-eye panes of Redford glass (made in nearby Redford, NY), assorted colonial-era tools, a cutter, a buggy, old postcards, and prints, are scattered throughout the restaurant.

The wine list is extensive, as is the choice of appetizers: baked brie, oysters Rockefeller, fried mushroom caps with mustard sauce, sautéed chicken livers, coquilles St. Jacques Mornay, to name a few. Entrees include selections you're not likely to find elsewhere in the region, like salmon croquettes with Newburgh sauce and Flaming Adirondack Sword, which honors the military motif with chicken breast, beef, ham, mushrooms, and tomatoes served on a saber. You'll also find excellent aged steaks, roast turkey, seafood combinations, chicken, and pasta dishes. For lighter appetites, there are dinner salads, sandwiches, and vegetarian platters.

Dennis Aprill

*Rustic decorative touches and antiques fill the Royal Savage Inn, Valcour.*

## *Westport*

**THE WESTPORT HOTEL**
518-962-4501.
Pleasant St. (Rte. 9N),
  Westport.
Closed: Tues. and Wed.
  Oct.—May.
Price: Moderate to
  Expensive.
Cuisine: American,
  French.
Credit Cards: MC, V.

Built in 1876, the gray-and-white clapboard Westport Hotel is conveniently located just east of the railroad station (only two trains a day) and the Depot Theater, which houses a regional repertory company. The hotel's owners, Rita and Ralph Warren, have fashioned the sprawling main floor into a series of cozy, inviting dining rooms and a comfortable cocktail lounge. In warm weather, meals are served on the patio and on the broad

Reservations: Suggested in summer and on holiday weekends.
Handicap Access: Yes.

porch that sweeps around two sides of the building.

Warm herb bread greets you at your table. The homemade soups are good; cream of spinach flavored with bacon is a delicious offering on a winter night. For entrees, there are several pasta dishes, such as seafood-and-ricotta-stuffed shells topped with a parsley-cream cheese sauce. The baked chicken breast stuffed with apple and sage dressing is flavorful and comforting; the bourbon shrimp is quite pleasurable, while the steak Dianne is tangy and tender.

The desserts, all prepared in-house, are up to the high standards of the rest of the meal. Selections change frequently, but we can heartily recommend the bread pudding with rum raisin sauce, and the brownie roofed with ice cream and fudge sauce.

*Enjoying a hearty dinner at the Westport Hotel.*

Joan Potter

## WESTPORT PIZZA AND PASTA

518-962-4878.
Pleasant St., at the intersection of Rtes. 9N and 22, Westport.
Open year-round.
Price: Inexpensive to Moderate.
Cuisine: Italian.
Serving: B, L, D in summer; D only in winter.
Credit Cards: None.
Handicap Access: Yes.

In an old red firehouse now outfitted with booths, oak tables, and chairs, and a forties jukebox, Kevin and Janice Lawson prepare an array of Italian specialties. The sourdough pizzas are available with the usual toppings, plus eggplant, pineapple, ham, anchovies, garlic, and artichoke hearts. The above items can also be stuffed into a calzone, along with ricotta and mozzarella cheese.

One evening, the linguine with clam sauce special came with one of the best salads we've ever eaten — oak-leaf lettuce straight from the garden, mushrooms, artichoke hearts, black olives, and crunchy croutons with a snappy pepper-Parmesan dressing. The eggplant Parmigiana was also a success — light and rich at the same time — and it came with a side order of spaghetti and a basket of garlic nuggets, little garlic-and-herb bread twists toasted to a golden brown.

In summer, diners can sit outdoors at tables set up in a brick courtyard, where they can observe Westport's attractive old buildings and leisurely traffic, and catch a glimpse of Lake Champlain sparkling in the background.

*A rustic bench marks the spot for great pizza in Westport.*

B. Folwell

## Willsboro

**INDIAN BAY MARINA AND RESTAURANT**
518-963-7858.
East Bay Rd., Willsboro Point, north of Willsboro on Rte. 27, west on Frisbie Rd., north on East Bay Rd.
Closed: Mid-Oct.—early May.
Price: Moderate.
Cuisine: American.
Serving: L, D.
Credit Cards: MC, V.
Handicap Access: Yes.

The Indian Bay Marina and Restaurant is housed in a red wooden building with a weathered cedar deck on the shore of Lake Champlain's Willsboro Bay. In the dining room, a wall of windows overlooks the water. From tables on the deck, customers can relax over drinks and food while observing the comings and goings of a variety of boats and their owners who, on hot summer days, are amazingly tanned and sparsely clad.

Chef Joe Wilkins cooks up delectable burgers — the kind whose juices drip down your chin — with toppings like mushrooms, onions, bacon, and cheese. Sandwiches, such as turkey and roast beef clubs, are served in neat baskets, as are Buffalo chicken wings accompanied by carrot and celery sticks and blue-cheese dressing. In keeping with the coastal ambience, dinners focus on seafood: broiled or fried scallops, deviled crabcakes, seafood au gratin, and linguine with steamed mussels. On a sunny day, the pleasant drive out to the marina, the nautical atmosphere, and the hearty food all add up to a very satisfying experience.

## HIGH PEAKS AND NORTHERN ADIRONDACKS

### *Au Sable Forks*

**D & H FREIGHTHOUSE EATERY**
518-647-8800.
Rte. 9N, Au Sable Forks.
Closed: Dec.—Apr.
Price: Inexpensive.
Cuisine: Pizza, sand-
  wiches, pastries.
Serving: B, L, D.
Credit Cards: None.
Handicap Access: Yes.

From the street, the old D & H freight house doesn't appear particularly promising, but don't let first impressions misguide you. Once you walk in, you'll find this down-home diner is friendly and appealing. Denise Potter bought the warehouse five years ago; underneath the crumbling beaverboard she discovered the original beaded-pine paneling. Searching around North Country barns and rummage sales, she's found assorted old railroad clocks, prints of D & H trackside scenery, and antique booths. The ticket window is where you pay your check, and a large slab of marble is the diner's counter. Even the ladies' room door is an antique.

The food here is good diner chow, plus excellent, inexpensive pizza. The meatball sub is enough to feed a crew of gandy dancers; there are five or so dinner choices, such as spaghetti (with or without meat), chicken Parmesan, and a Fisherman's Platter. Pies, cakes, and muffins are all made fresh every day.

On Saturday nights in the back of the freight house, there are antique auctions organized by Jon Kopp, a local dealer. The selection is usually quite eclectic; in September, at the annual sportman's auction, the focus is on fishing equipment, hunting gear, and so forth.

### *Dannemora*

**BILLY'S INN THE MIDDLE**
518-492-7144.
100 Cook St., Dannemora.
Price: Inexpensive.
Cuisine: Breakfast fare,
  specialty sandwiches,
  home-style dinners.
Serving: B, L, D, late night
  till 2 a.m.

Say it's late at night, you're headed off to a cottage on Chazy Lake or the Chateaugay lakes for the week, and everybody in the car is cranky and starving. Dannemora, the former address for Son of Sam and scores of other unsavory characters, is the next town along the way. What to do?

Located on Main Street, Billy's Inn the Middle faces the ever-present 32-foot-high prison wall that dominates the downtown Dannemora landscape.

Credit Cards: None.
Handicap Access: No.
Special Features: Late-
    night menu; live music
    occasionally.

However, once you're inside (the restaurant, that is), the wall seems barely noticeable; there are even some nice views of the Saranac River valley from the picture windows at the southern end of the dining area.

The food here is unpretentious and tasty. Entrees include juicy, cooked-the-way-you-want filet mignon and prime rib, Chicken Cordon Billy, which is stuffed with tangy herb-and-garlic cheese, and seasoned stir-fry. An assortment of Mexican and Italian dishes is also offered. Billy's has a complete breakfast, lunch, and late-night menu, all suitable family fare.

*Breakfast to late-night fare is available at Billy's.*

Dennis Aprill

## Keene

**THE BARK EATER**
518-576-2221.
Alstead Hill Rd., Keene.
Price: Expensive.
Cuisine: Gourmet
    American.
Serving: B, D.
Credit Cards: AE, MC, V.
Reservations: Required for
    nonguests.
Handicap Access: Yes.
Special Features: Old inn;
    fireplaces; antiques; polo
    games on Sundays in
    July and August.

Considering its small size, and the dips and doodles in the inn business, the Bark Eater has managed to attract some really good chefs and, thus, a loyal following. Folks who come to dinner pass over a menu listing wide variety in favor of a bounteous meal that is a cross between well-tested recipes and new adventures in the kitchen.

The activities galleyside are open to view by the guests, who can circulate to pick up a hot or cold drink or retrieve their own spirits from the refrigerator. The chef, therefore, must be amenable to dealing with people rather than hiding away behind the range, and, in fact, usually comes out to explain the evening menu. Dinner is prix fixe ($24.50 in summer 1992) for five courses served family style. A new chef came on board at the Bark Eater in June 1992.

The setting is an old farmhouse dating to the early 19th century; the size of the dining room is explained by the fact that the inn served as a way station for stagecoach lines in its day. Two natural-stone fireplaces, high ceilings, mahogany and walnut furniture, and lots of antiques make the public areas interesting.

**ELM TREE INN**
518-576-9769.
Intersection Rtes. 73 & 9N, Keene.
Closed: Tues.
Price: Moderate.
Cuisine: American.
Serving: L, D.
Credit Cards: MC, V.
Reservations: No.
Handicap Access: Yes

Tucked up under the eaves of this celebrated crossroads tavern is the date 1824; this is one of Keene's oldest buildings. Inside you won't find much evidence of the 19th century, but you will see memorabilia of the heyday of bobsledding, in posters, photos, patches, plaques, and a couple of early sleds. The inn is named for an enormous elm, measuring 20+ feet in circumference, that used to shade the front porch. The tree died nearly two decades ago; for a while, a tall stump marked the spot, but with recent renovations, that's gone, too.

Monty Purdy bought the inn just after World War II, and his son Ron now runs the place. Purdy's, as everyone in Keene calls the Elm Tree, serves plain, tasty food in a nice, no-frills setting. No matter how busy the dining room seems to be, the waitresses remain remarkably cheerful and speedy. The steak sandwich, with a large piece of sirloin, overhangs the platter; the cream of mushroom soup draws raves from customers. Occasionally you can get Mountain Steak, a northern version of chicken-fried steak: cube steak covered with cracker crumbs and fried in butter. The Purdyburger, a plump patty topped with a thick wheel of raw onion and melted cheese, has been written up in the *New York Times* as one of the all-time great North Country hamburgs.

**SPRUCE HILL LODGE**
518-576-9990.
Rte. 9N, 2 miles east of Rte. 73 between Keene and Elizabethtown.
Closed: Mon.
Price: Moderate to Expensive.
Cuisine: American.
Serving: L, D.
Credit Cards: None.
Handicap Access: Yes.

A year-round restaurant popular with local residents, who call the place Murphy's after the owner, Peter Murphy, Spruce Hill Lodge is also a favorite of the summertime crowd. On cold days, the darkish dining room adjacent to the big old bar is a pleasant spot to eat burgers, steaks, or various fried dishes, eavesdrop on taproom conversations, and watch habitués play the electronic dart game. In summer, the glassed-in porch with its view of fields and trees is a better choice.

For lunch, you can order homemade soup; sandwiches; baskets of deep-fried chicken, shrimp, or fish; and excellent hamburgers. The dinner entrees are heartier: filet mignon, T-bone steak, surf and turf, pork chops, and an open steak sandwich. Spruce Hill's dinner specials are a bargain, and depending on the evening, the offering could be spaghetti and meatballs, prime rib, or a surprisingly good lobster dinner. Jean Coolidge, the restaurant's cook, doesn't do her own dessert pastries, but Spruce Hill Lodge has found an excellent nearby bakery to provide pies and cakes.

## *Keene Valley*

**AUSABLE INN**
518-576-9986.
Main St. (Rte. 73), Keene
  Valley.
Closed: Mon.
Price: Moderate.
Cuisine: American,
  Continental.
Serving: D.
Credit Cards: MC, V.
Reservations: Only for parties of 6 or more.
Handicap Access: Yes.

The Ausable Inn's dining room is appealing at any time of year, but it's especially comforting on a gloomy evening with its pine-paneled walls, red leather chairs, and red tablecloths, and a fire blazing in the big stone fireplace. The waitresses are friendly and nurturing when you arrive, bringing out warm bread with a pot of herb butter to accompany crunchy, fresh green salads.

The menu offers light fare — hamburgers, chicken, and shrimp in a basket — but if you arrive with big appetites, there's Pasta Ausable, which is shrimp and scallops in a marinara sauce served over linguine, or another real winner, Hunter's Chicken, a tarragon-flavored combination of tender chicken breast, tomatoes, shallots, mushrooms, and wine. There's also steak, filet mignon, veal, and other seafood dishes.

The relaxed atmosphere of the Ausable Inn encourages diners to linger, sharing desserts chosen from a tray. Oftentimes, there's moist, flavorful carrot cake, or heavenly French Silk Pie, and excellent coffee to sip slowly.

**NOON MARK DINER**
518-576-4499.
Main St. (Rte. 73), Keene
  Valley.
Price: Inexpensive.
Cuisine: American diner.
Serving: B, L, D.
Credit Cards: None.
Handicap Access: Yes.

Truly the nerve center of Keene Valley, the Noon Mark is a great place to go just to experience the array of human beings, from hearty hikers and chic tourists to local business people and little kids. Named after Noonmark Mountain, a prominent nearby peak, the eatery has a front room with a counter plus a few tables, and an adjacent dining room lined with big windows, the preferred place to sit on a sunny day.

The service at the Noon Mark is friendly and efficient, and the menu is extensive. Breakfast, which can be ordered any time, includes egg dishes, pancakes, French toast, and various combinations (like scrambled eggs, sausage, and cheese) served on a roll. For lunch, hamburgers are a good choice, and the soups are always hearty and tasty; the chili is quite good, with chunks of beef rather than ground meat. Dinner items lean a little heavily on deep-fat frying, but you can get a broccoli quiche or a small sirloin

*A couple of Keene Valley coneheads at the Noon Mark Diner.*

Nancie Battaglia

steak. For dessert, there's ice cream in sundaes, floats, and milk shakes, or on top of a big wedge of great homemade pie.

The diner's owner, Lola Porter, is understandably proud of her homemade soups, gravies, doughnuts, pies, muffins, and breads; you can even buy baked goods to take home.

## *Lake Placid*

**ADIRONDACK ROOM**
518-523-2551.
At Whiteface Inn,
  Whiteface Inn Rd., Lake
  Placid.
Closed: Mar. 15—May 15,
  Oct. 30—Dec. 24.
Price: Expensive.
Cuisine: French,
  Contemporary.
Serving: B, L, D.
Credit cards: AE, CB, DC,
  MC, V.
Reservations:
  Recommended.
Handicap Access: Yes.
Special features: Lunches
  on the putting green.

A sophisticated menu in a not-so-sophisticated setting characterizes this centerpiece of the Whiteface Inn condominium-marina-sports complex. Because the smaller wing of the L-shape structure serves the needs of golfers and other sports people during the day, the attendant activity around the first tee does not lend itself to a quiet, candlelit setting in the main dining room until after dark. Nonsmokers, on the other hand, who are relegated to the rear section, may prefer to dine early to take advantage of the distant view of Lake Placid and Whiteface Mountain. Service is sometimes rather offhand.

A master chef presides over what is probably the most extensive listing of French cuisine north of Lake George. Appetizers alone could suffice for several courses — duckling breast tostada, mélange fumée (smoked fish and seafood with herbed cream cheese), calamari tempura, panzarotti (prosciutto-filled pastry), and jumbo shrimp in Dijon mustard sauce, for example. Light entrees featuring fish, fowl, and pasta are moderately priced. The tariff is higher for the more richly treated dishes, but again the choice is wide: beef (tournedos chasseur, steak au poivre, fillet), lamb, veal, poultry (chicken à la Oscar and half duckling à la Suedoise, a boneless portion napped with lingonberry sauce), and seafood, dressed up in haute cuisine. Specialties of the house are marinated quail and Veal Marcy, which is medallions of sautéed veal topped with prosciutto and mozzarella and finished in a sherry demi-glace. Desserts change daily, but white chocolate mousse, poire au Bourgogne (a fresh pear simmered in red wine and maple syrup caramel), and Chocolate Sin Pie are excellent choices.

**ALPINE CELLAR**
518-523-2180.
Rte. 86, beneath the Alpine
   Motor Inn, across from
   the Lake Placid Club
   Golf Course.
Price: Moderate.
Cuisine: German.
Serving: D.
Credit Cards: AE, DC, MC,
   V.
Reservations:
   Recommended.
Handicap Access: No.
Special Features: Fireplace;
   View of Olympic ski
   jumps.

German food served in a motel basement sounds downright awful, but the Alpine Cellar is a terrific place. Monique and Wolfgang Brandenburg have created a jolly rathskeller with bright white-plastered walls, an assortment of colorful steins, a collection of antique copperware, and cheerful dirndl-clad waitresses.

The list of appetizers is short: there's smoked trout, a house paté, and white asparagus vinaigrette, but you'll decidedly want to save room for the entrees, which come with the house salad plate (marinated beans, cucumbers in sour cream, and other vegetables), homemade bread, red cabbage, and spaetzel or potato pancakes. The menu's packed with meat, such as several schnitzels and home-stuffed wursts, goulash, venison, Kassler Ripchen (smoked pork chops), and the house specialty, Gebrotene Kalbhaxe (veal shanks, but order a day ahead). For dessert, it's apple strudel, of course.

The beer list is more impressive than the wine list, with 27 varieties of German brew, plus ales and lagers from Brazil, Norway, Russia, and elsewhere. The bar is rather dark, but it's friendly, too, and chances are you may find yourself seated next to a onetime Olympic skier or coach.

The Alpine Cellar is defintely not the place to take a vegetarian friend or someone who abhors accordion music. It is, however, one of the few ethnic restaurants in the Adirondacks that dishes out authenticity without airs.

**THE BOATHOUSE**
518-523-4822.
Lake Placid Club Drive,
   Lake Placid.
Open year-round.
Price: Inexpensive to
   Moderate.
Serving: D (winter); L, D
   (summer).

Subtitled "An American Bistro with Mediterranean Influence," Mike Nicola's waterfront place is a winner. The building used to be a boathouse for the enormous Lake Placid Club, which occupied the empty space just up the street. Completely redone with large picture windows, oak furniture, and see-in kitchen, the Boathouse is casual and comfortable. There's a sandy beach

Credit Cards: MC, V.
Handicap Access: Yes.
Special Features: Outdoor
   tables on lakeside deck.

below the dining room and a wraparound deck overlooking Mirror Lake.

The menu stays on the light side, with a variety of salads: Niçoise, spinach, Caesar, Mediterranean, and the Boathouse Salad (romaine, red onions, Gorgonzola cheese, apples, walnuts, and raspberry vinaigrette.) For hors d'ouevres, there are Greek specialties and frito misto. Individual hearth pizzas — which can actually serve two — come with imaginative toppings like roasted peppers, Kalamata olives, fresh rosemary and Gorgonzola, or pesto. Pastas with fresh, homemade sauces come in three sizes — appetizer, lunch, or dinner — so you can select the amount of food you'd like, and combine a small pasta with a large salad for a satisfying dinner.

Entrees include fresh grilled fish, steaks, burgers, and Spiedini, marinated pork cubes grilled shish-kebab style, served with roasted potatoes and Italian bread. All courses are served on the classic pine-cone china that used to grace Lake Placid Club tables. There's a small bar in an adjoining room, and a modest wine list.

*Alfresco dining at the Boathouse, Lake Placid.*

Nancie Battaglia

### CHARCOAL PIT RESTAURANT
518-523-3050.
Rte. 86 (1 mile from the Olympic Arena, near the Grand Union), Lake Placid.
Closed: Wed. in winter.
Price: Moderate to Expensive.
Cuisine: Continental, Greek, American.
Serving: D.
Credit Cards: AE, D, MC, V.
Reservations: Suggested.
Handicap Access: Yes.

Two generations and sixty years of restaurant experience are on tap at the Charcoal Pit. Chef Jim Hadjis absorbed everything he could from his late father, also Jim, who, with his wife Eugenia, built a solid reputation for good food. Now Jim earns the laurels with a mix of Greek, Continental, and American cuisine that is consistently excellent.

The seafood dishes — Greek shrimp Efrosini, served with feta cheese and plaki sauce; sea scallops Maria, in a red-bell-pepper sauce; and coquille St. Jacques Parisienne, to cite a few — are especially good, but Jim says that prime rib and rack of lamb are their best sellers. Individual loaves of delicious bread come with dinner, and there is a separate, complete dessert menu.

An arbor of hanging and standing greenery creates an area of privacy in the main room, and windows all around keep you in touch with the passing parade on the street and in a nearby mini-mall. On occasion, there is hustle and bustle inside as well, reflecting the popularity of the place.

At the opposite end of the building, the sometimes quieter greenhouse room has curved windows looking out on a lovely garden. In the bar, a copper-hooded fireplace adds interest and warmth, and there are large and small banquet rooms.

### THE GREAT ADIRONDACK STEAK AND SEAFOOD COMPANY
518-523-1629.
32 Main St. (near the Palace Theater), Lake Placid.
Open 7 days.
Price: Moderate to Expensive.
Cuisine: American, Cajun.
Serving: L, D.
Credit Cards: AE, DC, MC, V.
Reservations: None.
Handicap Access: Yes.

Farm tools and antiques, well placed with a touch of humor, plus heavy beams and barn wood create a rustic atmosphere to match this restaurant's name. The menu is pretty straight forward American, including some interesting appetizers (Cajun shrimp, scallops au gratin, and escargots, to name a few), with entrees leaning toward Cajun style for the seafood, "blackened" prime rib, and sea-steak combinations. There is pasta primavera or marinara, along with Cajun or Italian-style chicken dishes, and always daily specials.

Traffic along Main St. is the principal entertainment, as is conversation from the next table; the room is rather crowded and busy, so tête-à-têtes must be reserved for elsewhere.

Much the same menu is offered by the same owners at the Artists' Cafe, a tiny, downstairs spot at the beginning of Main St. There the crowding doesn't seem to bother, for some reason; a bonus is the view of Mirror Lake from the enclosed porch.

*In warm weather, the porch at the Interlaken Inn doubles as a dining area.*

Nancie Battaglia

**THE INTERLAKEN INN**
518-523-3180.
15 Interlaken Ave., Lake
  Placid.
Closed: Apr., Nov.; Sun.,
  Mon. May—Oct. and
  Dec.—Mar.
Price: Expensive.
Cuisine: Contemporary
  American.
Serving: D for nonguests.
Credit Cards: AE, MC, V.
Reservations:
  Recommended.
Handicap Access: No.
Special Features: Lovely
  old inn.

One of Lake Placid's fine old homes, operated as an inn for many years, has been turned into a Victorian hideaway by its present owners, the Johnson family. Whimsical furnishings, including period costumes, decorate the common rooms, which include a homey, small bar with wicker furniture overlooking the garden.

Only a limited number of outside diners are accepted beyond the house count and there is just one seating. Chefs Carol Johnson and her son Kevin Gregg lavish care upon the food they prepare. Much individual attention is given in the serving as well.

Five courses are offered, with choices only in entrees: these always include a red meat, two lighter meats, and a fish selection. Carol and Kevin prefer to call their style American, but they enjoy trying different combinations and subtle flavorings that add decided interest. The menu changes every day, but main-course possibilities may be filet mignon served with Jack Daniels cream sauce, chicken piccata, poached salmon with champagne dill sauce, or red snapper with Vera Cruz sauce. Fresh breads and desserts (Floating Islands, peach Melba, Chocolate Turtle Tart) are almost impossible to resist.

Mahogany paneling and high wainscoting lend formality to the mansion's original dining room. The enclosed porch areas have a more intimate feeling, and afford glimpses of Mirror Lake through the trees.

**JIMMY'S EATING AND DRINKING PLACE**
518-523-2353.
21 Main St., Lake Placid.
Open year-round.
Price: Inexpensive to Moderate.
Cuisine: Contemporary American.
Serving: L, D.
Credit Cards: AE, MC, V.
Reservations: No.
Handicap Access: Street-level entry.

In Lake Placid, dining spots overlooking Mirror Lake are relatively few, oddly enough. One of the most popular, Jimmy's 21, briefly Red's Eats, now Jimmy's once again, this local landmark sits nearly opposite the movie theater, tucked into a narrow building that extends back toward the lake from Main Street. The front room is a bar with rather subdued lighting — something of a disadvantage, especially when entering with small children.

A view of the lake opens up in the dining room at the rear of the building; at night the glow of lights ringing the shore is pretty. Some booths are situated between the dining area and the bar; they're cozy, but the service area is across the way, and it can be distracting. Kitchens are below, like in city watering holes around the world.

Tasty, unpretentious food, from pasta dishes, chicken, and quality steaks to homemade soups and plump deli-style sandwiches, comes trundling up on the dumbwaiter. As you munch your lunch, you'll find that Jimmy's is a popular watering hole and a good place to overhear the inside scoop on local affairs.

**LA VERANDAH**
518-523-2556.
1 Olympic Dr. (above the public parking lot on Main St.), Lake Placid.
Closed: Winter and spring.
Price: Expensive.
Cuisine: Continental.
Serving: D.
Credit Cards: AE, CB, DC, MC, V.
Reservations: Recommended.

An aptly titled grand old hotel that made Lake Placid famous around the turn of the century was the Grandview; today on the site is a Holiday Inn. Nearby is a handsome residence built by an early wealthy patron who wanted to summer next to his favorite dining establishment. Now, La Verandah fully occupies that house, operated by the Inn at the height of the tourist season, still in the style of a private retreat.

There are large and small rooms on two levels, each distinctively decorated with fabric wallpaper,

Handicap Access: No.
Special Features: Lovely old home; private parties.

rich colors, and fine furniture. On the main level, a small lobby serves as the cocktail lounge, augmented in good weather by tables on the porch outside. (The view of Mirror Lake from the veranda in summertime is quite lovely.) The Hearthside Room has a magnificent natural-stone fireplace and stained-glass windows. The Birch Room upstairs also has a stone fireplace and is attractively accented with birch trim.

Chef Claude specializes in nouvelle cuisine. Appetizers include smoked salmon, escargots, and homemade sausage with pistachios in a pastry shell. Salads and soups are limited but lush. Regular entrees range from pastas, like seafood vermicelli or fettucini with broiled scallops, to veal medallions with chanterelles, tournedos Rossini, rack of lamb, and sautéed chicken with marsala sauce. A separate children's menu is available.

The atmosphere may outweigh the presentation, but overall, the experience here generally merits the higher tariff.

**LAKE PLACID MANOR**
518-523-2573.
Whiteface Inn Rd., Lake Placid.
Closed: Apr.
Price: Expensive.
Cuisine: Continental.
Serving: B, L, D.
Credit cards: AE, MC, V.
Reservations: Recommended.
Handicap Access: No.
Special Features: Fireplaces; historic building.

Anyone who appreciates finesse in the preparation and presentation of food will seek out the Manor, tucked away on the shore of Lake Placid. A meal also provides the opportunity to see an authentic old Adirondack camp (circa 1882), with rustic furniture, a huge fireplace complete with moose head, and plenty of birchbark and bentwood furnishings in the common rooms. In good weather, the umbrella tables on the open porch frequently have to be reserved in advance; on rainy or chilly days, you can enjoy the cozy bar, with its forest-green walls and yellow-birch-log trim.

The dining room is airy and light; Windsor chairs add to the elegant effect. Whiteface Mountain is visible mainly from the front part of the room, but a raised area at the rear preserves the lake view for all tables. Glimpsed by candlelight, the lights from passing boats and nearby camps are intriguing.

The menu is not as extensive as those of many commercial establishments, but the ingredients are of the highest quality, are enhanced in the handling, and are so imaginatively put together that just remembering a Placid Manor meal starts the juices flowing. Appetizers change frequently, with spinach and wild mushroom strudel, lime and lager prawns, and escargots as winter and spring possibilities. Entrees often include exotic selections like red-deer loin or pheasant; poached and grilled fresh fish are always featured. Adventuresome at times, the Manor's menu may not be for those who are more comfortable with standard American fare.

**LINDSAY'S**
518-523-9470.
237 Main St. (across from
  the speed-skating oval),
  Lake Placid.
Closed: Thanksgiving and
  Christmas.
Price: Expensive to Very
  Expensive.
Cuisine: French.
Serving: D.
Credit Cards: AE, MC, V.
Reservations:
  Recommended.
Handicap Access: Yes.

The "back room" and alter ego at the Woodshed Restaurant, Lindsay's is a relatively small space wrapped around a garden alcove that is particularly pleasant on summer evenings. A feeling of space and elegance is created by the high, peaked ceiling, set off by big beams; a rich, dark green on the walls; and reproductions of Old Masters.

The room is uncrowded and the pace unhurried, allowing for relaxed enjoyment of a meal. Service is good, but the maître d' is sometimes oversolicitous.

Lindsay's cuisine is basically French and earns good to occasional rave reviews from diners. Appetizers include scallops Florentine, Gorgonzola-filled ravioli topped with fresh tomatoes, and sautéed quail. The list of entrees offers choice steaks and lamb; a half-dozen veal dishes, including sweetbreads in Madeira wine; chicken breasts under various sauces; imaginative seafood combinations such as shrimp Pomodora, with lobster, sautéed tomatoes, basil, and artichokes served over butterflied shrimp; or lobster Fra Diavolo. The dessert list is small but tempting.

**MIRROR LAKE INN**
518-523-2544.
5 Mirror Lake Dr., Lake
  Placid.
Open daily.
Price: Expensive to Very
  Expensive.
Cuisine: Continental.
Serving: B, D, Afternoon
  Tea.
Credit Cards: AE, CB, MC,
  V.
Reservations: Suggested.
Handicap Access: Yes.
Jackets required for men;
  proper dress for women.

When fire wrecked one of Lake Placid's fine old inns a few years ago, Ed and Lisa Weibrecht turned catastrophe into an opportunity to create in its place an elegant, modern resort with all the accoutrements.

The air of gracious comfort evident in beautifully appointed common rooms is continued in the dining room with a lighter touch. A split-level arrangement opens to all the tables a view of Mirror Lake and the distant High Peaks. Oil paintings by a nationally known artist that depict scenes from Lake Placid's early days lend the room special character. Lush greenery, fresh flowers, and candles complete the picture.

The menu choices are wide; a separate listing for health conscious diners — the Wellness Menu — features poached or grilled fish, low-fat pastas, and sautéed chicken, all without rich sauces. Fresh breads and soups with unusual flavors are bonuses. Entrees range from venison tenderloin to rainbow trout MacIntyre (sautéed trout topped with lemon, grapes, and walnuts), to pasta Adirondack style (sauced with smoked shrimp, smoked trout, fresh dill, and cream), plus steak, duckling, salmon, and lamb. The overall result is definitely above average but not always memorable. The desserts

Nancie Battaglia

*The Avrill Conwell dining room at the Mirror Lake Inn.*

will send anyone off happy, and the wine cellar is probably the most extensive in town.

The Cottage, a breezy little bar on the lake, is also owned by the Mirror Lake Inn; it's a popular spot for lunch, happy hour, and late snacks. The Inn also serves afternoon tea every day, to which the public is invited at no charge.

## NO. 1 CHINESE RESTAURANT

518-523-4800.
211 Main St. (across from the Olympic arena), Lake Placid.
Closed: Christmas.
Price: Inexpensive.
Cuisine: Chinese.
Serving: L, D.
Credit Cards: MC, V.
Reservations: Recommended for large parties.
Handicap Access: Yes.
Special Features: Take-out available.

Eating Chinese in the Olympic Village gets a bit confusing: on Main St., there's also the A-1 Chinese, with a very similar logo and food that does not compare, and in the same site as No. 1 (which was a gas station in its first incarnation), there used to be a not-too-terrific Oriental place known as the Golden Swan. You can skip the history and geography lessons if you just stick with No. 1.

For sure, the decor is a bit haphazard, with mismatched chairs, a fireplace, bits of artwork, and calendars showing Hong Kong harbor hung high on the walls, and the Chinese rock music can be peculiar to unappreciative ears, but the food's good and the price is right. No. 1 is open until 11 p.m. on Fridays and Saturdays all year.

The menu — proclaiming NO MSG in large letters — lists nearly 200 dishes, from Sing Ding Snow Dim, with chicken and pork, to bean curd Szechuan style. You can request that a dish be less sweet (some selections, like orange beef, do tend to be sugary), and you can ask the chef to turn up the heat. The service is fine and the Tsing Tao beer is always cold.

## Merrill

**HOLLYWOOD INN**
518-425-9994.
Rte. 374, Merrill.
Open daily in summer;
  closed Tues. in spring
  and fall.
Price: Moderate.
Cuisine: American.
Serving: L, D, SB.
Credit Cards: MC, V.
Reservations: No.
Handicap Access: Yes.

Camp owners on the Chateaugay lakes, residents along the northern rim of the park, and Montrealers who like to explore it have for years patronized a remarkably good, modest restaurant in Merrill, just inside the Blue Line. Russ and Joan Sawyer provide hearty country cooking at very reasonable prices.

The extensive menu comes as a surprise, given the place's size and location; seafood (the sampler plate includes broiled shrimp, scallops, crab, lobster, and a fresh fillet), fish, and chicken (broiled, barbecued, fried, or plumped with herb stuffing) just about balance in number the red meat dishes, and you'll find all the usual options there: pork chops, lamp chops, steaks, ham. At the height of the season, diners should go early and be prepared to wait, especially for the Sunday brunch.

Waiting can be made quite pleasant by a visit to the rustic bar in the center of this rambling farmhouse, which is amply decorated throughout with old photographs of the big, elegant camps that once lined the shores of the lakes. There are other pictures of life in the old days: besides hosting generations of tourists, the Chateaugay lakes held iron ore reserves, and some of the earliest Catalan forges were built here in the 1800s.

Located at the beginning of the narrows between the two lakes, the Hollywood has an airy porch with windows overlooking the water, where nonsmokers are seated. The public boat launch is next door, so you can go for a cruise and come back for dinner.

## Ray Brook

**TAIL O' THE PUP**
518-891-5092.
Rte. 86, Ray Brook, adjacent to the Evergreens.
Closed: Mid-Oct.—mid-May.
Price: Inexpensive.
Cuisine: Barbecue, hot dogs, burgers.

Back in 1945 when the Tail was just a pup, Adirondack highways were lined with similar roadside restaurants: places with black-and-white checkerboard linoleum floors, screens on the windows, brightly painted wooden tables with oilcloth tops, counters flanked with chrome-based stools, maybe a few picnic tables under the pines. Now

Serving: L, D.
Credit Cards: None.
Special Features: Take-out.

the Tail O' the Pup is the last of the breed, dishing out classic American road food with spunk.

There's a huge black contraption at the edge of the picnic grove where chicken and ribs (good-quality baby back ribs) are smoked. Then they're finished inside on the grill with a sweet but tangy barbecue sauce. Barbecue dinners come with waffle fries, fresh sweet corn, and cole slaw. Of course, you can get very good hot dogs here, too, dressed with chili and/or kraut, accompanied by plump, crunchy onion rings. To wash it all down, there's nice cold beer on tap, including Bass Ale and Killian's Red. You can eat inside, outside, or take it all home with you.

*Tail O' the Pup — more than just another roadside attraction — dishes out exemplary barbecue on Route 86.*

Nancie Battaglia

## Saranac

**BUD'S DINER**
518-293-8110.
Rte. 3, Saranac.
Price: Inexpensive.
Cuisine: American diner.
Serving: B, L, D.
Credit Cards: None.
Reservations: No.
Handicap Access: No.

The word "diner" usually conjures up images of an army of 16-wheelers parked in front of some greasy spoon. While truckers have discovered the honest home-cooked fare offered at Bud's, so have many local people and tourists, and for good reason: they get a reasonably priced, hot, tasty meal of ample portions. For example, the roast turkey sandwich comes complete with mounds of real turkey, homemade gravy, french fries, and crunchy cole slaw — all for a price of $4.75. You'll find all the usual cold sandwiches here, but at half the price you'd pay downstate. The coffee won't float horseshoes, and the pies are good.

Bud's decor can best be described as informal; it's the kind of place where you can keep your baseball cap on when you eat. There are booths for those who'd rather not eat at the counter.

## Saranac Lake

**THE BELVEDERE RESTAURANT**
518-891-9873.
57 Bloomingdale Ave.
  (Rte. 3), Saranac Lake.
Open year-round.
Price: Moderate.
Cuisine: Italian, American.
Serving: D.
Credit Cards: None.
Reservations: No.

For years, the "Bel" has been the place to go in Saranac Lake for Italian food. Since 1933, three generations of the Cavallo family have built this into one of the favorite restaurants in the area.

The bar is a local gathering place and, for patrons without children, serves as a lively "waiting room" for the restaurant, which wraps around it in an L-shape but has a quieter life of its own. Knotty pine in a diagonal pattern and large, curtained windows produce a clean, bright interior in the dining room.

Well-tested old-country recipes guarantee consistent and tasty standard entrees: chicken cacciatore, veal and peppers, lasagna with homemade noodles, spaghetti with several different sauces, plus steaks, ham, fried chicken, and pork chops. The hot sausage ("our own recipe," the menu states) is definitely worth trying. Meats and fish can be prepared without sauces if you choose. The bread here is a cut above the ordinary. Because the kitchen staff is small, service is not fast; if you're planning to see a film or Pendragon Theater production after dinner, come early.

**CASA DEL SOL**
518-891-0977.
154 Lake Flower Ave. (Rte.
  86), Saranac Lake.
Closed: 1 week in early
  Dec., 1 week in Apr.
Price: Inexpensive to
  Moderate.
Cuisine: Mexican.
Serving: L, D.
Credit Cards: None.
Reservations: No.
Handicap Access: Yes,
  with assistance; rest
  rooms are downstairs.

A recent visitor with a vacation home in the Southwest asserts that he hasn't found a Mexican restaurant east of the Mississippi to equal Casa del Sol. Certainly this small, colorful gem is one of the most popular restaurants in the region.

An outdoor patio and bar (covered) expands the waiting space in warm weather, but the policy is first-come, first-served, and no reservations are taken. Weekend nights can be very crowded, but the pub, with its mix of visitors and locals, makes the entertainment worth the wait.

Daily specials at both lunch and dinner are usually excellent and tempt regulars to vary from their favorite dishes. Sharing bountiful aperitivos is encouraged, and also opens up new possibilities —
Mexican Roulette, for example, is appetizer-portion chili rellenos, only some of the chilis are fiery jalapeños — as do combination plates of enchiladas, burritos, tostadas, and tacos with beef, bean, chicken, chili verde, chorizo, and combo stuffings, under red or green sauces. Corona, Dos Equis, and other Mexican beers are available.

Many selections are mild enough to satisfy anyone who might fear that this type of food is too spicy. In the evening, with only the Southwest colors and decor for visual influence, a definite mental change of pace is possible, an escape from mud season, if you will. Best of all, the prices are reasonable.

**LYDIA'S AND THE BOATHOUSE LOUNGE**
Hotel Saranac of Paul Smith's College
518-891-2200.
101 Main St. (across from the public library), Saranac Lake.
Closed: Thurs. eves. Sept.—June.
Price: Moderate.
Serving: B, L, D.
Credit Cards: AE, DC, MC, V.
Handicap Access: Yes.

The Hotel Saranac of Paul Smith's College is the social hub of the community and has a loyal following among its citizens who recognize the advantages of having a good, small hotel in their midst. As a training ground for students, this institution sometimes requires — and is granted — a certain forgiveness for occasionally uneven food and service.

A combination of booths and tables in Lydia's spacious main dining room, with windows fronting the street, makes for a pleasant and convivial daytime atmosphere. Subdued lighting and pastel colors create an interesting transition to more leisurely dining in the evening.

Three specials described as contemporary cuisine (scallops primavera; poached chicken and shrimp; duckling with apple, ginger, and green peppercorn sauce, for example) are featured each evening here, in addition to a dozen-plus regular items labeled "Adirondack," which really can be interpreted as hearty American (char-grilled steaks, pot roast, snow crab legs, broiled lemon-pepper sole). The Boathouse Lounge, a dark and cozy nook across the lobby from the main dining room, has a simpler menu with steak, fish, and sandwich offerings, plus the same lunch specialties as Lydia's. The Boathouse also serves late at night.

Thursday nights from Sepember to June the culinary arts students prepare theme buffets, highlighting international foods; these have a devoted local following. Note that fresh pastry and breads are available for sale here, in both dining rooms.

**PONTIAC CLUB**
518-891-5200.
94 Main St. (across from the Hotel Saranac), Saranac Lake.
Open year-round.
Price: Inexpensive.
Cuisine: American deli.
Serving: L, D. (Mon. L only).
Credit Cards: MC, V.
Handicap Access: Yes.
Special Features: Catering; private parties.

The Pontiac Club is an acclaimed spot right in the center of Saranac Lake village that emphasizes its "deli style." Diners are invited to be adventurous in creating sandwich combinations beyond the impressive list compiled by the Van Andens. For a more substantial meal, there is shrimp tempura, chicken wings, barbecue ribs, and steak sandwiches. All are available throughout the day and evening, with dinner specials added after 5 p.m.

Soups and salads above the ordinary are cooked up here, too. Seven different kinds of homemade bread add to the fun. Subs will satisfy those with the capacity or partners.

A handsome old building has been gutted and transformed into an attractive, modern setting with two personalities. The non-smoking section has a low ceiling and views of the sidewalk scene, enlivened by framed photos of early Saranac Lake people and pastimes. On another level, large windows and skylights open up the view of the village for smokers. A room for catered parties at the back sometimes takes overflow in the summer.

This is a happy choice for a family or anyone seeking good, hearty American fare. The quality is first-rate. Picnickers, note that the Van Andens also operate Lakeview Deli, near the boat-launch site on Lake Flower.

**THE RED FOX**
518-891-2127.
Rte. 3 west of the center of town, Saranac Lake.
Closed: Mon.—Wed. in winter, 2 weeks in Apr., Mon. in summer.
Price: Moderate.
Cuisine: American, Italian.
Serving: B, L in coffee shop; D in dining room.
Reservations: Suggested.
Handicap Access: No.

Harriet and Bill Walaski's Red Fox is a decent, pleasant spot. The food is good, the servings are ample, and local residents regard it as the place to go for all special occasions. An air of small-town friendliness permeates the somewhat over-decorated but warm and comfortable dining room.

The adventurous diner may have trouble finding something special about the food. A glimmer of hope is fresh seafood and homemade desserts, which our waitress said are offered during the summer months. In the dead of winter, however, the menu is heavy on beef — prime rib is a regular special, and steaks are abundant. Good steaks, as it turns out: the 14-ounce New York strip was charbroiled to perfection. The chicken special, which was a breast filled with bread stuffing, topped with melted cheese, and covered with a sauce that tasted too much like canned soup, left something to be desired. We had to be suspicious that it was prestuffed, frozen, and just souped up a little. There's an assortment of pastas, including lasagna.

Recently the Red Fox has added a coffee shop in a ground-level portion of the building, open for breakfast and lunch.

No doubt its very predictability makes the Red Fox popular. The formula is good food, good value, good service, with no pretensions and no surprises. For that, the Red Fox is a good bet.

## *Upper Jay*

**THE WOOD PARLOR AT HIGH PEAKS BASE CAMP**
518-946-2133.
Springfield Rd., 1 mile from the Rte. 9 bridge at Upper Jay.
Closed: Tues., Oct.—Apr.

If you've been skunked by the wily brook trout on the Ausable, you can catch your own dinner here, a meal-size Coho salmon. The pond-raised, yet tasty fish usually oblige, but you won't go hungry if you or your kids don't hook one; a member of the kitchen crew will net your dinner for you.

Price: Inexpensive to
   Moderate.
Cuisine: Continental.
Serving: B, L, D.
Credit Cards: AE, MC, V.
Handicap Access: Yes.
Special Features: Salmon
   pond; vegetarian dishes;
   occasional live music or
   theater performances.

The spacious Wood Parlor is open six days a week in the winter and daily in summer, for breakfast, lunch, and dinner, serving impressive sandwiches on good homemade bread, such as the Marcy Dam (ham or turkey with sautéed onions and peppers, topped with cheese). Pizzas feature nice chewy crusts, with Greek, vegetarian, white, and the usual toppings; soups are tasty, imaginative concoctions that change daily.

Dinners may include lamb shish kebab, grilled outdoors; Mexican or Greek specialties; stir fries; vegetarian platters. The service can be loopy and distracted — hence the local nickname "High Peaks Space Camp" — but be patient: the food here is fresh, simple, delicious, and well worth the wait.

## *Wilmington*

**THE COUNTRY BEAR**
518-946-2691.
Rte. 86, Wilmington.
Closed: Wed.
Price: Inexpensive.
Cuisine: American diner.
Serving: B, L.
Reservations: No.
Handicap Access: No.

A half-dozen booths, a few stools at the counter — the Country Bear is a tiny place, pretty much a one-woman show, with Gail Mitchell at the helm. She makes good homemade bread (white, whole wheat, and rye), slices it generously, and piles it high with cheese, meat, whatever, for honest sandwiches. The chili, which comes with or without meat, is properly spiced, and with a generous side of fries, that's a lunch that'll sustain you through a long afternoon of skiing, hiking, or visiting nearby Santa's Workshop. If you're planning a full day in the woods, the Bear has hearty, no-frills breakfasts, too.

**FOX FARM CAFE**
518-946-7770.
Rte. 86 and Fox Farm Rd.,
   Wilmington.
Price: Inexpensive.
Cuisine: Diner.
Serving: B, L.
Handicap Access: Yes.
No smoking throughout
   the restaurant.

For several years, this pale orange stucco building has lingered empty and forlorn, like some relic blown north off the Santa Fe Trail. After months of work, Jan and Alan Goodman, from Florida, hung out the "Open" sign again on this landmark eatery in May 1992.

Inside, the cafe is spruced up and very Adirondack-looking, with booths built from natural-finish wood slats, lumberjack memorabilia on the walls, white-birch curtain rods, and photos by the Goodmans. The menu is modern diner fare, with homemade biscuits, grits (this may be the only place inside the Blue Line that understands the mystery that is grits), bagels, hotcakes, hash, home fries, burgers, Reubens, soups, salads. The combinations for breakfast are dizzying: folks are encouraged to build their own meal from a list of possible eggs, meats, sides, and breads. Pancakes, waffles, and French toast come in tall and short stacks, and with real maple syrup. You can get breakfast right up to closing time, 3 p.m.

The chow here is consistently fresh and hearty, and the service is good. You can get a lunch to go to take up Whiteface Mountain — the scenic highway starts just a few miles away — or if it's winter, and you're downhilling at the Olympic mountain, you can forgo the assembly-line cafeteria ski-hill food and head for some home cooking instead.

**THE HUNGRY TROUT**
518-946-2217.
Rte. 86, Wilmington, at the Ausable River bridge.
Closed: Mid-Mar.—mid-May; Nov.
Price: Expensive.
Cuisine: Continental.
Serving: D.
Credit Cards: AE, MC, V.
Handicap Access: Yes.
Special Features: Fireplace; mountain and river views.

With a mile-long section of the legendary Ausable River wrapping around this motel-restaurant complex, and views of not one but two spectacular natural attractions — the Flume, a foaming cataract, and the summit of Whiteface Mountain — the Hungry Trout already promises a nice evening's expedition. Plan to arrive before dark in order to take advantage of the best of what this restaurant has to offer. While the food here is very good, it's the natural setting rather than the meal that is truly memorable.

The extensive menu lists seven different trout entrees (all of the trout is farm-raised, but still quite tasty), seafood, steaks, chicken, rack of lamb, grilled Norwegian salmon, and vegetarian pasta primavera. Appetizers include baked clams casino, steamed little necks, crab-stuffed mushrooms, and specials like barbecued venison riblets. The house salad is quite good, especially when dressed with balsamic vinaigrette. The dessert list features Ben and Jerry's ice cream in various rich and gooey combinations, along with chocolaty tortes, fresh-fruit pies, and nutty cakes.

Beneath the bar, on a lawn overlooking the river, is R.F. McDougall's, a brand-new but Victorian-looking pub. It's more casual than the main restaurant, has its own menu, and is a good place to head for imported beers and a light meal.

**WILDERNESS INN II**
518-946-2391.
Rte. 86, 1 mile west of Whiteface Memorial Highway, Wilmington.
Price: Moderate.
Cuisine: American.
Serving: D.
Credit Cards: DC, MC, V.
Handicap Access: No.
Special Features: Fireplace; children's menu.

This place is an unusual feast for the eyes as well as the alimentary canal. Autographed 8x10 glossies of Abbott and Costello, Desi Arnaz, Peter Lorre, Bill "Bojangles" Robinson, and dozens more line the walls of one dining alcove. The main dining room, containing just a half-dozen tables, has a massive stone fireplace with a mantle covered with wood carvings, candle holders, and seasonal knicknacks. The most startling vision, though, is of the glass-enclosed porch attached to the dining room that's a greenhouse-cum-diorama, with live plants, artificial birds, strings of colored lights, a train set, and sometimes a Christmas tree.

Owner Fran Walton serves decent charbroiled steaks, huge stuffed pork chops, spaghetti, chicken, and occasionally fresh fish. There's a salad bar with the requisite rabbit food plus tangy cold baked beans, pasta salads, and pickled beets. Think of Wilderness Inn II as a visit to Grandma's for dinner, only you should leave a tip.

## NORTHWEST LAKES REGION

### *Cranberry Lake*

**CRANBERRY LAKE INN**
315-848-3301.
Rte. 3, Cranberry Lake.
Closed: Apr.
Price: Moderate.
Cuisine: American.
Serving: B, L, D.
Credit Cards: MC, V.
Reservations: Not necessary.
Handicap Access: Inquire.
Special Features: Cold sandwiches available after 11 p.m.

A rarity in this remote area of the park, the Cranberry Lake Inn is a family restaurant offering full lunch and dinner menus. Here on the shore of one of the North Country's wildest lakes, guests can watch the changing seasonal panorama of the water and the surrounding hills.

The dining-room decor is rustically Adirondack, with antique snowshoes, traps, lumberjack tools, and various representatives of the local fauna in taxidermic settings adorning the walls. There's a small room off the main restaurant that's almost like a mini-museum of local memorabilia. In the publike barroom, hikers and snowmobilers gather to play pool and pinball and exchange tall tales.

For lunch, you can try a Philly-style cheese steak, a burger blanketed with Thousand Island dressing, chili, club sandwich, or Chicken O'Coleman — a chicken fillet with bacon, lettuce, and tomato. The dinner menu offers an assortment of seafoods, steaks, and chops; prime rib, available on weekends only, is a house specialty.

**WINDFALL HOUSE**
315-848-2696.
Tooley Pond Rd.,
   Cranberry Lake.
Open year-round.
Price: Moderate.
Cuisine: American.
Serving: D.
Credit Cards: None.
Handicap Access: No.

A bit off the beaten path in an already less-traveled corner of the park, the Windfall House is a nice family restaurant offering a complete menu of steaks, chicken, chops, and nightly specials. The salad bar draws very positive reviews from guests; desserts are good, too.

*A bull moose keeps watch over the dining room at the Lodge on Lake Clear.*

Nancie Battaglia

## *Lake Clear*

**THE LODGE ON LAKE CLEAR**
518-891-1489.
Rtes. 30 and 186, Lake Clear.
Closed: Tues. in Mar.—Apr.
Price: Expensive to Very Expensive.
Cuisine: German.
Serving: D.
Credit Cards: MC, V.
Reservations: Required.
Handicap Access: No.
Special Features: Old Adirondack inn.

The warmth and intimacy of an Adirondack inn enfold the visitor here in a relaxing, homey atmosphere that adds to the pleasure of a meal prepared as if every evening were a house party. Reservations are required; it's best to bring a group of friends rather than plan an intimate evening for two.

Knotty-pine woodwork and plenty of windows brighten the dining room, balanced by a low ceiling and exposed beams. A grand piano fills a back corner of the capacious room. Guests can relax by the fireplace in the rathskeller before or after dinner.

Cathy Fisher, who presides in the kitchen, continues to use many of the German recipes made famous by Mr. and Mrs. Hohmeyer, her fiance's parents. She displays her own love for cooking with original twists, flavorings, and combinations. Choices in soup and salad are limited (standbys are chicken, onion, or oxtail soup, and marinated cucumber or green salad), but a number of appetizers and desserts are available: smoked oysters, herring, artichoke, liver or vegetable paté, for starters; apple strudel, blueberry cake, Black Forest cake, or homemade ice cream to finish. For entrees, there are four to eight choices each night, with possibilities like Wiener schnitzel, roast pork, duckling, rabbit, venison, salmon, roulade, sauerbraten, lobster, or lamb. Everything is freshly made with a personal touch. A five-course meal prix fixe was $27.50 in 1992.

## *Oswegatchie*

**HILLSIDE DINER**
No phone.
Rte. 3, Oswegatchie.
Open year-round.
Price: Inexpensive.
Cuisine: Diner.
Serving: B, L, D.
Credit Cards: None.

You can always expect a genuine welcome from the locals and loggers when you walk into this diner, but what's unexpected is good, spicy Southwestern-style chili, courtesy of the new owners, who arrived here from Texas in 1990.

## *Star Lake*

**TWIN LAKES HOTEL
AND RESTAURANT**
315-848-2291.
Rte, 3, Star Lake.
Closed: Mon.
Price: Moderate.
Serving: D.
Credit Cards: None.
Handicap Access: No.

This attractive old house, one of the first in the region, was built in the late 1800s long before the first commercial ore was dug from nearby Benson Mines. For a time it served as a boarding-house for mine workers, and in the first decades of this century the hotel served the Orthodox Jewish summer community of Star Lake. Marc Chagall visited the area, although we can't say for certain if he ever dined at the Twin Lakes.

*The flower garden welcomes visitors at Twin Lakes Hotel, Star Lake.*

B. Folwell

Nowadays the menu here is traditional American cooking rather than strictly kosher. Entrees range from pizza to steaks and prime rib, with plenty of seafood dishes. The service is helpful, the atmosphere friendly, and in late spring, the roadside garden near the front porch is lovely.

### *Tupper Lake*

**THE PARK RESTAURANT**
518-359-7556.
320 Park St., Tupper Lake (Rte. 30, near Sunmount Developmental Center).
Open year-round.
Price: Moderate.
Cuisine: American.
Serving: L, D.
Credit Cards: AE, MC, V.
Handicap Access: Yes.

The cover of the Park's menu announces that your hosts are Bucky (Clark) and Leroy (Pickering), two pillars of Tupper Lake society, and there are no pretensions here, just good, solid family chow. The dining room is rather nondescript; what does attract your attention is a generous salad bar featuring homemade bread, all kinds of greenery, assorted toppings like pepperoni slices, black olives and cheddar cheese, plus tasty bean, potato, and macaroni salads.

On Thursday nights, there's an all-you-can-eat fried shrimp special, which is understandably quite popular. Sunday afternoons feature the Adirondack Buffet, beginning at 3 p.m., with baked turkey, roast pork, prime rib, and so forth. In late spring and through the summer, the Park's about the only place around where you can get honest-to-gosh fresh bullhead for dinner; if you've never tried it, think catfish from a cold, clear Adirondack lake, and you get the picture.

There's a wine list with a good assortment of reasonably priced German, French, and California wines to round out your meal.

**THE PINE GROVE**
518-359-6669.
166 Main St., Tupper Lake (Rte. 3, just past Leroy's Auto Sales).
Open year-round.
Price: Inexpensive to Moderate.
Cuisine: Italian, American, Mexican.
Serving: L, D.
Credit Cards: MC, V.
Handicap Access: Inquire.

For a dozen or so years, the Philippi family has run this cheerful little restaurant on the north edge of town. There's a pleasant barroom with tables, and nonsmokers eat in a modest wood-paneled room with a fireplace that looks and feels very much like someone's living room.

Homemade Italian food is the Pine Grove's strong suit, but the menu offers a surprising array of ethnic dishes, from Cajun shrimp to chicken fajitas, prepared with fresh ingredients and the right amount of zest. The veal cordon bleu Italiano comes with a side of spaghetti and homemade garlic bread; the peppery, slow-simmered tomato sauce is very good. Homemade soups are delicious, too. For dessert, there are big wedges of pie or squares of homemade cake, and you can savor real espresso served in a tiny glass mug with the correct twist of lemon on the side.

**THE ROSE RESTAURANT**
518-359-9621.
Cliff Ave., behind the
Bank of Tupper Lake.
Open year-round.
Price: Inexpensive to
Moderate.
Cuisine: American.
Serving: B, L, D.
Credit Cards: MC, V.
Handicap Access: Yes.

Formerly the Miss Tupper Diner, the Rose has recently been renovated into a nice-looking but rather narrow restaurant. Mirrors all along one wall help give a feeling of spaciousness, but the building still has that distinctly linear feel of a diner.

The food is a cut above the usual diner fare, though: when the waitress says the special is fresh scallops, she means it. You can get them lightly breaded and fried, and they're sweet and tasty. There are homemade Italian dishes on the menu, plus steaks, chicken, and fish. The plump burgers are a good choice for lunch and dinner, but save room for the pie. The coconut cream comes under a cloud of meringue, and it's heavenly.

*From the second-story deck at the Wawbeek, you can see down Upper Saranac Lake to Ampersand Mountain.*

Tom Warrington

**THE WAWBEEK**
518-359-2656.
Panther Mtn. Rd., off Rte.
30, Tupper Lake.
Closed: Mar.; weekdays in
winter and spring. Open
daily Memorial Day—
Labor Day.
Price: Expensive.
Cuisine: Country French,
Contemporary
American.
Serving: D year-round; B,
L July—Aug.
Credit Cards: MC, V.

The gorgeous view of Upper Saranac Lake from the upstairs deck at the Wawbeek would be reason enough to seek out the place; happily, the menu, service, and ambience of this out-of-the-way restaurant are every bit as appealing as the scenery.

The woodsy Adirondack-style lodge, once part of a boys' camp, was built in 1907. There are screen porches on two levels, a lovely dining room downstairs, and a cozy bar/lounge upstairs with its own fireplace. The architectural highlight is a huge stone fireplace with a downstairs hearth. It divides into two chimneys, forming a graceful arch as the stonework approaches the second floor; the stair-

Reservations:
  Recommended.
Handicap Access: Side door.
Special Features:
  Fireplaces; wonderful
  old Adirondack build-
  ing; lake view.

case leading to the lounge splits into two flights and intertwines with the fireplace, and there's a beautiful little window set into the wall behind the chimney so that natural light washes over all.

The menu is ambitious and imaginative. Appetizers, which change frequently, may include escargot Bourguignon, duck paté, or mushrooms stuffed with spinach and sausage. Entrees range from exotic offerings like barbecued quail, buffalo steaks, or venison to prime aged beef, chicken, and veal à la Bolognese or saltimbocca. Fresh fish and seafood are nicely done, and may appear on the evening's blackboard as grilled, blackened, sautéed, or poached, with a variety of sauces. The wine list contains an ample selection of domestic, French, and Italian wines. Rich desserts — tortes, tarts, cheesecakes, and strudels — are worth savoring slowly as the stars come out over the lake.

## *Wanakena*

**THE PINE CONE
  RESTAURANT**
315-848-2121.
Ranger School Rd.,
  Wanakena.
Closed: Mon.
Price: Moderate.
Cuisine: American.
Serving: L, D.
Credit Cards: None.
Reservations: No.
Handicap Access: Street-
  level entry.

**P**aul Alford is a graduate of the New York State Ranger School, and he's been back in the neighborhood for several years running a tavern/restaurant that offers plain but good cooking. The most popular entree is prime rib, and it's a generous portion; the menu also includes steaks, nice beer-battered haddock, and chicken. The service here is fleet and friendly. The Pine Cone sponsors barbecues and pig roasts in its lakeside pavilion; you can arrive by boat if you choose, and dock by the back door.

A tip: hang on to your hat when you walk in the door, or better yet, leave that favorite cap in the car. The ceiling here is festooned with hundreds (700? 900? lots of them, anyway) of hats, at least some of which, we assume, were gladly volunteered.

## CENTRAL AND SOUTHWESTERN ADIRONDACKS

### *Big Moose*

**BIG MOOSE STATION**
315-357-3525.
Big Moose Rd., Big Moose,
  about 8 miles north of
  Eagle Bay, off Rte. 28.
Closed: Mon.; Apr. and
  Nov.
Price: Inexpensive.
Cuisine: American diner.

**B**ig Moose Station is just that: the former railroad depot at Big Moose. And as the establishment's motto says, "The train may not stop here any longer, but you can." And you should.

Barbara and Jim Morgan run this charming breakfast-and-lunch place located about 10 miles north of Eagle Bay. They keep the menu simple and concentrate on quality; expect fresh-baked

Serving: B, L.
Credit Cards: None.
Handicap Access: No.

bread sliced at least half an inch thick, fresh fruit, and healthy portions for hearty appetites. The station's as near to the original as possible, decorated with memorabilia from the Adirondack Railroad's 90 years of service.

Jim's Louisiana boyhood surfaces every once in a while, and there'll be a Cajun special on the menu. Barbara's desserts are very good. You can get the usual breakfast fare here — eggs, home fries, flapjacks, French toast — and lunch things like homemade soup or chili, burgers, sandwiches.

The Morgans, who live above the restaurant in the old stationmaster's quarters, consider the entire building their home. When you come to eat, you've entered their house, and you'll be treated like a special guest, one they've been just waiting to see.

**BIG MOOSE INN**
315-357-2042.
Big Moose Rd., Big Moose, about 6 miles north of Eagle Bay, off Rte. 28.
Closed: Apr.
Price: Moderate to Expensive.
Cuisine: American, Seafood, Continental.
Serving: L, D.
Credit Cards: AE, MC, V.
Handicap Access: Yes.
Reservations: Recommended.

Ask anybody who lives between Otter Lake and Blue Mountain Lake where they go for anniversaries, birthdays, and celebratory dinners, and chances are they'll reply, "Big Moose Inn." Sometimes — in the dead of winter when the road seems endless, for example — it's an adventure getting here.

Bonnie and Doug Bennett run a nice place. The bar, which is festooned with thousands of credit cards on its ceiling, has quiet booths and nooks if you want to enjoy a sandwich; the living room has deep couches and a fireplace if you need to wait a moment for a table. In nice weather, you can linger on a deck near the water, which is staffed, it seems, by a flock of bold mallards who are happy to take a few pieces of bread in exchange for entertaining you. The dining room is big, with one section looking out over the lake and another that seems to be where larger groups end up. It can be noisy here, especially if the restaurant is full.

The extensive menu offers good steaks, lots of seafood (scallops, shrimp scampi, broiled crab claws, and combination platters), roast duck (no, not any local ones), veal Oscar, chicken cordon bleu, lamb chops, and seafood-and-beef combinations. Desserts are tasty, with peanut-butter pie a specialty of the house.

## Blue Mountain Lake

**POTTER'S RESTAURANT**
518-352-7664.
Rtes. 28 and 30, at the "Y" in the road, Blue Mountain Lake.
Closed: Sept.—June.

The dining room here is about as Adirondack as you can get: tucked under the rafters there are a mint-condition guideboat and a beautiful birch-bark canoe; a zooful of stuffed creatures, from moose to caribou to beaver to white-tail deer, inhabits the

Price: Moderate.
Cuisine: American.
Serving: B, L, D.
Credit Cards: AE, D, MC, V.
Reservations:
    Recommended for din-
    ner.
Handicap. Access: Yes.

walls. Here and there you'll find antique rustic furniture (check out the hallways), hand-colored photographs, historic maps, embroidered samplers, old Blue Willow china. Thanks to the cathedral ceiling, space is bright and breezy even on a muggy summer day. There are windows overlooking the lake on two sides, and you can arrive by boat if you choose. The dining room is so wonderful, in fact, that you leave wishing that the food was just a little bit better, so that you could wow a few friends with the whole experience.

Lunch is a good bet here; try the Reuben, turkey club, or French dip sandwiches; the cheeseburger; or the tasty, chunky New England clam chowder. The dinner menu hasn't changed in years, with filet mignon or prime rib being dependable choices. On Monday nights there's a buffet and a salad bar. Earnest and attentive college kids take good care of the tables.

## Indian Lake

**OAK BARREL RESTAURANT AND TAVERN**
518-648-5115.
Main St., Indian Lake (next
    to the Grand Union).
Closed: Nov.—Apr.
Price: Moderate.
Cuisine: American, Italian.
Serving: L, D.
Credit Cards: MC, V.
Handicap Access: Yes.

Princeton alumni take note: the famous Old Nassau bar has come to its final resting place in Indian Lake. Although the bar's been in town for years, its carved oak columns and arches were refinished only recently. It's a beaut. Once you've admired the bar, look up on the top shelf and you'll see another marvel — a cross-section of a tree that contains a horseshoe wrapped in a scarf. A local lumberjack cut the tree and discovered that wonder, which was featured in "Ripley's Believe It Or Not" back in the 1960s.

Cathy and Tom Scully offer an extensive menu at this old but pleasant roadhouse, a menu that presents a few new ideas each season, thanks to Tom's visits to workshops at the Culinary Institute of America. For appetizers there are portions of fettucini Alfredo and shrimp scampi, along with fried fare like stuffed mushrooms, chicken wings and potato skins.

Entrees include shrimp or chicken poached in wine and prepared without any added fat; veal dishes; grilled and sautéed fish and seafood; steaks and prime rib; and one of the house specialties, chicken Elegante, which is prepared with a breast of chicken, a petite piece of beef fillet, mushrooms, and sour cream. Marinated Black Diamond steak is another specialty. The Oak Barrel also dishes out a good pizza. There's a children's menu, too.

A few of the dinner offerings are available at lunch, along with juicy charbroiled burgers, club sandwiches, and homemade soups. Conversely, several of the lunch offerings are also an option for dinner. The dining room's not at all fancy so you can come as you are.

**WILDERNESS LODGE**
518-648-5995.
Starbuck Rd., off Big
  Brook Rd., off Rte. 30,
  Indian Lake.
Closed: Mon.—Tues. in
  summer; Mon.—Thurs.
  in winter.
Price: Moderate to
  Expensive.
Cuisine: American.
Serving: D, SB.
Credit Cards: AE, CB, D,
  DC, MC, V.
Reservations: Required.
Handicap Access: Street-
  level entry.
Special Features: Fireplace;
  vegetarian dishes.

Portion control, cholesterol, and the idea of eat-ing "light" are alien concepts here. Dinners are vast and rich, so Wilderness Lodge has a devoted following. Beef and seafood are the highlights, with nearly endless combinations of surf and turf: porterhouse steak and scallops, prime rib and stuffed shrimp, "Adirondack Cut" Delmonico steak (enormous!) with twin lobster tails. The seafood platters for two or more diners include frog legs, stuffed clams, fresh baked fish, sautéed shrimp, scallops, and rock lobster tail; the "plat-ters" are actually full-size serving trays.

There are appetizers on the menu, such as scal-lop and bacon bites, but unless you haven't eaten in weeks, skip the preliminaries. All meals come with a fruit cup (canned), salad bar (mainly iceberg lettuce), homemade soup (usually good), a basket of giant baking-powder biscuits, potato, family-style vegetables, and parfait for dessert. Service can be slow and stressed on a crowded night, but you may well appreciate a leisurely pace in order to digest your meal.

The dining room, dominated by a big stone fireplace, also doubles as a gallery for some unique art — pictorial windows and lamps made of thinly cut slices of native rocks that resemble stained glass, but with more complex colors and patterns. There's no liquor license at Wilderness Lodge, so guests are encouraged to bring their own wine and beer. Brunch, with excellent Belgian waffles, cheese omelets, puffy French toast, and luncheon fare, is available on some weekends in spring and fall, by reservation only.

## Inlet

**THE LOON SALOON**
315-357-5666.
Rte. 28 (on the South Shore
  Rd. corner), Inlet.
Closed: Wed.—Thurs. in
  fall and spring. Open
  daily in summer and
  winter.
Price: Inexpensive to
  Moderate.
Cuisine: American, Italian.
Serving: L, D. Late-night
  menu from 10 to mid-
  night.
Credit Cards: MC, V.

The Loon Saloon has no pretensions. What it does have is a pleasant dining room with a fireplace and food like Mother made before there were TV dinners and microwave ovens. The Loon's owners, Midge Daiker and Ann and Jim Dunn, have found a real gem in Theresa Taylor, the chef, who says she learned to cook from her grandmother, and no, she isn't interested in short-cuts.

Theresa bakes her own bread, like her grand-mother did, forming it into small loaves that diners pick up from the salad bar. For the homemade bread, there's homemade honey butter. The salad

Handicap Access: Ramp available in summer and fall (removed in winter).

bar has plenty of assorted fresh vegetables; the house dressing is a creamy peppercorn.

There's an extensive list of entrees, from pasta carbonara and various fettucini combinations to ribs, chops, steaks, and seafood. Some special treats offered from time to time include homemade lasagna, with a delicious slow-simmered sauce; spicy barbecued chicken and ribs; and moist roast turkey with homemade dressing, real mashed potatoes, and rich gravy. A superb dessert is Grandma's made-from-scratch Ambrosia Cake, three layers high, frosted with a cream cheese icing that melts in the mouth.

Way too much food, even for a cold winter's night, we discovered, and no one can leave the place without one of those styrofoam containers that says "Here's lunch for tomorrow!"

In case you devour tomorrow's lunch at midnight tonight, the Loon is open for lunch, too, with good burgers, homemade soups, some pasta dishes, and grilled chicken breast.

### SEVENTH LAKE HOUSE
315-357-6028.
Rte. 28, two miles east of Inlet.
Closed: Nov.—Christmas.
Price: Moderate to Expensive.
Cuisine: Contemporary American.
Serving: L (winter only), D.
Credit Cards: MC, V.
Reservations: Recommended.
Handicap Access: Street-level entry.
Special Features: Fireplace; vegetarian entrees; gourmet retail carry-out foods; catering.

Old-timers remember this place as the Beaver Lodge, a tavern marked by its parade of hundreds of shoes and boots nailed to the walls; for several decades, patrons gladly donated to the exhibit, then left the bar hours later in stocking feet. When chef/owner Jim Holt took over in 1989, the first thing he did was take all the dusty, stained footgear to the dump. It was a step in the right direction.

Holt came to the central Adirondacks after cooking at Vail's renowned Gasthof Gramshamer and Kira Club, and working as a private chef in California. With his experience and imagination, he's turned a grimy old joint into one of the best restaurants in the park. The place looks elegant but not prissy, with candles, fresh flowers, and linen on the tables; large picture windows face the lake. There's a canopied deck for dining out in the summer. The service is genuinely friendly and professional; the food is superb.

An especially nice touch is that the menus reflect the seasons. In spring and summer, there are blackened fish and grilled chicken dishes, cold soups, dinner salads, and fresh seafood pastas with light — but not trite — sauces. Winter brings heartier fare: plenty of aged steaks, broiled lamb chops, roast duck, roast pork with apple cider sauce, and fettucini with beef tenderloin, napped with a heavenly sauce of Gorgonzola cheese, tomatoes, garlic, and pine nuts. Appetizers include smoked trout with Dijon horseradish sauce,

*Your table is ready at Seventh Lake House, Inlet.*

Nancie Battaglia

shrimp ravioli, and different varieties of foccacia. The house dessert list usually features frozen amaretto mousse, chocolate gateau, apple strudel, and tarts baked on the premises. The wine list has a good selection of California wines at reasonable prices.

## *Long Lake*

**ADIRONDACK HOTEL**
518-624-4700.
Rte. 30, near the Long
   Lake bridge.
Closed: Christmas Day.
Price: Moderate.
Cuisine: American,
   Continental.
Serving: B, L, D.
Credit Cards: AE, DC, MC,
   V.

This rambling four-story hotel has been a Long Lake landmark since the 1870s; the lobby, with its turned-spindle clerk's booth, and the dining room, with a huge stone fireplace, crystal chandeliers, and stamped-tin ceiling, both date back to the turn of the century. There are not one, but two full-size stuffed black bears, plus myriad beavers, raccoons, deer, and other critters in various poses throughout the downstairs.

Reservations:
  Recommended for main
    dining room in summer.
Handicap Access: No.
Special Features: Historic
    building interior; fire-
    place.

For years the Adirondack suffered from peculiar management, and was open sporadically with a hit-or-miss menu. Now, the bar, dining room, and hotel have been taken in hand by veteran restaurateurs Art and Carol Young. The food and service are dependably good now.

There are two dinner menus, one offering mainly bar food, such as thick-crust pizzas from a brick oven, prime rib sandwiches, fish fry, spaghetti, and burgers. The other menu is more formal and substantial, but still not too fussy. The pork medallions with sautéed apples, the chicken breast served on a bed of spinach, and the scallops in puff pastry are the more imaginative selections from chef Anthony Liandarkis. On the appetizer list, the seafood fettucine is sizable enough for a meal.

Nancie Battaglia

*The sunny Victorian dining room at the Adirondack Hotel, Long Lake.*

A nice feature of the "Big A" is that you can have a complete dinner from the fancier menu brought to you in the cozy, pine-paneled bar, perhaps to your table next to the woodstove. Or, if you're feeling like making it an occasion, you can go for the Victorian-era dining room, linen tablecloths, fresh flowers, and all.

**THE COBBLESTONE**
518-624-6331.
Rte. 30, Long Lake.
Open year-round.
Price: Inexpensive to
  Moderate.
Cuisine: American, Italian.
Serving: B, L, D May—
  Oct.; D only Nov.—Apr.
Credit Cards: AE, DC, MC,
  V.
Reservations: No.
Handicap Access: Ramp in
  back.

This former roadhouse had a raucous past (strippers during hunting season, bar fights, etc.); but since 1983, Joe Tokarz and his family have turned the barn-red tavern into a quiet, respectable family restaurant. There are no surprises on tap at the Cobblestone: just good meals at reasonable prices in an airy, bright dining room.

In the summer, the 'Stone is open every single day, for every meal. Breakfast offerings include the usual eggs, hotcakes, and such; for lunch, there is a variety of cold and hot sandwiches, homemade soups, and salad plates. There's a full bar open from noon on.

The Friday night fish fry (haddock in light, crisp beer batter) is quite popular with locals and visitors alike; on Saturdays, the special is prime rib. At dinner you can also choose from lighter fare, such as hot sandwiches or burgers, pizza, or Buffalo-style chicken wings; Italian dishes, like baked manicotti; or full entrees, from steak to swordfish, salmon, and shish kebab. A favorite, filling meal is the Tavern Special: a mound of sliced roast beef covered with mozzarella cheese, sauteed peppers, and onions, resting on a platform of Italian bread. One of those, and you've got plenty of fuel for a day of skiing, hiking, or paddling.

**THE LAKESIDE**
518-624-9791.
Rtes. 28 and 30, Long
  Lake.
Open year-round.
Price: Inexpensive to
  Moderate.
Serving: B, L, D in sum-
  mer; D only fall—
  spring.
Credit Cards: MC, V.
Reservations: No.
Handicap Access: Street-
  level entry.
Special Features: Annual
  pig roast in Sept., occa-
  sional live music.

Go past the bar to the sunny dining room overlooking the lake, and don't sit near the jukebox unless you're prepared to talk loudly. With that advice in mind, you can enjoy decent family dining at the Lakeside. The pizza is quite good, but probably the best item on the menu is the Lakesider: a thick, juicy, charbroiled hamburg that comes with a fistful of curly fries and costs less than four bucks.

The menu includes lots of sandwiches, on "wheels" (Kaiser rolls) or "logs" (torpedo rolls), including the Fritzwich, a combination of ham, turkey, and roast beef on a grilled log, and a Monte Cristo. There's this, that, and the other fried and served in baskets, battered cheese sticks or mushrooms, and some barbecued entrees. The Lakeside has a half-dozen different beers on tap, with a Canadian brew a good complement to the Lakesider.

### North Creek

**COPPERFIELD INN**
518-251-2500.
224 Main St., North Creek.
Closed: Mon.—Tues. in
　winter and spring;
　month of Nov.
Price: Moderate to
　Expensive.
Cuisine: Contemporary,
　American.
Serving: B, L, D.
Credit Cards: AE, DC, MC,
　V.
Reservations:
　Recommended.
Handicap Access: Yes.

Step through the doorway of this brand-new, opulent hotel, and you get the distinct impression you're not in the Adirondacks anymore. Owner Eliot Monter has spared no expense at the Copperfield, which is evident in the marble floors, gleaming woodwork, chandeliers, and other details that seem more reminiscent of Williamsburg than the North Country.

The food's good, but not quite up to the standards set by the elegant foyer. Lunch is definitely a cut above other central Adirondack options, with hearty sandwiches and soups served in a subdued, tasteful setting.

Dinners range from prime beef to orange roughy Florentine, shrimp en brochette, and chicken with various herbs and sauces, competently prepared. On some week nights, special menus emphasizing German cuisine (sauerbraten, Wiener schnitzel) or pasta are offered. The salad bar, with marinated herring, red potato salad, hearts of palm, and other exotic trimmings, is probably the best in the central Adirondacks. The trademark dessert here is Mud Pie, a great big wedge of coffee ice cream with layers of fudge; it's more than enough for two.

There's a nice little bar with comfy couches and cocktail tables adjacent to the dining room, and a good selection of California and imported wines.

**SMITH'S RESTAURANT**
518-251-9965.
Main St., across from the
　Copperfield Inn, North
　Creek.
Open year-round.
Price: Inexpensive.
Cuisine: American,
　German.
Serving: B, L, D.
Credit Cards: CB, DC, MC,
　V.

Anna Smith, a young girl from Germany, landed in North Creek in the twenties because the town was the end of the line for the Delaware & Hudson. For half a century she presided over her Main Street restaurant, baking heavenly pies and rolls and introducing townspeople to good home cooking à la Anna. Now her son, Francis, a graduate of the Culinary Institute of America, is at the helm, and the food is still comfortable fare from an earlier era, as you'd expect when you walk in the door.

The walls are knotty pine, decorated with twenties-vintage lithographs of fish and fishermen. Booths line both sides of the main dining room. The light is bright, folks come and go, so this is not the place for a romantic dinner for two, but after an outdoorsy kind of day, Smith's satisfies.

The New England clam chowder is excellent. The knockwurst comes on a mountain of sauerkraut, with a plateful of buttery, peppery spaetzel; the sauerbraten is very good. Roast turkey and pork are the real items, with deep brown gravy smothering the authentic stuffing and mashed potatoes. Save room for at least one piece of pie: banana cream, chocolate cream, coconut cream, apple, raspberry, blueberry, or better yet, have pie for breakfast and get your day off to a good start.

### *North River*

**GARNET HILL LODGE**
518-251-2821.
Thirteenth Lake Rd.,
    North River, (4 miles off
    Rte. 28; follow the signs
    when you get to
    Thirteenth Lake).
Open year-round.
Serving: D.
Price: Moderate to
    Expensive.
Cuisine: Country,
    American, Continental.
Credit Cards: MC, V.
Handicap Access: Yes.
Special Features: Fireplace;
    ski lodge.

The Log House, which dates back to the 1930s, is the centerpiece of George and Mary Heim's cross-country ski complex near Thirteenth Lake. There are 50 km of groomed ski trails on the property, plus miles of trails on adjacent state lands, and after a day in the woods there's nothing like a hearty meal at Garnet Hill.

The lodge has an enormous garnet fireplace flanked by comfortable couches and Old Hickory chairs, with dining tables a few feet away. The building meanders on, with a ping-pong table in one room, a library in another, a pool table near the entry, and more dining tables on a glassed-in porch. This is a casual place where you don't need to change out of your ski togs for dinner.

Recently Garnet Hill's menu was revamped to offer some low-fat, lighter fare such as vegetables marinara served over whole-wheat pasta, and oven-broiled fresh fish. Entrees change frequently so that dinner visitors and guests at the lodge have several choices; on Fridays, for example, you can get New York strip steak, several seafood dishes, and basil lemon chicken. On Wednesdays, London broil, pork tenderloin, and fettucini Alfredo are among the entrees.

There's a full bar here, and service is usually good. On busy holiday weekends when the lodge is full, things can get a bit hectic, though, and food can be slow coming out of the kitchen. It's a good idea to call ahead.

**HIGHWINDS INN**
518-251-3760.
Barton Mines Rd., off Rte.
    28 at North River
    General Store, North
    River.

Driving up and up the Barton Mines Road you may start to wonder exactly where you're headed; after five miles of forest, you find yourself in a large clearing cradling New York's highest settlement, overlooking what was once the country's

Closed: Apr., Nov.
Price: Expensive.
Cuisine: Contemporary
American, Continental.
Serving: D.
Credit Cards: MC, V.
Reservations: Required.
Handicap Access: Yes,
with assistance.
Special Features: Fireplace;
sitting room for cock-
tails; mountain view.

largest garnet mine. The inn was built for the president of the company, and besides offering four wonderful rooms for overnight guests, dinner is available to nonguests on weekends in the winter and daily in the summer.

The menu changes frequently; the food is consistently excellent. (Families with small children may find the service, although quite competent, a bit slow.) Appetizers include escargots, shrimp with salsa and cream sauce, duck paté, eggplant crêpes, or a smoked fish plate. Usually there's a choice of four or five entrees each night, such as veal Barton (veal scallops filled with vegetable paté and napped with roasted red-pepper and brown veal sauces), Calvados chicken (breast of chicken with currants and apples in a Calvados cream sauce), fresh fish, steaks, duck, or pork. Desserts are prepared on the premises, with brownie sundaes and other heavenly chocolate concoctions that alone are worth the trip.

Highwinds Inn does not have a liquor license, but guests are encouraged to bring their own. Another bit of advice: plan to be at your table in the dining room well before sunset; the view to the west, over the Siamese Ponds Wilderness Area, is spectacular.

## *Mayfield*

**POUR JIM'S CHECK INN**
518-661-7635.
Rte. 30, Mayfield.
Open year-round.
Price: Inexpensive to
Moderate.
Cuisine: Tavern.
Serving: L, D.
Credit Cards: None.
Handicap Access: Street-
level entry.

The glass-block entryway gives you a clue as to Pour Jim's charms: the tavern is stuck in some pre-Jetsonian time warp, with curvilinear beige naugahyde booths, arched doorways, an acoustic tile ceiling that rises in several tiers, and a nifty back bar with colored lights. In some trendy yupscale neighborhood, folks would beat a path to a place like this simply for the decor. Pour Jim's does serve dinners (pork chops, steaks, and such), and the burgers are plump and juicy, but a highlight of the menu is the chicken wings. They're fresh, succulent, and thinly coated with a stingingly pungent hot sauce; a dozen will set you back $3.50, and that includes celery sticks and blue-cheese dressing to temper the heat.

**THE ROKADAGA**
518-661-6226.
Rte. 30, Mayfield.
Closed: Late Sept.—early
June.

From the terrace of the Rokadaga on a hazy summer day, the far shore of Great Sacandaga Lake shimmers in the distance. The water sparkles, the breezes blow — finally summer has come to the

Price: Moderate to
  Expensive.
Cuisine: American,
  Mexican.
Serving: L, D.
Credit Cards: MC, V.
Handicap Access: Yes.

North Country — and here's a lovely spot in which to enjoy it. There's ample seating on the terrace; the lakeside walls of the bar and dining areas are glass, with the best views to be had from the booths on the dining room's upper level. The Rokadaga is a new establishment, and its stylish ambience is a rarity in this part of the Adirondacks.

The menu is fairly simple: appetizers include Arizona cheese crisp (a flour tortilla topped with Colby Jack cheese, mild chili peppers, fresh tomatoes, and black olives), barbecue shrimp, nachos, skewered scallops wrapped in bacon with honey mustard sauce. For entrees, choices are London broil sandwich, fajitas, grilled chicken sandwich, seafood linguine, grilled pork tenderloin, steaks, and veal. The service is quite good.

## *Northville*

**ALHAMBRA DINER**
518-863-6367.
163 N. Main St.,
  Northville.
Open year-round.
Price: Inexpensive to
  Moderate.
Cuisine: American.
Serving: B (weekends only
  in winter, daily in sum-
  mer), L, D.
Credit Cards: None.
Handicap Access: No.

Originally a boxcar diner, the Alhambra opened in 1928. It was moved across the street and remodeled by its present owners, Phyllis and John Sullivan; the restaurant now contains several rooms, several levels, and several decors. The dining room is comfortable and clean; walk on through it and down a few steps to the cozy ski-lodge-style bar with its congenial booths and fireplace, then turn right to enter the pretty green-and-lavender garden room (often used for wedding parties).

Food and service are good, prices are reasonable (the average dinner entree costs $11.95), and Phyllis is on the premises, maintaining quality without cutting too many corners. "It's my kid," she says of the Alhambra, "and I love it." The homemade soup is good; the cheesecake is very, very good. Specials such as stuffed manicotti, grilled pork chops, or chicken Parmesan are offered daily. One caveat: there are stairs, tight corners, and very small bathrooms, making access difficult at best for mobility-impaired visitors.

Be sure to ask Phyllis about the ghost.

**NORTHAMPTON DINER**
518-863-2567.
Rte. 30, north of Mayfield,
  Northville.
Closed: Mon.
Price: Inexpensive.
Cuisine: American.

On the outside, the Northampton Diner looks like a prefab house. On the inside, it is a classic diner-car, with two long marble counters facing the grill and the stainless-steel wall behind it. The refrigerator case is cherry wood; the floor is made of little mosaic tiles. Your entrance is announced

Serving: B, L, D.
Credit Cards: None.
Handicap Access: Inquire.

by the sleigh bells hanging on the door, and it is immediately apparent that this is a family-run business. The Morehouses — Harold, Donna, Jim, and Darlena — seem to enjoy working together, and the atmosphere is friendly and warm, with much joking between the owners and the customers. This place obviously has a strong local following.

The food is typical diner fare, nothing special, but the prices are very low, and the coffee is good and generously poured. Breakfast is served all day, dinner until 7 p.m. on Thursday and Friday in the off-season and until 9 every night in the summer. There is a nonsmoking room in the back, but stay in the dining car — that's where the action is.

## *Old Forge/Thendara*

**THE FARM RESTAURANT**
315-369-6199.
Rte. 28, near the Moose
  River bridge, Old
  Forge/Thendara.
Closed: Mid-Mar.—May 1,
  late Oct.—mid-Dec.
Price: Inexpensive.
Cuisine: American.
Serving: B, L.
Credit Cards: None.
Handicap Access: Yes,
  bathrooms too.

The Farm got its start in the seventies as a fruit stand; for twenty years, Bev and Frank Burnap have presided over its transformation into a top-notch place to get a family meal. The restaurant is huge (it seats a hundred quite comfortably), but not cavernous; the walls and ceilings are covered with antique advertising art, obscure implements from logging and farming days, and historic prints and photographs.

Breakfast is available until 3 p.m., including big, cheesy omelets, blueberry pancakes, cinnamon

*The Farm Restaurant in Old Forge is like a museum with a menu.*

B. Folwell

French toast, and the usual eggs and home fries. For lunch, the soup's substantial and homemade, as is the chili, which comes topped with New York State cheddar. The bacon cheeseburger and Reuben are winners, but all the sandwiches are good. For kids, there are little pizzas and burgers and grilled hot dogs. Domestic wine and beer are available with lunch.

**THE MAPLE DINER**
No phone.
Main St., Old Forge.
Closed: Sun., Mon.
Price: Inexpensive.
Cuisine: Diner.
Serving: B, L.
Credit Cards: None.
Handicap Access: No.

Eating at the Maple Diner (which everyone knows as Jake's) is a trip back in time. It isn't manufactured nostalgia, it's just plain old, and the charm you find here is absolutely authentic.

There are maybe 15 stools at the counter. A small dining room at the rear has had a "This Section Closed" sign on the first table for as long as anyone can remember.

From early in the morning until about 11:30 a.m. is Shirley Berkowitz's shift. Singlehandedly she dishes out eggs, bacon, ham, sausage, French toast, and great repartee. When lunchtime rolls around, Jake comes down from the couple's upstairs apartment and takes over.

Jake knows his eggs and pea soup — quite possibly the best pea soup you'll find in the Adirondacks, or anywhere else. Shirley started it early in the morning, but Jake puts the finishing touches on it. To go with that soup, Jake will cut a fresh ham sandwich off the home-baked ham, or maybe a slab right off from-the-oven beef roast. Either way, it may remind you of the way you once took meat out of the refrigerator and made your own sandwich. None of this deli-sliced, shaved stuff.

Jake's about as crusty as they come; tales abound concerning his treatment of customers. It's said he once took a plate of scrambled eggs away from a diner and dumped them in the garbage just because that person had the nerve to put catsup on them. You don't mess with Jake's cooking. You don't rush

*Jake Berkowitz presides at the Maple Diner, Old Forge.*

Nancie Battaglia

Jake, either. At 82 years old, Jake could put many younger folks to shame with his efficient movements behind the counter, but he does things his way: one customer at a time, wait your turn. As we've heard Jake say to a group of tourists once, "You'd probably be happier down the street." And that was that.

## PINOCCHIO'S KITCHEN
315-369-3754.
Main St., Old Forge (in the Ferns Building).
Open year-round.
Price: Inexpensive to Moderate.
Cuisine: Italian.
Serving: L, D.
Credit Cards: None.
Reservations: No; you may have to wait for a table in summer.
Handicap Access: No.

Eating at Pinocchio's Kitchen is a little like going to your favorite uncle's house: you always know what to expect, and you're seldom disappointed. The food is going to be plentiful and tasty; you are going to recognize most of the guests.

Joe Petracca rules the place from his spot in the kitchen. He's in full view of the dining room, and he performs with a flourish as he drains hot pasta or ladles out his always fresh sauce. This is hearty Italian food, like homemade lasagna, ziti, manicotti. The white sauce is as good as the red, and if fresh clams aren't available, you won't find "Linguine with Clams" printed on the blackboard that serves as the menu at Joe's.

When it comes to pizza, Joe is a master. He also has a special trick of forming fresh pizza dough into good-size balls and baking it for his customers. A warm loaf arrives with the salads.

Service is efficient and when it's busy Joe often brings the food out himself. If it happens to be a quiet night, Joe may come out from his kitchen and sit down to discuss philosophy, theology, English literature, or any number of topics on his mind.

## SLICKERS
315-369-3002.
Rte. 28, Old Forge (next to Tourist Information Center).
Open: Daily.
Price: Inexpensive.
Cuisine: American, Tavern, Pizza.
Serving: L, D.
Credit cards: MC, V.
Special Features: Sandwiches and pizza available after 11 p.m.

Slickers is the kind of place you go to when you don't feel like dressing up, you aren't sure what you want to eat, and you wouldn't mind running into folks you know. The bright yellow building is a friendly welcome, and inside you find three different dining rooms with very different atmospheres. There's the porch, especially nice when the sun shines; a section of cozy booths facing out on Rte. 28; and the back room, which looks into the bar and also faces Old Forge Pond.

The food isn't fancy, but it's hearty, hot, and plentiful. If there is a better hamburger in the Adirondacks, we haven't found it yet. Forget your quarter-pounder: Slickers only deals in seven-ounce servings of aged, lean beef piled high with lettuce, tomato, and sweet onions. That's basic. There's also sautéed mushrooms, bacon, and a choice of provolone, cheddar, or blue cheese. Or consider the nacho platter: chili and cheddar cheese on a bed of tortilla chips, garnished with lettuce, tomatoes, sour cream, and jalapeños. On a recent visit, two diners were discussing the relative merits of chips with guacamole vs. salsa. The waitress settled the matter — try them both. She brought half orders of each, and plenty of chips to settle the debate.

Slickers is popular with nearly everyone in Old Forge and the surrounding area; during summer and on snowy winter days the place is jumping. There's a pool table out front that attracts novices and sharks. The tiny bar is often lined four- or five-deep. The ambience of the place is informal, chatty, loose. The food is first-rate, if not gourmet. Nouvelle cuisine has never threatened Slickers; you aren't likely to cross paths with a sun-dried tomato (and you aren't likely to miss it). One final tip: stay away from the "Bug Spray," a Slickers original concoction that combines Midori, rum, and cream of coconut. It's probably better applied to exposed skin to ward off the notorious blackflies.

## VAN AUKEN'S INNE

315-369-3033.
Forge St., Thendara (just off Rte. 28 by the railroad station).
Closed: Mar. 17—May 30; Oct. 15—Dec. 1.
Price: Expensive.
Cuisine: Contemporary American, Continental.
Serving: L, D.
Credit Cards: MC, V.
Handicap Access: Inquire.
Reservations: Recommended.

Just across from the Thendara station of the Adirondack Railroad is a huge old hotel, Van Auken's Inne. The long double-deck porch is inviting; the newly refurbished wood floors and tin ceilings hark back to the times when the train brought passengers every day. Jayne and George Taylor have spent four years restoring the building and fine-tuning the restaurant, creating a very pleasant place in which to have a meal.

Appetizers include smoked Norwegian salmon, baked brie encrusted with almonds, and spicy Cajun shrimp. Entrees from chef Rich Bell such as homemade pasta, excellent fresh fish, and red meats with robust sauces show imagination and flair, and he's currently composing a new menu for winter 1993 that will showcase his signature dishes. Sometimes at Van Auken's it may seem to take a long time for food to come out of the kitchen, but take heart — it means that every plate is getting individual attention.

After a meal, you can wander out on the capacious porch, drink or dessert in hand. If you've timed your visit right, you may be able to watch the train (revived in summer and fall 1992 for excursions in honor of the railroad's and the Adirondack Park's centennials) as it chugs into the station across the way, and get a nostalgic glimpse of how things used to be.

## *Speculator*

**KUNJAMUK CAFE**
518-548-3203.
Old Page Hill Road,
　Speculator (north on
　Route 30 1/4 mile from
　4 Corners, then right on
　Old Page Hill Road 1/2
　mile).
Open daily, year-round.
Price: Inexpensive.
Cuisine: American.
Serving: B, L, D.
Credit Cards: None.
Handicap Access: No.

Nancy Riley's Kunjamuk Cafe isn't the easiest place in the Adirondacks to find. After you turn onto Old Page Hill Road, a dirt road, from Rte. 30, you have to make another right onto another dirt road. The atmosphere is great, though. The place looks like an old Adirondack lodge, which it was, with high natural-wood ceilings and walls.

Food ranges from hamburgers to steaks and it's good home-cooking all the way. The service is excellent; the prices aren't going to break anyone. Kunjamuk breakfasts are huge, with unlimited fresh coffee. For lunch, a thick cheeseburger, accompanied by homemade french fries, tastes great.

After a meal like that, you can sit on the porch, soak up the outdoors, and plan your next adventure.

**HIGGINS HOUSE**
518 548-6445.
Rte. 8, Speculator (just east
　of Speculator 4 Corners).
Open year-round.
Price: Moderate.
Cuisine: American,
　Mexican, Seafood.
Serving: L, D.
Credit Cards: MC, V.
Handicap Access: No.

Higgins House is easy to find right in downtown Speculator, but only if you believe Speculator has a downtown. This quaint Adirondack village of 500 people overlooks aptly named Lake Pleasant, and has some spectacular mountain views.

Try one of the Mexican dishes on the menu for a change of pace from most Central Adirondack dining: the Mexican pizza (a flour tortilla covered

*Tom Higgins takes a break in front of the Higgins House, Speculator.*

Nancie Battaglia

with cheese, salsa, peppers, beans) is especially good, and is so large you probably won't want anything else. If ethnic food isn't to your taste, you'll find the scallops are fresh, tasty, and swimming in butter. Higgins House also dishes out a blue-cheese burger stacked on a Kaiser roll that's fully two inches high.

The service here is friendly and professional. Don't forget dessert — they usually have a selection of homemade treats. A piece of pecan pie topped with whipped cream is just the thing to end a pleasant meal at Higgins House.

**THE INN AT SPECULATOR**
518-548-3811.
Rte. 8, Speculator, 2 miles east of the 4 Corners on Rte. 8.
Open year-round.
Price: Moderate.
Cuisine: American, Seafood.
Serving: L, D.
Credit Cards: AE, MC, V.
Handicap Access: No.

The Inn is in a nice tree-lined grove, with plenty of off-road parking. Lunch here is excellent, and on Thursdays, when the county board is in session, you get free entertainment from the local pols. Try to get a table in the back near a window for some awesome views of Lake Pleasant.

The soups are homemade and quite good; appetizers include tavern-style fried veggies, like cauliflower, potato skins, and onion rings. The dinner menu features pasta dishes, like seafood capellini; several chicken entrees, such as chicken Cynara, which is a chicken breast served with artichoke hearts in a tarragon sauce; several veal specialties; a half-dozen beef offerings, including tenderloin Oscar, slices of tenderloin napped with béarnaise sauce and shrimp. Portions tend to be somewhat smaller than at other places in the neighborhood, so this isn't the place to go if you're ravenous; folks with big appetites may want to stick with something simple, like a steak.

**ZEISER'S**
518-548-7021.
Rte. 30, at the intersection of Rte. 8, Speculator.
Closed: Weekdays in winter.
Price: Expensive.
Cuisine: Continental.
Serving: L, D.
Credit Cards: MC, V.
Reservations: Recommended.
Handicap Access: Street-level entry.

John D. McDonald, the mystery writer, was a regular here, and it's easy to see why. With prints of champion racehorses on the walls, dark wood paneling, and a display of antique and rare Scotch whiskey bottles (including Hankey Bannister, Long John, and Sheep Dip), Zeiser's has the tasteful aura of an old-fashioned men's club. The late John Zeiser was the consummate host; his wife, Genevieve, is the chef and oftentimes the waitress, and the place runs at a seamless, relaxed pace. Zeiser's opened at the four corners in Speculator in 1954.

The menu is small, but the food is carefully prepared. When you're seated in the dining room (also small, with Empire-style chairs and maroon and white linens and drapes), chances are there will be homemade pickled beets or marinated white radishes at your table. Entrees include meltingly tender sauerbraten, aged steaks, half-chicken sauté Genevieve (sautéed in wine and herbs, then finished under the broiler), shrimp Dijonnaise, and pasta. Lamb chops are a frequent offering, and they are plump, succulent, and a very generous helping — far better than what you can get at the neighborhood butcher shop. The dessert list is short, but cakes are homemade.

Zeiser's is also open for lunch, offering a juicy burger, homemade soups, and well-stuffed sandwiches. And there are four guest rooms upstairs, in case you feel like moving in for a while.

### Wells

**THE COUNTRY**
**KITCHEN**
518-924-3771.
Main St. (Rte. 30), Wells.
Closed: Tues.
Price: Inexpensive.
Cuisine: American.
Serving: B, L, D.
Credit Cards: None.
Handicap Access: No.

In Wells, everyone goes to the Country Kitchen. The place could use better parking, but the food is hearty and the prices are low. The menu is mostly simple stuff like good old American hamburgers and apple pie, but everyone raves about it.

For dinner, the fried shrimp is very good, or you can sample a fresh fish fillet. The salads here are full of tomatoes and green peppers, unlike in many places that pad them with watery iceberg lettuce.

Eavesdrop on the natives sitting at the counter, and you'll hear all the local gossip you care to. The service is quick, and you can check out nearby Lake Algonquin following dessert.

## FOOD PURVEYORS

### BAKERIES

**THE BAKERY CAFE**
518-891-2763.
39 Woodruff St., Saranac
   Lake, around the corner
   from the A&P.

Reed VanDenBerghe bakes all kinds of bread, from down-home whole wheat to crusty French baguettes to bagels, plus assorted fruit pies, chocolate truffle cake, hazelnut torte, and almond tart. There's also a selection of lighter sweets including tofu cheesecake, cranberry mousse, and pumpkin chiffon pie, all less than 200 calories per serving.

You can enjoy lunch from the cafe, too, with sandwich choices such as ratatouille topped with provolone, smoked salmon on a bagel, falafel or hummus and vegetables stuffed in a pita pocket, all a cut above the usual. Rolls, pies, muffins, and breads are quite reasonably priced; in warm weather, you can enjoy your sweets or sandwiches in a sidewalk-cafe setting.

**BLUEBIRD BAKERY**
518-623-3301.
10 Hudson St.,

Cinnamon rolls, cheese fans, almond pockets, eclairs, crullers, brownies, doughnuts ... the Bluebird has all that a pastry lover can ask for, and

Warrensburg, near the bandstand.

less — for those of us who crave sugary buns yet feel guilty about gobbling them down, there are "mini meltaways," petite sweets with a cheese filling that offer a small yet satisfying amount of all that good bad stuff. If, on the other hand, you prefer more rather than less, there are big wedges of chocolate mousse cake for a dollar. Open year-round; closed Mondays.

*Currant scones and assorted muffins at Borne & Bread, Ray Brook.*

Nancie Battaglia

**BORNE & BREAD**
518-891-3333.
Rte. 86, Ray Brook.

A true gourmet bread shop perched on a busy highway, Borne & Bread offers a wide array of sweets and savories. The French bread pockets stuffed with pesto, sun-dried tomatoes, and ricotta, or artichokes, fresh tomato, and garlic make a perfect summertime supper; you can call ahead for delicious pizza on homemade foccacia covered with ratatouille, spinach, and other vegetable combinations. Fresh-baked breads such as basil-walnut, hot pepper-cheddar, olive-garlic, and oatmeal-currant are available on different days of the week. Pies, layer cakes, scones, muffins, cookies, croissants, and tea cakes in a kaleidoscope of flavors round out the selection. Prices here reflect the quality of the ingredients, which translates to $3 to $4 for a loaf of bread, but even at these premium rates, popular choices often sell out by late afternoon. Arrive early or call ahead if you've got a hankering for a specific thing. Borne & Bread also does catering for business lunches, tea parties, and dinners. Open daily mid-May—mid-Oct.

**THE DONUT SHOP**
315-357-6421.
Rte. 28, Eagle Bay.

A giant doughnut-shaped sign looms high above this drive-in located on the edge of Eagle Bay, home of the best doughnuts in the central Adirondacks. A couple of hot cinnamon-and-sugar-dipped sinkers and a steaming cup of black coffee make a terrific cheap breakfast. Open May— October; closed Tuesdays.

**JOHN MICHAEL'S OF NORTH CREEK**
518-251-4192.
Main St., North Creek, across from the Grand Union.

Deep, dark "blackout cake" is a specialty here. You can also get authentic prune, apricot, and almond Hamantachen, caraway-and-onion-flavored beer bread, Irish soda bread, brownies, butter cookies, cupcakes, and rolls at very reasonable prices — small cheesecakes are just $3. Closed Mondays.

**LESLIE'S PLACID BAKED GOODS**
518-523-4279.
99 Main St., Lake Placid.

A welcome new addition to Lake Placid's Main Street, Leslie's is a treat for the eyes, nose, and tastebuds: the window display changes often, with lots of seasonal ephemera, vintage clothing, and antique toys interspersed among the cookies, cakes, and pies; good smells are broadcast outdoors by a fan; the giant snickerdoodles, molasses crinkles, and chocolate chip cookies, priced at a buck apiece, are great to munch on when you're strolling. The baklava is flavorful, as is the traditional French Canadian Maple Oatmeal Pie. Leslie Birney bakes a variety of cakes and fruit pies, with most pies in the $10—$12 range; a buttermilk chocolate cake with walnut-fudge icing that serves 18 is $25. Closed in April.

**LILLY'S PLACE**
518-623-3194.
84 Main St., Warrensburg, at the Pillars.

Lilly Dinu worked as a pharmacist in Romania for 30 years and recently moved to Warrensburg, where her daughter is a dentist. Lilly's Place is a tiny patisserie in two spotless former motel rooms; there are a couple of tables for lunch, or you can take out your chicken or spinach crepe, ham-and-cheese croissant, Caesar salad, or fettucini. The pastries are heavenly; chocolate mousse cake, apple strudel, baclava, and Linzertorte are stand-out selections. If you'd like something with a more Adirondack flavor, try the warm bread pudding smothered with raspberry sauce or maple syrup. Open daily year-round.

**NATHAN'S ADIRONDACK BAKERY**
315-369-3933.
Crosby Blvd., Old Forge, around the corner from Old Forge Hardware.

Nathan's is the place for wonderful, chewy, better-than-New-York-City-style bagels and bialys; the dense, crusty eight-grain bread is good, too. Cinnamon buns, bran muffins, pizza slices, and special-occasion cakes are highly recommended. Open weekends during the school year; daily in July and August.

*Bagels and bialys join with North Country-style dough-nuts at Nathan's Bakery in Old Forge.*

Nancie Battaglia

**SPRUCE MOUNTAIN BAKERY**
No phone.
Rte. 9, Chestertown.

The roadside view of Spruce Mountain Bakery isn't exactly inviting: there's a derelict Fire Chief gas pump out front, and the bakery looks a bit dim and run-down, if not closed. Check it out, though: the Danishes and other gooey, sweet offerings are very good, and the light, buttery onion rolls are excellent.

**THE SUGAR BEAR BREAD & PASTRY SHOPPE**
518-946-7727.
Rte. 9N, Jay, just north of the village green.

Jay is a pretty, quiet little town, not generally the kind of place where you'd expect to find outstanding pastries. Arlie Adams, the former pastry chef at Lake Placid's Hilton, opened a bake shop in her home in May 1992. Her cakelike sour cream and onion dill bread is quite tasty. The sweets — brownies, turnovers, bear claws, and "cinnamon nuts," which are puff pastry sprinkled with almonds, cinnamon, and powdered sugar — are exceptionally good, and priced well below the competition. The chocolate cake crowned with white-chocolate icing is truly memorable.

## CANDY

**THE CANDY MAN**
518-946-7270.
Rte. 9, Jay.

Leonard and Charlene Matarese take their chocolate slowly and seriously, and hand-craft a full range of treats. There are no shortcuts here, no high-tech approaches; they even make the fillings in their shop and cover them with a generous layer of chocolate. In honor of Jay's major historic attraction, they concoct "covered bridge fudge," which is flavored fudge dipped in chocolate: for example, peanut-butter fudge dipped in dark chocolate, walnut fudge covered with white chocolate, and so on. The sugar-free candies concocted by Leonard get high marks for tasting remarkably like the real thing. Open year-round; mail orders available.

**WAGAR'S CONFECTIONARY**
518-668-2693/1-800-292-4277.
327 Canada St., Lake George.

Adirondack bear claws — oblong hunks of dark- or milk-chocolate-covered caramel spiked with giant cashews, almonds, or pecans — might be the best Adirondack invention of the 20th century. Actually, all of Wagar's chocolate is toothsome, and you can mail-order bear claws, almond butter crunch, hand-dipped apricots, or chocolate assortments from October to late March. It's worth a visit to the downtown Lake George shop, though, because it has a beautiful antique marble soda fountain that's open Memorial Day through Labor Day. Wagar's is also the place to get an excellent souvenir: they package yard-long pieces of saltwater taffy inside a box that has a campy map of Lake George.

**THE YUM YUM TREE**
518-891-1310.
46 Main St., Saranac Lake.

Home of the Spirited Truffles, rich, buttery, multi-bite hand-shaped candies that come in Irish Coffee, Amaretto, Grand Marnier, Raspberry Schnapps, White Russian, and other flavors, the Yum Yum Tree also offers croissants, breads, strudel, and rolls. For the chocoholic, there are chocolate-dipped chocolate chip cookies made on the premises. Open year-round; truffles can be shipped.

## DAIRIES

**CRYSTAL SPRING DAIRY**
No phone.
Rte. 86, Saranac Lake.

Nowadays, much of Crystal Spring's milk comes from outside the Adirondacks, but they still make cottage cheese, butter, and sour cream at the plant. The best product, though, is wonderful old-fashioned ice cream, available in July and August.

## DELICATESSENS AND GOURMET SHOPS

**ADIRONDACK
GENERAL STORE**
518-494-4408.
108 East Shore Dr.,
Adirondack.

Joan Lomnitzer makes 21 different soups, including tangy Reuben soup, excellent corn chowder, and spicy chili; the deli sandwiches are inexpensive and generous. Describing the store, located well off the beaten path on the east side of Schroon Lake, Joan says, "People come here if they live here, if they're visiting someone in town, or if they're lost." Besides serving good breakfast and lunch fare, the general store has local wild raspberry and blackberry jams, a full range of grocery items, and dry goods. Open year-round.

*The Country Gourmet, Keene Valley, features everything from imported pastas to fine coffees.*

Nancie Battaglia

**THE COUNTRY
GOURMET**
518-576-2009.
Rte. 73, Keene Valley.

Tracy Whitney and Jane Martin have developed a unique and successful shop in the shadow of the High Peaks, where they sell frozen homemade entrees like orange curry chicken, beef bundles, and various casseroles. Meals are designed to feed three or four adults, need to be heated in a conventional oven, and cost about $3 per serving, depending on the ingredients. The Country Gourment also has a full range of baked goods, from tasty muffins and cookies to celebration cakes, plus gourmet coffee beans, unusual pastas and sauces, and condiments. Closed April.

**JACK'S DELI & MEAT
MARKET**
518-648-6188.
Rtes. 28 and 30, Indian
Lake.

Jack Quintal, a veteran butcher, offers good-quality deli meats, sliced cheeses, aged steaks, roasts, and chops cut to order, and fresh fish. Sandwiches and subs are well stuffed; the chicken salad, loaded with big chunks of white meat and fresh vegetables in Italian dressing, is quite good. Stop here to stock your picnic cooler before you head for the Indian Lake islands. Open year-round.

**LAKEVIEW DELI**
518-891-2101.
102 River St., Saranac Lake.

**G**reat sandwiches, hearty cold salads, assorted gourmet treats, and exotic sodas are on tap at the Lakeview, just across the street from Lake Flower. Many folks come to this deli just to purchase Rock Hill Bake Shop's superb sourdough bread; you can find the big loaves of farm bread, whole-wheat sourdough, semolina, and rye in the freezer near the front of the store. Open year-round.

**LUIGI'S CAFE & DELICATESSEN**
518-946-2102.
Rte. 86, Wilmington, at the Ausable River dam.

**C**raving a smoked gouda and liverwurst, or kielbasa and kraut? Luigi's has an excellent array of deli meats, cheeses, and sausages, for sandwiches and subs, and makes a pretty good pizza, too. A house specialty pizza is the Adam and Eve — aged cheddar, mozzarella, and thin, fresh apple slices on a homemade crust. Open year-round.

**POTLUCK**
518-523-3106.
3 Main St., Lake Placid.

**U**ndoubtedly the most complete gourmet shop inside the Blue Line, Potluck has a good deli offering nearly infinite sandwich combinations. You can also get Green Mountain Coffee Roasters beans and blends here; imported beers, cheeses, and pastas; fancy ice cream; kitchen gifts and gadgets; and cupcake-size hand-dipped chocolates. Open year-round.

**ROSSI'S ITALIAN IMPORTS & DELICATESSEN**
518-532-9572.
Main St., Schroon Lake.

**O**pen every day, year-round, Rossi's is the real thing, not just some dabbler's idea of an Italian deli. You'll find all the right stuff here: sopressata, prosciutto, and homemade Italian sausage; fresh mozzarella; fresh ravioli; and good homemade salads and sauces. They even make hot, brown, seedy mustard that sells for a fraction of what Grey Poupon costs. Rossi's is a friendly little hole-in-the-wall that makes thick sandwiches perfect for packing on your Pharaoh Mountain hike, munching in the ice-fishing shanty, or enjoying on the town beach.

## FARM MARKETS AND ORCHARDS

**ADIRONDACK FARMER'S MARKET COOPERATIVE**
518-298-3755.
Box 136, Chazy.

**I**n 1987 a farmers' market was begun in Plattsburgh, and the weekly open-air affairs were so popular that other produce growers and other towns wanted to be part of the action, too. Now there are six Adirondack Park locations for the traveling markets, which feature native-grown fruits and vegetables, honey, maple syrup, jams and jellies, herbs and herbal teas, and all kinds of flowers.

In Elizabethtown the market is under a huge tent on the lawn in front of the Essex County Courthouse on Friday mornings, late May—late September. In Lake Placid, at the Horse Show Grounds on Rte. 73, the market is Saturdays from 3—6 p.m., late June—late September. At Paul Smiths, across from the entrance to the college, farmers meet Saturday mornings from late June—late September. In Port Henry, the market's on Friday afternoons beginning the last week in June, on Main Street. In Ticonderoga, look for the striped tent next to the Heritage Museum on Saturday mornings late June—late September. In Westport, market day is Thursday, starting at 10 a.m., near the Inn on the Library Lawn, July—September.

**BESSBORO ORCHARDS**
518-962-8609.
Rtes. 9N and 22, Westport.

Lou Gibbs has worked hard on this new orchard, and he offers good-quality Cortland, Empire, Paula Red, and MacIntosh apples that he sells as they're picked. In other words, the apples are fresh off the trees, and they go quickly in the fall.

**GUNNISON'S ORCHARDS**
518-597-3363.
Rtes. 9N and 22, Crown Point.

Honey from the bees that pollinate the trees, and all kinds of apples, including Spencer, Gala, Empire, Jonagold, and MacIntosh, are available right up until springtime at this impressive roadside orchard. Of course, October's the best time for a visit, but even if you're traveling the highway in the winter, stop in. Open Mon.—Sat. year-round.

**HARRINGTON'S GREENHOUSE**
518-597-3643.
Main St., Crown Point.

Fresh, luscious strawberries in June, and homemade jams and jellies, are available at this extensive greenhouse complex. The Harringtons also raise hardy perennials and propagate thousands of geraniums every spring.

**KING'S APPLE ORCHARD**
518-834-7943.
Mace-Chasm Rd., off Rte. 9, Keeseville.

This orchard opens in August, offering Tydemans and other early apples; later on in the fall, and through December, you can get Paula Red, MacIntosh, Cortland, Empire, and Red Delicious apples.

**LEDGETOP ORCHARDS**
518-597-3420.
Lake Rd., off Rte. 22, Crown Point.

Not too far from the Crown Point bridge, you pick your own sour pie cherries in July, gather drops from the apple orchard in late September, and select the perfect jack-o-lantern at the farm

*At Pray's, in Keesville, you can select a pint from the stand or pick your own berries — but don't mind the scarecrow.*

Nancie Battaglia

stand in October. The stand offers Cortland, Empire, Red Delicious, MacIntosh, and Kendall (think of a crunchier Mac) apples beginning in early September.

**PRAY'S FAMILY FARMS**
518-834-9130.
Rte. 9N, Keeseville.

People come from miles around when the strawberries ripen at Pray's, usually in mid-June. Besides the berries (there are blackberries and raspberries, too), the roadside stand sells home-grown vegetables of all kinds, right up to pumpkin season.

**RIVERMEDE**
518-576-4386.
Beede Rd., Keene Valley.

Brown eggs, maple syrup from the farm's sugar bush, and fresh beans, broccoli, leaf lettuce, new potatoes, scallions, squash, tomatoes, carrots, and more come from this High Peaks area farm.

**SEARS ORCHARD**
518-547-8224.
Rte. 22, Putnam.

A small orchard selling mainly to apple co-ops, Sears is worth a visit in the fall just to see the rolling Washington County hills in full color. This is a lovely part of the Adirondack Park that's often overlooked.

**SWEETWATER FARMS**
518-327-3566.
Rte. 86, between
  Bloomingdale and
  Saranac Lake.

One of the last remaining farms in the Saranac River valley, Sweetwater has a large roadside store offering organically grown produce. In July you're likely to find green beans, broccoli, lettuce, peas, cucumbers, and perhaps new potatoes; by mid-August, the corn is ready, along with tomatoes, zucchini, leeks, and lots of herbs. Prices are very reasonable; Hank and Lisa Duke's vegetables are indisputably fresh. Open late June—late September.

**TICONDEROGA
  ORCHARDS**
518-547-8424.
Old Wright Ferry Rd.,
  Putnam.

Macs, Jonamacs, Cortlands, Red Delicious, and Empires grow here; picking usually starts in late August. There isn't a farm stand as such, but you can call ahead to buy apples in quantity, or collect drops for cidering.

**VALLEY VIEW FARMS**
518-585-9974/6502.
Rte. 9, Ticonderoga.

Just south of the Ticonderoga Country Club you can enjoy another aspect of the country: pick-your-own strawberries in mid- to late-June, red raspberries in late July, and blueberries spanning both seasons. (Note that fruit ripening always depends on the weather; if spring is late and cold, it's best to call ahead to be sure the berries are ready for you.) There's also a farm stand with fresh vegetables open about June 20—late September.

## HEALTH FOODS

**J. B.'S HEALTH FOODS**
518-576-9864.
Rte. 73, Keene Valley.

Besides giant jars of dried beans, grains, herbs, pastas, and various mixes from which you can measure out your own portions, Julie Baird has a

*Granola, figs, nuts, and rice at J.B.'s in Keene Valley.*

Nancie Battaglia

good selection of packaged, dehydrated natural foods like hummus, tabouli, and black beans that are eminently suitable for backpacking. You'll also find an extensive assortment of healthy shampoos, cosmetics, soaps, sunscreens, bug dopes, and skin preparations. Prices here are quite reasonable. Open year-round; closed Tuesdays.

**LIVING WELL FOODS**
518-548-4710.
Rte. 30, at the 4 corners, Speculator.

Jeff Trudeau and Dacia Leonardo's brightly lit, well-stocked shop comes as quite a surprise, located as it is in the same concrete-block building as the Chamber of Commerce, a sweatshirt shop, and a paperback outlet. There's a goodly array of organic fruits and vegetables in the cooler and plenty of nuts, grains, herbal remedies, vitamins, mixes, dried fruits, books, and Rachel Perry cosmetics on the shelves. Closed in Apr.; open daily Memorial Day—Labor Day; open Tues.—Sat. the rest of the year.

**NORI'S NATURAL FOODS**
518-891-6079.
70 Broadway, Saranac Lake, near the post office.

Bins of grains and flours; jugs of oil, honey, and maple syrup; and canisters of herbs line the walls here — serve yourself. There's a selection of Kiss My Face lotions and insect-repellent potions, plus a cooler full of North Country cheeses and organically grown vegetables. The bulletin board is a good source for checking out local alternative-lifestyle happenings. Open year-round.

## MAPLE SYRUP

Upstate New York is a leading producer of high-quality maple syrup, and Adirondack syrup tastes no different from the Vermont stuff, which seems to get all the glory. Across the park, you can buy local syrup in craft shops, general stores, and farm stands; listed below is a sampling of a few syrup processors who sell directly from their homes and sugar bushes. There are many more folks who make syrup, and they advertise that fact with a large lithographed tin sign showing a maple leaf.

If you'd like to learn about sap, taps, and boiling off, the Uihlein-Cornell Maple Sugar Project (518-523-9137; Bear Cub Rd., Lake Placid, NY 12946), a joint project of the New York State College of Agriculture at Cornell University and Henry Uihlein, is open most weekday afternoons from spring through fall. Admission is free; in Mar. and Apr., you can observe the entire process from tree sap to finished product.

**Alstead Farms** (Patrick Whitney, 518-576-4793; Alstead Hill Rd., Keene) Wholesale and retail Adirondack maple syrup, 1/2 pint to 5-gallon drums.

Nancie Battaglia

*Gathering sap the old-time way at Frog Alley Farm, Keene Valley.*

**Vernon Balch** (518-251-3704; Minerva) Retail maple syrup.

**Frog Alley Farm** (518-576-9835; Rte. 73, Keene Valley) Retail maple syrup.

**Ginter's Maple Grove** (Art Ginter, 518-863-6796; Mountain Rd., Mayfield) Maple products — syrup, candy, etc. — shipped anywhere.

**Leadley's Adirondack Sugar Bush** (Jack Leadley, Sr., 518-548-7093; Rte. 30, Speculator) Retail maple syrup.

**Morningside Farm** (Sandy and Frank Labar, 518-251-2694; Minerva) Retail maple syrup.

**Toad Hill Maple Products** (Randy Galusha, 518-623-2272; Athol) Syrup, sugar, and a complete line of maple-syrup-making supplies.

## MEAT MARKETS

**DOTY'S COUNTRY ROAD BEEF HOUSE**
518-891-3200.
Lake Colby Dr., Saranac Lake.

The folks at Doty's make excellent breakfast and Italian sausages, and offer a full variety of aged beef cuts, lamb, pork, and deli meats. Open year-round.

**JACOBS & TONEY**
518-623-3850.
157 Main St., Warrensburg.

The front of the building proclaims "Meat Store of the North," and the folks here pride themselves on prime beef cut to order, fresh pork, chicken, lamb, and homemade fresh sausage. Open year-round.

**OSCAR'S HICKORY HOUSE**
518-622-3431/1-800-627-3431.
22 Raymond Lane (205 Main), Warrensburg.

For half a century, the Quintal family has been smoking up a storm — wonderful hams, sausages, cheese, some 165 different smokehouse products in all — in a shop just off Warrensburg's main street. You can get smoked catfish, boneless smoked chicken breast, smoked lamb, and eight kinds of bacon. Oscar's blends a variety of flavored cheese spreads, and the shop has gourmet crackers, condiments, and mixes. It's also a terrific butcher shop for fresh meat and bratwurst, weisswurst, knockwurst, all kinds of wursts. Open year-round; mail-order catalog available.

*Smokehouse products and more are available at Oscar's, Warrensburg.*

Nancie Battaglia

**SHAHEEN'S SUPER MARKET**
518-359-9320.
252 Park St., Tupper Lake.

A family-run store staffed by genuinely friendly folks who still carry grocery bags out to your car, Shaheen's is known for quality meats cut to order. Occasionally, homemade Lebanese specialties appear in the cooler; the kibbe is very popular and sells out within hours. Open year-round.

## SPECIAL EVENTS — BARBECUES AND COMMUNITY SUPPERS

Throughout the Adirondacks, civic organizations, fire departments, historical societies, and church groups put on a variety of public suppers. Don't be shy! Visitors are quite welcome at these affairs, and furthermore, the food is generally cheap and delicious.

A North Country favorite is the chicken barbecue — half-chickens marinated in a tangy lemon-based sauce and cooked outdoors over the coals. The trimmings are usually an ear of roasted sweet corn, potato salad, cole slaw or tossed salad, roll, watermelon wedge, and coffee; the price hovers around the $5 mark, less for kids' portions. There are also steak roasts, clambakes, pig roasts, and buffets. Listed below in chronological order are some of the annual feasts found in the Adirondacks; many of the winter carnivals and other events listed in Chapter Four, *Culture*, also have an important food component. Ask locally about others.

**Newcomb Lions Club Chicken Barbecue** (518-582-3211; Newcomb) Held on the Newcomb Town Beach on Lake Harris, off Rte. 28N, on the first Saturday in July.

**North Creek Fire Department Chicken Barbecue** (518-251-2612; North Creek) Held at the North Creek Ski Bowl, off Rte. 28, on the first Saturday in July.

*Blue Mountain Lake is one of the many communities offering summertime chicken barbecues.*

Nancie Battaglia

### Secret Recipe Chicken

Chances are if you asked a local grillmeister for the chicken-barbecue-sauce recipe, you'd be told it was a family heirloom not to be shared with casual visitors. Actually most of the Adirondack barbecues rely on variations of the Cornell University recipe; since 1949, the Poultry Science Department of the school has distributed close to a million copies of it. Below is that secret marinade so you can replicate smoky, lemony chicken at home.

   1 cup good cooking oil
   1 pint cider vinegar (some folks use lemon juice and vinegar)
   3 tb salt (or less, to taste)
   1 tb Bell's poultry seasoning
   1/2 tsp black pepper (or more, to taste)
   1 egg

Beat the egg vigorously. Then add the oil and beat again to emulsify the sauce. Add other ingredients. Dunk chicken halves in the sauce and let marinate in the refrigerator for a few hours. While grilling over hot coals, baste each side.

The sauce will keep in the refrigerator for about a week. Enough for 8 to 10 half-chickens. Leftover barbecued chicken makes superb chicken salad.

**Strawberry Festival** (518-251-2703; United Methodist Church, North River) Lots of strawberry shortcake, at the Methodist Church, Thirteenth Lake Rd., North River, off Rte. 28, on the second Saturday in July.

**Keene Valley Fire Department Open House and Chicken Barbecue** (518-576-4444; Keene Valley) Held at the fire hall on Market St., on the fourth Sunday in July.

**Newcomb Fire Department Steak Roast and Parade** (518-582-3211; Newcomb) Rib-eye steaks, burgers, corn, hot dogs, and salads, at the Newcomb Town Beach, on the last Sunday in July.

**Hague Fish & Game Club Barbecue** (518-543-6353; Hague) Held at the Fish and Game Club, off Rte. 9N, on the first Saturday in August.

**Inlet Volunteer Hose Co. Chicken Barbecue** (315-357-5501; Inlet) Held at the Fern Park pavilion on the second Saturday in August.

**Minerva Beach Party** (518-251-2869; Minerva) Steamed clams, hamburgers, hot dogs, sweet corn, and Italian-sausage-and-peppers sandwiches at the Minerva Lake beach, off Rte. 28N, on the second Saturday in August.

**Chilson Volunteer Fire Department Chicken Barbecue** (518-585-6619; Ticonderoga) Held at Elks Field, Rte. 22, on the second Sunday in August.

**Penfield Museum Heritage Day Chicken Barbecue** (518-597-3804; Penfield Homestead Museum, Ironville) Held on the museum grounds on the third Saturday in August.

**Keene Fire Department Open House and Chicken Barbecue** (518-576-4444; Keene) Held at the fire hall, on East Hill Rd., on the last Saturday in August.

**Plump Chicken Inn** (518-251-2229; Minerva Historical Society, Olmstedville) Chicken and biscuits, homemade pickles and salads, real mashed potatoes; held at Minerva Central School in Olmstedville on the last Saturday in August.

**Lewis Volunteer Fire Co. Ox Roast** (518-873-6777; Lewis) Held at the fire hall on the last Sunday in August.

**Indian Lake Pig Roast** (518-648-5112; Indian Lake Volunteer Fire Dept., Indian Lake) Succulent roast pork and stuffing, steamed clams, homemade clam chowder, corn, burgers, hot dogs, and beer; held at the Indian Lake fire hall, on Rte. 28, on the day before Labor Day.

**Bloomingdale Fire Department Field Day** (518-891-3189; Bloomingdale) Chicken barbecue and games, held at the fire hall, off Rte. 3, on the Sunday before Labor Day.

**Westport Marina Labor Day Lobsterfest** (518-962-4356; Washington St., Westport) Lakeside feeding frenzy at the Westport Marina, on the Sunday before Labor Day. Advance tickets are necessary.

**Fish & Game Club Lobster and Clam Bake** (518-532-7675; Schroon Lake) Held at the Fish and Game Club headquarters on the second Sunday in September.

**Raquette Lake Fire Department Clambake** (315-354-4228; Raquette Lake) Held at the Ole Barn, Limekiln Lake Rd., Inlet; advance tickets necessary; held on the second Sunday in September.

## WINE AND LIQUOR STORES

You can purchase wine and liquor in numerous stores throughout the park. Some of the smaller places are adjacent to taverns, or even the owners' homes; you may have to ring a buzzer to have them open the shop for you. Note that New York State liquor stores are closed on Sundays; beer and wine coolers are available in grocery stores, although you cannot buy beer until after noon on Sunday.

A handful of shops stand out for their good selection of domestic and imported wines and knowledgeable staff. In Lake Placid, **Terry Robards Wines and Spirits** (518-523-9072; 243 Main St.) is worth a visit; Robards was a columnist for the *Wine Spectator*, and occasionally sponsors wine tastings. If you're looking for a summery wine to go with a picnic, or a particular pressing from an obscure vineyard, he's the one to ask. Further south in the Adirondacks, Elizabeth Gillespie at **Speculator Spirits** (518-548-7361; Rte. 30, Speculator) knows her grapes, and her tiny shop offers an astonishing variety of wines.

*And for dessert, nothing beats a fresh cone from Donnelly's, just north of Saranac Lake on Rte. 86, at the Crystal Spring Dairy.*

Nancie Battaglia

# CHAPTER SIX
# *A Land for All Seasons*
## RECREATION

The wild Adirondack woods and waters beckoned the earliest visitors in the 19th century with promises of unlimited brook trout, scrappy smallmouth bass, wily northern pike, magnificent bull moose, abundant whitetail bucks, savage panthers, massive black bears: a veritable Noah's ark of fish and game filled to overflowing and there for the taking. These city "sports" relied on Adirondack guides to row them down the lakes, lead them through the forests, cook three

Nancie Battaglia

*Rowing a traditional Adirondack guideboat on a misty mountain lake.*

squares a day, and finally tuck them in balsam-bough beds at night. The popular press swelled with accounts of these manly Adirondack adventures, and by the 1870s the North Country was a great destination for thousands.

In those rough-and-tumble days, hunting and fishing were the prime recreational pursuits. Hiking through the woods was something done almost as a last resort: "If there is one kind of work which I detest more than another, it is *tramping*; how the thorns lacerate you! How the brambles tear your clothes and pierce your flesh! How the meshwork of fallen tree-tops entangles you!" wrote William H.H. Murray in *Adventures in the Wilderness*, published in 1869. Boating was simply a method of transportation, to row from one campsite to the next, or it was required by certain variations on a sport, as in "floating for deer" — pursuing a swimming buck while hunting on a lake. In the 1890s, recreational canoeing swept the nation (the idea of using native American watercraft for fun came over from England), and the Queen of American Lakes, Lake George, was the scene of American Canoe Association rendezvouses, with hundreds of paddling-, sailing-, and rowing-canoe enthusiasts gathering in jolly encampments.

The idea of hiking or mountain-climbing for recreation became acceptable with the growth of the grand hotels. Walking in the woods — dressed in long skirts, shirtwaists, high boots, wool stockings, long gloves, hats, veils — was fine for the ladies; they could hire their own guides, too, to take them up the High Peaks or into beautiful waterfalls. Hiking was healthful, too: breathing in pine-scented, ozone-laden air was regarded as a tonic for the frail, dyspeptic, or consumptive patient.

With the advent of the automobile, recreation in the Adirondack Park changed. No longer were the lake country and High Peaks remote and inaccessible to the masses; no longer did the exodus north take long days and lots of dollars. Vacations were within reach of almost every working person, and with the help of a reliable Ford or Buick, so were the Adirondacks. In the wake of this new, more democratic summer-vacation approach, the grand hotels closed one by one, replaced by motels and housekeeping cabins, and the New York State Department of Environmental Conservation responded to the demand by creating car-camping havens under the pines.

Today in the Adirondack Park, whether you come for health, adventure, solitude, or just plain fun, you'll find that outdoor recreation opportunities are limited only by your imagination. Nowhere else east of the Mississippi is there the opportunity for such a variety of sports: wilderness canoeing, backcountry hiking, rock climbing, downhill and cross-country skiing, fishing, big-game hunting ... the list goes on. If you want to get away from civilization, this is the place; there are 2.5 million acres of public lands to explore. In that regard, the Adirondack Park compares quite favorably with many of the national parks, and there's an added bonus: there's no entry fee when you cross the Blue Line. You may hike, canoe, ski-tour, whatever, in the forest preserve without having to fill out a form or buy a special permit.

On the other hand, if your taste runs to a genteel round of golf, or perhaps watching a chukker of polo, you'll find those here, too. There are tour boats to motor you around scenic lakes, pilots to hire for flying high above the mountaintops. The park might also be regarded as the birthplace of two of the mainstays of popular American culture: theme parks and miniature golf.

Outlined in this chapter you'll find descriptions of numerous diversions, along with suggestions on where to explore or play, where to buy or rent the proper equipment, whom to call for further details. What you won't find in this chapter is specific instructions on where to begin or end a particular hike, climb, or canoe trip; it's important that you take the responsibility to read the appropriate guidebooks and study the right maps. Each season, a few unprepared outdoors-folk become unfortunate statistics because of errors in judgment in a very wild place. The Blue Line encircles a park, but if you get lost, we can't "just turn the lights on" (as one urban-dweller suggested to forest rangers involved in a search) to find you.

# ADIRONDACK GUIDES

*Mitchell Sabattis (1824-1906), from Long Lake, was one of the best-known early Adirondack guides.*

Courtesy Adirondack Museum, Blue Mountain Lake, NY

An Adirondack guide is born, not made: that was the 19th-century sentiment. "He falls so to speak out of his log cradle into a pair of top boots, discards the bottle for a pipe, possesses himself of a boat and a jackknife and becomes forthwith a full-fledged experienced guide," wrote an observer in 1879. Ralph Waldo Emerson praised the guides as "doctors of the wilderness" in his poem "Red Flannel"; William H.H. Murray declared his usual guide, John Cheney, a paragon of virtue, and described the independent guides thusly: "A more honest, cheerful, and patient class of men cannot be found the world over. Born and bred, as many were, in this wilderness, skilled in all the lore of woodcraft, handy with the rod, superb at the paddle, modest in demeanor and speech, honest to a proverb, they deserve and receive the admiration of all who make their acquaintance." Of course, not all 19th-century visitors agreed with the preacher from Boston — one writer declared "a more impudent, lazy, extortionate, and generally offensive class ... would be hard to find" — but Murray's viewpoint became the popular ideal.

The Adirondack Guides' Association was established in 1891 as a sort of backwoods trade union, to adopt uniform pay for a day's work (then just a dollar or so), and to agree to obey the state's new game-protection laws.

Nowadays, the Department of Environmental Conservation (DEC) licenses hundreds of men and women as guides for all kinds of outdoor recreation, from rock-climbing and fly fishing to white-water rafting and bird-watching. Guides must pass a written exam that tests woods-wisdom and responses to weather or safety situations; they must also have current first-aid and CPR certification.

There are some 300 guides who are members of a select group within the DEC-licensees: the New York State Outdoor Guides Association (NYSOGA). These guides make a point of preserving wild resources as well as helping clients find the right places for hunting, fishing, camping, and climbing; many guides also practice low-impact camping and offer informal outdoor education.

Under the separate sports headings in this chapter, you'll find a sampling of licensed guides for different outdoor activities, but for a complete listing of all the NYSOGA guides and their specialties, you can contact Brian McDonnell at All Seasons Outfitters (518-891-1176; P.O. Box 916A, Saranac Lake, NY 12983).

## BICYCLING

*A bicycle club poses in the Devil's Oven at Ausable Chasm, 1890s.*

Courtesy Adirondack Museum, Blue Mountain Lake, NY

Adirondack highways, byways, and skidways offer challenges, variety, and great scenery for road and mountain bikers; May through October are the best months. In April, when warm temperatures beckon, road bikers might find that the snowbanks are gone, but a slippery residue of sand and gravel often remains on the road shoulders and in bike lanes. Likewise, springtime backcountry cyclists might discover patches of deep snow in shady areas of woods or stretches of muddy soup on sunnier trails. At the other end of the year, note that hunting season begins in October, and some of the best mountain-biking destinations are also popular hunting spots.

Currently there are no bicycling guidebooks, maps, or trip pamphlets readily available, either for suggested road loops or mountain-bike trails, although Backcountry Books, based in Vermont, plans to publish a guide to 25 Adirondack trips sometime in 1993. The annual Outdoor Guides published by *Adirondack Life* have listed dozens of bike trips; back issues are available (518-946-2191; Box 97, Jay, NY 12941). For other trip ideas, you can check at bike shops in Lake Placid or Saranac Lake or sporting-goods stores; there's also the *Adirondack Mountain Bike Club* (518-523-4339; 30 Bear Cub Rd., Lake Placid, NY 12946). A few possible road and backcountry trips are listed below.

All-terrain bicycles are barred from wilderness areas in the Adirondack Park, but generally speaking, most of the wilderness hiking trails are inappropriate for bikes anyway: too steep, too narrow, too wet, too rocky. In the state-land areas designated as wild forest, you'll find more old logging roads with bridges that make excellent bike routes, and in most of these places, you'll find far fewer other people.

Road cyclists will discover that many state highways have wide shoulders that are delineated as bike paths, such as Rtes. 28 and 30 from Indian Lake to Long Lake. You won't have to contend with much traffic in May and June or September and October, except for weekends, but be aware that the roads can become quite busy with all kinds of vehicles from log trucks to sight-seeing buses to RVs throughout the summer. Also, be well prepared for any long trips: check topographical as well as highway maps for significant hills on your proposed route, and always carry plenty of water, along with a good tool kit.

## BICYCLE DEALERS AND OUTFITTERS

### LAKE GEORGE AND SOUTHEASTERN ADIRONDACKS

**Bailey's Horses** (518-696-4541; Rte. 9N, Lake Luzerne, NY 12846) Mountain bike rentals.

**Friends Lake Inn** (518-494-4751; Friends Lake Rd., Chestertown, NY 12817) Mountain bike rentals, guided trips.

**Hull's Sporting Goods** (518-623-2116; 139 Main St., Warrensburg, NY 12885) New bike sales, repairs.

**Lake George Touring Co.** (518-668-4206; 204 Canada St., Lake George, NY 12845) Mountain bike rental and repairs, guided trips.

### HIGH PEAKS AND NORTHERN ADIRONDACKS

**Adirondack Adventure Tours** (518-523-1475; 126 Main St., Lake Placid, NY 12946) Mountain bike rentals, guided bike trips, trip planning.

*High Peaks Cyclery, Lake Placid.*

Nancie Battaglia

**Barkeater Bicycles** (518-891-5207; 43 Main St., Saranac Lake, NY 12983) New and used bike sales, repairs.

**Bear Cub Adventure Tours** (518-523-4339; 30 Bear Cub Rd., Lake Placid, NY 12946) Guided mountain bike trips.

**High Peaks Cyclery** (518-523-3764; Saranac Ave., Lake Placid) Road and mountain bike sales, repairs, and rentals.

**Sundog Ski and Sport** (518-523-2752; 90 Main St., Lake Placid; 518-891-5533; 157 Lake Flower Ave., Saranac Lake, NY 12983) Mountain bike sales, repairs, and rentals.

## CENTRAL AND SOUTHWESTERN ADIRONDACKS

**Adirondack Hut-to-Hut Tours** (518-251-2710; Minerva Hill Lodge, Minerva, NY 12851) Guided overnight mountain bike trips, road-bike tours.

**Cunningham's Ski Barn** (518-251-3215; Rte. 28, North Creek, NY 12853) Mountain bike rentals, guided trips.

**Garnet Hill Lodge** (518-251-2821; Thirteenth Lake Rd., North River, NY 12856) Mountain bike rentals for their wilderness trails only.

*Country roads throughout the Adirondack Park offer great scenery and little traffic.*

Nancie Battaglia

**Mountainaire Adventures** (518-251-2194; Rte. 28, Wevertown, NY 12886)
Mountain bike rentals.

**Sagamore Lodge** (315-354-5311; Sagamore Rd., Raquette Lake, NY 13436)
Mountain bikes available for guests, special mountain-bike weekends.

## BEYOND THE BLUE LINE

There are two excellent bike shops in Glens Falls: *Inside Edge* (518-793-5676;
624 Upper Glen St., Glens Falls, NY 12801) and the *Bike Shop* (518-793-8986;
Quaker Rd., Glens Falls). Just south of the park's boundary, in the Million
Dollar Half Mile, is *Syd and Dusty's Outfitters*, which rents mountain bikes
(518-792-0260; Rte. 149, Lake George, NY 12845). In Plattsburgh, *Wooden Ski
and Wheel* (518-561-2790; Rte. 9, Plattsburgh, NY 12901) is a professional shop
for new bikes, tune-ups, and equipment. In Gloversville, *R & G Bike & Sport*
(518-725-5548; 50 N. Main St.) is a full-service shop.

---

### *Rules of the Trail*

• **Ride on open trails only.** Respect trail and road closures and avoid trespassing on private lands. Federal and state wilderness areas are closed to cycling.

• **Leave no trace.** Even on open trails, you should not ride under conditions
where you will leave evidence of your passing. Practice low-impact cycling by
staying on the trail and not creating any new ones. Pack out at least as much as
you pack in.

• **Control your bicycle.** There is no excuse for excessive speed.

• **Always yield the trail** to hikers and others. Make your approach known well
in advance; a friendly greeting or a bell works well.

• **Never spook animals.** Give them extra room and time to adjust to your presence; use special care when passing horseback riders.

• **Plan ahead.** Know your equipment, your ability, and the area in which you
are riding, and prepare accordingly. Be self-sufficient; carry the necessary supplies
and tools you may need.

(From *The International Mountain Bicycling Association*)

---

## SELECTED CYCLING DESTINATIONS

Listed here are just a few suggestions for possible trips. There are many,
many more that you can learn about by asking local cyclists or guides or in
area bike shops. In **Lake George and Southeastern Adirondack**s, mountain bikers would do well to explore the 40 miles of carriage trails found on the old
Knapp estate, located on the east shore of Lake George. Some of these trails
lead you to magical abandoned gardens or mossy pools and defunct fountains. For some suggested itineraries, read *Discover the Eastern Adirondacks*
(Backcountry Books), one of a series of hiking guides written by Barbara

McMartin; trails that are old logging roads are described very clearly. Road bikers might want to try a 40-mile loop paralleling the Schroon River from Warrensburg to Brant Lake along county roads, or follow the "Dude Ranch Trail," a 40-mile route marked with big hat signs along Rtes. 418 and 9N. There's also the Warren County Bikeway leading from Lake George Village to Glens Falls.

For the *Champlain Valley*, you'll find the dirt roads north of Paradox leading to Johnson Pond or to Ironville are fun to explore on a mountain bike, as are old logging roads in the Hammond Pond Wild Forest. Consult *Discover the Eastern Adirondacks*, mentioned above, for specific trails. For road bikes, Rte. 22 between Crown Point and Willsboro offers plenty of possibilities and wonderful views, and the county road from Crown Point Center to Moriah to Elizabethtown is almost a roller-coaster of long hills; you can take a dip in Lincoln Pond if the going gets too hot.

Around the *High Peaks and Northern Adirondacks*, local cyclists know that the back roads out of Bloomingdale toward Union Falls Pond and Silver Lake are scenic and less traveled; from Saranac Lake village, there are loop trips possible to Rainbow Lake and Onchiota. For mountain bikers, the marked trail into Pine Pond, which begins off Averyville Rd. in Lake Placid, is a nice half-day trip; the old railroad route of the Adirondack Division of the New York Central, accessible off Rte. 86 between Lake Placid and Saranac Lake, is yet another possibility. Santanoni Preserve, located off Rte. 28N near Newcomb, is one of the best — and most popular — mountain-bike trips; you can take an easy 10-mile journey into the old Great Camp, or try the more difficult route into Moose Pond off the main trail.

North of Tupper Lake, in the *Northwest Lakes Region*, you'll find that Massawepie Cooperative Area, a large tract of land owned by the Boy Scouts, is open for recreational use in spring, fall, and winter (closed when camp is in session, June—August); mountain bikers can travel from Massawepie Lake to Horseshoe Lake on dirt roads, but do remember to sign in first. Also, there are numerous old logging roads that now serve as snowmobile trails near Cranberry Lake that may be suitable for bicycling; check locally on bridge conditions, though. Also, dirt roads in the St. Regis Canoe Area are open to cycling. Road bikers will find that Rte. 3, the major route in the region, has wide shoulders and gentle hills, suitable for long rides.

In the *Central and Southwestern Adirondacks*, the Moose River Plains Recreation Area, south of Indian Lake village, has many miles of dirt roads suitable for all-terrain biking, and ditto the region known as Perkins Clearing, off Rte. 30 between Indian Lake and Speculator. For road bikers, a 70-mile challenge is to go "around the horn," from Blue Mountain Lake to Long Lake, Newcomb, Minerva, North Creek, Indian Lake, and back to Blue Mountain, along Rte. 28N. There are three tough hills: at Blue Mountain, Minerva, and at North River; be sure your bike is geared for climbing!

# BOATING

**D**ozens of lovely Adirondack lakes have public launches for motor- and sailboats, operated by the New York State Department of Environmental Conservation, villages, or individual landowners. A short list of public boat ramps in the different regions follows; note that state campgrounds (listed under "Camping" later in this chapter) quite often have boat ramps. If you have a reserved campsite, there's no extra charge to launch a boat, and if you'd like to visit Lake Eaton, Buck Pond, or Eighth Lake, for example, you simply pay the day-use fee. Marinas and boat liveries offer yet another chance for folks with trailers to get their boats in the water. Many more options are open to canoeists and kayakers who can portage their boats a short distance, so look under "Canoeing and Kayaking" for some further suggested destinations.

*On the waterfront, 1906, at the Grand View Hotel's boathouse, Mirror Lake.*

Natalie and Maude Bryt

The *New York State Boater's Guide* contains the rules and regulations for inland waters, and is available from offices of the Department of Transportation. Some statewide laws for pleasure craft:

• You must carry one personal-flotation device for every passenger in your boat. Children under 12 are *required* to wear life jackets while on board.

• Any boat powered by a motor (even canoes with auxiliary small motors) and operated mainly in New York State must be registered with the Department of Motor Vehicles.

• When traveling within 100 feet of shore, dock, pier, raft, float, or an anchored boat, the speed limit is 5 mph. (Maximum daytime speed limits are 45 mph, and nighttime 25 mph, although on many lakes with rocky shoals or in water bodies which are also popular with nonmotorized craft, lower speeds are prudent.)

• Powerboats give way to canoes, sailboats, rowboats, kayaks, and anchored boats.

• The boat on your right has the right-of-way when being passed.

• Running lights must be used after dark.

• Boaters under 16 must be accompanied by an adult, or, if between 10 and 16 and unaccompanied, they must have a safety certificate from a NYS course.
• Boating under the influence of alcohol carries heavy fines and/or jail sentences.
• Littering and discharging marine-toilet wastes into waterways is prohibited.

---

### Zebra Mussels

A tiny, striped, barnacle-like mollusk from the Caspian Sea was accidentally introduced into Michigan's Lake St. Clair in the 1980s when a European freighter discharged its ocean-water ballast. From there, zebra mussels (*Dreissena polymorpha*) have been inadvertently spread by recreational boaters to Lake Erie, Lake Ontario, and elsewhere. Zebra mussels can clog water-intake pipes, attach themselves to navigational markers in such quantity that the buoys sink, and damage boat hulls. Besides affecting man-made objects, the nonnative mussels have the potential to drastically and irrevocably change a lake's ecology.

The mussels' free-swimming larvae are so small that thousands can be found in a boat's live well or cooling system, or even a bait bucket, and if this contaminated water is released into lakes and rivers, the mussels can spread into virgin territory. Research conducted by the Department of Environmental Conservation suggests that the interior Adirondack lakes are too acidic and lack the necessary calcium to encourage the mussels, but lakes George and Champlain may provide a habitat suited to them.

Canoes and car-top boats usually don't harbor the mussels because they're not left at anchor long enough for mussels to attach and usually don't carry water when transported from one lake to the next. Trailerable boats, especially inboards, pose a greater risk, but boat owners can minimize that by flushing the cooling system on land thoroughly before launching in a new lake, and by rinsing the boat hull and trailer. To be doubly safe, you can use a mild bleach solution for the rinse, or let the boat and trailer dry completely on a hot, sunny day.

---

## PUBLIC BOAT LAUNCHES

## LAKE GEORGE AND SOUTHEASTERN ADIRONDACKS

Note that motorboats (over 10 hp) and sailboats (longer than 18 feet) used on Lake George must have a boating-usage sticker, available from local marinas or from the Lake George Park Commission (518-668-9347; Box 749, Lake George, NY 12845).

### Brant Lake

**Brant Lake Boat Launch** (Rte. 8, Brant Lake).

### Lake George

**Million Dollar Beach** (518-623-3671; Beach Rd., Lake George) Ramp closed during the beach's busiest season, one week before Memorial Day to one week after Labor Day.

**Hague Town Beach** (Lake Shore Dr., Rte. 9N, Hague) Access to northern portion of Lake George.

### Schroon Lake

**Horicon State Launch Facility** (518-494-2220; River Rd., 1/2 mile east of Rte. 9, Schroon Lake).

**Town Dock** (Dock St., off Main St., Schroon Lake).

## CHAMPLAIN VALLEY

### Lake Champlain

**Fort Ticonderoga** (518-585-2821; Rte. 74, Ticonderoga) Follow the signs to the ferry.

**New York State Boat Launch: Port Douglas** (off County Rte. 17, 2 miles south of Port Kent), **Port Henry** (off Rte. 9), **Westport** (Rte. 22), **Willsboro** (518-963-7266; Point Rd).

## HIGH PEAKS AND NORTHERN ADIRONDACKS

### Chateaugay Lakes

**Upper Chateaugay Lake** (off Rte. 374, 1/2 mile south of Merrill).

### Franklin Falls Pond

**NYS Boat Launch** (off County Road 48, Franklin Falls).

### Lake Flower

**Lake Flower** (off River St., Rte. 86, in the center of Saranac Lake village).

### Lake Placid

**NYS Boat Launch-Lake Placid** (off Mirror Lake Dr., Lake Placid).

**Village Boat Launch-Lake Placid** (off Victor Herbert Dr., Lake Placid).

### Saranac Lakes

**Lower Saranac Lake** (518-891-3170; off Rte. 3 at the highway bridge southwest of Saranac Lake village).

**Middle Saranac Lake** (off Rte. 3 at South Creek Fishing Access Site) Car-top boats only.

**Upper Saranac Lake** (dirt road off Rte. 3, east of Rte. 30) Car-top boats only. Also at Saranac Inn for north end of lake, off Rte. 30, car-top boats only.

## NORTHWEST LAKES REGION

### *Cranberry Lake*

**Cranberry Lake Boat Launch** (Columbia Rd., off Rte. 3, in Cranberry Lake village).

### *Big Tupper Lake*

**Tupper Lake Public Launch** (Rte. 30, south of Tupper Lake village).

*Tying up to the public dock at the Tupper Lake boat launch.*

Nancie Battaglia

## CENTRAL AND SOUTHWESTERN ADIRONDACKS

### *Canada Lake*

**Canada Lake Public Launch** (off Rte. 10, Canada Lake).

### *Caroga Lake*

**Caroga Lake Public Launch** (off Rte. 10, Caroga Lake).

### *Fulton Chain of Lakes (First through Eighth lakes)*

**Fourth Lake Public Launch** (off Rte. 28, Inlet).

**Old Forge Public Launch** (off Rte. 28, Old Forge) Access to First through Fourth Lakes.

## Great Sacandaga Lake

**Great Sacandaga Lake Public Launch** (off Rte. 30, south of Northville).

## Lake Pleasant

**Lake Pleasant** (off Rte. 8 between Speculator and Lake Pleasant).

## Long Lake

**Long Lake Boat Launch** (Town Dock Rd., off Rte. 30, Long Lake).

## Piseco Lake

**Piseco Lake** (Piseco Lake Rd. near the airport, Piseco).

## Stillwater Reservoir

**Stillwater Reservoir** (off Stillwater Rd. near Stillwater Hotel).

## BOAT LIVERIES AND MARINAS

Dozens of privately owned marinas and boat liveries offer a variety of services; complete listings are available from the tourist information booklets published by Warren, Essex, Clinton, Franklin, and Hamilton counties (see Chapter Eight, *Information*). Listed below you'll find a sample of marinas and liveries, which may rent motorboats, sailboats, or canoes; offer parts and service for boat engines; or have deep-water launch ramps.

## LAKE GEORGE AND SOUTHEASTERN ADIRONDACKS

### Brant Lake

**Palmer Bros. Marina** (518-494-2677; Palisades Rd., Brant Lake).

### Lake George

**Bay View Marina Boat Launch** (518-644-9633; Rte. 9N, Bolton Landing).

**Beckley's Boat Rentals and Sales** (518-668-2651; Rte. 9N, Diamond Point).

**Boardwalk** (518-668-4828; Lower Amherst St., Lake George).

**Castaway Marina** (518-656-3636; Rte. 9L, Cleverdale).

**Chic's Marina** (518-644-2170; Rte. 9N, Bolton Landing).

**Gilchrist Marina** (518-668-2028; Rte. 9N, Diamond Point).

**Norowal Marina** (518-644-3741; Sagamore Rd., Bolton Landing).

**Yankee Yacht Sales** (518-668-2862; Rte. 9N, Diamond Point).

**Ward's Dockside Marina and Boat Rentals** (518-543-8888; Rte. 9N, Hague).

**Werner's Boat Rentals** (518-543-8866; Rte. 9N, Silver Bay).

*Loon Lake*

**Loon Lake Marina** (518-494-3410; Jct. Rtes. 8 and 9, Chestertown).

*Schroon Lake*

**Maypine Marina** (518-532-7884; off Rte. 9, Schroon Lake).

## CHAMPLAIN VALLEY

*Lake Champlain*

**Essex Marine Base** (518-963-8698; off Rte. 22, Essex).

**Essex Shipyard Point** (518-963-7700; off Rte. 22, Essex).

**Headwater Marina** (518-585-7066; off Rte. 22, Ticonderoga).

**Indian Bay Marina** (518-963-7858; East Bay Rd., off County Rd. 27, Willsboro).

**Monitor Bay Marina** (518-597-3035; Rte. off Rte. 22, Crown Point).

**Snug Harbor Marina** (518-585-6685; off Rte. 22, Ticonderoga).

**Van Slooten Harbour Marina** (518-546-7400; 140 S. Main St., Port Henry).

**Velez Marina Service** (518-546-7588; Lake Shore Dr., Port Henry).

**Westport Marina** (518-962-4356; Washington St., Westport).

**Willsboro Bay Marina** (518-963-4472; Point Rd., off Rte. 22, Willsboro).

*Westport Marina, on Lake Champlain.*

B. Folwell

## HIGH PEAKS AND NORTHERN ADIRONDACKS

### *Lake Placid*

**Lake Placid Marina** (518-523-9704; Mirror Lake Dr., Lake Placid).

**Capt. Marney's Boat Rentals** (518-523-9746; 3 Victor Herbert Rd., Lake Placid).

### *Saranac Lakes*

**Ampersand Bay Resort** (518-891-3001; Ampersand Bay Rd., off Rte. 3, Saranac Lake) Lower Saranac Lake.

**Crescent Bay** (518-891-2060; off Rte. 3, Saranac Lake) Lower Saranac Lake.

**Swiss Marine** (518-891-2130; 7 Duprey St., Saranac Lake) Lower Saranac Lake.

## NORTHWEST LAKES REGION

### *Big Tupper Lake*

**Blue Jay Campsite** (518-359-3720; Rte. 30, Tupper Lake).

**McDonald's Boat Livery** (518-359-9060; Rte. 30, Tupper Lake).

### *Cranberry Lake*

**Cranberry Lake Boat Livery** (315-848-2501; Rte. 3, at Robinson's IGA, Cranberry Lake).

**The Emporium** (315-848-2140; Rte. 3, Cranberry Lake).

### *Fish Creek Ponds*

**Hickok's Boat Livery** (518-891-0480; Rte. 30, Fish Creek Ponds, Tupper Lake) For Fish Creek Ponds and Upper Saranac Lake.

## CENTRAL AND SOUTHWESTERN ADIRONDACKS

### *Big Moose Lake*

**Dunn's Boat Service** (315-357-3532; Big Moose Rd., Big Moose).

### *Blue Mountain Lake*

**Blue Mountain Lake Boat Livery** (518-352-7351; Rte. 28, Blue Mountain Lake).

### *Fulton Chain of Lakes (First through Eighth lakes)*

**Clark's Marine Service & Boat Rentals** (315-357-3231; Rte. 28, Eagle Bay) On Fourth Lake.

**Inlet Marina** (315-357-4896; South Shore Rd., off Rte. 28, Inlet) On Fourth Lake.

**Palmer Point Boats** (315-357-5594; off Rte. 28, Old Forge).

**Rivett's Boat Livery** (315-369-3123; off Rte. 28, Old Forge) On First Lake.

### *Great Sacandaga Lake*

**Bobilin's Marina** (518-661-5713; Lakeside Dr., Mayfield).

**Edinburg Marina** (518-863-8398; County Rte. 4, Edinburg).

**Montoney's Marine** (518-661-6473; Rte. 30, Mayfield).

**Northampton Marine (**518-863-8127; Rte. 30, Northville).

**Park Marine Base** (518-863-8112; Sacandaga Park, off Rte. 30, Northville).

### *Lake Pleasant*

**Lake Pleasant Marine** (518-548-7711; Rte. 8, Lake Pleasant).

**Lemon Tree** (518-548-6231; Rte. 30, Speculator).

**Paul's Bait Shop** (518-548-3321; Rte. 8, Speculator).

### *Indian Lake*

**Lakeside Marina** (518-648-5459; off Rte. 30, Indian Lake).

### *Long Lake*

**Coddington's Boat House** (518-624-2090; Rte. 30, Long Lake).

**Deerland Marina** (518-624-3371; Rte. 30, Long Lake).

**Long Lake Marina** (518-624-2266; Rte. 30, Long Lake).

### *Piseco Lake*

**Piseco Lake Lodge** (518-548-8552; Old Piseco Rd., Piseco).

### *Raquette Lake*

**Bird's Marine** (315-354-4441; Rte. 28, Raquette Lake).

**Burke's Boat Livery** (315-354-4623; Rte. 28, Raquette Lake).

**Raquette Lake Marina** (315-354-4361; off Rte. 28, Raquette Lake).

*Stillwater Reservoir*

**Stillwater Shop and Boat Launch** (315-376-6470; Stillwater Rd., off Big Moose Rd., Stillwater Reservoir, Lowville).

## BOAT TOURS

If you'd like to experience some of the 2800 Adirondack lakes but you haven't got a clue how to be your own helmsman, practically every lake of significant size has its resident fleet of sight-seeing vessels. Prices vary widely, depending on the length of the tour and what frills come with it (music, dancing, and champagne, for example, on a Lake George moonlight cruise). The season usually runs from early May through October, although this depends on the individual operator as well as when the ice goes out of a particular lake. Note that many of the boats are enclosed, so this is an activity you can still try on a misty, drizzly day. Regardless of whether you choose sunshine, clouds, or evening for your cruise, it's a good idea to call ahead for a reservation.

*The* Minne-Ha-Ha *heads out on a Lake George cruise.*

Nancie Battaglia

## LAKE GEORGE AND SOUTHEASTERN ADIRONDACKS

**Lake George Shoreline Cruises** (518-668-4644; Kurosaka La., Lake George) Several different enclosed boats to choose from, including the jaunty wooden *Horicon*, narrated daytime and dinner cruises, special events.

**Lake George Steamboat Cruises** (518-668-5777; Beach Rd., Lake George) Three enclosed boats, including the paddlewheeler *Minne-Ha-Ha*, narrated cruises from 1 to 4 hours long, snack bar, cocktail lounge, dinner cruises.

**Sagamore Resort** (518-644-9400; Sagamore Island, Bolton Landing) Two enclosed boats, with gourmet dinner cruises aboard the elegant *Morgan*.

## CHAMPLAIN VALLEY

**Fort Ticonderoga Ferry** (802-897-7999; Rte. 74, Ticonderoga; mailing address: Shorewell Ferries, Shoreham, VT 05770) Inexpensive, scenic, quick trip across Lake Champlain.

**Lake Champlain Scenic & Historic Cruises** (802-897-5331; Fort Ticonderoga, Ticonderoga; mailing address: Larrabee's Point, Shoreham, VT 05770) Operates the *Carillon*, which offers a narrated tour between forts Ticonderoga and Crown Point.

**Lake Champlain Ferries** (518-963-7010; Rte. 22, Essex) Car ferry between Essex, NY and Charlotte, VT with hourly trips. Also 518-834-7960; Rte. 22, Port Kent. Car ferry between Port Kent and Burlington with hourly trips. Passengers without cars are welcome.

## HIGH PEAKS AND NORTHERN ADIRONDACKS

**Lake Placid Marina Boat Tours** (518-523-9704; Lake Dr., Lake Placid) Scenic trips on Lake Placid aboard the enclosed, classic wooden boats *Doris* (1950) and *Lady of the Lake* (ca. 1929).

**Lorraine's Pedal Boats** (518-891-2241; Saranac Lake Village) Regularly scheduled narrated historic tours on Lake Flower; cocktail cruises on Lake Flower and Oseetah Lake aboard the *Pelican*, an open pontoon boat.

## CENTRAL AND SOUTHWESTERN ADIRONDACKS

**Bird's Marina** (315-354-4441; Rte. 28, Raquette Lake) Daily (except Sunday) rides on the mail-delivery boat.

**Blue Mountain Lake Boat Livery** (518-352-7351; Rte. 28, Blue Mountain Lake) Scenic cruises through the Eckford Chain of Lakes aboard two restored wooden launches, the *Neenykin* and the *Osprey*, accommodating 18 or fewer passengers.

**Norridgewock II** (315-376-6200; Number Four Rd., Stillwater Reservoir. Mail: Beaver River, Lowville, NY 13367) Tours on Stillwater Reservoir; access to Beaver River, the most remote community in the park.

**Old Forge Lake Cruises** (315-369-6473; Rte. 28, Old Forge) Scenic, narrated 28-mile cruise on the Fulton Chain of Lakes, aboard the *Uncas* or the *Clearwater*. Evening "showboat" cruises, dinner cruises by reservation.

**Raquette Lake Navigation Co.** (315-354-5532; Town Dock, Raquette Lake) Lunch, brunch, and dinner cruises (by reservation) aboard the new *W.W. Durant*, an enclosed replica of a 19th-century boat.

# BOWLING

Many of the Great Camps and magnificent 19th-century hotels featured outdoor bowling alleys, and many a North Country youngster earned a few bits setting pins for the summer folk in olden times. Nowadays, prime Adirondack woods are made into the best bowling pins and bowling alleys at the AMF factory just outside the Blue Line, in Lowville, so why not commemorate this continuing tradition with a gutter ball or two at a regional keglers' hall? Bowling isn't a bad idea for physical activity on a gloomy day, either, and most bowling alleys offer drinks and snacks, too.

In *Lake George and Southeastern Adirondacks*, options are *Lake George Bowl*, 518-668-5741; Rte. 9, Lake George, and the *Lake Luzerne Community Center*, 518-696-4545; 2505 Lake Ave., Lake Luzerne. For the **Champlain Valley** towns, try *Adirondack Lanes*, 518-585-6077; Hague Rd., Ticonderoga, and *Keeseville Bowling Center*, 518-834-7777; 4 Main St., Keeseville. Around the **High Peaks and Northern Adirondacks**, lanes are found at the *Saranac Lake Bowling Alley*, 518-891-1860; 8 Bloomingdale Ave., Saranac Lake, or *Riverside Hotel and Bowling Alley*, 518-647-9905; Rte. 9N, Au Sable Forks. Rain or shine, in the **Northwest Lakes Region** you can try the *Tupper Bowl*, 518-359-2234; Moody Rd., Tupper Lake. In the **Central and Southwestern Adirondacks**, the alleys are open year-round at the *North Street Inn*, 315-369-3970; on North St., just off Rte. 28 in Old Forge.

# CAMPS

A surprising assortment of famous folks spent their summers at Adirondack camps: Vincent Price was a counselor at Camp Riverdale, on Long Lake; Bonnie Raitt spent many summers at Camp Regis, on Upper St. Regis Lake; G. Gordon Liddy is an alumnus of Brant Lake Camp; Arlo Guthrie and his mother, a dance instructor, enjoyed many seasons at the Raquette Lake camps; Lionel Trilling edited the newsletter at a boys' camp in the southern Adirondacks; and the list goes on.

Throughout the Adirondacks summer camps offer a wide range of programs. There are high-adventure camps, with the emphasis on self-reliance in the wilderness through extended canoe trips, backpacking treks, or rock-climbing lessons. There are also very posh, comfortable camps, with nice cabins, good food, and fine-arts programs. Some camps are truly Great Camps — in the architectural sense of the phrase — magnificent, rustic old waterfront estates. And several camps offer family sessions so that everyone can share in the fun.

The following list is a sampling of many summer camps, with both winter and summer addresses and phone numbers. Note that camps owned by the Boy Scouts of America are generally open only to members of certain troops; Girl Scout camp enrollment policies are usually open to all girls, with a modest fee to join as a scout (for insurance coverage). Likewise, YMCA camps are open to all youngsters who pay dues.

If you're in the Adirondacks during July or August, and would like to visit a particular camp with your prospective happy camper, we recommend that you call ahead; also, many camps will send videos to give you a sight-and-sound taste of the the action.

## LAKE GEORGE AND SOUTHEASTERN ADIRONDACKS

**Brant Lake Camp** (Boys) Directors: Karen Meltzer, Robert Gersten, Richard Gersten. 518-494-2406; Brant Lake, NY 12815. Winter office: 212-734-6216; 19 E. 80th St., New York, NY 10021. Established in 1915, and still run by the same family. Programs include a full range of team sports (baseball, basketball, wrestling, soccer, hockey), water sports (canoeing, waterskiing, swimming, sailing), computers, crafts, music, theater. Ages 7—16 in different divisions. Also, **Brant Lake Camp** (Girls), with emphasis on dance, arts, and sports, for ages 12—16.

**Camp Chingachgook** Director: George W. Painter. 518-656-9462; Pilot Knob Rd., Pilot Knob, NY 12844. Winter office: 518-374-9136; 13 State St., Schenectady, NY 12305. Established in 1913 on the east side of Lake George; YMCA-affiliated. Coed. Program includes sailing, waterskiing, canoeing, hiking, art, drama, team sports, ropes course.

**Camp Somerhill** Directors: Lynn Teper-Singer, Lawrence Singer, Bruce Singer. 518-623-9914; Athol, NY 12810. Winter office: 914-793-1303; 20 Huntley Rd., Box 295, Eastchester, NY 10709. Coed; on private lake. Programs in athletics, science, horseback riding, creative arts, water sports; overnight backpack and canoe trips; flying lessons; trips to museums, Tanglewood, or Saratoga Performing Arts Center.

**Hidden Lake Camp** Director: Susan Spencer. 518-696-2244; RD 2, Box 2769, Lake George, NY 12845. Winter office: 518-374-3345; 945 Palmer Ave., Schenectady, NY 12309. Girls; operated by Mohawk Pathways Girl Scout Council. Highlights include a self-esteem-building ropes course; 2-week canoe program with 4-day trips to Raquette and Blue Mountain lakes; mountain-biking overnights; plus swimming, hiking, crafts, nature study.

**Luzerne Music Center** Directors: Bert Phillips and Toby Blumenthal. 518-696-2771; Lake Rd., Lake Luzerne, NY 12846. Winter office: 1-800-874-3202; 4739 Harvest Bend, Sarasota, FL 34235. Coed, ages 11—19; excellent chamber music program led by members of the Philadelphia Orchestra.

**Point O' Pines Camp for Girls** Directors: Sue and Jim Himoff. 518-494-3213; Brant Lake, NY 12815. Winter office: 212-288-0246; 40 E. 78th St., New York, NY 10021. Girls; on Brant Lake; 8-week session; full program.

**Skye Farm Camp and Retreat Center** Director: Debi Paterson. 518-494-3432; Sherman Lake, Bolton Landing, NY 12814. Winter office: 518-494-7170; HCR 2, Box 103, Warrensburg, NY 12885. Boys; girls; adults. Operated by United Methodist Church; full summer program for children; special fall hiking and canoeing weekends for adults; winter cross-country skiing and snowshoeing days.

**Sonrise Lutheran Outdoor Ministry** Directors: Larry and Ruth McReynolds. 518-494-2620; Pottersville, NY 12860. Boys; girls; coed; adults. Affiliated with Missouri Synod. On Schroon Lake; full program; conference center open year-round.

**Word of Life Fellowship** Directors: Jack Wyrtzen and George Theis. 518-532-7111; Rte. 9, Schroon Lake, NY 12870. Sessions for girls; boys; coed; adults. Nondenominational Christian camp and conference center. Full range of indoor and outdoor sports; horseback riding. Snow camp for ages 12—19 with skiing, snowmobiling, sleigh rides, ice fishing.

## CHAMPLAIN VALLEY

**Camp Dudley** Director: Dr. William Schmidt. 518-962-4720; Camp Dudley Rd., Westport, NY 12993. Established in 1885; the oldest boys' camp in the country. Affiliated with the YMCA, but operated independently. On Lake Champlain; activities include all water sports, hiking, backpacking, golf, soccer, arts, photography, tennis, wrestling. Ages 10—15.

**North Country Camps: Lincoln** (Boys) and **Whippoorwill** (Girls) Directors: Peter Gucker and Nancy Gucker Birdsall. 518-834-5527; Auger Lake, Keeseville, NY 12944. Winter office: 201-768-6198; 36 Wellwood Rd., Demarest, NJ 07627. Eastablished by the Gucker family in 1920. Strong camping-trip program with backpacking, canoeing, sailing, horseback riding, mountain climbing; in-camp programs in swimming, windsurfing, kayaking, soccer, science, crafts, aerobics, ropes, dance, music, arts.

**Pok-O-MacCready Camps: Pok-O-Moonshine** (Boys), **MacCready** (Girls), and 1812 Homestead (coed outdoor education center). Director: Jack Swan. 518-963-8366; Mountain Rd., Willsboro, NY 12996. Winter office: 203-775-9865; Box 5016, Brookfield, CT 06804. Established in 1905; on Long Pond. Summer-camp sessions highlight horseback riding, sailing, backpacking, gymnastics, lacrosse, tennis, canoeing, rock climbing, archery, crafts, dance, drama. During fall, winter, and spring, the campus is an outdoor education center open to school groups, featuring traditional skills and crafts in the homestead; earth studies; programs for "at-risk" students.

## HIGH PEAKS

**Camp Chateaugay** Directors: Hal Lyons and Laurie Roland. 518-425-6888; Upper Chateaugay Lake, Merrill, NY 12955. Winter office: 303-674-3115; 28587 Clover La., Evergreen, CO 80439. Coed. Wilderness program for ages 14—16, water sports, horseback riding, tennis, soccer, climbing, lacrosse, woodcraft, photography, arts.

**Camp Treetops** Director: Jeff Jonathan. 518-523-9329; North Country School, Rte. 73, Lake Placid, NY 12946. Coed; ages 7—13. Besides horseback riding, overnight canoeing and camping trips, rock climbing, sailing, and a full range of nature and arts programs, the camp is also a working farm, where kids take care of the animals and gardens.

*Taking the plunge at Camp Treetops, Lake Placid.*

Nancie Battaglia

**Eagle Island** 518-891-0928; Eagle Island, Upper Saranac Lake, Lake Clear, NY 12944. Winter office: Girl Scout Council of Greater Essex County, NJ, 201-746-8200; 120 Valley Rd., Montclair, NJ 07042. Sessions for girls, families, and women. Located on an island with a rustic Great Camp estate; strong program in water sports; open to non-Girl Scouts, too.

**Woodsmoke** Director: Kris Hansen. 518-523-3868; Lake Placid, NY 12946. Winter office: 518-523-9344; Box 628, Lake Placid, NY 12946. Coed; ages 7—15; maximum 45 campers per session; log cabins. Program includes swimming, sailing, canoeing, tennis, backpacking, mountain climbing, riflery, woodcraft, environmental studies.

**Young Life Saranac Village** Director: C. L. Robertson. 518-891-3010; Star Rte. Box 88, Saranac Lake, NY 12983. Coed, nondenominational Christian camp for teens. Located in the rustic Great Camp, Prospect Point. Programs include all water sports, team sports, Bible studies.

## NORTHWEST LAKES REGION

**Adirondack Scout Reservation** Director: David Boshea. 518-359-2281; Massawepie Lake, Tupper Lake, NY 12986. Winter office: 716-244-4210; 474 East Ave., Rochester, NY 14607. Three boys' camps operated by the Hiawatha Council (Syracuse) and Otetiana Council (Rochester): Camp Forester on Deer Pond, Camp Mountaineer on Massawepie Lake, and Camp Sabattis. Programs include sailing, canoeing, hiking, woodcraft, nature, rock climbing, ecology. Adirondack Treks, with extended backcountry excursions to many regions of the park, are open to any Boy Scout troops.

**Camp Regis-Applejack** Director: Michael Humes. 518-327-3117; Rte. 30, Paul Smiths, NY 12970. Winter office: 914-997-7039; 107 Robinhood Dr., White Plains, NY 10605. Coed; ages 7—17; Quaker philosophy. Based at a former estate on the shore of Upper St. Regis Lake; canoeing, kayaking, sailing, waterskiing, hiking, team sports, arts and crafts, photography, performing arts, wilderness overnight trips for senior campers.

**Star Lake Computer Camp** Director: Dick Leroux. 315-267-2167. Star Lake SUNY Campus, Star Lake, NY 13690. Winter office: 1-800-458-1142; Raymond Hall, SUNY, Potsdam, NY 13676. Coed; ages 9—14. Campers explore the natural world around Star Lake, then create data bases to develop a guidebook and map; outdoor activities include canoeing, hiking, camping.

## CENTRAL AND SOUTHWESTERN ADIRONDACKS

**Adirondack Woodcraft Camps** Directors: John and David Leach. 315-369-6031; Rondaxe Rd., Old Forge, NY 13420. Established in 1925; coed. Two private lakes; all water sports; extended backpacking and canoeing trips throughout the Adirondacks; crafts, sciences, academic enrichment.

**Camp Baco** (Boys) and **Camp Che-Na-Wah** (Girls) Directors: Robert and Ruth Wortman. 518-251-2929; Lake Balfour, Minerva, NY 12851. Winter office: 516-374-7757; 80 Neptune Ave., Woodmere, NY 11598. Ages 6—16. Camp Baco established in 1923; on private lake. Activities include swimming, canoeing, sailing, waterskiing, tennis, lacrosse, archery, photography, drama, music, crafts.

**Camp Eagle Cove** Director: Paul Turner. 315-357-2267; South Shore Rd., Inlet, NY 13360. Winter office: 1-800-251-2267; Box 1066, Boca Raton, FL 33429-

1066. Coed; on Fourth Lake. Program includes all water sports, horseback riding, tennis, wilderness canoeing and camping trips, computers, crafts, drama, and English as a second language.

**Camp Gorham** Director: Barbara Fisher. 315-357-6401; Darts Lake, Eagle Bay, NY 13331. Winter office: 716 E. Main St., Rochester, NY 14604. Coed; ages 8—15. Affiliated with YMCA of Greater Rochester; 1100-acre facility on Darts Lake. Activities include all water sports, horseback riding, hiking, nature study, overnight camping and canoeing trips. Campers must be members of YMCA of Greater Rochester; summer-camp memberships are $20. Family-camping week in August.

**Camp Russell** Director: Carl Sahre. 315-392-3290; Woodgate, NY 13494. Winter office: 315-866-1540; Box 128, Herkimer, NY 13350. Boys. Established in 1918; affiliated with the Boy Scouts. Programs include water sports, forestry, overnight canoeing and camping trips.

**4-H Camp Sacandaga** Director: Cornell Cooperative Extension. 518-548-7993; Page St., Speculator, NY 12164. Winter office: 518-623-3291; Cooperative Extension, HCR 02, Box 23B, Warrensburg, NY 12885. Coed; ages 8—19. Originally a Civilian Conservation Corps camp. Programs include environmental education, creative arts, horseback riding, water sports.

**Cedarlands Scout Reservation** Director: Kevin Bishop. 518-624-4371; Walker Rd., Long Lake, NY 12847. Winter office: 315-735-4437; Oneida Council BSA, 1400 Genesee St., Utica, NY 13501. Boy Scouts only. Water sports, crafts, overnight wilderness trips.

**Deerfoot Lodge** Director: Charles Gieser. 518-548-5277; Whitaker Lake, Speculator, NY 12164. Winter office: 518-966-4115; RD 2,Box 159B, Greenville, NY 12083. Boys, ages 8—16. Owned by Christian Camps, Inc. Activities include water sports, hiking, overnight canoeing and camping trips, special 12-day backcountry Voyageur trips. Also **Tapawingo**, for girls, at Camp of the Woods; 518-548-5091; Rte. 30, Speculator.

**Fowler Camp and Conference Center** Director: Kent Busman. 518-548-6524; Sacandaga Lake, Speculator, NY 12164. Winter office: 518-374-4573; 1790 Grand Blvd., Schenectady, NY 12309. Coed; ages 9—18. Affiliated with Reformed Church in America. Some older Great Camp-style rustic and log buildings. Activities include water sports, hiking, crafts, nature study, overnight canoeing and camping trips. Special late summer and fall sessions for adults and seniors exploring Adirondack history and environment.

**Long Lake Camp** Directors: Marc and Susan Katz. 518-624-4831; Walker Rd., Long Lake, NY 12847. Winter office: 1-800-767-7111; 33 Western Dr.,

Ardsley, NY 10502. Coed; on Long Lake. Emphasis on drama, dance, music, circus skills, video; programs include horseback riding, canoeing, gymnastics, martial arts, water sports, and overnight canoeing and camping trips.

**Northern Frontier** Director: Rev. Bruce Baker. 518-251-2322; North River, NY 12856. Winter office: 914-564-2567; 83 Coach La., Newburgh, NY 12550. Boys. Affiliated with the Christian Service Brigade. Located on private lake. Activities include horseback riding, rock climbing, canoeing, hiking, fishing, swimming, crafts, archery, and overnight trips. Special sessions for fathers and sons.

## CAMPING

Sleeping out under the stars on a remote island, or in the posh comfort of a recreational vehicle, or nestled within the cozy confines of a backpacking tent deep in the forest — camping possibilities in the Adirondacks cater to all tastes. The Department of Environmental Conservation (DEC) operates 40-some public campgrounds here, most of which are on beautiful lakes or peaceful ponds, all of which are open from just before Memorial Day through Labor Day. Some campgrounds are open earlier, for fisher-folk, and some are open later into the fall.

The smaller places (those with 100 sites or fewer) often tend to be quieter; some campgrounds accommodate upwards of 400 families, and can be like visiting little cities in the woods. However, camping in the North Country is still very much a family-oriented experience; the crime problems you might have read about at the national parks are not found here. The only hassles you might encounter are from persistent chipmunks and red squirrels who regard your picnic table as their lunch counter, too. Facilities at these campgrounds include a picnic table and grill at each site, water spigots for every ten sites or

*Backcountry camping by an Adirondack lake.*

Nancie Battaglia

Michael Trivieri

*An Adirondack lean-to near Eagle Bay.*

so, and lavatories; however, not every state campground has showers. Several campgrounds have sites for mobility-impaired campers, with hard-surface areas, water spigots at wheelchair height, and ramps to the restrooms.

Camping is also permitted year-round on most of the 2.5 million acres of state land, but keep in mind that you need a permit to stay more than three days in one backcountry spot, or if you are camping in a group with more than 10 people. These permits are available from local forest rangers. Some locations, like Stillwater Reservoir, Lows Lake, or Lake Lila, have designated primitive camping spots, with fire rings or privies, but you may camp elsewhere provided you pitch your tent at least 150 feet from any trail, stream, lake, or other water body. (Check the information on low-impact camping, below.) Also, along the Northville-Lake Placid Trail and on popular canoe routes you'll find lean-tos for camping. These three-sided log structures are a trademark of the Adirondack wilds, and custom calls for you to share a lean-to with other campers.

Reservations can be made for a site in the state campgrounds by calling MISTIX (1-800-456-CAMP), a computerized reservation service based in California. It's a handy convenience to be able to call ahead, but don't expect the person on the other end of the line to know which individual sites at which campgrounds have the nicest views or best swimming. You can reserve a site for anywhere from a single night to three weeks and charge it to your charge card; if you change your mind, however, getting a refund can be complicated. The DEC campgrounds will cheerfully take you on a first-come, first-served basis if space is available; before July 4 and after September 1, it's usually easy to find a nice site without a reservation. Campsites cost between $7 and $13 per night in 1992.

Note that DEC public campgrounds do not supply water, electric or sewer hookups; for these amenities, there are privately owned campgrounds in many communities, attached to properties with housekeeping cabins or free-standing. Check individual listings in Chapter Three, *Lodging*, for these facilities. Also, some towns offer public camping; check with local tourist-information offices, listed in Chapter Eight, *Information*.

If you'd like to try camping, but don't know where to begin or don't own a single bit of equipment, the Beginner Camper Program sponsored by recreational equipment companies and DEC is an easy way to learn the ropes. At Fish Creek Pond Campground, on Rte. 30 about 10 miles from Tupper Lake, you can rent all the necessities — tent, cook set, sleeping bags, cooler, backpacks, and such — and secure a campsite for $13 per day. There are staff people to help you set up camp and planned activities to introduce you to this new environment. You have to supply your own chow, and clothing for cool nights and warm days, but the rest is there waiting for you.

## PUBLIC CAMPGROUNDS

### LAKE GEORGE AND SOUTHEASTERN ADIRONDACKS

**Eagle Point** (518-494-2220; US Rte. 9, 2 miles north of Pottersville) 3-day minimum stay for reserved sites; boat launch, showers, swimming.

**Hearthstone Point** (518-668-5193; Rte. 9N, 2 miles north of Lake George Village) On Lake George. 3-day minimum for reserved sites; showers, swimming.

**Lake George Battleground** (518-668-3348; Rte. 9, 1/4 mile east of Lake George Village) Historic site. 3-day minimum for reserved sites; showers.

**Lake George Islands** (518-668-5441; 400 sites on Narrows Islands, Glen Islands, Long Island groups) Access by boat; tents only; swimming. No dogs allowed.

**Luzerne** (518-696-2031; off Rte. 9N, Lake Luzerne) On Fourth Lake. 3-day minimum for reserved sites; showers, swimming, canoe and rowboat launch; no powerboats allowed.

**Rogers Rock** (518-585-6746; Rte. 9N, 3 miles north of Hague) On Lake George. Historic site. 3-day minimum for reserved sites; boat launch.

## CHAMPLAIN VALLEY

**Ausable Point** (518-561-7080; Rte. 9, north of Port Kent) On Lake Champlain. 3-day minimum for reserved sites; showers, swimming, boat launch.

**Crown Point Reservation** (518-597-3603; off Rte. 9N, near the bridge to Vermont north of Crown Point) On Lake Champlain. Showers, boat launch.

**Lincoln Pond** (518-942-5292; County Rte. 7, 6 miles south of Elizabethtown) 3-day minimum for reserved sites; swimming, showers, canoe or rowboat rentals, no powerboats allowed.

**Paradox Lake** (518-532-7451; Rte. 74, 2 miles east of Severance) Swimming, showers, canoe or rowboat rentals, boat launch.

**Poke-O-Moonshine** (518-834-9045; Rte. 9, 6 miles south of Keeseville) Showers, access to Poke-O-Moonshine Mountain for rock climbers.

**Putnam Pond** (518-585-7280; off Rte. 74, 6 miles west of Ticonderoga) Swimming, showers, canoe or rowboat rentals, boat launch.

**Sharp Bridge** (518-532-7538; Rte. 9, 15 miles north of Schroon Lake) Showers, access to Hammond Pond Wild Forest for fishermen, mountain bikers, or hikers.

## HIGH PEAKS AND NORTHERN ADIRONDACKS

**Buck Pond** (518-891-3449; off Rte. 30 near Onchiota) Swimming, showers, canoe or rowboat rental, boat launch.

**Lake Harris** (518-582-2503; Rte. 28N, Newcomb) Swimming, showers, boat launch.

**Meacham Lake** (518-483-5116; Rte. 30, 9 miles north of Paul Smiths)

*Campers at Wilmington Notch.*

Nancie Battaglia

Swimming, showers, horse trails and barn, some primitive sites accessible by foot only, boat launch.

**Meadowbrook** (518-891-4531; Rte. 86 near Ray Brook) Showers.

**Saranac Lake Islands** (518-891-3170; off Rte. 3 near highway bridge southwest of Saranac Lake Village) Access by boat, tents only.

**Taylor Pond** (518-647-5250; Silver Lake Rd., 9 miles northwest of Au Sable Forks) Boat launch.

**Wilmington Notch** (518-946-7172; Rte. 86, 3 miles west of Wilmington) Showers; on the Ausable River.

## NORTHWEST LAKES REGION

**Cranberry Lake** (315-848-2315; off Rte. 3, 1 mile south of Cranberry Lake village) 2-day minimum stay for reserved sites. Swimming, showers, rowboat or canoe rentals.

**Fish Creek Pond** (518-891-4560; Rte. 30, 12 miles east of Tupper Lake) 3-day minimum for reserved sites. Swimming, showers, canoe or rowboat rentals, boat launch, nature programs.

**Rollins Pond** (518-891-3239; Rte. 30, near Fish Creek Pond campsite) 3-day minimum for reserved sites. Showers, canoe or rowboat rentals, boat launch.

---

### The Bear Truth

Just as some humans have become acclimated to sleeping out in the wilds, some wild animals have become attuned to human habits and have learned to recognize coolers, thermoses, packs, and tents as possible food sources. When in doubt about the presence of hungry black bears or pesky raccoons, take all precautions. If your campsite has a metal footlocker for food storage, use it. Otherwise, stash your food and cooking gear well away from your tent; put it in a pack or several strong plastic bags and suspend it between two trees with a sturdy rope at least 20 feet off the ground. Tie it off by wrapping several times around one tree and tie a complicated knot; bears have been known to swat down food packs within their reach, climb saplings, and even bite through ropes. Don't try to outsmart Bruin by putting your food in an anchored boat away from shore; bears can swim. The campsite caretaker can give you an update on the bear situation at a particular place and offer more advice.

Actual bear attacks are extremely rare in the Adirondacks. If a bear does visit your camp, usually lots of noise (yelling, banging on pots or pans, a loud whistle) scares him or her off. Do keep your dog under control in the event of a close encounter of the ursine kind.

## CENTRAL AND SOUTHWESTERN ADIRONDACKS

**Alger Island** (315-369-3224; off South Shore Rd., west of Inlet) 2-day minimum stay for reserved sites; on Fourth Lake; access by boat, tents only.

**Brown's Tract Ponds** (315-354-4412; Uncas Rd. west of Raquette Lake hamlet) 2-day minimum for reserved sites. Swimming, canoe or rowboat rentals, no powerboats allowed.

**Caroga Lake** (518-835-4241; Rte. 29A south of Caroga Lake hamlet) 2-day minimum for reserved sites. Swimming, showers, boat launch.

**Eighth Lake** (315-357-3132; Rte. 28, between Raquette Lake and Inlet) 3-day minimum for reserved sites. Swimming, showers, canoe or rowboat rentals, boat launch.

**Forked Lake** (518-624-6646; North Point Rd., off Rte. 30 southwest of Long Lake hamlet) 2-day minimum. Primitive walk-in or canoe-in sites, launch for car-top and small powerboats.

**Golden Beach** (315-354-4230; Rte. 28, 3 miles east of Raquette Lake hamlet) On Raquette Lake. Swimming, showers, boat or canoe rentals, boat launch.

**Indian Lake Islands** (518-648-5300; off Rte. 30, 11 miles south of Indian Lake hamlet) 3-day minimum for reserved sites. Access by boat, tents only, boat launch.

**Lake Durant** (518-352-7797; Rte. 28/30, 3 miles east of Blue Mtn. Lake) 3-day minimum for reserved sites. Swimming, showers, canoe rentals, boat launch, handicap-access campsite.

**Lake Eaton** (518-624-2641; Rte. 30, 2 miles north of Long Lake bridge) 2-day minimum for reserved sites. Swimming, showers, canoe or rowboat rentals, boat launch.

**Lewey Lake** (518-648-5266; Rte. 30, across from Indian Lake Islands access road) 2-day minimum for reserved sites. Swimming, showers, canoe or rowboat rentals, boat launch.

**Limekiln Lake** (315-357-4401; Limekiln Lake Rd., off Rte. 28 east of Inlet) 2-day minimum stay for reserved sites. Swimming, showers, canoe or rowboat rentals, boat launch.

**Little Sand Point** (518-548-7585; Piseco Lake Rd., off Rte. 30) 2-day minimum for reserved sites. On Piseco Lake. Swimming, canoe or rowboat rentals, boat launch.

**Moffit Beach** (518-548-7102; off Rte. 8, 4 miles west of Speculator) 3-day minimum for reserved sites. On Sacandaga Lake. Swimming, showers, canoe or rowboat rentals, boat launch.

**Northampton Beach** (518-863-6000; Rte. 30, 2 miles south of Northville) 3-day minimum for reserved sites. On Great Sacandaga Lake. Swimming, showers, canoe or rowboat rentals, boat launch.

**Point Comfort** (518-548-7586; Piseco Lake Rd.) 2-day minimum for reserved sites. On Piseco Lake. Swimming, showers, canoe or rowboat rentals, boat launch.

**Poplar Point** (518-548-8031; Piseco Lake Rd.) 2-day minimum for reserved sites. On Piseco Lake. Swimming, canoe or rowboat rentals, boat launch.

**Sacandaga** (518-924-4121; Rte. 30, 4 miles south of Wells) 2-day minimum for reserved sites. On Sacandaga River. Swimming, showers, no powerboats.

**Tioga Point** (315-354-4230; Raquette Lake) 2-day minimum for reserved sites. On Raquette Lake. Access by boat; tents only.

## CANOEING AND KAYAKING

Paddlers agree: the Adirondack Park offers some of the best canoeing and kayaking in the Northeast; some might argue that the region rivals the Boundary Waters Canoe Area in Minnesota for excellent backcountry tripping. Within the Blue Line, there are some 2800 lakes, ponds, flows, and still-waters, and thousands of miles of rivers and streams. For thrill seekers, there's serious white water (up to Class V) on the Upper Hudson, the Moose, portions of the Schroon, and other rivers; for flat-water fans, there are long trips linking lakes and watersheds, such as the 44-mile route from Long Lake to Tupper Lake, the 35-mile trip from Old Forge to Blue Mountain Lake, or the 25-mile trip from Osgood Pond to Lake Kushaqua, near Paul Smiths. In the St. Regis Canoe Area, it's possible to paddle for weeks on end and visit a different pond

*Enjoying a peaceful morning paddle on Second Pond, near Saranac Lake.*

Nancie Battaglia

or lake each day. There's even a 3-day race, the Adirondack Canoe Classic, in September, that covers 90 miles of water in a long diagonal from the Fulton Chain of Lakes to Saranac Lake village (see the listing of "Races and Seasonal Sports Events" later in this chapter).

Given that the possibilities are almost unlimited, how does a newcomer choose where to go? Two guidebooks cover Adirondack destinations for human-powered watercraft: *Adirondack Canoe Waters: North Flow* by Paul Jamieson and Donald Morris (Adirondack Mountain Club, 1991) and *Adirondack Canoe Waters: South and West Flow* by Alec Proskine (Adirondack Mountain Club, 1989). Of the two, *North Flow* is more informative and a joy to read, thanks to Jamieson's lovely descriptions; *South and West* is workmanlike, with helpful maps locating carries (the Adirondack word for portage), water-falls, and put-ins. Both *Adirondac* and *Adirondack Life* magazines publish fre-quent articles describing canoe trips; check a local library for back issues, or contact the publications directly (listed in Chapter Eight, *Information*). There's also a fine map, *Adirondack Canoe Waters*, published by Adirondack Maps in Keene Valley, that shows several routes; you can purchase the chart in region-al bookstores, sporting goods stores, or outfitters.

The Department of Environmental Conservation has published pamphlets describing various canoe routes, including the Bog River area near Tupper Lake, Stillwater Reservoir, and many others. Canoeing on Niagara Mohawk Power Company's hydroelectric impoundments on the Beaver, Raquette, Sacandaga, and Oswegatchie rivers is outlined in a free brochure available at information booths or by calling NiMo (315-474-1511). Some tourist informa-tion offices, such as the Saranac Lake Chamber of Commerce (518-891-1990), offer useful brochures and maps, too; ask for *Canoe Franklin County*. Note that these simplified maps are not suitable for navigating; always consult U.S. Geological Service topographic maps for the area you're traveling through.

When you're planning for any trip, allow an extra day in case the weather doesn't cooperate. Remember that you're required to carry a life jacket for each paddler; lash an extra paddle in your canoe, too. Bring plenty of food and fuel, a backpacker stove, and rain gear. A poncho makes a good coverall for hiking, but you're far better off with rain jacket and pants in a canoe, since a poncho can become tangled if you should dump the canoe. Do sign in at the trailhead registers when you begin your trip.

If you're still overwhelmed by making a decision about where to go, consult one of the outfitters listed below. (These are folks specializing in canoeing or kayaking with good-quality equipment; many boat liveries and marinas also rent aluminum or Coleman canoes.) And if you're anxious to try canoeing but just aren't sure of your abilities, there are plenty of places to get informal instruction in flat-water or white-water techniques. Your local Red Cross office may schedule water safety and basic canoe instruction, or you can contact the Tri-Lakes office of the American Red Cross (518-891-3280; 52 Broadway, Saranac Lake, NY 12983) for their workshop dates.

## CANOE OUTFITTERS AND TRIP GUIDES

### LAKE GEORGE AND SOUTHEASTERN ADIRONDACKS

**Adirondack Mountain Club** (518-668-4447; Luzerne Rd., Lake George, NY 12845) Spring, summer, and fall canoe workshops in different locations; guided canoe tours for women, youth, and Elderhostel groups.

**W.I.L.D./W.A.T.E.R.S.** (518-494-7478; Rte. 28, The Glen, Warrensburg, NY 12885) Canoe and kayak instruction for youth and adults, white-water clinics, kayak camp for youth, lodging available.

### HIGH PEAKS AND NORTHERN ADIRONDACKS

**Adirondack Adventure Tours** (518-523-1475; 126 Main St., Lake Placid, NY 12946) Guided canoe trips; complete trip outfitter.

**Adirondack Rock and River Guide Service** (518-576-2041; Alstead Hill Rd., Keene, NY 12942) White-water kayaking instruction, guided trips, lodging.

**All Seasons Outfitters** (518-891-3548; 168 Lake Flower Ave., Saranac Lake, NY 12983) Guided day and overnight canoe trips, flat-water canoe lessons, complete trip outfitter.

**Bear Cub Adventure Tours** (518-523-4339; 30 Bear Cub Rd., Lake Placid) White-water canoe and kayak instruction, guided trips.

**Birchbark Tours** (518-891-5704; 32 Glenwood, Saranac Lake) Guided canoe trips.

**Jones Outfitters Ltd.** (518-523-3468; 37 Main St., Lake Placid) Canoe rentals and sales.

**Middle Earth Expeditions** (518-523-9572; HCR 01, Box 37, Lake Placid) Guided wilderness canoe and fishing trips.

**Jim Sausville** (518-891-2062; 3 Beaver Pond Rd., Saranac Lake) Flat-water and free-style canoe instruction.

**Tahawus Guide Service** (518-891-4334; Box 424, Lake Placid) Guided canoe and traditional guideboat trips.

**Wilderness Recreation Leadership Program** (518-891-2915; North Country Community College, Saranac Lake) Complete trip outfitter; guide and wilderness-leadership training.

**Young's Foothills** (518-891-1221; Box 345, Saranac Lake) Guided canoe trips.

## NORTHWEST LAKES REGION

**Raquette River Outfitters** (518-359-3228; 9 High St., Tupper Lake, NY 12986) Complete trip outfitter; guided trips, car shuttles.

**St. Regis Canoe Outfitters** (518-891-1838; Floodwood Rd., Lake Clear, NY 12945) Complete trip outfitter; guided trips, canoe instruction, car shuttles.

**Trillium Guide Service** (518-891-2484; Box 133, Lake Clear) Guided canoe trips.

---

### Don't Drink the Water

Sure, the water's cool and clear, and looks like it should be the ideal thirst quencher — but please, resist the temptation to drink freely from Adirondack lakes, rivers, ponds, and streams. Sadly, due to careless campers and occasional animal pollution, these wild waters may harbor a microscopic parasite known as *Giardia lamblia*, which often causes bloating, diarrhea, cramping, vomiting, and other discomforts. Giardiasis — also known as Beaver Fever — is easily diagnosed (with a stool sample) and easily treated (with quinicrine or Flagyl), but it's better to avoid the ailment in the first place. Practice good campsite sanitation. Treat all drinking water by boiling 10 minutes, by using a specially designed giardia-proof filter, or with chlorine or iodine tablets.

---

## CENTRAL AND SOUTHWESTERN ADIRONDACKS

**Adirondack Hut-to-Hut Tours** (518-251-2710; Rte. 28N, Minerva Hill Lodge, Minerva, NY 12851) Canoe rentals; guided backcountry canoe trips; guided "inn-to-inn" canoe tours.

**Adirondack Outfitters of Long Lake** (518-624-5998; Rte. 30, Long Lake, NY 12847) Canoe rentals; sporting goods shop.

**Blue Mountain Outfitters** (518-352-7306/352-7675; Box 144, Blue Mountain Lake, NY 12812) Complete trip outfitter; guided trips; car shuttles; sporting goods shop, canoe rental and sales.

*Blue Mountain Outfitters, Blue Mountain Lake.*

Nancie Battaglia

**Mountainaire Adventures** (518-251-2194; Rte. 28, Wevertown, NY 12886) Guided canoe trips, lodging.

**Stillwater Shop** (315-376-2110; Stillwater Rd., Stillwater Reservoir. Mail: Star Rte., Lowville, NY 13367) Canoe rentals, camping supplies for sale.

**Tickner's Moose River Canoe Outfitters** (315-369-6286; Rte. 28, Old Forge, NY 13420) Complete trip outfitter; canoe instruction, canoe rentals and sales.

**Trailhead Lodge** (518-863-2198; Washburn Rd., Benson Center, Northville, NY 12134) Guided canoe trips, lodging.

## DOGSLEDDING

Since the mid-1970s, the Saranac Lake-Tupper Lake area has been a haven for nationally regarded sled-dog racers; several weekends in January and February are packed with top-quality meets. For about a decade Alpo had sponsored the races, held on the trails at Paul Smith's College and at Massawepie Scout Reservation, but it looks like Yukon Jack may take over in winter 1993. For an updated schedule, contact the Saranac Lake Chamber of Commerce (518-891-1990).

Nancie Battaglia

*A racing dog team heads for the finish line near Saranac Lake.*

If you'd like to try the sport, the Lake George Winter Carnival (518-668-5755), spread over the February weekends, has held dogsled rides on a casual basis. At the Best Western Golden Arrow Motel on Main St. in Lake Placid

(518-523-3353), there are dogsled rides on frozen Mirror Lake. The most authentic and exciting dogsled trips are available from *XTC Horse & Sled Dog Adventures* (518-891-5684; Forest Home Rd., Saranac Lake, NY 12983). You can reserve a day-long or overnight trek in nearby wilderness areas, and even drive the team yourself. A tip: don't holler "Mush!" near the huskies, unless you want the dogs to think you're a real bonehead. Most lead dogs respond to "Let's go!" or other similar commands spoken by their owners.

## FAMILY FUN

**B**esides millions of acres of pristine natural attractions, the Adirondack Park offers plenty of man-made amusements and accessible gorges and caves. Ausable Chasm, a spectacular gorge of carved sandstone cliffs near the far northeastern corner of the park, is one of the country's oldest privately owned tourist attractions. Since the 1930s, visitors have filled their pockets with glittering garnets at the Barton's Mines tour. Santa's Workshop, near Whiteface Mountain, is the oldest theme park in the world, dating back to 1946, and it is the place to mail your Christmas cards from, since the postmark reads "North Pole, NY." Frontier Town, near North Hudson, combines Adirondack historic sites, like a working iron forge and a gristmill, with Wild West zest. On the other end of the spectrum, there are new-wave fun parks, too, with towering water slides and outdoor pools that generate their own whitecaps.

You'll find miniature golf courses listed under a separate heading, Olympic spectator events outlined under "Olympic Sports," and annual races and competitions toward the end of this chapter. Described below is a potpourri of places to go and things to do.

**Price Codes**

| Admission price for an adult: | under $8 | $9 to $13 | over $13 |
| --- | --- | --- | --- |
| (children's tickets are less) | Inexpensive | Moderate | Expensive |

### LAKE GEORGE AND SOUTHEASTERN ADIRONDACKS

**Natural Stone Bridge & Caves** (518-494-2283; Stone Bridge Rd., Pottersville) 5 caves, stone archway, mineral shop. Open daily Memorial Day—Columbus Day. Price: Inexpensive.

**Water Slide World** (518-668-4407; Rtes. 9 and 9L, Lake George) Wave pool, water slides, bumper boats. Daily June 20—Labor Day. Price: Expensive.

**House of Frankenstein Wax Museum** (518-668-3377; Canada St., Lake George) From the Phantom of the Opera to modern horrors. Open daily Memorial Day—Columbus Day. Inexpensive.

**Magic Forest** (518-668-2448; Rte. 9, Lake George) Rides and games, entertainment, Santa's Hideaway. Open daily late June—Labor Day. Moderate.

**Movieworld Wax Museum** (518-668-3077; Canada St., Lake George) Elvis and Batman in the lobby; lots of other life-size wax figures and movie memorabilia. Open daily Memorial Day—Labor Day. Inexpensive.

### CHAMPLAIN VALLEY

**Ausable Chasm** (518-834-7454; Rte. 9, Ausable Chasm) Deep gorge, known as a tourist attraction since the 1870s; boat ride. Daily mid-May—mid Oct. Moderate.

*Shooting the rapids at Ausable Chasm.*

Nancie Battaglia

**Frontier Town** (518-532-7181; off exit 29 of I-87; North Hudson) Wild West theme park, historic exhibits, rodeo, rides, entertainment. Daily Memorial Day—Labor Day. Moderate to Expensive.

### HIGH PEAKS AND NORTHERN ADIRONDACKS

**High Falls Gorge** (518-946-2278; Rte. 86; Wilmington) Gorge and waterfalls on the Ausable River. Daily July—August. Moderate.

**Santa's Workshop** (518-946-2212; Rte. 431, Wilmington) Real reindeer, crafts demonstrations, Santa, rides, entertainment. Daily Memorial Day—

*At North Pole, New York, Santa is always in season.*

Nancie Battaglia

Columbus Day, some winter weekends. This is the only place in the Adirondacks where you can buy a personalized magic wand. Moderate.

**Whiteface Mountain Chairlift Ride** (518-946-2223; Rte. 86, Wilmington) Recommended during fall foliage season. Daily late June—Columbus Day. Inexpensive.

### CENTRAL AND SOUTHWESTERN ADIRONDACKS

**Adirondack Centennial Railroad** (315-369-6290: Rte. 28, Thendara) After a long hiatus, a portion of the Adirondack Railroad is once again in service in summer and fall 1992, with excursions from Thendara to Minnehaha, about four miles away. Call for information about 1993 trips. Inexpensive to Moderate. The station has been recently restored as a railway museum, too.

**Barton Garnet Mine Tours** (518-251-2706; Barton Mines Rd. (off Rte. 28), North River) Tours of open-pit mines, rock collecting, mineral shop. Inexpensive.

**Enchanted Forest/Water Safari** (315-369-6145; Rte. 28, Old Forge) Water slides, rides, entertainment. Daily Memorial Day—Labor Day. Expensive.

**Gore Mountain Gondola Rides** (518-251-2411; Peaceful Valley Rd., North Creek) Fri—Sun August 31—Oct. 8. Inexpensive.

**McCauley Mountain Chairlift Ride** (315-369-3225; McCauley Mtn. Rd., off Bisby Rd., Old Forge) Double chairlift ride, whitetail deer to watch. Daily June 25—Labor Day; weekends Memorial Day—June 24; Labor Day— Columbus Day. Inexpensive.

**Sherman's Amusement Park** (518-835-2020; off Rte. 10, Caroga Lake) Wonderful century-old carousel, beach, picnic grounds, and pavilion. Open daily July—Aug.; some weekends in spring and fall. Inexpensive.

**BEYOND THE BLUE LINE**

New York's largest theme park — *Great Escape Fun Park* (518-798-1084 or 518-792-8227 Rte. 9, Lake George) — is just south of Lake George village. It's an awesome complex with 100 rides, shows, and attractions; the Screamin' Demon roller coaster provides quite an adventure for the strong of stomach. Open daily June 10—Labor Day, plus some fall weekends, and weekends only Memorial Day—June 10.

# FISHING

**B**rook trout, lake trout, landlocked salmon, muskellunge, great northern pike, pickerel, walleye, smallmouth bass, largemouth bass, bullhead, whitefish, and panfish by the boatload are all native to Adirondack waters; toss in the introduced exotics and hybrids like brown trout, rainbow trout, splake, tiger musky, and kokanee, and the fisherman's options are a veritable North Country Neptune's harvest.

Of course, we offer no guarantees that you'll actually catch anything. But with a bit of preparation — like reading a guidebook, calling one of the hot-lines, perhaps a day with a guide or a fly-fishing lesson, or a well-planned trip to remote, lightly fished waters — you may be able to tell the story about the big one that didn't get away. As to geographical directions for finding lunker-land, we can only recall the response of a local old-timer to a visitor's query about where to fish on a certain lake: "Anywhere it's flat."

Begin your fishing education with the *New York State Fishing Regulations Guide*, published by the Department of Environmental Conservation (DEC) and available at DEC offices, sporting goods stores, tourist information centers, or by mail (DEC, 50 Wolf Rd., Albany, NY 12233) The free booklet out-

*Checking the chart for lunkers near the North Branch of the Saranac River.*

Nancie Battaglia

lines all the seasons and limits for various species, fishing-license information, special trout lakes and streams where you may use only artificial lures, and a list of endangered and threatened fish that are illegal to possess. Everyone over age 16 who fishes in the Adirondacks must have a New York fishing license, which can be purchased at sporting goods stores and town offices. Nonresidents can get special 5-day licenses; state residents over 70 are eligible for free licenses.

In general, trout season runs April 1—September 30; bass season from the third Saturday in June—November 30; northern, walleye, and pickerel from the first Saturday in May—March 15. There are some wonderfully helpful hotlines for fishing tips, describing what's hitting where on which kind of bait. For the southern part of DEC Region 5, including Lake George, lower Lake

*The little one that didn't get away, on Long Pond in the St. Regis Canoe Area.*

Nancie Battaglia

Champlain, Schroon Lake, and central Adirondacks, call 518-623-3682; for the High Peaks and northwestern lakes area, call 518-891-5413.

If you'd like to read about fishing, Warren County (518-761-6366) has a booklet describing Lake George, Schroon Lake, and other southeastern Adirondack waters. Franklin County (518-483-6788) publishes a fold-out four-color map listing species prevalent in major streams, ponds, and lakes. Tupper Lake Chamber of Commerce (518-359-3328) offers a handout that even tells you which brands of lures catch local fish. Hamilton County (518-648-5239) lists hunting and fishing information on a brochure with a map. There are a couple of books that you can find in local libraries or bookstores: *Good Fishing in the Adirondacks* (Stackpole Books, 1990) by Dennis Aprill and *Fishing in the Adirondacks* (Adirondack Sports Publications, 1982) by Francis Betters.

---

### Catch-and-Release Fishing

Angling for fun rather than for the fry pan is catching on across the country, especially in trout waters. If you'd like to match wits with a wild piscine and then send him or her back for another day, here are some tips for catch-and-release fishing.

Use a barbless hook; or take a barbed hook and file down, or bend down, the barb with a pair of pliers. The hook should usually just go through the fish's lip rather than lodge deep in the throat. Be gentle landing your fish; some anglers go so far as to line their nets with a soft cotton bag. When removing the hook, it's best not to handle the fish at all, since you can disturb the protective coating on the skin. If you have to touch the fish, wet your hands first, don't squeeze the body, and don't touch the gills. If you can, remove the hook without touching the fish, by holding the hook's shank upside down and removing it, with the fish near the water. Usually, the creature will swim away happily. But if your trout is tired, you can cradle it gently, facing it upstream so that water flows through the gills, or if you're in a lake, move the fish back and forth slowly, as a kind of artificial respiration.

Even catch-and-release fish have a tendency to grow after their close encounter of the piscatorial kind, and *Mountain Taxidermy Studio* (1-800-231-1716; RD 1, Box 141, Elizabethtown) can make a custom, hand-painted replica of the fish you let go. Take accurate measurements, a snapshot, and estimate the weight, and they'll be able to send you back a trophy to hang on the wall; the price is about $10 per inch.

---

To get in the proper frame of mind for fishing, nothing beats a trip to a local fish hatchery. In *Lake George and Southeastern Adirondacks*, the *Warren County Fish Hatchery* (518-623-4141; Hudson St., Warrensburg) is open daily, with a chance to see plenty of trout, and a special film, and picnic. In the *Champlain Valley*, the *Essex County Fish Hatchery* (518-597-3844; Creek Rd., Crown Point) is also open every day, and there's no admission charge. The only fish ladder in the park is on the Boquet River (518-963-

7266; School St., Willsboro); if you time it just right in the fall, you can watch salmon — big salmon — ascending the watery staircase. In the *Northwest Lakes Region,* the *Adirondack Fish Hatchery* (518-891-3358; Rte. 30, Saranac Inn), which is open daily, specializes in raising landlocked salmon for stocking lakes.

Acid rain has had an effect on fishing in some parts of the Adirondack Park, especially in the southwestern quadrant, where there's more precipitation (the spring snow melt can be extremely acidic and shocking to a lake's ecosystem), and thinner, less buffered soils. About 200 lakes and ponds that once supported fish are now dead; research has shown that it's not the direct effects of low pH levels, but rather acidic waters leaching minerals such as aluminum from the soil, that causes the damage. Efforts to combat acidification by applying lime or other chemicals are still in the experimental stages. Fisheries biologists are also breeding trout that can survive in more acidic waters, but as yet these creatures have not been widely stocked. The good news is that more than 2500 lakes and ponds, and countless miles of rivers and streams, have stabilized at pH levels that support fish and all kinds of wildlife. For more information about acid rain, its effects, and what you can do to offset its spread, contact your local chapter of Trout Unlimited, or the DEC.

## FISHING GUIDES AND OUTFITTERS

### LAKE GEORGE AND SOUTHEASTERN ADIRONDACKS

**Adirondack Fishing Adventures** (518-623-9979; Cameron Rd., Athol, NY 12810) Hudson River float trips for trout fishing, guided trips to remote streams and ponds.

**Adirondack Gun & Tackle** (518-532-7089; Main St., Schroon Lake, NY 12870) Charter boat service, guided trips to remote ponds, ice fishing, bait and tackle.

**Ann's Bait & Tackle Shop** (518-644-9989; Norowal Rd., Bolton Landing, NY 12814) Bait and tackle.

**Ellsworth Fishing Guide Service** (518-668-4624; Rte. 9, Lake George, NY 12845) Charter boat for landlocked salmon, lake trout, or bass on Lake George, bait and tackle shop.

**Gibaldi Guide Service** (518-494-7059; Schroon River Rd., Warrensburg, NY 12885) Guided trips on Lake George, Lake Champlain, or to wilderness lakes and ponds.

**Lake George Camping Equipment** (518-644-9941; Rte. 9N, Bolton Landing) Charter boat for salmon, trout, or bass on Lake George.

**Lake Luzerne Guide Service** (518-696-4646; 2101 Lake Ave., Lake Luzerne,

NY 12846) Charter boat for salmon and lake trout on Lake George; guided fishing on wilderness lakes.

**Northeast Adventure Charters** (518-793-6307; Bay Rd., Lake George) Charter boat for salmon, lake trout, bass, tackle shop, overnight trips.

**The Outdoorsman Sport Shop** (518-668-3910; Rte. 9N, Diamond Point, NY 12824) Bait and tackle.

**Remington's Garage and Sport Shop** (518-494-3260; Rte. 8, Brant Lake, NY 12815) Bait and tackle, guided trips.

**Sand n' Surf Charter Service** (518-668-4622; Rte. 9N, Diamond Point) Charter boat for salmon, lake trout, bass on southern Lake George; free lodging with full-day spring or fall charter.

**Ted's Charter Fishing Service** (518-668-5334; Rte. 9N, Diamond Point) Charter boat for salmon, lake trout, bass on southern Lake George; free lodging with full-day spring or fall charter.

## CHAMPLAIN VALLEY

**Adirondack-Champlain Guide Service** (518-963-7351; RR 297, Willsboro, NY 12996) Guided fishing trips on Lake Champlain and backcountry lakes.

**Bailey's Boat Charters** (518-834-7965; Rte. 9, Keeseville, NY 12944) Charter boat for lake trout, salmon, and bass on Lake Champlain.

**Peaked Hill Guide Service** (518-532-7953; Box 154, Severance, NY 12872) Guided fishing trips for northern pike, lake trout and bass on Paradox Lake and nearby ponds; ice fishing shanty rentals.

## HIGH PEAKS AND NORTHERN ADIRONDACKS

**Adirondack Bass & Camping** (518-946-7362; Glen Rd., Jay, NY 12941) Guided wilderness fishing trips.

**Adirondack Mountain Club** (518-523-3441; Adirondak Loj, Loj Rd., Lake Placid, NY 12946) Fly-fishing workshops.

**Ausable Angler** (518-946-7274; Box 68, Wilmington, NY 12997) Fly-fishing trips on the west branch of the Ausable River; fly-fishing and fly-tying instruction.

**Blue Line Sport Shop** (518-891-4680; 82 Main St., Saranac Lake, NY 12983) Fishing tackle, canoes, camping equipment.

**Francis Betters Guide Service** (518-946-2605; Rte. 86, Wilmington) Fly-fishing guide on the Ausable River, fly-fishing and fly-tying instruction, tackle shop.

*Fran Betters (center), writes about fishing, ties flies especially for the Ausable River, offers guide service, and runs a sport shop in Wilmington.*

Nancie Battaglia

**Deerspring Guides** (518-425-6685; Wampep Acres, Merrill, NY 12944) Remote fishing trips, traditional guideboat trips.

**Pat Gallagher Guide Service** (518-523-9727; Box 306, Lake Placid) Guided wilderness fishing trips.

**Jones Outfitters** (518-523-3468; 37 Main St., Lake Placid) Fly-fishing instruction, guide service, rod and reel repairs, Orvis shop.

**Placid Bay Ventures Guide & Charter Service** (518-523-1744; 70 1/2 Saranac Ave., Lake Placid) Charter boat on Lake Placid, guided wilderness fishing trips.

**River Road Bait & Tackle** (518-891-2128; off Rte. 3, Bloomingdale, NY 12913) Fishing tackle, hand-tied flies, rods and reels.

**Tahawus Guide Service** (518-891-4334; Rte. 86, Ray Brook, NY 12977) Guided fishing trips to remote streams; corporate retreats.

**Young's Foothills** (518-891-1221; Box 345, Saranac Lake, NY 12983) Guided trips for trout, bass, and pike; ice fishing; rod and reel repairs.

## NORTHWEST LAKES REGION

**Tip Top Sport Shop** (518-359-9222; 40 Park St., Tupper Lake, NY 12986) Fishing equipment and licenses.

## CENTRAL AND SOUTHWESTERN ADIRONDACKS

**Adirondack Hut-to-Hut** (518-251-2710; Minerva Hill Lodge, Minerva, NY 12851) Guided fishing trips, fly-fishing clinics, lodging.

**Adirondack Mountain & Stream Guide Service** (518-251-3762; Hardscrabble Rd., Olmstedville, NY 12857) Guided wilderness fishing trips, ice fishing.

**Adirondack Outdoor Enterprises** (518-648-5684; Sabael Rd., Indian Lake, NY 12842) Fly-in fishing trips; guided wilderness trips.

**Ed's Fly Shop** (518-863-4223; Rte. 30, Northville, NY 12134) Trout flies and fishing tackle.

**Garnet Hill Lodge** (518-251-2821; Thirteenth Lake Rd., North River, NY 12856) Guided trout-fishing trips, lodging.

**Tom Kravis Guide Service** (518-863-4988; Benson Rd., Northville) Guided fishing trips to remote ponds and streams.

**Mountainaire Adventures** (518-251-2194; Rte. 28, Wevertown, NY 12886) Guided fishing trips, lodging.

**Moose River Company** (315-369-3682; Main St., Old Forge, NY 13420) Fishing tackle and fly-fishing gear, general line of outdoor equipment.

*Moose River Company, Old Forge, has a complete line of outdoor gear.*

Nancie Battaglia

**North Country Sports** (518-251-4299; Thirteenth Lake Rd., North River) Guided wilderness fishing trips, fishing tackle, fishing books and videos, hand-tied flies.

**Pepperbox Outfitters** (Beaver River Station, Box 258L, Lowville, NY 13367) Wilderness fishing trips.

**Charles Reynolds** (315-826-7934; Rte. 8, Morehouseville. Mail: HCR 325, Cold Brook, NY 13324) Custom trout flies.

**Traditional Adirondack Outings** (315-369-3978; Big Otter Camp, Otter Lake, NY 13427) Guided wilderness fishing trips, lodging.

**Wharton's Adirondack Adventures** (518-548-3195; Box 544, Lake Pleasant, NY 12108) Guided wilderness fishing trips.

## GOLF

*Two duffers at Loon Lake, one of the oldest courses in the Northeast.*

Nancie Battaglia

Take in the rolling green hills, craggy peaks, deep blue lakes, and bracing air, and the Adirondacks do recall Scotland's landscape just a wee bit. Perhaps, then, it's no surprise that there are dozens of courses tucked amongst mountain valleys throughout the park. Once upon a time there were even more golf clubs than are open today, courses that were attached to the grand hotels and luxurious private clubs.

At the turn of the century, Adirondack visitors could play at beautifully designed courses at the Lake Placid Club (where pro Seymour Dunn had a golf-club factory); at the St. Regis Golf Course, associated with Paul Smith's Hotel; at the Ampersand Hotel Golf Course, on Lower Saranac Lake; at the Childwold Park Hotel's course, north of Tupper Lake on a huge estate. Long Lake had three active nine-hole courses at various times until 1968; the Eagles Nest Country Club near Blue Mountain Lake opened with an exhibition by golf immortal Harry Vardon in 1900, and closed in 1928. The Stevens House Golf Course in Lake Placid asked golfers to wear the traditional red coats to warn hotel guests to watch for sailing balls, but by 1947 there was little left of this quaint practice, or the course itself. The first black member of the PGA, Dewey Brown, ran the Cedar River club outside Indian Lake. There's a paper-back book, *Adirondack Golf Courses ... Past and Present* (Adirondack Golf, 1987), compiled by Peter Martin, that outlines the history of Blue Line golf with dozens of old photographs and anecdotes.

Adirondack golf courses today range from informal, inexpensive, converted cow pastures to challenging, busy, championship links. At most places you don't have to reserve a tee time, and at only one are golfers required to rent carts. You can stroll about, take in the scenery, and enjoy your own kind of hiking. Most courses also offer informal tournaments that visitors may join. An added benefit: many of the golf courses have decent restaurants or snack bars where you can enjoy a sandwich or a beer after the round.

## GOLF COURSES

**Price Codes**

| Greens Fees (9 holes): | under $10 | $10 to $15 | Over $15 |
|---|---|---|---|
| | Inexpensive | Moderate | Expensive |

### LAKE GEORGE AND SOUTHEASTERN ADIRONDACKS

**Bend of the River Golf Course** (518-696-3415; Rte. 9N, Hadley) 9 holes; par 35; 2700 yards. Inexpensive. One of the first Adirondack courses to open in the spring.

**Cronin's Golf Resort** (518-623-9336; Golf Course Rd., Warrensburg) 18 holes; par 70; 6121 yards. Inexpensive.

**Green Mansions** (518-494-7222; Darrowsville Rd., Chestertown) 9 holes; par 36; 2700 yards. Moderate.

**Sagamore Resort & Golf Club** (518-644-9400; French Mt. Rd., Bolton Landing) 18 holes; par 70; 6900 yards. Very expensive. Designed by Donald Ross; challenging.

**Schroon Lake Municipal Golf Course** (518-532-9359; Hoffman Rd., Schroon Lake) 9 holes; par 36; 2958 yards. Inexpensive.

**1000 Acres Golf Club** (518-696-5246; Rte. 418, Stony Creek) 9 holes; 3900 yards. Inexpensive.

**Top of the World** (518-668-2062; Lockhart Mt. Rd., Lake George) 9 holes; par 36; 2900 yards. Inexpensive.

### CHAMPLAIN VALLEY

**Cobble Hill Golf Course** (518-873-9974; Rte. 9, Elizabethtown) 9 holes; par 35; 3000 yards. Inexpensive. Completed in 1897, views of the High Peaks.

**Moriah Country Club** (518-546-9979; Broad St., Port Henry) 9 holes; par 32; 3000 yards. Inexpensive.

**Port Kent Golf Course** (518-834-9785; Rte. 373, Port Kent) 9 holes; par 30; 2047 yards. Inexpensive.

**Ticonderoga Country Club** (518-585-2801; Hague Rd. Ticonderoga) 18 holes; par 71; 6300 yards. Moderate. Designed by Seymour Dunn.

**Westport Country Club** (518-962-4470; Liberty Rd., Westport) 18 holes; par 72; 6200 yards. Moderate. Challenging back nine, beautiful views, nice restaurant.

**Willsboro Golf Club** (518-963-8989; Point Rd., Willsboro) 9 holes; par 35; 3100 yards. Moderate.

## HIGH PEAKS AND NORTHERN ADIRONDACKS

**Ausable Club** (518-576-4411; Ausable Club Rd., St. Huberts) 9 holes; unusual Scottish links-type course. Inexpensive. Open to nonmembers in September only, Mon.—Thurs. Beautiful views of the High Peaks.

**Ausable Valley Country Club** (518-647-8666; Golf Course Rd., Au Sable Forks) 9 holes; par 34; 2700 yards. Inexpensive.

**Craig Wood Country Club** (518-523-9811; Cascade Rd., Lake Placid) 18 holes; par 72; 6544 yards. Moderate. Named after Lake Placid native Craig Wood, who won both the U.S. Open and Masters in 1941.

**Lake Placid Club Resort** (518-523-3361; Mirror Lake Dr., Lake Placid) 2 18-hole courses. Expensive. Courses from the formerly posh Lake Placid Club, beautiful views of the High Peaks.

**Loon Lake Golf Club** (518-891-3249; Rte. 99, Loon Lake) 18 holes; par 70; 5600 yards. Inexpensive. Completed in 1895, one of the oldest courses in the Adirondacks. Adjacent buildings designed by Stanford White.

**Saranac Inn Golf & Country Club** (518-891-1402; Rte. 30, Saranac Inn) 18 holes; par 70; 6500 yards. Moderate. Designed by Seymour Dunn in 1910.

**Saranac Lake Golf Club** (518-891-2675; Rte. 86, Saranac Lake) 9 holes; par 36; 6100 yards. Moderate.

**Whiteface Inn Resort Golf Course** (518-523-2551; Whiteface Inn Rd., Lake Placid) 18 holes; par 72; 6500 yards. Moderate. Designed by Walter Hagen and John VanKleek; beautiful views.

## NORTHWEST LAKES REGION

**Clifton-Fine Golf Course** (315-848-3570; Rte. 3, Star Lake) 9 holes; par 36; 2854 yards. Inexpensive.

**Tupper Lake Golf & Country Club** (518-359-3701; Country Club Rd., Tupper Lake) 18 holes; par 71; 6250 yards. Inexpensive.

### CENTRAL AND SOUTHWESTERN ADIRONDACKS

**Brantingham Golf Course** (315-348-8861; Brantingham Rd., off the Greig-Lyons Falls Rd., Brantingham Lake) 18 holes; par 71; 5300 yards. Inexpensive — you can play one round or all day for the same fee.

**Cedar River Golf Course** (518-648-5906; Rtes. 28/30, Indian Lake) 9 holes; par 36; 2700 yards. Inexpensive.

**Inlet Golf Course and Country Club** (315-357-3503; Rte. 28, Inlet) 18 holes; par 72; 6000 yards. Inexpensive to Moderate.

**Lake Pleasant Golf Course** (518-548-7071; Rte. 8, Lake Pleasant) 9 holes; par 35; 2900 yards. Inexpensive.

**Sacandaga Golf Club** (518-863-4887; Rte. 30, Sacandaga Park, Northville) 9 holes; par 36; 3000 yards. Inexpensive.

**Nick Stoner Golf Course** (518-835-4211; Rte. 10, Caroga Lake) 18 holes; par 70; 5800 yards. Inexpensive to Moderate.

**Thendara Golf Club, Inc.** (315-369-3136; Rte. 28, Thendara) 18 holes; par 72; 6000 yards. Moderate. Designed by Donald Ross; great scenery along the Moose River.

**Wakely Lodge & Golf Course** (518-648-5011; Cedar River Rd., Indian Lake) 9 holes; par 34; 2600 yards. Inexpensive.

## HIKING AND BACKPACKING

*Hikers ascending Avalanche pass, 1888.*

Seneca Ray Stoddard, Courtesy
Adirondack Collection,
Saranac Lake Free Library

Take a walk on the wild side. The Adirondack Park has more than 2000 miles of marked hiking trails that lead to pristine ponds, roaring waterfalls, spectacular peaks, ice caves, and hidden gorges; perhaps the toughest choice for an Adirondack visitor is selecting where to go. There are 20-some guidebooks to help you make that decision. The *Discover the Adirondacks* series (Backcountry Publications), by historian and hiking maven Barbara McMartin, divides the park into 11 geographical regions describing the natural and human histories of dozens of different destinations; besides marked trails, McMartin suggests some easy-to-moderate bushwhacks to reach great views and little-known gems. The guidebooks published by the Adirondack Mountain Club (ADK) slice the Adirondacks into six regions; there's also a volume dedicated to the 132-mile Northville-Lake Placid Trail. Both guidebook publishers offer a couple of volumes that sample trips from all corners of the park. For details on these books, check the bibliography in Chapter Eight, *Information*, and for local sources, consult the bookstores section in Chapter Seven, *Shopping*.

For even more reading on tramps and treks, there's *Adirondac* magazine, published by ADK; *Adirondack Life*, especially the annual Guide to the Outdoors, outlines plenty of good long walks; and the Department of Environmental Conservation has brochures and maps for trails in the various wilderness and wild forest areas. Some towns are even accommodating enough to offer free hiking maps; for example, if you're in the Blue Mountain Lake vicinity, ask for the trail map at the post office; or at the Tupper Lake Chamber of Commerce, ask for their sheet on nearby mountains to hike.

*On the summit of Pitchoff Mountain, High Peaks.*

Nancie Battaglia

The Adirondack woods are fairly free of the hazards that you need to worry about in other locales. There's some poison ivy in the Champlain Valley, but very little in the High Peaks, Northwest Lakes, and Central Adirondacks. Poison oak doesn't thrive in this climate. Rattlesnakes are found only in isolated parts of the Tongue Mountain range near Lake George, and rarely in the

### *Buzz Off*

Springtime in the Adirondacks can be lovely, as the wildflowers unfold in the woods, songbirds sing in the trees, and speckled trout rise in shady pools, but all this earthly paradise has a power squadron of tiny, persistent insects to keep us humans from overwhelming the countryside. We speak here of blackflies, not much bigger than a fruit fly, with an annoying habit of swarming around your head, and a bite that leaves a painful red welt. Bug season is usually late May through June, although its duration depends on the weather: a dry spring can mean relatively few days of winged botheration, and a few weeks of rain can keep the rivers flowing swiftly, nurturing batch after batch of larvae. "The venomous little wretches are quite important enough to spoil many a well planned trip to the woods and it is best to beat them from the start," wrote Nessmuk, the 19th-century outdoor author who traveled extensively in the Adirondacks.

Take heart. Many towns are using BTi, a bacteria that attacks blackfly larvae, to control the insects, and the program seems to be working well while not harming other species. If you are planning an extended hike, golf outing, streamside fishing trip, horseback ride, or other slow-moving activity in the woods, you'll want to apply a good-quality insect repellent, wear light-colored clothing (blue, especially dark blue, seems to attract blackflies), and tuck in your pantlegs, shirts, and such: the Adirondack red badge of courage is a bracelet of bites around the ankles or waist. Avoid wearing scented hairspray, perfume, or sweet-smelling shampoo, as these products broadcast "free lunch!" to hungry little buggers.

There's a pharmacy of lotions and sprays that use varying amounts of DEET (diethyl-meta-toluamide) as the active ingredient, but note that products containing more than 25% DEET should not be used on children. DEET should not be used on infants at all. Avon's Skin-So-Soft bath oil has remarkable powers of insect repellency without mysterious chemical additives. Folks also swear by Save the Baby, a eucalyptus-based ointment for infants. Fabric softener sheets, like Bounce, can be tucked into your hatband to keep flies away from your face. Some Adirondackers prefer pine-tar-based bug dopes, like Old Woodsman, that also have the lasting aroma of authenticity; after a good dose of Old Woodsman, your pillows and sheets will be scented, too. Nessmuk offered this recipe for blackfly repellent in 1880: "Three ounces pine tar, two ounces castor oil, one ounce pennyroyal oil. Simmer all together over a slow fire, and bottle for use.... Rub it in thoroughly and liberally at first, and after you have established a good glaze, a little replenishing from day to day will be sufficient. And don't fool with soap and towels where the insects are plenty." Of course, you can garb yourself from crown to the ground in head nets and bug-repellent jackets and trousers.

Blackflies usually don't travel too far over water, so canoeists on lakes aren't often bothered until they reach an island or it's time to put the canoe back on the roof rack. Bicyclists — if they travel fast enough — only have to contend with removing dead bugs from their helmets and sunglasses and trying not to ride with their mouths open.

After blackflies come the punkies and mosquitoes, which seem a minor hassle once you've endured the May clouds. Punkies and mosquitoes are basically nighttime creatures; a citronella candle may deter them, and if you're sleeping with the windows open, spray the screens with bug dope before you go to bed.

Champlain Valley; keep your eyes open when crossing rock outcrops on warm, sunny days. These eastern timber rattlers are quite shy and nonaggressive, but do take care not to step on or surprise one.

In some parts of the park, you can leave the trailhead and not see another person until you return to your car and look in the rearview mirror. The Five Ponds Wilderness Area, between Stillwater Reservoir and Cranberry Lake, is especially remote. Try the Red Horse Trail, which goes north from Big Trout Pond (which is a bay on the reservoir), past Salmon, Witchhopple, Clear, and Crooked lakes, and you'll find yourself in big-timber climax hardwood forest. Or you can make a two- or three-day circuit through the High Peaks, entering from Elk Lake and hiking through Panther Gorge, and rarely encounter other hikers.

Parts of the Northville-Placid trail are many miles from the nearest road; passing through the West Canada Lakes or Cold River areas, you might go several days with just the cry of the loon or howl of the coyote for company. Going end-to-end on this long trail requires a minimum of 10 days and a solid amount of backcountry knowledge, but you can pick shorter sections of the trail for three-day junkets. It's possible to find solitude even in the middle of the busy summer season if you select the right destination.

Lest we make it sound too daunting, there are plenty of easy hikes in the two- to five-mile length that traverse beautiful terrain. If you'd rather take a walk in the company of other people, destinations like Crane (near Johnsburg), Bald (near Old Forge), Owl's Head (near Long Lake), or Goodnow mountains (near Newcomb) present great views, but you probably won't be alone at the top. If you'd like to visit an accessible vestige of old-growth forest, the Pine Orchard, outside Wells, comprises many, many acres of enormous white pines and giant spruces along a well-marked, fairly level trail. Chimney Mountain, near Indian Lake, is a unique rock formation that hides several deep caves; it's an easy walk to the summit, but exploring the caves is something for experienced spelunkers.

Wherever you choose to go, be prepared. Your pack should contain a flashlight, matches, extra food and water, map, compass, and some extra clothes. At most trailheads, there's a register for signing in. Forest rangers use this data to estimate how much use a particular area receives, and in the unlikely event that you get lost, the information about when you started, where you were planning to go, and whom you were with would be helpful to the search team.

But if even these kinds of excursions are not for you, the trails at the Visitor Interpretive Centers at Newcomb and Paul Smiths are ingeniously designed to offer a wide range of nature in a relatively short distance, and you won't be too far from the building no matter how long you travel. You can even go out on a guided trip to explore wildflowers, mushrooms, trees, or birds. There are also wheelchair-accessible trails at both centers.

Several organizations and guide services lead trips and offer map-and-compass, woodcraft, and low-impact-camping workshops.

## Low-Impact Camping

Setting up a wilderness campsite in the not-too-distant past relied on techniques like digging deep trenches around tents, cutting balsam boughs for backwoods beds, sawing armloads of firewood, and burying garbage and cans. For camp cleanup, we thought nothing of washing dishes in the lake and scrubbing ourselves vigorously with soap and shampoo as we cavorted in the shallows. All these activities often left a lasting mark on the woods and waters; today, especially when traveling off the beaten path, it's important to leave no trace of your visit.

Low-impact camping is perhaps easier than old-fashioned methods, once you know a few of the basics. Most of the relevant skills are simply common sense; think of the consequences and cumulative effects of your actions when you set up camp, and you're on your way to becoming a responsible wilderness trekker.

Choose a site at least 150 feet away from the nearest hiking trail or water source, and try to select a place that will recover quickly after you leave. Separate your tent from your cooking area, to avoid attracting animals to your bedside and to distribute the impact of your stay. When you leave, tidy up. Be sure the spot is absolutely clean of any trash — even stuff we commonly regard as biodegradable — and spread soil or dead leaves around any trampled spots.

Rely on a portable stove for backcountry cooking rather than expecting to find ample dry wood. (You can only use dead and down wood in the forest preserve anyway; cutting trees on state land is prohibited.) Plan your meals ahead so that you don't have extra cooked food to store or dispose of; if no one in the party can assume the role of "master of the clean plate club," then pack out all your leftovers. Wash your dishes and your body well away from streams and lakes using a mild vegetable-based soap.

How to s—t in the woods is something to consider, too; nothing kills that "gee, isn't it terrific out here in the woods" feeling more than finding unmistakable evidence of other humans. Bring a little shovel or trowel and bury that hazardous waste at least six inches down, and at least 150 feet from the nearest water. Lean-tos and some designated backcountry campsites have privies; use them.

## HIKING GUIDES AND ORGANIZATIONS

**Adirondack Discovery** (315-357-3598; Box 545, Inlet, NY 13360) Guided day hikes to places of historical and geological interests, in July and August throughout the park.

**Adirondack Mountain Club** (518-668-4447; Luzerne Rd., Lake George, NY 12845) Interpretive hikes with naturalists, guided fall foliage hikes, wilderness backpack tours, special weekends for women, youth, and senior citizens. Many programs in the High Peaks at Adirondak Loj, (518-523-3441).

**Adirondack Visitor Interpretive Centers** (518-327-3000; Rte. 30, Paul Smiths, NY 12970; 518-582-2000; Rte. 28N, Newcomb, NY 12851) Guided hikes, marked nature trails, nature-study workshops.

### Tick, Tick, Tick

In the early 1990s, a few cases of Lyme Disease have been recorded in the Adirondacks, and hikers should take precautions against exposing themselves to deer ticks (*Ixodes dammini*), which can carry the spirochete. The ticks can be found in deep woods, on moss, ferns, or trees, although they prefer to stay on their host animals, whitetail deer and deermice. Dogs — especially exuberant ones which go crashing through the brush — are more at risk than humans; it's a good idea to have your pet inoculated against Lyme Disease by your regular veterinarian.

New York State has just approved the sale of Permanone, a tick repellent that can be applied to clothing. Be careful! It's a very strong material that should not be placed on your skin or your pets. You can minimize your exposure to ticks by wearing long pants (with cuffs tucked into your boots) and long-sleeved shirts, using a good insect repellent, and staying on the trail. If you wear light-colored clothing, the ticks are easier to spot, and you can check yourself and your kids for the bugs while you're in the woods.

Deer ticks are very tiny, no bigger than a sesame seed. They don't fly. If you find another eight-legged crawling creature on your body, it could be a spider, a wood tick (not a carrier of Lyme), or an arachnid locally called a "ked," which, despite its scary-looking crablike pincers, is harmless.

June and July are the months when humans face the highest risk of tick contact. A tick must feed for several hours before the disease is transmitted. If you find a tick attached to your skin, pull it out steadily and firmly with a pair of tweezers or your fingers, grasping as close to the tick's mouth as you can. Save the creature in a jar — your doctor will probably want to see it. Apply a topical antiseptic to the bite if it's sore.

If you see on your skin a clear area encircled by a red rash, and are feeling flu-like symptoms, you may have been exposed to Lyme Disease. You should visit your family doctor or a local medical center for a Lyme test, but be aware that it takes several weeks after exposure for your body to show the Lyme antibodies that will register on the test. Lyme symptoms mimic many other ailments so it is difficult to get an accurate diagnosis; most medical practitioners will begin a course of antibiotics if they feel you've been exposed.

**All Seasons Outfitters** (518-523-3548; 168 Lake Flower Ave., Saranac Lake, NY 12983) Guided backpack trips.

**Birchbark Tours** (518-891-5704; 32 Glenwood, Saranac Lake) Wildflower and bird hikes, special-needs backpack trips, historical trips.

**Dr. Anne LaBastille** (315-357-6561; Box 135, Ray Brook, NY 12977) Guided backpack trips, day hikes for women and small family groups.

**McDonnell's Adirondack Challenges** (518-891-1176; Box 855, Saranac Lake) Backpack trips, outfitter.

**Middle Earth Expeditions** (518-523-9572; HCR 01 Box 37, Lake Placid, NY 12946) Backpack trips or day trips.

**Sagamore** (315-354-5301; Sagamore Rd., Raquette Lake, NY 13436) Guided hikes for guests, nature-hike weekends with lodging.

**Trillium Guide Service** (518-891-2484; Box 133, Lake Clear, NY 12945) Backpack and day trips for women and families.

**Wilderness Education Association** (518-891-2915; North Country Community College, Saranac Lake) Wilderness-leadership training programs.

**Sheila Young** (518-891-1221; Box 345, Saranac Lake) Guided hikes.

## HORSEBACK RIDING, POLO, AND WAGON TRIPS

*Cooling off in Chateaugay Lake after a ride through the woods.*

Nancie Battaglia

The North Country may not hold the wide, open spaces of the Wild West, but there are hundreds of miles of wilderness horse trails to explore and plenty of outfitters to help you find a suitable mount. The possibilities range from hour-long rides to two- or three-day guided backcountry overnights. If you own your own horse, the Department of Environmental Conservation (DEC) has several free trail networks across the park, and even operates special campgrounds that accommodate man and beast. For a handy booklet with maps of the trail systems, contact the DEC, 518-891-1370; Ray Brook, NY 12977. One rule applies for bringing out-of-state horses in: proof of a negative Coggins test is required. If you plan to camp more than three nights in the forest preserve, or in a group of 10 or more, you'll need a permit from the local forest ranger.

Hayrides, sleigh rides, and wagon trips are available in many communities. You can ride a carriage through Lake George village or around Mirror Lake, in Lake Placid; there's no need to make a reservation. Listed below are some outfitters and teamsters who offer wagon trips, and places to ride. In general, local stables are open only during warm weather.

If you enjoy just watching horses, there are two excellent annual horse shows in Lake Placid, located a walk, trot, and canter away from the Olympic ski jumps: the *Lake Placid Horse Show* in late June, and the *I Love NY Horse Show* (518-523-9625; North Elba Town Hall, Lake Placid, NY 12946) in early July. At both, the emphasis is on international Olympic-level competition for hunters, jumpers, and riders. Also for spectators, there are Sunday afternoon polo games at the Bark Eater Inn (518-576-2221; Alstead Hill Rd., Keene, NY 12942) starting in late June. Admission is free; the Adirondackers play against teams from Saratoga Springs and Vermont. If you're an accomplished rider, you may even be able to join in a pickup game.

A legacy of the dude-ranch days in the southeastern Adirondacks, *Painted Pony* (518-696-2421; Howe Rd., Lake Luzerne, NY 12846) offers professional rodeo competitions Wednesday, Friday, and Saturday nights every week from July 1 to Labor Day, rain or shine. This is the home of the country's oldest weekly rodeo, complete with trick riding and roping, clowns and novelty acts; and there's more rodeo action, too, at *1000 Acres* (518-696-2444; Rte. 418, Stony Creek, NY 12878).

Nancie Battaglia

*Git along little dogie, at Painted Pony, a Lake Luzerne rodeo.*

## LAKE GEORGE AND SOUTHEASTERN ADIRONDACKS

**Bailey's Horses** (518-696-4541; Rte. 9N, Lake Luzerne, NY 12846) Western trail rides, lessons, hay wagon or carriage rides around Lake Vanare, winter trail rides, trips to Lake George horse trails by reservation.

**Bennett's Riding Stables** (518-696-4444; Rte. 9N, Lake Luzerne) Western trail rides, lessons.

**Bit n' Bridle Ranch** (518-696-2776; Rte. 418, Stony Creek, NY 12878) Western trail rides.

**Harrisburg Lake Club & Resort** (518-696-3461; Harrisburg Rd., Stony Creek)

**Pine Hill Riding Stables** (518-668-2711; Rte. 9N, Lake George, NY 12845)

**Stock Farm** (518-494-4074; Stock Farm Rd., Chestertown, NY 12817) Wagon, sleigh, and hay rides.

## CHAMPLAIN VALLEY

**Buck Mountain Carriage** (518-597-3759; Buck Mt. Rd., Crown Point, NY 12928) Carriage and sleigh rides.

**Steve Sayward** (518-963-4032; Middle Rd.,Willsboro, NY 12996) Wagon rides.

**Stonehill Farm** (518-834-9594; Port Douglas Rd., Keeseville).

**Willow Hill Farm** (518-834-9746; Edwards Corners, Keeseville).

## HIGH PEAKS AND NORTHERN ADIRONDACKS

**Breezy Hollow** (518-946-7036; Hesseltine Rd., Jay, NY 12941) Trail rides.

**Circle 7** (518-582-4011; Rte. 28N, Newcomb, NY 12852) Wagon trips to Santanoni Preserve, by reservation only; camp outfits for hunters and fishermen taken in by wagon.

**Greenwood Riding Stable** (518-425-6688; off Rte. 374, Chateaugay Lake, Merrill, NY 12955) Hourly rides, English only; lessons.

**Sentinel View Stables** (518-891-3008; Harrietstown Rd., Saranac Lake, NY 12983) English and Western lessons, jumping instruction, bridle trails.

**XTC Ranch** (518-891-5684; Forest Home Rd., Saranac Lake) Conestoga wagon trips with Western-style cookout, wilderness trail rides, sleigh rides, dogsled trips.

**Wilson's Livery Stable** (518-576-2221; Alstead Hill Rd., Keene, NY) Western or English trail rides by the hour or day, wagon and sleigh rides, open year-round.

## NORTHWEST LAKES REGION

**Cold River Trail Rides** (518-359-7559; Rte. 3, Tupper Lake, NY 12986) Minimum 1-day ride, by reservation; packhorse trips for fishing, hunting, and camping; no children under 14.

## CENTRAL AND SOUTHWESTERN ADIRONDACKS

**Adirondack Saddle Tours** (315-357-4499; Uncas Rd., Inlet, NY 13360) Packhorse trips for fishing, hunting, and camping.

**Adirondack Wilderness Stables** (518-548-5454; Rte. 8, Lake Pleasant, NY 12108) Hourly, half- or full-day rides, English or Western; lessons; overnight trips available; open year-round.

**T & M Equestrian Center** (315-357-3594; Rte. 28, Inlet) Guided trail rides, Western only; hay and sleigh rides by reservation, ponies for kids, overnights to Moose River Recreation Area.

## PUBLIC HORSE TRAILS

### LAKE GEORGE AND SOUTHEASTERN ADIRONDACKS

**Lake George Trail System** East side of Lake George, off Pilot Knob Rd., 41 miles of carriage roads on an old estate; lean-tos.

**Lake Luzerne** Off Rte. 9N near Lake Luzerne hamlet, on Fourth Lake. Department of Environmental Conservation campsite (518-696-2031) with corral; 5 miles of trails on state land that connect with many miles of privately owned dude-ranch trails.

**Pharaoh Lake Horse Trails** Pharaoh Lake Wilderness Area, east of Schroon Lake. 12 miles of woods roads; lean-tos.

### HIGH PEAKS AND NORTHERN ADIRONDACKS

**Cold River Horse Trails** 6 miles east of Tupper Lake off Rte. 3. 13- and 32-mile-loop dirt trails; lean-tos and corral. Connects with Moose Pond Trail and Santanoni trails.

**Meacham Lake** 3.5 miles north of Paul Smiths off Rte. 30. 10 miles of trails; lean-tos and barn.

**Moose Pond Trail** just north of Newcomb off Rte. 28N. 10 miles.

**Raquette Falls Horse Trail**. Branches off Cold River Trail. 2 miles.

**Santanoni Trail** North of Newcomb off Rte. 28N. 10-mile round-trip.

### NORTHWEST LAKES REGION

**Saranac Inn Horse Trail System** Off Rte. 30 near Saranac Inn. Several short trails to ponds in the St. Regis Canoe Area; 11-mile round-trip on the dirt Fish Pond Truck Trail.

### CENTRAL AND SOUTHWESTERN ADIRONDACKS

**Moose River Recreation Area** Between Indian Lake and Inlet off Rte. 28. 28-mile dirt road plus many miles of old logging roads; campsites.

**Independence River Wild Forest** Off Number Four Rd., near Stillwater Reservoir; assembly area at Chases Lake Rd., off Rte. 12, Greig. 28 miles of sand roads; connects with Otter Creek; barn.

**Otter Creek Trails** Near Greig, off Rte. 12. 15 miles of sand roads; connects with Independence River.

## HUNTING

The Adirondacks have long been regarded as happy hunting grounds. Early accounts describe shooting bucks and does year-round, for daily camp consumption and for swank Manhattan restaurants. Old pictures show small groups of men displaying dozens of deer; the moose — never truly abundant in the Adirondacks — probably disappeared in part due to overhunting. (Other factors were loss of habitat and diseases transmitted by deer.) Market hunting has been outlawed for a century, as have practices like hounding (hunting deer with dogs), jacking (night hunting with a lamp), and floating (pursuing swimming deer with a boat). The Adirondack Guides Association was a major force in pushing the state to enact and enforce hunting laws that would ensure that deer would not face the same fate as the moose.

*A successful Adirondack hunt in the 1890s.*

Courtesy Adirondack Museum, Blue Mountain Lake, NY

Many Adirondack counties now hold more resident whitetail deer than year-round humans, and hunting is a popular, regulated pursuit each fall. Besides deer, there are seasons for black bear (the 1991 bear take for the Adirondack Park was more than 600), snowshoe hare, coyote, bobcat, and other small mammals, plus ruffed grouse, woodcock, wild turkey, and waterfowl. The booklet and maps describing large- and small-game seasons are available from local Department of Environmental Conservation (DEC) offices, or by writing to DEC, 50 Wolf Rd., Albany, NY 12233; licenses can be purchased from sporting goods stores, town offices, or the DEC. Nonresidents may purchase special five-day licenses. If you have never had a New York State hunting license, you must show proof that you have attended a hunter education course. Turkey hunting requires a special stamp from DEC; waterfowl hunters must possess a Federal Migratory Bird Hunting Stamp.

In general, the big game season begins with early bear (mid-September—mid-October); archery for deer or bear (late September—mid-October); muzzle-loading for deer or bear (one week in mid-October); and regular big-game season (third Saturday in October through the first Sunday after Thanksgiving) Bow and black-powder hunters may take antlerless deer; during regular season, it's bucks only in the Adirondack Park.

Wilderness, primitive, and wild forest areas of the forest preserve are all open to hunting, more than 2.5 million acres of land. Paper companies, which own about a million acres more, also offer memberships and leases for hunting and fishing privileges; contact Finch Pruyn & Co. (518-793-2541; 1 Glen St., Glens Falls, NY 12801) or the Empire State Forest Products Association (518-463-1297; 123 State St., Albany, NY 12207) for information. While hunting, please respect the boundaries of private, posted lands.

Listed below are some gun shops and licensed guides who specialize in hunting. One annual event that hunters may want to keep in mind is the annual *NEACA Gun Show* at the Saranac Lake Civic Center (518-891-3800; Ampersand Ave., Saranac Lake, NY 12983), held in mid-July.

## GUN SHOPS

### LAKE GEORGE AND SOUTHEASTERN ADIRONDACKS

**Adirondack Gun and Tackle** (518-532-7089; Main St., Schroon Lake) Guns and ammunition, general line of sporting goods.

**Ellsworth's Sport Shop** (518-668-4624; Rte. 9, Lake George) Guns and ammunition, sporting goods.

**Nemec's Sport Shop** (518-623-2049; 263 Main St., Warrensburg) Guns and ammunition, sporting goods.

**Remington's Garage & Sport Shop** (518-494-3260; Rte. 8, Brant Lake) Guns and ammunition, sporting goods.

**T-Bar-T Sport Shop** (518-793-1044; Rte. 9L, Lake George) Guns and ammunition, gunsmithing, black powder supplies.

### CHAMPLAIN VALLEY

**Keegan Firearms Sales & Service** (518-585-7370; 8 Colonial Hgts., Ticonderoga) Guns and ammunition, gunsmithing.

## HIGH PEAKS AND NORTHERN ADIRONDACKS

**Blue Line Sport Shop** (518-891-4680; 82 Main St., Saranac Lake) Guns and ammunition, sporting goods.

**M & M Guns** (518-647-5369; Palmer St., Au Sable Forks) Guns and ammunition, gunsmithing.

**Paul Robinson** (518-946-2270; Rte. 9N, Upper Jay) Guns and ammunition.

## NORTHWEST LAKES REGION

**Randall Gearsbeck** (315-848-2758; Rte. 3, Oswegatchie) Guns and ammunition, sporting goods.

**Fortune's Hardware** (518-359-9471; 61 Main St., Tupper Lake) Guns and ammunition, sporting goods.

**Tip Top Sport Shop** (518-359-9222; 40 Park St., Tupper Lake) Guns and ammunition, sporting goods.

## CENTRAL AND SOUTHWESTERN ADIRONDACKS

**Adirondack Sportsman** (518-863-4525; 221 Bridge St., Northville) Guns and ammunition, sporting goods.

**Moose River Company** (315-369-3682; Main St. Old Forge) Guns and ammunition, gunsmithing, sporting goods.

**Pumpkin Mountain Gun Shop** (518- 352-7772; Rte. 28, Blue Mountain Lake) Guns and ammunition, gunsmithing, black powder supplies.

## HUNTING GUIDES

## LAKE GEORGE AND SOUTHEASTERN ADIRONDACKS

**Lake Luzerne Guide Service** (518-696-4646; 2101 Lake Ave., Lake Luzerne, NY 12846) Guide for big game.

**Trout Brook Guide Service** (518-532-7089; Main St., Schroon Lake, NY 12870) Guide for big and small game.

## CHAMPLAIN VALLEY

**Adirondack-Champlain Guide Service** (518-963-7351; Long Pond, Willsboro, NY 12996) Guide for big game, grouse, and rabbits.

## HIGH PEAKS AND NORTHERN ADIRONDACKS

**Adirondack Bass & Camping** (518-946-7362; Glen Rd., Jay, NY 12941) Guide for big game.

**Middle Earth Expeditions** (518-523-9572; Cascade Rd., Lake Placid, NY 12946) Guide for big game, lodgings.

**Placid Bay Ventures** (518-523-2001; 70 Saranac Ave., Lake Placid) Guide for big game, lodging.

**Smith's Taxidermy & Guide Service** (518-891-6289; 41 Broadway, Saranac Lake, NY 12983) Guide for big game.

**Stillwaters Guide Service** (518-523-2280; Cascade Rd., Lake Placid) Guide for big game, bow hunting, snowshoe hares with hounds.

**Young's Foothills** (518-891-1221; Box 345, Saranac Lake) Guide for black powder and bow hunting.

## NORTHWEST LAKES REGION

**Cold River Ranch** (518-359-7559; Rte. 3, Tupper Lake, NY 12986) Pack-horse hunting trips.

## CENTRAL AND SOUTHWESTERN ADIRONDACKS

**Adirondack Hut to Hut** (518-251-2710; Minerva Hill Lodge, Rte. 28N, Minerva, NY 12851) Guide for big game, pack-horse trips.

**Adirondack Mountain & Stream Guide Service** (518-251-3762; Hardscrabble Rd., Olmstedville, NY 12857) Guide for big game, snowshoe hares with hounds.

**Adirondack Range Guide & Outfitter** (315-826-7416; Rte. 8, Hoffmeister, NY 13353) Hunting guide for big and small game, pack-horse trips.

**Adirondack Saddle Tours** (315-357-4499; Uncas Rd., Inlet, NY 13360) Pack-horse hunting trips.

**Pepperbox Outfitters** (Beaver River Station, Box 258L, Lowville, NY 13367) Guide for big game, bow hunting.

**Mark Shoemaker** (315-369-3978; Big Otter Camp, Otter Lake, NY 13427) Guide for big game, lodging.

**Wharton's Adirondack Outfitters** (518-548-3195; Box 544; Lake Pleasant, NY 12108) Guide for big game.

# ICE SKATING

Considering that Adirondack waters exist more months of the year in a solid rather than liquid state, it's no wonder that ice skating is a popular

*A fairy princess on skates, 1901*

The Barry Collection, Courtesy Lake Placid Center for the Arts

pastime in the park. The modern sport of speed skating was launched in Saranac Lake and Lake Placid: in the early 1900s, more world records were set here — and broken — by local bladesmen than at any other wintry place. Nowadays, there's backcountry skating possible on remote lakes and ponds, skating on plowed rinks in the towns, and indoor figure skating or hockey on Zamboni-maintained ice sheets.

If you'd like to try wilderness skating, wait until late December at least. Cold, clear, still weather produces the most consistent ice. Ice that is two inches thick will support one person on skates, but it's better to wait for at least three inches to form, since currents and springs can create weak spots. Ice is thinner near shore; steer clear of inlets, outlets, and other tributaries where currents are strong. Ponds in the High Peaks are often good for skating by New Year's Day, especially if there's been little snow. You can scout Chapel Pond, off Rte. 73 south of Keene Valley, or the Cascade lakes, on the same road, north of Keene, or Heart Lake, at the end of the Adirondak Loj Road. Ask locally for more favorite places.

Many towns offer lighted rinks with warming huts; check with local tourist offices for hours. Long Lake's public rink is one of the better ones, and it's conveniently located on Rte. 30 between a diner and a restaurant. There's free skating under the lights in Fern Park, in Inlet (315-357-5501), and in Old Forge, on North Street (315-369-6983). Many towns along Lake Champlain, such as Ticonderoga and Westport, often have good (or not so good, depending on winds and weather) skating. In Lake Placid, you can enjoy terrific ice outdoors most evenings at the *Olympic Speed Skating Oval*, on Main St., or you can skate in the Olympic Arena (518-523-1655) at scheduled times for a small charge. Tupper Lake (518-359-2531; McLaughlin St., behind the A&P) maintains indoor rinks for hockey and skating; Saranac Lake's Civic Center (518-891-3800) also has good ice indoors.

A few shops in Lake Placid specialize in hockey and figure skates, outfits, and equipment: *Skater's Patch Pro Shop* (518-523-4369; inside the Olympic Arena); the *Cobbler's Shop* (518-523-3679; Main St.), and the *Edge in Sports* (518-523-9430; in front of the Olympic Arena, on Main St.). You can rent skates from the latter two for gliding around the speed oval, and from *High Peaks Cyclery* (518-523-3764; Saranac Ave.). Also, many of the general-purpose sporting goods stores throughout the region stock skates for children and adults.

## MINIATURE GOLF

**P**erhaps the thought of all that wild country to explore makes your kids crave more familiar entertainment, and perhaps one of the many mini-golf places can fill the bill. Throughout the Adirondacks, there are opportunities to sink little bitty putts after avoiding windmills, Vikings, and loop-de-loops; several are listed below, but you may want to call ahead for hours. Historians take note: the oldest miniature golf course in the world is called, fittingly enough, *Miniature Golf*, and it is located at the intersection of Beach Rd. and Rte. 9 in Lake George.

Elsewhere in **Lake George and Southeastern Adirondacks**, you can try *Around the World in 18 Holes* (518-668-2531; Rte. 9, Lake George), *Fort Mini Golf*

*Negotiating a putt through the Viking ship under Paul Bunyan's watchful gaze at Round the World Golf, Lake George.*

B. Folwell

(518-668-5471; Fort William Henry Commons, Rte 9, Lake George), or *Gooney Mini Golf* (518-668-2700; at the Haunted Castle, Rtes. 9 and 9N, also Lake George). Further up the road, it's the *Narrows Pizza Miniature Golf Course* (518-532-7591; Rte. 9, Schroon Lake), and you won't have to worry about what's for dinner after the round.

For the **High Peaks and Northern Adirondacks** area, mini-golf is an international affair at *Around the World in 18 Holes* (518-523-9065; Saranac Ave., Lake Placid). Within the **Northwest Lakes Region** is *Tupp Putt* (Park St., Tupper Lake). In the **Central and Southwestern Adirondacks,** you can choose from the unique indoor course, *Tropical Paradise* (315-369-3290; Main St., Old Forge), or *Nutty Putty Miniature Golf* (315-369-6636; Main St., Old Forge), or *Pa'Mella's Main Course* (315-357-3807; Rte. 28, Inlet), or the new course located at the **Adirondack Trail** (518-648-5533; Rtes. 28 and 30, Indian Lake).

## OLYMPIC SPORTS

L ake Placid is the only place in North America that has hosted two Winter Olympic Games, in 1932 and 1980. During the '32 games, the American team won the bobsledding events and took silver and bronze medals in speed-skating, hockey, figure skating, and bobsledding, and thus was regarded the unofficial Olympic champion. In 1980, Eric Heiden garnered five gold medals in speed skating, and the U.S. hockey team won the tournament following a stunning upset over the Russians in the semifinal round. The legacy of Olympic glory lives on here, at the brand-new training center on Old Military Road, where hundreds of athletes eat, sleep, and work out in a high-tech setting, and in several specialized sports facilities in and around Lake Placid. From season to season, many different competitors come to town for coaching and practice: on Mirror Lake, in the summer, you can glimpse the U.S. rowing, canoeing, and kayaking teams working out in the morning mist.

*J. Hubert Stevens drove his brother Curtis to the Olympic gold medal for the two man bobsled in the 1932 Olympics.*

Nancie Battaglia

*You, too, can ride through Zig Zag and Shady Corner on a real bobsled at Mount Van Hoevenberg.*

There's just one place in the country where you, too, can ride a bona fide bobsled on an Olympic run: Mount Van Hoevenberg, on Rte. 73 just a few miles from downtown Lake Placid. This thrill does not come cheap; it's $25 for the longest minute you'll ever spend. (Note that the sleds are piloted by experienced professional drivers.) Rides are available Tuesday—Sunday afternoons from Christmas through early March, depending on the track conditions, and it's a good idea to call ahead. *The Olympic Regional Development Authority* (ORDA) is the place to call for details on all of the Olympic venues and winter sports schedules (518-523-1655; Olympic Center, Lake Placid, NY 12946).

Watching international luge and bobsled competitions is almost as exciting as trying it yourself, and considerably easier on the wallet and the heart rate. There are races nearly every weekend beginning in late December. Dress warmly for spectating; you'll want to walk up and down the mile-long course in order to see and hear the sleds zoom through Shady Corner or spiral down the Omega Curve. At some vantage points, the sleds fly by nearly upside-down, and the roar of the runners is a rackety lesson in the Doppler effect. You'll definitely want to see several starts, too, where track stars have a decided advantage in launching the sleds.

In the Olympic Arena in the center of Lake Placid, you can watch Can/Am ice hockey tournaments, professional exhibition games, figure skating compe-

*For the annual Independence Day Ski Jump, skiers zoom down specially designed porcelain rails rather than snow and ice.*

Nancie Battaglia

titions (collegiate, I.S.I.A., and invitational), and skating exhibitions, year-round. An annual highlight is the *Gus Lussi International Figure Skating Championships* in mid-February. There are speed-skating races next door at the outdoor oval, and you can usually watch Olympic hopefuls training on winter afternoons.

Ski jumping on the 70- and 90-meter jumps is decidedly something to see; watching men fly through the air overhead is far more impressive in person than the sport appears on television. The annual *New Year's and Master's Ski Jump* takes place the last weekend in December, and world-team trials and meets are later in the winter; contact ORDA for a schedule. Dress warmly for spectating here too, since the bleachers are exposed to the elements. Surprisingly, this is one winter event that you can also enjoy in the summer: you can ride a chairlift to the base of the 90-meter jump, then go up the elevator to the top, for a small fee. The jump tower is open mid-May to early October, and the view is great. An annual favorite is the *Independence Day Ski Jump* sponsored by ORDA (518-523-1655); this is a Lake Placid spectator event you don't have to dress warmly for. Also, at the jumping complex (known as Kodak Sports Park), you can watch the U.S. freestyle skiers training in summer and fall. The skiers go off jumps, twirl and tumble through the air, and land in a huge tank of water, with their skis still attached.

At Whiteface Mountain, you can see the ballet and mogul portions of the *Subaru Freestyle World Cup* in late January, and occasional international downhill and slalom races. Or you can try the Olympic Mountain for yourself — look further in this chapter for skiing inspiration.

## RACES AND SEASONAL SPORTS EVENTS

E vents are listed in chronological order within each region.

### LAKE GEORGE AND SOUTHEASTERN ADIRONDACKS

**Prospect Mountain Road Race** (518-668-2195; Prospect Mt. Memorial Highway, Lake George, NY 12845) 5.5 miles uphill all the way, in early May.

**N.Y.S. Bass Federation Tournament** (518-543-6353; Hague, NY 12836) On Lake George in late June.

**Adirondack Distance Run** (518-793-9848) 10-mile road race from Lake George to Bolton Landing, in early July.

**Summerun** (518-532-7675; Box 741, Schroon Lake, NY 12870) 5k and 10k run through downtown Schroon Lake, on the first Saturday in August. Kids' fun run in the early morning.

### CHAMPLAIN VALLEY

**Red-Nose Race** (518-962-4446; Westport, NY 12993) 5k footrace through town, in early February.

**Rotary International Fishing Classic** (518-561-5030) Sponsored by Plattsburgh Rotary Club, covering all of Lake Champlain; weigh stations at Port Henry, Westport, and Willsboro; in late May.

**Pleasant Valley Run** (518-873-6408; Elizabethtown Social Center, Box 205, Elizabethtown, NY 12932) 7k footrace from Lewis to Elizabethtown, on the second Saturday in May.

**Lake Champlain International Fishing Derby** (802-862-7777; P.O. Box 4384, South Burlington, VT 05406) Covering all of Lake Champlain, weigh stations in Willsboro and Ticonderoga, in mid-June.

**Fourth of July Race** (518-962-4446; Westport) 7k footrace from Wadhams to Westport, on July 4th.

**Montcalm Mile Run** (518-585-6619; Ticonderoga, NY 12883) Footrace down Ticonderoga's main street, on July 4th.

**Fort to Fort Race** (518-585-2821; Fort Ticonderoga) 30k race from Fort Crown Point to Fort Ti; qualifier for the New York City Marathon; held in early October.

**24-hour Marathon & Ultramarathon** (518-962-4446; Westport) Ten-person relay teams, with each member running a mile every hour; ultramarathon for solo runners; from noon Saturday to noon Sunday, at the Essex County Fairgrounds racetrack in Westport, on the third weekend in July.

## HIGH PEAKS AND NORTHERN ADIRONDACKS

**Lawrence Loppet** (518-523-1655; Olympic Regional Development Authority, Lake Placid, NY 12946) 25k and 50k citizens' races at Mount Van Hoevenberg (the Olympic cross-country ski course); sponsored by the Lawrence Insurance Group, in early February.

**Empire State Winter Games** (518-523-1655; ORDA, Lake Placid) Citizens' competitions in figure skating, luge, bobsled, speed skating, ski jumping, cross-country skiing, and other events, around Lake Placid in early March.

**Lake Colby Ice Fishing Derby** (518-891-2197; Saranac Lake Fish & Game Club, Saranac Lake, NY 12983) Held on Lake Colby, off Rte. 86 north of Saranac Lake village, in early March.

**Whiteface Mountain Cocoa Butter Open** (518-523-1655; Whiteface Mt. Ski Area, Wilmington, NY 12993) Citizens' downhill, slalom, and fun races, in late March.

**Ice Breaker Canoe Race** (518-891-1990; Saranac Lake Chamber of Commerce, Saranac Lake) 5-mile race on the Saranac River, in late March.

**Pedal, Paddle, Pole Race** (518-523-9605; Cascade Ski Touring Center, Lake Placid) Four-person teams mountain-bike, canoe on the Ausable River, and cross-country ski, in early April.

**Ausable River Whitewater Derby** (518-946-7200; Sponsored by the Ausable Valley Jaycees, Jay, NY 12941) 6-mile downriver canoe race on the east branch of the Ausable River, from Keene to Upper Jay; on the last Sunday in April.

**'Round the Mountain Canoe Race** (518-891-1990; Saranac Lake Chamber of Commerce, Saranac Lake) 10-mile canoe race on Lower Saranac Lake and the Saranac River, in early May.

**West Branch Derby** (518-523-2591; Lake Placid) 6-mile downriver canoe race on the west branch of the Ausable River, in late May.

**Saranac Lake Area Chamber of Commerce Golf Tournament** (518-891-1990; Saranac Lake Golf Club, Rte. 86, Saranac Lake) Two-person scramble in early June.

Nancie Battaglia

*A welcome drenching at the annual Whiteface Mountain Uphill Footrace.*

**Whiteface Mountain Uphill Footrace** (518-946-2255; Wilmington) 8.3-mile race up the Whitetace Mountain Veterans' Memorial Highway, on the second Sunday in June.

**Tour of the Adirondacks** (518-523-2752; Sundog Ski and Sport, 90 Main St., Lake Placid) Bike races of varying lengths on challenging back roads, and criteriums in town, in late June.

**Willard Hanmer Guideboat and Canoe Races** (518-891-1990; Saranac Lake Chamber of Commerce, Saranac Lake) Races on Lake Flower for guideboats, canoes, rowing shells, war canoes, and kayaks in early July.

**Casio Triathlon** (518-523-1655; ORDA, Lake Placid) 1.2-mile swim, 46-mile bike race, 12-mile run, near Lake Placid, in early August.

**Can-Am Rugby Tournament** (518-891-1990; Saranac Lake Chamber of Commerce, Saranac Lake) North America's largest rugby meet, with more than 100 teams competing in fields throughout Lake Placid and Saranac Lake, in early August.

**Mike Flanagan Memorial Bike Race** (518-523-3764; High Peaks Cyclery, Saranac Ave., Lake Placid) 53- and 70-mile road races near Lake Placid, on the second weekend in August.

**International Lacrosse Tournament** (518-523-2591; North Elba Park District, Lake Placid) At the North Elba Horse Show Grounds in mid-August.

**Lake Placid Mountain-Bike Classic** (518-523-1655; ORDA, Lake Placid) Gymkana events, obstacle course, and dirt races at Whiteface Mountain in mid-August.

**Adirondack Canoe Classic** (518-891-1990; Saranac Lake Chamber of Commerce, Saranac Lake) 90-mile three-day marathon canoe race from Old Forge to Saranac Lake village, in early September.

*The 90-mile Adirondack Canoe Classic, in September, sends solo and tandem racers from Old Forge to Saranac Lake.*

Nancie Battaglia

**Adirondack Century Ride** (518-523-3764; High Peaks Cyclery, Saranac Ave., Lake Placid) 100-mile one-day bike tour from Lake Placid to Old Forge, in mid-September.

## NORTHWEST LAKES REGION

**Lumberjack Scramble and Little Logger Marathon** (518-359-3328; Tupper Lake Chamber of Commerce, Park St., Tupper Lake, NY 12986) 10k and 25k cross-country ski races, in late January.

**Genesee Flatwater Weekend** (518-359-3328; Tupper Lake Chamber of Commerce) 11-mile canoe race on the Raquette River on Saturday, 44-mile canoe race from Long Lake town beach to Tupper Lake village on Sunday, on the second weekend in June.

**Tin Man Triathlon** (518-359-3328; Tupper Lake Chamber of Commerce) 1.2-mile swim, 56-mile bike, 13.1-mile run beginning at the Tupper Lake Municipal Park, on the third weekend in July.

**St. Regis Invitational Canoe Race** (518-891-1990; Paul Smith's College, Paul Smiths, NY 12970) Flat-water race in the St. Regis Canoe Area, in early August.

**24-Hour Marathon** (518-359-3328; Tupper Lake Chamber of Commerce) Ten-person relay teams each run 1-mile laps; at the Tupper Lake High School track on the second weekend in August.

**Mini Triathlon** (518-359-3328; Tupper Lake Chamber of Commerce) Road bike, canoe, and footraces at the Tupper Lake Rod & Gun Club, in Sepember.

**Spud Harvest Quadrathlon** (518-327-6370; Paul Smith's College, Paul Smiths) 18-mile road bike, 5-mile canoe, 9-mile mountain bike, and 5-mile run, in late September.

## CENTRAL AND SOUTHWESTERN ADIRONDACKS

**Jeff Meneilly Memorial Cross-Country Ski Race** (315-357-5501; Inlet Chamber of Commerce, Inlet, NY 13360) 5k citizens' cross-country ski race; Empire State Games qualifier; in late January.

**Piseco Airport Race** (518-548-4521; Speculator Chamber of Commerce, Speculator, NY 12164) 10k citizens' race in Piseco, on the first Saturday in February.

**Kunjamuck Kick** (518-548-4521; Speculator Chamber of Commerce) 10k citizens' race near Speculator, sponsored by the International Paper Company, in late February.

**Sisu Cross Country Ski Race** (518-863-4974; Lapland Lake Cross Country Ski Center, Storer Rd., Northville, NY 12134) 25k citizens' race at Lapland Lake, in late February.

**Snowflake Derby** (315-369-3225; McCauley Mt. Ski Area, Old Forge, NY 13420) Community downhill ski races, in early March.

**Whitewater Derby** (518-251-2612; North Creek Chamber of Commerce, Main St., North Creek, NY 12853) Slalom race for canoes and kayaks on the Hudson River Saturday, downriver canoe race from North Creek to Riparius on the Hudson on Sunday, on the first weekend in May.

**Return of the Chimney Swifts** (1-800-676-FULT; Hubbell's Chimney, Second St., Northville) Inexplicably, a flock of chimney swifts always returns to this old factory on the same day each year, after wintering in Brazil. Look at dusk on May 6, or visit the site any evening thereafter to see them come flying out.

**Mud Season Miniature Golf Classic** (315-357-5501; Inlet Chamber of Commerce, Inlet) For adults and children, at Pa'mella's main course on Rte. 28, in early May.

**Piseco Triathlon** (518-548-4521; Speculator Chamber of Commerce) Swim, road-bike and run, circumnavigating Piseco Lake, on the third Saturday in July.

**Lane Lake Run** (518-548-4521; Speculator Chamber of Commerce) 10k footrace around Lake Pleasant, on the second Sunday in August.

**Great Sacandaga Lake Triathlon** (1-800-676-FULT; 18 Cayadutta St., Gloversville, NY 12078) 10k run, 23-mile bike, and 4-mile canoe race on Great Sacandaga Lake, on the third Sunday in August.

**Reindeer Roundup** (518-863-4974; Lapland Lake Cross Country Ski Center, Storer Rd., Northville) 10k citizens' cross-country ski race; Empire State Games qualifier, before Christmas.

## ROCK AND ICE CLIMBING

Despite the sculpting effects of glaciers and the wearing forces of the weather, plenty of steep, challenging rock walls remain in the High Peaks, and scattered cliff faces can be found in the central Adirondacks. Possibilities for rock and ice climbers abound, from non-technical scrambles up broad, smooth slides to gnarly 700-foot pitches in the 5.11+ difficulty range. Adirondack climbers, from wannabes to veterans, all depend on a sturdy green guidebook, *Climbing in the Adirondacks: A Guide to Rock and Ice Routes in the Adirondacks* by Don Mellor (Adirondack Mountain Club, 1988). Since the approaches to many of the best climbs involve a hike or bushwhack to the base, this book is indispensable. It also outlines hundreds of climbs and explains the local ethic of clean climbing in the wilderness: leave as few traces as possible (don't cut brush or scrub off lichens), and place a minimum of bolts, on the lead only.

Climbers can get word-of-mouth tips in a few places in the High Peaks. *The Mountaineer* (518-576-2281; Rte. 73, Keene Valley, NY 12943) sells climbing gear, topo maps, and guidebooks; the advice is free. Hardware and software for climbing can also be found at *Eastern Mountain Sports* (518-523-2505; 51 Main St., Lake Placid, NY 12946) and *High Peaks Cyclery* (518-523-3764; Saranac Ave., Lake Placid).

To learn the basics of climbing, or polish your skills if you've had some experience, a handful of guide services specialize in helping you climb higher.

*Learning the ropes of Adirondack rock-climbing with Don Mellor.*

Nancie Battaglia

## CLIMBING INSTRUCTION

**Adirondack Alpine Adventures** (518-576-9881; Rte. 73, Keene, NY 12942). Rock- and ice-climbing guide service; instruction for women, small groups, or individuals, with video critiques.

**Adirondack Mountain Club** (518-523-3441; Adirondak Loj, Loj Rd., Lake Placid, NY 12946). Weekend workshops for beginners and intermediates, lodging.

**Adirondack Rock and River** (518-576-2041; Alstead Hill Rd., Keene). Rock- and ice-climbing guide service, instruction for beginners to experts, natural indoor climbing wall, lodging.

**Don Mellor** (518-523-3984; Mirror Lake Dr., Lake Placid). Rock- and ice-climbing guide, instruction for all levels. Don wrote the book on Adirondack climbing.

### The High Peaks

The Adirondack Park holds dozens of mountaintops rising 4,000 feet or more above sea level. You don't need to be a technical climber to enjoy the views, but you should be an experienced, well-prepared hiker capable of putting in at least a twelve-mile round trip. For trail descriptions and access points, consult the *Guide to Adirondack Trails: High Peaks Region* (Adirondack Mountain Club, 1990) or *Discover the Adirondack High Peaks* (Backcountry Publications, 1989). The following "Forty-Six" can be found in the area bounded by Newcomb on the south, Elizabethtown on the east, Wilmington on the north, and the Franklin County line on the west.

| Peak | Elevation | | |
|---|---|---|---|
| 1. Mount Marcy | 5344 feet | 24. Mount Marshall | 4363 |
| 2. Algonquin Peak | 5115 | 25. Seward Mountain | 4331 |
| 3. Mount Haystack | 4961 | 26. Allen Mountain | 4347 |
| 4. Mount Skylight | 4925 | 27. Big Slide Mountain | 4232 |
| 5. Whiteface Mountain | 4865 | 28. Esther Mountain | 4239 |
| 6. Dix Mountain | 4823 | 29. Upper Wolf Jaw | 4203 |
| 7. Gray Peak | 4826 | 30. Lower Wolf Jaw | 4173 |
| 8. Iroquois Peak | 4849 | 31. Phelps Mountain | 4160 |
| 9. Basin Mountain | 4826 | 32. Street Mountain | 4134 |
| 10. Gothics Mountain | 4734 | 33. Sawteeth Mountain | 4134 |
| 11. Mount Colden | 4715 | 34. Mount Donaldson | 4108 |
| 12. Giant Mountain | 4626 | 35. Cascade Mountain | 4098 |
| 13. Nippletop Mountain | 4593 | 36. Seymour Mountain | 4091 |
| 14. Santanoni Peak | 4606 | 37. Porter Mountain | 4068 |
| 15. Mount Redfield | 4606 | 38. Mount Colvin | 4068 |
| 16. Wright Peak | 4587 | 39. South Dix Mountain | 4068 |
| 17. Saddleback Mountain | 4528 | 40. Mount Emmons | 4039 |
| 18. Panther Peak | 4442 | 41. Dial Mountain | 4003 |
| 19. Table Top Mountain | 4413 | 42. East Dix Mountain | 4006 |
| 20. Rocky Peak Ridge | 4383 | 43. Blake Peak | 3970 |
| 21. Hough Peak | 4409 | 44. Cliff Mountain | 3871 |
| 22. Macomb Mountain | 4390 | 45. Nye Mountain | 3871 |
| 23. Armstrong Mountain | 4429 | 46. Couchsachraga Peak | 3793 |

(Elevations from *Of the Summits, Of the Forests*, Adirondack Forty-Sixers, 1991)

The *Adirondack Forty-Sixers* is an organization dedicated to these High Peaks. To earn the member's patch, you must have climbed all of the mountains listed above. The group also does volunteer trail work and education projects; for information, write to Adirondack Forty-Sixers, RFD 1, Box 390, Morrisonville, NY 12962.

## And More Peaks

In other parts of the park there are mountains nearly as high, with sweeping vistas of vast forests and wild lakes. A short list follows of lofty peaks with well-marked trails and open summits or fire towers. Note that there are plenty more mountains in the park; ask locally for favorite vantage points.

| Peak | Elevation | Closest Town |
|------|-----------|--------------|
| Snowy Mountain | 3899 feet | Indian Lake |
| McKenzie Mountain | 3832 | Lake Placid |
| Lyon Mountain | 3830 | Chazy Lake |
| Boreas Mountain | 3776 | North Hudson |
| Wakely Mountain | 3770 | Indian Lake |
| Blue Mountain | 3759 | Blue Mt. Lake |
| Hurricane Mountain | 3678 | Elizabethtown |
| Pillsbury Mountain | 3597 | Speculator |
| Ampersand Mountain | 3552 | Saranac Lake |
| Vanderwhacker Mountain | 3386 | Minerva |
| Crane Mountain | 3254 | Johnsburg |

*Taking a break at Lake Tear of the Clouds, source of the Hudson River, with Mount Marcy's peak in the distance.*

Nancie Battaglia

## ROWING

The Adirondack guideboat is the preeminent rowing machine for the region, and you'll find a selection of boatbuilders in Chapter Seven, *Shopping*. For sources of modern rowboats, such as Alden shells, consult *Adirondack Rowing* (518-585-7870; 306 Lake George Ave., Ticonderoga, NY 12883) or *Pete Smith* (518-251-3632; River Rd., North Creek, NY 12853).

Most of the small-to-medium-size Adirondack lakes are very suitable for rowing. Quieter lakes, like Indian Lake, Paradox Lake, Forked Lake, Star Lake, Lake Pleasant, Long Lake, and many others offer several miles of open water, yet have less powerboat traffic than Lake George or Schroon Lake. You'll also find that early morning or early evening, when the winds are relatively calm, are the best times to row. Mirror Lake, on the backside of downtown Lake Placid, is not open to motorboats, so that's another possibility for rowers. You might even be able to match a few strokes with Olympic athletes as they train.

## SAILING

The big lakes — Champlain and George — offer some nice sailing in the midst of beautiful scenery, and have plenty of marinas for an evening's

*Coming back from a catamaran cruise on Upper Chateaugay Lake.*

Nancie Battaglia

rest or equipment repairs. Also any lakes with public launches are open to sailboats; the most suitable craft for bouldery-bottomed Adirondack lakes are those without deep keels and with centerboards you can pull up readily. Even then, remember to keep an eye out for unmarked rocks and shoals! Sailing on these mountain-valley lakes with their many islands can be tricky, since in the lee of an island you stand a good chance of being becalmed. Wind can whip shallow lakes into whitecapped mini-oceans, too. A portable weather radio should be included in your basic kit; Adirondack forecasts (out of Burlington, Vermont) can be found at 162.40 megahertz.

You can purchase Coast Guard charts for Lake George and Lake Champlain, but not for any of the smaller, interior lakes. Some of the topographical maps have troughs and some shoals marked, but these maps are of limited use to sailors. Your best bet may be to ask at local boat liveries for lake maps, or at least ask for advice about where to find the best water or how to avoid the worst shoals.

For hardware, lines, and other equipment you may need, check in the beginning portion of this chapter for a list of some marinas. Also, in the Lake George area, *Yankee Yacht Sales* (518-668-2862; Rte. 9N, Diamond Point) is well stocked with everything from the essentials to brand-new boats. They also offer sailing instruction and rent day-sailers and cruisers. On Lake Champlain, *Westport Marina* (518-962-4356; Washington St., Westport) has a good selection of sailing supplies.

## SCENIC FLIGHTS

**M**aybe climbing a mountain isn't for you, yet you still seek a bird's-eye-view of the territory. In that case, why not charter a small plane to soar over the hills and valleys, lakes and rivers? Several pilots offer sight-seeing flights at a surprisingly reasonable cost; a 15- to 20-minute flight covering about 50 miles of territory costs far less than the average evening out. You can make special arrangements for longer flights, but a typical short trip costs about $45 for a family of four. Other companies charge a rate of about $150 per hour, and can accommodate five adults. Seaplane services are also equipped to take canoeists, fishermen, and hunters into several remote ponds and lakes.

Listed below are a few fixed-wheel and seaplane services available for private charters; you must call ahead for a reservation.

**Adirondack Flying Service** (518-523-2473; Cascade Rd., Lake Placid, NY 12946) Scenic flights over the High Peaks, glider rides, air taxi.

**Bird's Seaplane Service** (315-357-3631; Sixth Lake, Inlet, NY 13360) Scenic seaplane flights, hunting and fishing charter.

*A float plane on Long Lake.*

Nancie Battaglia

**Helms Aero Service** (518-624-3931; Rte. 30, Long Lake, NY 12847) Scenic seaplane flights, hunting and fishing charter.

**Nancy Lake Flying Service** (518-924-2122; Park Rd., Wells, NY 12190) Scenic flights, hunting and fishing charter.

**North Country Aviation** (518-891-1262; 4 Beechwood Dr., Saranac Lake, NY 12983) Scenic flights over the High Peaks and Saranac Lakes, air taxi, photographic flights.

**Payne's Air Service** (315-357-3971; Seventh Lake, Inlet) Scenic flights, hunting and fishing charter.

**"Feets" Shelton** (315-848-3400; Cranberry Lake, NY 12927) Scenic flights around the Cranberry-Star Lake area; charters.

## SCENIC HIGHWAYS

Most of the Adirondack highways and byways are pretty darn scenic: even the interstate known as the Northway, I-87, won an award as

*A Sunday drive on Whiteface Mountain, 1930s.*

Courtesy Natalie and Maude Bryt

"America's Most Beautiful Highway" in 1966-67. Here, though, we're talking specifically about roads up mountains with great views from the summit. In the Lake George area, the *Prospect Mountain Memorial Highway* (518-668-5198; Northway Exit 21, off Rte. 9 near Lake George village) snakes up a small mountain to offer a terrific 100-mile view stretching from the High Peaks to Vermont and the Catskills. Not too far from Lake Placid, the *Whiteface Mountain Veterans Memorial Highway* (518-946-7175; off Rte. 431, Wilmington), has a great view, too, looking down on other mountaintops and silvery lakes. Both are state-operated toll roads open daily from mid-May through the fall.

# SKIING (CROSS COUNTRY) AND SNOWSHOEING

The Adirondack Park is paradise for cross-country skiers. Most winters there's plenty of snow, especially in the higher elevations or west of the Champlain Valley. There's a wide range of ski destinations, from rugged trails for mountaineering expeditions in the High Peaks to gentle, groomed paths suitable for novices, with hundreds and hundreds of miles of intermediate trails in between. Many of the marked hiking trails on state land are not only suitable for cross-country skiing or snowshoeing, they're actually better, since swampy areas are frozen and ice-bound ponds and lakes can be easily crossed.

For suggestions on backcountry ski trails, consult any of the books in the *Discover the Adirondacks* series (Backcountry Publications) by Barbara McMartin; below the name of each trail is a list of appropriate activities along the route, like skiing, picnicking, camping. Both *Adirondack Life* and *Adirondac*

*Considering the route on a backcountry tour near Whiteface Mountain.*

Nancie Battaglia

magazines often outline ski treks in their winter issues; if your local library has back issues, a treasure trove of potential ski trips is at your fingertips. Just a few favorite intermediate-level trips are Santanoni Preserve, near Newcomb; Avalanche Lake, from Adirondak Loj; Cascade Lake, near Big Moose; and sections of the Northville-Lake Placid Trail between the Cedar River Road and Long Lake. Many of the designated wilderness areas (described below) offer great ski touring on marked but ungroomed trails. The Centennial Challenge, a hiking-canoeing-skiing program sponsored by the Visitor Interpretive Centers (518-327-3000), describes several trips in a handy brochure. There are many, many more trip possibilities. Another option for exploring the wild, wintry woods is to hire a licensed guide; check under "Hiking and Backpacking" earlier in this chapter for guides who specialize in backcountry trips.

Before setting out on any of these wilderness trips, prepare your pack with quick energy food; a thermos filled with hot tea or cocoa; extra hat, socks, and gloves; a topo map and compass; matches; flashlight; and a space blanket. Dress in layers of wool, polypropylene, or synthetic pile. Don't travel alone. Sign in at the trailhead register. Let friends know your destination and when you plan to return.

Many towns maintain free public cross-country ski trails, and the Visitor Interpretive Center (VIC) at Paul Smiths (518-327-3000; Rte. 30) has many miles of beginner-to-intermediate trails. At the Newcomb VIC (528-2000; Rte. 28N), the marked trails are not quite so adaptable to skiing, but you can try snowshoeing at no charge; the Tubbs company has donated 50 pairs of state-of-the-art snowshoes for the public to enjoy. Traveling softly on the snow through the old-growth forest at Newcomb is a special treat.

The *Jackrabbit Trail* (518-523-1365; Box 843, Lake Placid, NY 12946) is a superb local resource, some 25 miles of groomed trails connecting Keene with Lake Placid and Saranac Lake. The trail combines old logging roads and hiking trails, and is named for Herman "Jack Rabbit" Johannsen, who laid out many of the routes between 1916 and 1928. From some of the hotels in downtown Placid, you can strap on your skis and just head out for the woods. There's even guided inn-to-inn skiing sponsored by some lodgings; ask your host if you're staying in the High Peaks. The Jackrabbit Trail joins with many of the commercial ski-touring areas and traverses the McKenzie Mountain Wilderness Area between Whiteface Inn and Saranac Lake. Be sure to get the free map published by the Adirondack Ski Touring Council for details on sections of the route. Note that dogs are not welcome on groomed portions of the Jackrabbit Trail, nor at the privately owned ski centers.

Besides wilderness trails and informal town ski trails, there are some excellent cross-country ski areas with meticulously groomed tracks and rental equipment. You'll find a variety of ski areas listed below, and we do suggest calling ahead for current information about snow cover. Many of the touring centers offer lessons, and the *Adirondack Mountain Club* (518-523-3441; Adirondak Loj, Loj Rd., Lake Placid, NY 12946) schedules numerous backcountry and telemark workshops for beginning and intermediate skiers. Citizens' races are listed above, under "Races and Seasonal Sports Events"; a tabloid newspaper, *On the Trail* (315-437-9296; 6450 Pheasant Rd., E. Syracuse, NY 13057) lists many upstate New York races and clinics.

## CROSS-COUNTRY SKI CENTERS

### LAKE GEORGE AND SOUTHEASTERN ADIRONDACKS

**Harrisburg Lake Resort** (518-696-3461; Harrisburg Lake Rd., Stony Creek, NY 12878) Groomed trails, connects to backcountry trails in Wilcox Lake Wild Forest, food, lodging.

**Rogers Rock State Campsite** (518-585-6746; Rte. 9N, Hague, NY 12836) Ungroomed trails.

**Schroon Lake Ski Trails** (518-532-7675; Box 726, Schroon Lake, NY 12870) Backcountry skiing in Pharaoh Lake and Hoffman Notch Wilderness areas.

**Top of the World** (518-668-2062; Lockhart Mt. Rd., Lake George, NY 12845) 10k groomed trails, rentals, lessons, food, lodging.

### CHAMPLAIN VALLEY

**Ausable Chasm** (518-834-9990; Rtes. 9 and 373, Ausable Chasm, NY 12911) 26k groomed trails, night skiing, rentals, food.

### HIGH PEAKS AND NORTHERN ADIRONDACKS

**Adirondak Loj** (518-523-3441; Adirondak Loj Rd., Lake Placid, NY 12946) 12k backcountry trails, connects with numerous wilderness trails, guided tours, lessons, food, lodging.

---

### *Cold, Cold, Cold*

In the old days, folks caught unprepared in the wilds occasionally died of "exposure." Today, we call that same condition hypothermia (literally, "low temperature"), and it remains a serious concern in cool, moist climates year-round. Even on a summer day, a lightly clad hiker can suffer from hypothermia after being caught by a cool rain or in a steady breeze. In winter, unaccustomed strenuous exercise coupled with the wrong kind of clothing can lead to hypothermia.

Hypothermia is caused when the body loses heat faster than it can produce it. The normal body-core temperature of 98.6 degrees decreases to a dangerous and even life-threatening level. This heat loss occurs when the body is inadequately insulated by clothing, usually garb that's ineffective against wet, wind, or cold. Precipitating events can be a dunking in cold water or a soaking in steady drizzle.

To compensate for this heat loss, the body tries to produce more warmth, which burns up energy and requires extra work by the body's muscles. As the energy reserve dwindles and muscles become exhausted, hypothermia sets in.

The signs of hypothermia arrive in stages: first, the person feels and acts cold. He or she may be shivering, having some trouble with manual dexterity, or even showing bluish skin color. Next, shivering may become uncontrollable, and the person starts to behave erratically. These behavioral changes can include sluggishness, apathy, irritability; physically, the person may be staggering or having difficulty with balance. Some outdoors people refer to the "Umble Rule" — watch out when a companion begins to stumble, mumble, grumble, and fumble.

The final stage of severe hypothermia is a true medical emergency. The person feels cold to the touch; shivering has stopped; limbs may be frostbitten. The victim may be stuporous and obviously uncaring about his or her survival. The treatment of all stages of hypothermia is basically the same — add warmth. Warm the person with your hands, body-to-body contact, a fire. Provide hot liquids: tea, soup, cocoa, or any nonalcoholic drinks are good. For a person in severe hypothermia, try to prevent further heat loss (adding heat is best accomplished in a hospital setting) and get the victim to a medical facility as quickly as possible.

A few ounces of prevention go a long way in avoiding hypothermia. Dress in layers, especially clothing made of wool, polypropylene, or synthetic pile, all of which still insulate when wet. (As the forest rangers say, "Cotton kills.") Bring spare hats, mittens, socks, overpants, extra windbreaker. Bring along plenty of high-energy food and warm liquids in a thermos. Put an "instant heat" packet or two in a pocket. Watch out for your friends, and be honest about your abilities. Know when to turn back rather than pushing beyond your limits.

Frostbite and its cousin, frostnip, are not hypothermia. The terms refer to flesh actually freezing, and it's usually portions of fingers, toes, ears, nose, or chin that are affected. Frostbite can occur quickly, especially on skin surfaces exposed to the wind; watch for the skin looking waxy or mottled. One test for frostbite is to pinch the affected part gently and watch for the color to change. Unaffected flesh will change back to its normal color, but frozen parts will remain whitish. They feel hard and cold, too.

At the first sign of frostbite, warm the affected part at body temperature. You can warm your hands by sticking fingers in your mouth, by placing them in an armpit or between your legs; ears and cheeks can be warmed with a dry hand; feet can be warmed up with the help of a buddy's body. Do not rub a frostbitten part; you can cause severe tissue damage because there are real ice crystals in the cells. Don't use temperatures above 110 degrees for warming, as excessive heat can cause greater damage. (In other words, be very careful using a pocket hand-warmer.) Avoid refreezing any frostbitten parts.

Deep frostbite should not be thawed. It sounds grim, but it's better to walk out on frozen feet than it is to thaw them and then try to shuffle along. Severe frostbite is a medical emergency that will need evacuation and lengthy hospitalization to help repair circulatory damage.

**Bark Eater X-C Ski Center** (518-576-2221; Alstead Hill Rd., Keene, NY 12942) 20k groomed trails, connects with Jackrabbit Trail, rentals, lessons, guided tours, lodging.

**Cascade Ski Touring Center** (518-523-9605; Rte. 73, Lake Placid) 15k groomed trails, connects with Jackrabbit Trail, night skiing, rentals, lessons, full ski shop, food and drink.

**Craig Wood Golf Course** (518-523-2591; Rte. 73, Lake Placid) 10k trails, connects with Jackrabbit Trail, night skiing.

**Cunningham's Ski Barn** (518-523-4460; Main St., Lake Placid) Groomed trails on Lake Placid Club property, connects with Jackrabbit Trail, rentals, lessons, full ski shop.

**Dewey Mountain X-C Ski Trails** (518-891-2697; Rte. 30, Saranac Lake, NY 12983) 12k groomed trails, night skiing, lessons, guided tours.

**Mount Van Hoevenberg** (518-523-2811; Rte. 73, Lake Placid) 50k groomed trails (the Olympic trails), connects with Jackrabbit Trail, rentals, lessons, full ski shop, food.

**Whiteface Inn Resort** (518-523-2551; Whiteface Inn Rd., Lake Placid) 15k groomed trails, connects with Jackrabbit Trail, rentals, lessons, food, lodging.

## NORTHWEST LAKES REGION

**Big Tupper Ski Area** (518-359-3651; Rte. 30, Tupper Lake, NY 12986) 15k groomed trails, rentals, ski shop, food and drink.

**Cranberry Lake Trail** (315-386-4000; Rte. 3, Cranberry Lake, NY 12927) Backcountry trails.

**Deer Pond Loop** (518-359-3328; Rte. 30, Tupper Lake) 15k loop of backcountry trails.

## CENTRAL AND SOUTHWESTERN ADIRONDACKS

**Adirondack Hut-to-Hut Tours** (518-251-2710; Minerva Hill Lodge, Rte. 28N, Minerva, NY 12851) Guided backcountry ski trips, lodging.

**Adirondack Woodcraft Ski Touring Center** (315-369-6031; Rondaxe Rd., Old Forge, NY 13420) 10k groomed trails, night skiing, rentals, full ski shop, lodging.

**Fern Park Recreation Area** (315-357-5501; South Shore Rd., Inlet, NY 13360) 20k groomed trails, night skiing.

**Garnet Hill Cross-Country Ski Center** (518-251-2821; 13th Lake Rd., North River, NY 12856) 50k groomed trails, connects with trails in Siamese Ponds Wilderness Area and with trails at High Winds, rentals, lessons, guided tours, full ski shop, food, lodging.

**Gore Mountain** (518-251-2411; Peaceful Valley Rd., North Creek, NY 12853) 10k groomed trails, rentals, ski shop, food.

**High Winds Ski Touring Center** (518-251-2706; Barton Mines Rd., North River) 20k groomed trails, connects with Garnet Hill, rentals, guided tours, food, lodging.

**Lapland Lake** (518-863-4974; Storer Rd., Northville, NY 12134) 40k groomed trails, rentals, lessons, full ski shop, food, lodging.

*Having a blast at Lapland Lake.*

Nancie Battaglia

**Long Lake** (518-624-3077; Rte. 30, Long Lake, NY 12847) 80k backcountry trails, excellent map available for Long Lake and Raquette Lake area trails.

**McCauley Mountain** (315-369-3225; McCauley Mountain Rd., Old Forge) 20k groomed trails, rentals, lessons, food.

**Sagamore Lodge** (315-354-5311; Sagamore Rd., Raquette Lake, NY 13436) Special weekend and week-long cross-country ski programs, 35k trails, lodging.

**Speculator Cross-Country Ski Trails** (518-548-4521; Elm Lake Rd., Speculator, NY 12164) Backcountry trails.

## CROSS-COUNTRY SKI OUTFITTERS AND SHOPS

### HIGH PEAKS AND NORTHERN ADIRONDACKS

**All Season Outfitters** (518-891-6159; 168 Lake Flower Ave., Saranac Lake, NY 12983) Cross-country ski and snowshoe rentals, shuttle service.

**Blue Line Sport Shop** (518-891-4680; 82 Main St., Saranac Lake) Ski rentals and sales, sporting goods, maps.

**Eastern Mountain Sports** (518-523-2505; 51 Main St., Lake Placid, NY 12946) Ski rentals and sales, telemark and backcountry equipment, outdoor gear, guidebooks, maps.

**High Peaks Cyclery** (518-523-3764; 18 Saranac Ave., Lake Placid) Ski rentals and sales, telemark and backcountry equipment, snowshoe and skate rentals, outdoor gear.

**The Mountaineer** (518-576-2281; Rte. 73, Keene Valley, NY 12943) Ski sales, telemark and backcountry equipment, outdoor gear, guidebooks, maps.

**Sundog Ski & Sport** (518-523-2752; 90 Main St., Lake Placid) Downhill and cross-country ski sales, backcountry and telemark equipment. Also at 518-891-5533;157 Lake Flower Ave., Saranac Lake.

### NORTHWEST LAKES REGION

**Tip Top Sport Shop** (518-359-9222; 40 Park St., Tupper Lake, NY 12986) Downhill and cross-country ski equipment, skates.

### CENTRAL AND SOUTHWESTERN ADIRONDACKS

**Blue Mountain Outfitters** (518-352-7675; Rte. 30, Blue Mountain Lake, NY 12812) Cross-country ski rentals.

**Cunningham's Ski Barn** (518-251-3215; Rte. 28, North Creek, NY 12853) Downhill and cross-country ski sales and rentals, clothing.

**Sporting Propositions** (315-369-6188; Rte. 28, Old Forge, NY 13420) Downhill and cross-country ski sales and rentals, clothing.

### BEYOND THE BLUE LINE

**Fall Line Ski Shop** (518-793-3203; Quaker Rd., Glens Falls, NY 12801) Downhill and cross-country ski sales and rentals.

**Infinity Ski and Sport** (518-587-6500; 67 Weibel Ave., Saratoga Springs, NY 12866) Downhill and cross-country ski equipment.

**Inside Edge** (518-793-5676; 624 Upper Glen St., Glens Falls) Downhill and cross-country ski sales and rentals.

**Syd & Dusty's Outfitters** (518-792-0260; Rtes. 9 and  149, Queensbury, NY 12804) Downhill and cross-country ski equipment, outdoor gear.

**Wooden Ski and Wheel** (518-561-2790; Rte. 9, Plattsburgh, NY 12901) Cross-country ski equipment, outdoor gear.

## SKIING (DOWNHILL)

Schussers and snow bunnies alike flock to the North Country for downhill thrills, and skiing has been a part of Adirondack life since the 1930s. Weekend ski trains from New York's Grand Central once brought thousands of folks to North Creek, where they could "ride up and slide down." The "ride up" was in school buses, with wooden racks for skis mounted on the outside, and the "slide down" was on twisty trails carved out of the forest near Barton's Mines, across from the present-day slopes at Gore Mountain.

*Ski-joring behind a motor-cycle, a schusser could go uphill, downhill, or even snowplow down Broadway in Saranac Lake.*

Courtesy Adirondack Collection, Saranac Lake Free Library

Today there are a couple of high-profile mountains with challenging slopes and extensive snowmaking: Whiteface and Gore, both operated by the Olympic Regional Development Authority, a state agency. There are also a number of nice, little mountains where the emphasis is on family fun rather than on the latest Day-Glo outfits and state-of-the art equipment. A few towns, like Indian Lake and Newcomb, operate free downhill areas for residents and guests. Of course you won't find man-made snow there, and you'll have to remember dormant skills for managing a poma lift or a rope tow, but you can have a blast with the kids and beat the crowds.

Downhill season in the Adirondacks depends a great deal on the weather, naturally. Often, snowmaking begins in November, and some trails may open

*Whiteface Mountain in Wilmington boasts 65 trails and the highest vertical in the Northeast.*

Nancie Battaglia

in mid-December, but it can be Christmas week before the snow is reliable throughout an entire ski area. In the Northeast, you won't find deep powder like you can in the Rockies; skiing is just plain different here. Many people prefer spring conditions, when there's loose "corn" snow and bright sunshine. Whatever the weather, it's not a bad idea to call ahead for the ski conditions before you go.

Compared to ski areas in Vermont or the Rockies, the Adirondacks are quite undeveloped. The emphasis at the hills is on skiing, not on hot-tub lounging, nightlife, or aprés-ski ambience. You won't find condos or restaurants at the base of a mountain (outside of the base lodge); for fancier meals and lodging, you have to go into town. Listed below are some downhill ski areas within the Adirondack Park.

## DOWNHILL SKI AREAS

**Price Codes**

| Weekend lift tickets for an adult: | Under $15 | $15 to $25 | Over $25 |
|---|---|---|---|
| | Inexpensive | Moderate | Expensive |

## LAKE GEORGE AND THE SOUTHEASTERN ADIRONDACKS

**HICKORY HILL**
518-623-2825.
Hickory Hill Rd., off Rte. 418, Warrensburg, NY 12883.
Summer address: Box 9004, Schenectady, NY 12309.
Trails: 14 (1 beginner, 7 intermediate, 6 expert.)
Lifts: 1 rope tow, 1 T-bar, 2 poma-lifts.

Just after World War II, Hans Winbaur and some friends began carving out ski slopes on a steep, conical mountain overlooking the Schroon and Hudson rivers, near Warrensburg. Today, Hickory retains a folksy, hand-hewn approach, and in fact, it's the only ski area in the country that's owned and operated by its stockholders — kind of a cooperative skiing enterprise. Volunteers still work on the trails, service the lifts, and raise money to keep the hill afloat.

Vertical drop: 1200 ft.
Snowmaking: No.
Tickets: Inexpensive.
Open: Sat.—Sun. 9—4.

Runs named Winfall, Hare, Grand Teton, and Topnotch, from the summit, are expert slopes, but there are gentler ridge trails and traverses for intermediates. There's a certified ski school, a base lodge with hot food and cold drinks, and a professional patrol on duty. Hickory Hill depends on natural snow cover, so be sure to call ahead.

## HIGH PEAKS AND NORTHERN ADIRONDACKS

**MOUNT PISGAH**
518-891-0970.
Mt. Pisgah Rd., off
   Trudeau Rd., Saranac
   Lake, NY 12983.
Trails: 1 main trail, some
   side trails.
Lifts: 1 T-bar.
Vertical drop: 300 ft.
Snowmaking: Yes.
Tickets: Inexpensive.
Open: Tues.—Sun.; week-
   days 3—9 p.m., Sat. 9—
   6, Sun. 12—6.

Sylvia Plath skied Mount Pisgah back in the fifties and chronicled her spectacular downhill tumble in *The Bell Jar*. Since then, the hill has been operated on-again, off-again until a couple of years ago, when volunteers took the initiative to rebuild the hill and by their efforts encouraged town and village officials to revitalize the slope. The mountain today is still very much a family ski area, with a friendly atmosphere and slopes geared to intermediate skiers. One section called "Suicide" falls somewhere between a modest drop-off and a mini-headwall; ten-year-olds think it's awesome.

There's snowmaking over most of the hill here, thanks to local fund-raising efforts, and a ski school, patrol, and base lodge with hot food and nonalcoholic drinks. Pisgah is one of the few places left in the Adirondacks where you can still enjoy night skiing; local residents often hit the slopes after work, when a lift ticket (good from 6—9 p.m.) costs just $6.

**WHITEFACE**
   **MOUNTAIN**
518-946-2233.
Rte. 86, Wilmington, NY
   12997.
Trails: 65 (17 expert, 25
   intermediate, 17 novice).
Lifts: 9 chairlifts (7 double-
   chairs, 2 triple-chairs).
Vertical drop: 3216 ft.
Snowmaking: 93%.
Tickets: Expensive.
Open: daily 9—4.

New York governor Averell Harriman dedicated Whiteface Mountain, a state-owned facility, in 1958; the event was marred slightly when the chairlift he was riding came to a dead halt and Harriman had to be rescued by ladder from his lofty perch. Not to worry, modern skiers — Whiteface lifts are quite reliable now.

The Olympic mountain has the longest vertical drop in the East, and lots of intense, expert-level skiing. Cloudspin, one of the black-diamond trails, is long and hard with beaucoup big bumps; Wilderness, another toughie, is the site of international mogul competitions. Intermediate skiers have dozens of challenging trails, too, with the three-mile-long Excelsior at the top of the list. Whiteface is big enough — but not a place you can get lost in — to accommodate scads of skiers without long lift lines building up.

For families, there's an excellent play-and-ski program for tots and a first-rate ski school led by Ed Kreil. Whiteface also sponsors races from low-key fun events like the Cocoa Butter Open to Olympic qualifiers.

There are three lodges for food, drink, and discussing the slopes, plus a full ski shop with rentals for skiers of all sizes and abilities. Although a weekend adult ticket is more than $30, there are sizable midweek discounts, special promotions, and ladies' days.

## NORTHWEST LAKES REGION

**BIG TUPPER SKI AREA**
518-359-3651.
Country Club Rd., off Rte. 30, Tupper Lake, NY 12986.
Trails: 23.
Lifts: 4 (2 double-chairs; rope tow, T-bar).
Vertical drop: 1152 ft.
Snowmaking: 60%.
Tickets: Moderate.
Open: Daily 9—4.

On Mount Morris, overlooking Big Tupper Lake, is a solid family ski area that's had a roller-coaster history. Since the early sixties, when the mountain was first developed, Big Tupper has been through several owners and operators, from the town government to a New Jersey millionaire.

The mountain is mostly intermediate terrain, with a headwall beginning many runs, leading to a long, gentle run-out. When there's good snow cover, skiers looking for more difficult pitches can try from the top of the number-one chair for steep and narrow chutes. At the base lodge, there's a cafeteria, bar, ski shop, ski-school office, picnic tables, and a fireplace; the rental shop is located in a separate building.

Big Tupper was among the first Blue Line hills to welcome telemark skiers and snowboarders, and sponsors informal races on weekends. The Molson Brewing Company frequently sponsors competitions and special Fridays with reduced lift tickets (all day for just $12 in 1992); check locally for details.

*Big Tupper Ski Area often has excellent natural snow and is rarely crowded.*

Nancie Battaglia

## CENTRAL AND SOUTHWESTERN ADIRONDACKS

**GORE MOUNTAIN**
518-251-2441.
Peaceful Valley Rd., off
  Rte. 28, North Creek,
  NY 12853.
Trails: 41.
Cross-country trails: 11
  km.
Lifts: 9 (1 4-person gondo-
  la, 1 triple-chair, 5 dou-
  ble-chairs, 1 J-bar).
Vertical drop: 2100 ft.
Snowmaking: 90%.
Tickets: Expensive.
Open: Daily 9—4.

Near North Creek, the cradle of North Country Alpine skiing, is the state's other Adirondack ski hill: Gore Mountain, which opened in the early sixties. Since 1984 Gore has been managed by the Olympic Regional Development Authority (ORDA), as is Whiteface Mountain, and since then, snowmaking has been installed over much of the mountain and trails have been widened.

Gore is intermediate heaven, with wide-open cruising runs, such as Showcase, Sunway, and Twister, on the lower part of the mountain, accessible from the high-speed triple chair. Mogul mavens and expert skiers can find good sport on Chatiemac and Hawkeye. Gore is home to New York's only gondola; folks agree it's a real blessing on a blustery winter day.

For families, the mountain has an excellent nursery, a ski-and-play program for tots ages 3—6, and a ski school for all ages. The base lodge has a nice, cozy lounge, while the cafeteria is a bit cavernous. There's a full ski shop and rentals on the ground floor. Citizen racers can join in NASTAR competitions every weekend, while wannabe boarders can take lessons in the new rage of snowboarding.

Gore offers discounts on midweek and early-season tickets, with special promotional offers through soft-drink manufacturers.

**MCCAULEY
  MOUNTAIN**
315-369-3225.
McCauley Mt. Rd., off
  Bisby Rd., Old Forge,
  NY 13420.
Trails: 14 (3 expert, 5 inter-
  mediate, 6 novice).
Cross-country ski trails: 20
  km.
Lifts: 5 (1 double-chair, 2
  T-bars, 1 rope tow, 1
  pony lift).
Vertical drop: 633 ft.
Snowmaking: Yes.
Tickets: Inexpensive.
Open: Daily 9—4.

Hank Kashiwa, the international racing star and ski inventor, learned his first snowplow turns here; his brilliant career is something folks in Old Forge still talk about. Actually, the local high school has produced three U.S. Olympic ski-team members, thanks to good coaches and the welcoming intermediate slopes at the nearby hill.

This little mountain has heaps of natural snow, thanks to a climate that can produce 200 inches or more during an average winter, and there's snowmaking, too. Helmers and Olympic, both of which have snowmaking, are the most difficult slopes. Intermediates can sample Upper God's Land, a ridge trail; Sky Ride, a wide route serviced by the double chair; or the gentle, sweeping Challenger. The lift crew feeds the deer here, so even nonskiers can enjoy a visit. You'll find all the amenities at McCauley: a ski school, rentals, food, and drink.

**OAK MOUNTAIN**
518-548-7311.
Elm Lake Rd., off Rte. 30,
   Speculator, NY 12164.
Trails: 13.
Lifts: 3 T-bars.
Vertical drop: 650 ft.
Snowmaking: No.
Tickets: Inexpensive.
Open: Fri.—Sun. 9—4.

Just a wedeln away from Speculator's busy corner is Oak Mountain, built in 1948. Norm and Nancy Germain run an exemplary family ski hill here that offers diverse slopes for intermediates and novices. There are steep woodland trails, broad gentle runs, and a few options in between.

Townsfolk work as lift attendants in exchange for skiing privileges; the nearby public schools offer free ski lessons here for students. There's a base lodge that resembles an overgrown cabin, with dozens of wooden picnic tables, and overall, the philosophy of the place — that downhill skiing is for everybody — is as clear today as it was 40 years ago.

## SNOWMOBILING

Plenty of snow, miles of old roads, active clubs, and support from town trail-maintenance programs add up to excellent snowmobiling in many parts of the park. A hub of snowmobile activity is Old Forge, which issues more than 12,000 snowmobile permits each winter. (Permits are available from the Tourist Information Center on Rte. 28 in the center of town.) Trails in Old Forge spread out like a river with numerous tributaries. You can connect with Inlet trails to the east, or Independence River Wild Forest and Big Moose trails to the north, and Forestport and Boonville routes to the south. These trails meet still other trails, so that you can continue further east from Inlet to Indian Lake or Speculator, and then from Speculator to Wells, or you can go from Inlet to Raquette Lake, and then on to Long Lake. Confused? There's information listed below to help you track down the right maps and brochures, or even hire a guide.

Besides the Old Forge-Inlet area, which gets blanketed by more than 15 feet of snow during an average winter, there are more than 400 miles of snowmobile trails in the Tupper Lake-Saranac Lake-Lake Placid area, and near Cranberry Lake there are scores of miles of trails. Many trail networks throughout the park cross private timberlands as well as the state forest preserve. Public lands designated as Wild Forest areas are open to snowmobiling; Wilderness Areas are not. (You'll find descriptions of these areas near the end of this chapter.)

As with any winter pursuit, planning and preparation help make a successful outing. Know your machine; carry an emergency repair kit and understand how to use it. Be sure you have plenty of gas. Travel with friends in case of a breakdown or other surprise situation. Never ride at night unless you're familiar with the trail or are following an experienced leader. Avoid crossing frozen lakes and streams unless you are absolutely certain the ice is safe. Some town or county roads are designated trails; while on such a highway, keep right, observe the posted snowmobile speed limit, and travel in single file.

Your basic pack should contain a topographic map and compass as well as a local trail map; survival kit with matches, flashlight, rope, space blanket, quick-energy food, and something warm to drink; extra hat, socks, and mittens. Although a sip of brandy or other alcoholic beverage can give the illusion of warming you up, alcohol actually impairs circulation and can hasten hypothermia. And an arrest for snowmobiling under the influence carries with it severe penalties.

## SNOWMOBILE RENTALS AND GUIDES

Guided snowmobile tours are a relatively new service in the Adirondacks, and for getting around unfamiliar territory during a full day's riding, a knowledgeable leader is a real asset. In some communities you can rent a sled, but this service is not widespread. For example, in the *High Peaks and Northern Adirondacks*, you can rent snowmobiles in Lake Placid from *Adirondack Snowmobile Rentals* (518-523-1388) and *Lake Placid Sports Unlimited* (518-523-3596); *Adirondack Adventure Tours* (518-523-1475) offers guided expeditions.

In the *Central and Southwestern Adirondacks*, *Snowmobile Escort Service* (315-369-6205), based in Old Forge, takes small groups along less-traveled routes to Beaver River, Brantingham, Long Lake, and many more places. Around Old Forge, several dealers rent snowmobiles: *Old Forge Sports Tours* (315-369-3796), *Snowland Snowmobile Rentals* (315-369-3115), and *Big Moose Yamaha* (315-357-2998, Eagle Bay) In Long Lake, the folks at *Mt. View Farms Bed & Breakfast* (518-624-2521) rent snowmobiles and lead half- and full-day trips down the lake and into Sabattis.

## SNOWMOBILE TRAIL INFORMATION

### LAKE GEORGE AND SOUTHEASTERN ADIRONDACKS

**Warren County Tourism** (518-761-6366; Municipal Center, Lake George, NY 12845) Snowmobile trail information.

### HIGH PEAKS AND NORTHERN ADIRONDACKS

**Department of Environmental Conservation** (518-891-1370; Rte. 86, Ray Brook, NY 12977) Snowmobile trail booklet.

**Essex County Tourism** (518-942-7794; Court House, Elizabethtown, NY 12932) Snowmobile trail information.

**Franklin County Tourism** (518-483-6788; 63 W. Main St., Malone, NY 12953) Trail information for northern Adirondacks.

**Lake Placid Visitors Bureau** (518-523-2445; Main St., Lake Placid, NY 12946) Trail information, sled rentals and guide information.

**Saranac Lake Chamber of Commerce** (518-891-1990; Main St., Saranac Lake, NY 12983) Trail information.

## NORTHWEST LAKES REGION

**Cranberry Lake Information** (315-848-2900; Cranberry Lake, NY 12927) Snowmobile trail information.

**Tupper Lake Chamber of Commerce** (518-359-3328; Park St., Tupper Lake, NY 12986) Trail information, special events.

## CENTRAL AND SOUTHWESTERN ADIRONDACKS

**Central Adirondack Association** (315-369-6983; Main St., Old Forge, NY 13420) Information on Old Forge-Inlet-Big Moose area trails; 500+ miles of groomed trails; connections with Hamilton, Lewis, and Fulton county trail networks; excellent snow cover.

**Hamilton County Tourism** (518-648-5239; White Birch Lane, Indian Lake, NY 12842) 750 miles of connecting trails.

**Long Lake Recreation Department** (518-624-3077; Rte. 30, Long Lake, NY 12847) Groomed trails connecting with Raquette Lake trails, trail map, sponsors annual Long Lake 100 race in February.

**Speculator Snowmobile Trails** (518-548-4521; Rte. 30, Speculator, NY 12164) Groomed trails on International Paper Company lands, connections with Indian Lake and Wells trails, trail map.

**Wells Snowmobile Trails** (518-924-2455; Rte. 30, Wells, NY 12190) 60 miles of trails, connections with Speculator and Old Forge systems.

## SWIMMING

There are so many fine places to swim in the Adirondacks it's almost easier to list where you can't swim: Ausable Chasm and High Falls Gorge spring to mind. Most of the hundred-plus towns in the park offer clean, safe, free beaches with lifeguards on duty in July and August, and many of the public campgrounds described earlier in this chapter have excellent swimming areas with guards. If you want to visit a state campground just for swimming and

*Taking a dive, Mirror Lake, 1900.*

Courtesy Natalie and Maude Bryt

picnicking, the day-use fee is about $5 per carload. Off the beaten path, there are pools beneath foaming falls, and deep spots in fast rivers, but you'll find the best way to find a particular community's favorite swimming spot is to ask locally.

## WHITE-WATER RAFTING

The upper Hudson River provides some of the East's most exhilarating white water: nearly 17 miles of continuous Class III-V rapids. From about 1860 to 1950, river drivers sent logs downstream every spring to sawmills and pulp mills, and they followed along behind the churning, tumbling timber in rowboats to pry loose logjams. Since the mid-1970s, the Hudson's power has been rediscovered for recreational purposes, with several rafting companies making the trip from the Indian River, just south of Indian Lake, to North River, where Rte. 28 is close to the Hudson.

The Hudson Gorge is wild and remote, miles from the nearest road. The river passes beneath the Blue Ledges, a 400-foot-high cliff, and around rolling, green mountains. Names of the rapids and pools date back to the loggers' time: Osprey Nest, Harris Rift, the Black Hole, and OK Slip, where it was okay to make camp for the night on a river drive.

Reliable water levels are provided by a daily dam release below Lake Abanakee, courtesy of the Town of Indian Lake. Releases begin about April 1 and last through Memorial Day, and most years there is a short fall season with dam releases on weekends only.

Although you don't need white-water paddling experience to enjoy a trip down the Hudson, you do need to be over age 14, in good physical condition,

*Powering through the rapids in the Hudson Gorge.*

Nancie Battaglia

and a competent swimmer. The outfitters supply you with an 8-person raft, wetsuit, paddle, life jacket, and helmet; they also shuttle you to the put-in, give onshore instructions in safety and paddling techniques, and supply lunch or dinner (usually a steak cook-out) at the end of the trip. Rafters should bring polypropylene underwear to wear under the suits; wool hats, gloves, and socks; sneakers; and dry, warm clothing for after the trip. (Springtime Adirondack air can be pretty chilly, and the water temperature is truly frigid).

A licensed guide steers each raft and directs the paddlers. This trip is not for passive passengers; you're expected to paddle — sometimes hard and fast — as the guide instructs. The Hudson Gorge is an all-day adventure, including four to five hours of strenuous exercise. The 1992 price for a trip ran from $65 to $85 per person.

Several rafting companies also offer a short, fun, family-type trip on the Sacandaga River at Lake Luzerne. These junkets float 3.5 miles and last about an hour. Dam releases make the Sacandaga floatable all summer long, and the cost is about $10 per person. This is one river you can float in the comfort of your own bathing suit. At the other end of the spectrum is the Moose River from McKeever to Port Leyden; this is a 14-mile bear absolutely for experienced white-water paddlers only. The Moose is only runnable after spring ice-out, and the charge is about $80 to $95 per person.

## WHITE-WATER OUTFITTERS

**ARO** (1-800-525-RAFT; Box 649, Old Forge, NY 13420) Trips on the Hudson and Moose rivers in spring, Black River and Sacandaga in summer.

**Adirondack Wildwaters Inc.** (1-800-933-2468 or 518-696-2953; Box 801, Corinth, NY 12822) Hudson River trips in spring, Moose River trips in April.

**Adventure Sports Rafting Company** (1-800-441-RAFT; Main St., Indian Lake, NY 12842) Hudson River trips in spring and fall.

**Hudson River Rafting Company** (1-800-888-RAFT or 518-251-3215; Rte. 28, Cunningham's Ski Barn, North Creek, NY 12853) Hudson River trips in spring and fall, Sacandaga River trips in summer, Moose River trips in April.

**Middle Earth Expeditions** (518-523-9572; HCR 01 Box 37, Lake Placid, NY 12946) Hudson River trips in spring, overnight float-in fishing trips in fall.

**Unicorn Expeditions** (1-800-UNICORN; P.O. Box T, Brunswick, ME 04011) Hudson River trips in spring, Moose River in April.

**Whitewater Challengers** (1-800-443-RAFT; White Haven, PA 18661) Hudson River trips in spring, Moose River trips in April.

**Whitewater World** (1-800-472-2386; Main St., North Creek, NY 12853) Hudson River trips in spring and fall, Moose River trips in April.

**W.I.L.D./W.A.T.E.R.S. Outdoor Center** (518-494-7478; Rte. 28, The Glen, Warrensburg, NY 12885) Hudson River trips in spring, Moose River trips in spring and fall as water levels allow, Sacandaga River trips in summer.

## WILDERNESS AREAS

"Where man is only a visitor who does not remain," is a phrase contained within the legislation that defined the 15 wilderness areas of the Adirondack Park in the early 1970s. These portions of the forest preserve are 10,000 acres or larger, and contain little evidence of modern times. Wilderness areas are open to hiking, cross-country skiing, hunting, fishing, and other similar pursuits, but seaplanes may not land on wilderness ponds, nor are motorized vehicles welcome. Listed below are Adirondack wilderness areas.

### LAKE GEORGE AND SOUTHEASTERN ADIRONDACKS

**Pharaoh Lake** 46,000 acres, east of Schroon Lake village. Extensive trail system, 36 lakes and ponds, lean-tos, views from Pharaoh and other nearby mountains. Popular with hikers and fishermen.

### HIGH PEAKS AND NORTHERN ADIRONDACKS

**Dix Mountain** 45,000 acres, southwest of Keene Valley. Adjacent to High Peaks wilderness, rock climbing at Chapel Pond, views from Noonmark, Dix, and many other mountains.

**Giant Mountain** 23,000 acres, between Elizabethtown and Keene. Roaring Brook Falls, extensive hiking trails, views from Rocky Peak Ridge, Giant, and other mountains.

Michael Trivieri

*View of Mount Marcy and Indian Pass from South Meadow.*

**High Peaks** 193,000 acres, between Lake Placid and Newcomb. Excellent trail network, rock climbing at Wallface and other peaks, small lakes and ponds, views from Mount Marcy, Algonquin, and numerous other summits. Some interior destinations (Lake Colden and Marcy Dam) and peaks are very popular, to the point of being overused; more than 10,000 people climb Mount Marcy every year.

**Jay Mountain** 7100 acres, east of Jay. Difficult access due to surrounding private lands; no state-marked trails at this writing.

**McKenzie Mountain** 38,000 acres, north of Ray Brook. Trails for hiking and cross-country skiing, fishing and canoeing on the Saranac River, views from McKenzie and Moose mountains.

**Sentinel Range** 23,000 acres, between Lake Placid and Wilmington. Small ponds for fishing, few hiking trails, views from Pitchoff Mountain. This area is quite remote and little used.

### NORTHWEST LAKES REGION

**St. Regis Canoe Area** 20,000 acres, west of Paul Smiths. 58 lakes and ponds for canoeing, views from St. Regis and other mountains, trail network for hiking and cross-country skiing. (Although not technically a wilderness area, the canoe area is managed in similar ways.)

## CENTRAL AND SOUTHWESTERN ADIRONDACKS

**Blue Ridge** 46,000 acres, south of Blue Mountain Lake. Contains several miles of the Northville-Lake Placid Trail for hiking and cross-country skiing; Cascade, Stephens, Wilson, Mitchell, and other trout ponds.

**Five Ponds** 101,000 acres, between Cranberry Lake and Stillwater Reservoir. Numerous ponds (some of which are sterile due to acid rain), canoeing on the Oswegatchie River, many acres of old-growth forest, some hiking trails. This area receives little use.

**Ha De Ron Dah** 27,000 acres, west of Old Forge. Small ponds and lakes; hiking and cross-country ski trails around Big Otter Lake. This area receives little use.

**Hoffman Notch** 36,000 acres, between Minerva and the Blue Ridge Rd. Ponds and trout streams, a few hiking trails. This area is used mostly by fishermen and hunters.

**Pepperbox** 15,000 acres, north of Stillwater Reservoir. Few trails, difficult access, mostly wetlands, excellent wildlife habitat.

**Pigeon Lake** 50,000 acres, northeast of Big Moose Lake. Numerous lakes, ponds, and streams; trails for hiking and cross-country skiing.

Nancie Battaglia

*A loon with two chicks eyes a pair of canoeists on a northwestern Adirondack lake.*

**Siamese Ponds** 112,000 acres, between North River and Speculator. Canoeing on Thirteenth Lake; Sacandaga River and numerous trout ponds; trails for hiking and cross-country skiing.

**Silver Lake** 105,000 acres, between Piseco and Wells. Silver, Mud, and Rock lakes; southern end of the Northville-Placid trail. This area receives little use.

**West Canada Lakes** 157,000 acres, west of Speculator. Cedar, Spruce, West Canada lakes, and 160 other bodies of water; portions of the Northville-Placid trail and other hiking trails. One of the largest roadless areas in the Northeast.

---

### Waterfalls

Throughout the Adirondacks, the combination of streams and rivers and mountainous terrain provides numerous waterfalls. Some are spectacularly high, like T-Lake, which is taller than Niagara; others, like Buttermilk Falls, near Long Lake, are a two-minute walk from the car. Listed below are just a few of the hundreds of cascades on forest preserve lands that you can visit.

| Falls name | Description | Nearest town |
| --- | --- | --- |
| Auger Falls | Gorge on the Sacandaga River, easy hike from Rte. 30 | Wells |
| Blue Ridge Falls | On the Branch, visible from Blue Ridge Rd. | North Hudson |
| Bog River Falls | 2-tier falls at Big Tupper Lake, visible from County Rd. 421 | Tupper Lake |
| Buttermilk Falls | Raquette River, easy hike | Long Lake |
| Cascade Lake Inlet | Rock falls above Cascade Lake, 4-mile hike from Big Moose Rd. | Big Moose |
| Falls Brook | 1-mile hike | Minerva |
| The Flume | On West Branch Au Sable River, visible from Rte. 86 | Wilmington |
| Hanging Spear Falls | Opalescent River, remote wilderness | High Peaks |
| High Falls | Oswegatchie River, remote | Cranberry Lake |
| Raquette Falls | Raquette River, remote | Tupper Lake |
| Rockwell Falls | Hudson River | Lake Luzerne |
| Shelving Rock | On Knapp estate, 4-mile hike | Pilot Knob |
| Split Rock Falls | Boquet River, access from Rte. 73 | Elizabethtown |
| T-Lake Falls | Steep, remote | Piseco |
| Wanika Falls | Chubb River, remote | Lake Placid |

*Blue Ridge Falls, near North Hudson.*

B. Folwell

## WILD FOREST AREAS

More than a million acres of public land in the park are designated as wild forest and are open to snowmobile travel, mountain biking, and other recreation. Some wild forest areas are listed below.

### LAKE GEORGE AND SOUTHEASTERN ADIRONDACKS

**Lake George.** Located on both the east and west shores of the lake, north of Bolton Landing. Contains the Tongue Mountain Range on the west and the old Knapp estate, with 40+ miles of hiking and horse trails, on the east.

**Wilcox Lake.** West of Stony Creek. Miles of snowmobile trails and old roads; ponds and streams for fishing.

### CHAMPLAIN VALLEY

**Hammond Pond.** Between Paradox and Moriah, with old roads for hiking and ponds for fishing.

## HIGH PEAKS AND NORTHERN ADIRONDACKS

**Debar Mountain.** Between Loon Lake and Meacham Lake. Horse trails; hiking, fishing in the Osgood River.

**Saranac Lakes.** West of Saranac Lake village. Excellent canoeing; island camping.

## NORTHWEST LAKES REGION

**Cranberry Lake.** Between Cranberry Lake and Piercefield. Snowmobile and hiking trails, trout ponds.

## CENTRAL AND SOUTHWESTERN ADIRONDACKS

**Black River.** Between Otter Lake and Wilmurt. Ponds and streams.

**Blue Mountain.** Northeast of Blue Mountain Lake. Contains part of the Northville-Placid trail; Tirrell Pond; views from Blue Mountain.

**Ferris Lake.** Between Piseco and Stratford. Dirt roads for mountain biking and driving through by car, numerous ponds and streams.

**Independence River.** South of Stillwater Reservoir. Dirt roads, fishing on the Independence River, snowmobile trails, beaver ponds.

**Jessup River.** Between the south end of Indian Lake and Speculator. Miami and Jessup rivers, Lewey Lake, views from Pillsbury Mountain; trails for snowmobiling, hiking, and mountain biking.

**Moose River Plains.** Between Indian Lake and Inlet. Dirt roads; numerous ponds and streams, Cedar River and Cedar River Flow, primitive car-camping sites, snowmobile trails.

**Sargent Ponds.** Between Raquette Lake and Long Lake. Trout ponds, hiking trails, canoe route between Raquette Lake and Blue Mountain Lake.

**Shaker Mountain.** East of Canada Lake. Dirt roads; hiking, cross-country skiing, and mountain-biking routes.

**Vanderwhacker Mountain.** Northwest of Minerva. Fishing on the Boreas River, views from Vanderwhacker Mountain.

# WILDLIFE

The Adirondack Park offers a great variety of wildlife in their natural habitats to observe, from bull moose to butterflies.

With marsh and mountain, field and forest to explore, experienced birders might be able to see a hundred different species in a day. (Back in the 1870s, a very young Theodore Roosevelt and a friend compiled and published a bird guide to the northern Adirondacks, listing some 90+ native birds they had observed.) In late spring, warblers in all colors of the rainbow arrive, and the best place to watch for them is along edges where habitats meet, such as woods on the border of a wetland or along the edge of a brushy field. A variety of songbirds, including kingbirds, flycatchers, grosbeaks, waxwings, thrushes, wrens, and sparrows, all nest here.

Bird-watchers looking for an unusual event should note that on May 6, as regular as can be, the chimney swifts return to Hubbell's old chimney, the remnant of a factory in Northville. Somehow they make the return trip from Brazil on the same date every single year.

Many of the interior lakes and ponds are home to kingfishers, ducks, herons, and loons; listen and watch for the great northern diver in the early morning and at dusk. Peregrine falcons and bald eagles, absent from the park for much of the 20th century, have been reintroduced in remote places. Cliffs in the High Peaks are now falcon eyries, and you may be able to spot a bald eagle or two in the Northwest Lakes part of the park. In the evening, listen for owls: the barred owl, which calls "Who cooks for you, who cooks for you," is quite common. In the fall, look up to see thousands of migrating Canada and snow geese.

Small mammals are numerous: snowshoe or varying hares, weasels, mink, raccoons, fisher, pine martens, otters, bobcats, porcupines, red and gray foxes. Coyotes, with rich coats in shades of black, rust, and gray, can be seen in fall, winter, and spring, and their yips and yowls on a summer night can be thrilling to the backcountry campers' ears. About 50 lynx from the Northwest Territories have been released in the High Peaks in the past few years, in an attempt to restore the big cats to their former range.

---

### Don't Touch That Critter!

In recent years an increasing number of rabies cases have been reported in the far northern corner of the Adirondacks. The disease seems to be spread mainly by raccoons, foxes, and skunks in upstate New York.

If you come across a wild animal acting unafraid or lying passively, by all means stay away from the creature. Don't touch dead animals you may find. Humans are not at great risk for rabies exposure since contact with sick wildlings can be avoided.

Dogs should be inoculated against rabies. Keep your pet under control when traveling through the woods, and don't let Fido run loose.

---

Whitetail deer are seemingly everywhere, especially in the early spring before the fawns are born. A few dozen moose (mainly bulls) have wandered into the park; plans are on the drawing board to reintroduce the big creatures from a herd in northern Canada.

Many of the state campgrounds are good places to observe wildlife, especially aquatic birds and mammals. Ask the caretaker about where to see resident otters, ducks, loons, and ospreys, and you may be rewarded with a wonderful vacation experience.

Nancie Battaglia

*A whitetail doe in the deep woods.*

# CHAPTER SEVEN
# *Woodsy Whimsy to Practical Gear*
## SHOPPING

Long before Ralph Lauren sold his first tweedy socks and country-plaid bed ensembles, that certain Adirondack look was thriving here, favored by ordinary folks who chose substance over style and function over form. Today, in general stores and old-fashioned haberdasheries throughout the park, you can get buffalo-plaid woolens and other practical gear without worrying whether you're setting — or following — the trend.

Courtesy Natalie and Maude Bryt

*D.C. Wells, a pioneer Adirondack peddler, makes a sale by the shores of Lake Placid.*

If your acquisitive desires run to more permanent things, the ever-comfortable, always-in-season Adirondack chair is readily available from woodworkers found on highways and byways. You can get the country seat in basic pine or beautiful native hardwoods, with rockers or anatomically curved backs, as a settee or porch swing, or even with hinges so the whole thing folds for traveling or storage. (We'd like to think that an Adirondack chair strapped to the roof rack of a visitor's car is the kinder, gentler version of that ubiquitous Maine souvenir, the lobster trap.)

Rustic furniture, from four-square, utilitarian tables to fanciful, sculptural headboards and coat racks, is still an authentic product made by local artisans who range the woods looking for that right piece of crooked yellow birch, the perfect shaggy cedar sapling. For a song (almost), you can purchase a rustic picture frame or framed mirror, or you can spend a small fortune on a custom collector's piece. Adirondackana, a real term used as a catchall for housewares with a suitably woodsy motif, historic collectibles, prints, books, and native crafts, is the specialty of a handful of fine shops that have been in business since the 1950s.

For the past 20 years, handcrafts have enjoyed a renaissance inside the Blue Line, as our tastes have turned from mass-produced things to well-made objects stamped with the maker's personality. Adirondack crafts range from traditional packbaskets woven from ash splints to chunky hand-knit sweaters depicting northwoods wildlife to whimsical contemporary jewelry featuring miniature oars for the ears. Some artisans rely on local wood to fire their kilns, or Adirondack wool for their yarns, or even quills from resident porcupines for their jewelry. Other craftspeople are here for the quiet lifestyle and the inspiration they get from woods and waters. Crafts can be purchased in select shops and galleries, at the artisans' studios, and at local festivals and fairs, all of which are described further on in this chapter.

For book lovers, there are a number of shops offering contemporary novels, trashy paperbacks for a rainy day in the cabin, nice stories to read to the kids, and a wide range of how-to, where-to, and why-to publications. If you can't find it on the shelves, just ask — the staffs at these independently owned bookstores are quite willing to order almost any book in print. For out-of-print books there are several shops, and there's even a mail-order seller who specializes in words of the weird — horror and fantasy fiction. In some emporiums you'll find books combined with other things, from gourmet foods to tobacco to hardware, making for an excellent afternoon's browsing.

There are dozens of antique shops in the park, with concentrations around Warrensburg, Chestertown, and the Gore Mountain region, and in the Champlain Valley. From second-Empire settees to postcards, moose antlers to Georgian silver, squeeze boxes to cheese boxes, there's bound to be the dealer who has just what you're looking for, and at a fair price. Besides the shops, there are a couple of first-rate antique shows, which you'll find listed under "Fairs and Festivals" further in this chapter, and occasional auctions, providing bargains, entertainment, and lunch.

General stores are still the real item in many North Country towns, supplying the goods for daily life, from fresh milk to rain ponchos to crescent wrenches, and maybe even a wedding present. We like to think that the definition of a true general store is a place where you could buy truly everything —

*Norman's, a classic Adirondack general store in Bloomingdale, has been serving customers for 90 years.*

Nancie Battaglia

*Guideboat and packbasket: traditional Adirondack crafts.*

Nancie Battaglia

from socks on up to dessert — you'd need for a week in the wilds or a few days at the cottage.

The watery side of the Adirondack Park attracts its fair share of small-craft aficionados (otherwise known as "boat nuts") to special gatherings and the fine traditional small-craft exhibit at the Adirondack Museum (which are described in Chapter Four, *Culture*). Boatbuilders who make elegant guideboats — the sleek, speedy native rowboat — along with craftspeople who design and make everything from ultralight pack canoes to Gold Cup racer replicas are listed in this chapter. As with all the self-employed artisans, it's best to call ahead before going to check out the goods.

The one thing you won't find inside the Blue Line of the Adirondack Park is the modern suburban shopping mall. For that consumer experience you need to go south, to Aviation Mall (off I-87, Glens Falls), or north, to Champlain Centres (off I-87, Plattsburgh), or west, to Watertown, Utica, Syracuse, and beyond. Schroon Lake, Lake Placid, and Saranac Lake have old-fashioned main streets that you can stroll for serious window shopping. Canada Street, Lake George's main drag, is a Day-Glo kaleidoscope of T-shirt shops, ice-cream stands, and souvenir galleries; the leather shop offers what may be the park's perhaps ... um ... tackiest gift item — a lucite toilet seat with barbed wire imbedded in it. A few towns like Ticonderoga, Tupper Lake, Saranac, and Placid have plazas with grocery, discount, liquor, and hardware stores, but in general, Adirondack shopping is a quiet, folksy kind of thing.

## ADIRONDACKANA

We can't claim to have invented the word that defines all kinds of material things that complement the countryside. The term evokes textures: bark, woodgrain; smells: balsam, cedar; tastes: maple, apple; forest colors: deep green, gold, sienna. For a real sampling of Adirondackana, you need to travel to the heart of the park, the High Peaks and the Central Adirondacks.

## HIGH PEAKS

### *Keene Valley*

**The Birch Store** (518-576-4561; Rtes. 9N and 73, Keene Valley, near the Noonmark Diner) Christine Evans and Marion Jeffers are just the fourth owners in the shop's century of business; they combine antiques, hip new clothing and jewelry with traditional Adirondack camp furnishings: blankets, birchbark baskets and frames, chairs, balsam pillows, and wickerware. Open daily June 15—Labor Day, and weekends from Labor Day to Columbus Day.

*Outdoors at the Birch Store, Keene Valley.*

Nancie Battaglia

### *Lake Placid*

**The Adirondack Store and Gallery** (518-523-2646; 109 Saranac Ave., Lake Placid, west of Cold Brook Plaza) This place wrote the book on Adirondackana. If you're looking for anything — pottery, table linens, wrapping papers, doormats, sweaters, stationery, cutting boards — emblazoned with loon, trout, pine-cone or birch motifs, search no further. There's an excellent selection of Adirondack prints by Winslow Homer and Frederic Remington; antique baskets and rustic furniture; camp rugs and blankets; gorgeous handwoven jackets by Atwood, a local designer; and woodsy ornaments for the Christmas tree, including minute Adirondack chairs. The store is also the prime source for the elegant Lake Placid Club china, available by the place setting or open stock. Open daily year-round.

*A contented bear guards the door at the Adirondack Store.*

Nancie Battaglia

**Adirondack Trading Company** (518-523-3651; 91 Main St., Lake Placid, between With Pipe and Book and Bookstore Plus) is chockablock full of little doodads from the woods, like cedar-scented soaps and sachets; reasonably priced pine-cone-covered picture frames and twig clothing racks; silk-screened totebags shaped like fish. Carrying the animal look even further, there are flannel night shirts printed with leaping deer and moose silhouettes, and goofy bear-foot slippers. Tables, bookshelves, and dressers with painted tops and white-birch legs and trim are reasonably priced. Open daily year-round. Also, there's an Adirondack Trading store in Saranac Lake (518-891-6278; 48 Broadway), open Mon.—Sat. year-round.

## CENTRAL AND SOUTHWESTERN ADIRONDACKS

### *Old Forge*

**Moose River Trading Company** (315-369-6091; Rte. 28, Thendara) Packbaskets, stylish waterproof canvas hats, Duluth packs, wanigans, maps, compasses, bug dope, camp cookware and blankets, Adirondack chairs, and Guide's Coffee — what more could you need for an Adirondack expedition or for assembling your own Great Camp room at home? Open year-round; mail-order catalog, too.

**Wildwood** (315-369-3397; Main St., Old Forge, 1 block from Old Forge Hardware) Proprietor Sarah Cohen, whose grandfather founded Old Forge Hardware, sells ash-splint baskets, beautiful postcards, stuffed animals representing every Adirondack mammal, imported chocolate, Portmeirion porcelain, guideboat paddles, rustic furniture, Navajo rugs, hand-carved bird earrings, wooden toys, and has in stock just about every book that men-

Inside Wildwood, in downtown Old Forge.

Nancie Battaglia

tions the Adirondacks, from Upton Sinclair's autobiography to Ian Fleming's *The Spy Who Loved Me*. There are rooms full of regional antiques, including prints, postcards, and photographs, and lots of old books. Two tastefully redone storefronts are full of stuff, and it's easy to spend hours here. Open daily Memorial Day—Columbus Day; Mon.—Sat. fall, winter, and spring.

### BEYOND THE BLUE LINE

**Sutton's Farm Market** (518-798-0133; Lake George Rd., Queensbury, NY) Upscale country store with many unusual Adirondack gift items.

## ANTIQUES

Driving along rural routes in no matter what part of the country we find ourselves, we just expect to find barns full of milk-painted country furniture, salt-glazed crocks, and graceful, yet functional hand tools. But these artifacts don't always relate to the territory we're traveling through, for reasons of history, culture, and climate. When you're antiquing in the Adirondacks, keep a thumbnail sketch of the region's past in your mind and that will guide you to old things true to the countryside.

You can expect to find artifacts from logging and farming days, and plenty of good-quality, mass-produced 19th-century furniture. Local pottery, except in the far southern part of the park is quite rare; Redford glass, made in the Saranac River valley in the far northern Adirondacks in the early 1800s, is highly prized and extremely hard to find. Antique, locally made rustic furniture, which was discarded willy-nilly in the fifties as camp owners modernized, is scarce, but Old Hickory chairs and tables, made in Indiana and popular in the Northeast, have the right look and feel, and are widely available. If you're looking for the right pair of snowshoes or antlers to hang on your walls at home, you shouldn't have any trouble finding them here.

Many shops stock wood engravings and hand-tinted etchings of Adirondack scenes from old books; these prints — many of them by Winslow Homer or Frederic Remington — appeared in *Harper's Weekly, Every Saturday,* and other magazines, and are usually relatively inexpensive. Stereo views of the grand hotels, postcards from the 1890s-1930s, and photographs by George Baldwin, H.M. Beach, "Adirondack" Fred Hodges, and others are charming, but not too dear. For photographs by Seneca Ray Stoddard, a contemporary of William Henry Jackson and Mathew Brady, you can expect to pay a bit more, but the images are exceptional. Another name on the collectible list for ephemera fans is Verplanck Colvin: mountain panoramas, diagrams, and maps from his 1870-90 surveys are meticulous and curious at the same time.

Another aspect of the Adirondack past to keep in mind is that the area has been a tourist destination since the Civil War. There's a brisk trade in historic souvenirs and small things relating to bygone transportation networks; the embossed brass luggage tags from old steamboat and stagecoach lines are but one example. Besides items designed to catch a visitor's eye or track his or her property, you can find objects that the summer folk brought with them from back home or from around the world to decorate all camps great and small. These 19th-century part-time residents amassed an eclectic variety of knickknacks, musical instruments, rugs, silver, china, and amusements that have become part of the antique scene as properties changed hands or as families sent away the elephant-foot humidors, the inlaid-wood boxes, and all those wonderful things the Victorians adored.

A couple of publications can help you find antique dealers. The *Warren County Antique Dealers Association* (518-494-3948; Box 21, Warrensburg, NY 12885) offers a free map and brochure for the region from Lake George to Lake Luzerne to North Creek, listing about three dozen shops. The *Gore Mountain Region Chamber of Commerce* (518-251-2612; Main St., North Creek, NY 12853) has an antiques brochure for the North Creek-Riparius-Olmstedville area. A 32-page booklet, *1992 Antiquing in Northern New York* (published by auctioneer Greg Walsh; 315-265-9111; 150 Maple St., Potsdam, NY 13676) is quite useful for antique hunting in northern New York, Ontario and Quebec; you don't need to confine your search within the borders of the Adirondack Park. Likewise, consult the brochure *Crafts and Antiquing* (518-563-1000; Plattsburgh and Clinton County Chamber of Commerce, Box 310, Plattsburgh, NY 12901), which describes 30 northern-tier shops. And once you've decided to look outside the Blue Line, consider a trip south, to Fulton County (information 1-800-676-3858), where there are numerous shops in the Sacandaga and Mohawk basins. In Glens Falls, not too far away from I-87 (east of Exit 19), is *Glenwood*

*Manor* (518-798-4747; Quaker Rd.), a group undertaking with 40 dealers, who've filled three dozen rooms with quality antiques; the mansion is open year-round, daily in July and August.

Antique auctions are not as frequent in the Adirondacks as they are in the St. Lawrence and Hudson valleys or the Catskills. *Jon Kopp* (518-647-8039), a dealer in Au Sable Forks, holds Saturday night auctions at the D & H Freight House from May through October. Usually in September he has a special "sportsmen's sale" with lots of antique fishing gear, packbaskets, and so on. In Keene, *Adirondack Public Auctions* (518-576-4664) schedules occasional sales in their barn and handles estate auctions. Check the classifieds in the daily papers from outside the Blue Line (*Glens Falls Post Star* and the *Plattsburgh Press-Republican* are good bets) for weekend auction listings, which usually appear by the Thursday before the sale. Otherwise, look around for posters and flyers, or ask in the shops.

The best local fair is unquestionably the *Adirondack Antiques Show*, held at the Adirondack Museum (518-352-7311; Rte. 28/30, Blue Mt. Lake) in late September. Also highly recommended is the July show and sale (518-891-1990; Harrietstown Town Hall, Saranac Lake) sponsored by the Adirondack Medical Center. Both shows feature dozens of booths packed with primitive furniture, books, boats, prints, glass, rugs, decoys, and of course, Adirondackana. Ephemera buffs would enjoy the *Adirondack Memorabilia Show* (518-585-2696), held in Ticonderoga in early August.

Described below are a sampling of the antique shops you'll find in the Adirondack Park. Most are open several days a week in July and August, and on weekends in spring and fall; some are open year-round. Many dealers travel to shows in search of materials to add to their inventory as well as to sell, so it's always a good idea to call ahead if you're planning to drive a great distance in search of something special, or just for a day of browsing.

## LAKE GEORGE AND SOUTHEASTERN ADIRONDACKS

### Adirondack

**Country Cottage Antiques and Gifts** (Carl Pratt; 518-494-2051; 9 Church St., off East Shore Dr.) Oriental rugs, country furniture and accessories; reproductions, all in a pre-Civil War-era cottage. Open daily July—Aug.; weekends only May—June, Sept.—Oct. Call ahead.

### Chestertown

**Atateka Books and Collectibles** (Donna and Mark Walp; 518-494-4652; Friends Lake Rd.) Mainly old and rare books, but there are plenty of nostalgic and amusing souvenirs, toys, and advertising art. Open weekends May—Oct., or by appointment.

**The Attic Antiques** (Ruth and Bill Aiken; 518-494-2078; Rte. 9 at Loon Lake, 2.5

miles west of Chestertown) A big shop with kitchen primitives, art and Depression glass, china, books, lots of paper ephemera, some furniture. Open daily July—Aug; by chance or appointment June, Sept.—Oct.; call ahead.

**Stuff & Things Antiques** (John Eagle; 518-494-3948; Friends Lake Rd.; mailing address: Box 21, Warrensburg, NY 12885) Country furniture, American Indian items, unusual American and international folk art pieces. Open May—Nov.

## *Lake George*

**Antiques and Such** (Jeff Schaap; 518-668-4710; Rte. 9) Specializing in European armoires, kitchen hutches, and other furniture; an assortment of smalls including clocks, antique lighting fixtures, jewelry. Open Mon.—Sat., Oct.—June; daily July—Sept.

## *Lake Luzerne*

**Homespun** (Kay Fazio; 518-696-3289; Rte. 9, Lake Luzerne) Oak and pine furniture; table linens; collectibles; folk art. Open year-round; daily in summer.

## *Schroon Lake*

**Many Tribes Indian Collections** (Walter and Doris Cohen; 518-532-7334; Skylark Lane) Native American baskets, rugs, pottery, jewelry from around the country. By appointment only.

**Purple Raven** (518-532-7178; Main St.) General line of antiques and collectibles. Open daily July—Aug.; weekends in fall.

## *Warrensburg*

**Antiques and Decorative Arts** (518-623-3426; 84 Main St., at The Pillars) Furniture, prints, china and glassware, international folk art, in a group shop. Open year-round; daily in summer.

**Donegal Manor** (John Wright; 518-623-3549; 117 Main St.) Behind Donegal Manor Bed and Breakfast, the barn offers Irish linen, furniture, coins, Adirondack postcards, books, pocket watches, Victorian jewelry, glass, prints. Open year-round; daily in summer.

**Field House Antiques** (Virginia Field; 518-623-9404; 179 Main St.) In the carriage house behind the main house you'll find furniture, country ware, toys, china, and glass. Open year-round; daily in summer; call ahead for spring or fall hours.

**Fine Finish** (Peter and Pam Bombard; 518-623-2428; Rte. 28, 2.5 miles northwest of Warrensburg) Assortment of antique furniture and some horse-drawn vehicles. Open year-round.

**Ed and Pearl Kreinheder** (518-623-2149; 197 Main St.) Extensive selection of used and rare books; country furniture and accessories. Open year-round, Mon.—Sat. Call ahead in spring and fall.

**Paradox Mountain Strings** (Alex Gray; 518-494-7670; 84 Main St., at The Pillars). Vintage guitars, banjos, and mandolins; repairs. Open year-round.

**Riverside Gallery** (Lenore Smith; 518-623-2026; 2 Elm St., 1 block west of Rtes. 9 and 28) Selection of Adirondack and 19th-century prints, paintings, reproduction furniture, picture framing. Open year-round Mon.—Sat.

**Tamarack Shoppe** (518-623-3384; 148 Main St., at the bandstand) Decorative arts, Fiesta ware, jewelry, glass, kitchen items, books, and some furniture, mixed in with new brass, table linens, rugs, and imported china. Open daily, year-round.

**Time and Again Antiques** (Sharon and Roger Gibbs; 518-623-3893; 90 River St.) Group shop featuring vintage clothing, toys, china, glass, books and music, furniture, "bargain room," clocks and clock repair. Closed: Nov.—Apr. Open weekends May—June, Sept.—Oct.; daily July—Aug. One of the few shops with handicap access.

## CHAMPLAIN VALLEY

### Elizabethtown

**Pleasant Valley Collectibles** (Janice and Conrad Hutchins; 518-873-2100; Upper Water St.) "Interesting old stuff from a pack rat's attic — everything priced to sell." Open by chance or appointment.

### Essex

**Margaret Sayward's Antiques & Untiques** (518-963-7828; South Main St.) Furniture, glassware, collectibles, refinishing and reupholstery. Open daily June—Oct., winter and spring by chance or appointment.

**Summer Shop** (Colin Ducolon; 518-963-7921; Rte. 22) Painted furniture, early pressed glass, 19th-century textiles, coin silver. Open June—Oct.

### Keeseville

**Bosworth Tavern Antiques** (Andrea Knight; 518-834-7736; Rte. 9) General line of furniture and antiques. Open year-round; call ahead.

**Running Rabbitt Antiques Et Caetera** (Elaine LaPlant; 518-834-7017; Rte. 9, south of Keeseville) Furniture, Maxfield Parrish prints, wicker, tinware, rag rugs, dishes. Open year-round by chance or appointment.

### Ticonderoga

**Lonergan's Red Barn Antiques** (Craig Lonergan; 518-585-4477; Rte. 9N) That creaky old roadside shop packed to the roof beams with things that you've been looking for — lots of books, china, furniture, photos, prints, Lake Champlain souvenir plates, Fiesta ware, crocks, tinware, trunks, farm implements, horse-drawn equipment, old guns — or, as the flyer says, "Useful Stuff for Man and Beast." Open daily Memorial Day—Columbus Day; weekends in spring and fall, or by appointment.

### Westport

**The Inn on the Library Lawn** (518-962-8666; corner Rte. 22 and Washington St.) Quilts, country and oak furniture, country pottery, glass, toys, prints, jewelry, books. Open daily Memorial Day—Oct.

### Willsboro

**Ben Wever's Farm** (Dare Van Vree Wever; 518-963-8372; 221 Mountain View Dr.) Ten rooms of antiques in a restored farmhouse on a 500-acre working farm, specializing in pine, cherry, walnut, and mahogany furniture; fine china, porcelain, and silver; rugs; paintings; lamps; glass; Adirondackana, Americana and Victoriana. Open daily late June—Labor Day; also Memorial Day weekend.

**Brown House Antiques** (Suzanne Medler; 518-963-7396; Main St.) Six rooms of linens, prints, pine and mahogany furniture, china, books, Fiesta ware, toys and dolls, wicker, Adirondack collectibles. Open late June—Aug. Tues.—Sat; weekends in Sept. by chance.

## HIGH PEAKS AND NORTHERN ADIRONDACKS

### Au Sable Forks

**Don's Antiques** (Marge and Don Denette; 518-647-8422; North Main St.) Furniture, Depression and patterned glass, clocks, stoneware, postcards, "ancestral paraphernalia." Open year-round by chance or appointment.

### Bloomingdale

**Buyer's Paradise** (Gerald Yelle; 518-891-4242; Rte. 3) Old roadhouse filled with oak and Victorian furniture, tools, primitives, glass and china, Adirondackana. Open weekends in fall and spring; daily in July—Aug.

**Germaine Miller** (518-891-1306; Rte. 3) Country and small Adirondack furniture, painted cupboards, Majolica and Quimper, china, glass, silver. By chance or appointment.

Buyer's Paradise, Bloomingdale, is just that.

Nancie Battaglia

**Sign of the Fish Studio & Gallery** (Henry and Virginia Jakobe; 518-891-2510; Rte. 3) Furniture, books, paintings and prints, glass, china. Open July— Aug., or by appointment.

### Clayburg

**Peg's Antiques** (Peg and Bob Defayette; 518-293-7062; Rte. 3) Furniture, kitchenware, tools, primitives, jewelry, lamps, dolls, Shaker reproductions. Open by chance or appointment.

### Jay

**Country Classics Furniture** (Lou Hoyt; 518-946-7960; Rte. 9N) Antique furniture; fine-furniture repairs and refinishing. Open year-round Fri.—Mon.

### Keene Valley

**George Jaques Antiques** (518-576-2214; Main St.) Old and new rustic furniture, advertising art and signs, antique taxidermy, porch furniture. Open Memorial Day—Columbus Day.

Bentwood and baskets at George Jaques Antiques, Keene Valley.

Nancie Battaglia

## Lake Placid

**Cassidy's Antiques North** (Linda Cassidy; 518-523-9482; Alpine Mall, 120 Main St.) Old rustic furniture, jewelry, carvings, camp-style decorative items, prints. Open year-round.

**Heritage Hill Antiques** (Mrs. A.E. Dunn; 518-523-2435; Crestview Plaza, Rte. 86) Antique jewelry and estate items, postcards, prints. Open year-round; weekends only in January.

**Lake Placid Antique Center** (Robert Peacock; 518-523-3913; 103 Main St.) Group shop with five dealers, selling furniture, books, prints, Adirondackana, musical instruments, toys, woodenware. Open daily year-round.

*Log Cabin Antiques, Lake Placid, is open year-round.*

Nancie Battaglia

**Log Cabin Antiques** (Greg Peacock; 518-523-3047; 86 Main St.) Furniture, prints, kitchenware, Adirondackana. Open year-round.

**Alan Pereske** (home phone 518-891-3733; shop address 81 Saranac Ave.) Oak, pine, and rustic furniture; paintings and prints of local interest; glass, toys; ephemera. Open weekends spring and fall. Mon.—Sat. July and Aug.

## Loon Lake

**The Old Art Gallery** (518-891-3249; at Loon Lake Golf Course, Onchiota Rd.) Bins of 19th-century engravings and lithographs plus some framed pieces, in a building designed by Stanford White, at one of the oldest golf courses in the country. Open daily mid-May—Oct.

**Red Barn Antiques** (Jay Friedman; 518-891-5219; Onchiota Rd.) Furniture, oil lamps, glassware, tools, postcards and prints, jewelry, clocks. Open July—early Sept.

## Saranac

**William J. Sackett, Jr.** (518-293-8844; Rte. 3) Old bottles, jars, and insulators; 8

rooms and garage full of antiques and collectibles. Open by chance or appointment.

## Saranac Lake

**Christina's Place** (518-891-6052; Broadway) Glass, porcelain, furniture, rugs, paintings; also jams and jellies; reproduction vintage clothing by Lynn Cameron. Open year-round Tues.—Sat.

## Upper Jay

**Janie's Antiques** (Janie Fitton; 518-946-2485; Rte. 9N) Furniture, kitchenware, advertising art, toys — "mostly wholesale." Open mid-Apr.—mid-Sept. by chance or appointment.

**Old Seed Store** (518-946-7055; Rte. 9N) Oak, pine, wicker, and mahogany furniture; tools, pottery, china and glass; advertising art; horse-drawn vehicles. Open late May—Sept.

## Wilmington

**Olde Fox Farm Galleries** (518-946-2332; Rte. 86 and Fox Farm Rd.) Furniture, glass, porcelain, toys. Open July—August by chance or appointment.

## NORTHWEST LAKES REGION

## Childwold

**William J. Wilkins** (518-359-3808; Rte. 3) Specializing in fishing, hunting, boating, and other outdoor-related antiques and ephemera, plus twig and bark camp furniture and native American collectibles. By appointment only.

## CENTRAL AND SOUTHWESTERN ADIRONDACKS

## Inlet

**North Woods Antiques** (315-357-4722; Rte. 28) General line of antiques and collectibles. Open late June—Sept.; call ahead.

## Lake Pleasant

**Tamarack Shoppe** (518-548-7637; Rte. 8) Antique books, jewelry, china, glass, primitives, furniture. Open spring and fall weekends; daily July 4—Labor Day, or by appointment.

## Long Lake

**Ethel's House** (Ann Stewart; 518-624-4242; Rte. 28) Jewelry, glass, kitchen-

*The inviting entrance to Ethel's House, Long Lake.*

B. Folwell

ware, quilts, vintage clothing, linens, baskets, tools, prints; homemade breads, jams, jellies, and chocolates; flower shop. Open Apr.—Christmas; daily Memorial Day—Columbus Day, weekends after.

### Minerva

**Mountain Niche Antiques** (John and Kathy Feiden; 518-251-2566; Rte. 28N, 2 miles north of Minerva post office) Country and Victorian furniture, textiles, books, prints, tools, pottery, glassware. Open most days, year-round; call ahead.

### Mayfield

**The Antique Lover** (Terry and Dick Peters; 518-661-6424; Rte. 30) Not much furniture, but lots of kitchenware, glass, china, woodenware, postcards, dolls. Open spring—fall, by chance or appointment.

### Northville

**Iron Horse Antiques** (518-863-8022; Rte. 30) Furniture, dolls, toys, vintage clothing, ephemera. Open spring—fall, by chance or appointment.

**The Red Barn** (518-863-4828; 202 N. Main St.) Furniture, prints, collectibles, baskets. Open spring—fall, by chance or appointment.

### Old Forge

**Antiques & Articles** (Ed Diamond; 315-369-3316; 19 Main St.) Oak, wicker, rustic, and pine furniture; baskets, books, Fiesta ware, Depression glass and collectibles, toys. Appraisals and house sales. Open daily July—Aug.; fall weekends.

**Wildwood** (Sarah Cohen; 315-369-3397; Main St.) Adirondack postcards, prints, fishing tackle, maps, lots of old books, regional ephemera, advertising art, toys, glass and china. Open year-round Mon.—Sat.; daily in summer.

### Olmstedville

**Board 'n Batten** (Floss and Bob Savarie; 518-251-2507; Main St.) Furniture, country items, Adirondack postcards, buttons, steins; focus on quality glass and pottery. Open daily July—Aug.; other times by chance or appointment.

### Riparius

**Clen's Collectibles** (Donalda and Clennon Ellifritz; 518-251-2388; River Rd., off Rte. 8; mailing address: Box 13, Wevertown, NY 12886) General line of antiques and smalls; Adirondack postcards and prints. Open year-round by chance or appointment.

### Speculator

**Newton's Corners Antiques** (Pam and Rick Murray; 518-548-8972; Rte. 8) Kitchen cupboards and tables, hoosiers, linens, pottery and glass, jewelry, prints, quilts. Open year-round; closed Sun. and Wed. Call ahead in fall and spring.

## ART GALLERIES AND PAINTERS' STUDIOS

The best 19th-century American painters came to the Adirondacks to interpret the wild northern scenery on paper and canvas, and today many artists still rely on the great outdoors for subject matter. Listed here you'll find local artists in residence as well as art galleries representing painters from different eras and regions.

### CHAMPLAIN VALLEY

### Elizabethtown

**The Gallery** (Nancy Dawson; 518-873-6843; River St., across from the Hand House) Exclusive representative for the works of Clifford Jackson (1924-1985) and Jossey Bilan (1913-1980), both acclaimed Adirondack landscape artists. Living local artists represented include Ruth Rumney and others. By appointment only.

**Mountain View Gallery** (Nan Stevens; 518-873-7376; Ray Woods Rd., off Rte. 9) This pleasant private gallery is decidedly off the beaten path, but it's surely worth a visit. More than two dozen of the region's finest painters, printmakers, and photographers are represented here, including Nathan Farb, Gary Randorf, Nancie Battaglia, Pat Reynolds, Terry Young, Bruce Mitchell, Gary Casagrain, Anne Lacy, and Elfriede Abbe. Nan also arranges special exhibitions and does custom matting and framing. Open Tues.—Sat. June—Sept., or by appointment.

## Essex

**Atea Ring Gallery** (Atea Ring; 518-963-8620; Elm St., in the 1867 Schoolhouse) A modern professional fine-arts gallery like you'd expect to find in a major city, located instead in a quiet historic village. The gallery features one-person and group exhibitions of paintings, quilts, prints. Past shows have included works on paper by Harold Weston, primitive paintings by Edna West Teall (who was the Grandma Moses of Essex County), and quilts from the Kentucky Quilt Project. Open June—Aug.

## Willsboro

**Patricia Reynolds** (518-963-8356; 390 Point Rd.) Watercolor and oil landscapes of Lake Champlain and the Adirondacks; lovely flower paintings from the artist's extensive perennial gardens; usually a hundred or so works on hand. Also, the Westport Yacht Club holds a one-day show for Patricia every July. Open by chance or appointment year-round.

## HIGH PEAKS AND NORTHERN ADIRONDACKS

## Bloomingdale

**Fortune Studio** (Timothy Fortune; 518-891-0918; RR 1, Box 37A) Oil and watercolor Adirondack landscapes by an internationally regarded artist; "Marzipan and Company" hand-knit sweater kits with nifty Adirondack wildlife designs. Open year-round, by appointment only.

## Keene

**Heritage Gallery** (Bruce and Annette Mitchell; 518-576-2289; corner Spruce Hill and Hurricane Rds.) Oil and watercolor paintings of Adirondack and Vermont scenes; limited-edition wildlife, floral and landscape prints, by talented members of the Mitchell family. Open Mon.—Sat. June—Nov. 14.

## Wilmington

**Little Cottage in the Woods** (June Clow; 518-946-7152; off Rte. 86) Adirondack scenes in oil, pencil, watercolor; prints; paintings for children, all by June. Open afternoons, year-round.

**NORTHWEST LAKES REGION**

*Cranberry Lake*

**End of the Pier Studio** (Jean Reynolds; 315-848-2900; Rte. 3, at The Emporium) Watercolor paintings of the Cranberry Lake area and Adirondack vistas, limited edition four-season prints, notecards by the artist. Open by chance or appointment.

*Tupper Lake*

**Casagrain Studio and Gallery** (Gary Casagrain; 518-359-2595; Rte. 3, across from Massawepie Cooperative Area, 10 miles west of Tupper Lake Village) Oil paintings and limited edition prints of Adirondack scenes and native wildlife by Gary. Open year-round, by chance or appointment; call ahead.

**CENTRAL AND SOUTHWESTERN ADIRONDACKS**

*Northville*

**Commonground Gallery** (518-863-4693; Bridge St.) Adirondack landscapes by Anne M. Miller. Open year-round; call ahead.

*Old Forge*

**Gallery North** (315-369-2218; Main St., at the Ferns Emporium) Limited-edition wildlife and Adirondack prints and posters by nationally acclaimed artists; picture matting and framing. Open year-round.

# BOATBUILDERS

The interconnected waterways of the region led to the development of a specialized craft, the Adirondack guideboat. Traditional guideboats, which first appeared after the Civil War, are smooth-skinned rowboats with quartersawn cedar and pine planks, and have naturally curved spruce roots for the ribs. These delicate-looking craft were meant to be fast on the water and easy to carry between ponds, lakes, and rivers. In the 19th century, a sportsman could buy a handmade boat for $30 or $40; nowadays, a handmade, authentic guideboat costs just a bit more.

Besides guideboats, a number of local boatbuilders have developed their own special designs, from ultralight pack canoes to sleek mahogany runabouts. Listed below you'll find a variety of water craftsmen; note that it's always a good idea to call ahead if you'd like to see a particular boat. Also, if you expect to make a cash-and-carry purchase of an old-fashioned guideboat, you may find that there is already a waiting list of other prospective buyers. Beautiful things take time to create.

## HIGH PEAKS AND NORTHERN ADIRONDACKS

### *Keene*

**Pisces Paddles** (Dave Kavner; 518-576-2628; Rte. 73, opposite Owl's Head Mountain) Traditional beaver-tail-shape or modern bent-shaft wooden canoe paddles ($75-$85); meticulously detailed model guideboats and canoes for your mantel or curio cabinet ($300-$700).

**Renaissance Woodworks** (Carl Mancini; 518-576-2028; Rte. 73, opposite Stewart's Shoppe) New wooden canoes replicating classic J. Henry Rushton designs, and Adirondack guideboats built to order; boat restoration, seat caning, other custom woodworking. Price range for 16-foot traditionally built guideboat with oars and yoke: $7,000; wooden canoes $2,000 and up.

### *Saranac Lake*

**Hathaway Boat Shop** (Christopher Woodward; 518-891-3961; 9 Algonquin Ave., Rte. 3 west of town) A long line of Saranac Lake boatbuilders have occupied this shop on the edge of town, including Willard Hanmer, whose boats are on permanent display at the Adirondack Museum. Chris learned the trade from Carl Hathaway, who learned from Willard himself. Traditional wooden Adirondack guideboats; boat repairs. Price range for traditional guideboats with oars and yoke: $7,500-$10,000.

**Spencer Boatworks** (Spencer Jenkins; 518-891-5828; 13 Edgewood Rd., off Rte. 3) Inboard wooden boats, built along classic runabout lines with modern epoxy lay-up. Models include cruisers, sport, and utility boats 18 to 26 feet long; prices $38,000-$92,000. Spencer boats look fast just sitting on their trailers. Also wooden-boat and inboard-motor repairs.

## NORTHWEST LAKES REGION

### *Tupper Lake*

**Frenette Boatbuilders** (Rob Frenette; 518-359-3228; 9 High St.) Rushton-design wooden canoes and rowboats, traditional Adirondack guideboats, and sailboats all built to order; wooden boat repairs, seat caning. New boats start at $3,000; traditional guideboats with complete outfit: $7,000 and up.

### *Upper St. Regis Lake*

**Boathouse Woodworks** (James Cameron; 518-327-3470; Upper St. Regis Lake)

*Jim Cameron, on Upper St. Regis Lake, is one of several craftspeople who still make traditional Adirondack guideboats.*

Lynn Cameron

Traditional wooden Adirondack guideboats built to order; price range for 16-foot traditional guideboat with oars and yoke: $6,000-$7,000. Seat caning; boat restoration.

## CENTRAL AND SOUTHWESTERN ADIRONDACKS

### *Indian Lake*

**John B. Spring** (518-648-5455; Rte. 28) New wood-and-canvas canoes in 15-foot Rushton designs and 17-foot traditional models; price range $3,000 and up. Wooden boat repairs; seat caning.

### *Long Lake*

**Adirondack Goodboat** (Mason Smith; 518-624-6398; Deerland Rd., 1 mile from Rte. 28/30) The goodboat, which won the "Great Versatility Race" at Mystic Seaport's annual small boat gathering, is a car-toppable, multipurpose (row, sail, or motor) wooden boat, built with modern techniques and materials for easy maintenance and strength without excess weight. Other models are the Lakesailer and the Chipmunk canoe; kits available. Price range: $1,700-$5,500.

### *Northville*

**James Anthony Powerboat Company** (James A. Lombard; 518-863-2626; 222 Reed St.) A great idea for the boater who loves the look of wood but doesn't like the idea of taking care of it: James Anthony's Gentleman's Runabout has a fiberglass hull with mahogany deck planking. The design is 1930s classic all the way, with a plumb bow and barrel-back stern. Price range: $38,000-$65,000.

*An ultralight Hornbeck pack canoe on an Adirondack pond.*

Nancie Battaglia

### Olmstedville

**Hornbeck Boats** (Peter Hornbeck; 518-251-2764; Trout Brook Rd.) Nessmuk (George Washington Sears) pioneered the go-light outdoor movement in the 1880s, and Pete has brought his designs into the 20th century. Kevlar pack canoes in 9-, 10 1/2-, and 12-foot lengths, perfect for tripping into remote ponds, weigh only 12 to 19 pounds; kevlar guideboats are available by special order. Price range: $495-$2,000.

## BOOKS

Within the Adirondack Park, there are about a dozen independently-owned bookstores, each with its own personality. Some highlight children's or nature books; others offer art supplies and crafts alongside paperbacks and hard covers. Note that the local college bookstores are open to the public, too.

### CHAMPLAIN VALLEY

#### Elizabethtown

**L.W. Currey, Inc.** (Lloyd Currey; 518-873-6477; Water St.) Regarded as the world's largest dealer of rare science fiction, horror, and fantasy books. For serious collectors — by appointment only or mail order.

## *Ticonderoga*

**Dragonfly Books and Crafts** (Bonnie Davis; 518-585-7543; 214 Montcalm St.) Lots of children's books, regional guidebooks and histories, used books, antiques and crafts. Open year-round.

**Fort Ticonderoga** (518-585-2821; off Rte. 74) In a huge log cabin at the entrance to the museum, if you go beyond the bins of child-size peace pipes and souvenir headdresses, you'll find books, prints, monographs, maps, and audiotapes pertinent to 18th-century military history. Open daily mid-May—mid-Oct.

**North Country Community College** (518-585-6095; 202 Montcalm St.) College bookstore; general titles, magazines. Open year-round, except for college vacations, Mon.—Sat.

## *Westport*

**Billy Goat Books** (518-962-8666; Washington St., at the Inn on the Library Lawn) Children's books. Open Memorial Day—Labor Day.

## HIGH PEAKS AND NORTHERN ADIRONDACKS

### *Keene Valley*

**Bashful Bear** (518-576-4736; Rte. 73, across from the diner) Rambling farmhouse with a surprisingly good selection (10,000 titles) of regional titles and children's books, contemporary novels, how-to's, nature guides, and cheerful service. Adirondack folk music tapes and CDs, too. Open daily in summer; call for hours fall—spring.

**The Mountaineer** (518-576-2281; Rte. 73) Good selection of outdoor, adventure-travel, nature and Adirondack titles; topographical maps. Open year-round Mon.—Sat.

### *Lake Placid*

**The Bookstore Plus** (518-523-2950; 89 Main St.) Racks and racks of paperbacks, good assortment of how-to guides, contemporary fiction, regional histories and guidebooks, cookbooks, children's books, coffee-table books, art supplies, stationery and cards. Buy a book here, and you get a bonus — crisp, new $2 bills in change. Open year-round Mon.—Sat.

**Eastern Mountain Sports** (518-523-2505; 51 Main St.) Adirondack and outdoor guidebooks, camping cookbooks, and adventure travel tales; topographical maps; all kinds of gear and garb. Open year-round Mon.—Sat.; daily in summer.

**A New Leaf** (518-523-1847; Hilton Plaza, Main St.) New Age and self-help books; cards and stationery; tea, coffee, and cappucino. Open daily year-round.

**With Pipe and Book** (Julie and Breck Turner; 518-523-9096; 91 Main St.) A Main Street landmark shop with new and rare Adirondack books; a huge selection of used books, including bargains; antique postcards, prints, and maps; pipe tobaccos and imported cigars. Open year-round Mon.—Sat.

*Julie Turner, at With Pipe and Book, offers fine tobaccos along with rare books and prints.*

Nancie Battaglia

### Saranac Lake

**North Country Community College** (518-891-2915; Winona Ave.) College bookstore; general interest, magazines. Open fall—spring Mon.—Sat.

**A Novel Experience** (Mary Blake; 518-891-1242; 52 Broadway) A very good city-style bookshop that happens to be in a small town. Contemporary fiction and nonfiction, children's books, books of regional interest, cookbooks, magazines, Adirondack music on tape and CD. Open year-round Mon.—Sat.

## NORTHWEST LAKES REGION

### Paul Smiths

**Adirondack Life Store** (518-327-3000; Rte. 30, Adirondack Park Visitor Interpretive Center) Adirondack histories and guidebooks, magazines, maps, posters. Open daily late May—Oct.

**Paul Smith's College Bookstore** (518-327-6314; Rte. 30, Paul Smith's College, below the snack bar) Good selection of regional guides and histories, forestry books, topographic maps, magazines. Open year-round Mon.—Sat.

### Tupper Lake

**Hoss's Country Corner** (Christine Black, Manager; 518-359-2092; 111 Park St.) Many Adirondack titles, outdoor recreation and natural history guidebooks, cookbooks, Christian books, topographical maps, clothing, gifts. Open year-round Mon.—Sat.

## CENTRAL AND SOUTHWESTERN ADIRONDACKS

### Blue Mountain Lake

**Adirondack Museum Gatehouse Shop** (Victoria Verner; 518-352-7311; Rtes. 28 and 30) Excellent assortment of Adirondack history and guidebooks, books on antique boats and furniture, children's books, Adirondack folk music and storytelling on tape and CD, prints, postcards, stationery, and gifts. Open daily late May—Columbus Day.

**Cedarwood Gift Shop** (Kimball LaPrairie; 518-352-7306; Rte. 28 next to post office) Adirondack books, posters, and cards; unusual regional craft items for all ages. Open daily June—September.

### Long Lake

**Hoss's Country Corner** (John and Lorrie Hosley; 518-624-2481; Rte. 30) Adirondack histories and guidebooks, Christian books and tapes, children's nature books, general store. Hoss's sponsors Adirondack book-signing evenings in July and August with dozens of regional authors. Open year-round Mon.—Sat.

### Old Forge

**Old Forge Hardware** (Mirnie Kashiwa, Manager; 315-369-6100; Main St., Old Forge, NY 13420) Tucked way in the back of this enormous emporium is a good bookstore, with Adirondack histories and guidebooks, cookbooks, nonfiction, children's books, paperbacks, and art supplies. Open year-round Mon.—Sat.; daily in summer.

**Wildwood** (Sarah Cohen; 315-369-3397; Main St.) Many Adirondack titles, cookbooks, books on collecting furniture, baskets, etc.; natural history books, novels, photography books, maps, posters, art postcards, shelves and shelves of old books. Open year-round Mon.—Sat.; daily in summer.

*Adirondack and outdoor books are a specialty at Hoss's Country Corner, Long Lake.*

Nancie Battaglia

## Speculator

**The Knappsack** (no phone; Rte. 30, in the Lane Emporium) New and used paperbacks. Open year-round: weekends in fall, winter, and spring; Mon.—Sat. in summer.

### BEYOND THE BLUE LINE

Aviation Mall, on Aviation Road just off Exit 19, I-87, in Glens Falls, has both *B. Dalton Bookseller* (518-793-3897) and *Waldenbooks* (518-798-4517). Both places have an excellent selection of regional books right up front, as well as the latest best-sellers, extensive reference books, cookbooks, children's books, and books on tape. Open daily, year-round.

On Rte. 9 south of Lake George, known as the "Million Dollar Half Mile," you'll find the *Book Warehouse* (518-793-0231), with lots of popular titles, remaindered books, magazines, children's books, and reference books. Open daily, year-round.

In Saratoga Springs, *Bookworks* (518-587-3228; 456 Broadway) stocks some 20,000 titles, along with maps, magazines, and cards; the regional section features folklore, history, guides, and natural history. The store sponsors book-signings with authors like William Kennedy, Bill McKibben, and Sue Halpern. Open year-round Mon.—Sat. Also in Saratoga, *Nahani* (518-587-4322; 482 Broadway) has a large self-help selection, plus many books of upstate interest.

North of the park, in Plattsburgh's Champlain Centre North mall, you'll find *Waldenbooks* (518-561-5349) and *Lauriat's* (518-562-0343), which are open daily year-round. In Watertown, beyond the northwestern edge of the park, off I-81, Salmon Run Mall has both *Lauriat's* (315-782-7744) and *Waldenbooks* (315-788-9398), and downtown you'll find *Book World* (315-782-6350; 9 Public Square). To the southwest of the Adirondacks, Sangertown Square on Rtes. 5 and 5A in Utica has *B. Dalton* (315-797-5621) and *Waldenbooks* (315-797-5915).

Several regional publishers specialize in books of local interest and have mail-order catalogs: *Adirondack Mountain Club* (518-668-4447; RR 3, Box 3055, *Lake George, NY 12845), Backcountry Publications* (802-457-1049; Box 175, Woodstock, VT 05091), *North Country Books* (315-735-4877; 18 Irving Place, Utica, NY 13501), *Syracuse University Press* (315-443-5534; 1600 Jamesville Ave., Syracuse, NY 13244-5160), and *Purple Mountain Press* (1-800-325-2665; Box E-3, Fleischmanns, NY 12430).

## CLOTHING

L ooking for designer labels, bargains, and special-occasion wear in the modern "shop till you drop" mode is an entertainment best pursued outside the Adirondack Park. Here inside the Blue Line you'll find mainly classic woolens, or practical stuff, or T-shirts. Lake Placid's Main Street, which has a pleasant parade of shops, is described here; listed below you'll also find a handful of the old-fashioned haberdasheries, plus some interesting new places and clothing designers.

If for some unforeseen reason, you need to outfit an entire family from the ground up in a hurry, and at minimal cost, *Ames*, a discount department chain, has stores in Saranac Lake (518-891-2850; Rte. 86) and Tupper Lake (518-359-3325; Demars Blvd). They're open every day except Thanksgiving, Christmas, and New Year's Day.

### LAKE GEORGE AND SOUTHEASTERN ADIRONDACKS

*Bolton Landing*

**Bolton Babies** (518-644-2826; Rte. 9N) Handmade infants' and toddlers' clothing, toys, and educational games. Open Memorial Day—Labor Day.

**Bolton Bay Traders** (518-644-2237; Main St., across from Frederick's Restaurant) Quality sportswear for men and women, including Merrill and Nike hiking boots; Columbia, Big Dog and Sierra Designs jackets, shirts, pants, and shorts; Adirondack and outdoor guidebooks. Open year-round.

## Lake George

**Janet Vito Boutique** (518-668-2601; 283 Canada St.) Batik and tie-dye imported summer dresses; Danskin leotards; sportswear for women. Open Wed.—Mon. year-round.

## Warrensburg

**Blue Heron Designs-Fine Wearables** (Charlene Leary; 518-623-3189; Truesdale Hill Rd.) Handwoven natural-fiber sweaters, vests, coats, shawls, and bags; hand-painted silk scarves, tunics, and jewelry; other fiber artwork. Open year-round: daily June 1—Sept. 1; Thurs.—Mon. Sept.—May.

## HIGH PEAKS AND NORTHERN ADIRONDACKS

## Lake Placid

**The Adirondack Store & Gallery** (518-523-2646; 109 Saranac Ave.) Terrific hand-knit sweaters with wildlife designs by Marzipan and Co.; hand-woven jackets, classic Pendleton woolen shirts and jackets. Open Mon.—Sat. year-round; daily Memorial Day—Labor Day.

**Bass Shoe Factory Outlet** (518-523-2718; 340 Main St.) Shoes, boots, and socks for men and women. Open Mon.—Sat. year-round; daily in summer.

**The Bear Haus** (518-523-3848; 23 Main St.) Men's and women's clothing, including swimwear and skiwear; Royal Robbins and other well-known brands. Open Mon.—Sat. year-round.

**Benetton** (518-523-1951; 53 Main St.) The United Colors thereof; natural-fiber clothing for men, women, and children. Open Mon.—Sat. year-round.

**The Country Store** (518-523-3335; 71 Main St.) Quality men's clothing; formal wear rental and sales. Open Mon.—Sat. year-round.

**Dexter Shoe Factory Outlet** (518-523-4452; Saranac Ave., across from Cold Brook Plaza) Casual and dress shoes for men and women, boots, socks. Open Mon.—Sat. year-round; daily in summer.

**Eastern Mountain Sports** (518-523-2505; 51 Main St.) Outdoor clothing and footgear by Woolrich, Patagonia, Merrill, Nike, and EMS. Open Mon.—Sat. year-round; daily in summer.

**Far Mor's Kids** (518-523-3990; 1 Main St.) "Far Mor" means grandmother in Swedish; imagine an indulgent, tasteful granny and you've got a glimpse of this shop. Designer infant and children's clothes; educational toys and puzzles; quilts. Open year-round.

**Fashion Factory Outlet** (518-523-1961; 324 Main St., next to Bass Factory Outlet) Underwear, swimwear, shirts, and sportswear for men and women;

*Eastern Mountain Sports, Lake Placid.*

Nancie Battaglia

Hathaway, White Stag, and other brands. Open Mon.-Sat. year-round; daily in summer.

**Hocus Pocus Boutique** (518-523-2111; 8 Main St.) Sleepware, lingerie, classic women's clothing. Open Mon.—Sat. year-round.

**The In Step** (518-523-9398; 35 Main St.) Designer shoes, stockings, and bags. Open Mon.—Sat. year-round.

**Ruthie's Run** (518-523-3271; 11 Main St.) Men's and women's clothing, including Polo, Boston Traders, and other quality brands. Open Mon.—Sat. year-round.

**The Summit** (518-523-2881; 111 Main St.) Hip seasonal clothing for men and women, including Ocean Pacific, Gotcha, and other labels. Open Mon.—Sat. year-round.

**Two Harts** (518-523-3840; 117 Main St.) Imported clothing from India and Central America for women; imported jewelry and gifts. Open Mon.—Sat. year-round.

**Where'd You Get That Hat?** (518-523-3101; 155 Main St.) The question friends back home are bound to ask. New and used men's and women's hats of all descriptions. Great selection of colorful Converse high-top sneakers. Open year-round.

### Saranac Lake

**Altman's** (518-891-3850; 16 Broadway) No, not that Altman's.... Jockey underwear for women, sleepwear, and conservative ladies' clothing. Open Mon.—Sat. year-round.

**Cinderella's** (518-891-4431; 44 Broadway) Handmade and designer fashions for infants to teenagers, First Communion and confirmation dresses. Open Mon.—Sat. year-round.

**T.F. Finnigan** (518-891-1820; Main St., near the Adirondack Bank) Men's clothing, including Cross Creek, Nautica, B.D. Baggies; formal wear rental and sales. Open Mon.—Sat. year-round.

**Parnell Shoe Salon and Boutique** (518-891-3530; 82 Main St.) Ladies' clothing and shoes, including Clark's sandals and practical walking shoes. Open Mon.—Sat. year-round.

## NORTHWEST LAKES REGION

### *Tupper Lake*

**Hoss's Country Corner** (518-359-2092; 111 Park St.) From outerwear to underwear for men, women, and children, plus a full range of outdoor supplies and books. Open Mon.—Sat. year-round.

**Together Fashions** (518-359-3191; 68 Park St.) Casual wear for young women and ladies; imported and American labels. Open Mon.—Sat. year-round.

### *Upper St. Regis*

**Lynn Cameron Collections** (518-327-3470) Looking for the perfect gown for some enchanted evening? Lynn designs and sews meticulous reproductions of antique clothing, specializing in dance attire. She also makes jackets for men and women; suits, skirts, and dresses for women and children; plus doll clothing and furniture. Open by appointment only; her designs can also be seen at Christina's Place, on Broadway in Saranac Lake.

*Blouse, skirt, and hats by Lynn Cameron.*

Lynn Cameron

## CENTRAL AND SOUTHWESTERN ADIRONDACKS

### *Indian Lake*

**Spring's General Store** (518-648-6105; Main St., across from Stewart's Shop) Johnson Woolen Mills jackets and vests; work clothes. Open year-round.

## Old Forge

**Adirondack Apparel** (315-369-6070; Main St.) Family clothing by Lee, Woolrich, and other brands. Open Mon.—Sat. year-round.

**Sporting Propositions** (315-369-6188; Mini Mall, Rte. 28) Tennis, golf, ski, and sports apparel by Izod, Black Diamond, and other brands. Open Mon.—Sat. year-round.

## Speculator

**Speculator Department Store** (518-548-6123; Rte. 8) One-stop shopping for timeless woolens here: men's Pendleton "topsters" (unlined jackets that can be dressed up or down), ladies' suits, Chief Joseph and Hudson Bay blankets, anything you could need or want in buffalo plaid. Open year-round.

*At the Speculator Department Store, wool is always in season.*

Nancie Battaglia

## BEYOND THE BLUE LINE

They call it the "Million Dollar Half Mile," and it's just a quick toss of the credit card from Lake George Village. Four separate plazas on both sides of US Rte. 9 (near its intersection with Rte. 149 off Exit 20, I-87) add up to outlet heaven for the dedicated shopper. Most stores are open every day, year-round; on Memorial Day weekend nearly 70 stores participate in the annual Sidewalk Sale.

On the west side of the road, toward I-87, is the *Dexter Shoe Factory Outlet* (518-792-4202). Continuing south on the same side of the street is *French Mountain Commons Outlet Center* with Jonathan Logan, Country Road/Australia, Reebok, Lady Leslie, and 9 West, plus houseware outlets such as Fieldcrest/Cannon, Pier 1, Oneida, Pfaltzgraff, and Welcome Home.

On the east side of the road starting from the Rte. 149 intersection, *Log Jam Factory Stores* (518-792-5316) houses Gitano, Maidenform, Carter's Children-wear, Banister Shoes, Colonial Sportshoe, Famous Brand Housewares, the Leather Loft, and L'Eggs/Hanes/Bali store, among others. South of the Days Inn, you'll find the *Adirondack Factory Outlet Mall*, with Converse, Champion, Barbizon Lingerie, Bugle Boy, Manhattan, Socks Galore, Polly Flinders, Swank, and B.D. Baggies, plus the Book Warehouse, Corning/Revere, Kitchen Collection, Lots of Linens, and the Clock Center. The *Lake George Plaza Factory Stores* has a cluster of more upscale shops: Harve Benard, London Fog, Ralph Lauren, Geoffrey Bean, Anne Klein, Micki Designer Separates, Crazy Horse, Van Heusen, Timberland, Helly Hansen USA, Cape Isle Knitters, Dansk International, and Fenn, Wright & Manson.

At this writing, plans are underway to develop an outlet mall in Plattsburgh at Champlain Centre South (518-561-866) on Rte. 3, with London Fog, Macy's Close-Out, T.J. Maxx, and many clothing shops. Several stores should be open by fall 1992.

## CRAFT SHOPS

**H**andmade functional items have always been part of Adirondack life; in the last few decades, the region has attracted many contemporary crafts people from outside, and has at the same time encouraged local folks to rediscover old-time products. This renaissance has been nurtured by the

*The Adirondack North Country Association craft gallery, in Lake Placid.*

Nancie Battaglia

Adirondack North Country Association (ANCA), a nonprofit business group that published the first "Craft Trails" map highlighting studios and stores more than a dozen years ago. In the early 1980s, ANCA took over the former library of the Lake Placid School of Art to create a shop featuring some 250 regional artisans. Crafts accepted by the ANCA shop undergo close scrutiny for quality; you won't find mass-produced items or anything made from a kit here. A panel of craftspeople and artists makes sure that the artifacts selected for display and sale are made within the region, too.

The ANCA shop offers quite a potpourri, ranging from the funky to the very traditional, displaying everything from earrings to dining room tables, all of consistently high quality. You'll find more details on the shop further on in this section; a new version of the Craft Trails map, which features dozens of Adirondack artists and crafts people whose studios are open to the public, is available by sending a stamped, self-addressed envelope to ANCA, 93 Saranac Ave., Lake Placid, NY 12946.

Listed below you'll find an assortment of craft shops and studios representing a variety of media. Many of the studios are in private homes, so it's a good idea to call ahead before you plan a long trip. Further on in this chapter under separate headings, you'll find fiber and fabric artists and basket makers; carvers of wood, plaster, and other materials; and furniture makers.

## LAKE GEORGE AND SOUTHEASTERN ADIRONDACKS

### Bolton Landing

**Trees** (518-644-5756; Rte. 9N) Adirondack chairs, wooden toys, baskets, balsam items, books of regional interest. Open mid-June—Columbus Day.

### Brant Lake

**Carl Heilman** (518-494-3072; RR 1, Box 213A) Custom, handcrafted snowshoes.

### Chestertown

**Miss Hester's Emporium** (518-494-7940; Corner Main and Church Sts.) Sharing an entryway with the Main St. Ice Cream Parlor, Miss Hester's has primitive painted songbirds made by local wood-carvers, quilted wallhangings in batik and metallic fabrics by Katherine Tennyson, baskets, antiques, cards, and gifts. Open year-round.

### Diamond Point

**Hearthside Artisans II** (Priscilla Hauser; 518-668-2172; Rte. 9N) Quilts, pottery, woodenware, toys, Christmas items, and many more handcrafted goods made by some 65 area artisans. Closed Jan.; open Thurs.—Sun. spring and fall; daily June—Oct.

### Schroon Lake

**Many Tribes Indian Collection** (Walter and Doris Cohen; 518-494-7334; Skylark Lane) A log cabin filled with Native American masks, rugs, dolls, baskets, and pottery. Visiting the Cohens' house is like going to a museum where everything is for sale. Open by appointment only.

### Warrensburg

**Queen Village Gifts** (Jane LeCount; 518-623-2480; 38 Main St.) Adirondack, Amish, and antique quilts; pine furniture, Adirondack chairs. Open year-round.

## CHAMPLAIN VALLEY

### Essex

**The Store in Essex/The American Bird and Craft Studio** (Kay and Will Lake; 518-963-7121; 1 Main St.) Both shops are in an 1810-vintage stone building next to the Lake Champlain ferry slip. The store has quilts, afghans, woodenware, furniture, antiques, and such; the bird studio features woodcarvings, jewelry, stained glass, baskets, copper sculpture, prints, paintings, and photographs. Open daily mid-May—late Oct.

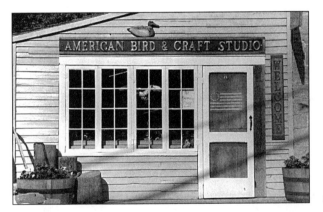

Nancie Battaglia

**Sugar Hill Pottery** (Judith Koenig; 518-963-7068; Main St.) Hand-thrown stoneware pottery. Open daily late May—Columbus Day.

### Port Kent

**Northern Expressions** (Jessica Northrup; 518-834-2093; at the Lake Champlain ferry slip) All kinds of pottery, textiles, jewelry, woodenware, dried floral pieces, baskets, paintings, stencilling, stained glass, and prints. Crafts demonstrations and workshops scheduled occasionally. Open daily May 15—Oct. 19.

*Sugar Hill Pottery, Essex.*

Nancie Battaglia

## Ticonderoga

**Dragonfly Books** (Bonnie Davis; 518-585-7543; 214 Montcalm St.) Local wood-enware, fabric crafts, baskets, plus books. Open year-round; Wed.—Sat. fall—spring; daily July—Aug.

**Hancock House Gallery** (518-585-7868; Moses Circle) Works by local artists, historical souvenir items. Open Wed.—Sat. year-round.

## Westport

**Westport Trading Co.** (Kip Trienens; 518-962-4801; Main St.) Kip's a master stained-glass artist, making scenic, floral, Art Deco, and beveled windows, panels, and mirrors; his shop also sells bark and twig baskets, pottery, jew-elry, contemporary furniture, and eclectic crafts from here and there. Open year-round, most of the time.

## Willsboro

**Adirondack Folk Art Crafts** (Dorothy Harris; 518-963-4405; Rte. 22) Paintings on antique saws, woodworking, animal art. Open May—Dec.

**Kaleb's Korner** (Ray and Janine Provost; 518-963-7210; 7 Main St.) Carved and painted fish decoys, furniture, custom woodworking. Open year-round; call ahead.

## HIGH PEAKS AND NORTHERN ADIRONDACKS

## Jay

**Jay Crafts Center** (Lee Kazanas and Cheri Cross; 518-946-7824; Rte. 9N) Pottery lamps, bowls, vases, and dinnerware made by Lee and Cheri, wooden toys, ash-splint baskets, silver jewelry, prints, custom matting and

*Pottery at Jay Crafts Center.*

Nancie Battaglia

framing, wrought-iron hooks in barnyard animal cut-out designs. Open Apr.—Dec.

**Youngs' Studio and Gallery** (Sue and Terrance Young; 518-946-7301; Rte. 86) Functional and tasteful hand-thrown pottery made by Sue; beautiful limited-edition metal etchings of Adirondack landscapes by Terry; other local crafts. Open year-round Tues.—Sat.

### *Keene*

**North Country Taxidermy** (Bud Piserchia; 518-576-4318; Rte. 73) You can't miss this place — there's usually a full-size, stuffed whitetail buck scratching his antlers on a sapling out front. If you'd like to buy a souvenir antler or two, there are boxes full of them, and they're very reasonably priced. The bearskin rugs are a specialty. Open year-round.

### *Lake Placid*

**ANCA Crafts Center Store** (Eileen Kurtz; 518-523-2062; 93 Saranac Ave.) More than 250 upstate New York crafts people are represented here. There's jewelry made of silver, porcupine quills, semiprecious stones, butterfly wings, and feathers; designer clothing for dolls, children, and adults; handsome leather bags and backpacks; quilts; handmade paper; wood carvings of fish, birds, folk figures; baskets; pottery; rustic and contemporary painted furniture; prints; photographs; stationery. Open Mon.—Sat. year-round; daily in July—Aug.

**Caribou Trading Co.** (518-523-1152; Hilton Plaza, Main St.) Contemporary pottery, jewelry, kites and mobiles, woodenware, handwovens, hand-painted T-shirts by artisans from all over the country. Open daily year-round.

**Guadalupe's Mexican Imports** (518-523-4827; 47 Saranac Ave., near McDonald's) Tinware, glass, textiles, pottery, sweaters, and jewelry from Mexico and Central America. Open Mon.—Sat. year-round.

**Po Polsku** (Elliott and Joan Verner; 518-523-1311; 12 Saranac Ave., at the Ramada Inn) Folk crafts imported directly from Poland: embroidered clothing; carved, painted, and inlaid wooden boxes and plates; dolls and toys; textiles; paper cutouts. Open year-round; daily in summer. Catalog available.

**The Studio** (518-523-3589; 15 Main St.) Satiny-finish burl bowls and canisters; inlaid and exotic wooden desk accessories and frames; paintings, watercolors, and prints of Adirondack scenes and wildlife by many regional artists; local pottery; textiles; stationery. Open Mon.—Sat. year-round, daily in July—Aug.

### Loon Lake

**Kate Mountain Pottery** (518-891-0049; Kate Mountain Lodge) Functional stoneware and miniature pottery by three potters. Open Tues.—Sat. afternoons June—Labor Day; fall weekends.

### Saranac Lake

**North Country Originals** (518-891-1245; 45 Main St.) Adirondack paintings, drawings, and prints; new rustic frames; picture matting and framing. Open Mon.—Sat. year-round.

**Princess Pine Gift Shop** (518-891-5170; 136 River St.) Baskets, dried floral arrangements, wreaths, toys, and dolls. Open Mon.-Sat. year-round.

### Wilmington

**Handycraft Store** (518-523-2966; Rte. 86) Rustic furniture, pine-cone baskets and figures, Adirondack chairs, animal puppets, wallhangings, quilts. Open daily Memorial Day—Labor Day; weekends in fall.

**Pottery by Kathy Daggett** (518-946-2445; Hardy Rd.) Functional stoneware pottery in forest-color glazes. By appointment only.

**Riverbend Gallery** (Joe and Stevie Capozio; 518-946-2319; off Rte. 86) Copper enamel jewelry and large pictorial pieces; watercolor, acrylic and oil paintings and prints. Open Tues.—Sun. July—Labor Day.

## NORTHWEST LAKES REGION

### Childwold

**Leather Artisans** (Tom Amoroso; 518-359-3102; Rte. 3) Classic, beautifully made leather handbags, wallets, belts, and backpacks; quality local crafts. Open year-round: daily Memorial Day—Labor Day; open Thurs.—Mon. Jan.—May.

**The Wood 'n' Basket Shop** (Paul Benton; 518-359-0607; Rte. 3, next to Leather Artisans) Adirondack chairs made by Paul, Peruvian hand-knit sweaters, imported baskets, deerskin moccasins, and lots of kitschy vacationland souvenirs. Open year-round; daily Memorial Day—Labor Day. Canadian money accepted at par.

### *Paul Smiths*

**Adirondack Life Store** (518-327-3000; at the Adirondack Park Visitor Interpretive Center, Rte. 30) Ash-splint baskets; porcupine-quill jewelry; Adirondack cards, posters, and prints; regional books, magazines, and calendars. Open daily Memorial Day—Labor Day; fall weekends.

## CENTRAL AND SOUTHWESTERN ADIRONDACKS

### *Blue Mountain Lake*

**Adirondack Lakes Center for the Arts** (518-352-7715; Rte. 28, next to the Post Office) A tiny shop, but packed with unusual local crafts: birchbark origami birds, funky jewelry, cloth rabbits and bears for kids, pottery, paintings, prints, and handwovens. Open daily late June—Labor Day; some weekends in spring and fall.

*Rustic clock made by Tom Phillips.*

Nancie Battaglia

*Rustic home furnishings at Blue Mountain Designs.*

Nancie Battaglia

**Adirondack Museum Gatehouse** (Victoria Verner; 518-352-7311; Rtes. 28 and 30, at the Adirondack Museum entrance) Handwoven coverlets, guideboat models, rustic and camp-style miniatures, baskets and other items by Judy and Tom Phillips, decoys and cutting boards by Dux Dekes, jewelry, balsam pillows, plus Adirondack books, maps, prints, and stationery. Open daily late May—Oct. 15.

**Blue Mountain Designs** (Lory Wedow; 518-352-7361; Rte. 30) Lory is a contemporary jewelry designer, and besides his lean and classy silverwork, this old schoolhouse is full of fine-quality rustic and camp-style furniture, wrought iron, woodenware, pottery, handwovens, silk-screen prints, photographs, etchings, stationery, and clothing. Open daily mid-May—mid-Oct., some weekends before Christmas.

**Red Truck Clayworks** (Bill Knoble; 518-352-7611; Rtes. 28 and 30, south of the Blue Mt. Lake Service Center) Bill is a potter who digs his own glaze materials from a secret Adirondack source; the glaze is an elegant, deep pearly black. The shop, a former diner, features his platters, bowls, vases, and place settings in a variety of glazes and polychrome geometric designs, plus large-format photographs by Amanda Means, pastel landscapes by Charles Atwood King, and works by other local artists. Open daily mid-June—Labor Day. For special orders, Bill's studio is in Chestertown (518-494-2074).

### *Indian Lake*

**The Village Shop** (Fran Wells; 518-648-5375; Rtes. 28 and 30, near the Cedar River bridge) Adirondack chairs, woodenware, paintings and prints by

Adirondack artists, quilts and pillows. Open spring and fall weekends; daily July—Aug.

**Wilderness Lodge** (518-648-5995; Starbuck Rd., off Big Brook Rd., off Rte. 28) Paintings and photographs by local artists, plus unusual lamps and pictorial panels made of thin slices of native rocks. By appointment only, or check out the crafts during dinner; Wilderness Lodge is a restaurant open year-round.

### Lake Pleasant

**Cabin Clayworks** (Barbara Higgins; 518-548-4506; Rte. 8) Hand-thrown functional pottery; demonstrations. Open June—Aug.; call ahead.

### Long Lake

**Mountain Medley** (Ed Wight; 518-624-4999; Rte. 30, between Hoss's Country Corner and the Cobblestone) Adirondack chairs and benches, functional stoneware pottery, rocking horses, loon and Canada goose planters, lamps, and more, all made by Ed, plus assorted baskets, quilts, dolls, toys, candles, and so on from nearly a hundred regional artisans. Open daily mid-June—mid-Oct.

### Mayfield

**Havlick Snowshoe Co.** (Richard Havlick; 518-661-6447; Rte. 30) Handmade snowshoes and snowshoe furniture, Adirondack packbaskets, and outdoor gear. Open daily, year-round.

### Northville

**Adirondack Country Store** (Joyce Teshoney; 518-863-6056; 252 N. Main St.) A rambling old farmhouse filled with quality local crafts: hickory and oak rockers made by local Amish woodworkers, quilts, handwovens, jewelry, hand-spun yarns, baskets, pottery, toys, decoys, Adirondack books. Open daily Memorial Day—Labor Day; Wed.—Sun. spring and Sept.—Dec.; Sat. only Jan.—Mar.

### Old Forge

**The Artworks** (315-369-2007; Main St.) Cooperative crafts gallery featuring North Country artisans exclusively, with ash-splint baskets, stained glass, hooked rugs, woodcarvings, patchwork quilts and pillows, toys, and jewelry; a mini version of the ANCA gallery in Lake Placid. Open year-round.

**The Broom Man** (315-369-6503; 1146 Main St.) Handmade brooms, rakes, and pitchforks; hand-loomed wool and cotton rugs; Adirondack sweaters; baskets; wagons. Open daily Memorial Day—Labor Day; weekends in spring and fall.

Nancie Battaglia

*The Artworks, Old Forge.*

**Hand of Man Gallery** (315-369-3381; Main St., near the Town of Webb school) Watercolors by Lloyd Schafer, glass, pottery, jewelry, handmade lampshades, turned woodenware, patchwork, and craft and basket-making supplies. Open daily Memorial Day—fall.

**Mountain Peddler** (315-369-3428; Main St.) Quilts, tinware, baskets, woodenware, gifts. Open year-round; daily Memorial Day—Columbus Day.

### Olmstedville

**Knits & Stitches** (Elizabeth LeMay; 518-251-3481; at the Four Corners) Where else can you find a wood-duck house ready to put out by your pond? Lots of good-quality hand- and machine-knit woolens, from socks to sweaters, plus ash-splint baskets, quilts, toys, pottery, woodenware. Open Tues.— Sun. July—Sept.; weekends rest of the year.

### Raquette Lake

**Sagamore Bookstore** (315-354-9905; at Sagamore Lodge, Sagamore Rd., 4 miles off Rte. 28) Rustic furniture and miniatures; ash-splint baskets, stained glass, wrought iron, carved and painted shelf fungus, handmade paper. Open daily Memorial Day—Labor Day; spring and fall weekends.

### Speculator

**Mrs. B's Apple Basket** (518-548-6367; Rte. 8) Baskets, pottery, quilts, rag rugs, stained glass, toys. Open daily Memorial Day—Labor Day; fall weekends.

## FAIRS AND FLEA MARKETS

For a shopping experience that combines fresh-air hiking, adventure, and occasional bursts of comedy or drama, consider these outdoor extravaganzas: from May through Columbus Day, many Adirondack communities sponsor crafts fairs and flea markets. At one end of the spectrum are juried craft shows with consistently high-quality items, at the other are the time-honored flea markets and town-wide garage sales that escape succinct categorization as to just what you can expect to find. But that's the fun of those affairs — nosing past the Elvis-on-velvet paintings and bags of tube socks to discover a cut-glass bud vase or stereo views of Ausable Chasm. Listed below are some annual events arranged by region and date; check local newspapers for information about other festivals. The "Inside & Out" calendar of events in *Adirondack Life* is another good source of information.

### LAKE GEORGE AND SOUTHEASTERN ADIRONDACKS

**Arts Festival of Beauty Sidewalk Arts & Crafts Show** (518-623-9814; Main St., Warrensburg) Paintings and crafts of all kinds, held in early July.

**Hobby Fair** (518-532-7675; Town Park, off Rte. 9, Schroon Lake) 50+ crafts booths, music by Seagle Colony students, rustic-furniture building and other demonstrations, held on the third Saturday in July. Also that day in Schroon Lake, the Community Church Bazaar, on Rte. 9.

**Riverview Arts & Crafts Festival** (518-696-3423; Lakeside Park, Lake Luzerne) Crafts fair, held the third Saturday in July.

**Bolton Library Book Sale** (518-644-2233 or 644-3831; Rte. 9N, Bolton Landing) Large assortment of books for children and adults, held in late July.

**Quality Antique Show-Under the Big Top** (518-644-3831; Bolton Central School Ballfield, Bolton Landing) Antique show with 30+ dealers, held the first weekend in August.

**Hiho Fair** (518-532-7675; St. Andrew's Episcopal Church, Rte. 9, Schroon Lake) Large book sale, antiques, crafts, homemade baked goods and jellies, and white elephant surprises, held on the second Saturday in August.

**Antique Car Show** (518-623-4881; County Fairgrounds, Warrensburg) Flea market and car show, held on the third weekend in August.

**Craft Fair** (518-644-3831; Bolton Central School Ballfield; Bolton Landing) Adirondack crafts and music, held on Labor Day weekend.

**World's Largest Garage Sale** (518-623-2161; throughout Warrensburg) The traffic backs up to Northway Exit 23 for this town-wide blowout; more than

*The World's Largest Garage Sale is held every October in Warrensburg.*

Nancie Battaglia

500 dealers, plus many local families, offer a bewildering array of stuff for sale. Plan to walk once you get to town; there are special parking lots and shuttle buses. Held the first weekend in October.

## CHAMPLAIN VALLEY

**Marigold Festival** (518-962-8383; Main St., Westport) Crafts fair on the library lawn, games and events for children. Memorial Day weekend.

**Old-Time Folkcraft Fair** (518-963-4478; Payne Memorial Library) Crafts fair held on the last Saturday in July.

**Adirondack Memorabilia Show** (518-585-2696; Heritage Museum, Ticonderoga) Ephemera and antiques show, flea market, crafts fair, held on the first Saturday in August.

**Champ Day** (518-546-7261; Main St., Port Henry) A craft and food fair with games and programs for children celebrating "Champ," Lake Champlain's legendary monster of the deep, held on the first Saturday in August.

**Downtown Essex Days** (518-963-4287; Main St., Essex) Crafts fair, games, and races, held on the first Saturday in August.

*Lake Placid Antiques, Arts, and Crafts Show, at the Olympic Speed-Skating Oval.*

Nancie Battaglia

## HIGH PEAKS AND NORTHERN ADIRONDACKS

**Lake Placid Antiques, Arts, and Crafts Show** (518-523-1583; Speed-Skating Oval, Main St., Lake Placid) More than 200 vendors, held on the first Saturday in July.

**Asplin Craftfest** (518-891-5783; Asplin Tree Farms, Saranac Lake) Juried crafts show featuring furniture, pottery, baskets, jewelry, stained glass, and more. Held on the third weekend in July.

**Peak of Summer Country Fair** (518-946-2255; Wilmington Town Park, off Rte. 86, Wilmington) Crafts fair and games for children, held on the third Saturday in July.

**Adirondack Antiques Show and Sale** (518-891-4141; Harrietstown Town Hall, Main St., Saranac Lake) Quality antique show, held in late July.

**Kiwanis Crafts Fair** (518-946-2551; Village Green, Rte. 9N, Jay) Outdoor crafts fair, held the second weekend in August.

**Artisans' Studio Tours** (518-946-2445) Artists and craftspeople in the Jay-Wilmington-Upper Jay area open their studios to the public, in mid-August.

## NORTHWEST LAKES REGION

**Backwoods Craft Fair and Flea Market** (315-848-2391; Rte. 3, Cranberry Lake) Dozens of local artisans selling their wares and demonstrating their skills, plus assorted flea market bargains, held the third weekend in July.

**Eastern Star Flea Market** (518-359-2542; Municipal Park across from the A&P, Tupper Lake) More than 200 dealers with everything from Adirondack ephemera to good used furniture to imported footwear, plus fried dough, sausage-and-pepper sandwiches, and other cholesterol-laden yet delicious carnival-style chow, held on third weekend in August.

## CENTRAL AND SOUTHWESTERN ADIRONDACKS

**Neighbor Day** (315-369-6411; Arts Center, Rte. 28, Old Forge) A crafts fair with music, special exhibitions, chicken barbecue, and events for children, held on the second Sunday in June.

**Central Adirondack Craft Fair** (315-369-6411; sponsored by the Arts Center/Old Forge) At the North Street Pavilion in downtown Old Forge, a crafts fair with 75+ exhibitors, held on the first weekend in July.

**Caroga Historical Museum Craft Fair** (518-835-4400; Caroga Historical Museum, London Bridge Rd., off Rte. 10, Caroga Lake) Annual outdoor crafts fair, held on the second Saturday in July.

**Antique Show and Sale** (518-624-3077; Town Hall, Long Lake) Adirondack antiques show and sale, with occasional special exhibits (a previous year featured gold items salvaged from the *Nuestra Senora de Atocha*, a Spanish shipwreck off Florida); sponsored by Long Lake Parks and Recreation, held in mid-July.

**Morehouse Craft Fair** (315-826-7109; Morehouse Firehall, Rte. 8, Morehouseville) Crafts fair sponsored by the fire department auxiliary, held in mid-July.

**Arts in the Park Craft Fair** (315-357-5501; Arrowhead Park, Inlet) Outdoor crafts fair sponsored by the Inlet Chamber of Commerce, held on the third weekend in July.

**Speculator Flea Market** (518-548-4521; Ballfield, Rte. 30, Speculator) 50+ vendors; sponsored by the chamber of commerce, held on the third Saturday in July.

**Piseco Craft Fair** (518-548-8732; Piseco Community Hall, Old Piseco Rd., Piseco) 50+ crafts booths; sponsored by the Piseco Women's Club, held on the last Saturday in July.

**Adirondack Gem and Mineral Show** (518-251-2612; Gore Mt. Ski Area Lodge, Peaceful Valley Rd., North Creek) 20+ gem dealers, plus gem-cutting demonstrations and lectures, held the first weekend in August.

**Heart of the Park Craft Fair** (518-624-3077; Mount Sabattis Park Pavilion, Rte. 30, Long Lake) Crafts fair "under the big top," sponsored by Long Lake Parks and Recreation, held the first Sunday in August.

**TWIGS Arts and Crafts Show** (518-548-4521; Ballfield, Rte. 30, Speculator) 75+ craftspeople; sponsored by the local branch of the Amsterdam Memorial Hospital Auxiliary, held on the second Thursday in August.

**Town-wide Garage Sale** (518-624-3077; throughout Long Lake) Long Lake introduces drive-by shopping on the third Saturday in August.

**Adirondack Antiques Show** (518-352-7311; Adirondack Museum, Blue Mountain Lake) Ephemera, quilts, furniture, photographs from some 50 dealers, on the grounds of the Adirondack Museum, held on the last weekend in September. Call to confirm date; admission charge required for show visitors.

**Antique Show & Sale** (315-369-6411; Arts Center/Old Forge) Featuring Adirondack and upstate New York antique and ephemera dealers, held on the first weekend in October.

**Rustic Furniture Makers' Fair** (518-352-7311; Adirondack Museum, Blue Mt. Lake) Displays by more than 40 rustic-furniture builders on the grounds of the Adirondack Museum, held the first Saturday in October. Museum admission required for fair visitors.

## FIBER AND FABRIC; BASKETS AND BALSAM

The fiber arts these days go beyond things made exclusively of thread and yarn; handmade paper relies on wood and other plant fibers, while traditional and modern baskets also use wood splints, grasses, ropes, and other natural materials. The needle arts in the true Adirondack sense of the word include native sweet-smelling pillows and sachets; the needles of balsam fir (*Abies balsamea*) are gathered, dried, and stuffed into calico fabric bags, sometimes in whimsical wildlife shapes. Listed below you'll find an assortment of quilters, basket makers, papermakers, weavers, and balsam crafters from across the park.

North of the Adirondack Park border, on the St. Lawrence River, is Akwesasne, home of many Mohawk families, the place to look for superb traditional baskets woven of ash splints and sweet grass. The *Akwesasne Cultural Center Museum* (315-346-2240; Rte. 37, Hogansburg, NY 13655) has a shop selling all kinds of baskets, from tiny thimble cases to full-size packbaskets, plus moccasins decorated with beadwork and porcupine quills. Call ahead for hours and directions.

Also north of the park is basket maker Bill Smith (315-262-2436; Colton, NY 13625), who learned traditional Akwesasne basket-making years ago; he and his wife Sal make melon, apple, and packbaskets, and teach basket making at community arts centers (look under "Crafts Instruction" in Chapter Four, *Culture*, for locations).

### LAKE GEORGE AND SOUTHEASTERN ADIRONDACKS

#### *Warrensburg*

**Blue Heron Designs** (Charlene Leary; 518-623-3189; Truesdale Hill Rd.) Fine handwoven clothing and accessories. Open daily June 1—Sept. 1; Thurs.—Sun. spring and fall. Call ahead.

**Queen Village Gifts** (Jane LeCount; 518-623-2480; 38 Main St., at the traffic light) Large inventory of Amish, Adirondack, and antique quilts. Open year-round.

## CHAMPLAIN VALLEY

### Essex

**The Essex Weaver** (Anna Folkesson; 518-963-4412; Rte. 22) Fine handwoven throws, rag rugs, blankets, shawls, and clothing; antique looms and spinning wheels; spinning and weaving supplies. Call ahead.

### Lewis

**Sofbags Factory Store** (Michael and Rebecca Baker; 518-873-2666; Rte. 9) High-quality Cordura, nylon, and canvas book bags, backpacks, duffel bags, luggage, wallets, and equipment cases made on site. Open Mon.—Fri. year-round, Mon.—Sat. July and August.

## HIGH PEAKS AND NORTHERN ADIRONDACKS

### Au Sable Forks

**Woods Run Baskets** (Elizabeth Rogers; 518-647-5451; Star Rte. 2 Box 112) Shaker-design baskets "with an Adirondack flair." By appointment only.

### Gabriels

**Paperworks** (Myrna Bendett; 518-327-3294; Bert LaFountain Rd.) Marbled paper, decorative frames, checkbook covers, and boxes; Adirondack paper designs — loons, herons, bears, deer, and pine trees — on boxes and frames. By appointment only.

### Newcomb

**Upper Hudson Woolery** (Judy Blanchette; 518-582-2144; Rte. 28N) Hand-spun yarns from Judy's own sheep, hand-knit sweaters, spinning wheels, spinning lessons. Open daily year-round.

### Saranac Lake

**Asplin Tree Farms** (Charlene Dunham; 518-891-5783; Rte. 86) When the Dunhams purchased the tree farm several years ago, they found many of the balsams unsatisfactory for Christmas-tree market. But even crooked balsam firs smell lovely, so they began to process the needles for sachets and for the fragrance industry. On sale here you'll find everlasting balsam pillows and sachets in all kinds of shapes and sizes. Open daily June 1—Dec. 24.

# NORTHWEST LAKES REGION

## *Paul Smiths*

**Timberdown Handcrafts** (Tracy Santagate; 518-327-3665; Rte. 30) Willow and reed baskets; traditional Adirondack ash-splint pack baskets. By appointment only.

## *Tupper Lake*

**Edith Mitchell** (518-359-7830; 4 Wawbeek Ave.) Beautiful quilts from crib-size to king-size in a variety of traditional and contemporary patterns by special order. Edith was the driving force behind Blue Mountain Designs for many years and is regarded today as the foremost quilter in the Adirondack Park. Her reputation doesn't end at the Blue Line — her quilts have been featured in several traveling national exhibitions and she has taught quilting workshops all over the world. By appointment only.

**Genevive Sutter** (518-359-2675; Raquette River Dr.) Lovely pictorial quilts of Adirondack scenery and historic buildings; one of Genevive's pieces was presented to Governor Cuomo for the Adirondack Park Centennial in May 1992. By appointment.

**Thomas and Judy Phillips** (518-359-9648; Star Rte. 2) Ash-splint melon, apple, and potato baskets in various sizes; packbaskets. By appointment only.

# CENTRAL AND SOUTHWESTERN ADIRONDACKS

## *Indian Lake*

**Homemade Quilts and Crafts** (Kathleen Herrick; 518-648-5360; Rte. 28) Traditional Adirondack tied quilts in various sizes, patchwork pillows, dolls, baskets, balsam pillows. Open daily Memorial Day—Columbus Day; other times by chance or appointment.

## *Long Lake*

**Mountain View Farm** (Donna Adams; 518-624-2521; Adams Park Rd., off Walker Rd., Long Lake, NY 12847) Hand-spun yarns from Donna's sheep and angora rabbits; sweaters, vests, and afghans; spinning lessons and demonstrations. Open year-round; call ahead.

**The Spinning Wheel** (518-624-9900; Rtes. 28 and 30) Hand-spun yarns, hand-knit sweaters and mittens, handwoven pillows, jewelry, gifts. Open daily July-Aug.; weekends in spring and fall.

## *Olmstedville*

**Knits and Stitches** (Elizabeth LeMay; 518-251-3481; Four Corners) Quilts, hand- and machine-knit wool sweaters, baskets, and other crafts. Open Tues.—Sun. July—Sept.; weekends in spring and fall.

# FURNITURE

Regional woodworkers create furniture in a variety of styles, from Shaker-inspired modern designs, to rugged rustic sculptural pieces, to the simple, straightforward Adirondack chairs that now come in an infinite range of permutations and combinations. You can find camp and home furniture in many of the craft shops described above, or you can go to the workshops and specialty stores listed below. Several of the rustic workers have brochures or catalogs that you can request by mail; if you're planning to visit an individual's shop, it's always a good idea to call ahead.

If you think you'd like to try to build your own rustic furniture, several arts centers listed in Chapter Four, *Culture*, offer hands-on workshops in which you can make a simple twig-and-bark stand. Also, Ed Smith, a woodworker from Diamond Point, has collected rustic furniture plans from early-20th-century magazines and published them in a 64-page booklet, *How to Build Rustic Furniture*. The book is $7.95 plus $1.00 shipping and handling, from Smith Brook Press, RR 1 Box 217D, Diamond Point, NY 12824.

Besides individual furniture craftsmen and local factories, you can find full-service furniture stores in many towns such as *Casier Furniture* (518-891-2400; 10 Bloomingdale Ave., Saranac Lake, NY 12983 and 518-359-2327; Park St., Tupper Lake, NY 12986), *Futterman's Furniture* (518-359-3681; 110 Park St., Tupper Lake), and *Helms Village Store* (518-624-3566; Rte. 30, Long Lake, NY 12847). Check the yellow pages in local phone books for other furniture stores.

## LAKE GEORGE AND SOUTHEASTERN ADIRONDACKS

### *Bolton Landing*

**Thomas W. Brady, Furnituremaker** (518-644-9801; 87A North Bolton Rd., Bolton Landing, NY 12814) Elegant contemporary furniture in cherry, walnut, and figured maple: screens, bedsteads, desks, blanket chests, tables, and chairs, some with painted motifs or in Shaker designs. Color flyer available; open year-round by appointment only.

### *Diamond Point*

**Pine Plank** (Don Farleigh; 518-644-9420; Box 37, Diamond Point, NY 12824) Adirondack chairs, benches, and tables in pine. Open year-round Tues.—Sun.

*Don Farleigh relaxes in one of his Adirondack chairs.*

Nancie Battaglia

### Schroon Lake

**Adirondack Rustics** (Barry Gregson; 518-532-9384; Charley Hill Rd., Schroon Lake, NY 12870) Rustic tables, chairs, settees, beds, corner cupboards, and sideboards, made of burls, cedar, white-birch bark, and assorted woods. Barry's furniture has been featured in *Fine Woodworking, Country Living,* and the *Old House Journal*; he occasionally can be seen demonstrating his craft at Schroon Lake fairs and folk festivals, which you'll find listed in this chapter. Color brochure available; open year-round Tues.—Sat.; call ahead.

*Barry Gregson of Adirondack Rustics works on a butternut settee.*

Nancie Battaglia

**The Bear's Hand** (Bill Bresnahan; 518-532-7636; South Schroon Rd.) Twig-style furniture; oak, hickory, and cherry rocking chairs; high chairs, lamps, and tables; refinishing and restoration. Open year-round; call ahead.

### CHAMPLAIN VALLEY

### Keeseville

**Willsboro Wood Products** (518-834-5200; S. Ausable St., Keeseville, NY 12944) Indestructible yet attractive and comfortable beds, tables, chairs, dressers, mirrors, benches, and settees made of northern white cedar; featured in the L.L. Bean catalog. Color catalog available; open Mon.—Fri. year-round.

*The "Warrensburg Dresser" and "Silver Lake Mirror" from Willsboro Wood Products.*

Nancie Battaglia

## *Mineville*

**Essex Industries** (518-942-6671; Pelfisher Rd., Mineville, NY 12956) Canoe and guideboat accessories: backrests, caned seats, yokes; folding canvas camp stools and shopping bags. Flyer and price list available; open Mon.—Fri. year-round.

## HIGH PEAKS AND NORTHERN ADIRONDACKS

### *Keene*

**Adirondack Rustic Furnishings** (Ronald Sanborn; 518-576-9593; Hulls Falls Rd., Keene, NY 12942) "Sculpture from the forest" is how Ron describes his whimsical twig-style chairs, étagères, bookshelves, dining sets, headboards, and frames. Free price list and brochure available; color brochure $7.00; open year-round by appointment only.

### *Keene Valley*

**John Van Hazinga** (518-576-9864; Box 548, Keene Valley, NY 12943) Daybeds, headboards, and bookshelves in a pine-tree silhouette design can be seen at J.B.'s Health Goods Store, Rte. 73, which is open Wed.—Mon. year-round.

### *Lake Placid*

**Free Flow Creations** (Dave Hall; 518-523-2697; Corner Rte. 86 and Whiteface Inn Rd.) Cherry, maple, and birch tables, chairs, desks, dressers, beds, picture frames, and mirrors. Open Wed.—Sat. year-round, or by appointment.

### Saranac Lake

**Forest Murmurs** (Glenn Bauer; 518-891-5104; 32 McClelland St., Saranac Lake, NY 12983) Custom birchbark and twig signs for your home or camp; lamps, mirrors, frames, and sconces. Price list and brochure available; open Mon.-Fri. year-round; call ahead.

### Upper Jay

**Country Corners** (518-946-7960; Rte. 9N, Upper Jay, NY 12987) Reproduction Windsor chairs, quality pine country furniture. Open year-round.

## NORTHWEST LAKES REGION

### Paul Smiths

**Train Brook Forest** (David Woodward; 518-327-3498; Easy Street, Paul Smiths, NY 12970) Ornate 18th-century-style travel trunks and document boxes made of wood and leather and lined with marbled paper; wrought-iron fireplace screens with silhouette designs of trees or wildlife; fireplace accessories; iron lighting fixtures in Arts and Crafts period designs. Open year-round; by appointment only.

### Tupper Lake

**Thomas Phillips** (518-359-9648; Star Rte. 2, Tupper Lake, NY 12986) Ash-splint baskets with sculptural branch handles; twig-style and birchbark chairs, tables, benches, and beds; cedar outdoor furniture; rustic furniture restoration. Price list available; open by appointment only.

## CENTRAL AND SOUTHWESTERN ADIRONDACKS

### Blue Mountain Lake

**Bud Hayes** (518-352-7784; Durant Rd., Blue Mountain Lake, NY 12812) Adirondack chairs for children and adults by special order. Call ahead.

### Indian Lake

**Backwoods Furnishings** (Ken Heitz; 518-251-3327; Rte. 28; Indian Lake, NY 12842) A Paul Bunyan-size log chair arches over Ken's driveway, marking the home of one of the originators of the Adirondack rustic revival. Twig, birchbark, and cedar beds, tables, sideboards, settees, rockers, and custom orders. Ken's furniture has been featured in *House Beautiful, House and Garden, Gourmet,* and many other publications. Color brochure available; open year-round by appointment only.

**Chimney Mountain Craftsmen** (518-648-5722; Big Brook Rd., off Rte. 30) Pine furniture factory making beds, cabinets, gun cases, bookshelves in stock or special order. Open daily year-round.

### Long Lake

**Cold River Gallery** (Jamie Sutliffe; 518-624-3581; Deerland Rd., Rte. 30, Long Lake, NY 12847) Painted arch-top trunks; carved furniture, mirrors, and frames with wildlife designs; custom doors and signs. Open year-round by appointment only.

**Mountain Medley** (Ed Wight; 518-624-4999; Rte. 30) Curved back, classic, and child-size Adirondack chairs in stock or by special order. Open daily late June—Columbus Day.

### Old Forge

**Old Forge Woodmaker** (315-369-3535; Main St., Old Forge, NY 13420) Adirondack chairs and benches; pine tables, bookshelves, and rockers. Open Wed.—Mon. Memorial Day—Labor Day; weekends in spring and fall.

### Speculator

**Jerry's Wood Shop** (518-548-5041; Rte. 30, Speculator, NY 12164) Folding and rigid Adirondack chairs and settees; picnic tables; swing sets and lawn furniture in stock. Open daily year-round.

## GENERAL STORES

Up north, in a town that shall remain nameless, there's an abandoned cobblestone building with a sign proclaiming that it's the "Shop of Three Wonders: Wonder Where It Came From, Wonder What It Costs, and Wonder How Long It's Been Here." Actually, it's just that kind of intellectual exercise that makes an expedition to a bona fide Adirondack general store fun. Chances are you'll find some odd-shaped old things like nail pullers and chick-feeding troughs right alongside the mixing bowls, glass percolator tops, and sugar shakers, and maybe an aisle over from the fire-engine-red galluses and boot socks, but a ways from the chips and salsa. Don't worry about the dust; don't be afraid to ask the price. If you can't find it here, you can probably live without it.

There are also those general stores that really take the word "general" to heart, so that you can pick out a nice wedding present as well as the fixings for an afternoon picnic, including sunglasses, bug dope, and wholesome food. Each place has its own personality and style, and they all have their merits and place within the community. Listed below are some of the more general stores found throughout the park.

## LAKE GEORGE AND SOUTHEASTERN ADIRONDACKS

### *Adirondack*

**Adirondack General Store** (Joan and Dick Lomnitzer; 518-494-4408; East Shore Dr., on the east side of Schroon Lake) There's a fine line between country-looking places that try too hard and end up cutesy, and those real country stores that mix the antique and the modern, the dry goods and the foodstuffs — and end up completely charming. This place, which was the company store for a tannery dating back to the 1850s, hits the nail on the head. You can hang out by the woodstove when it's cold, read the paper on the porch when it's warm, buy a nice gift for someone, or get milk, eggs, bread, and such for camping in Pharaoh Lake Wilderness Area. There are a few tables for eating breakfast or lunch; the deli is very good, and Joan's homemade soups are substantial and scrumptious. Open year-round.

### *Brant Lake*

**Daby's General Store** (518-494-4039; Rte. 8) Mixed in with the Freihofer's doughnuts, videos, cold beer, and wristwatches are display cases and shelves with 1940s-vintage dolls, old bottles and toys, and fancy knives, for looking at, not for sale. You can find just about everything here, and even if you only buy some Popsicles, the view down Mill Pond toward the cobblestone library perched out over the water is worth the trip on its own. Open year-round.

## HIGH PEAKS AND NORTHERN ADIRONDACKS

### *Bloomingdale*

**Norman's Wholesale Grocery** (518-891-1890; Rte. 3) Norman's has been in the same family since it opened in 1902, and some of the display drawers and cases still have ornate hardware and lettering declaring "Socks and Mittens" or "Silks and Laces." For retail customers, the stock is mainly convenience-store items, but the place still feels very much like the old times when the stagecoach stopped here. Open year-round.

## NORTHWEST LAKES REGION

### *Cranberry Lake*

**The Emporium** (315-848-2140; Rte. 3) A tiny place crammed with souvenirs, maps, fishing tackle, announcements of coming attractions, canned goods, frozen treats, and T-shirts, but there's even more — the Emporium is a marina, too, with gas pumps and a big long weathered wooden dock. Although there probably aren't many bargains here, it's worth a visit if you're in the neighborhood. This kind of place used to be common in the Adirondacks,

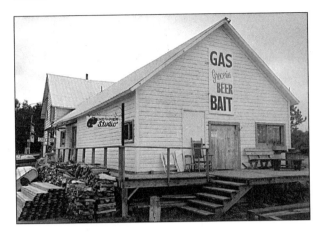

*Everything you need is at The Emporium, on Cranberry lake.*

Nancie Battaglia

and the Emporium is one of the few lakeside general stores that remains. Open daily year-round.

## CENTRAL AND SOUTHWESTERN ADIRONDACKS

### Long Lake

**Hoss's Country Corner** (John and Lorrie Hosley; 518-624-2481; corner Rtes. 30 and 28N) An exemplary modern general store with aisles of groceries, fresh meats, and deli items; Woolrich clothing for men and women, from long underwear to jumpers to winter jackets; camp furnishings; stuffed animals by Gund; quilts, rugs, and baskets galore; cold beer; topo maps; Adirondack, outdoor, children's, and Christian books; gift items; jewelry; scented soaps and candles; out-of-town newspapers; film ... the list is nearly endless, as is the rambling frame building that goes up, down, and around. The week before Christmas Lorrie puts nearly everything on sale, and customers get to pick their own discount from a hat. Open Mon.—Sat. year-round.

### Minerva

**Murdie's General Store** (518-251-2076; Rte. 28N) If you're on the Teddy Roosevelt Memorial Highway retracing his midnight ride to the presidency in 1901, and find that you need gas, nightcrawlers, a buffalo-plaid hat, a six-pack, transmission fluid, ice cream, spaghetti, or maps, well, look no farther. Open year-round.

### Old Forge

**Old Forge Hardware** (315-369-6100; Main St.) A visit to Old Forge Hardware is to Adirondack shopping what a trip to the Adirondack Museum is to regional history. This coliseum-size landmark bills itself as the "Adiron-

*A bird's-eye view of Old Forge Hardware.*

Nancie Battaglia

dacks' Most General Store," a title with which we can't argue. Need a pack-basket? Bamboo steamer for your wok? Man O' War brand spar varnish? Snowshoes? Inflatable pool? Reflective dog collar to fit a Newfoundland? Authentic shade for your antique Aladdin lamp? Squirrel-baffling bird feeders? Spiles for maple sugaring? Replacement handle for your peavey? You can spend an entire day here. Open year-round.

## Raquette Lake

**Raquette Lake Supply** (315-354-4301; downtown Raquette Lake) The Dillon family has owned Raquette Lake Supply in one manifestation or another for more than a century. The building is huge, with the post office, a bakery, and the Tap Room on one side, a laundromat on another, and (defunct) hotel rooms upstairs; the store takes up most of the floor space facing the water. There's a soda fountain, meat counter, dairy case, and groceries, plus toy tomahawks, vintage postcards, and fish poles. This is the only place in the park where you can get honest-to-gosh, cut-from-the-lake ice for your cooler. The huge bluish blocks come with a frosting of sawdust that a quick plunge in the lake rinses off. Open year-round, mornings from Columbus Day to late May; daily from Memorial Day—Oct. If you're around in February for the annual ice-cutting weekend, drop by for a glimpse of a time-honored process.

## Sabael

**The Lake Store** (Eris and Bill Thompson; 518-648-5222; Rte. 30) Lots of toys, gifts, sports gear, souvenirs, and clothing, plus a great summertime soda fountain, year-round deli, and all the major food groups; worth a visit especially if you're looking for a surprise for someone who has everything. Open year-round.

### Wells

**Perry's General Store** (518-924-2156; Rte. 30) If you can get past the glass case full of old-fashioned penny candy, you'll find yarn, greeting cards, groceries, insulated rubber boots, wool clothing, gifts, antiques, and baskets. You can also get hunting and fishing licenses here, in a handsome 1890s storefront across from Lake Algonquin. Open year-round.

## GLASS

A handful of glass workers ply their transparent trade in the Adirondacks, making custom beveled or stained-glass windows or blown-glass decorative items. You'll find their studios listed below; since many crafts people work out of their homes, it's always a good idea to call ahead.

### LAKE GEORGE AND SOUTHEASTERN ADIRONDACKS

### Chestertown

**Handblown Glass by Beth Melecci** (518-494-2066; Stagecoach Rd.) Blown glass Christmas-tree ornaments, lamps, vases in subtle, swirling colors; fine crystal decorative pieces. Open year-round, by appointment only.

### Lake Luzerne

**Lori Lochner Art Glass** (518-654-6545; Gailey Hill Rd.) Glass jewelry and accessories from conservative to outrageous; traditional architectural stained glass. Open year-round by appointment only.

### CHAMPLAIN VALLEY

### Westport

**Westport Trading** (Kip Trienens; 518-962-4801; Main St.) Architectural stained-glass windows, panels, and mirrors in stock or made to order; repairs for antique stained glass. Shop open most of the time, year-round; drop-ins welcome.

### HIGH PEAKS AND NORTHERN ADIRONDACKS

### Bloomingdale

**Almekinder Glass** (Leisa Almekinder; 518-946-2565; Star Rte. 37A) Etched and leaded-glass windows, signs, cabinet doors, room dividers, and door

Nancie Battaglia

*Kip Trienens hangs a stained-glass window at Westport Trading.*

panels; restoration and repairs. Color brochure available. Open year-round, by appointment only.

### *Upper Jay*

**Epic Glassware** (Nick Ferro; 518-946-7100; Rte. 9N, Upper Jay, NY 12987) Etched glass in hundreds of freehand designs, on pitchers, plaques, wine glasses, plates; the pine-cone and pine-tree motifs have a nice Adirondack look to them. Custom orders for commemorative designs. Shop open Thurs.—Mon., year-round; drop-ins welcome.

## CENTRAL AND SOUTHWESTERN ADIRONDACKS

### *North Creek*

**Visions** (Scott Evans; 518-251-2026; Main St.) Carved windows and mirrors in stock or custom made; attractive wildlife and forest designs. Shop open weekends in spring and fall; daily in summer.

### *Old Forge*

**Meyda Stained Glass Studio** (315-369-6636; Main St.) Tiffany-style shades, mirrors, planters, jewelry boxes. Open daily Memorial Day—Labor Day.

## JEWELRY

Many of the crafts shops listed above carry silver, gold, or porcelain jewelry by local artisans; the jewelers and mineral shops described below specialize in contemporary designs or native gemstones.

### HIGH PEAKS AND NORTHERN ADIRONDACKS

#### Lake Placid

**Darrah Cooper Jewelers** (518-523-2774; 10 Main St., next to the Hilton) Delightful sterling silver and gold charms and earrings representing miniature North Country objects: packbaskets, canoe paddles, guideboats, oars, pine cones, and Adirondack chairs. Also rings, bracelets, and necklaces in precious stones, silver, and gold. Open Mon.—Sat. year-round.

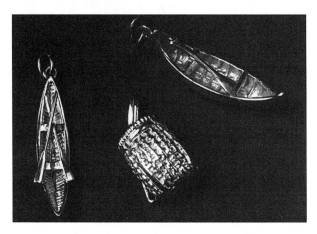

*Adirondack charms by Darrah Cooper, Lake Placid.*

Nancie Battaglia

**Arthur Volmrich** (518-523-2970; 99 Main St.) Fun earrings and necklaces mixing antique charms, buttons, and stones with modern components; turquoise bracelets and watchbands; custom rings; repairs and resettings. Open Mon.—Sat. year-round.

### CENTRAL AND SOUTHWESTERN ADIRONDACKS

#### Blue Mountain Lake

**Blue Mountain Designs** (Lory Wedow; 518-352-7361; Rtes. 28 and 30) Classic contemporary cast and hand-fabricated silver and 14k gold: rings, earrings, handmade chains, pins, bracelets, and necklaces. Open daily Memorial Day—Columbus Day, plus fall weekends until Christmas.

### North River

**Gore Mountain Mineral Shop** (518-251-2706; Barton Mines Rd., 5 miles off Rte. 28) Garnet jewelry, faceted gem stones, rocks and minerals from around the world, gem cutting demonstrations on Sundays and Mondays. Open daily late June—Labor Day.

**Jasco Minerals** (518-251-3196; Rte. 28 and Barton Mines Rd.) Specializing in native garnet, plus semiprecious stones from around the world; custom jewelry orders; rocks and minerals. Open year-round, daily Memorial Day—Labor Day.

## OUTDOOR GEAR

Many shops in the Adirondack Park offer sports equipment, outdoor clothing, and camping supplies; you'll find them listed in Chapter Six, *Recreation*, under specific headings like Camping, Fishing, Rock and Ice Climbing, or Skiing.

## SCULPTURE AND WOOD CARVINGS

Architectural-design elements, folk-art figures, realistic decoys, and modern concrete sculpture are just a few of the things shaped by Adirondack hands. Listed below you'll find a sampling of decorative items for indoors and out.

### CHAMPLAIN VALLEY

### Essex

**American Bird & Craft Studio** (Kay and Will Lake; 518-963-7121; Main St., by the ferry slip) Carved shorebirds and waterfowl; other crafts. Open daily late May—Oct. 31.

**The Weeping Cherub** (Loy Kempster; 518-963-8952; on the alleyway to the Old Dock House Restaurant, off Main St.) The Kempsters travel throughout the Northeast restoring and re-creating ornate plasterwork in museums and historic homes. Their shop offers plaster mantels, friezes, ceiling medallions, wall sconces, planters, garden benches, and table supports reproduced from Greek and Roman antiquities, Della Robia sculptures, and 16th- and 17th-century homes. Catalog available. Open Mon.—Sat. May—Oct.

## HIGH PEAKS AND NORTHERN ADIRONDACKS

### *Bloomingdale*

**Ralph Prata** (518-891-2417; West Main St.) Since 1978, Ralph has been creating hauntingly abstract concrete carvings: freestanding sculptures, wall reliefs, and framed limited-edition works. Brochure available; open by appointment only.

*Rick Bütz carves a loon in his Blue Mountain Lake workshop.*

## CENTRAL AND SOUTHWESTERN ADIRONDACKS

### *Blue Mountain Lake*

**Rick and Ellen Bütz, Woodcarvers** (518-352-7737; 1/4 mile north of the Adirondack Museum on Rtes. 28 and 30) If you know anything at all about whittling, chances are you are familiar with these Adirondack carvers: Rick is host of the nationally broadcast PBS television series "Woodcarving with Rick Bütz," and author of several popular books on the subject. The shop features wildlife woodcarvings from songbirds to whitetail deer, figures from Adirondack folk tales, and historic St. Nicholas carvings; special commissions are welcome. Open Mon.—Sat. May—Oct.; call ahead.

### *Morehouseville*

**Shore Birds & Decoys** (Charles Reynolds; 315-826-7934; mailing address HCR Box 325, Cold Brook, NY 13324) Life-size decoys and woodcarvings of loons, ducks, sea gulls and shore birds; hand-tied wet, dry, terrestrial, and nymph flies. Open year-round; call ahead.

# CHAPTER EIGHT
# *Nuts, Bolts, and Free Advice*
## INFORMATION

*Got a question? Don't be afraid to ask at the Post Office.*

Nancie Battaglia

This chapter supplies common-sense advice plus a metaphorical map and compass to get you to the right places to find the answers to your additional questions. These services and subjects are included in this chapter:

## AMBULANCE, FIRE, STATE AND LOCAL POLICE

There is no unified emergency-assistance system that operates throughout the Adirondack Park. In Warren County, which includes Lake George, Warrensburg, North Creek, Lake Luzerne, Pottersville, Johnsburg, and several other communities, you can dial 911 for help. (Note that cellular phones work in the Lake George region, but not particularly well — or at all — in other parts of the park.) There are solar-powered emergency phones spaced about every two miles along the shoulders of I-87, the Northway.

In the Champlain Valley, High Peaks, Northwest Lakes, and Central Adirondacks, you can dial 0 to reach the operator; stay on the line and you'll be connected to the appropriate agency. If you're lucky enough to have a telephone book nearby when you run into trouble, check the inside front cover for emergency listings for individual towns.

The New York State Police has offices throughout the Adirondacks. If no local officer is available calls are forwarded to a 24-hour central dispatcher. Numbers are:

| | | | |
|---|---|---|---|
| **Chestertown** | 518-494-3201 | **Keeseville** | 518-834-9040 |
| **Schroon Lake** | 518-532-7611 | **Ray Brook** | 518-897-2000 |
| **Westport** | 518-962-8235 | **Indian Lake** | 518-648-5757 |
| **Willsboro** | 518-963-7400 | **Old Forge** | 315-369-3322 |

The number for the Poison Control Center is 1-800-336-6997.

## AREA CODES

The area code for the eastern two-thirds of the Adirondacks, including Lake George, Warrensburg, Schroon Lake, Elizabethtown, Westport, Keene, Lake Placid, Saranac Lake, Tupper Lake, Long Lake, Blue Mountain Lake, Indian Lake, North Creek, Speculator, Wells, and Northville, is 518. For communities in the northwestern and west-central Adirondacks, such as Cranberry Lake, Star Lake, Raquette Lake, Inlet, Eagle Bay, Big Moose, and Old Forge, the area code is 315.

## BANKS AND AUTOMATIC TELLER MACHINES

Many Adirondack banks still keep the proverbial "banker's hours," so don't count on transactions after 3 p.m. A few local banks are locally owned and independent; some are members of the Norstar, Key Bank, Marine

Midland, or First American chains, and will honor checks drawn on accounts from member banks.

For a vacation cash crunch, some banks may advance money on charge cards. Automatic teller machines are not associated with every bank, as they often are in urban areas; in much of the central Adirondacks, ATMs are quite rare. You can find NYCE Cashere terminals at Stewart's Shops throughout the park (see "Late-Night Food and Fuel" in this chapter for a list of locations). These booths honor NYCE or Cirrus cards, or can give you an advance on VISA, Mastercard, American Express, or Discover cards, but don't expect the machine to spit out greenbacks at you. The NYCE terminal dispenses a paper receipt that you present to the cashier, who then gives you the money.

## LAKE GEORGE AND SOUTHEASTERN ADIRONDACKS

**First National Bank of Glens Falls** (an Evergreen Bank)
Main St., Bolton Landing, 518-644-3421
Canada St., Lake George, 518-668-5486
137 Main St., Warrensburg, 518-623-2666
These banks have NYCE Cashere and Cirrus ATMs.

**Glens Falls National Bank** (an Arrow Bank)
Main St., Chestertown, 518-494-2691
Canada St., Lake George, 518-668-5461
Main St., Schroon Lake, 518-532-7121

**Grand Union**
Rte. 9, Chestertown, has a NYCE and Cirrus ATM near the front doors.

**Norstar Bank**
2097 Main St., Lake Luzerne, 518-696-3181
138 Main St., Warrensburg, 518-623-2801
These banks are connected with NYCE, Cirrus, and Metroteller ATM services.

## CHAMPLAIN VALLEY

**Albany Savings Bank**
Montcalm St., Ticonderoga, 518-585-6066
This bank has a 24-hour ATM in the foyer for Cirrus and NYCE cards.

**Essex County Champlain National Bank**
Main St., Crown Point, 518-597-3322
Court St., Elizabethtown, 518-873-6347
18 Main St., Westport, 518-962-8216
Point Rd., Willsboro, 518-963-4201. This branch has a NYCE and Cirrus ATM.

**Keeseville National Bank**
Main St., Keeseville, 518-834-7331

**Key Bank of Eastern New York**
Main St., Au Sable Forks, 518-647-8136

**Norstar Bank**
S. Main St., Port Henry, 518-546-3311
Montcalm St., Ticonderoga, 518-585-2815

## HIGH PEAKS AND NORTHERN ADIRONDACKS

**Adirondack Bank**
60 Main St., Saranac Lake, 518-891-2323
53 Church St. Extension, Saranac Lake, 518-891-2323
Cold Brook Plaza Extension, Lake Placid, 518-523-3344
All branches have ATMs connected to the NYCE, Pulse, Discover, Cashere, and Plus systems.

**Essex County Champlain National Bank**
Rte. 73, Keene, 518-576-9515

**Key Bank of Central New York**
Saranac Ave., Lake Placid, 518-523-9535
55 Broadway, Saranac Lake, 518-891-2900
Both branches have 24-hour ATMs for NYCE, Plus, and Cirrus systems.

**Key Bank of Eastern New York**
Emmons and Cook St., Dannemora, 518-492-2561

**Key Bank of New York**
Rte. 28N, Winebrook Hills, Newcomb, 518-582-2711

**Marine Midland Bank**
70 Main St., Saranac Lake, 518-891-3711

**National Bank & Trust Co.** (formerly Bank of Lake Placid; owned by NBT Bankcorp of Norwich)
81 Main St., Lake Placid, 518-523-9544. This branch only has a 24-hour ATM for NYCE, Plus, Metroteller, and Mac cards.
Cold Brook Plaza, Lake Placid, 518-523-9544
2 Lake Flower Ave., Saranac Lake, 518-891-2050
Rte. 86, Wilmington, 518-946-2121

## NORTHWEST LAKES REGION

**Key Bank of Central New York**
402 Park St., Tupper Lake, 518-359-2917

53 Church St. Extension, Saranac Lake, 518-891-2323
Cold Brook Plaza Extension, Lake Placid, 518-523-3344
All branches have ATMs connected to the NYCE, Pulse, Discover, Cashere, and Plus systems.

**Essex County Champlain National Bank**
Rte. 73, Keene, 518-576-9515

**Key Bank of Central New York**
Saranac Ave., Lake Placid, 518-523-9535
55 Broadway, Saranac Lake, 518-891-2900
Both branches have 24-hour ATMs for NYCE, Plus, and Cirrus systems.

**Key Bank of Eastern New York**
Emmons and Cook St., Dannemora, 518-492-2561

**Key Bank of New York**
Rte. 28N, Winebrook Hills, Newcomb, 518-582-2711

**Marine Midland Bank**
70 Main St., Saranac Lake, 518-891-3711

**National Bank & Trust Co.** (formerly Bank of Lake Placid; owned by NBT Bankcorp of Norwich)
81 Main St., Lake Placid, 518-523-9544. This branch only has a 24-hour ATM for NYCE, Plus, Metroteller, and Mac cards.
Cold Brook Plaza, Lake Placid, 518-523-9544
2 Lake Flower Ave., Saranac Lake, 518-891-2050
Rte. 86, Wilmington, 518-946-2121

**NORTHWEST LAKES REGION**

**Key Bank of Central New York**
402 Park St., Tupper Lake, 518-359-2917
**Community Bank**

# BIBLIOGRAPHY

Rte. 3, Star Lake, 315-848-3344

**Grand Union**
Ames Plaza, Tupper Lake, 518-359-9197. NYCE cardholders can receive cash at the service desk between 9 a.m. and 9 p.m.

**Tupper Lake National Bank**

L. Sprague DeCamp's horror-fantasy *The Purple Pterodactyls* has a definite Adirondack flavor. Mystery writer John D. McDonald, of Travis McGee fame, even wrote a book about his cats spending their summers in Piseco.

The two lists that follow are not a trivial pursuit of Adirondack literature, but collections of recent (and readily available) books and important, out-of-print historical volumes that may be read at several local libraries. The latter books don't circulate; an appointment may be necessary in order to peruse a special collection. For a list of libraries with special sections of Adirondack literature, consult Chapter Four, *Culture*. For where to buy Adirondack books, check Chapter Seven, *Shopping*.

## BOOKS YOU CAN BUY

### *Literary Works*

Banks, Russell. *The Sweet Hereafter*. NY: Harper Collins, 1991. 257 pp., $20.

Cooper, James Fenimore. *The Last of the Mohicans*. Numerous paperback editions. NY: Bantam Classics, 1982. 384 pp., $3.50.

Doctorow, E. L. *Loon Lake*. NY: Random House, 1980. 258 pp., $11.95.

Dreiser, Theodore. *An American Tragedy*. Paperback editions available. NY: Signet Classics, 1964. 832 pp., $4.95.

Jamieson, Paul. *Adirondack Pilgrimage*. Glens Falls: Adirondack Mountain Club, 1986. 248 pp., $15.95.

Oates, Joyce Carol. *Bellefleur*. NY: E. P. Dutton, 1980. 558 pp., $13.95.

White, William Chapman. *Adirondack Country*. Reprint. Syracuse, NY: Syracuse University Press, 1983. 368 pp., illus., $16.95.

### *Anthologies*

Bruchac, Joseph; Craig Hancock, Alice Gilborn, and Jean Rikhoff, eds. *North Country*. Greenfield Center, NY: Greenfield Review Press, 1986. 458 pp., $12.95. Contemporary fiction and poetry about the region.

Jamieson, Paul. *The Adirondack Reader*. 2d ed. Glens Falls: Adirondack Mountain Club, 1982. 544 pp., $18.50. An excellent introduction to the region, with selections spanning nearly 400 years of Adirondack history, literature, and commentary.

Tefft, Tim, ed. *Of the Summits, Of the Forests*. Morrisonville, NY: Adirondack Forty-Sixers, 1991. 352 pp., photos, index, $18.50.

## *Architecture*

Gilborn, Craig. *Durant: The Fortunes and Woodland Camps of a Family in the Adirondacks.* Sylvan Beach, NY: North Country Books, 1981. 170 pp., photos, maps, index, $19.95.

Howard, Hugh. *The Preservationist's Progress.* NY: Farrar, Straus & Giroux, 1991. 320 pp., $22.95.

Kaiser, Harvey. *Great Camps of the Adirondacks.* Boston: David Godine, 1986. 240 pp., color photos, maps, index, $35.

## *Folklore*

Bruchac, Joseph. *Hoop Snakes, Hide Behinds and Side-Hill Winders.* Freedom, CA: Crossing Press, 1991. 115 pp., $10.95. Tall tales.

Carr, Harvey. *I Was on the Wrong Bear.* Greenfield Center, NY: Bowman Books, Greenfield Review Press, 1992. 166 pp., $9.95. Tall tales from a Blue Mountain Lake storyteller.

Ward, Vaughn. I *Always Tell the Truth (Even When I Have to Lie to Do It!)* Greenfield, NY: Greenfield Review Press, 1990. 116 pp., $9.95. Tall tales by members of the Adirondack Liars' Club.

## *Local Histories*

Durant, Kenneth and Helen. *The Adirondack Guide-Boat.* Camden, ME: International Marine Publishing Co., 1980. 250 pp., illus., photos, index, $30.

Everest, Allan S. *Rum Across the Border.* Reprint. Syracuse, NY: Syracuse University Press, 1992. 172 pp., photos, $9.95.

Graham, Frank. *The Adirondack Park: A Political History.* New York: Alfred A. Knopf, 1978; Syracuse, NY: Syracuse University Press, 1991. 330 pp., index, $14.95.

Hochschild, Harold. *Township 34.* Blue Mountain Lake, NY: Adirondack Museum Book, 1980s. Slipcase set of seven volumes on railroads, lumberjacks, steamboats, hotels, mines, and 19th-century life around Blue Mountain Lake. $35.95 for set; individual volumes also available.

Manley, Atwood. *Rushton and His Times in American Canoeing.* 1968. Reprint. Syracuse, NY: Adirondack Museum Book. 1989. 200 pp., photos, $16.95.

Murray, William H.H. *Adventures in the Wilderness*. 1869. Reprint. Syracuse, NY: Syracuse University Press/Adirondack Museum Book, 1989. 352 pp., illus., $13.95.

Steinberg, Michael. *Our Wilderness*. Glens Falls, NY: Adirondack Mountain Club, 1991. 112 pp., photos, $18.95. Billed as a history for ages 10 and up, this book is also an excellent summary for adults.

Warner, Charles Dudley. *In the Wilderness*. 1878. Reprint. Syracuse, NY: Syracuse University Press/Adirondack Museum Book, 1990. 134 pp, $9.95.

### Natural History

North Country Books, in Utica, publishes a series of four Adirondack field guides for native mammals, trees and shrubs, wildflowers, and mushrooms. All of the books are paperbacks with numerous color photos; prices are $12.95 each for the mushroom and wildflower guides and $13.95 each for the mammal and tree guides.

*Nature lovers in their element at the Visitor Interpretive Center, Paul Smiths.*

Nancie Battaglia

DiNunzio, Michael. *Adirondack Wildguide*. Elizabethtown, NY: Adirondack Conservancy/Adirondack Council, 1984. 160 pp., illus., $14.95.

Jaffe, Howard and Elizabeth. *Geology of the Adirondack High Peaks Region*. Lake George, NY: Adirondack Mountain Club, 1986. 216 pp., photos, $12.95.

Saunders, D. Andrew. *Adirondack Mammals*. Syracuse, NY: Adirondack Wildlife Program, 1988. 216 pp., illus., $11.95.

## Photographic Studies

Farb, Nathan. *100 Views of the Adirondacks*. NY: Rizzoli Press, 1988. 168 pp., color photos, $45.

Oppersdorff, Mathias. *Adirondack Faces*. Syracuse, NY: Syracuse University Press/Adirondack Museum Book, 1991. 108 pp., $34.95.

Wuerthner, George. *The Adirondacks: Forever Wild*. Helena, MT: American Geographic Publishing Co., 1988. 102 pp., guidebook, color photos, $15.95.

## Recreation

There are two main sources for Adirondack guidebooks for hiking, snow-shoeing, and cross-country skiing: the Adirondack Mountain Club (ADK), based in Lake George, NY, and Backcountry Publications, out of Woodstock, VT. *The Forest Preserve Series* by different ADK authors covers seven different regions of the park, from the High Peaks to the Northville-Lake Placid Trail; these $14.95 pocket-size paperbacks have plenty of detail and each comes with a separate topo map with trail overlays. The *Discover the Adirondacks Series*, published by Backcountry Publications and written by historian/hiker Barbara McMartin, divides the park into eleven regions. These offer notes on the human and natural history of a particular destination, and cost between $9.95 and $14.95. If you can't decide on which region to trek, Barbara McMartin has also written *Fifty Hikes in the Adirondacks: Short Walks, Day Trips, and Extended Hikes Throughout the Park*, published by Backcountry ($12.95). And ADK publishes two Adirondack samplers, one on day hikes and one on backpacking trips, at $8.95 each.

Aprill, Dennis. *Good Fishing in the Adirondacks*. Harrisburg, PA: Stackpole Books, 1990. 224 pp., photos, maps, $14.95.

Betters, Francis. *Fishing the Adirondacks*. Wilmington, NY: Adirondack Sports Publications, 1982. 114 pp., illus., maps, $14.95.

Jamieson, Paul, and Morris, Donald. *Adirondack Canoe Waters: North Flow*. Lake George, NY: Adirondack Mountain Club, 1991. 368 pp., maps, index, $15.95.

Mellor, Don. *Climbing in the Adirondacks: A Guide to Rock & Ice Routes*. Lake George, NY: Adirondack Mountain Club, 1990. 318 pp., photos, maps, index, $24.95.

Nessmuk [George Washington Sears]. *Woodcraft and Camping*. 1920. Reprint. NY: Dover Publications, 1963. 105 pp., illus., index, $3.95.

## Travel

Stoddard, Seneca Ray. *The Adirondacks Illustrated*. 1874. Reprint. Glens Falls, NY: Chapman Historical Museum, 1983. 204 pp., illus., index, $15.

Vesty, John. *Adirontreks: Places and People in the Adirondacks*. Indian Lake, NY: Crossroads Publications, 1990. 268 pp., photos, $16.95.

## BOOKS YOU CAN BORROW

Barnett, Lincoln. *The Ancient Adirondacks*. NY: Time-Life Books, 1974. 184 pp., photos, index. An excellent introduction to the Adirondack Park by a Westport resident and former *Life* magazine editor.

Bethke, Robert. *Adirondack Voices: Woodsmen and Woods Lore*. Urbana, IL: University of Illinois Press, 1981. 148 pp., photos, music.

Colvin, Verplanck. *Report on a Topographical Survey of the Adirondack Wilderness of New York*. Albany, 1873. Sounds dull, but it reads like an adventure story. Many engraving and maps.

Cutting, Edith. *Lore of an Adirondack County*. Ithaca, NY: Cornell University Press, 1944. Essex County folklore.

Deming, Philander. *Adirondack Stories*. Boston, MA: 1880. Gritty short stories.

Donaldson, Alfred L. *A History of the Adirondacks*. 2 vols. NY: 1921. The most complete regional history.

Engels, Vincent. *Adirondack Fishing in the 1930s: A Lost Paradise*. Syracuse, NY: Syracuse University Press, 1978.

Everest, Allan S. *Our North Country Heritage: Architecture Worth Saving*. Plattsburgh, NY: Tundra Books, 1972. 143 pp., photos. Historic buildings in Clinton and Essex counties.

Headley, Joel Tyler. *The Adirondacks, or Life in the Woods*. NY: 1849. Early travelogue.

Kirschenbaum, Howard, Susan Schafstall and Janine Stuchin, eds. *The Adirondack Guide: An Almanac of Essential Information and Assorted Trivia*. Raquette Lake, NY: Sagamore Institute, 1983. 200 pp., maps, photos, index.

Porter, Eliot. *Forever Wild: The Adirondacks*. NY:1966. Lovely coffee-table book of large-format photos.

Thompson, Ernest Seton. *Rolf in the Woods*. Garden City, NY: 1921. Children's adventure story set in early-19th-century Adirondacks.

Thomas, Howard. *Folklore from the Adirondack Foothills*. Prospect, NY: Prospect Books, 1956. 150 pp.

Thompson, Harold W. *Body, Boots and Britches*. Syracuse, NY: Syracuse University Press, 1979. 538 pp. Folklore and folk music of northern New York.

Todd, John. *Long Lake*. Pittsfield, MA: 1845. Glimpses of pioneer life.

Van Diver, Bradford. *Rocks and Routes of the North Country*. Geneva, NY: W. F. Humphrey Press, 1976. 204 pp. Roadside geology.

Weston, Harold. *Freedom in the Wilds*. St. Huberts, NY: Adirondack Trail Improvement Society, 1971. 230 pp. Adirondack memoirs of a renowned 20th-century painter.

## CLIMATE AND WEATHER INFORMATION

An Adirondack year has been described as "nine months of winter and three months of poor sledding." Winter does seem long, especially to residents, with an average of 190 days with subfreezing temperatures annually. The western Adirondacks, including Old Forge, Eagle Bay, Big Moose, Inlet, Cranberry Lake, and Star Lake, get considerably more snow than the eastern Adirondacks, with about 10 feet falling in an average winter from lake-effect storms. Winters in the Champlain Valley have had little snow in recent years.

*Enjoying the snow and ice has always been part of the Adirondack experience.*

Courtesy the Barry Collection, Lake Placid Center for the Arts

Spring in the Adirondacks can be rather elusive. March is winter, despite the date of the vernal equinox. April weather bounces between brief flashes of hot and dry, sustained snow and cold, and mixtures of mild and moist; whatever the weather, it's prime time for white-water rafting on the Hudson River. (See Chapter Six, *Recreation*, for a list of rafting outfitters). May tends to be reliably above freezing during the daytime, although in 1976 nearly two feet of snow fell on May 19. June temperatures can be sweltering, with plenty of bug activity.

July and August days are usually in the 70s and 80s, with occasional hotter spells, but evenings cool off pleasantly. Usually early September brings the finest dry weather for outdoor activities, with highs in the 70s and lows in the 50s.

Fall can be brilliantly sunny, providing great leaf-peeping opportunities from about September 20 through October 15, depending on the elevation. Or autumn can be dismally rainy, with the only chance to see fall colors provided by looking in mud puddles. There's a toll-free hotline for fall foliage reports, 1-800-CALL-NYS.

General advice about the weather is one thing; getting an accurate forecast is another. There is no nearby National Weather Service station to help meteorologists; temperature forecasts for Albany or Syracuse need be adjusted downward by five or ten degrees, with a corresponding adjustment for precipitation. Rain and 40 degrees for the Capital District usually means sleet or snow in the Adirondacks.

The Lake Placid radio station, WIRD (105.5 FM), has a weatherman on staff who provides good information for the area from Tupper Lake to Keene; there's a 24-hour telephone weather report available at 518-523-1363. The "Eye on the Sky" weather update from Vermont Public Radio, WVPR (107.9 FM), is fairly reliable for the eastern Adirondacks. The Albany television station, WRGB, also has a weather forecast at 518-476-WRGB, which covers the southern Adirondacks.

## GUIDED TOURS

There are hundreds of licensed Adirondack Guides for fishing, hunting, hiking, and climbing; you'll find information about two-legged guides in Chapter Six, *Recreation*. Several communities in the Champlain Valley have self-guided walking and driving tours for historic-preservation buffs; check "Architecture," in Chapter Four, *Culture*, for the details.

Only a few companies offer guided tours by bus in the Adirondacks. *Lake Placid Sightseeing Tours*, on Mirror Lake Drive 518-523-4431, provides a narrated trip through the Olympic village. *Flack Tours* offers day trips to Cranberry Lake and Star Lake for organized groups, and may be expanding their services to other destinations in late 1992. Call the office at 1-800-842-9747. *Adirondack Trailways* occasionally schedules special guided tours originating in Albany and points south. Call 1-800-225-6815. *Change O' Pace Tours,* based in Melrose, NY, offers Adirondack caravan tours with recreational vehicles; call 1-800-289-7886.

## HANDICAPPED SERVICES

D isabled New York residents can get free passes to state-operated camping, swimming, and golf facilities and historic sites. Write to Office of Parks and Recreation, Agency Building 1, Empire State Plaza, Albany, NY 12238 for an application.

Some of the nature trails at the Visitor Interpretive Centers, at Paul Smiths and Newcomb, are designed for the mobility-impaired. The Adirondack Mountain Club (see "Bibliography," above) plans to add appendices on appropriate trails for wheelchairs in each of its hiking guidebooks, in new editions slated for 1993. Also, Pinto Press in Elizabethtown is compiling a park-wide guide to accessible fishing, camping, sight-seeing, and hiking for publication possibly in 1993.

Cultural institutions, such as the Adirondack Museum, libraries, and arts centers, are generally accessible; some historic buildings are not. Chapter Four, *Culture,* provides more information. Restaurants that are accessible are described in Chapter Five; lodgings with handicapped facilities are listed in Chapter Three.

## HEALTH CENTERS AND HOSPITALS

### LAKE GEORGE AND SOUTHEASTERN ADIRONDACKS

**Bolton Health Center**, 518-644-9471; Cross St., Bolton Landing.
**Chester Health Center**, 518-494-2761; Main St., Chestertown.
**Glens Falls Hospital**, 518-792-5261; 100 Park St., Glens Falls.
**Warrensburg Health Center**, 518-623-2844; Main St., Warrensburg.

### CHAMPLAIN VALLEY

**Champlain Valley Physicians Hospital Medical Center**, 518-561-2000; Beekman St., Plattsburgh.
**Elizabethtown Community Hospital**, 518-873-6377; Park St., Elizabethtown.
**Mineville Health Center**, 518-942-6661; Hospital Rd., Mineville.
**Moses-Ludington Hospital**, 518-585-2831; Wicker St., Ticonderoga.

## HIGH PEAKS AND NORTHERN ADIRONDACKS

**Adirondack Medical Center**, 518-523-3311; Church St., Lake Placid (formerly Placid Memorial Hospital).

**Adirondack Medical Center**, 518-891-4141; Lake Colby Dr., Saranac Lake (formerly Saranac Lake General Hospital).

**Mountain Health Center**, 518-576-9771; Rte. 73, Keene.

## NORTHWEST LAKES REGION

**Clifton-Fine Hospital**, 315-848-3351; Rte. 3, Star Lake.

**Mercy Health Care**, 518-359-3355; 115 Wawbeek Ave., Tupper Lake.

**Piercefield Medical Center**, 518-359-7120; Town Hall, Piercefield.

## CENTRAL AND SOUTHWESTERN ADIRONDACKS

**Indian Lake Health Center**, 518-648-5707; Rte. 28, Indian Lake.

**Long Lake Medical Center**, 518-624-2301; Rte. 28N, Long Lake.

**Nathan Littauer Hospital**, 518-725-8621; 99 E. State St., Gloversville.

**North Creek Health Center**, 518-251-2541; at Adirondack Tri-County Nursing Home, Ski Bowl Rd., North Creek.

**Town of Webb Health Center**, 315-369-6619; South Shore Rd., Old Forge.

## LATE-NIGHT FOOD AND FUEL

### LAKE GEORGE AND SOUTHEASTERN ADIRONDACKS

**Cumberland Farms** (food and fuel), open all night. Rte. 9N, Lake Luzerne, 518-696-0043; 112 Main St., Warrensburg, 518-623-9857.

**Grand Union** (food), open all night. Main St., Warrensburg.

**Nice 'N Easy** (food and fuel), open till 11 p.m. Main St., Chestertown, 518-494-2032.

**Prospect Mtn. Diner** (food), open all night during summer. Rte. 9, Lake George, 518-668-5889.

**Stewart's Shops** (food and fuel), open till 11 p.m. Main St., Bolton Landing, 518-644-9078; Brant Lake Rd., Chestertown, 518-494-3208; Rte. 9, Lake George, 518-668-9378; Main St., Schroon Lake, 518-532-9095; Main St., Warrensburg, 518-623-9848.

**Warrensburg Mobil Service** (fuel), open all night. Main St., Warrensburg, 518-623-9492. Near Exit 23 of I-87.

## CHAMPLAIN VALLEY

**Stewart's Shops** (food and fuel), open till 11 p.m. Rte. 9, Au Sable Forks, 518-647-9900; Park St., Elizabethtown, 518-873-9946; Front St., Keeseville, 518-834-5918; S. Main St., Port Henry, 518-546-9992; Montcalm St., Ticonderoga, 518-585-9777.

## HIGH PEAKS AND NORTHERN ADIRONDACKS

**Nice 'N Easy** (food and fuel), open till 11 p.m. 70 River St., Saranac Lake, 518-891-5418.

**Sugar Creek Convenience Stores** (food and fuel), open till 11 p.m. Lake Flower Ave., Saranac Lake, 518-891-5817; Rte. 86, Wilmington, 518-946-7680.

**Stewart's Shops** (food and fuel), open till 11 p.m. 122 Cook St., Dannemora, 518-492-4885; Rte. 73, Keene, 518-576-2056; 315 Main St., Lake Placid, 518-523-9905; Bloomingdale Ave., Saranac Lake, 518-891-9892.

## NORTHWEST LAKES REGION

**Stewart's Shops** (food and fuel), open till 11 p.m. Park St., Tupper Lake, 518-359-9845.

**Wawbeek Quick Stop** (food and fuel), open till midnight. 36 Wawbeek Ave., Tupper Lake, 518-359-2311.

## CENTRAL AND SOUTHWESTERN ADIRONDACKS

**Conway's Country Store** (food and fuel), open till 10 p.m. Rte. 28, Wevertown, 518-251-2283.

**Nice 'N Easy** (food and fuel), open till 11 p.m. Rte. 28, North Creek, 518-251-3667.

**Stewart's Shops** (food and fuel), open till 11 p.m. Rte. 28, Indian Lake, 518-648-5992; Rte. 28, North Creek; 192 S. Main, Northville, 518-863-2475.

# MAPS

On a standard road-atlas page showing New York State, the Adirondack Park isn't much bigger than a postage stamp, making it tough to navigate through unfamiliar territory. The Adirondack North Country Association

(ANCA) publishes an excellent full-size road map that shows just the park and adjacent counties; send $1.25 (check or money order) and a stamped, self-addressed legal-size envelope to ANCA, 183 Broadway, Saranac Lake, NY 12983 to receive one. JiMapco, in Round Lake, NY, publishes individual county maps that are generally available in grocery stores and book shops. *The New York State Atlas and Gazetteer* ($12.95) published by De Lorme Mapping Co., Freeport, ME, uses a topographical map format to show areas in still greater detail; these can be found in most area bookstores.

# MEDIA

## *Magazines and Newspapers*

**Adirondac** (518-668-4447; RR 3, Box 3055, Lake George, NY 12845) Bimonthly magazine. Published by the Adirondack Mountain Club, with articles on local history, outdoor recreation, and environmental issues.

**Adirondack Life** (518-946-2191; Box 97, Jay, NY 12941) Bimonthly magazine, plus annual Guide to the Outdoors. Known for excellent color photography; publishes essays, short stories, columns, and features on history, outdoor recreation, architecture, culture, local life, regional products, politics, and environmental issues by nationally known writers.

**Blueline** (315-267-2000; c/o English Dept., Potsdam College, Potsdam, NY 13676) Annual literary magazine devoted to the North Country.

### LAKE GEORGE AND SOUTHEASTERN ADIRONDACKS

**Adirondack Journal** (518-623-9786; 5 Woodward Ave., Warrensburg, NY 12885) Weekly newspaper for Chestertown, Pottersville, Lake Luzerne, Warrensburg, and vicinity. Also publishes the **Adirondack Trader**, with scads of ads for garage sales, vehicles, pets, real estate, and services throughout the southeastern and central Adirondacks.

**Adirondack Mountain Times** (518-623-3411; 166 Main St., Warrensburg, NY 12885) Weekly newspaper for Warren County. Also publishes the **Warrensburg-Lake George News.**

**The Chronicle** (518-792-1126; 286 Glen St., Glens Falls, NY 12801) Excellent weekly coverage of northern New York events.

**Glens Falls Post Star** (518-792-3131; Lawrence and Cooper Sts., Glens Falls, NY 12801) Daily newspaper covering the Adirondacks from Lake George to Long Lake.

## CHAMPLAIN VALLEY

**Essex County Republican** (518-873-6368; Denton Publishing, Elizabethtown, NY 12932) Weekly newspaper for Keeseville and northern Essex County.

**Plattsburgh Press-Republican** (518-561-2300; Cornelia St., Plattsburgh, NY 12901) Daily paper covering Ticonderoga to Saranac Lake to Plattsburgh. *North Country Living* is a weekly tabloid supplement with a calendar of events and features.

**Times of Ti** (518-585-6204; 26 1/2 Father Jogues Place, Ticonderoga, NY 12883) Weekly paper for Ticonderoga, Port Henry, and Crown Point.

**Valley News** (518-873-6368; Denton Publishing Co., Elizabethtown, NY 12932) Weekly paper for Elizabethtown, Westport, Essex, Keene, and Keene Valley.

## HIGH PEAKS AND NORTHERN ADIRONDACKS

**Adirondack Daily Enterprise** (518-891-2600; 61 Broadway, Saranac Lake, NY 12983) Daily paper for Lake Placid, Saranac Lake, Paul Smiths, and Tupper Lake area; the *Weekender* has a good regional calendar of events plus local history features.

**Lake Placid News** (518-523-4401; Mill Hill, Lake Placid, NY 12946) Weekly paper for Lake Placid, Keene, Keene Valley, and Wilmington.

**Tri-Lakes Free Trader** (518-891-0561; 41 Broadway, Saranac Lake) Weekly classifieds-only paper.

## NORTHWEST LAKES REGION

**Tupper Lake Free Press** (518-359-2166; 136 Park St., Tupper Lake, NY 12986) Weekly paper covering Tupper Lake, Piercefield, Cranberry Lake, and Long Lake.

**Watertown Daily Times** (315-782-1000; 260 Washington St., Watertown, NY 13601) Daily newspaper with an Adirondack bureau based in Tupper Lake.

## CENTRAL AND SOUTHWESTERN ADIRONDACKS

**Adirondack Express** (315-369-2237; Box 659, Old Forge, NY 13420) Weekly newspaper covering Raquette Lake to Otter Lake.

**Edinburg Newsletter** (518-863-2075; Star Rt., Box 330, Hadley, NY 12835) Monthly news for Northville and Great Sacandaga Lake area.

**Hamilton County News** (518-548-6898; Rte. 30, Speculator, NY 12164) Weekly newspaper for Long Lake, Blue Mountain Lake, Indian Lake, Speculator, Wells, Piseco, and Benson.

**North Creek News** (518-251-3012; Ski Bowl Rd., North Creek, NY 12853) Weekly paper for Johnsburg, Bakers Mills, Minerva, Olmstedville, North Creek, and North River.

## Radio Stations

**National Public Radio**. Three NPR affiliates reach different parts of the Adirondacks:

**WAMC-FM**, 90.3, 518-465-5233; Albany, NY; also translator WANC, 103.9 (Ticonderoga).

**WSLU-FM**, 91.7 (Blue Mountain Lake, Lake Placid, Tupper Lake), 91.5 (Long Lake), 90.5 (Saranac Lake), 88.3 (Peru) 315-379-5356; Canton, NY. The best news and feature coverage for the entire Adirondack Park by any media outlet.

**WVPR**, 107.9, 802-674-6772; Windsor, VT. News coverage for the eastern Adirondacks and relatively reliable weather forecasts.

## Commercial Radio Stations

**WENU-FM**, 101.7, 518-793-7733. Glens Falls. General.

**WIRD-FM**, 105.5, 518-523-3341. Lake Placid. General.

**WKBE-FM**, 1005, 518-798-8634. Glens Falls. Rock.

**WSCG-FM**, 93.5, 518-654-9058. Corinth. Country.

**WIPS-AM**, 1250, 518-585-2868. Ticonderoga. General.

**WNBZ-AM**, 1240, 518-891-1544. Saranac Lake. General.

## Television Stations

There are no television stations broadcasting from the Adirondacks, and TV reception in areas not covered by cable or translator can be terrible. The Plattsburgh NBC-affiliate, WPTZ, does report news from Lake Placid, Saranac Lake, and elsewhere in the eastern Adirondacks during the Today Show and in evening slots. The PBS-affiliate, WCFE-TV, also based in Plattsburgh, produces special programs on Adirondack people, places, and things from time to time. For the 1985 Forest Preserve Centennial, they produced a highly acclaimed hour-long special, "Forever Wild"; for the 1992 Adirondack Park Centennial, a look at wilderness philosophy is the theme of a program currently in production. Check local cable listings or call the station (518-563-9770; Sesame St., Plattsburgh, NY 12901) for news about historical and environmental programing on the North Country.

# REAL ESTATE

Since the population of the region has been fairly stable over the last century, there are often older farmsteads and village homes for sale, as families build new houses to meet their needs. If you're not afraid of the "handyman's special," the Adirondacks could provide some challenges and rewards for you. Backcountry cabins here can be wonderful, or rustic in the worst sense of the word, but if all you're looking for is shelter from the storm, you may be able to find a bona fide bargain. Townhouses and condominiums are a new local phenomenon, and after intense initial speculation prices have stabilized at a level that shouldn't be too shocking to a typical New England urbanite. Waterfront — on just about any lake, river, or pond inside the Blue Line — tends to be scarce, and dear: the going rate can be as high as $1000 per running foot of shoreline, just for the land. Add a summer cottage, or a real winterized house, plus a decent driveway, a boathouse, or a garage, and the figures start to climb. The Adirondack real-estate market hit a peak in late 1988, with frenzied buyers spreading their money around generously. Now prices have adjusted to reflect more accurately the true values of different properties, but lakefront property continues to hold its worth.

Even crossroads that don't have grocery stores have real-estate offices. Check the local phone book, ask at the post office, look on the bulletin board at the laundromat, or stop in at the nearest chamber of commerce. Weekly newspapers usually have some real-estate listings, especially in July and August; there's also a monthly publication called *North Country Real Estate Guide* put together by Glebus Enterprises in Lewis, NY, with offerings from a dozen or more realtors. *Adirondack Life* magazine has a large real-estate section in each issue. Also, *Adirondack Properties*, published by Tri-Lake 3hree Press in Tupper Lake is printed each month with numerous listings by real estate offices located across the park. There's a good mix of undeveloped acreage, luxury summer homes, year-round houses, and businesses.

Once you find your dream place, and you've looked at it through the driving sleet of November as well as in the peach-colored August twilight, it's time to locate a lawyer. Most Adirondack attorneys are seasoned veterans at working with local zoning authorities or the Adirondack Park Agency (APA), which regulates development in the many communities that don't have town planning boards. For general information about zoning laws in the park, contact the APA, in Ray Brook, at 518-891-4050.

# RELIGIOUS SERVICES AND ORGANIZATIONS

Churches throughout the Adirondacks anchor the communities and provide a network of help and social life along with spiritual guidance.

Several local churches are interesting for their architecture, and are listed in the National Register of Historic Places; a few seasonal chapels are located on lovely islands accessible only by boat. Some churches even put on great, inexpensive dinners (see Chapter Five, *Restaurants & Food Purveyors*, for advice on chicken barbecues and church suppers). Check the papers for listings of church services. Inside the park, Lake Placid has the only active synagogue; Temple Beth Joseph, in Tupper Lake, is open as a historic building and only occasionally offers services.

## ROAD SERVICE

For **AAA** members, there are local offices in Glens Falls, 518-792-0088; Gloversville 518-725-0811; and Plattsburgh 518-563-3830. For non-AAA members, some 24-hour towing and automotive services are listed below:

### LAKE GEORGE AND SOUTHEASTERN ADIRONDACKS

| | |
|---|---|
| **Lakeview Automotive**, Lake George | 518-668-9267 |
| **Thomson's Garage**, Lake George | 518-668-5337 |
| **Pottersville Garage**, Pottersville | 518-494-3631 |
| **Warrensburg Car Care**, Warrensburg | 518-623-2135/1-800-540-2997 |

### CHAMPLAIN VALLEY

| | |
|---|---|
| **Chesterfield Truck Stop**, Keeseville | 518-834-7407 |
| **Pierce's Service Station**, Lewis | 518-873-2065/962-8971 evening |
| **R.B. Motors**, Ticonderoga | 518-585-7774 |

### HIGH PEAKS AND NORTHERN ADIRONDACKS

| | |
|---|---|
| **Central Garage**, Lake Placid | 518-523-3378 |
| **John's Sunoco Service**, Saranac Lake | 518-891-5938 |
| **Wilmington Service Station**, Wilmington | 518-946-7138/946-7478 |

### NORTHWEST LAKES REGION

| | |
|---|---|
| **Counter's Garage**, Tupper Lake | 518-359-9846 |

### CENTRAL AND SOUTHWESTERN ADIRONDACKS

| | |
|---|---|
| **Joyce's Body Shop**, Blue Mountain Lake | 518-352-7343 |
| **Central Adirondack Garage**, Indian Lake | 518-648-5565 |

| | |
|---|---|
| **Chambers Garage**, Inlet | 315-357-2051 |
| **C & H Citgo**, Old Forge | 315-369-3678 |
| **Speculator Auto**, Speculator | 518-548-8102 |
| **Brussel's Thendara Garage**, Thendara | 315-369-3755 |

## TOURIST INFORMATION

By now nearly every adult from Boston to Philadelphia can hum the annoying, persistent tune, "I LOVE NY," but the legacy of that television campaign is some very informative and attractive county tourism publications. Warren County publishes an annual colorful guide with a calendar of events and lists of hiking trails, boat-launch sites, museums, libraries, roadside attractions, campgrounds, pharmacies, and much more; call 518-761-6366 for a free copy. Likewise, Essex County has a helpful town-by-town guide listing motels, golf courses, marinas, antique shops, stables, and special events, available by calling 518-942-7794. Franklin County has a four-color booklet with general background information, plus another publication detailing businesses and services; these are available from the tourism office at 518-483-6788. Clinton County offers a magazine-size guide, available by calling 518-563-1000. Hamilton County has printed a series of pamphlets with information on hunting and fishing, snowmobiling, crafts shops, and dining and lodging, available by calling 518-648-5239.

Some local chambers of commerce and visitor-information centers are listed below:

*Tourist information office in Bolton Landing.*

B. Folwell

## LAKE GEORGE AND SOUTHEASTERN ADIRONDACKS

**Bolton Landing** (Rte. 9N, Bolton Landing, NY 12814; 518-644-3831).
**Chestertown-Brant Lake-Pottersville** (Main St., Chestertown, NY 12817; 518-494-2722).
**Hague-Silver Bay** (Rte. 9N, Hague, NY 12836; 518-543-6353).
**Lake George** (Rte. 9, Lake George, NY 12845; 518-668-5755).
**Lake Luzerne** (Box 222, Lake Luzerne, NY 12846; 518-696-3500).
**Schroon Lake** (Main St., Schroon Lake, NY 12870; 518-532-7675).
**Stony Creek** (Box 35, Stony Creek, NY 12878; 518-696-2395).
**Warrensburg** (136 Main St., Warrensburg, NY 12885; 518-623-2161).

## CHAMPLAIN VALLEY

**Moriah-Port Henry-Mineville** (Box 34, Port Henry, NY 12974; 518-546-7261).
**Ticonderoga-Crown Point** (Box 70, Ticonderoga, NY 12883; 518-585-6619).
**Westport** (General Delivery, Westport, NY 12992; 518-962-8383).
**Willsboro** (Box 124, Willsboro, NY 12996; 518-963-8668).

## HIGH PEAKS AND NORTHERN ADIRONDACKS

*A friendly farewell from Onchiota.*

Nancie Battaglia

**Lake Placid Visitors Bureau** (Main St., Lake Placid, NY 12946; 518-523-2445).
**Saranac Lake** (30 Main St., Saranac Lake, NY 12983; 518-891-1990 or 800-347-1992).
**Whiteface Mountain** (Rte. 86, Wilmington, NY 12993; 518-946-2255).

## NORTHWEST LAKES REGION

**Cranberry Lake** (Box 506, Cranberry Lake, NY 12927; 315-848-2900).
**Tupper Lake** (55 Park St., Tupper Lake, NY 12986; 518-359-3328).

## CENTRAL AND SOUTHWESTERN ADIRONDACKS

**Blue Mountain Lake Association** (Rte. 28, Blue Mountain Lake, NY 12812; 518-352-7659).

**Central Adirondack Association** (Main St., Old Forge, NY 13420; 315-369-6983).

**Gore Mountain Region** (Main St., North Creek, NY 12853; 518-251-2612).

**Indian Lake** (Main St., Indian Lake, NY 12842; 518-648-5112).

**Inlet** (Rte. 28, Inlet, NY 13360; 315-357-5501).

**Long Lake** (Rte. 28N, Long Lake, NY 12847; 518-624-3077).

**Northville Civic Association** (Box 255, Northville, NY 12134),

**Speculator-Lake Pleasant-Piseco** (Rte. 30, Speculator, NY 12164; 518-548-4521).

# Index

# LODGING BY PRICE CODE

**Price Codes:**

| | |
|---|---|
| Very Inexpensive | Under $35 |
| Inexpensive | $35-$65 |
| Moderate | $65-$95 |
| Expensive | $95-130 |
| Very Expensive | Over $130 |

**VERY INEXPENSIVE**
Corner Birches B&B Guest House
Lake George American Youth Hostel

**VERY INEXPENSIVE–INEXPENSIVE**
Adirondack Loj
Schroon River Ranch Motel

**INEXPENSIVE**
Abner Greenfield's Country Inn
Ark/Constitution Trail Inn, The
Bonnie View Acres B&B
Charlie's Inn & Junction Campground
Cinnamon Bear, The
Country Road Lodge
Cranberry Lake Inn
Deer Meadows
1852 Inn
1870 B&B
Elms Waterfront Cottages & Lodge
Fairview House
Geandreau's Cabins
High Peaks Base Camp
Hillman's Cottages

Hilltop Cottage B&B
Inn at Speculator, The
Inn on the Hill
Kastner's
Long View Lodge
McCane's
Melody Lodge
Murdie's B&B
Peebles Indian & Mountain View Lake Cottages
Pine Tree Inn B&B
Piseco Lake Lodge
Porches, The
Right Eye Cottages
Rolling Hill B&B
Schroon Lake Place, The
Snowshoe Hill Cottages
Stillwater
Stoneleigh B&B

# RESTAURANTS BY PRICE CODE

## RESTAURANTS BY CUISINE

# About the Author

Since moving to the mountains in 1976, Elizabeth Folwell has worked in a variety of Adirondack places, serving as education coordinator of the Adirondack Museum in Blue Mountain Lake, and as executive director of the Adirondack Lakes Center for the Arts, also in Blue Mountain Lake. Currently she is senior editor of *Adirondack Life* magazine, based in Jay, New York. She also had a brief career as manager of a general store, and worked as a project coordinator for Travelers Aid during the 1980 Winter Olympics in Lake Placid.

While at *Adirondack Life*, she has written numerous pieces on local history, outdoor recreation, and the environment; her freelance articles on adventure travel in the Northeast and the Carribean have appeared in national publications. She is co-author of *Cultural Resources in New York's North Country*, published by the Adirondack Museum in 1979.

She lives in Blue Mountain Lake with her husband, Tom Warrington, and two dogs.

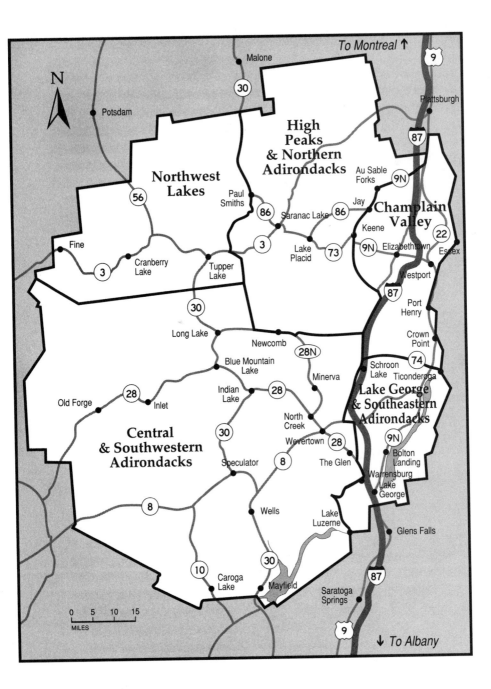